ART FUNDAMENTALS

Theory and Practice

ELEVENTH EDITION

ART FUNDAMENTALS

Theory and Practice

ELEVENTH EDITION

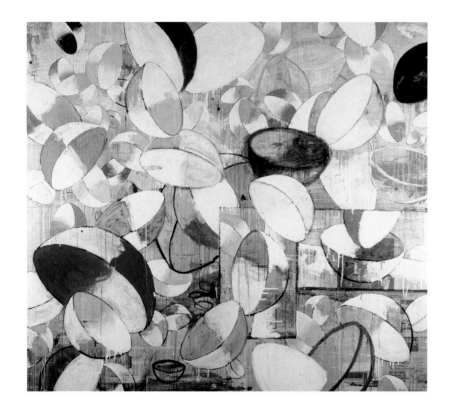

Otto G. Ocvirk

Robert E. Stinson

Philip R. Wigg

Robert O. Bone

David L. Cayton

School of Art
Bowling Green State University

Mc
Graw
Hill **Higher Education**

Boston   Burr Ridge, IL   Dubuque, IA   New York   San Francisco   St. Louis
Bangkok   Bogotá   Caracas   Kuala Lumpur   Lisbon   London   Madrid   Mexico City
Milan   Montreal   New Delhi   Santiago   Seoul   Singapore   Sydney   Taipei   Toronto

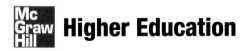

Published by McGraw-Hill, an imprint of The McGraw-Hill Companies, Inc., 1221 Avenue of the Americas, New York, NY 10020. Copyright © 2009, 2006, 2002, 1998 by The McGraw-Hill Companies, Inc. All rights reserved. No part of this publication may be reproduced or distributed in any form or by any means, or stored in a database or retrieval system, without the prior written consent of The McGraw-Hill Companies, Inc., including, but not limited to, in any network or other electronic storage or transmission, or broadcast for distance learning.

4 5 6 7 8 9 0 RRD/RRD 0

ISBN: 978-0-07-352652-2
MHID: 0-07-352652-5

Editor-in-Chief: *Michael Ryan*
Publisher: *Lisa Moore*
Developmental Editor: *Betty Chen*
Editorial Assistant: *Meredith Grant*
Marketing Manager: *Pamela Cooper*
Media Project Manager: *Thomas Brierly*
Production Editor: *Anne Fuzellier*
Art Director: *Preston Thomas*
Art Manager: *Robin Mouat*
Design Manager: *Ashley Bedell*
Interior Designer: *Glenda King*
Photo Manager: *Brian J. Pecko*
Photo Researcher: *Emily Tietz*
Production Supervisor: *Randy Hurst*
Production Service: *The Left Coast Group, Inc.*
Composition: *10/12 Palatino by Lachina Publishing Services*
Printing: *70# Sterling Ultra by R.R. Donnelley Willard*

Cover image: *Eiso* by Paul Manes. Oil on canvas, 60 × 66 in. (152.4 × 167.6 cm). Courtesy of Paul Rogers/9W Gallery, New York, NY.

Library of Congress Cataloging-in-Publication Data
Art fundamentals: theory and practice / Otto G. Ocvirk … [et al.].—11th ed.
    p. cm.
  Includes bibliographical references and index.
  ISBN-13: 978-0-07-352652-2 (acid-free paper)
  ISBN-10: 0-07-352652-5 (acid-free paper)
  1. Art—Technique. 2. Art. I. Ocvirk, Otto G.
  N7430.A697 2009
  702.8—dc22
                            2008036000

www.mhhe.com

CONTENTS

v

CHAPTER EIGHT

Space   223

CHAPTER NINE

Time and Motion   258

The original textbook that set the standard for introduction to art courses across the country, *Art Fundamentals* has guided generations of students through both the essential elements of art and the rich and varied history of their uses. We have organized *Art Fundamentals* to assist with "knowing" and "feeling" the fundamental concepts of refined creation. Numerous visual examples elevate the lessons beyond mere discussion to demonstrating instead of telling. As always, our intent is to stimulate without locking students into a restricted mind-set or mechanical copying of ideas.

The demand for this eleventh edition of *Art Fundamentals* proves that the study of art foundation is as vital as ever, and this edition aims to meet that need with comprehensive coverage of the art elements, clarity, plentiful illustrated examples, carefully chosen color images, and well-defined concepts. The elements and the principles that aid in their application, as in the past, are still employed by all artists, with the evolution of technologies having expanded and modified the way in which the elements can be put to use. *Art Fundamentals* looks at aspects of the components individually and in context. While no individual component can be developed in isolation, for all must work in unison, our intent is for the student to become so familiar with each element that it may be used subconsciously and integrated with the others without struggle.

HALLMARK FEATURES

To help students understand the concepts and apply them, these proven features have been revised and updated:

- A list of keywords, arranged alphabetically, appears at the beginning of each chapter. This placement allows students to preview the keywords before beginning the chapter and reference them while reading the words in context; the keywords are also boldfaced within the text.
- Numerous color illustrations representing a broad array of media and diverse artists, such as Käthe Kollwitz, Amir Nour, Yasuo Ohba, and Ismael Rodriguez Rueda, demonstrate the various concepts and show how other artists have applied them to their work. The eleventh edition of *Art Fundamentals* contains over 400 images that include Pablo Picasso's *The Bull*, states I–XI; Alexander Calder's *Myxomatose*; Robert Rauschenberg's *Canyon*; David Hockney's *Mother I, Yorkshire Moors, August, 1985, #1*; and Katherine D. Crone's *Tokyo Sunday*. Allow these images to spark curiosity, and have students try to understand what the artists have done in each piece to make it work.

NEW TO THE ELEVENTH EDITION

In the eleventh edition, we have also included the following revisions and new features:

- A chapter on the art elements of time and motion (Chapter 9) has been added to this edition.
- A visually enriched timeline replaces former Chapter 10, "Content and Style." The timeline is titled "After Images: A Visual Timeline of Artistic and Stylistic Comparisons," which comes from the common practice among artists to title their works as "after" the works of other artists, such as Vincent van Gogh's *Japonaiserie: Bridge in the Rain (after Hiroshige)*. "After Images" enhances visual learning, providing side-by-side images for comparison and study into how art elements are developed.
- Chapter 1 now includes a section on critical thinking to help students think about, view, and make art that is relevant to contemporary issues and to facilitate their understanding of art and its historical development.
- Advances in technology and new applications of media are incorporated throughout the text, although we still present the work of contemporary artists alongside the old masters. Extended

discussions on film and video and advances in computer and camera techniques have been added along with visual examples.

- The art elements chapters have been developed and expanded by the presentation of both two- and three-dimensional examples and applications. Content from the former Chapter 9 on the third dimension has been integrated accordingly throughout the book.

SUPPLEMENTS

Additional resources to supplement *Art Fundamentals,* eleventh edition, can be found online at **www.mhhe.com/ocvirk11e.** The student section of the Online Learning Center (OLC) contains study materials such as quizzes, key terms, and flash cards. Content from the previously published *Core Concepts in Art* CD-ROM is available through the OLC by clicking on *MyArtStudio,* an interactive site that allows students to study and experiment with various elements and principles of art and to view videos of techniques and artists at work. Exercises on the OLC guide students to *MyArtStudio* at appropriate points in the text.

The instructor section includes sample student projects and a link to *The Image Vault,* McGraw-Hill's Web-based presentation manager. A list of images on *The Image Vault* that correspond to images from the textbook is available on the instructor site. Instructors can incorporate images from *The Image Vault* in digital presentations that can be used in the classroom (no Internet access required), burned to CD-ROM, or embedded in course Web pages. See **www.mhhe.com/theimagevault** for more details.

ACKNOWLEDGMENTS

We would like to express our gratitude to Ms. Carrie Anne Cayton for the countless hours spent editing and helping to bring this edition to life and to Dr. Andrew Hershberger for all his work in developing the new section, "After Images: A Visual Timeline of Artistic and Stylistic Comparisons." And, as ever, we send immeasurable thanks to our reviewers, whose thorough commentary helped us evaluate our delivery of information. The diversity of our reviewers—from longtime fans to instructors who had never before used the book—provided us a broad perspective and great insight. Like any artwork, revision and critique must be utilized until the text effectively conveys what the author wants to communicate. Our deep appreciation also goes out to the artists, museums, galleries, and art owners for providing us with permissions and materials for the numerous visual reproductions of their artwork. In addition, we are grateful for the hard work done by our publisher, McGraw-Hill, and its Higher Education staff, who have finalized all the details necessary for publication to go forward. Finally, we must thank our many readers and instructors—we hope this edition serves you well.

REVIEWERS

James Baken, Rocky Mountain College
Laurence J. Bradshaw, University of Nebraska–Omaha
Michael J. Buono, Drury University
Derrick Burbul, University of Nebraska–Kearney
Carolyn Castano, Long Beach City College
Ron Clark, El Paso Community College
Jennifer Costa, Illinois Central College
Dwayne Crigger, Missouri State University
Kathleen Driscoll, Mount Ida College
Alison Gates, University of Wisconsin–Green Bay
Kay A. Klotzbach, Camden County College
Robert McCann, Michigan State University
Christine McCullough, Youngstown State University
Isaac Powell, Northwestern State University
Liz Roth, Oklahoma State University
Sherry M. Stephens, Palm Beach Community College
Anne Toner, Northwest College
Jason Travers, Lehigh University
Cathy Wilkin, Northern Virginia Community College

Introduction

CHAPTER ONE

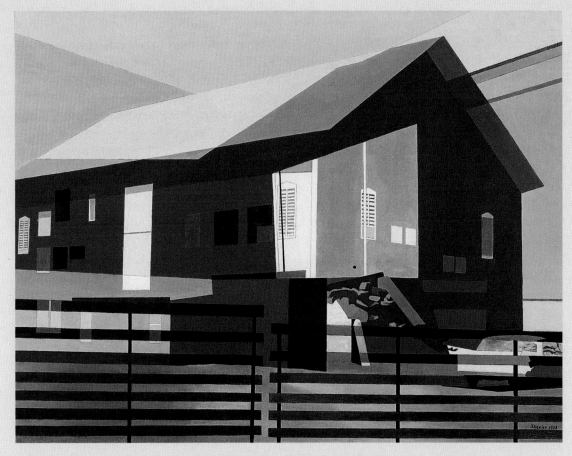

Charles Sheeler, *Composition around Red (Pennsylvania)*, 1958. Oil on canvas, 26 × 33 in. (66.1 × 83.9 cm). Montgomery Museum of Fine Arts. The Blount Collection of American Art.

INTRODUCTORY TERMS

Art —"The formal expression of a conceived image or imagined conception in terms of a given medium."—Sheldon Cheney

abstraction
A process or visual effect characterized by the simplification and/or rearrangement of the image.

addition
A sculptural term that means building up, assembling, or putting on material.

aesthetic, aesthetics
1. Sensitive to art or beauty. "Aesthetically pleasing" implies intellectual or visual beauty (i.e., creative, eloquent, or expressive qualities of form, as opposed to the mere recording of facts in visual, descriptive, or objective ways). 2. The study or theory of beauty—traditionally a branch of philosophy but now a compound of the philosophy, psychology, and sociology of art—dealing with the definition, inspiration, intent, forms, and psychological effects of art and beauty.

art
"The formal expression of a conceived image or imagined conception in terms of a given medium" (Sheldon Cheney).

assemblage
A technique that involves grouping found or created three-dimensional objects, which are often displayed *in situ*—that is, in a natural position or in the middle of the room rather than on a wall.

Bauhaus
Originally a German school of architecture that flourished between World War I and World War II. The Bauhaus attracted many leading experimental artists of both two- and three-dimensional fields.

casting
A sculptural technique in which liquid materials are shaped by being poured into a mold. This technique is also known as **substitution.**

concept
1. A comprehensive idea or generalization.
2. An idea that brings diverse elements into a basic relationship.

Conceptual artists
Artists who focus on the idea, or "concept," of the work and are much more concerned with conveying a message or analyzing an idea than with the final product.

conceptual perception
Creative vision derived from the imagination; the opposite of **optical perception.**

content
The expression, essential meaning, significance, or aesthetic value of a work of art. Content refers to the sensory, subjective, psychological, or emotional properties we feel in a work of art, as opposed to our perception of its descriptive aspects alone.

craftsmanship
Aptitude, skill, or quality workmanship in the use of tools and materials.

Cubism
The name given to the painting style invented by Pablo Picasso and Georges Braque between 1907 and 1912, which uses multiple views of objects to create the effect of three-dimensionality while acknowledging the two-dimensional surface of the picture plane. Signaling the beginning of abstract art, Cubism is a semiabstract style that continued the strong trend away from representational art initiated by Cézanne in the late 1800s.

decorative (art)
The two-dimensional nature of an artwork or any of its elements, which emphasizes the essential flatness of a surface; also has generically referred to the ornamentation or enrichment of a surface.

descriptive (art)
A type of art that is based on adherence to actual appearances.

design
The underlying plan on which artists base their total work. In a broader sense, *design* may be considered synonymous with the term **form.**

elements of art
Line, shape, value, texture, and color—the basic ingredients the artist uses separately or in combination to produce artistic imagery. Their use produces the visual language of art.

expression
1. The manifestation through artistic form of thought, emotion, or quality of meaning. 2. In art, expression is synonymous with the term **content.**

form
1. The total appearance, organization, or inventive arrangement of all the visual elements according to the principles that will develop unity in the artwork; composition. 2. In sculpture, can also refer to the three-dimensional shape of the work.

glyptic
1. The quality of an art material like stone, wood, or metal that can be carved or engraved.
2. An art form that retains the color, tensile, and tactile qualities of the material from which it was created. 3. The quality of hardness, solidity, or resistance found in carved or engraved materials.

graphic (art)
Two-dimensional art processes such as drawing, painting, photography, printmaking, and so on that generally exist on a flat surface and can create the illusion of depth. Commercial applications include posters, newspapers, books, and magazines.

installations
Interior or exterior settings of media created by artists to heighten the viewers' awareness of the environmental space.

manipulation
The sculptural technique of shaping pliable materials by hand or with the use of tools—also known as **modeling.**

mass
1. In graphic art, a shape that appears to stand out three-dimensionally from the space surrounding it or that appears to create the illusion of a solid body of material. 2. In the plastic arts, the physical bulk of a solid body of material.

medium, media (pl.)
The material(s) and tool(s) used by the artist to create the visual elements perceived by the viewer.

modeling
A sculptural term for shaping a pliable material.

Naturalism
The approach to art that is essentially a description of things visually experienced. Pure naturalism would contain no personal interpretation introduced by the artist.

negative area
The unoccupied or empty space left after the positive images have been created by the artist. Consideration of the negative areas is just as important to the organization of form as the positive areas.

nonobjective, nonrepresentational art
A type of art that is completely imaginative, in which the elements, their organization, and their treatment are entirely personalized and the image is not derived from anything visually perceived by the artist.

objective
That which is based on the physical reality of the object and reflects no personal interpretation, bias, or emotion; the opposite of **subjective.**

optical perception
A purely visual experience with no exaggeration or creative interpretation of that which is seen; the opposite of **conceptual perception.**

organic unity
A condition in which the components of art (subject, form, and content) are completely interdependent. Though not a guarantee of "greatness," the resulting wholeness is vital to a successful work.

picture frame
The outermost limits or boundary of the picture plane.

picture plane
The actual flat surface on which the artist executes a pictorial image. In some cases, the picture plane acts merely as a transparent plane of reference to establish the illusion of forms existing in a three-dimensional space.

plane
1. An area that is essentially two-dimensional, having height and width. 2. A two-dimensional pictorial surface that can support the illusion of advancing or receding elements. 3. A flat sculptural surface.

plastic (art)
1. The use of the elements to create the illusion of the third dimension on a two-dimensional surface. 2. Three-dimensional art forms such as architecture, sculpture, ceramics, and so on.

positive area
The subject—whether representational or nonrepresentational—which is produced by the art elements (shape, line, etc.) or their combination. (See **negative area.**)

principles of organization
Concepts that guide the arrangement and integration of the elements in achieving a sense of visual order and overall visual unity. They are harmony, variety, balance, proportion, dominance, movement, and economy.

Process artists
Artists who focus on the execution, or "process," of the work and are much more concerned with the technique they employ in creating the work than with the final product.

realism, Realism (art movement)
A style of art that emphasizes universal characteristics rather than specific information (e.g., a generalization of all "motherhood" rather than an extremely detailed portrait of a specific woman). As a movement, it relates to painters like Honoré Daumier in nineteenth-century France and Winslow Homer in the United States in the 1850s.

relief sculpture
An artwork, graphic in concept but sculptural in application, utilizing relatively shallow depth to establish images. The space development may range from very limited projection, known as *low relief*, to more exaggerated space development, known as *high relief*. Relief sculpture is meant to be viewed frontally, not in the round.

representational art
A type of art in which the subject is presented through the visual art elements so that the observer is reminded of actual objects (see **naturalism** and **realism**).

sculpture
The art of shaping three-dimensional materials to express an idea.

shape
An area that stands out from its surroundings because of a defined or implied boundary or because of differences of value, color, or texture.

space
The interval, or measurable distance, between points or images; can be actual or illusionary.

style
The specific artistic character and dominant trends of form noted during periods of history and art movements. Style may also refer to artists' expressive use of media to give their works individual character.

subject
1. In a descriptive approach to art, refers to the persons or things represented. 2. In more abstract applications, refers to visual images that may have little to do with anything experienced in the natural environment.

subjective
That which is derived from the mind, instead of physical reality, and reflects a personal bias, emotion, or innovative interpretation; the opposite of **objective.**

substitution

In sculpture, replacing one material or medium with another. (See also **casting**.)

subtraction

A sculptural term meaning the carving or cutting away of material.

technique

The manner and skill with which artists employ their tools and materials to achieve an expressive effect.

three-dimensional

Possesses the dimensions of (or illusions of) height, width, and depth. In the graphic arts, the feeling of depth is an illusion, while in the plastic arts, the work has actual depth.

two-dimensional

Possesses the dimensions of height and width, especially when considering the flat surface, or picture plane.

unity

The result of bringing the elements of art into the appropriate ratio between harmony and variety to give a sense of oneness.

volume

The measurable amount of defined or occupied space in a three-dimensional object.

THE EVOLVING NATURE OF ART

The desire to create is not a new phenomenon. It appears to be a fundamental yearning that can be traced back to the earliest recesses of history. Our prehistoric ancestors crawled through dark cave passages, where, by flickering torchlight, they created amazing images of bison and horses, engraved on antler, and sculpted bulbous figures (figs. 1.1 and 1.2). Why did they work in grottos of protruding rock with such limited access? Were the images meant to be shared with others? Were they part of a shaman's ritual to ensure a successful hunt, worship the spirits of bison and horses, or ensure fertility and the continuation of the tribe? Although we may speculate about their purposes, these early images reveal something as old as humanity itself—the magical urge and need to create.

Even now, during the current epoch of manned and robotic space exploration, we seem as driven as the ancients to interpret the workings of the universe and our immediate environment through art (fig. 1.3). In fact, the amount of artwork being created today is unrivaled. Art presents the ordinary in an extraordinary way and gives meaning to the mundane. It provides the subtext that brings vitality to everyday experiences and transports us to somewhere

1.1 *Running Horse Attacked by Arrows.* Paleolithic cave painting, c. 15,000–10,000 B.C.E., Lascaux, France. In the context of fine art, one meaning of the word *fundamental* is the essential or basic urge to create art. Erich Lessing/Art Resource, NY.

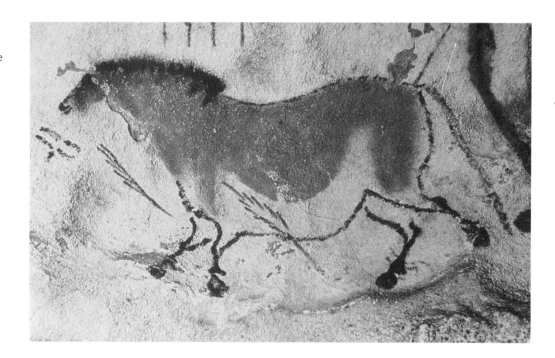

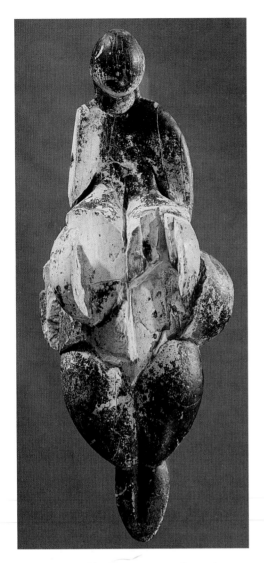

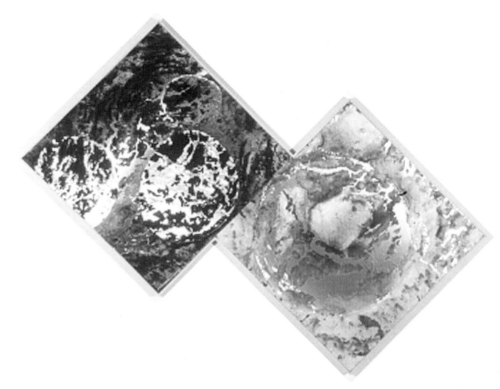

1.3 Dorothea Rockburne, *Copper, Paper Pulp, and Dieu Donné #8*, 2003. Paper pulp and paint on two copper panels mounted on wood, joined, 57 × 35 × 1¾ in. installed. Often inspired by images of our solar system and distant nebulae, Rockburne explores the workings of our universe through her work. © 2008 Dorothea Rockburne/Artists Rights Society (ARS), New York.

1.2 *Venus of Lespugue*, carving from the Aurignacian Period, c. 25,000–18,000 B.C.E., found in Rideaux Cave of Lespugue in the foothills of the Pyrenees, France. 5¾ in. high. Possibly used as a magical fertility fetish, the *Venus of Lespugue* was carved from a mammoth tusk during the Aurignacian Period. SCALA/Art Resource, NY.

beyond. With art, we can convey complex emotions, soothe the soul, or provoke thought and action; its language expresses our feelings and communicates our ideas like no other. This may be why the fundamental urge to create art objects can be traced back to the earliest recesses of history, and it is certainly why the urge persists in humans yet today.

But what exactly *is* **art**? Its multiple definitions are complex and nearly elusive. The term is often synonymous with **craftsmanship,** which implies knowledge of materials and their skillful handling. In fact, any creative and variable

skill can be labeled an art. During the fourteenth, fifteenth, and sixteenth centuries, the craft guilds (or unions) that upheld the standards and traditions of the artists' trades were designated as "Arti." Today, the term *the arts* refers to branches of learning that study creative skills—such as the musical arts, visual arts, performing arts, and so on. The terms *art* and *works of art*, therefore, also refer to *products* of such skills—products that commonly display intentional structure, unusual perception, and creative intuition. According to some people, a work of art is only achieved when the creation goes beyond simple function

Many philosophers over the years have offered their opinions on the purposes and qualifications of art:

- the formal [structured] expression of a conceived image in terms of a given medium (Cheney)

- the making of a form produced by the cooperation of all the faculties of the mind (Longman)

- significant form (Bell)

- eloquence (Burke)

- unexpected inevitability of formal relations (Fry)

- a unified manifold which is pleasure giving (Mather)

- a diagram or paradigm with a meaning that gives pleasure (Lostowel)

- that which gives pleasure apart from desire (Thomas Aquinas)

- objectified pleasure (Santayana)

- imitation [reflection of life or other ideas]

- propaganda [emphasis on communication rather than expression, implying an effort to influence conduct]

1.4 These philosophical descriptions of "art" exemplify a constant effort to decipher the real nature of art and suggest that it is a different thing for different people. Note that several of these definitions stress "pleasure" as a component of art, although some art seems to have no intention of provoking pleasure. Whatever the definition, art can be a relaxant or stimulant; for the artist, it can also produce frustration—but in most cases, finally, a sense of achievement.

or utility and takes on more than ordinary significance. For others, anything creative counts, regardless of skill level. The purposes and qualifications of art vary with every individual, culture, and time period, so in some sense, the definition of *art* is still developing (fig. 1.4).

Think about your own definition of art . . . and be aware that your opinion may change. Take, for example, the image of a flower. When is it art, and when is it not art? Does it matter if the image is a drawing or a print, a child's finger painting or a paint-by-number picture? What if you can barely recognize the flower?

Certain audiences feel that quality artwork must be "beautiful" (i.e., visu-ally or intellectually pleasing), or else the work is just "craft" instead of "art." Fine craftsmen, however, would surely argue that their crafts are indeed beautiful. In any case, beauty is **subjective** and depends partly on the viewer's expectations. The public often likes and expects images that are familiar, recognizable, sentimental, or pleasant to experience. However, not all people, even of similar backgrounds, would agree on the beauty of a given subject matter, much less its visual treatment. What happens if a work contains an emotional image but is badly executed? Is it still considered beautiful? What if a work lacks a compelling image but is expertly executed?

Aesthetics, the philosophical appreciation of the "beautiful," is a complex study that is still evolving, in part because the **concept** of beauty has changed radically over the course of the last several generations. While searching for new means of self-expression, every generation of artists alters the nature of art. Since the eras of ancient civilizations, techniques and ambitions have changed radically, and today we have an array of different approaches to art. Regardless of the time or place of creation, art has always been produced because an artist has wanted to say something and has chosen a particular way of saying it. For each piece, the artist makes choices

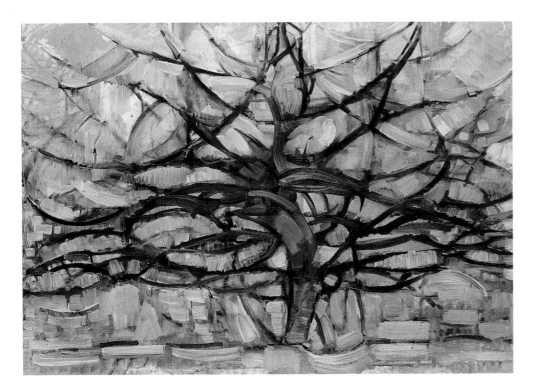

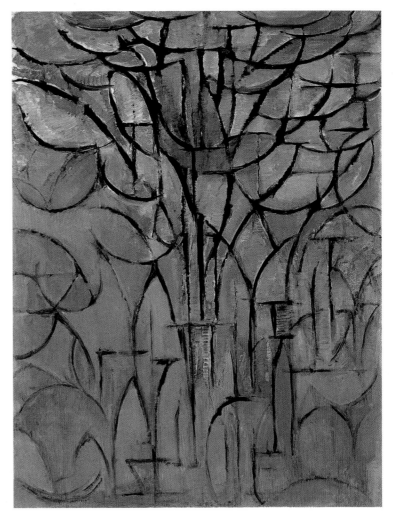

about the structure, media (materials and tools), techniques (methods of using the media), and treatment of subject matter that will best express his or her idea. Over time, an artist's body of work can reveal an expressive character unique to the individual artist, like a signature. This expressive quality is known as an artistic **style.** Some styles, once unique to individual artists, have been adopted by generations of artists and have broader historical application. In many cases, a single artist's style changes as his or her body of work develops and grows. One prime example is the work of Piet Mondrian (figs. 1.5, 1.6, 1.7, and 1.8), whose final style has influenced artists

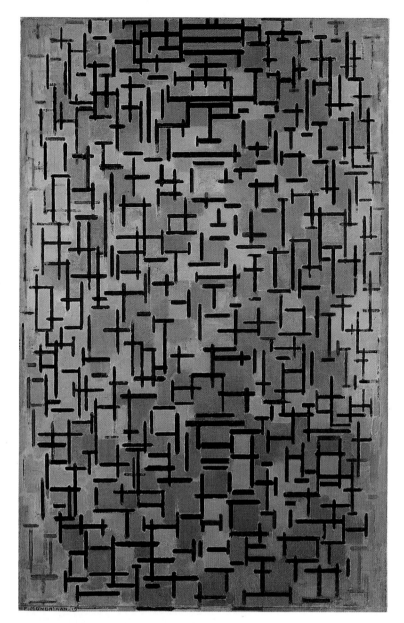

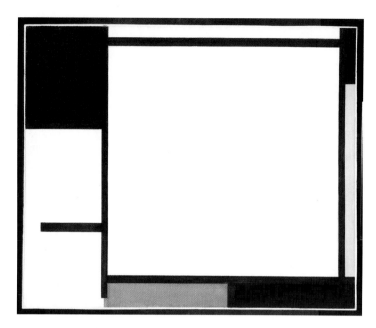

1.8 Piet Mondrian, *Composition with Blue, Black, Yellow and Red,* 1922. Gouache on paper, 41 × 49 cm. The primary colors divided by block lines, all in a two-dimensional grid, are typical of Mondrian's later work. This is the style that has generated so much influence through the years. Nationalgalerie, Berlin, Photo © Bildarchiv Preussischer Kulturbesitz/Art Resource, NY. © 2008 Mondrian/Holtzman Trust c/o HCR International Warrenton Virginia

1.7 Piet Mondrian, *Composition,* 1916. Oil on canvas and wood strip, 47¼ × 29½ in. (120 × 74.9 cm). As a follow-up to figs. 1.5 and 1.6, this later work can be seen as even closer to the severity of Mondrian's final style in fig. 1.8. Solomon R. Guggenheim Foundation, New York (FN 4/9.1229). © 2008 Mondrian/Holtzman Trust c/o HCR International, Warrenton, Virginia.

in other fields (figs. 1.9, 1.10, and 1.11). Young artists are often tempted to prematurely impose a style on their work, instead of allowing it to mature naturally. However, they must remember—just like a signature—one's expressive style truly only develops through time and repeated practice.

Often, the evolution of style and purpose results in artwork that pushes the boundaries of public acceptability. During the nineteenth and twentieth centuries, artists often confounded the public by the increasingly abstract treatment of subject matter. Contemporary artists, too, make expressive choices that the public often doesn't understand or find personally relevant. As a result, many people who want to be actively engaged in art find that much of what they see is not meaningful to them. Unfortunately, their creative inhibitions can be magnified by the enormous diversity of our world. Before the twentieth century, people often had a better understanding and greater acceptance of what they saw because their exposure was limited. Unlike those more insular periods, today's sophisticated printing and distribution techniques have made most of the art of

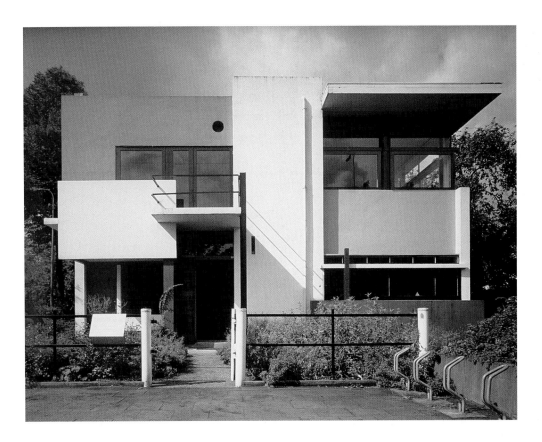

1.10 Gerrit Rietveld, *Red/Blue Chair,* designed 1918 (made c. 1950 by G. van de Groenekan). Pine, ebonized and painted, $34\frac{7}{8} \times 23\frac{5}{8} \times 29\frac{3}{4}$ in. ($88.4 \times 60 \times 75.5$ cm). The relationships between horizontals and verticals and the juxtapositions of color within an asymmetrical grid are features shared by this chair and the paintings of Piet Mondrian. Toledo Museum of Art, Toledo, OH. Purchased with funds from the Florence Scott Libbey Bequest, in memory of her father, Maurice A. Scott (1985.48); © 1998 Beeldrecht Amsterdam.

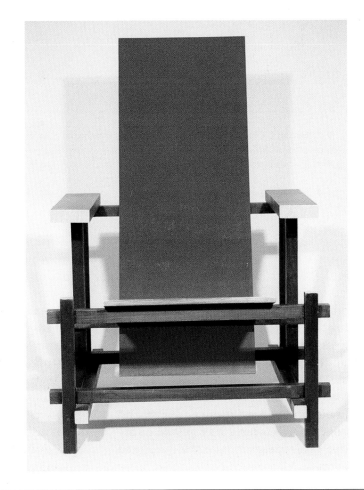

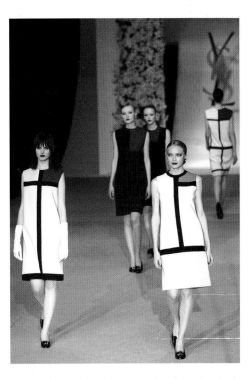

1.11 Yves Saint Laurent, Mondrian-inspired dresses. Models present dresses motivated by painter Piet Mondrian during French legendary fashion designer Yves Saint Laurent's farewell show Tuesday, January 22, 2002, at the Georges Pompidou Center in Paris. © AP Photo/ Remy de la Mauviniere

both the past and present available to us. In addition, television, the Internet—with its instant global interactive communications—radio, and air travel have contributed to a great cultural mixing.

In order to appreciate the many forms of art to which we have access today, we must understand the basics from which they have grown. This book seeks to provide such an understanding by examining the nature of the many factors involved in producing artwork, including the principles that govern those factors.

THE THREE COMPONENTS OF ART

Subject, form, and content have always been the three basic components of a work of art, and they are wed together in a way that is inseparable. In general, *subject* may be thought of as the "what" (the topic, focus, or image); *form*, as the "how" (the development of the work, composition, or the substantiation); and *content*, as the "why" (the artist's intention, communication, or meaning behind the work).

Subject

The **subject** of visual art can be a person, an object, a theme, or an idea. Though there are many and varied ways of presenting the subject matter, it is only important to the degree that the artist is motivated by it.

Objective images, which represent people or objects, look as close as possible to their references' actual appearance and can be clearly identified (see figs. 6.1, 6.24, and 8.11). These types of images are also called **representational.**

Artists who explore the process of abstraction (simplification and rearrangement) create images that look less like the object on which they are

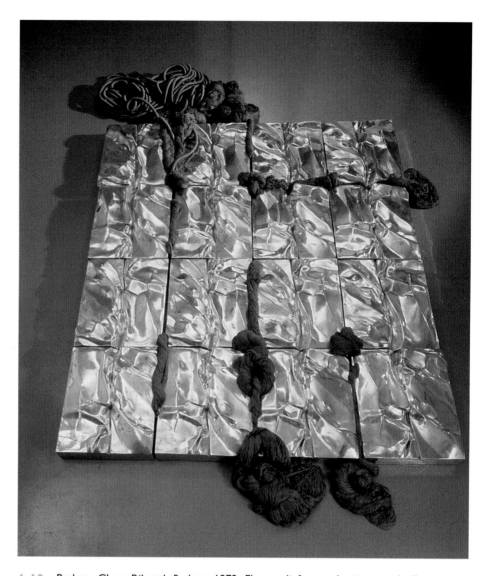

1.12 Barbara Chase-Riboud, *Bathers*, 1973. Floor relief, cast aluminum and silk in sixteen pieces, 400 × 400 × 12 cm. Barbara Chase-Riboud does not limit her image to a superficial presentation of subject (bathers). She reveals deeper meanings through the form of the work, with the repetition of cast undulating surface folds and the contrast of metal against flowing silk coils. Courtesy of the artist and Jernigan Wicker Fine Arts, CA.

based, although they may still be recognizable (fig. 1.12; see also figs. 1.5, 4.20, 5.25, 9.9, and 9.13).

In the most advanced type of abstraction, the subject has no reference to any physical object, and this **nonrepresentational** image is thus considered **nonobjective** (see figs. 1.8, 7.25, and T.71). Here, the subject may be difficult for the observer to identify, since the image is only a particular configuration of art elements instead of people or objects. This type of subject often refers to

the artist's idea about energy and movement, which guides the use of raw materials, and it communicates with those who can read the language of form. (Abstraction will be discussed in more detail later in this chapter.)

Music, like art, deals with subjects and provides an interesting comparison. In the visual arts, the subject is often a particular thing viewed and reproduced by the artist. But at other times, art presents a nonrecognizable subject—an idea rather than a thing.

Likewise, music sometimes deals with recognizable sounds—thunderstorms and birdsongs in Beethoven's *Pastoral* Symphony or taxi horns in Gershwin's *An American in Paris*. While represented rather abstractly, these are the musical equivalents of recognizable subjects in an artwork. By contrast, Beethoven's Fifth Symphony and Gershwin's Concerto in F are strictly collections of musical ideas. In the medium of dance, choreography often has no specific subject, but dancing in Copland's ballet *Rodeo* is, to a degree, subject oriented. In all of the arts, subjects obviously should be judged not alone but by what is done with them.

Regardless of the type of art, the way the subject is formed to give it **expression** is the important consideration; all of the fine arts have subjects that obviously should not be judged alone but by what is done with them (fig. 1.13).

Form

As a component of art, the word **form** refers to the total overall arrangement or organization of an artwork. It is the result of the use of the elements of art and the principles of organization, which are used to give them order and meaning. When studying a work's form—the total organization or composition—we are analyzing how the piece was created. More specifically, we are examining how the artist's choices relate to each other and interact to form the artwork's final appearance. In this sense, the word *form* may actually be thought of as a verb rather than a noun.

The **elements of art,** which include *line, texture, color, shape,* and *value,* are the most basic, indispensable, and immediate vehicles or building blocks for expression. Their characteristics, determined by the artist's choice of media and techniques, can communicate a wide range of complex feelings. All artists must deal with the elements singularly or in combination, and their organization can heighten a work's interest.

Based on the intended expression, each artist can arrange the elements in any manner that builds the desired character into the piece. However, the elements are given order and meaningful structure when arranged according to the **principles of organization,** which help integrate and organize the elements. These principles include *harmony, variety, balance, proportion, dominance, movement,* and *economy.* They help create *spatial* relationships and effectively convey the artist's intent. The principles of organization are flexible, not dogmatic, and can be combined and applied in numerous ways. Some artists arrange intuitively, and others are more calculating, but with experience, all of

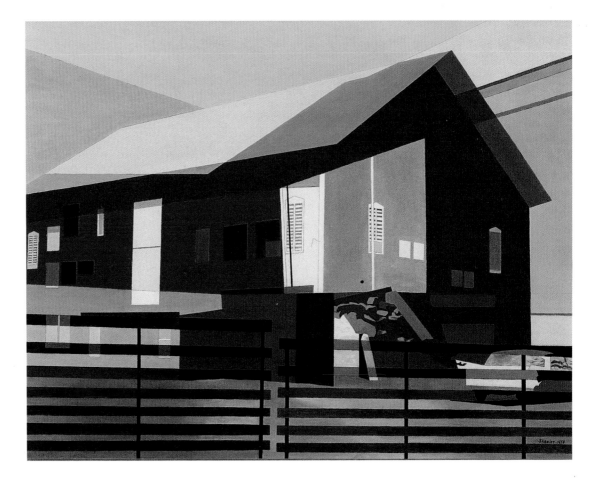

1.13   Charles Sheeler, *Composition around Red (Pennsylvania),* 1958. Oil on canvas, 26 × 33 in. The subject—a man-made structure—is clear enough. However, a work of art should be judged not by its subject alone but rather by how that subject is treated. Montgomery Museum of Fine Arts. The Blount Collection of American Art.

them develop an instinctive feeling for organizing their work. So important are these concepts, that a chapter on form will focus on the principles of organization, and separate chapters will cover each of the elements.

Content

The emotional or intellectual message of a work of art is its **content**—a statement, expression, or mood developed by the artist and interpreted by the observer. Of the three components of art, content may be the most difficult to identify, because the audience, without direct communication with the artist, must decipher the artist's thoughts by observing the work's subject and form. For example, in *Young Girl in the Lap of Death* (fig. 1.14), the striking emphasis of the left-to-right diagonals, the sharp contrasts of light and dark values, and the aggressive and powerful drawing strokes give us some insight into Käthe Kollwitz's concern for life, though we may not understand the depth of her passion.

Ideally, the viewer's interpretation is synchronized with the artist's intentions. However, the viewer's diversity of experiences can affect the communication between artist and viewer. For many people, content is determined by their familiarity with the subject; they are confined to feelings aroused by objects or ideas they know. A much broader and ultimately more meaningful content is not utterly reliant on the image but is reinforced by the form. This is especially so in more abstract works, in which the viewer may not recognize the image as a known object and must, therefore, interpret meaning from shapes and other elements. Images that are hardly recognizable, if representational at all, can still deliver content if the observer knows how to interpret form.

Occasionally, artists may be unaware of what motivates them to make certain choices of image or form. For them, the content of the piece may be subconscious instead of deliberate. For example, an art-

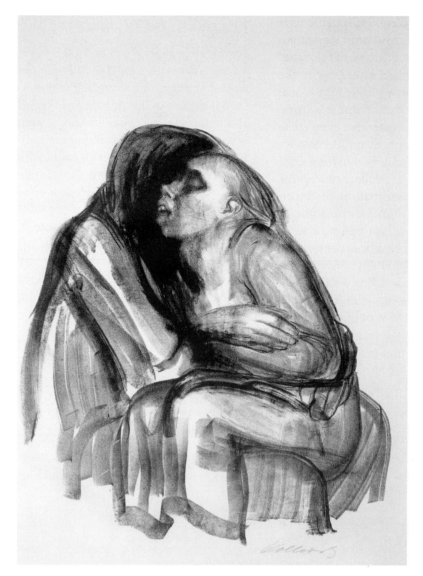

1.14 Käthe Kollwitz, *Young Girl in the Lap of Death*, 1934. Crayon lithograph, 42 × 38 cm. Käthe Kollwitz's natural talent for drawing was encouraged by her father, who arranged private lessons before sending her to an art school for women in Berlin. After her study of Edvard Munch's work, she boldly confronted emotionally charged images. Hunger and death were not strangers in her home because of her husband's medical practice, but the theme of death became an obsession after her son Peter was killed in WWI and her grandson Peter in WWII. It is reinforced in this composition by sharp diagonal movements, extreme contrasts of value, and the boldness of the drawing. Art © 2008 Artists Rights Society (ARS), New York/VG Bild-Kunst, Bonn. Photo © Käthe Kollwitz Museum Köln.

ist who has a violent confrontation with a neighbor might subconsciously need to express anger (content) and is thus compelled to work with sharp jagged shapes, bitter acrid reds, slashing agitated marks (form) and exploding images (subject). Sometimes the meaning of the nonobjective shapes is born in the artist's mind only after they seem to evolve and mutate on the canvas.

Although it is not a requirement for enjoying artwork, a little research about the artist's life, time period, or culture can help expand viewpoints and lead to a fuller interpretation of content. For example, a deeper comprehension of Vincent van Gogh's use of personalized color may be gained by reading Van Gogh's letters to his brother Theo. His letters expressed an evolving belief that color conveyed specific feelings and attitudes and was more than a mere optical experience. He felt that his use of color could emit power like Wagner's music. The letters also reveal a developing personal color iconography, in which red and green eventually symbolized the terrible sinful passions of humanity; black contour lines provided a sense of anguish; cobalt blue signified the vault of heaven, and yellow symbolized love. For Van Gogh, color was not strictly a tool for visual imitation but an instrument to transmit his personal emotions (fig. 1.15). Color symbolism may not have been used in all of his paintings, but an understanding of his intent helps explain some of his choices and the power in his work.

ORGANIC UNITY

If an artist is successful in wedding all three of the components (subject, form, and content) in a work, they become inseparable, mutually interactive, and interrelated—as if they were a living organism. When this is achieved, we can say the work has **organic unity,** containing nothing that is unnecessary or distracting, with relationships that seem inevitable (fig. 1.16).

A well-made television set might be used as an illustration of organic unity because it has a complex but minimum number of parts necessary to function, and these parts work only when properly assembled with respect to each other. When all the parts are activated, they become organically unified. As in the case of sophisticated engineering, this sense of reciprocal "wholeness" is also sought in art. Organic unity does not guarantee the work to be judged a "great work of art," but it does help give the work a vital feeling of completeness.

In figure 1.17A and B, we see the beginning and end state of an intaglio print by Rembrandt. Many of us would have been happy achieving the first state, but Rembrandt continued adjusting areas in

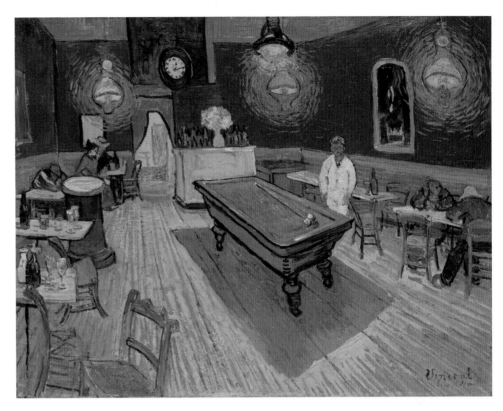

1.15 Vincent van Gogh, *The Night Café,* 1888. Oil on canvas, 27½ × 35 in. Van Gogh used color to transmit his personal emotions and not as a tool strictly for visual imitation. He saw in the provincial café the sinful obsessions of humanity, which he expressed with reds. He used greens to represent the powers of darkness, contrasted by an atmosphere of pale sulfur like the devil's furnace. His personal symbolic application of color was constantly evolving. © Yale University Art Gallery/Art Resource, NY.

1.16 This diagram illustrates the interrelationship of subject, form, and content as described in the text. Any of these components may be the starting point for a work. For example, the inspiration for a work could begin after observing an object (subject), which might stir up passionate feelings within the artist (content) and give rise to the developing composition (form). Or, it could begin with an artist's playful manipulation of shapes and color on a canvas (form), which suggests a feeling or emotion to develop (content) and eventually becomes an image (subject). An artist's personal sadness or passion for a social issue (content) could also be the starting idea that becomes expressed through color choices (form) and results in a pattern of nonobjective marks (subject). Whatever the evolution, progression, or emphasis of the components—subject, form, and content—organic unity is the desired end.

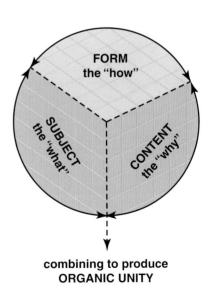

FORM
the "how"

SUBJECT
the "what"

CONTENT
the "why"

combining to produce
ORGANIC UNITY

1.17 Rembrandt Harmenszoon van Rijn, *Christ Presented to the People,* first state and last state, 1655. Print (dry point). Rembrandt searched for the most interesting and communicative presentation of his idea. In doing so, he made dramatic deletions and changes, which in this case involved scraping out a portion of the copper plate. Figure A is the first version of the work, and figure B is the last.
The Metropolitan Museum of Art, Gift of Felix M. Warburg and His Family, 1941. (41.1.36). Image © The Metropolitan Museum of Art.

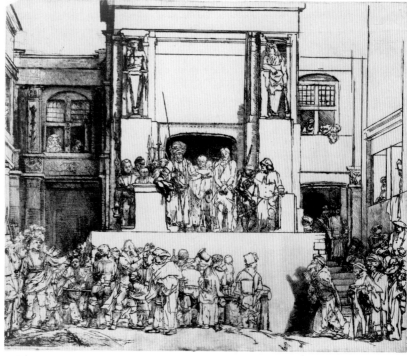

A

Subject: Rembrandt has chosen to depict the moment when Christ is presented to the Jewish chief priests, rulers, and the common people. He includes a range of figures, from the wealthy to the beggars, and the scene takes place in the courtyard of the palace or praetorium of Pilate the governor. (However, Rembrandt probably based the architecture and figures on his sketches done in the Jewish sections of Amsterdam, since Rembrandt's travels did not include Palestine.)

Form: Rembrandt's organization draws focus on the figures near the center, and the changes between the first print (A: stage 1) and the last print (B: stage 5) emphasize the Christ figure, enhance the scene's complexity, and draw the viewer into the picture. Rembrandt seems to take delight in solving compositional problems which allow him to present information in dichotomous ways. For example, could he place an image in the center of a composition and yet have that object feel higher or lower in the composition? How could the verticality be emphasized in a horizontal layout? Could it be possible to make a composition that appears to be similar and dissimilar at the same time, on both sides of a central axis? Could he darken an area to make it recede and at the same time make the object next to it advance? If an object is lightened or darkened to make it join a larger area, how could he do it without losing

the object—could the object still be made to stand out?

In the first print (A), the horizontal layout is established by the plate size and the row of people moving across the bottom. But the horizontal emphasis changes to vertical in the last print (B). To do this, Rembrandt emphasizes an upward thrust in the composition by the creation of a low point of view (known as a worm's eye view), located slightly above the left sewer tunnel (notice how the angles of the lines defining the extreme right side wall appear to be pointing across in the first print (A) but more downward in the last (B). With the low viewpoint, the viewer has the feeling of looking **up** at the remaining composition. To further reinforce the verticality, he scrapes out the people in the center foreground of the first print (A) and replaces them with sewer tunnels and a dark shape that runs across the bottom of the picture (B). This emphasizes the vertical direction of the five wall units in the composition by allowing the central area to flow from top to bottom uninterrupted.

In addition, Rembrandt draws attention to the picture's bottom edge by creating a tension between it and the area immediately above it—due to their relative closeness and the dark shading. He anchors the dark tunnel shapes by emphasizing the ground plane under the people on either side. These ground plane lines

subconsciously extend across the darkened center of the image, which helps to tie them visually to the bottom edge. The new open wall plunges to an unknown depth—further emphasizing the feeling of height.

Having emphasized the bottom of the plate (B) to increase the feeling of height, Rembrandt does the same to the top edge. Although the composition now appears even more horizontal because some of the top of the print has been removed, additional architectural detail is added across the central section, even with the top of the two recessed walls—which keeps the verticality strongly emphasized. This clustering of visual detail helps visually activate the very top of the porch area and helps make the central porch area even more important. By the last stage (B), this upward thrust is aided by the addition of an arching shape over the door immediately behind the central figures. Rembrandt has enlarged and darkened the whole area to make the central figures feel higher in the composition and more important than they were earlier.

Although this composition might appear at first glance to be similar on both sides of an imaginary vertical center line, Rembrandt works at finding ways to make all the areas similar and dissimilar at the same time. The recessed wall areas immediately to the left and right of the central area are approximately the same width,

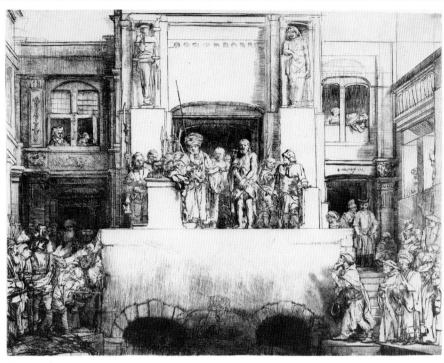

B

yet the left side is in deep shadow and the right is bathed in light. Both sides have second-story arched window units, but to strengthen the dissimilarity, the windows on the right are noticeably higher. By the last state of the print (B), the top and bottom of the right windows have been lowered to the level of those on the left, but by removing all the glass above the figures and completely opening the window area, the windows on the right are noticeably dissimilar and still feel higher than those on the left side of the picture. All four windows contain female viewers, but the woman in the far right window is hanging out of the window frame.

Also, the extreme left and right sidewalls originate from the same point on the back wall, but they are different widths and different heights. By the last state (B), the top of the right sidewall is raised considerably with building detail. By lightening the figures in the foreground and shading the entire area with a similar gray tone, Rembrandt pulls the entire area together, making the right side of the composition more competitive visually with the left side, and does so without developing the same size or type of darkness.

After successfully stretching the composition vertically, Rembrandt works at the problem of manipulating space by pulling some areas forward and pushing others back. In the final stage, Christ is pulled forward as the space to his right is darkened and recedes. The doorway on the ground floor to the left is deepened by the addition of five additional archways and the hint of an emerging figure in the darkest area. In the opposite doorway, emerging figures are lightened against the surrounding darkness, and the contrast of dark and light pulls them forward as they descend the stairway. The two statues above the central figures have been lightened, which pushes them back behind the central figures. The development of darks on both sides of the central balcony, even though dissimilar, also helps to bring the entire middle area forward.

Furthermore, Rembrandt's ingenious use of the balcony as a visual device allows him to create a metaphorical and physical separation between the ruling class and the common people while focusing on the main figures. With the removal of the line of people across the foreground of the first state (A), the balcony, wall, and central figures are thrust forward as if the viewer is invited to become a participant in the ongoing event. The feeling of looking **up** also places the viewer on the ground level with the common man.

Content: Although observers can read a number of meanings into the piece, it is impossible to say with certainty what motivated Rembrandt to create this print. While the picture draws the viewer into the moment when Christ is presented to the people, it does so without endorsing any specific religious point of view.

We know that the print was made during a time of economic crisis in Rembrandt's life, and it reflects his lifelong interest in biblical themes. Considering the great diversity of religious doctrines of the period, it is possible that his intent was simply to develop an image with mass appeal and make a profit from the sale of this edition. However, considering Rembrandt's waning popularity, it is strange that even for the sake of increased sales, he is unwilling to provide what the buyers were finding in the work of competing printmakers—straightforward, unadorned presentation of the image. Unwilling to compromise, he seems driven to explore the use of light and dark and the solution of personal compositional problems.

"If I be lifted up" is a reoccurring scriptural theme usually associated with the concept of the crucifixion and certainly known to Rembrandt. He seems motivated, if not by that scripture, then by the idea of trying to place the main figures in the center of a horizontal composition and at the same time denying that location by emphasizing the verticality and optically elevating the platform.

search of an organic unity. As we study the two images and consider the three components of a work of art, we can almost hear his critical dialogue that led to the compositional changes.

During the creative process, the initial idea that inspires the work could originate in any of the three components. Once found, it must then be developed in union with the other two components. The work can develop in any order; none is more "correct" than another.

The sense of unity may be difficult to detect in the works of some contemporary artists who blur the components. In their works, the distinctions between subject, form, and content are hazy, "muddied," or lost because these components are sometimes treated as identical. This break with tradition requires a shift of gears in our thinking.

In **Conceptual Art,** for example, the *concept* is foremost (the product is considered negligible) and the *content and subject* seem to be the same thing. The artist using this style often denies the use of common media and form in order to convey a message or analyze an idea (e.g., using combinations of words, photography, and "found" objects of human construction). In **Process Art,** the *act* of producing is the only significant aspect of the work, thus reducing *form and content* to one entity. These two groups of artists are more concerned with their ideas and techniques, respectively, than the "look" of the final product, and although they might consider their work to be intellectually "beautiful," they would probably not use this term. Styles that embrace such goals can be quite puzzling if the aims of the artist are not understood by the viewer

How does the artist know when organic unity is really achieved? It is an intuitive sensation—often in the pit of the stomach—a knowledge that all the pieces fit together instinctively and intellectually. The work is finished—or is it? Having given the best of themselves, art-

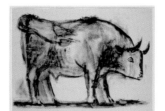
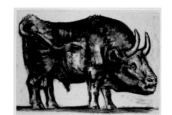
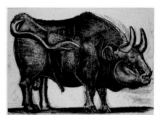
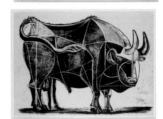
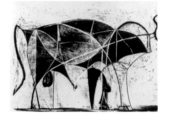
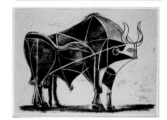
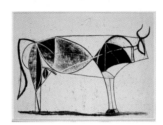
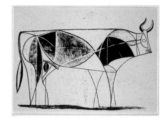
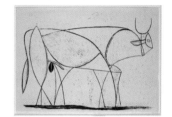
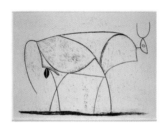
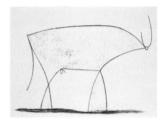

1.18 Pablo Picasso, *Bull*, states I–XI, 1945. Engraving. This illustration shows the progression of abstraction from the first state of the work to the eleventh as Picasso distills his image down to the bare essence of subject. Réunion des Musées Nationaux/Art Resource, NY © 2008 Estate of Pablo Picasso/Artists Rights Society (ARS), New York. Photo: R. G. Ojeda.

ists are often never sure of this. Perhaps the perspective of a few days, months, or even years will give the answer.

ABSTRACTION

Let us study for a moment a process for simplifying and reorganizing information known as **abstraction.** It allows the treatment of subject matter to evolve from a purely descriptive image to one that has no reference to the natural world. For centuries, artists worked at creating representational images for the church or wealthy patrons. Artists' opportunity for self-expression was somewhat limited to what their patrons would support. Eventually, the industrial age, the rise of a well-to-do middle class with a desire for fine things, and the advance of scientific discovery altered the parameters and purpose of the artwork. After the invention of the camera in the nineteenth century, many artists began to feel that they no longer "needed" to record nature with great accuracy (the camera could do that); instead, they felt free to reflect on and interpret their experiences in artistic terms. A new scientific investigation of color theory, which played various colors against each other, further removed the artist from a strictly responsive interpretation of nature. Artists simplified images and rearranged or stripped parts down to better communicate the essentials of what they were experiencing. This process came to be known as abstraction, and as it evolved, artwork became a greater tool for self-expression.

To be sure, all visual artwork requires some degree of abstraction, however minute. The very nature of capturing life in an artist's medium makes the image abstracted from reality. Even the most naturalistic rendering of a butterfly is an image that has been simplified from its three-dimensional existence—and captured on a flat surface. Further abstraction occurs when artists embrace the freedom and expressive qualities of the process and increase the amount of changes to the image. Sometimes the subject remains a recognizable image; sometimes it just becomes a designed pattern or a block of elements that resembles nothing visually experienced. For observers conditioned to expect a literal copying of a physical subject, a greater degree of abstraction makes a work more difficult to understand and appreciate. However, the simplification and rearrangement is intended to make the deeper meaning more accessible, not less profound (fig. 1.18). The degree of abstraction should not deter the viewer from looking more carefully at the artwork. Whether recognizable or not, the subject is just one component; the way it is presented or formed to give it expression is an equally important consideration in the search for meaning (fig. 1.19).

The diagram in figure 1.20 illustrates the evolution of abstraction and shows how the treatment of subject matter developed from a purely descriptive image to one that has no reference to the natural world. (This change will be demonstrated using the work of historical periods in art, but such a progression could also happen over the lifetime of an individual artist or perhaps within the process of developing one work itself.)

In the style known as **Naturalism,** the subject has a physical reference,

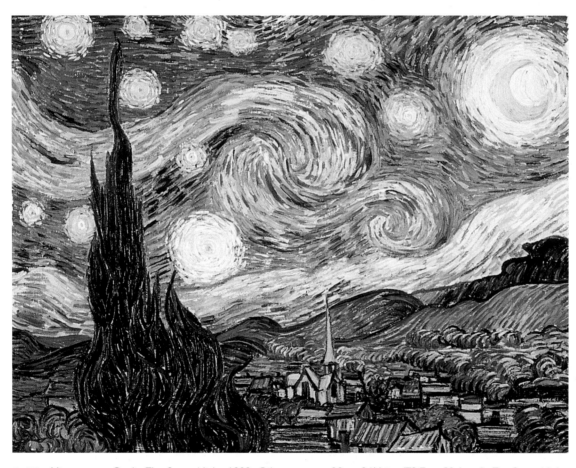

1.19 Vincent van Gogh, *The Starry Night,* 1889. Oil on canvas, 29 × 36¼ in. (73.7 × 92.1 cm). *The Starry Night* was completed near the mental asylum of Saint-Remy, thirteen months before Van Gogh's death at the age of 37. His letters indicate that he wanted to create, from his imagination, a more exciting and comforting nature than one might observe from a single glimpse of reality. He was interested in exaggerated lines—warped as in old woodcuts. The compelling stylization, the staccato-like brushstrokes, the circular and swirling movement of the cosmic members, and the flamelike cypress keep the viewer actively engaged. The Museum of Modern Art, New York. Acquired through the Lillie P. Bliss Bequest (472.1941) The Museum of Modern Art, New York, NY, U.S.A. Digital Image © The Museum of Modern Art/Licensed by SCALA/Art Resource, NY.

The Evolution of Abstraction

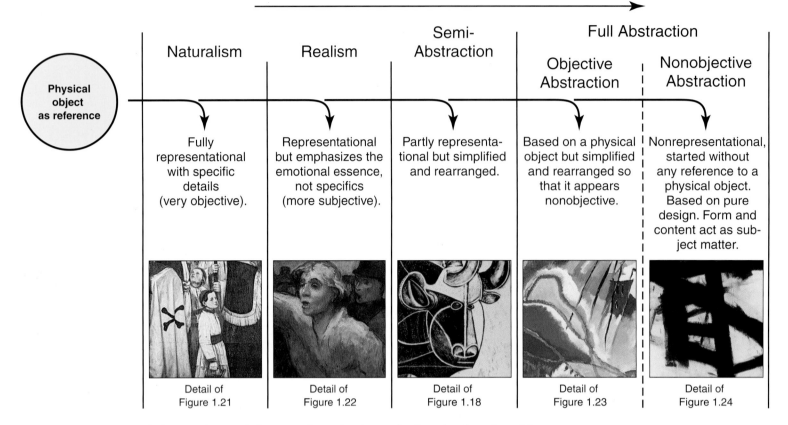

Physical object as reference

Naturalism	Realism	Semi-Abstraction	Full Abstraction	
			Objective Abstraction	Nonobjective Abstraction
Fully representational with specific details (very objective).	Representational but emphasizes the emotional essence, not specifics (more subjective).	Partly representational but simplified and rearranged.	Based on a physical object but simplified and rearranged so that it appears nonobjective.	Nonrepresentational, started without any reference to a physical object. Based on pure design. Form and content act as subject matter.
Detail of Figure 1.21	Detail of Figure 1.22	Detail of Figure 1.18	Detail of Figure 1.23	Detail of Figure 1.24

1.20 Abstraction is a relative term because it is present in varying degrees in all works of art, from full representation to complete nonobjectivity. This diagram briefly illustrates such degrees of abstraction through various historical periods—from the very descriptive to the development of nonobjective abstraction. Such progression could also happen over the lifetime of an individual artist or within the process of developing one work itself.

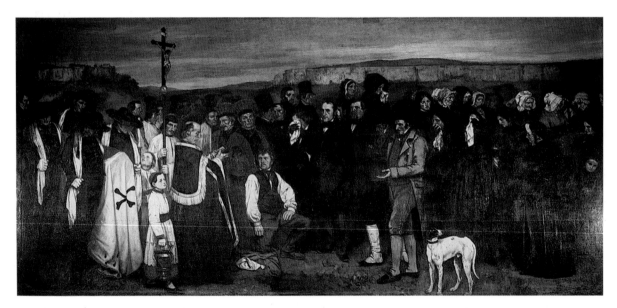

1.21 Gustave Courbet, *Burial at Ornans*, 1849. Oil on canvas, 10 × 22 ft. (3 × 6.7 m). Courbet was the leading early exponent of the naturalist leanings of some Realist painters. Critics harshly condemned him for painting "ugly" pictures of average people at their mundane activities. Collection of the Louvre, Paris. Photo: AKG, Berlin/SuperStock.

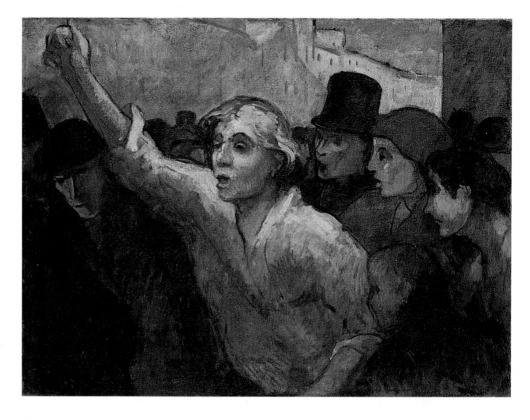

1.22 Honoré Daumier, *The Uprising*, c. 1852–58. Oil on canvas, 34 × 44 in. Influenced by a climate of scientific positivism, the artists of the Realist movement tried to record the world as it appeared to the eye, but they also wished to interpret it so as to record timeless truths. This painting by Daumier shows his broadly realist renderings of a political protest. Acquired 1925/The Phillips Collection, Washington, D.C.

which the artist reproduces as close to optically perceived as possible (fig. 1.21; see also fig. 1.20). The artists that produced this style were very objective in the development of their subject matter, making the image very specific, with no room for personal interpretation. They used a very **descriptive** approach, much like the effect of the camera, stressing precise details and individual characteristics of the objects. Such was the reliance on observable detail for a particular likeness that Gustave Courbet, one of the leading artists of the movement, once said, "Bring me an angel and I will paint you an angel."

The approach became more subjective, or inventive, with the work of Honoré Daumier and those working with **Realism.** With this style, the work is still somewhat representational but not as reliant on specific detail. The subject was simplified or abstracted from what was optically seen, and it was developed to emphasize an emotional response (fig. 1.22; see also fig. 1.20). The Realists would try to present universal meanings rather than specific information—for example, they would paint an image that represents the conditions, the drudgery, and the hardships faced by all women of the period rather than a portrait of a specific woman with her unique traits. A Realist's approach is less responsive and more innovative, uses more experimental brushwork, and sacrifices some specific information to gain universal impressions.

As the work of artists became even more subjective, they began to simplify and rearrange what they had visually experienced to an even greater degree. The image, still somewhat perceivable, was stripped down to expressive and communicative rudiments while reordering and emphasizing those essentials. The image became *semiabstract,* although it was still reliant on an initial object (see figs. 1.18 [the first bull in the second row], 7.32, 8.44, and T.54). The intent was often to make a deeper meaning more accessible, like the **Cubists'** desire to show the surface facets and the superimposed multiple views of an object—even if at the expense of the object's recognizability (see fig. T.51).

As artists continued to search for new ways to express themselves, some discovered the excitement of simply organizing the various elements into nonrecognizable works of complete abstraction. Within this group, two types may be found. In appearance, they are often indistinguishable unless the intent of the artist is known. The first type, *objective abstraction,* occurs when artists base their work on a physical object, but during the working process, the finished image becomes so abstracted that it no longer resembles or even appears to represent the initial reference (fig. 1.23; see also fig. 1.20). For these artists, the effect is not always foreseen while the work is in progress.

For those working with the second type, *nonobjective abstraction,* the image starts out as a nonrepresentational statement that is purely invented, having no physical reference to anything experienced visually (fig. 1.24; see also figs. 1.20, 1.55, and 7.25). Sometimes a

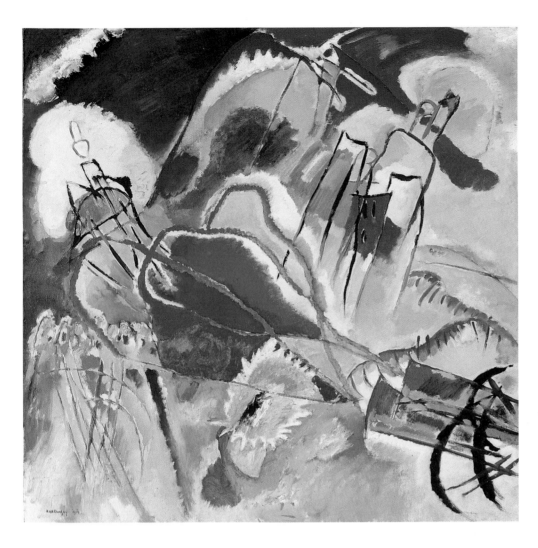

About 1910, the Russian Wassily Kandinsky began to paint freely moving biomorphic shapes in rich combinations of hues. His characteristic early style can be seen in this illustration. Such an abstract form of expression was an attempt to show the artist's feelings about object surfaces rather than to describe their outward appearances.

The artist was more interested in the actual physical action involved in this type of expression than in the character of the resulting painting.

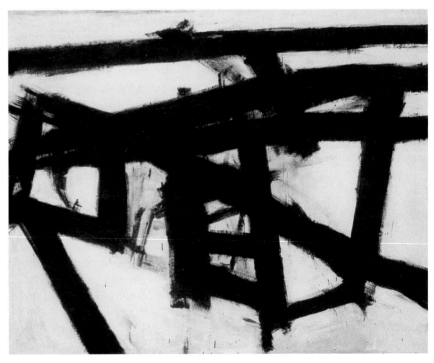

work suggests a meaning to the artist as it evolves; sometimes the meaning is purely the pleasure of working with the elements and the expression of the artist's personal feeling or emotion. For both types of abstraction, observers must interpret content from only the artist's use of media, techniques, elements, and principles of organization.

EXPANDING PERSONAL AWARENESS

When an artist views an object—a tree branch, for example—and is inspired to reproduce the original as seen, he or she is using and drawing inspiration from **optical perception.** The artist who reproduces only what he or she perceives in the "real world" is thought of as a "perceptual" artist. However, some artists see the tree branch but envision a crying child or rearing horse. When the imagination triggers this creative vision and suggests additional images, the artists are employing **conceptual perception.** Artists who are inspired by imaginative concepts are called "conceptual" artists. Leonardo da Vinci, writing in his *Treatise on Painting,* recorded an experience with conceptual perception while studying clouds. "On one occasion above Milan, over in the direction of Lake Maggiore, I saw a cloud shaped like a huge mountain made up of banks of fire. . . ." Elsewhere, he recommends staring at stains on walls as a source of inspiration. Following Leonardo, author and painter Victor Hugo found many of his ideas for drawings by studying coffee stains on tablecloths.

By attempting to see the uniqueness in everything around us, we can expand our sensitivity and response to art. The author Gertrude Stein wrote, "A rose is a rose is a rose." A literal interpretation would lead us to expect all roses to be identical, but we know that every rose has a different character, even with identical breeding and grooming. Every object is ultimately unique, be it a chair, a tree, or a person. One of the major characteristics that sets the artist apart is the ability to see (and experience) the subtle differences in things. By exposing those differences, the artist can make the ordinary seem distinctive, the humdrum exciting (fig. 1.25).

1.25 Patricia Nix, *La Primavera,* 1992–94. Mixed media on canvas, 72 × 80 in. Patricia Nix's *La Primavera* presents roses as a repeated theme, but subtle differences in texture, color, and treatment keep them fresh and unique. From the collection of Ivan Blinoff, London. Courtesy of the artist.

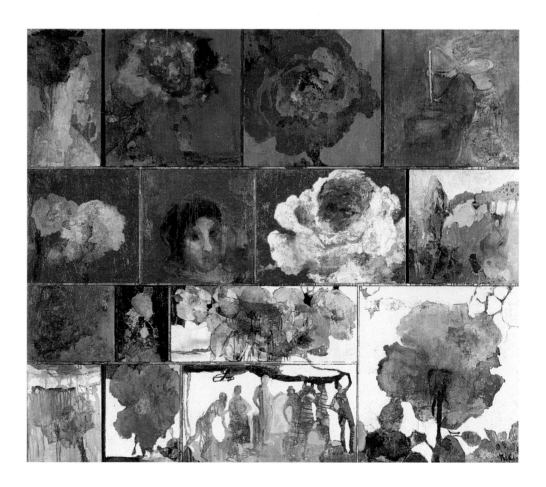

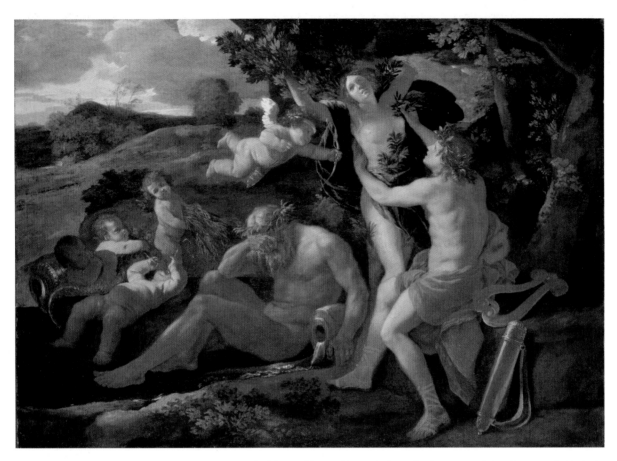

1.26 Nicolas Poussin, *Apollo and Daphne*, 1627, 97 × 131 cm. This painting tells the story of Apollo, a mythological deity. While walking on Mount Olympus, he spotted a beautiful nymph named Daphne. Smitten, he pursued her until she cried out for help to her father Peneus, the river god. As Apollo reached out, her feet turned to roots, her hands were covered with leaves, and her body became the trunk of a laurel tree. As a memento of his lost love, Apollo fashioned a laurel wreath—later given as the highest prize at competitions all over Greece. Alte Pinakothek © ARTOTHEK.

All art is illusory to some extent, and some artwork is more successful than others at drawing us out of our standard existence into a more meaningful state. Frames, galleries, stages, exaggerated costumes or makeup, and so on all serve to set the artwork apart from the everyday world. This "aesthetic distance" helps the audience focus on the ideas presented and seems to transport them beyond the mundane, into a hypersensitized world of greater values. Thus, in art, the "real" can supersede mere optics; artwork does often involve things seen but, more importantly, includes our reactions to those things.

Our ability to respond to artwork depends on maintaining an open mind. By ridding ourselves of the expectation that all forms of art should follow the same rules or have the same qualities, we can appreciate more of what we see (and be less restricted when developing ideas for our own pieces). For example, some people expect art to tell a story in a descriptive manner (fig. 1.26). Many fine works contain elements of storytelling, but not all artists have a need or an obligation to narrate. In addition, we know that many people judge a work of art by how closely it looks like something. It is true that skillful **plastic** and **graphic** artists can create amazing resemblances, but even the best perceptual artists try to incorporate more into the work than replication alone. Most artists feel that considerations of form are equally important to the outcome of the work, and therefore, making a "like-ness" is not the only key to art. Many of the best photographers are not content to simply point and shoot, although the camera can capture the world with great accuracy; instead, they look for the best compositional view (angle and framing), create or wait for the right lighting conditions, use filters, alter the depth of field, or make adjustments in developing (fig. 1.27).

When the artist reaches below the surface appearances and uses unfamiliar ways to find unexpected truths, the results can often be distressing. Such distress frequently follows exposure to a new art experience. Under these conditions, the artist may be accused of being incompetent or a charlatan. Much of what we value in art today was once decried in this way. General acceptance

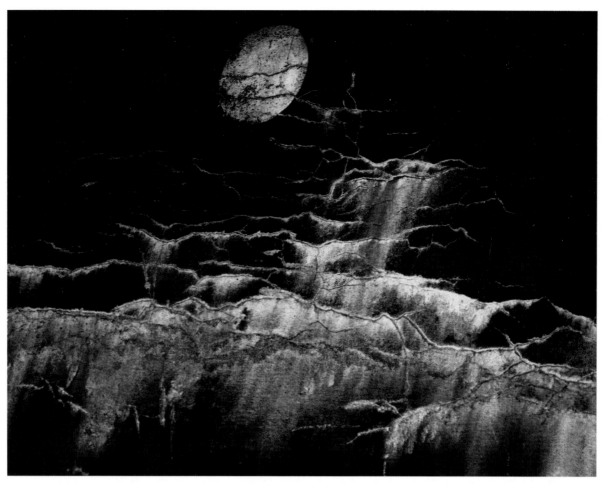

1.27 Minor White, *Moon & Wall Encrustations,* 1964. Gelatin silver print. Photographers may have the edge on other visual artists when it comes to recording objective reality, but many photographer-artists are not satisfied with obvious appearances and use complex technical strategies to structure or enhance the final image. Minor White Archive, Princeton University. Bequest of Minor White. (MWA64-6). Reproduced with permission of the Minor White Archive, Princeton University Art Museum. © Trustees of Princeton University.

of the new comes about only when enough time has passed for it to be re-evaluated. Then, the new begins to lose its abrasiveness. Thus, there is no need for embarrassment at feeling confused or defiant about an artwork that seems "far out"; instead, we need to strive for continued exposure, thought, and study (fig. 1.28).

Much of the public, for example, is curious about **installations.** By creating or altering an interior or exterior setting with various media, the artist's intention is to heighten the viewer's awareness of the environmental space—to see and think of that space in a new way (fig. 1.29). The work is usually,

but not always, nonfigurative and ranges from the relatively small to the enormous in scale. Some materials that have been used include sheet metal, fiberglass, wood, bronze, steel, plastic, plaster, stone, lasers, sound, and computer-controlled projection. Actually, any available materials are eligible, including mixed media. If placed outdoors, an installation may be simple (but frequently quite large) and often sits in an easily viewable civic location. When set in an interior location, most frequently in a gallery, installations are often composed of multiple pieces, sometimes flooding the floors and/or walls. The positioning of the pieces may

be simple but dominating or even seemingly haphazardly spread out.

Observers react in different ways—some excited, others perplexed, some having their vision altered, and others delaying judgment. In the recent past, some installations have been accused by the populace of being inconsequential, dehumanized, or irrational, and some have even provoked violent reactions. This is not surprising, as the installation is a relatively new art form, and unusual styles of art have many times produced a general outcry. Richard Serra, a veteran of installations that are generally minimalist in nature, has had some of his work dismantled or defaced;

THE GATES, PROJECT FOR CENTRAL PARK, NEW YORK

Christo's and Jeanne-Claude's Plans for Their Temporary Work of Art (1979–2005)

Artistic Statement

For those who walked through *The Gates*, following the walkways, the saffron-colored fabric was a golden ceiling creating warm shadows. When seen from the buildings surrounding Central Park, *The Gates* seemed like a golden river appearing and disappearing through the bare branches of the trees and highlighting the shape of the meandering footpaths.

The sixteen-day-duration work of art was free to all, and will be remembered as a joyous experience for every New Yorker as a democratic expression that Olmsted invoked when he conceived a "central" park. The luminous moving fabric underlined the organic design of the park, while the rectangular poles were a reminder of the geometric grid pattern of the city blocks around the park. *The Gates* harmonized with the beauty of Central Park. The work of art remained for sixteen days; then the gates were removed and the materials industrially recycled.

The Gates

Number of gates: 7,500
Height of gates: 16 feet
Width of gates: varying from 5 ft. 6 in. to 18 ft.
Placement: following the edges of walkways, perpendicular to the selected 23 miles of footpaths
Spacing of the gates: 10- to 15-ft. intervals

Materials (Recycled)

Steel: 5,290 U.S. tons of steel
Vinyl tube 5 in. × 5 in.: 315,491 linear ft.
Cast aluminum reinforcements: 15,000
Steel leveling plates: 15,000
Bolts and self-locking nuts: 165,000
Vinyl leveling plate covers: 15,064
Nylon thread: woven into 1,092,200 square ft. of fabric and sewn into 7,500 fabric panels (46 miles of hems)

Work Force

Employment: hundreds of NYC residents for manufacturing and assembling the gate structures, installation workers, maintenance teams in uniform with radios working around the clock

As Christo and Jeanne-Claude have always done for their previous projects, *The Gates* was entirely financed by the artists through C.V.J. Corp. (Jeanne-Claude Javacheff, President) with the sale of studies, preparatory drawings and collages, scale models, earlier works of the fifties and sixties, and original lithographs on other subjects. The artists do not accept sponsorship of any kind.

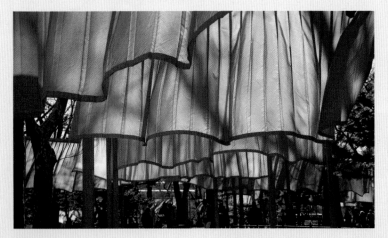

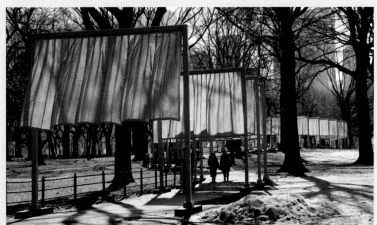

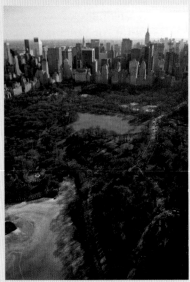

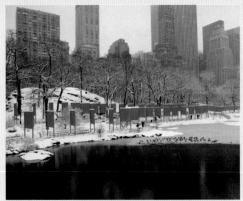

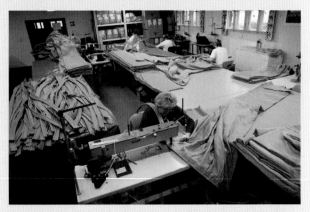

1.28 **Christo and Jeanne-Claude,** *The Gates,* **project for Central Park, New York, 1979–2005.** *The Gates* represents the culmination of years of planning and hard work, spent not only in designing and organizing but also in securing the legal arrangements necessary for such a large and integrated work of art to be installed in only five days and unfurled on the same day. The photos show the saffron-colored gates installed and their earlier fabrication. © Christo and Jeanne-Claude 2005. Photographs: Wolfgang Volz/laif/Redux.

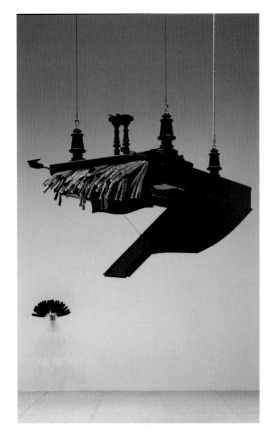

1.29 Rebecca Horn, *Concert for Anarchy,* Berlin 1994. Grand piano and mixed media, variable dimensions. Horn's use of a piano in defiance of gravity makes the space within her installation an intimidating and overwhelming three-dimensional setting. Photograph by Attilio Marazano. © Rebecca Horn. All rights reserved. © 2008 Artists Rights Society (ARS), New York/VG Bild-Kunst, Bonn.

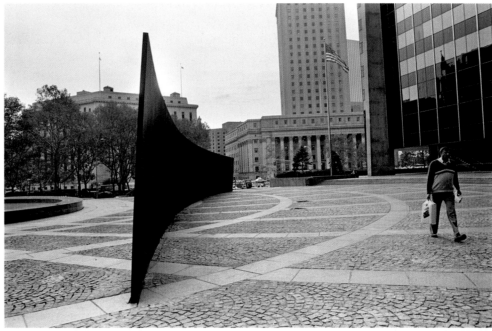

1.30 Richard Serra, *Tilted Arc,* 1981. Cor-Ten steel (73 tons), 120 ft. long × 12 ft. high with 12/1 ft. slope toward the Federal Building. This site-specific installation was erected in Federal Plaza in New York City, commissioned by the Arts-in-Architecture program of the U.S. General Services Administration. It split the space of the Federal Plaza in half, forcing onlookers to become more aware of their own movements through the space. Unfortunately, it was not appreciated by many workers at the plaza, who complained that it interfered with the public use of the space, restricted views and access to government buildings, promoted crime, and attracted litter and rats. Many felt that "public sculpture" should be more inviting, regardless of the artist's right to create. After eight years of controversy, the sculpture was dismantled and destroyed. © 1985 David Aschkenas.

his *Tilted Arc* was removed as the result of protests (fig. 1.30). In return, these protestations have drawn the wrath of many artists who feel, as artists always have, that art should be given free rein, because art forms that have produced widespread criticism in the past have become accepted with the passage of time.

Despite the ridicule sometimes visited on them, installations are now firmly fixed on the art scene. There is little doubt that they enhance viewer involvement and produce a different outlook on the spaces in which they are placed. Some significant artists in this area are Ann Hamilton (see fig. 8.50), whose work is generally sensuous; Sandy Skoglund (fig. 1.31), who sets up dreamlike environments; Rebecca Horn (see fig. 1.29), whose work is presented in surreal architectural settings; Patrick Dougherty, who twists and tilts cut branches into towering walk-through works (see fig. 6.21); and Jennifer Steinkamp (see fig. 7.4), who creates interactive video/sound/space installations. These works sometimes require a great deal of laborious effort—no doubt, to their creators, a labor of love—and if these artists make us think of an environment in a new way, they have succeeded.

We all have the capacity to appreciate the beautiful or expressive, as evidenced by the aesthetic choices we make every day. But we must enlarge our sensitivity and taste, making them more inclusive. This may mean accepting the possibility that what is unfamiliar or disliked may not necessarily be poorly executed or devoid of meaning. However, the quality of art is always subjective and questionable. Even with training, people's tastes, like Stein's roses, do not turn out to be identical. Perhaps the most reliable proof of quality comes only with time and the eventual consensus of sensitive people.

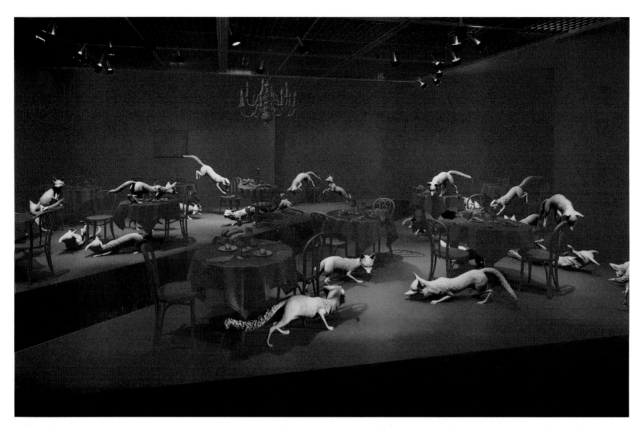

1.31 Sandy Skoglund, *Fox Games,* 1990. Polyester resin sculptures, tables, chairs, painted tableware, painted bread, chandelier, cloth napkins, and tablecloths, approx. 30 × 30 × 12 ft. high. In this installation, Sandy Skoglund presents a personal environment of red tables and gray foxes, which confronts the viewers, causing them to see the spatial setting in a new way. This version was installed at the Denver At Museum in Colorado in June of 1990. Denver Art Museum Collection, 1991.36. Photograph by Bill O'Connor. © Denver Art Museum. Sandy Skoglund, FOX GAMES © 1989.

DEVELOPING IDEAS

Creativity emanates from ideas. For the artist, a creative idea may be an all-encompassing plan, a unique set of relationships, an attitude to be conveyed, or a solution to a visual problem. An idea may come as a "bolt from the blue," or it may be the end product of much thoughtful effort, as reflected in notes, sketches, and repeated overhauls of the artwork.

All creative enterprises are occasionally plagued by idea blocks, but they seem to afflict the fledgling artist most often. For the beginner, the initial idea for artwork is sometimes conceived at a rather pedestrian level, being equated with subject matter ("I don't know *what* to do!"). Although a familiar object or experience is usually the best starting point in such situations, the following approaches, suggested by artists, are ways to develop ideas or overcome the creative block. You may wish to expand the list.

Look for stimulating ideas around you. Take a bus ride across town, or visit a restaurant and observe how people relate to each other. Study the life and heartbeat of your city or town. Look closely at nature—notice shapes, values, textures, and patterns. Remember the flattened frog skeleton you spotted on the way out of the parking lot—could it be used as a symbol for a special theme? Supplement an impulse by brainstorming anything remotely related. Doodle or experiment with any available media.

Think of a pressing social issue. Make lists of all the verbs, adverbs, or adjectives that could be associated with that issue, and add color notations associated with each term. Write down a single sentence or phrase that catches your attention during a news report, poetry reading, or argument with a friend. You should note as many variations on the idea or its presentation as possible; include *visual metaphors*—ways of expressing the idea without actually depicting it directly. And, as with any good debate team, try to express an opposing concept, feeling, or setting in terms of image, color, and emotional character. In short: observe, explore, and expand. Generate as many ideas as you can—the last few may be the best.

Existing artwork can also serve as a stimulus for ideas. Try to imagine what another artist's work was trying to develop. Think about the concept or the "problem" that was being solved visually, and think about how the artist's form choices reinforced the content. It doesn't matter if you correctly pinpoint the original artist's problem or not. You can try to apply the same concept to your own subject matter. Or create a new direction to explore by altering the problem or combining several problems. Maybe you will even discover an aspect that the original artist has failed to address, and you can attempt to solve it in your own way. See how many different solutions you can develop for the same problem.

Unfortunately, the artist's block sometimes occurs right in the middle of creating the image. Some artists, when they can't quite build the bridges between nearly finished areas, feel that they must sacrifice an acceptable portion of the work in order to find the freedom to continue with the development of the remaining image. Before doing this, maintain an ongoing dialogue with yourself. Do whatever it takes to see your work with fresh eyes or from a new vantage point. Try looking at the work in a mirror, holding up your hands and blocking out portions to see sections in isolation, squinting, or turning the image upside down. Often, troublesome areas stand out when you can see them in a new way.

While most studio artists generate their own ideas, the majority of artists in commercial industries are given an initial concept. Graphic designers, product designers, architects who have client demands, or even artists working on specific commissions, are required to use a predetermined subject or content. For them, the search for ideas does not end after being given the initial goal. Quite the contrary—it is just the beginning. To expand and develop the idea, they may need to consider all the variables of the **design** of the product; study the competition; identify the age demograph-

ics to which the item must appeal; find typeface, color schemes, and layouts that reinforce most effectively the appeal to that demographic; run sample market studies of concept, design, and color; and lay out multiple strategies for reaching their potential audience and making their product irresistible. New and exciting ideas that challenge the established paradigms for each step along the process are the backbone of a successful campaign. This search for ideas can be very logical, almost scientific, and can be used in both commercial and studio application.

CRITICAL THINKING AND ANALYSIS

At some point in the creative process (or in truth, at many points), there will come a need for analysis and evaluation. Critical-thinking skills will play a vital role in achieving a unified and successful work. Whether formal or informal, this review process, also known as a critique, identifies what works well and helps to find constructive ways to improve troublesome areas in the work.

Critiques are not restricted to any discipline and may occur in either individual or group settings. For example, after a full day's production of coffee mugs, studio potters will often pick out their five best pieces, analyze them, and try to discover those special qualities that make those five jump out as the best of the group. The same thing could be done comparing preliminary sketches for a work or studying appealing masterpieces. It is important to remember that "to critique" does not mean "to blame." Analysis and evaluation of work is not about faulting the artist for "mistakes." Unfortunately, many beginning artists let the fear of making errors prevent them from creating anything at all. Don't stop before you start.

When applied to ongoing work, critiques can happen at any point and

can be repeated until the idea and creation are fine-tuned. These times of reflection and critique will become easier and more beneficial as you study and become more familiar with the vocabulary, principles, and elements of art. If possible, participate in class critiques and/or discussions—or at least, maintain an internal dialogue. The benefits are twofold: you will learn to identify and articulate visual or conceptual problems in a work, and the experiences will become a resource for ideas. When a previously analyzed problem occurs later in your work, the solution for the stumbling block will present itself much sooner and may even be applied subconsciously.

How does one begin a critique? Unfortunately, there are no formulas. You may want to identify the three components of the work (subject, form, and content), evaluate them separately, and then examine how they work together as a whole. Analysis may seem awkward in the beginning, but asking some of the following questions may help.

- What areas feel most successful and why?
- What areas feel incomplete or troublesome, and what is the cause?
- How is the subject presented?
- Are there visual or symbolic metaphors that could have helped expand the image?
- If the image is nonobjective, what suggests the meaning?
- How are the elements used to support or destroy the image compositionally (e.g., color choices, line quality, etc.)?
- Have the principles of organization been observed (e.g., harmony versus variety, balance, etc.)?
- What is the intention behind the work?
- What is being communicated—a feeling, an idea, a personal aesthetic?
- Is it too esoteric?
- Is it too obvious?

- Where does the work succeed in integrating these components, and where is it less successful?

You may want to begin with your own feeling about each issue but then ask yourself what sets up that response and how it could be altered—are there other interpretations, viewpoints, or relationships that could have been presented? As you become more skilled at analysis, you may find it becomes less necessary to *consciously* explore a list of questions. The most relevant may simply rise to the subconscious.

BASIC CONCEPTS OF TWO-DIMENSIONAL ART

Artists who work with two-dimensional art generally begin with a flat surface. The flat surface is the **picture plane** on which artists execute their pictorial im-ages. A piece of paper, a canvas, a board, or a copper plate may be representative of the picture plane. This flat surface may also represent an imaginary plane of reference on which an artist can create spatial illusions.

For example, the raw elements can be manipulated to produce either a **two-dimensional** effect (having the dimensions of height and width—like a circle, triangle, or square) or a **three-dimensional** effect (having the dimensions of height, width, and the illusion of depth—like a sphere, pyramid, or cube). In a two-dimensional work, the elements and image seem to lie flat on the picture plane, but when the elements are three-dimensional, penetration of that **plane** is implied (fig. 1.32A).

When the elements cling rather closely to the artistic surface (picture plane) and do not leap toward or away from us dramatically in the format, we can say they are **decorative.** Although this term can also refer to ornamentation, here it refers to a spatial condition. When elements are of this nature, collectively we can say that the **space** created by them is decorative—relatively flat or shallow.

However, when the images or elements appear to exist in front of or behind the picture plane and we feel that we could dive into the picture and weave our way around and behind the art elements, the space is said to be plastic. Whether working with decorative or plastic space, the picture plane is used as a basis for establishing both two- and three-dimensional pictorial space.

Although graphic artists may create plastic space, they are not necessarily plastic artists. Graphic artwork (drawing, painting, printmaking, photography, etc.) generally exists on a flat surface and relies on the *illusion* of the third dimension. The products of the plastic arts (sculpture, ceramics, architecture, etc.), on the other hand, have tangible mass and occupy *actual* space. With three-dimensional works of art, the artist begins with the material—metal, clay,

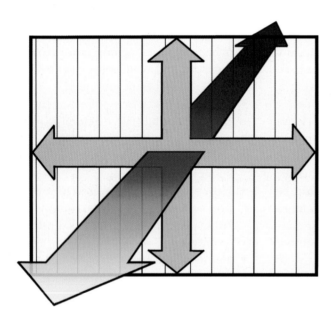

1.32A **The picture plane.** Movement can take place on a flat surface, as indicated by the vertical and horizontal light-blue arrows. The vertical black lines represent an imaginary plane through which a picture is seen. The artist can also give the illusion of advancing and receding movement in space, as shown by the large yellow-to-dark-blue arrow.

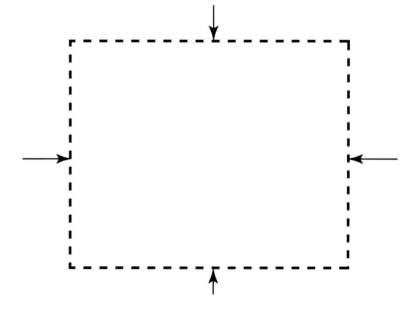

1.32B **The picture frame.** The picture frame represents the outermost limits, or boundaries, of the picture plane. These limits, indicated here by a broken line, represent the edges of the canvas or paper on which the artist works. The size and direction of the pictorial frame is one of the first considerations made in the composition of the work and is sometimes indicated by a drawn margin in preparatory sketches.

stone, glass, and so on—rather than with the picture plane, and works it as a total form against the surrounding space, without the limitations of the flat surface.

The defined boundary around the working area (or picture plane) is generally called the **picture frame** (fig. 1.32B). The picture frame should be clearly established before beginning the composition. Once its shape and proportion are defined, all of the art elements and their employment will be influenced by it. The problem for the pictorial artist is to organize the elements of art within the picture frame, on the picture plane.

The proportions and shapes of frames used by artists are varied. Squares, triangles, circles, and ovals have been used as frame shapes, but the most popular is the rectangle, which in its varying proportions offers the artist an interesting variety within the two-dimensional space (figs. 1.33, 1.34, 1.35). Many artists select the outside proportions of their pictures on the basis of geometric

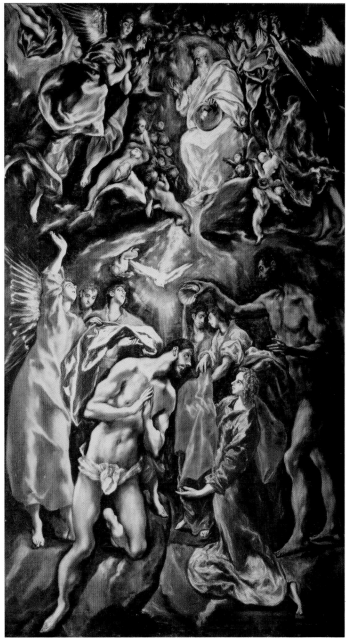

1.34   El Greco, *Baptism of Christ*, 1608–14. Oil on panel, 330 × 211 cm. The rectangular frame shape, by its proportions, emphasizes the verticality and creates an earthly and a heavenly plane. El Greco has elongated his figures and shapes to repeat and harmonize with the vertical character of the picture frame. The use of bright color and the zigzagging diagonals help tie the heavenly and earthly realms together. Hospital de Tavera, Toledo, Spain/The Bridgeman Art Library.

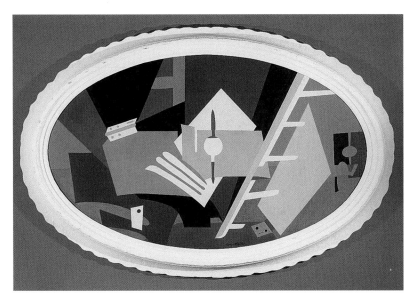

1.33   Esphyr Slobodkina, *Composition in an Oval*, c. 1953. Oil on gesso board, 32½ × 61½ in. (82.5 × 156.2 cm). Slobodkina has used an unusual frame shape to emphasize an angular abstract painting. Now used less frequently, such frame shapes were employed more often in the past with traditional religious subjects. Grey Art Gallery. New York University Art Collection. Gift of Mr. and Mrs. Irving Walsey, 1962.

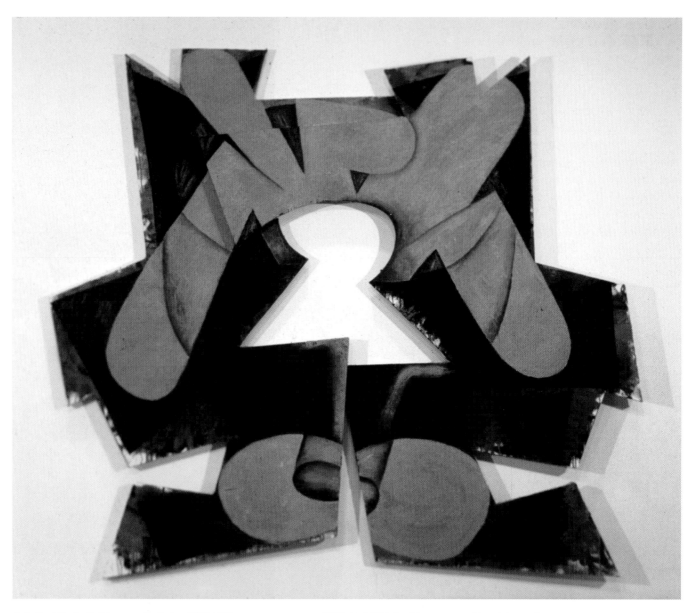

1.35 Elizabeth Murray, *Keyhole*, 1982. Oil on two canvases, 99½ × 110½ in. Murray uses the picture plane as physical space. The shapes that make up the picture plane contribute movement and a 3-D element to her paintings. This potentially chaotic aspect of her work is kept under control by the flattened, abstracted shapes that she uses in her imagery. © Elizabeth Murray, Courtesy PaceWildenstein, New York; Courtesy Paula Cooper Gallery, New York; Courtesy the Collection of Agnes Gund.

ratios (see the "Proportion" section in Chapter 2). These rules suggest selecting lengths and widths of odd proportions (such as 2:3 or 3:5) rather than equal relationships. The results are visually pleasing spatial arrangements. Most artists, however, rely on their instincts rather than on a mechanical formula. After the picture plane has been established, the direction and movement of the elements of art should be in harmonious relation to this shape. Otherwise, they will tend to disrupt the goal of pictorial unity.

Those areas that are occupied by the objective or nonobjective images are called **positive areas**. Unoccupied spaces are termed **negative areas** (fig. 1.36A and B). Negative areas might be considered as those portions of the picture plane that remain after the positive areas have been positioned (fig. 1.37). Although the positive areas may seem tangible and more explicitly laid down, the negative areas are just as important to total picture **unity.** The concept of positive and negative is important for beginners investigating art organization,

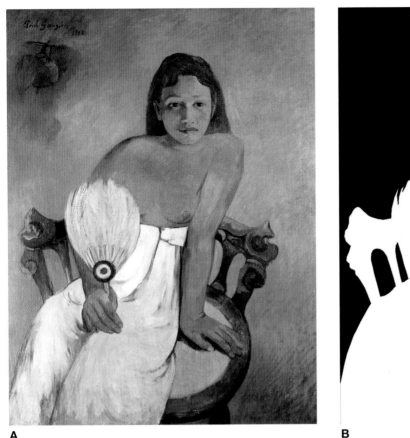

A

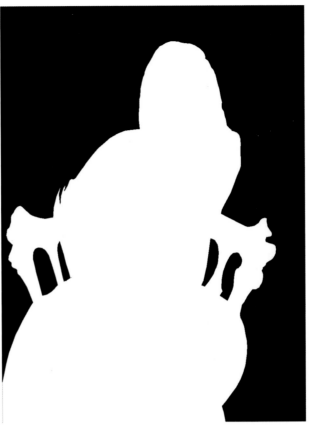

B

1.36 Paul Gaugin, *Girl with a Fan,* 1902. Oil on canvas. The subject in figure A represents a positive shape that has been enhanced by careful consideration of the negative area, or the surrounding space. In figure B, the dark areas indicate the negative shapes, and the white area designates the location of the positive image. Museum Folkwang, Essen, Germany/The Bridgeman Art Library.

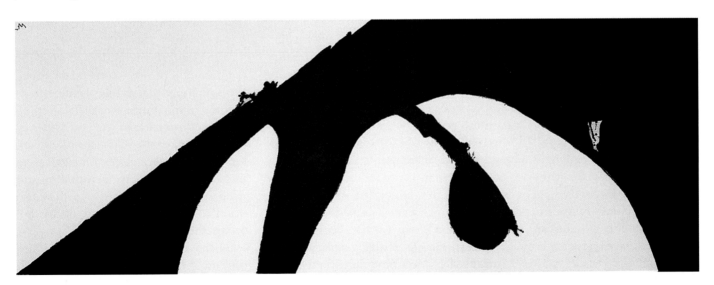

1.37 Robert Motherwell, *Africa,* 1965. Acrylic on Belgian linen, 81 × 222½ in. In this nonfigurative or nonobjective work, some areas have been painted and others not. It is very simple, perhaps deceptively so. To the viewer, the darks seem to be the positive shapes, although after some looking, the effect may be reversed. The Baltimore Museum of Art. Gift of the Artist. BMA 1965.012.
© Dedalus Foundation, Inc./Licensed by VAGA, New York, NY.

because they usually direct their attention to positive images and fail to consider the surrounding negative areas. As a result, their pictures may seem boring, overcrowded, busy, and/or confusing. Composing with both the positive and negative areas will help alleviate these problems.

Traditionally, the *figure* and *foreground* positions were considered positive, while the *background* areas were considered negative. The term *figure* probably came from the human form, which was used as a major subject in artwork and implied a spatial relationship, with the figure occupying the position in front of the remaining background (see fig. 1.36A and B). Recently, abstract painters have adopted the terms *field* to mean positive and *ground* to mean negative. For example, they speak of a color field on a white ground and a field of shapes against a ground of contrasting value (see figs. 2.59 and 7.25).

TWO-DIMENSIONAL MEDIA AND TECHNIQUES

Each art **medium** (materials and tools), along with the **technique** used to control or shape it, has intrinsically unique characteristics that affect the feeling of the work. Many artists select their media and tools because of those very nuances—for example, a photograph has a different look than a woodcut, and a brush makes a different type of line or mark than an ink pen. Depending on what the artist wants to communicate, the choice of material and technique can fantastically enhance the expression of the work.

Artists also derive much stimulation from their interaction with the media and the various techniques. Painters are attracted by the smell and feel of fresh plaster resisting the brush in fresco and

secco painting. Oils and watercolors provide a different tactile excitement from gouache and tempera, as do wet or dry surfaces. For the draughtsman, the difference between a heavy pressure and a light touch can be just as compelling as the textural quality of the drawing surface. Graphite, charcoal, colored pencils, pastels, or chalk can all be blended, erased, or used aggressively (fig. 1.38). Inks, whether applied by brush, crow quill, speedball steel point, sharpened bamboo stick, or cardboard, can be exciting because of how they react to dry or dampened surfaces. For printmakers, watching the physical surface change is intriguing: in lithography, the drawing comes to life on the stone or plate as water magically resists the application of ink (see fig. 1.14); intaglio plates are etched in acid until the topography reveals the image below the plate's surface (see fig. 3.15); in woodcuts and wood engraving, the resistance of the wood provides a unique texture (see fig. 3.18); stencil or serigraphic images can be flat in decorative color and surface quality or dissolve into transparency and overlapping texture (see fig. 4.1). The examples are endless.

Over the years, many of the media and techniques have developed into standard fare. However, artists are not restricted to such materials or uses. With advances in technology, a deluge of new processes and materials have become available for experimentation and development. Some are extensions of traditional approaches, while others, like digital-generated imagery, are without precedent. The photographic innovations of such artists as Edward Steichen, Alfred Stieglitz, and Ansel Adams (fig. 1.39) have led to creative filmmaking, videos, xerography, and the artistic employment of other photographically related media. Very often, the traditional and nontraditional are intermixed, especially in multidisci-

plinary works. Regardless of refinement or simplicity, all innovations have broadened the artist's vision.

BASIC CONCEPTS OF THREE-DIMENSIONAL ART

In the two-dimensional graphic arts (drawing, painting, photography, printmaking, graphic design, etc.), images generally have two dimensions (height and width), exist on a flat surface, and can generate the *illusion* of space. In the three-dimensional arts, the added dimension is that of *actual* depth. This depth usually allows multiple positions and/or views for the observer and increases the physical impact of the work. Because actual depth is fundamental to 3-D art, one must be in the presence of the artwork to fully appreciate it. In this text, photographic reproductions are the most convenient means of conveying the 3-D experience, but words and graphic representations of 3-D art are not substitutes for actual sensory experience. The reader is therefore strongly encouraged to put actual observation into practice.

Subject, form, and content—the components of art—function in much the same manner in the plastic arts as they do in the graphic arts. The emphasis placed on each of the components, however, may vary. For example, sculptors use the components for expressive purposes; architects, ceramists, and metalsmiths, while expressive, may also interpret form for the sake of utility and ornamentation.

Formal organization is more complex in three-dimensional art than in the graphic arts. Materials, developed in actual space through physical manipulation, exist in a tactile as well as visual sense. The resulting complexities expand the content or meaning of the

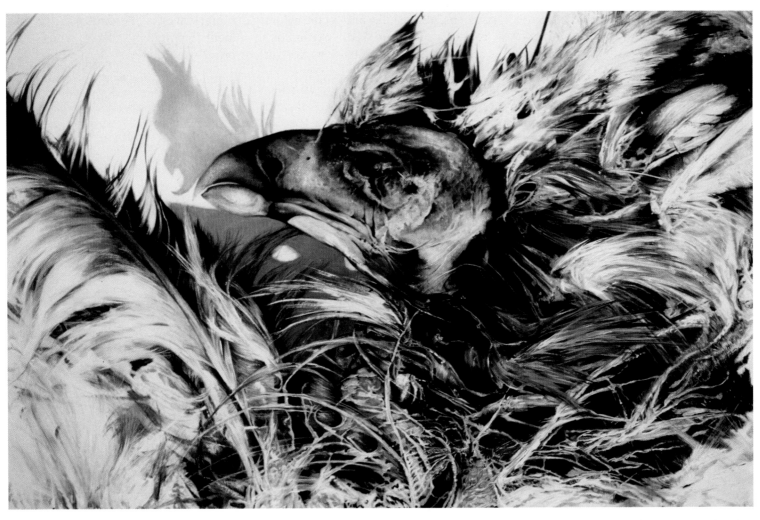

1.38 Thomas Hilty and Tamara Monk, *Phoenix,* 2006. Graphite, pencil, and acrylic, 36 × 48 in. (91.4 × 121.9 cm). This mixed-media work shows the collaborative effort of two artists. They have skillfully blended the applications of graphite, pencil, and acrylic to produce the expressive and texturally varied surfaces. Courtesy of the artists.

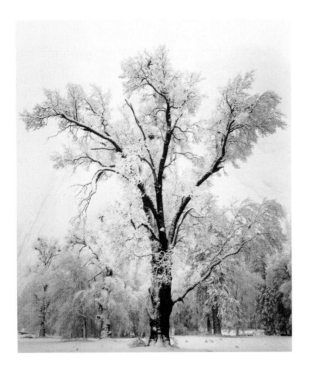

1.39 Ansel Adams, *Oak Tree, Snowstorm, Yosemite National Park, California,* 1948. Gelatin silver print. The invention and development of photography added an important new medium to the repertoire of artists. The accomplishments of such photographers as Ansel Adams rank with those of well-known painters, sculptors, and architects. Collection Center for Creative Photography, University of Arizona © The Ansel Adams Publishing Rights Trust.

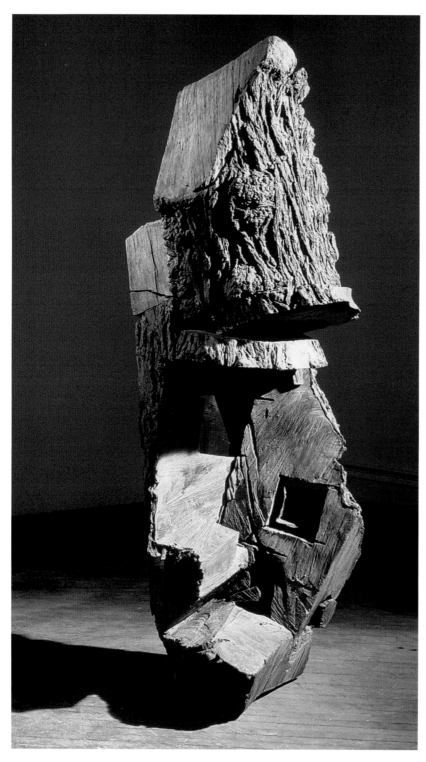

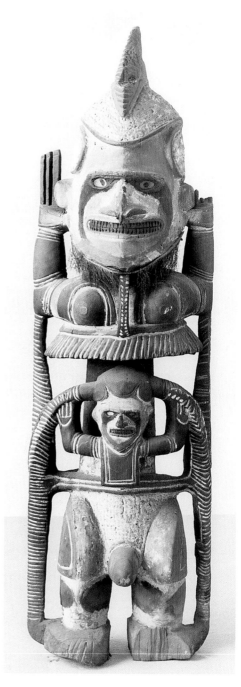

1.41 Uli figure, New Zealand. Painted wood, 59 in. (152 cm) high. To illustrate the different meanings of the term *form*, we may say that the forms in this piece of sculpture are the open and solid individual shapes, or that the form of the work consists of the total assembly of those individual parts. Hamburgisches Museum für Völkerkunde.

1.40 Mel Kendrick, *Bronze with Two Squares*, 1989–90. Bronze (edition of three), 73 × 28 × 28 in. (185.4 × 71.1 × 71.1 cm). Meant to be experienced visually and tactilely, this sculpture is deceiving because it looks like wood but was created by manipulation and cast in bronze. The sculptor has to know his or her materials well to create this kind of trompe l'oeil effect. Courtesy of the artist.

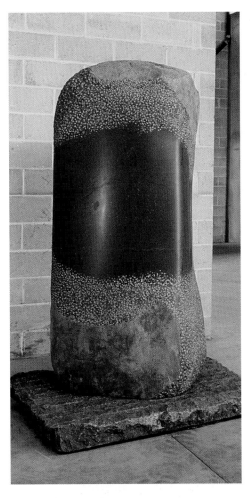

1.42 Isamu Noguchi, *The Stone Within*, 1982. Basalt, 75 × 38 × 27 in. (190.5 × 96.5 × 68.6 cm). The sculptor Noguchi has subtracted just enough stone in this work to introduce his concept of minimal form while preserving the integrity of the material and its heavy, weighty mass. © 2008 The Isamu Noguchi Foundation and Garden Museum, New York/Artists Rights Society (ARS), New York.

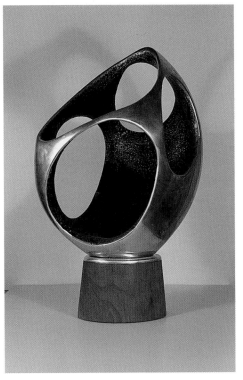

1.43 John W. Goforth, *Untitled*, 1971. Cast aluminum, 15¾ in. (40 cm) high with base. The volume incorporates the space, both solid and empty, that is occupied by the work. Collection of Otto Ocvirk. Courtesy of Carolyn Goforth.

form (fig. 1.40). It is important to note the difference between the definition of *form* as "organizing or organization" (as previously defined) and its common usage meaning the "shape" of a two- or three-dimensional object. Sculptors often use *form* to refer to their sculpture's **shape,** defined by cavities (open negative areas) and protuberances (positive shapes; fig.1.41). Such pieces have both mass and volume. **Mass** invariably denotes a sculpture's implied weight or bulk. Mass may also refer to a solid physical object of relatively large weight or a coherent body of matter, like clay or metal, that is not yet shaped, modeled, or cast. Stone carvers, accustomed to working with **glyptic** materials, tend to think of a heavy, weighty mass (fig. 1.42); modelers, who manipulate clay or wax, favor a pliable mass. On the other hand, **volume** would be the three-dimensional space defined by an object's borders. A teapot and an empty room have a measurable volume; a brick has mass within its volume. The sculptor who assembles materials may enclose negative volumes by adding positive mass to form unique relationships (fig. 1.43). Both mass and volume indicate the presence of the sculpture's three-dimensionality, or form.

THREE-DIMENSIONAL MATERIALS AND TECHNIQUES

Over the past 100 years, the range of 3-D materials has expanded from basic stone, wood, and bronze to steel, plastic, fabric, glass, laser beams (holography), fluorescent and incandescent lighting, and so on. Such materials have revealed new areas for free exploration within the components of subject, form, and content, but the basic methods for working with them remain the same. There are four primary technical methods

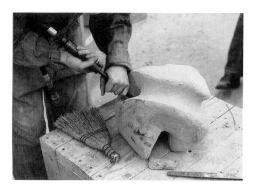

1.44 **Subtracting stone.** In the subtractive process, the raw material is removed until the artist's conception of the form is revealed. Stone can be shaped manually or with an air hammer, as shown here. Photograph courtesy of Ronald Coleman.

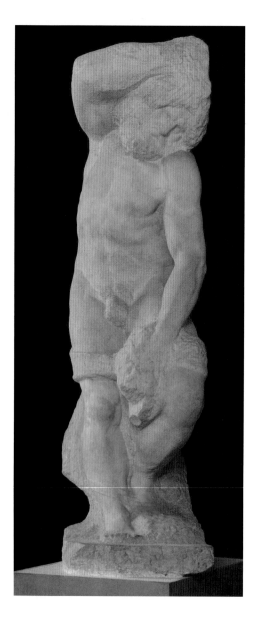

1.45 Michelangelo Buonarroti, *The Bearded Captive,* c. 1516–27. Marble, 8 ft. 8¼ in. (2.65 m) high. Michelangelo created heavy, massive sculpture and enlarged the sizes of human body parts for expressive purposes. The tectonic composition was in keeping with the intrinsic nature of the stone. Accademia, Florence, Italy. © Arte & Immagine srl/Corbis.

for creating three-dimensional forms: **subtraction, manipulation, addition,** and **substitution.** Although each of the technical methods is developed and discussed separately in the following sections, many three-dimensional works are produced using combinations of the four methods.

Subtraction

Artists cut away materials capable of being carved (glyptic materials), such as stone, wood, cement, plaster, clay, and some plastics. They may use chisels, hammers, torches, saws, grinders, and polishers to reduce their materials (fig. 1.44). It has often been said that when carvers take away material, they "free" the image frozen in the material, and a sculpture emerges. The freeing of form by the subtraction method produces the unique qualities of the act of carving (fig. 1.45).

Manipulation

Widely known as **modeling,** manipulation is a direct method for creating form. Clay, wax, and plaster are common media that are pliable during their working periods. Because they respond directly to human touch, they may be manipulated by hand into the finished product, leaving the artist's imprint. These manipulable materials may also be mechanically shaped to imitate other materials. Special tools such as wedg-

ing boards, wires, pounding blocks, spatulas, and modeling tools (wood and metal) are used for additional control (fig. 1.46). Because most common manipulable materials are not durable, they usually undergo further technical change. For instance, clay may be fired in a kiln (fig. 1.47) or cast in a more permanent material like bronze. Obviously, the selected techniques and materials are important, because both contribute their own special quality to the final form.

Addition

Methods of addition involve the assembling of materials like metal, wood, and plastic with the aid of welding torches, soldering guns, staplers, bolts, screws, nails, rivets, glue, and even rope (fig. 1.48; see also fig. 1.50). Methods of addition may also involve relatively sophisticated technology and, in terms of nonfunctional sculpture, may take advantage of the most recent innovations in epoxies, resins, and welding techniques. To accommodate the physical distribution of weight, stress, and tension, many sculptures also employ the use of wire armatures and other supports onto which materials may be affixed.

Substitution

Substitution, or **casting,** is a technique for reproducing an original three-dimensional model in a new material

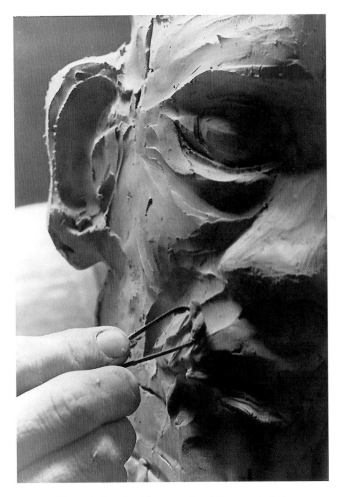

1.46 **Manipulation.** In this example of the manipulation technique, clay is removed with a loop tool. Clay may be applied to the surface with fingers, hands, or other tools. Photograph courtesy of Ronald Coleman.

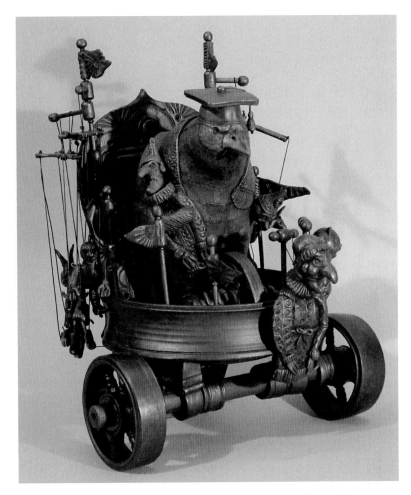

1.47 David Cayton, *The Last Performance,* Ceramics, primitive firing, 18 in. (45.7 cm) high. This is an example of clay that has been fired in a primitive kiln. The heavy reduction firing has caused the clay surfaces to turn black. Courtesy of the artist.

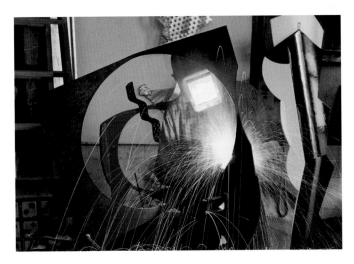

1.48 **Welding.** In the additive process, pieces of material are attached to each other, and the form is gradually built up. Welded pieces, such as the one illustrated, are often, though not always, more open than other sculptural techniques. Sculptor John Mishler welding at his Old Bag Factory Studio, Goshen, IN. Photograph courtesy of John Mishler.

through the use of a mold. Typically, the purpose is to duplicate the original in a more permanent material. For example, a clay or wax model can be exchanged for a bronze, fiberglass, or cement cast (fig. 1.49). This may be accomplished through a variety of processes (sand casting, plaster casting, or lost-wax casting), using a variety of molds ranging from waste molds and piece molds to flexible molds. Substitution is the least creative or inventive of the technical methods because it is imitative; the creativity lies in the creation of the original, not in the casting process. Regardless of which process they employ, three-dimensional artists know that materials, tools, and techniques are not ends in themselves but necessary means for developing a three-dimensional work (see fig. 1.40).

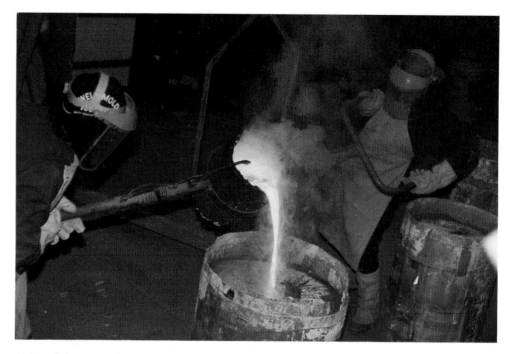

1.49 **Substitution**. In this illustration of the substitution process, molten metal is poured into a sand mold that was made from a model. Photograph courtesy of Ronald Coleman.

AREAS OF THREE-DIMENSIONAL APPLICATION

Sculpture

The term **sculpture** has had varied meanings throughout history. The word derives from the Latin verb *sculpere,* which refers to the process of carving, cutting, or engraving. The ancient Greeks' definition of *sculpture* also included the modeling of such pliable materials as clay or wax to produce figures in **relief** (with shallow depth) or in the round (freestanding). With these materials, the Greeks developed an ideal standard of beautiful proportions for the sculptured human form (see fig. 2.43). Contemporary sculptors are no longer limited to carving and modeling because of the diverse newfound materials and techniques that have led to greater individual expression and artistic freedom. They now combine all types of materials and explore more open spatial relationships (fig. 1.50). Sculptors weld, bolt, rivet, glue, weave, sew, hammer, and stamp

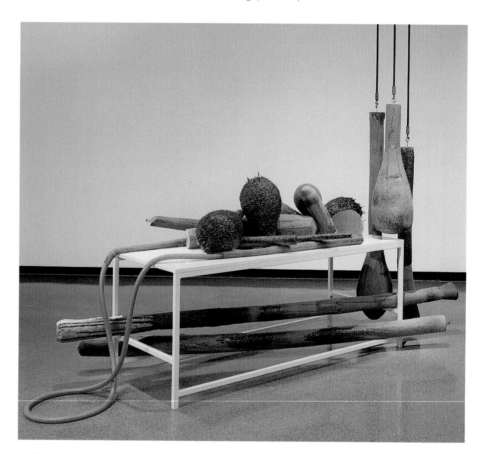

1.50 Joan Livingstone, *Seeped,* 1997–2000. Felt, stain, resin, pigment, and steel, 112 × 36 × 96 in. (284.5 × 91.4 × 243.8 cm). Modern sculpture exploits every conceivable material that suits the intentions of the artist. Courtesy of the artist and the SYBARIS Gallery, Royal Oak, MI. Photograph by Michael Tropea.

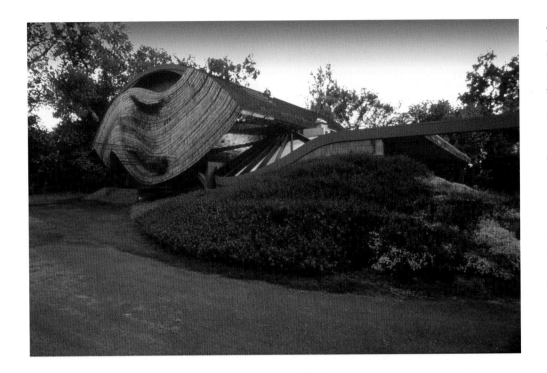

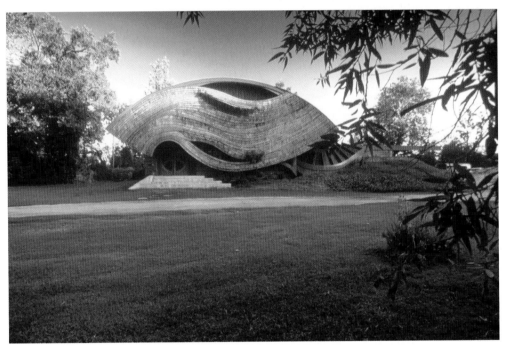

1.51 Arthur Dyson, *Lencioni Residence in Sanger, CA*, 1985. Architect Arthur Dyson designs structures that incorporate free-flowing curves and other architectural elements that integrate the residential structure with the natural environment. Courtesy of Arthur Dyson and Associates, Architects. Photo by Scot Zimmerman.

assorted materials such as steel, plastic, wood, and fabric. Many images challenge the boundaries between media, as in the case of **assemblage,** where the lines between two- and three-dimensional art are crossed (see fig. 6.22).

Architecture

The architect Louis Sullivan made the oft-repeated remark that "form follows function." This concept has influenced several decades of design, changing the appearance of architecture, tools, telephones, silverware, and even furniture. Sometimes this concept is misapplied. The idea of streamlining is practical when applied to the design of such moving objects as trains and cars, because it has the function of reducing wind resistance. However, streamlining has less logical application in the design of lamps and spoons. Although streamlining is helpful in eliminating irrelevancies from design, even simplification can be overdone. The **Bauhaus** notion of the house as a "machine for living" helped architects rethink architectural principles, but it also introduced a cold and austere style against which there was an inevitable reaction.

Technological innovations and new building materials have given architects greater artistic flexibility. Thanks to technical developments in steel and concrete, buildings can be large in scale without projecting massive, weighty forms. Vast interior spaces can be illuminated, and buildings can be completely enclosed or sheathed in glass, thanks to air-conditioning. Cantilevered forms can be extended into space. Freeform shapes can be created with the use of precast concrete. All of these structural improvements have allowed architects to think and plan more freely. In many ways, architects today are "building sculptors," and their designs require a thorough grounding in artistic principles as well as an understanding of engineering concepts (fig. 1.51).

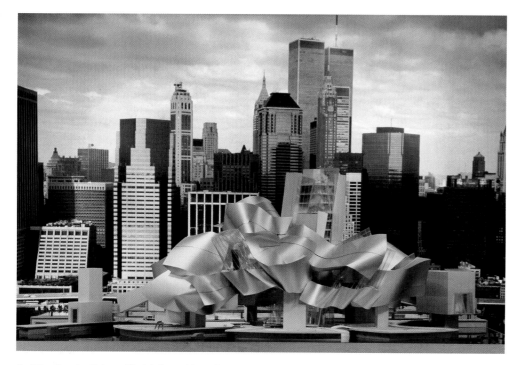

1.52 Frank Gehry, *Model for a New Guggenheim Museum in New York City,* **2000.** Architect Frank Gehry proposed this free-flowing sculpturelike design to house art from the twentieth century. Frank O. Gehry & Associates. Photograph by David Heald. © Solomon R. Guggenheim Foundation, New York.

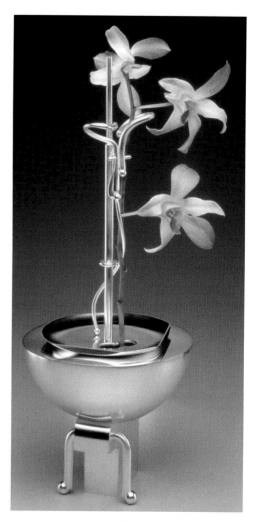

1.53 Tom Muir, *Orchid Vase,* 1997. Sterling silver, 11½ × 4¾ in. (28.9 × 11.8 cm). In this beautiful presentation, organic and geometric shapes are delicately integrated. The geometric shapes of the base contrast with the flowing organic stem support which subtly balances the piece, draws the viewer's eye around the work, and highlights the presence of the orchids. Courtesy of the artist. Photograph by Tim Thayer.

Furthermore, computer-aided design has allowed for the structural engineering of highly idiosyncratic buildings that could otherwise not be calculated. This may be seen in Frank Gehry's Guggenheim Museum in Bilbao, Spain, and the models for the Guggenheim South Street Seaport project (fig. 1.52).

Metalwork

Most of the changes in metalworking (jewelry, decorative and functional ware, etc.) have been in concept rather than technique. Traditional techniques (such as hand-welding, forging, soldering, riveting, and lost-wax or open casting) are still in use, although modern equipment has made procedures simpler and more convenient. To a large degree, fashion determines the character of metalwork, but it is safe to say that contemporary work is larger and more oriented toward sculpture than most work of the past. Constant cross-fertilization occurs among the various areas of art, and metalwork is not immune to these influences. The metalworker benefits from studying the concepts of both two- and three-dimensional art (fig. 1.53).

Glass Design

Glassworking is similar to metalworking now that modern equipment has simplified traditional techniques.

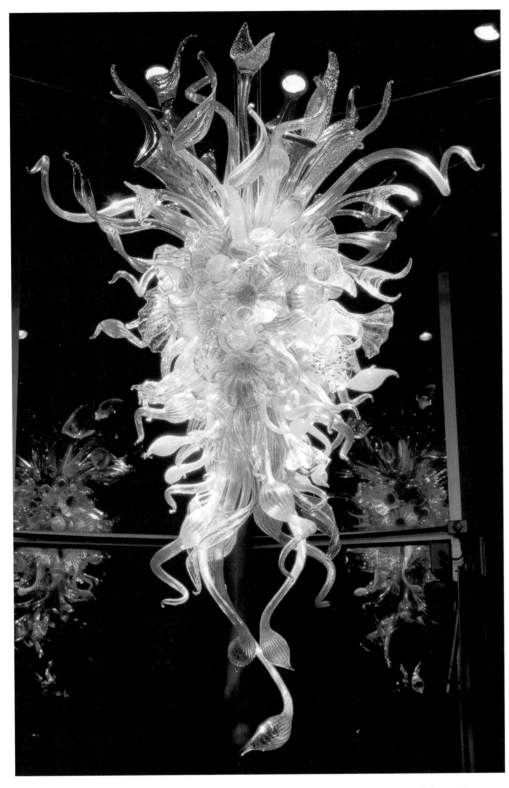

1.54 Dale Chihuly, *Nepenthes Chandelier*, 2004. Blown glass, size 111 × 68 × 54 in. This magnificent glass piece is most unusual and creative in its scale, coloring, shape definition, and ability to control an environmental setting. © 2008 Dale Chihuly.

Designing glass objects, however, is very much an art form of recent times. Many freeform and figurative pieces have the look of contemporary sculpture. Colors augment design in a decorative, as well as an expressive, sense. Thus, the principles of art structure are integrated with the craft of the medium (fig. 1.54).

Ceramics

In recent years, as ceramic work has become, in many cases, less functional, the basic shape of the ceramic object has become more sculptural. The ceramist must be equally aware of three-dimensional considerations and of the fundamentals of graphic art, because individual surfaces may be altered by incising, painting with colored slips, fuming, or glazing (fig. 1.55).

Fiberwork

Fiberwork has undergone a considerable revolution recently. Three-dimensional forms are becoming increasingly more common, particularly as the traditional making of rugs and tapestries by hand has diminished. Woven objects now include a vast array of materials incorporated into designs of considerable scale and bulk. Traditional as well as contemporary concepts of fiberwork require a fundamental understanding of both 2-D and 3-D concepts (fig. 1.56).

Product Design

Relative newcomers to the art scene, contemporary designers create forms that are aesthetically pleasing and yet still fulfill their functional requirements. The same abstract quality of expressive beauty that is the foundation for a piece of sculpture underlies such functional forms as automobiles, television receivers, telephones, industrial equipment, window and interior displays, and

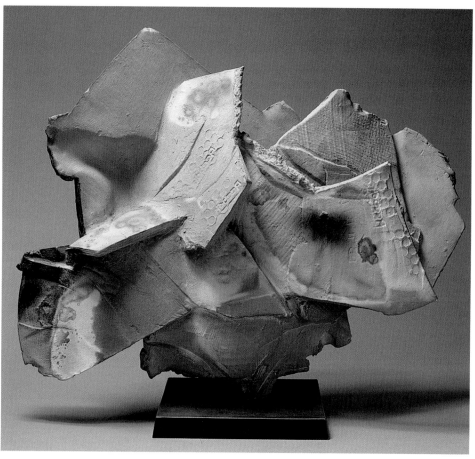

1.55 Paul Soldner, *Pedestal Piece (907)*, 1990. Thrown and altered clay with slips and low-temperature salt glaze, 27 × 30 × 11 in. (68.6 × 76.2 × 27.9 cm). The coloring resulting from the controlled firing process enhances the sculptural composition of the clay piece. Scripps College, Claremont, CA. Gift of Mr. and Mrs. Fred Marer, 92.1.154.

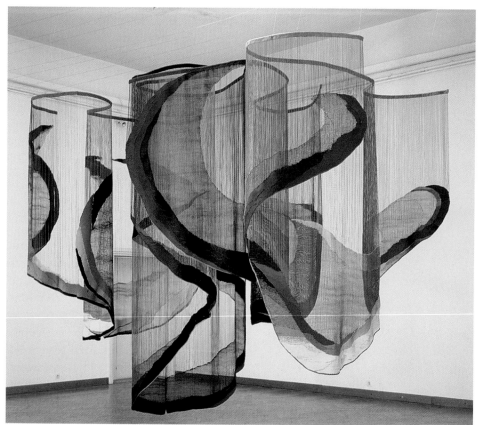

1.56 Eta Sadar Breznik, *Space*, 1995. Woven rayon, 157½ × 137⅞ × 137⅞ in. (400 × 350 × 350 cm). Contemporary textile design frequently goes beyond its largely two-dimensional traditions. Ljubljana, Slovenia. Photo © Boris Gaberščhek.

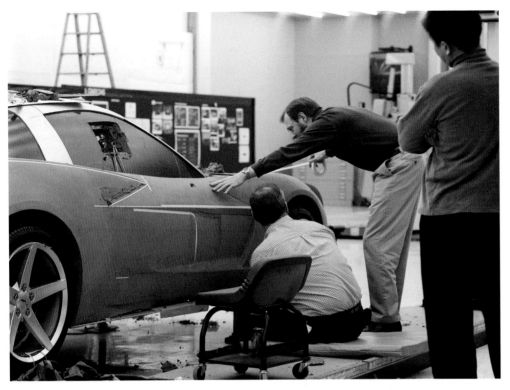

1.57 General Motors Corporation prototype, 2007. **Mixed media, full scale.** Artists are shown here working on a clay mockup for a new model. Developing concepts in automotive design are determined by advances in technology, engineering, economics, and visual appearance. © GM Corp.

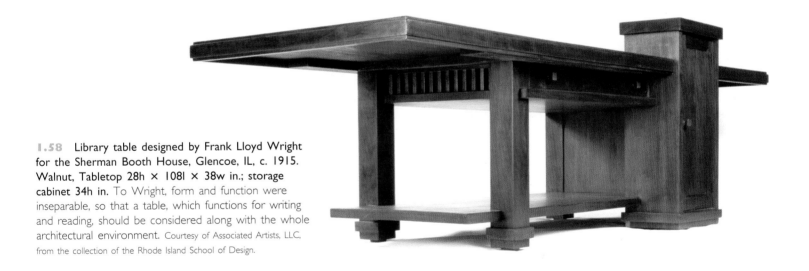

1.58 Library table designed by Frank Lloyd Wright for the Sherman Booth House, Glencoe, IL, c. 1915. Walnut, Tabletop 28h × 108l × 38w in.; storage cabinet 34h in. To Wright, form and function were inseparable, so that a table, which functions for writing and reading, should be considered along with the whole architectural environment. Courtesy of Associated Artists, LLC, from the collection of the Rhode Island School of Design.

furniture (fig. 1.57). Artist-designers of these 3-D products organize elements like shapes, textures, colors, and space according to the same principles of harmony, variety, balance, proportion, and so forth as are used in the fine arts.

Frank Lloyd Wright, the celebrated American architect, combined architecture with engineering and art in shaping his materials and their environment. The unity of his ideas is expressed in the table he designed for the Sherman

Booth House (fig. 1.58). The sophisticated design and formal balance that Wright incorporated into this ordinary object can be seen in his highly selective repetitions, proportional relationships, and refinement of details.

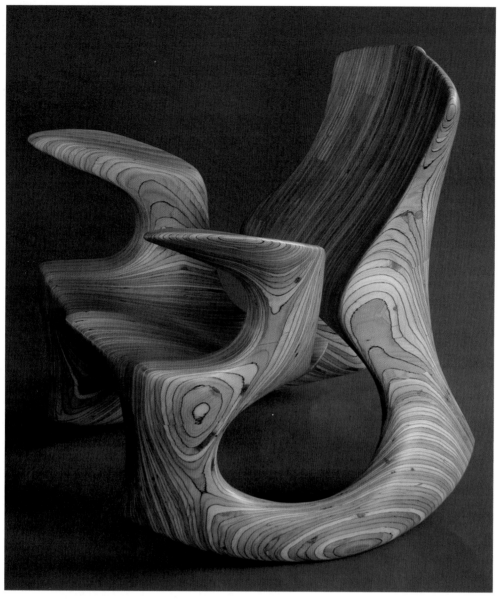

1.59 David Delthony, *Lotus (rocking chair)*, 2002. Laminated plywood, 40 × 29 × 35 in. Delthony combines ergonomics and aesthetic appeal to create organic furniture that transcends function and becomes sculptural form. Courtesy of Artist-Craftsman David Delthony.

shape. This unique piece of furniture resembles a freely expressed contemporary sculpture. Expressive form follows function in a new and creative way.

COMBINING THE INGREDIENTS: A SUMMARY

In this chapter, we have mentioned some of the means by which an artist's emotions may be brought to the surface. You have been introduced to the components, elements, and principles involved in making visual art. You have some idea of how these factors enter into analyzing and diagnosing problems in an ongoing work, and you should be able to view your own work and the work of the "masters" with greater awareness. In the next few chapters, the fundamentals will become more detailed, and their application will prove even more relevant to the creation of your own artwork.

Aside from satisfaction, one of the dividends gained by a better understanding of the visual arts is that it puts us in touch with some remarkably sensitive and perceptive people. We always benefit from contact, however indirect, with the creations of great geniuses. Einstein exposed relationships that have reshaped our view of the universe. Mozart created sounds that, in an abstract way, summed up the experiences and feelings of the human race. Though not always of this same magnitude, visual artists also expand our frames of reference, revealing new ways of seeing and responding to our surroundings. When we view artwork knowledgeably, we gain insight into the problems and solutions before us and can gather a new sense of direction for our own images.

The balance that exists between design, function, and expressive content within an object varies with example. For instance, when designing his rocking chair, David Delthony placed strong emphasis on expressive form without sacrificing the function of reclining comfort (fig. 1.59). At first glance, we are drawn in by the chair's dominant outer contour and its open

Form

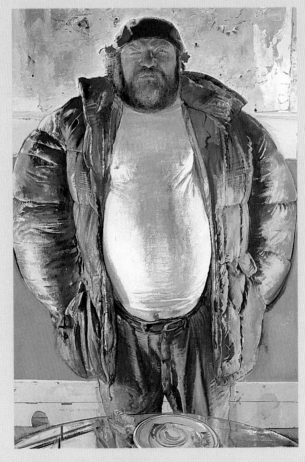

Jerome Paul Witkin, *Jeff Davies*, 1980. Oil on canvas, 6 × 4 ft. (1.83 × 1.22 m).
Palmer Museum of Art, Pennsylvania State University. Gift of the American Academy
and Institute of Arts and Letters (Hassam and Speicher Purchase Fund).

THE VOCABULARY OF
FORM

Form — 1. The total appearance, organization, or inventive arrangement of all the visual elements according to the principles that will develop unity in the artwork; composition. 2. In sculpture, form can also refer to the three-dimensional shape of the work.

accent
Any stress or emphasis given to the elements of a composition that brings them more attention than other features that surround or are close to them. Accent can be created by a brighter color, darker value, greater size, or any other means by which a difference is expressed.

allover pattern
A design that is formed through the systematic repetition of smaller designed units over an entire surface.

approximate symmetry
The use of similar imagery on either side of a central axis. The visual material on one side may resemble that on the other but is varied to prevent visual monotony.

asymmetry
"Without symmetry"; having unequal or non-corresponding parts. An example: a two-dimensional artwork that, without any necessarily visible or implied axis, displays an uneven distribution of parts throughout.

atectonic
Three-dimensional work characterized by considerable amounts of space; open, as opposed to massive (or tectonic), and often with extended appendages.

balance
A sense of equilibrium between areas of implied weight, attention, attraction, or moments of force; one of the principles of organization.

closure
A concept from Gestalt psychology in which the mind perceives an incomplete pattern or information to be a complete, unified whole; the artist provides minimum visual clues, and the observer brings them to final recognition.

composition
The arranging and/or structuring of all the art elements, according to the principles of organization, that achieves a unified whole. Often used interchangeably with the term **design.**

design
The organizing process or underlying plan on which artists base their total work. In a broader sense, *design* may be considered synonymous with the terms **form** and **composition.**

dominance
The principle of organization in which certain visual elements assume more importance than others within the same composition or design. Some features are emphasized, and others are subordinated. Dominance is often created by increased contrasts through the use of isolation, placement, direction, scale, and character.

economy
The distillation of the image to the basic essentials for clarity of presentation; one of the principles of organization.

form
1. The total appearance, organization, or inventive arrangement of all the visual elements according to the principles that will develop unity in the artwork; composition. 2. In sculpture, form can also refer to the three-dimensional shape of the work.

Gestalt, Gestalt psychology
A German word for "form"; an organized whole in experience. Around 1912, the Gestalt psychologists promoted the theory that explains psychological phenomena by their relationships to total forms, or *Gestalten,* rather than their parts. In other words, our reaction to the whole is greater than our reaction to its individual parts or characteristics, and our minds integrate and organize chaotic stimuli so that we see complete patterns and recognizable shapes.

golden mean, golden section
1. Golden mean—"perfect" harmonious proportions that avoid extremes; the moderation between extremes. 2. Golden section—a traditional proportional system for visual harmony expressed when a line or area is divided into two sections so that the smaller part is to the larger as the larger is to the whole. The ratio developed is 1:1.6180, or roughly 8:13.

harmony
A principle of organization in which parts of a composition are made to relate through commonality—repeated or shared characteristics, elements, or visual units. Harmony is the opposite of **variety.**

interpenetration
The positioning of planes, objects, or shapes so that they appear to pass through each other, which locks them together within a specified area of space.

kinetic (art)
From the Greek word *kinesis,* meaning "motion"; art that involves an element of random or mechanical movement.

mobile
A three-dimensional, moving sculpture.

moments of force
The direction and degree of energy implied by the art elements in specific compositional situations; amounts of visual thrust produced by such matters as dimension, placement, and accent.

motif
A designed unit or pattern that is repeated often enough in the total composition to make it a significant or dominant feature. Motif is similar to "theme" or "melody" in a musical composition.

movement
Eye travel directed by visual pathways in a work of art; one of the principles of organization. Movement is guided by harmonious connections, areas of variety, the placement of visual weights, areas of dominance, choices in proportions, spatial devices, and so on.

pattern
1. Any artistic design (sometimes serving as a model for imitation). 2. A repeating element and/or design that can produce a new set of characteristics or organization.

principles of organization
Concepts that guide the arrangement and integration of the elements in achieving a sense of visual order and overall visual unity. They are harmony, variety, balance, proportion, dominance, movement, and economy.

proportion
The comparative relationship of size between units or the parts of a whole. For example, the size of the Statue of Liberty's hand relates to the size of her head. (See **scale.**) Proportion is one of the principles of organization.

radial
Emanating from a center.

repetition
The use of the same visual effect—and/or similar visual effects—a number of times in the same composition. Repetition may produce the dominance of one visual idea, a feeling of harmonious relationship, an obviously planned pattern, or a rhythmic movement.

rhythm
A continuance, a flow, or a sense of movement achieved by the repetition of regulated visual units; the use of measured accents.

scale
The association of size relative to a constant standard or specific unit of measure related to human dimensions. For example, the Statue of Liberty's scale is apparent when she is seen next to an automobile. (See **proportion.**)

symmetry *typ of Balance*
The exact duplication of appearances in mirrorlike repetition on either side of a (usually imaginary) straight-lined central axis.

tectonic
The quality of simple massiveness; three-dimensional work lacking any significant extrusions or intrusions.

transparency
A visual quality in which a distant image or element can be seen through a nearer one.

variety
Differences achieved by opposing, contrasting, changing, elaborating, or diversifying elements in a composition to add individualism and interest. Variety is an important principle of organization; the opposite of **harmony.**

visual unity
A sense of visual oneness—an organization of the elements into a visual whole. Visual unity results from the appropriate ratio between harmony and variety (in conjunction with the other principles of organization).

FORM AND VISUAL ORDERING

A work of art always has three essential components: subject, form, and content. These components may vary in degree of emphasis, but their interdependence is so great that no single one can exist without the others, nor can it be fully understood in isolation from the others. The entire artwork should be more important than any one of its components (fig. 2.1). In this chapter, we explore the component **form** in order to investigate

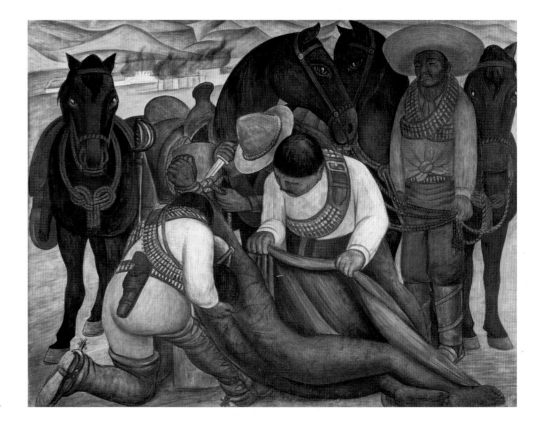

2.1 Diego Rivera, *The Liberation of the Peon,* 1931. Fresco, 6 ft. 2 in. × 7 ft. 11 in. (1.88 × 2.41 m). Here we see a political artist making use of appropriate and expected subject material. Without the effective use of form, however, the statement would be far less forceful. Philadelphia Museum of Art, PA. Gift of Mr. and Mrs. Herbert Cameron Morris. © Philadelphia Museum of Art/Corbis Media. Reproduction authorized by National Institute of Fine Art and Literature of México and Banco de México. © 2008 Banco de México Diego Rivera and Frida Kahlo Museums Trust. Av. Cinco de Mayo No. 2, Col. Centro, Del. Cuauhtémoc 06059, México, D.F.

the structural principles of creating visual order. Here, the term *form* refers to the total arrangement of the composition and to the very act of organizing and composing it.

When we see images, we take an active part in making sense of what we see. Our minds are flooded with visual information, so we instinctively and subconsciously look for visual connections and relationships to create order out of the confusion. A group of horizontal and vertical lines might be interpreted as a chair, a detailed shape might be recognized as a figure instead of the background, and a series of shapes in different positions might be seen as a moving object. This instinct for order is the basis of our appreciation of structure, and it is only natural that an artist should apply it to his or her creative process.

THE PRINCIPLES OF ORGANIZATION

It is often said that an artist's task is to bring order out of chaos. Whether the imagery is figurative or nonobjective, the artist's intent is to develop an integrated and unified visual whole out of diverse elements. This process is diagramed in figure 2.2. Having selected the appropriate media, the artist begins by subjecting the elements (line, shape, value, texture, and color) to the application of the seven **principles of organization**—harmony, variety, balance, proportion, dominance, movement, and economy. These principles guide the artist in developing the various elements and creating a sense of space. If the artist's plan is successful, the sum total equals **visual unity**—a sense of visual oneness. The artist, in working with the elements, has created an organization of parts that fits into an ordered visual whole where every element has become vital to it.

These principles of organization are not laws with only one possible interpretation or application; rather, they are flexible guides to organizing the elements. Their use or integration is highly intuitive or subjective for each work. Although we will study the principles separately, they do not *function* separately within the overall structure of a composition; instead, they actually affect and influence each other (for example, an area's degree of dominance affects the whole composition's sense of balance). Principles can be combined or omitted as necessary, as long as the artist understands what effect that choice may have on development of the other principles. Incorporating any particular one may not be enough to guarantee a successful work, since principles are not ends in themselves.

The organizing process, which can be variously termed **composition** or **design,** is usually a mix of intuition and intellect. By applying the various principles of organization, the visual artist controls and integrates the art elements—building relationships that are harmonious and yet varied enough to create excitement. He or she also imparts a certain feeling of balance or visual equilibrium, appropriate relationships of size and scale, areas with varying degrees of dominance or emphasis, and pictorial movement. This is done as efficiently as possible and establishes a spatial relationship between objects. The work may undergo much change as it progresses, but the final arrangement (image) should effectively communicate the artist's feeling.

To some extent, the structure of visual elements leads the viewer's experience much like a musical score guides musicians. Just as the musical blueprint (the score) indicates the tempo (the speed or pace of the music), the placement and movement of the notes, the location of rests, and the degree of sound to be produced, so the visual composition controls eye movements in both

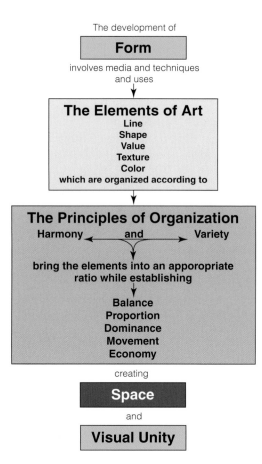

2.2 This diagram illustrates how the components of *form* relate to each other. Although the process of composing artwork may sometimes occur in this order, artists can begin their work by focusing on any of these items and can continue in any sequence.

speed and direction, provides pauses, and, in a sense, manipulates the volume (by using loud or soft colors, clashing lines, or softly related shapes).

The individual characteristics of each element are also so integral to this organizational process that they really cannot be separated from it. However, for the sake of clarity, we will first address the guiding principles and then discuss the elements individually in the chapters that follow, along with an explanation of how the principles of organization may be applied to each. In view of this interconnectedness, the principles should be reviewed repeatedly to

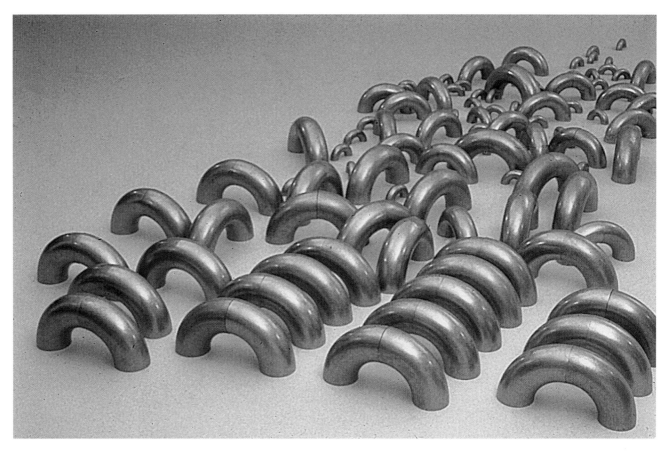

2.3   Amir Nour, *Grazing at Shendi*, 1969. Steel (202 pieces), 119 × 161 in. (variable). The repeated semicircular shapes not only reflect Nour's memories of grazing goats and sheep, but they also relate all the pieces of his sculpture to each other. The various sizes and positions then give the work a sense of variety similar to the nature of a moving flock. Courtesy of the artist. Private Collection.

fully understand how each element and its attributes can be developed through and yet used to achieve harmony, variety, balance, proportion, dominance, movement, and economy.

Harmony

Harmony, the first of the principles of organization, may be defined as a pleasing relationship between different sections of a composition. It occurs when elements or independent parts have characteristics in common—such as repeated colors, similar textures, shared edges, and so forth. These areas become vitally linked; their commonality makes them visually related or "pulls them together." Harmony, then, may be thought of as the factor of cohesion that relates the various parts of a composition to each other.

Even vastly different areas or images will begin to harmonize if they are treated in a similar manner. For example, an artist can begin to relate two different kinds of lines, vertical and horizontal, by making them all straight. If they were all the same length, they would harmonize even more, and if they were all drawn with an ink pen on damp paper, their similar character would relate them even further. We will look individually at the many ways an artist may create harmony, including the repetition of an element, the creation of rhythm, the repetition of a pattern or motif, and the creation of visual groupings through closure, visual linking, and linking through extensions.

Repetition

A primary way of creating harmony or harmonious relationships in a composition is through the use of **repetition.** As the term implies, certain things are repeated or used more than once in the composition, such as an *element* of art (for example, the color green), an element's *characteristic* (its intensity), or a *design* produced by a combination of the elements (see fig. 7.16A).

Repetition does not require exact duplication—just similarity or near likeness. Slight variations will add subtle interest to an image that might otherwise be tiring (figs. 2.3, 2.4, and 2.5).

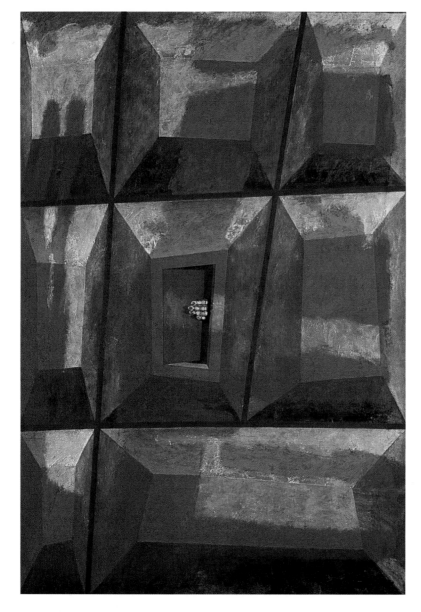

2.4   Pauline Gagnon, *Secret Little Door*, 1992. Mixed media on canvas, 48 × 72 in. Repetition is introduced in this image by the theme of architectural surface and shape. But, by repeating those items in differing ways, the artist creates variety, and a potentially monotonous composition is greatly enlivened. Courtesy of the artist and Jain Marunouchi Gallery.

Repetitive similarities are like our genetic predisposition to resemble our parents, expressing relatedness. In art, the relationships created by such resemblances give a work a degree of harmony. Carefully handled repetition can also produce links to induce the eye travel of the observer. Repeated elements may create small areas of emphasis that draw attention from one location to another. Even as those similarities are reduced, the *least* related elements may achieve subtle emphasis and draw attention to their dissimilarity.

Rhythm

One attribute of repetition is the ability to produce **rhythm.** Rhythm is a continuance, a flow, or a sense of movement that results from repeated beats, some-times regular, sometimes more eccentric. Walking, running, wood chopping, and hammering are all human activities that have a constantly repeated movement and beat. In visual art, that "beat" is a visual unit (an element, characteristic, or design). Consequently, the repetition of visual units will result in rhythm when strategically placed and, if necessary, suitably accented (fig. 2.6; see also fig. 9.1). These also serve to direct eye movement from one part to another.

Depending on how they are used, repetition and rhythm can confer on an artwork both excitement and harmony. The rhythm of visual movement may be smoothly flowing, or it may be less regular and rather jerky, as dictated by the artist. A gentle, smoothly flowing rhythm may instill a sense of peace, as in a quiet landscape (see fig. 2.63), while a very active rhythm, as in a stormy landscape, may feel rougher or suggest violent action (see fig. 4.3). The type of rhythm will depend on how regularly the units are repeated and how similar they seem. This includes the likeness of their character (e.g., rough versus smooth surface textures), their direction (horizontal versus diagonal lines), their type (regular versus irregular shapes), their value (dark versus light), their size (large versus small), and so forth. Repeating a series of extreme contrasts will create a strong beat, while subtler variations will create a quieter pulsing.

The creation of rhythm also relies on the repetition of pauses between repeating units. When a drummer taps out the old "shave and a haircut . . . two bits," all the drumbeats are of the same duration, so the variation in the negative spaces—or intervals of silence *between* the beats—helps create the rhythmic pattern. Added emphasis (**accents**) on certain beats then adds to the flavor of the rhythm. In the visual arts, the "pause" is a negative visual space or less-accented visual unit. Unfortunately, artists often overlook these negative intervals—but the pauses are

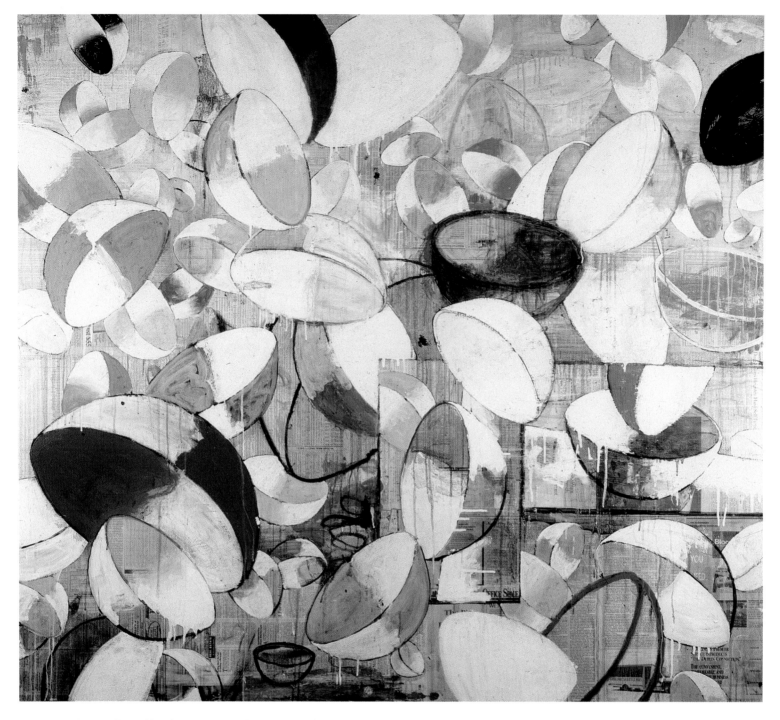

2.5　　Paul Manes, *Eiso*, 1995. Oil on canvas, 60 × 66 in. (152.4 × 167.6 cm). The visual units in Manes's painting are ovoid saucer shapes. The repetition of this shape creates harmony. Variety develops out of differences in the shape's size and color. Courtesy of Paul Rogers/9W Gallery, New York, NY.

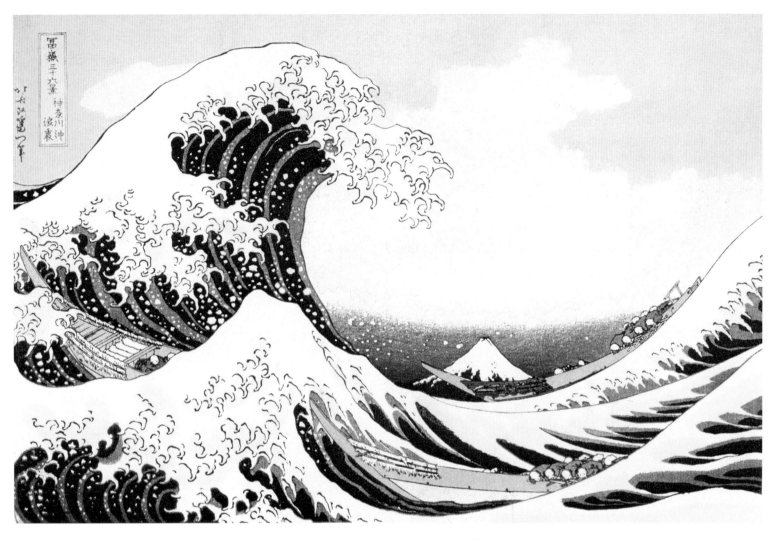

2.6 Katsushika Hokusai, *Under the Wave off Kanagawa* (from the series *The Thirty-Six Views of Fuji*), 1829–33. Colored woodblock print, 10½ × 15 in. (26.7 × 38.1 cm). The rhythmic surging of the driving sea is established by the repeated zigzag and curving diagonals of the waves and boats, the recurring pattern of the rolling sea-foam motif, and the blue and black stripes of the waves. Takahashi Collection. Sakamoto Photo Research Laboratory/ Corbis Media.

just as responsible for creating rhythm as the repeating element(s). The importance of spacing (visual silence) can be seen in the sculpture of Alexander Calder (fig. 2.7) or in the intervals between the heads in Andrew Stevovich's *Internet Café* (see fig. 5.24). A great variety of rhythms can be created by changing the size or character of the visual units (see fig. 3.9) and the duration of the pauses (see fig. 3.24). Bridget Riley successfully charges her painting *Evoë 1* with interesting rhythmical order; she uses several different rhythms simultaneously and ties the picture together by repeating curvilinear shapes, relating their direction, and using colors of modified value and intensity (fig. 2.8).

Pattern

Pattern is another important concept that involves harmony as established through repetition. At the most elementary level, pattern may be seen as any arrangement, design, or organized series of elements, and it may function as the model for some sort of imitation—like the pattern a dressmaker uses to make a skirt. If the basic pattern (model) is repeated numerous times, then that basic pattern can be referred to as a **motif.** The repetition of a motif then creates a new design, called an **allover pattern,** which is only seen when the entire whole can be viewed. For example, the *smallest* repeating design in wallpaper is the *motif,* whereas the *larger* design seen when viewing the entire wall is the *allover pattern.*

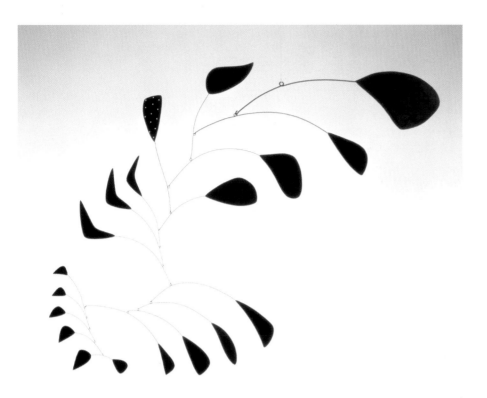

2.7 Alexander Calder, *Vertical Foliage,* 1941. 157.5 × 167.6 × 142.2 cm. Calder liked to think of his mobiles as paintings in motion. In this view, rhythm is obvious in the interplay between the repeating positive shapes and negative intervals. As the mobile begins to turn, those relationships change and create a great variety of new rhythms. Art © 2008 Calder Foundation, New York/Artists Rights Society (ARS), NY. Photo © Art Resource, NY. Private collection.

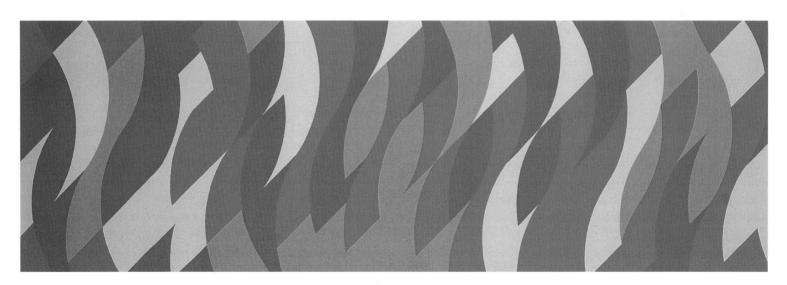

2.8 Bridget Riley, *Evoë 1,* 1999–2000. Oil on linen, 6 × 19 ft. (194 × 580 cm). Shapes related in color, value, and curving edges create a dramatic sweep across the composition. Interest is added to the rhythmic movement and ordered beat by changing the size and type of shape and the diagonal accents. Courtesy Karsten Schubert, London. © 2000 Bridget Riley. All rights reserved. Photograph by Prudence Cumming, London.

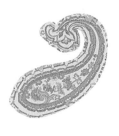

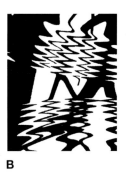

2.9 (A) This basic pattern has a paisley shape (see fig. 2.11). (B) This pattern is created by an arrangement of lines and positive and negative shapes based on an abstraction of tree reflections (see fig. 2.10).

A   **B**

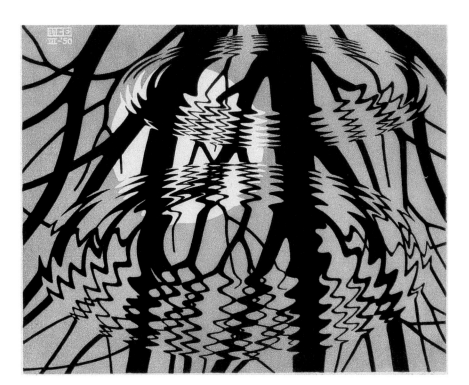

2.10 M. C. Escher, *Rippled Surface*, 1950. Although the subject is trees, the distinctive pictorial characteristic of this work is the pattern produced by the rippling reflections of the trees—a pattern that is developed, though not identically, in all areas of the work, creating unity. © 2008 The M. C. Escher Company-Holland. All rights reserved. www.mcescher.com.

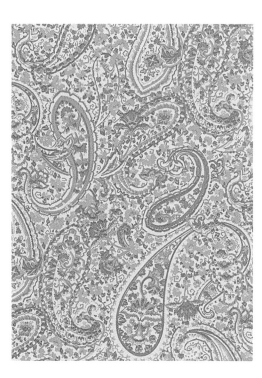

2.11 The paisley is repeated casually to achieve an overall pattern of rather irregular design. Courtesy of Fashion Wallcoverings, Distributors, Cleveland, OH.

Patterns and motifs may be composed of arranged elements, from simple marks to more complex relationships of line, shape, value, texture, or color. They may be totally invented, suggested by natural objects, or inspired by man-made objects (fig. 2.9A and B). When the repetitions are irregular, the total organization may appear casual, as in the reflected-tree pattern and the wallpaper pattern in figures 2.10 and 2.11. The composition can also be more controlled when more regulated repetitions are used, as in the soup-can artwork of Pop artist Andy Warhol (see fig. T.74). Here, the motif is easy to identify, and the allover pattern is quite regular and geometric.

However, systematic and regulated repetition does not always have to result in a predictable allover pattern. Quiltmakers often rotate their motifs and change the color, value, texture, and placement to allow a new pattern of diagonals, squares, or diamonds to emerge from the allover pattern (fig. 2.12). In a similar manner, Chuck Close alters his repeating design unit (a diamond with circular internal shapes) by changing the color and value in each cell (motif block),

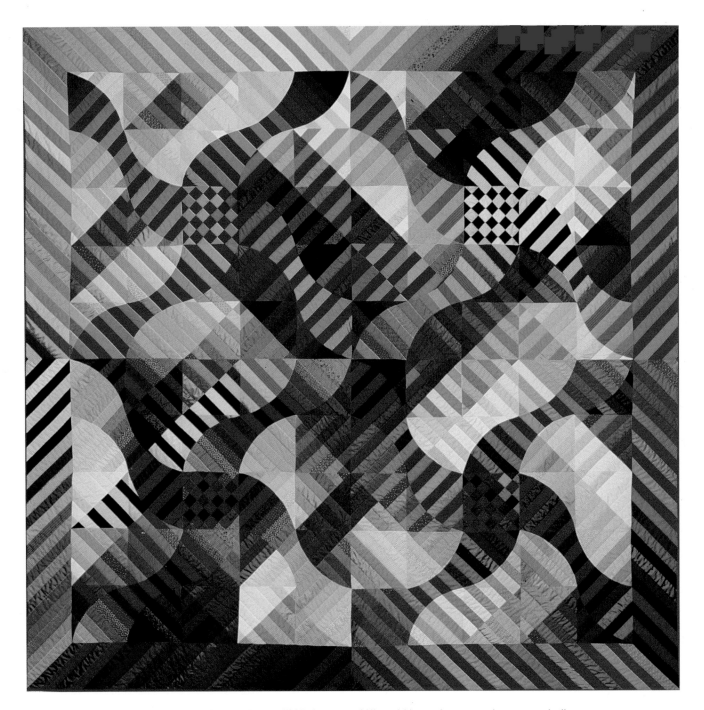

2.12   Michael James, *Rhythm/Color: Spanish Dance,* 1985. Somerset Village, MA, machine-pieced cotton and silk, machine quilted. 100 × 100 in. (254 × 254 cm). Using traditional quilting techniques, Michael James has repeated the basic design unit four times. However, the unusual allover pattern becomes more important than the repeating motif after color, value, and texture are changed within the units to accentuate and emphasize new space relationships. Collection of the Newark Museum, Newark, New Jersey. Photograph by David Caras.

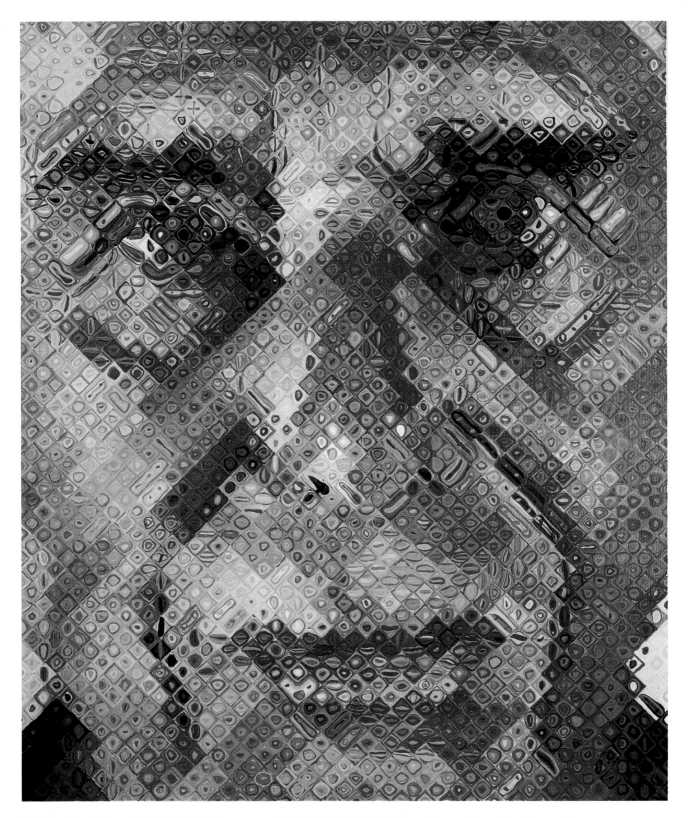

2.13 Chuck Close, *Paul III,* 1996. Oil on canvas, 102 × 84 in. (259.1 × 213.4 cm). A very interesting allover pattern emerges as a larger-than-life portrait. Because of the changing treatment in color and value, the allover pattern dominates the repeating motif, or design unit—a diamond with a series of internal circles. Image © The Cleveland Museum of Art, Mr. and Mrs. William H. Marlatt Fund, 1997.59. Photograph by Ellen Page Wilson, courtesy PaceWildenstein.

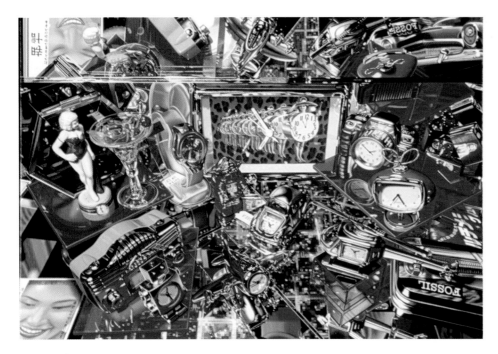

2.14   Don Jacot, *What Makes You Tick?* 2003. Oil on linen, 28 × 40 in. In this painting, clocks are a repeating theme, although the motif is really the *idea* of "clock" instead of one particular image that is identically duplicated numerous times. Notice the variety of style, size, and shape involved with the repetition. Courtesy of Louis K. Meisel Gallery.

and as a result, the allover pattern is a portrait of Paul III (fig. 2.13). Here, it is quite obvious that the allover pattern (a face) would be impossible if the motif were repeated without alteration.

Many studio artists prefer an even subtler use of motif. Instead of repeating similar patterns, these artists repeat an *idea* or *theme*. For example, in Don Jacot's *What Makes You Tick?* the clocks are the repeating theme (fig. 2.14). The clocks are not repeated over and over exactly alike but rather are constantly changed and accented in differing ways. This is similar to the "ta-ta-ta-TUM" in Beethoven's Fifth Symphony, which is repeated throughout the composition but constantly changes in terms of tempo, pitch, volume, and the voice of the instrument playing it.

Sometimes the theme (motif) develops for an artist over a long series of work. Consider thirty paintings by an artist, each of which deals with a cat in some different attitude or position. In

each individual painting, the cat would be the subject, but in considering the total series, the cat becomes the artist's repeating theme, idea, or motif. Two examples from a larger series may be seen in Impressionist artist Claude Monet's *Waterloo Bridge* paintings (see figs. 7.27 and 7.28) and the work of Piet Mondrian (see figs. 1.5–1.8).

Closure (Visual Grouping)

In the early part of the twentieth century, Max Wertheimer, a German **Gestalt** psychologist, began to investigate how the viewer sees form, pattern, or shape as configurations in terms of group relationships rather than as individual items. He discovered that several factors, such as nearness, size, and shape relatedness, help the mind relate objects visually. When the arrangement of visual units suggests that they are part of a larger pattern or shape, people mentally "fill in" missing gaps and tend to see incomplete patterns as complete

or unified wholes. We will be referring to this mental process of assembling to create pattern as **closure**.

This "closure tendency" occurs when an artist provides a minimum of information or visual clues and the observer provides the closure or imposes an understanding of the patterns with final recognition. The following examples demonstrate this concept. In figure 2.15A, some viewers will see an *X* formed by the black circles, and others will see a + created by the blue squares. In figure 2.15B, the mind connects those objects that help us see the configuration of an arrow. The four triangles with concave hypotenuses in figure 2.15C seem to create a complete circle, but remove some triangles or move them out of alignment and the circle becomes harder to "see" or is destroyed completely. (These four shapes also demonstrate how negative areas can become "positive" shapes: when the positive black shapes appear to connect into a circle in figure 2.15C, the negative central area becomes important, and we see the central area as a positive circle.) However, the same small shapes that created the circle can be rearranged to suggest a serpentine line instead (figure 2.15D).

With the concept of closure, the whole (the collective pattern or organization) is greater than its individual parts. In practice, this simply means that when images are evenly spaced across a pictorial field, they must be experienced individually—such as the circles, rectangles, and triangles in figure 2.16A. But as they are moved closer together and the negative intervals are adjusted, they begin to join together as visual units, and it becomes easier to see a developing circular grouping in the upper half and a lower horizontal line (fig. 2.16B and C). At this stage, the growing awareness of the larger groupings becomes more important than any one individual triangle, circle, or rectangle. As the individual shapes are moved closer, they appear to "bond" together

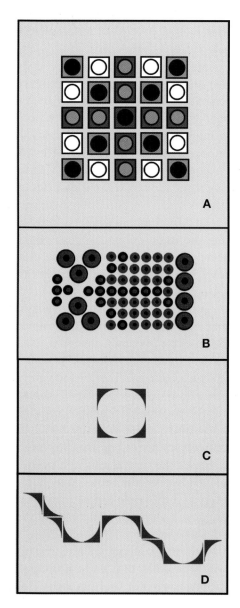

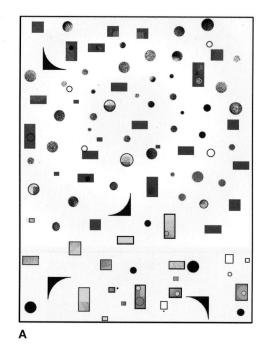

A

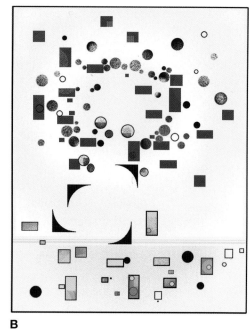

B

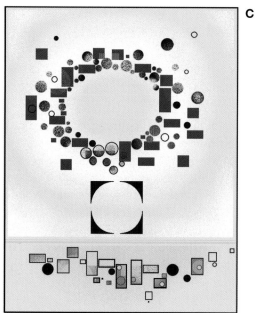

C

2.15 **Examples of closure.** The total configuration is more important than the individual components, as our minds "see" incomplete patterns as complete wholes. (A) The similar shapes are mentally connected to see an X or a + instead of small circles and squares. (B) The similar shapes optically join to form an arrow. (C) The shapes seem to form a circle within a square. (D) The shapes optically connect into a serpentine object.

2.16 (A) Individual shapes without any implied organization. (B) Individual shapes moving closer together and beginning to establish a visual grouping. (C) Shapes close together, with closure suggesting patterns of an oval, a circle, and a horizontal bar.

at some point *before* they physically touch each other (fig. 2.16C). How close do the objects have to come before they optically link? Recognition of the visual connection is a matter of experience that improves with practice but requires an awareness of the adjusted negative space. (Try to discover how the mind fills in the missing information. Determine at what point shapes begin to join visually. Can a third shape be made to join a grouping of two? Is more or less space needed between the units to do so? Try to determine what spacing creates the most tension between the units and if any particular spacing becomes too static.)

In the final image (fig. 2.16C), all of the various shapes have a harmonious relationship because of their spacing. The individual circles, rectangles, and triangles have become related, although variations in the negative intervals between shapes allow the new groupings to appear dense in one location while fading away in another. The sense of harmony may be further enhanced by similarity in color, surface texture, shapes, direction, linear quality, and the like. Shapes also visually join more easily wherever their edges are made to align.

Admittedly, with closure there are many factors at work, including proximity and similarity. For Wertheimer, this visual ordering helped explain how artists organize structure and create pattern in their work.

Visual Linking

While closure unifies shapes that share an implied group relationship, bringing these elements so close together that they physically touch suggests other ways of unifying a composition. When this occurs, the shared space itself becomes the cohesive factor. We will study the concept as it applies to shared edges, overlapping, transparency, and interpenetration.

Shared Edges

Shapes that share a common edge (contacting, touching, or butting together) are often united because the shared edge imposes common spatial relationships that help draw them together. For example, shapes with shared edges tend to be on the same limited spatial plane or share a similar spatial or pictorial depth. The Cubists and some contemporary artists like Gunther Gerzso (fig. 2.17, see also fig. T.51) have used this idea quite successfully. Shapes of the same size and related color or value will further unite compositions dealing with flat or limited space.

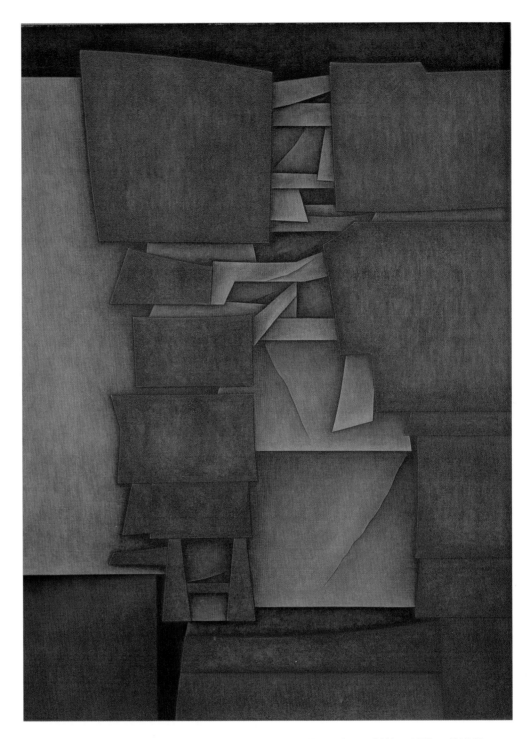

2.17 Gunther Gerzso, *Personage in Red and Blue,* 1964. Oil on fabric, 39⅜ × 28¾ in. (100.33 × 73 cm). In this painting, shapes are united by shared edges as well as similar color and textural development. Though the sense of space is shallow, it is heightened by the contrast of value. Courtesy of the Gene C. Gerzso 1999 Trust.

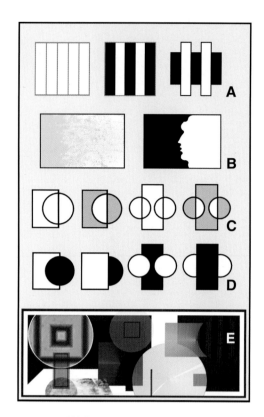

This harmonizing technique, however, can somewhat restrict the development of illusionistic or three-dimensional images. When connected shapes are of the same size and value, they limit the ability to create spatial references (fig. 2.18A, *left*). Changing the value makes them more distinct, but their spatial depths become more ambiguous—sometimes advancing, sometimes receding (fig. 2.18A, *center*). However, altering both the value and size of the connected shapes begins to establish a spatial reference in which the shapes more easily pass behind or in front of each other (fig. 2.18A, *right*). Additional variations in shading also serve to enhance the illusion of depth, however shallow (see fig. 2.17). (When connected shapes no longer share the same depth, harmony can be further established, if needed, through some other method—such as similar use of texture or color.)

Although sharing spatial relationships will pull areas of a composition together, there may be additional complications with using shared edges. When shapes with a common border share a similar value level or color, the dividing edge where they merge is often obscured—visually they become one new shape (fig. 2.18B, *left*). In addition, connected shapes seem to retain their individual character when the common dividing edge is rather nondescript, but when the edge begins to suggest something recognizable, the suggested image becomes a positive shape, and a specific spatial reference is created that forces the remaining shape to recede as a negative area (fig. 2.18B, *right*). Differences

2.18 (A) Denied or implied spatial references involving *shared edges*. (B) Dissolved and altered spatial references involving *shared edges*. (C) Little spatial reference created by *overlapping shapes*. (D) Greater spatial reference created by *overlapping shapes*. (E) Shapes related by *transparency*.

2.19 M. C. Escher, *Day and Night*, 1938. Woodcut in two colors, 15½ × 26¾ in. (39.3 × 67.9 cm). In this print, Escher effectively incorporates shapes with shared edges, structured ambiguity, and stable figure/ground relationships in the transition from light to dark. His use of variety (separation and elaboration) helps make the light and dark ducks stand out as figures against the opposite-value background. © 2008 The M. C. Escher Company-Holland. All rights reserved. www.mcescher.com.

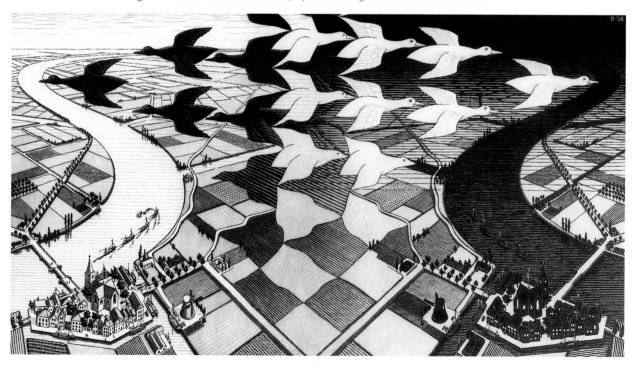

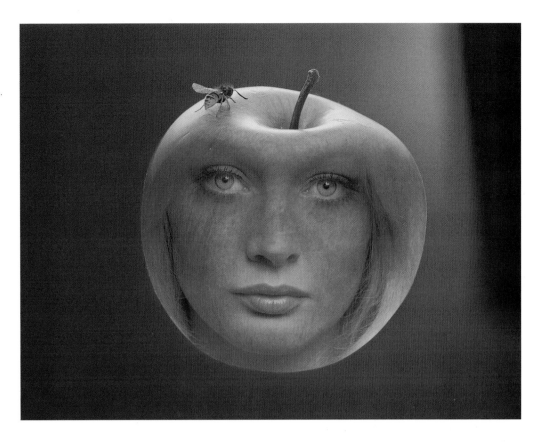

2.20 Sam Haskins, *Apple Face,* from the book *Haskins Posters,* 1973. Photograph. In this image, two distinctly different naturalistic images convincingly share the same shape and space.
© Sam Haskins Partnership. (Website URL: www.haskins.com).

in value or texture further exacerbate the situation. M. C. Escher explored this phenomenon, using it to his advantage when he made patterns of dark ducks fly through patterns of light ducks (fig. 2.19). As the ducks fly farther away from the central part of the image, the detail becomes more and more distinct, whereas the "duck" shapes toward the middle take on the imagery of the landscape.

Overlapping

With overlapping, the areas involved are also drawn together by a common relationship, and the shared item is a bit more involved than a simple edge; it becomes a shared area. As long as the colors, values, and textures are the same or related, the overlapping tends to unite the areas involved (fig. 2.18C). However, the space defined may be shallow and rather ambiguous—one time the circle is seen on top; the next time

the square is seen on top. The Futurists often achieved this effect by overlapping multiple views of the same object (see fig. 9.9).

Overlapping does not always mean limited space or cohesive relationships. A difference in treatment may cause visual separation of the two shapes and deeper spatial references, in which the overlapped object is seen as the receding shape (fig. 2.18D). Color and value choices may exaggerate or minimize the spatial effect.

With a more figurative application, independent symbolic information cannot only overlap but even occupy the same shared physical space. In this manner, entirely different symbols or image areas can be brought into a plausible harmonious context. If we study Sam Haskins's photo *Apple Face* (1973), the face is quite believably contained within the shape of the apple (fig. 2.20, see also fig. 4.5).

Transparency

An artist can also add harmony to images that occur in the same area through the use of **transparency** (see fig. 2.18E; see also figs. 1.56 and 8.9). When a shape or image is seen through another, the relating visual devices that create harmony and unite those two areas include the shared area itself, the layers of space they both pass through, and the surface treatment of all the images (highlights, shading, color, texture). Like simple overlapping, this technique tends to limit the visual depth that the artist may introduce but still serves as another harmonious device.

Interpenetration

When several images not only share the same area but also appear to pass through each other, they are brought into a harmonious relationship not only by the common location but also by the physical depth of the space in which they all appear (see figs. 8.10 and 8.11). Whether shallow or deep, illusionistic or stylized, the space itself pulls the various images into a visual harmony. Notice that in figure 2.21 there are two series of shapes. Some seem to plunge toward the left end and the rest toward the right end of the composition. Even though the two sets of planes are treated in very different textures and colors, the sharing of the internal space created by the **interpenetration** of shapes helps unify this work.

Linking through Extensions (Implied and Subjective Edges/Lines/Shapes)

A wide variety of dissimilar images and shapes can be made to relate by being visually linked through the use of *extensions*. Like the invisible lines of a surveyor's instrument that helps map out and organize cities, roads, and contours of the land, the extensions in a composition help the artist organize and bring all parts of that structure into a harmonious relationship.

While we have seen harmony achieved through shared edges, overlapping shapes, transparency of surface, or forms passing through each other, the inherently related items are relatively close to each other. However, the concept of extensions—implied edges, lines, or shapes—provides the artist with a system of visual alignment that can relate shapes much farther apart from each other.

By simply extending the edge of a shape across the composition, the artist can establish new objects, images, or shapes in locations some distance away.

Placing new shapes along the implied extended edge links distant shapes, thereby harmonizing the areas. Artists often use such alignment to integrate an entire composition and create space by implied tension.

Extensions reveal "hidden" relationships. They harmonize by setting up related directional forces, creating movement, and repeating predictable intervals between units. The directional impulse of these invisible, implied lines or shape edges suggests—sometimes subconsciously—an expectation that something will be discovered in a new area and pulls the eye toward this new location. These impulses integrate a work as they wind through the composition along the contours of information (fig. 2.22A and B).

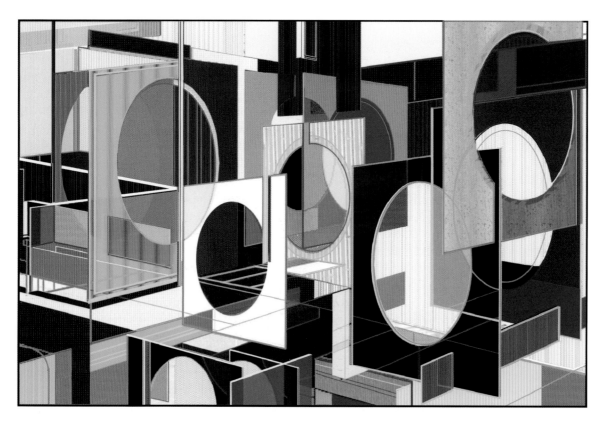

2.21 Clouret Bouchel, *Passing Through*, 2001. Digital imagery, 7 × 10½ in. (17.8 × 26.7 cm). This is an example of interpenetration, with lines, shapes, and planes passing through one another. Courtesy of the artist.

2.22A Johannes Vermeer, *Diana and the Nymphs,* c. 1655–56. Oil on canvas, 33½ × 41 in. (97.8 × 104.6 cm). Here, Vermeer uses extended edges to interlock the images, find the location for new forms, relate shapes, and create directional movement across the painting. Royal Cabinet of Paintings, Mauritshuis. The Hague, Netherlands, Scala/Art Resource.

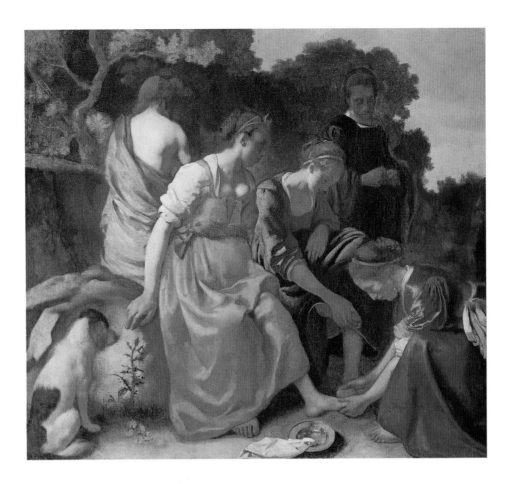

2.22B This overlay shows some of the extended edges with solid lines of various weights and their extensions by dots and dashes. Notice how the implied direction is often interrupted or disguised by subtle changes.

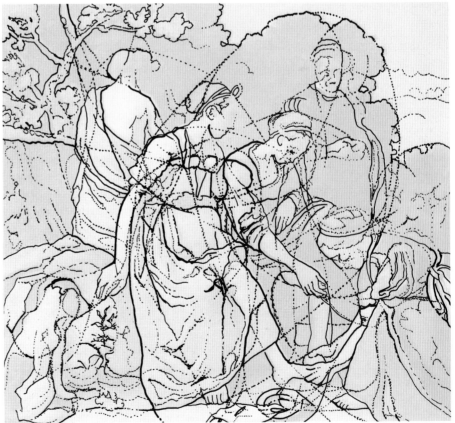

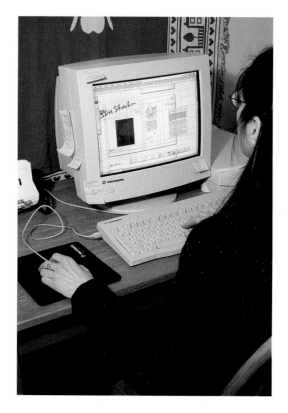

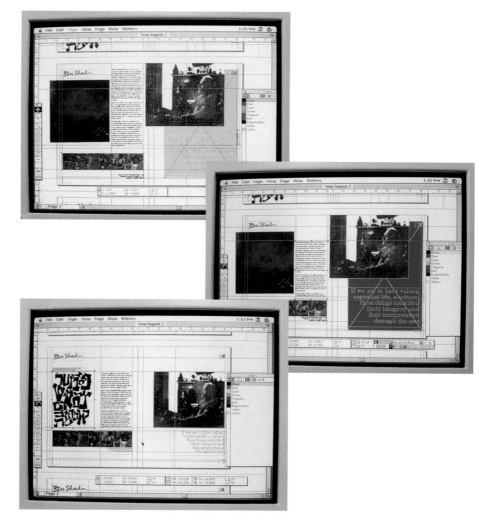

2.23 Designers often use a grid system to help with the layout and organization of text and visual information. The system can be applied to one image or made to relate a whole corporate campaign. © Erv Schowengerdt.

As an element in its own right, line draws all sectors of an arrangement together (see figs. 3.10 and 3.11). This line may be clear and dominant or less emphasized, fading away to a dissolved contour (see figs. 5.24 and 5.25). As strong indicators of direction, new lines introduced anywhere along the extension of a first line may relate the original to the new by implied direction. Invisible linear extensions (subjective lines) are exceedingly strong devices for relating compositional areas, and designers usually rely on them in the form of grid systems for the layout and organization of blocks of type, logos, and graphic information (fig. 2.23).

Like line, shape can create a strong directional movement and, as an organizational tool, create cohesive (harmonious) relationships with other shapes. Shape can create directional force or visual movement in two ways: (1) when the shape points in a general direction (for example, a long triangle points in the direction of the narrow end), it directs the viewer across the composition; and (2) when the outside edges of that pointing shape can be extended by hidden lines, they will direct the viewer in two other directions. Each of these implied or subjective edge extensions may be used to locate new shapes or objects all across the composition that

can be harmonized by the same directional force. Irregular shapes can also be brought into harmonious relationship by moving them around until their subjective edges (invisible extended edges) intersect or align. In this way, a grouping of shapes in one part of the composition can create tension or subconscious closure with other groupings or individual shapes some distance away.

The use of subjective edges, lines, and shapes allows eye movement to be controlled and directed anywhere, even rotating volumes in space and returning the viewer to the picture plane. Extensions may cross over areas enclosed by other images and shapes as well as across open areas of color and texture. Thus, while many concepts used to create harmony may limit the depth of pictorial space, the unifying concepts of extension may be applied equally well to plastic space and to decorative space, and they are not restricted to any particular degree of abstraction.

Because extensions are such an important tool of organization, great care must be taken so that their use does not become too obvious. Therefore, artists delight in hiding directional forces by interrupting them with countermovements, accents, or subtle misalignments.

Excessive Use of Harmony

To briefly summarize the first principle of organization: areas of a composition harmonize when they exhibit similar elements, characteristics, or designs and/or when they share the same grouping, space, or alignment.

Although harmony brings a vital cohesion to the work, it is potentially dangerous if overused. When commonality is employed to an inappropriate extreme, the composition may be plagued with an overwhelming feeling of monotony. In those situations, the problem may be relieved by slightly reducing the degree of similarity or by establishing harmony in a different manner. When the proper adjustments have been made, the individual relationships will be pleasantly interactive, and the overall composition will not feel monotonous.

Variety

Variety is the counterweight to harmony, the other side of organization essential to unity. While an artist might bring a work together with harmony, it is variety that imparts individuality. Variety arouses the viewer's curiosity and holds his or her attention. It is a factor of visual contrast—an isolation of elements and images. Like a good

sheepdog that singles out one animal from the flock, the introduction of variety actively separates areas or images to make them more exciting and let them stand apart.

If an artist achieves complete equality of visual forces, the work may feel static, lifeless, and unemotional. Visual boredom is a sign of an overly harmonious composition. By adding degrees of variation, the artist introduces essential ingredients (such as diversion or change) for sustaining attention.

Visual interest, then, results directly from adding variety to the pictorial components. Variety causes visual separation—a pulling apart of related elements or images, differentiating and disassociating the components. This separation is achieved through the use of contrast and elaboration.

Contrast

Contrast, by definition, means "opposition or dissimilarity," and it occurs wherever elements with opposing characteristics are placed in the same area. When artists repeat elements in a way that makes them appear unrelated—such as a few wide lines in a group of narrow ones—the differences, or contrasts, stand out. Dissimilarities are exaggerated when opposing elements and/or their characteristics are juxtaposed or placed in close proximity, such as red against green or dark against light. As contrasts are heightened, the areas involved become less harmonious but more visually exciting.

It is through the introduction of contrasts that an area, image, or shape is made to become emphasized or more dominant. A varying level of interest will help move the eye through the composition, so it may be necessary to make some contrasts stronger than others. Subtle contrast obviously occurs when the difference between elements is less extreme, and it is important to note that even slight changes in texture, color, value, size, spacing, or alignment

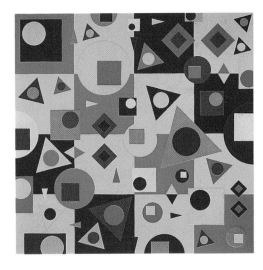

2.24 Franklin Jonas, *Geostructure I*, 1998. Acrylic on linen, 200 × 200 cm. Variety is achieved by making repeated units dissimilar. Here, Franklin Jonas repeats a series of triangles, circles, and squares, but all are different in size, color, value, and placement. The balance between harmony and variety can be tipped to favor either principle. In this case, making all the colors lighter and not as intense could swing the composition toward harmony but compromise the visual interest. With study, the viewer will continue to discover new relationships and varied patterns within the work. Courtesy of the artist. Photo by Kerry Bowman.

can draw a viewer's attention, however briefly.

In figure 2.24 Franklin Jonas has repeated circles, squares, and triangles, but they are different in size, color, value, and placement. These contrasts, which include shapes placed at varied and interesting angles, make the composition quite stimulating.

Elaboration

Another way to increase variety is to elaborate certain areas that lack visual interest. Elaboration may be thought of as embellishment, or the enhancement of the surface with subtle (sometimes contradictory) information, minute details, and pattern. Although this may sound like *repetition,* the intent is not to increase relatedness but, quite the opposite, to gradually introduce visual difference or opposition in order to attract attention. In figure 2.19, notice how M. C. Escher added more and more detail to the duck shapes as they move away from the center, making them stand apart from the opposite-colored area, which slowly becomes background. Artists rework areas persistently, to elaborate their expression until a satisfactory resolution is reached. Surfaces enriched by such changes impart the artist's concept with dramatic strength and purposeful meaning.

Picture surfaces become more exciting as variations are introduced. In music, the greater the number of vibrations, the higher the pitch. Similarly, in art, as contrasts are introduced, the visual "pitch" or excitement is increased; reduction in contrasts lowers the "vibration." (The frequency of contrasts in an artwork might also be compared to contrasts of volume in a musical composition.) In art, contrasts and elaboration are necessary to give some parts greater emphasis than others. However,

if they are overused, the excessive variety causes a feeling of visual chaos. But something just short of that point can be quite exciting.

The Dualism of Harmony and Variety

Visual unity and organization in art depend on an intricate relationship of similarity and contrast—a dualism of harmony and variety. For the sake of clarity, we have tried to present harmony and variety separately; however, in actual practice, they are opposite sides of the same coin and must be considered at the same time (fig. 2.25).

When organizing a composition, a subjective balance is required between harmony and variety, for one cannot be altered without affecting the other. As areas decrease in harmony, they increase proportionately in visual excitement. Likewise, making certain areas more related will reduce the amount of variety in those areas and increase the feeling of harmony. To hold contrasts together, some harmonious relationships are necessary, but these two principles do not have to be of equal

proportions; harmony might outweigh variety, or variety might outweigh harmony (fig. 2.26; see also fig. 2.24).

In music, if the composition needs more variety, a composer may intentionally introduce discord (not normally pleasant to the ear) and resolve it later in the composition with more harmonious tones (multiple notes that produce a pleasing sound when played together). Discord in art results when unrelated parts are put together so that variety far outweighs harmony. This may produce too much visual excitement, which like the musical counterpart, must be resolved with harmonious relationships sufficient to keep the composition from being completely chaotic.

As artists work at maintaining a compositional balance between harmony and variety, one of the most difficult concepts to grasp is that of applying harmony and variety at the same time by using the same element. Consider the use of shape. In *Orion,* Victor Vasarely uses circles as a unifying device to create a harmonious relationship (fig. 2.27). However, to avoid monotony, the artist seeks all the different

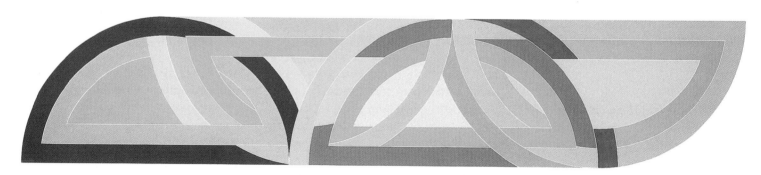

2.25 Frank Stella, *Damascus Gate Stretch Variation,* 1968. Acrylic on canvas, 60 × 300 in. (152.4 × 763.9 cm). Stella has harmonized the painting through his inventive and repeated use of the curve and straight-edged shapes, light shades of most colors, and the same flat surface texture; he has provided variety by using shapes of varied size and direction, contrasting colors and intensity, and accents of darker red and black against the remaining light shades of color. Collection Walker Art Center, Minneapolis. Gift of Mr. and Mrs. Edmond R. Ruben, 1969. © 2008 Frank Stella/Artists Rights Society (ARS), NY.

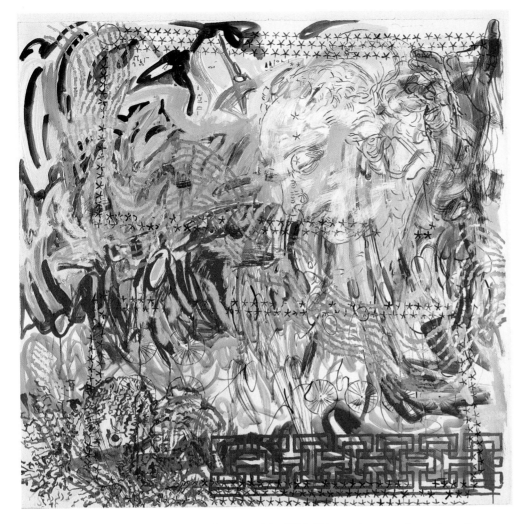

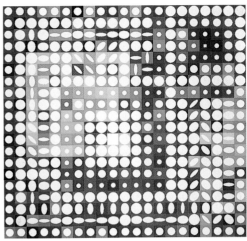

2.26 Nancy Graves, *Perfect Syntax of Stone and Air.* 1990. Watercolor, gouache, and acrylic on paper, 48½ × 48⅜ in. (123.2 × 122.9 cm). So many colored brushstrokes and color marks are repeated that some degree of relatedness (harmony) is apparent, but variety is by far the dominant factor because of the array of complementary colors (yellow/violet, red/green, blue/orange) and the introduction of elaborated patterns. Though dynamic in presentation, every inch has some rich detail awaiting discovery. Photo courtesy of Gerald G. Peters Gallery. Art © Nancy Graves Foundation/licensed by VAGA, New York, NY.

ways that circles can be introduced by changing their size, point of view, and angle. Thus, he has introduced variety by the very same element used to create harmony—circular shapes. The same thing could be done with any of the elements. Red, for example, could be used to make a series of shapes relate, providing harmony. Changing the red's character, by making it lighter or darker or by changing its brilliance or intensity, could vary the design while adding interest. Again, variety and harmony are developed by the thoughtful use of the same basic component.

A sensitive use of harmony and variety will become a means by which the other principles of organization are expanded and given vitality. Each choice in the blending of similarity with contrast will affect the development of balance, appropriate proportions, varying degrees of dominance or emphasis, pictorial movement, economy, and spatial order (see fig. 2.2).

Balance

Gravity is universal, and we spend our daily lives resisting its influence.

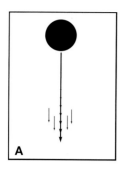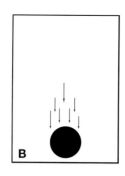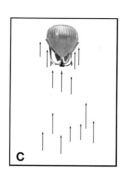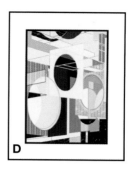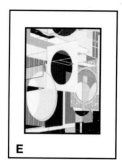

2.28 Balance: gravitational forces and the resulting pictorial tensions. (A) Objects placed high in the pictorial field often create a sense of tension with the bottom, top, and sides because of the expectation that gravity will cause the objects to drop. (B) Objects placed low in the pictorial field often create a sense of peace or resolution because of the feeling that gravity has already acted on the objects. (C) The expected effect of gravity on recognizable objects can be altered by their placement; unusual locations can add to psychological tension. (D) Equal dimensions of a mat around pictorial artwork may make the work feel unstable. (E) Increasing the width at the bottom of the mat will help stabilize the picture.

While walking, standing on one leg, or tipping back in a chair, we experience its effect and intuitively seek a state of balance. When we are off balance, we have a strong fear that gravity will pull us over and we will fall down. Those expectations are so strongly ingrained in our subconscious that they also have an effect on the art we experience and produce. Most artwork is viewed in an upright orientation—in terms of top, sides, and bottom. As a result, gravity affects the visual components. For example (fig. 2.28A), a shape (here, a circle or ball) placed high in the pictorial field creates a sense of tension between the shape and the baseline of the picture plane. This is caused by the expectation that gravity will cause the shape to drop. When it does not, a tension is created. On the other hand, a shape placed low or on the baseline creates less tension. With gravity having acted on the shape, the expectation of movement is resolved (fig. 2.28B). When a shape becomes figurative, we have an understanding of the image, which includes an estimate of its mass, weight, and function. All of what we know about an object affects

how we judge balance on a picture surface. For example, if the shape in figure 2.28A becomes a hot-air balloon, a large negative area under that shape will tend to support or balance it—we may even have the sensation of the balloon lifting up from that area (fig. 2.28C). But, if that shape is a floating grand piano, the viewer has the opposite expectation (see fig. 1.29). Whether objective or nonobjective components are used, the influence of psychological weight/tension and its compositional adjustment are endless (fig. 2.29).

Artists often mat their work to gain an "aesthetic distance" or separation from the everyday world. The hope is that we will see the work in a new context. But, even here, psychological factors can affect the visual weight and balance. In the case of a mat with two-inch top, sides, and bottom, the bottom may have the illusion of being pinched or smaller than the other sides (see fig. 2.28 D). This is an optical illusion that would make the artwork appear to be unstable, even rising on the wall. To compensate, the bottom measurement is generally made wider than that of the

top and sides so that the whole image seems stabilized or balanced (see fig. 2.28 E).

Balance is so fundamental to unity that it is impossible to consider the principles of organization without it. At the simplest level, balance implies the gravitational equilibrium of a single mark on a picture plane. Try placing a single colored shape on a white surface anywhere *but* in the center. The final location will involve a balance between the object and the amount of open space around it. Balance can also refer to the gravitational equilibrium of pairs or groups of units (such as lines or shapes) that are arranged on either side of a central axis. This concept is best illustrated by simple scales like a horizontal beam poised on a fulcrum (or pivot point), much like a child's teeter-totter. The forces are balanced horizontally, left and right, with respect to the supporting balance beam. If more weight is applied to the beam on either side of the fulcrum, that side will tip down. The beam is balanced when the weights and fulcrum are positioned so that neither side of the beam tips (fig. 2.30A–C).

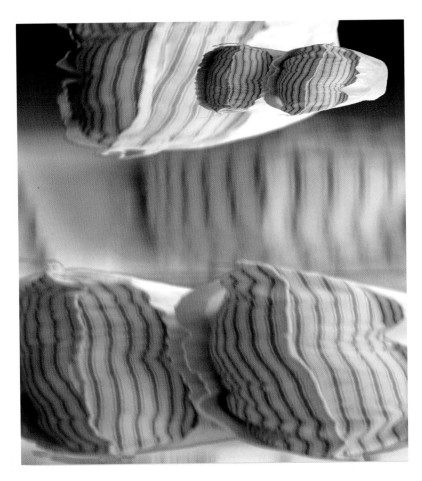

2.29 Deborah Oropallo, *Sleep*, 2005. Permanent pigment print and acrylic canvas, 42 × 37 in. (106.7 × 94 cm). Our normal expectation for images placed high in the picture plane is for them to drop. Pictorial shapes that resist gravity create visual tension and interest. In this image, there is a subtle adjustment in our psychological expectations. Because of the strategic placement of the high pillows, they psychologically join through closure with the top edge of the picture frame. The surrounding value contrasts reinforce the attraction to the area, with the net effect being a sense of the pillow shapes drifting away. Courtesy of the artist.

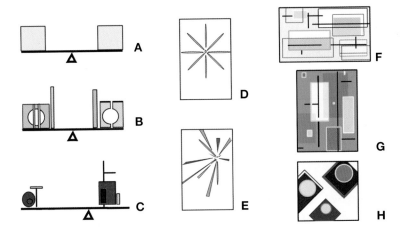

2.30 Diagrams A, B, and C illustrate the basic concept of balance by using horizontal balance beams and pivot points (fulcrums). Diagrams D and E illustrate balance that radiates around a central point. Diagrams F, G, and H show components balanced horizontally, vertically, and diagonally. The pictorial layout can have a bearing on which system is emphasized.

When we apply this concept to art, balance does not result from the actual physical weighing process. The visual weight or force of any area within an artwork depends on the amount of attention that area draws—its level of visual impact. Such judgments are based on the experience of the artist and his or her intuitive grasp of the principles of physics. In art, compositions are not restricted to balancing elements on the left with elements on the right. Instead, balance may be established radially (around a fixed point), horizontally, vertically, and diagonally (fig. 2.30 D–H).

In graphic composition, balance refers to the optical equilibrium felt among all parts of the work. The artist balances forces horizontally, vertically, and diagonally in all directions and positions (fig 2.31). Several factors, when combined with the elements, contribute to balance in a work of art. These factors or variables are position or placement, size, proportion, character, and direction of the elements. Of these factors, position plays the lead role. If two shapes of equal physical qualities are placed near the left side of a picture frame, the work will appear out of balance with the right side. Such shapes should be positioned to contribute to the total balance of all the picture parts involved. Similarly, the other factors can put a pictorial arrangement in or out of balance according to their use.

As the eye travels over the picture surface, it pauses momentarily at the significant picture parts—areas where there is an increased degree of visual impact due to the contrast of an element's size, color, texture, and so forth relative to its surroundings. These points of interest represent moving and directional forces that may be termed **moments of force.** In seeking balance, the artist should recognize that the varied elements create the moments of force, and their discriminating placement will result in controlled tension. Such forces should be positioned to

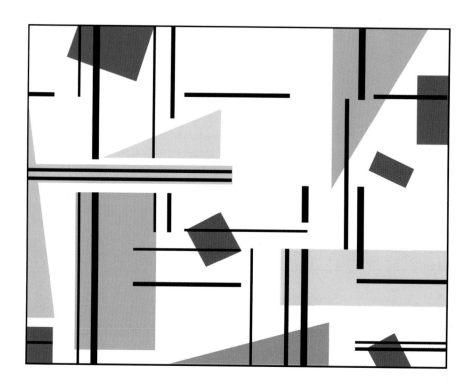

2.31 In this illustration, the visual weights and directional forces are equalized in all directions—horizontally, vertically, and diagonally.

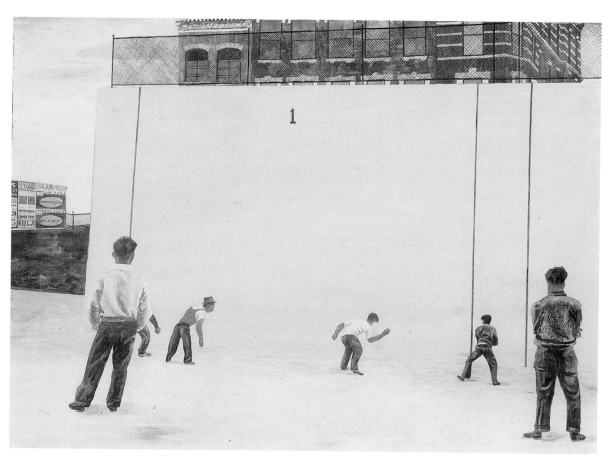

2.32 Ben Shahn, *Handball*, 1939. Tempera on paper over composition board, 22¾ × 31¼ in. (57.8 × 79.4 cm). The figures, numbers, and buildings may be seen as moments of force. The artist strategically arranges them to establish tension between areas within the composition and create a sense of balance. The Museum of Modern Art, New York, Abby Aldrich Rockfeller Fund. Photo © The Museum of Modern Art/Licensed by SCALA/Art Resource, NY. © Estate of Ben Shahn/Licensed by VAGA, New York, NY.

contribute to the *total balance* of all the picture parts involved. In the painting *Handball* (fig. 2.32), Ben Shahn creates tension between the two figures in the foreground and the number 1 at the top of the wall. These forces together support one another. The darker values of the building above the large wall are balanced by those of the dark wall and billboard on the left and of the figures in the lower portion of the painting.

Symmetrical Balance (Formal Balance)

A symmetrical image represents the simplest form of artistic balance. It has elements and visual units repeated on both sides on an imaginary central axis in mirrorlike fashion (fig. 2.33). When those visual units are exactly the same on both sides, *pure* **symmetry** is created.

Symmetrical images can be confrontational; they can stare directly at us in an intimidating manner. This frontality captures our attention, but its hold on us is usually short-lived because of the static quality of the composition. However, secondary features may tend to alleviate this somewhat. Because of the nature of symmetry, unity can be readily achieved, but the artist is challenged to maintain our interest with details and contrasts.

Approximate Symmetrical Balance

The potential monotony of pure symmetry can be reduced by subtly varying the nature of the repetition to achieve **approximate symmetry.** Balance is still the objective, and the solution is similar, but the artistic components, instead of being identical, are different. With approximate symmetry, the parts on either side of the imaginary central axis are positioned in the same manner, but they are slightly altered in size, color, number, and so on so that both sides are similar without being exact replicas. Approximate symmetry requires more sensitivity from the artist regarding the

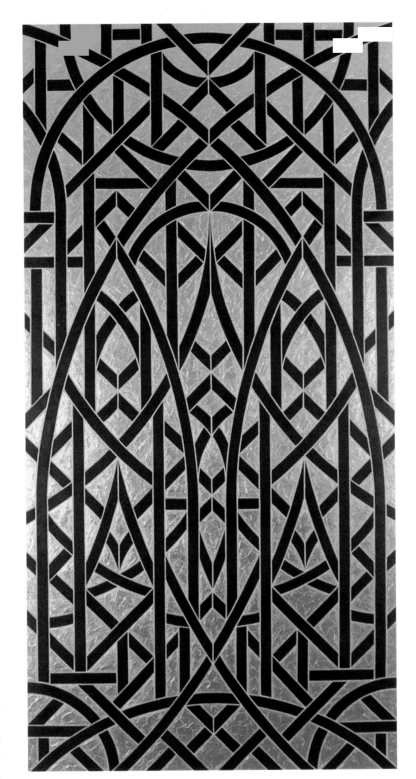

2.33   Valerie Jaudon, *Big Springs*, 1980. Gold leaf and oil on canvas, 96 × 48 in. (243.8 × 121.9 cm). This symmetrical composition is divided equally by a subtle vertical axis. Each side of this center line is repeated in mirrorlike duplication. The active interlacing pattern helps prevent this work from being visually static. © Valerie Jaudon/Licensed by VAGA, New York, NY.

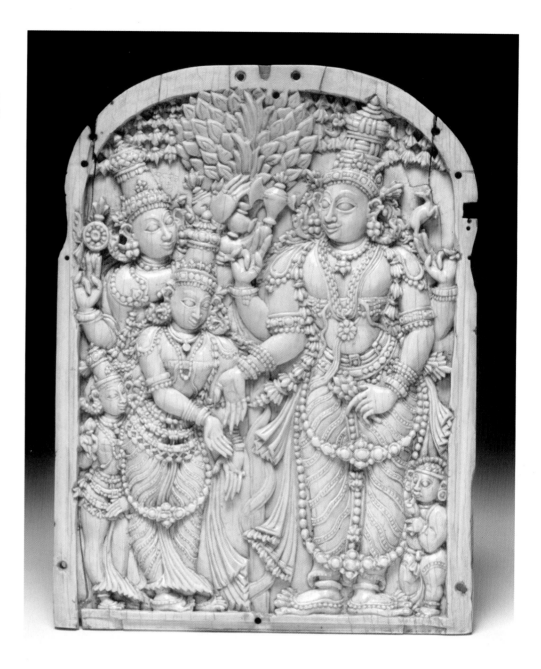

2.34 Unknown artist, *The Marriage of Shiva and Parvati: The Wedding of the Charming One,* South India (Madurai), 1766. Carved ivory with traces of tamarind juice, 16 × 11 cm. This Hindu ivory carving has approximate symmetrical balance. Relatively equal visual weights are placed on either side of a subtle vertical axis, although neither side is exactly the same. © V&A Images, Victoria and Albert Museum.

various weights of the components, for both sides must still balance out. Overall, compositions with approximate symmetry are potentially more interesting than those with pure symmetry—the differences produce more interest and may thereby hold viewer attention. With approximate symmetry, the potential monotony of pure symmetry is somewhat relieved, although the image is still fairly static (figs. 2.34 and 2.35; see also figs. 4.20 and 8.45).

Radial Balance

Another type of arrangement, called **radial** balance, can create both *true* and *approximate* symmetry. In radial balance, however, the visual forces are distributed around a central point and often radiate from it. The rotation of these forces results in a visual circulation, adding a new dimension to what might otherwise be static, symmetrical balance. Pure radial balance balances

opposing forces, but interesting varieties can be achieved by modifying the spaces, numbers, and directions of the forces (figs. 2.36 and 2.37).

Radial balance is widely used in the applied arts. For instance, jewelers often use radial patterns for stone settings on rings, pins, necklaces, and brooches. Architects have featured this principle in quatrefoils and "rose" windows, where the panes of glass are radially arranged like flower petals. Plates and vessels of

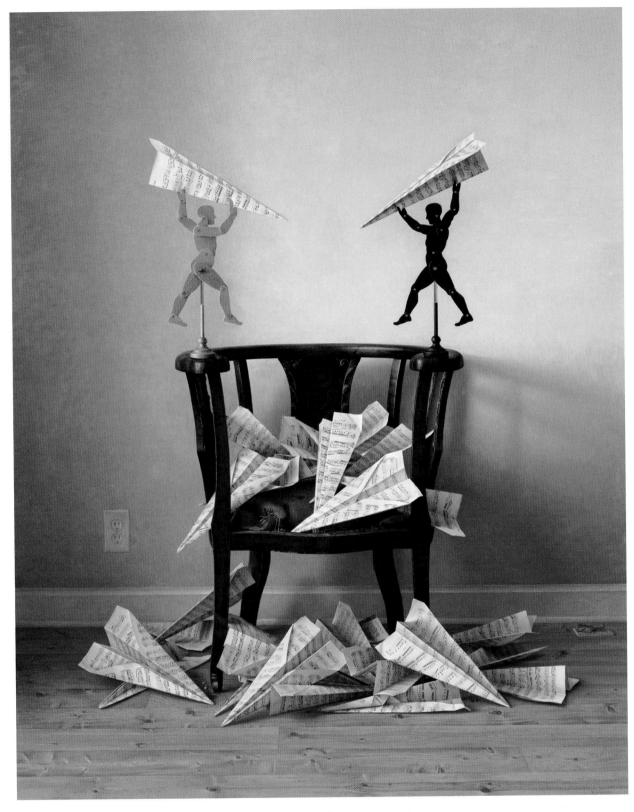

2.35 Scott Fraser, *Black and White,* 2004. Oil on board, 75 × 59 in. *Black and White* makes effective use of approximate symmetry. At first glance, the left and right sides of the painting may appear to be mirror images, other than the obvious value contrasts of the human figurines. However, note the wall socket, the shadows, and the variety of paper-airplane positions on the floor and the chair. Private collection. Courtesy of Scott Fraser.

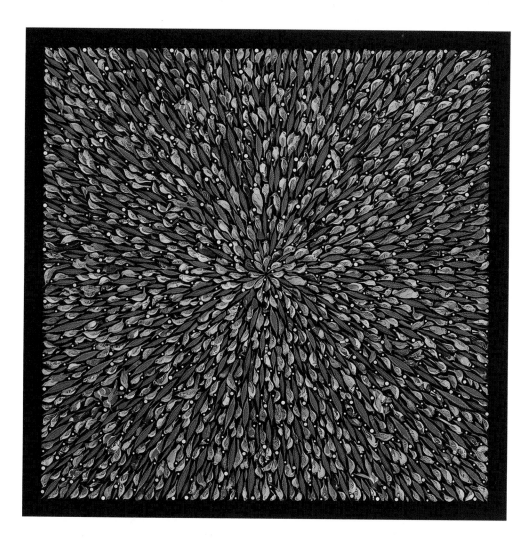

2.36 Fred Tomaselli, *Bird Blast,* 1997. Pills, hemp leaves, photocollage, acrylic, resin on wood panel, 60 × 60 in. (152.4 × 152.4 cm). With radial balance, there is frequently a divergence from some (usually central) source. Here, too, the linear development of the red leaves and the birds seems to explode from the center of the composition. Gift of Douglas S. Cramer. The Museum of Modern Art, New York, NY. U.S.A. Digital image © The Museum of Modern Art/Licensed by SCALA/Art Resource, NY.

2.37 Marc Chagall, *I and the Village,* 1911. Oil on canvas, 6 ft. 3⅝ in. × 4 ft. 11⅝ in. (1.92 × 1.51 m). The fairy-tale world of the imagination is found in this example by an artist who evades fixed classification. Recent technological concepts (X-rays and flight) are reflected in the freely interpreted transparent objects and in the disregard for gravity. © 2008 Artists Rights Society (ARS), New York/ADGP, Paris. The Museum of Modern Art, New York, NY. U.S.A. Mrs. Simon Guggenheim Fund. Digital image © The Museum of Modern Art/ Licensed by SCALA/Art Resource, NY.

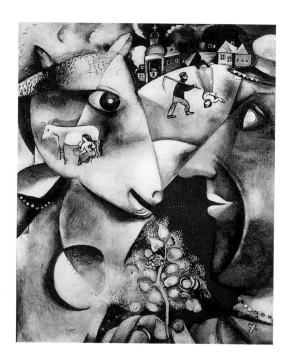

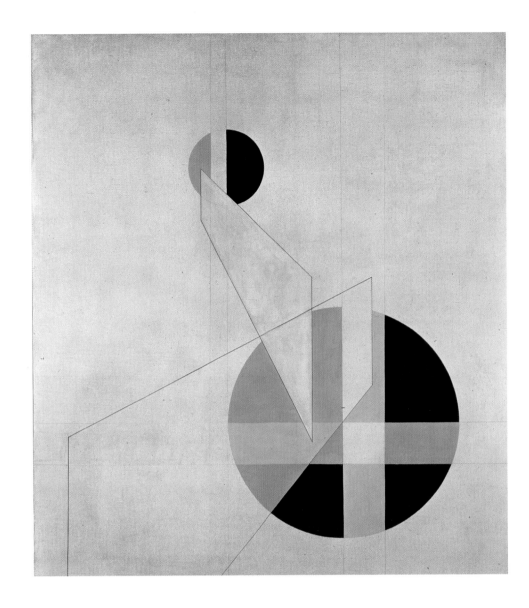

2.38 László Moholy-Nagy, *A XX*, 1924. Oil on canvas, 53⅜ × 45¼ inches (135.5 × 115 cm). This asymmetrical painting relies on an equilibrium that is felt between the visual weights and forces of the shapes, colors, lines, and surrounding negative area. Each element is strategically placed and accented to balance another. Art © Artists Rights Society (ARS), New York, VG Bild-Kunst, Bonn. Photo © CNAC/MNAM/Dist. Réunion des Musées Nationaux/Art Resource, NY.

all kinds evolve on the potter's wheel in a radial manner and frequently give evidence of this genesis. Radial balance may be seen in two-dimensional work as well, and the visual material producing the radial effect can be either non-objective or figurative.

Asymmetrical Balance (Informal/Occult Balance)

Balance created through **asymmetry** achieves an optical equilibrium of the elements that is "felt" or implied among all parts of the work. Asymmetry is also sometimes referred to as an *informal* or *occult* balance because it is hidden, somewhat mysterious, and intended to be experienced across the entire composition (figs. 2.38 and 2.39; see also figs. 2.32 and 8.42).

As the name suggests, asymmetry does not involve a central axis or any degree of symmetry but rather balances forces horizontally, vertically, and diagonally in all directions. Visual units that have very different moments of force (degrees of emphasis) may be made to balance each other depend-ing on the position of the units, and the visual center of balance may thus be in any location. For example, a "felt" balance might be achieved between a small area of strong color and a large empty space. The placement of that colored area would depend on its qualities like size, shape, and so forth, as well as the size of the negative area around it. There are no rules for achieving asymmetrical balance. If, however, the artist can establish the opposing forces and their tensions so that they seem to balance each other within a total concept

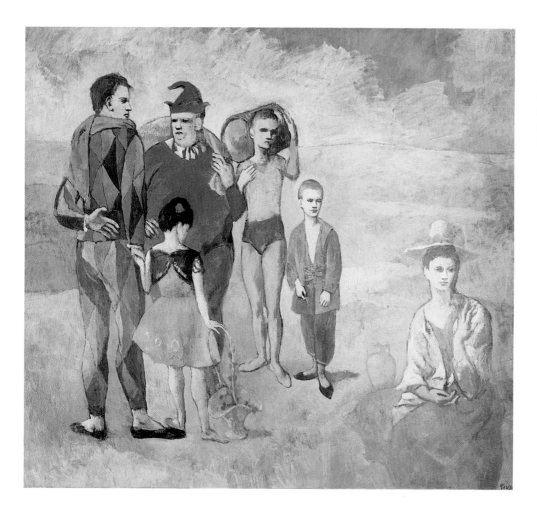

2.39 Pablo Picasso, *Family of Saltimbanques*, 1905. Oil on canvas, 6 ft. 11¾ in. × 7 ft. 6⅜ in. (2.13 × 2.30 m). An intuitive balance is achieved through the asymmetrical distribution of varying shapes, similar values, and related colors. Chester Dale Collection. © 2008 Board of Trustees, National Gallery of Art, Washington. Photo: B. Grove © 2008 Estate of Pablo Picasso/Artists Rights Society (ARS), New York.

(contributing to the allover balance of the total picture), the result will be vital, dynamic, and expressive.

While working on the image, the sense of compositional balance changes each time an element is added, subtracted, or altered—so one adjustment may require subsequent modification in other areas. Asymmetrical artwork entails an intricate balancing act for the artist, but the potential compositional arrangements are varied and countless.

Proportion

Proportion deals with the ratio of individual parts to one another or to the whole. For example, the length of an arm in comparison to the length of the whole body is a proportional relationship. In works of art, appropriate proportions are often difficult to determine and the relationships of parts are hard to compare with accuracy because proportion is often a matter of personal judgment. When the ratios of parts to the whole seem logically related, the proportions create harmony and balance. Those parts that are disproportionately enlarged or diminished create variety that can aid in expressing an idea. The term **scale** is used when proportion is related to size and refers to a standard gauge or "norm" in order to judge the relationship between objects. For example, the human figure is a norm used by architects for scaling buildings as well as by artists for representing scale in artworks.

Artists have been seeking an ideal standard for proportional relationships since ancient times. Classical Greek philosophy expressed the view that mathematics was the controlling force of the universe and established the **golden mean,** sometimes called the **golden section,** to represent the ideal standard for proportion and balance in life and art. The Greek mathematician Euclid held that the golden mean was the "moderation of all things," a place between two extremes. The golden section, as it applies to works of art, states that a smaller part relates to a larger part as the larger part relates to the whole. It may be seen in a geometric relationship when a line is divided into what is called the mean and extreme ratio (fig. 2.40). When a line AB is sectioned at point C, AC is the same ratio to AB as CB is to AC; that is, AC: AB = CB:AC. This extreme and mean ratio has a numerical value of 0.6180. Any new unit will be this much smaller or larger than the original unit, making those units in a ratio of 1 to 1.6180. Applying this concept to geometry, the Greeks sought the most beautifully proportioned rectangle that could be created out of a square. They arrived at what is

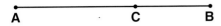

2.40 This line is divided into a geometric relationship known as the mean and extreme ratio. This is sometimes referred to as the golden mean or golden section.

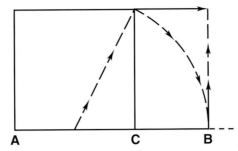

2.41A A golden rectangle may be found by extending the baseline of a perfect square in one direction. With a compass point fixed on the center of the square's baseline, draw an arc from the upper corner of the square down to the extended baseline. Having thus located the length of the new rectangle, draw a line upward to the line extended from the top of the square.

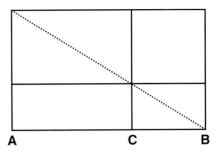

2.41B A diagonal line drawn across the new rectangle will cross the original square where the golden mean should be drawn parallel to the baseline. Measuring the sides of the golden rectangle will expose some interesting mathematical relationships. Comparing the original length of the square (AC) to the length of the new rectangle (AB) will reveal the same ratio as that of the length of the new addition (CB) to the original square (AC). That ratio will be 1:1.6180. (See the discussion of the Fibonacci series in this chapter.)

referred to as the golden rectangle (figs. 2.41A and B and 2.42A and B).

Holding the human figure in highest esteem, the ancient Greeks devised special proportional standards for their figurative works. We find these standards in their sculpture. The scale was based on certain mathematical canons, or rules, that established ideal relations of human parts. A figure, for example, was determined to be seven and one-half heads tall, and the distance from the top of the head to the chest was said to be one-quarter of the total height. The Greek sculptor Polyclitus is thought to be the first to have issued such a canon in the form of a written treatise (which has since been lost). The bronze copy of his sculpture of a spear bearer (the original also lost) is sometimes called "the canon" because it best demonstrates his standard for figure proportions (fig. 2.43). The idea of affording keenly pleasing proportional relationships extended into all areas of daily Greek life.

Historically, these ancient Greek ideals had continuing effects, influencing generations of artists. Leonardo Fibonacci, a medieval mathematician of the thirteenth century, discovered a series of related numbers. The sequence was created by adding together the two previous numbers to arrive at each new number: 0, 1, 1, 2, 3, 5, 8, 13, 21, 34, 55, and so on. Published in *Liber Abaci (Book of the Abacus)* in 1202, this sequence is called the Fibonacci series and also demonstrates an increasing ratio of approximately 1:1.6180. Indeed, one may start with any number. Using 10 as an example, one can multiply by

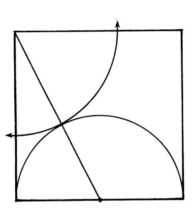

2.42A A golden mean may also be established *inside* of a square. From the center of the base of the square, draw a semicircle inside the square. Next draw a line from the center of the baseline to the square's upper corner. Where the diagonal crosses the first circle, establish a radius from the upper corner, and draw an arc to the top and side of the square.

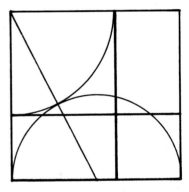

2.42B Lines drawn parallel to the top and side of the square from the points of intersection by the second arc will subdivide the square into golden rectangles with the mathematical ratio of 1:1.6180. This process may be done again from the opposite side or repeated in the new squares just created. This subdivision could continue on indefinitely revealing the same ratio of 1:1.6180. (See the discussion of the Fibonacci series in this chapter.)

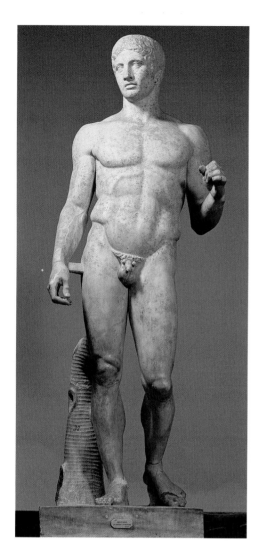

2.43 Polyclitus of Argos, *Doryphoros* (Roman copy), 450–440 B.C.E. Marble, 6 ft. 11 in. (212 cm) high. Polyclitus wrote a theoretical treatise and demonstrated a new system of ideal proportions in a sculpture, which took the form of a young man walking with a spear (the spear is no longer extant). The Greeks called the figure "Doryphoros" (spear carrier). The Polyclitus style was characterized by harmonious and rhythmical composition, and it influenced Roman culture. Museo Archeologico Nazionale, Naples, Italy. Scala/Art Resource, New York.

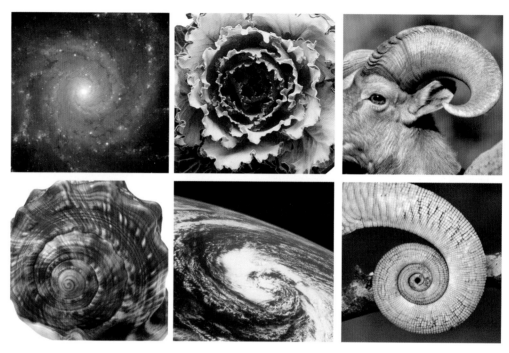

2.44 Examples of spiraling curves taken from nature. From top left to bottom left: © Gemini Observatory-GMOS Team. © C Squared Studios/Getty Images. © Brand X Pictures. © Nicole Duplaix/NGS/Getty Images. © StockTrek/Getty Images. © Martin Harvey/Getty Images.

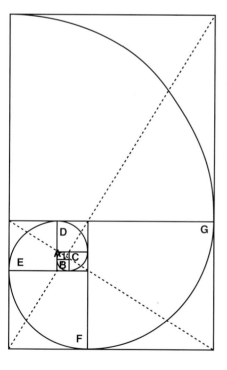

2.45A The spiraling curve is created by the continuing projection of the golden section and may be drawn with the aid of a compass. The inside corner of the square locates the compass point, which scribes an arc from corner to corner. This line is continued into the next square with a new compass point located on the inside center corner of that square. The process continues from square to square until the spiral is completed.

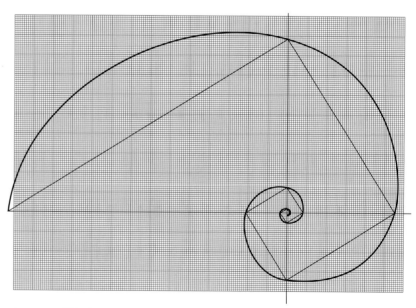

2.45B This diagram illustrates the same spiral, created by plotting the numbers from the Fibonacci series (1, 1, 2, 3, 5, 8, 13, 21, 34, 55, 89, 144) on a horizontal and vertical axis.

1.6180 to get the number 16. From that point, simply adding the previous two numbers will provide the next number (10, 16, 26, 42, 68 . . .), and consecutive numbers in the growing sequence will have the same ratio as the golden section.

Today, scientists recognize this relationship in nature. It is found in the expanding curve of the nautilus shell, the curve of a cat's claw, the spiral growth of a pinecone, the seed patterns in a sunflower's head, and the center of a daisy (fig. 2.44). Botanists study this spiral arrangement (called phyllotaxy) in leaves, scales, and flowers. This spiraling curve may be demonstrated in the continuing projection of the golden rectangle into progressively larger and larger units (fig. 2.45A and B).

During the Renaissance, artists like Leonardo da Vinci renewed interest in mathematically formulated proportional scaling. This can be found, for example, in Leonardo's drawing *Proportions of the Human Figure* (fig. 2.46).

Modern artists also have composed pictures that conform to the standard frame shape of the golden rectangle. The French painter Georges Seurat is known for his scientifically measured use of the Post-Impressionistic technique of Pointillism and his use of light and simultaneously contrasted colors. He was also intrigued with the mathematical proportions of the golden rectangle. In the painting *Circus Sideshow (La Parade)*, Seurat used subtle variations of golden rectangles and squares (fig. 2.47A and B). Notice how he strategically placed the softly rounded figures, the tree, the geometric forms, and the various decorative motifs at golden-section points.

Most artists seek balance and logical proportions. The dimensions of the images reproduced in this book would reinforce this claim. However, some artists choose to disregard the essentials of proportions—that is, harmonious and balanced relationships—in order to

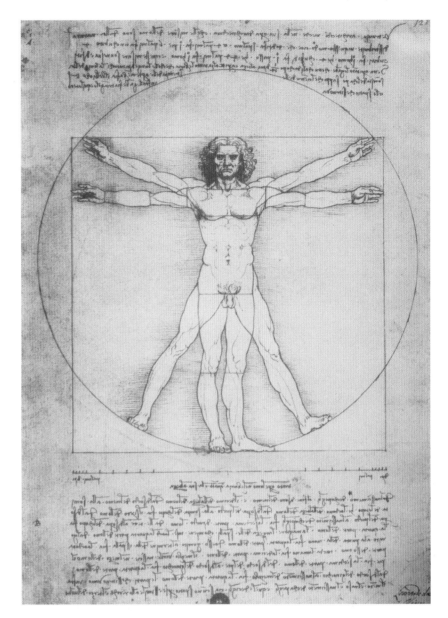

2.46 Leonardo da Vinci, *Proportions of the Human Figure* (after Vitruvius), c. 1485–90. Pen and ink, 13½ × 9¾ in. (34.3 × 24.8 cm). Here, Leonardo demonstrates his interest in human anatomy. By positioning a male figure within a circle and a square, Leonardo was investigating the proportional relationships of the head, body, arms, and legs. Note that the figure's height is equal to its outstretched arms and that the square's center is located where the legs join while the circle's center is the navel. Accademia, Venice, Italy. Corbis-Bettmann.

emphasize the extremes of scale. When a very large shape is placed alongside a much smaller one in an artwork, the effect is disproportionate. A spectator may register some dismay when confronted with extreme examples of disproportionate scale. Common objects become unsettling when made monumental (fig. 2.48). When making judgments in determining proportions, most artists will rely on an educated intuition and will adjust and readjust the sizes of their elements until they relate well to the whole work.

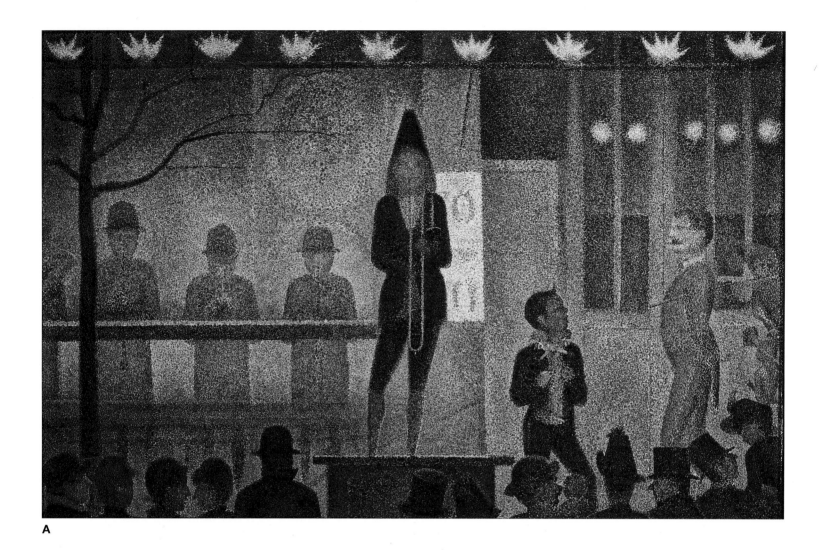

A

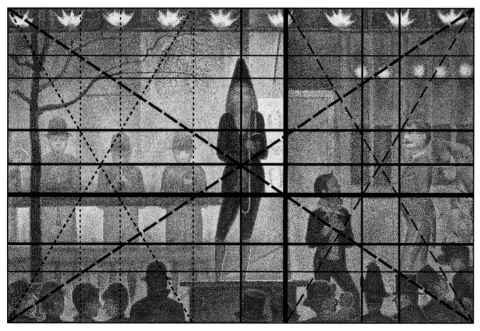

B

2.47 Georges Seurat, *Circus Sideshow (La Parade)*, 1887–88. Oil on canvas, 39¼ × 59 in. (99.7 × 149.9 cm). (B) When this Seurat painting is divided by a diagonal from upper left to lower right (large dashes), it crosses the large square where a golden rectangle would be subdivided by a heavy horizontal line. Smaller golden rectangles are created in the vertical rectangle on the right. These small rectangles may be further divided by intersecting diagonals. This could continue indefinitely. In addition, when another large square is established on the right side of the picture (small dotted lines) and a diagonal is drawn from lower left to upper right, the left side may be broken down into smaller golden rectangles that mirror those on the right side of the diagram. Notice how Seurat has used these lines and their intersections for the strategic placement of figures and imagery. The Metropolitan Museum of Art, Bequest of Stephen C. Clark, 1960. (61.101.17) Photograph © The Metropolitan Museum of Art.

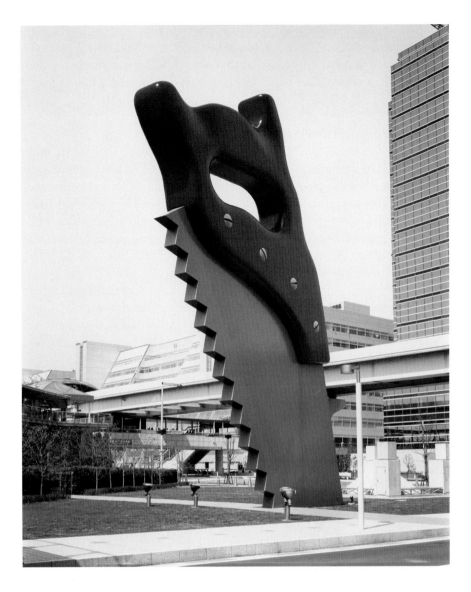

2.48 Claes Oldenburg and Coosje van Bruggen, *Saw, Sawing*, 1996. Steel, epoxy resin, fiber-reinforced plastic, urethane and polyvinylchloride foams, painted with polyester gelcoat, 50 ft. 8 in. × 4 ft. 9 in. × 40 ft. (15.4 × 1.5 × 12.2 m). This clearly recognizable object far surpasses the scale expected of it. Courtesy Oldenburg van Bruggen Studio. Photography by Spatial Design Consultants Co., Ltd., Yokohama.

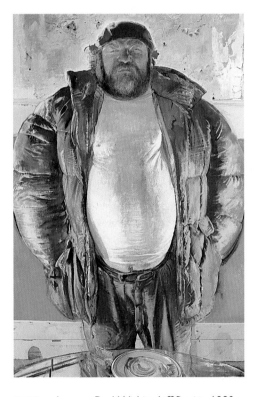

2.49 Jerome Paul Witkin, *Jeff Davies*, 1980. Oil on canvas, 6 × 4 ft. (1.83 × 1.22 m). If there was ever a painting in which one subject dominated the work, this must be it. Most artworks do not need this degree of dominance, but Witkin evidently wanted a forceful presence—and he got it. Palmer Museum of Art, Pennsylvania State University. Gift of the American Academy and Institute of Arts and Letters (Hassam and Speicher Purchase Fund).

Still, many artists find a need for enlarging and/or diminishing the sizes of certain elements to aid the expression of an idea or as a means of creating emphasis or dominance. When using changes in scale for emphasis, the artist will find that he or she can harness and sustain the observer's attention. In the Jerome Witkin painting *Jeff Davies* (fig. 2.49), the artist uses enlargement as a means of emphasizing the presence of his figure. The subject, a large, physically imposing man, is presented with a bulky torso in simple, light values, surrounded by the darker forms of the head, arms, jacket, and pants. The art-ist has positioned the white torso in the center of the composition for primary attention and has sized the figure's image so that it seems to burst the limits of the painting's format. Witkin's exaggerated enlargement and relative scaling came from his perceptions of the actual figure he was to represent. The result is an overpowering portrait.

Another way artists have used inordinate proportion or scaling is to indicate rank, status, or importance of religious, political, military, and social personages. *Hierarchical scaling* is a term used to describe this system, whereby figures of greatest importance are made

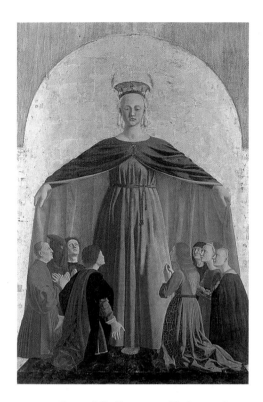

relatively larger to denote their status. In the painting *Madonna of Mercy*, Piero della Francesca doubled the size of his Madonna figure in order to elevate her to a lofty object of reverence (fig. 2.50). The proportions in this painting, and others like it, are subjective in their intent rather than representational (fig. 2.51).

The physical size of the work in comparison to human scale can also be utilized for expressive purposes. The artist Chuck Close tends to overwhelm us with paintings of enormous human heads (fig. 2.52). Resulting from their overall size—the portraits range from five to eight feet in height—there is a proportional enlargement of facial details, such as hairs and skin pores. The view of the artist in his studio illus-

trates the overpowering scale of these enlargements (see fig. 2.13). The heads, at first heroic, become intimidating and, in some respects, even frightening.

Dominance

While developing an image, an artist strives for interest by creating differences that emphasize the degrees of importance of its various parts. These differences result from compositional considerations within the medium—some features are emphasized, and others are subordinated. This creates both primary focal points and secondary areas of interest that help move the eye around the work.

Areas become dominant when they are emphasized by contrasts that make

2.50 Piero della Francesca, *Madonna of Mercy* (center panel of triptych), 1445–55. Oil and tempera on wood, height about 4 ft. 9 in. (1.44 m). The figure of Mary extends her arms to make a shelter of her cape for the smaller figures at her feet. The positioning of the worshipful figures who surround the central columnar form helps give a sense of depth to the scene. The artist's use of hierarchical scaling also strengthens the feeling of the maternal and merciful power of the Madonna. Italian Civic Museum, Sansepolcro, Italy/SuperStock.

2.51 Nancy Spero, *Artemis, Acrobats, Divas and Dancers*, 1999–2000. Glass and ceramic mosaic. Comparing the *Madonna of Mercy* (fig. 2.50) from 1445–55 with the female figure in Spero's *Artemis, Acrobats, Divas and Dancers* reveals a variety of ways to impart dominance. Even though the *Madonna* was made for a sacred space while Spero's *Artemis* resides in the profane space of a New York City subway stop, both use centrality to establish dominance. Francesca's *Madonna* also uses scale relationships within the painting to establish her importance. Staring directly at the viewer, Artemis spreads her arms in a gesture of independence, using her cape as an extension of her body. Gazing downward, the Madonna also spreads her arms but to envelop her dependents in a gesture of protection, making her cloak a refuge. While different, each pose expresses dominance. Public commission for MTA Arts for Transit, New York, NY. © Nancy Spero. Courtesy Galerie Lelong, New York.

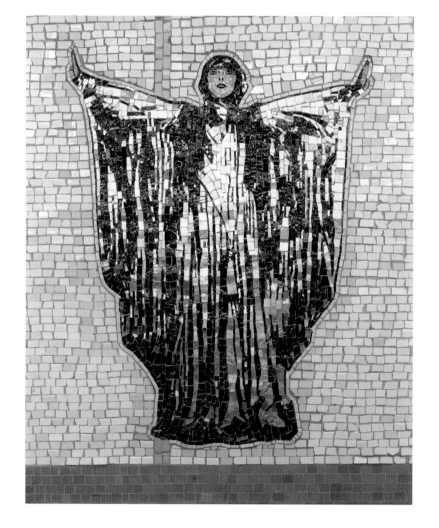

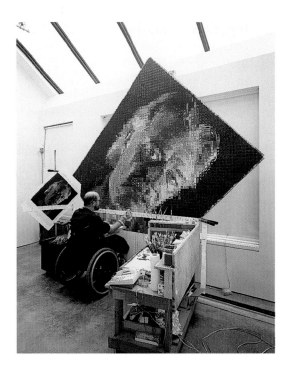

2.52 Chuck Close working on *John*, 1992. Oil on canvas, 100 × 84 in. The colossal size of the head in Close's painting requires an examination and interpretation of every textural and topographical feature of the model's face. Courtesy of PaceWildenstein. Photograph by Bill Jacobson.

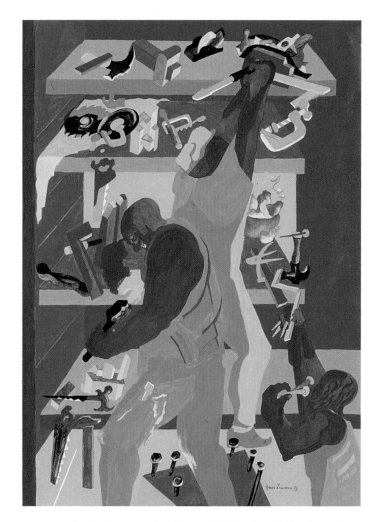

2.53 Jacob Lawrence, *Builders in the Workshop*, 1993. Gouache on paper, 28½ × 19 in. (72.3 × 47.7 cm). The human figures here become the focal points, or optical units of greatest importance, because of their size and activity. The dominant area is where the two central figures merge. The other figure directs attention toward the center, and the tables and tools are less dominant still. © 2008 The Estate of Gwendolyn Knight Lawrence/Artists Rights Society (ARS), New York.

them stand out from the rest. Contrast draws attention like the spotlight in a dramatic production or crescendo in a musical piece. In general, the greater the contrast, the greater the emphasis and the more dominant the area becomes.

The following methods of emphasis can be used to achieve **dominance:** (1) *isolation*—a separation of one part from others; (2) *placement*—"center stage" is most often used, but another position can be dominant, depending on the surroundings; (3) *direction*—a movement that contrasts with others draws focus; (4) *scale or proportion*—larger sizes normally dominate, but unusual scale or proportion also attracts attention; (5) *character*—a significant difference in general appearance is striking (such as a change in line quality). All of these are heightened by contrasts in the other elements used in their creation—color, value, texture, and so forth.

Artwork that neglects varying degrees of dominance seems to imply that everything is of equal importance, resulting in a confusing image that gives the viewer no direction and fails to communicate. This does not mean that areas of secondary dominance are insignificant to an overall composition. Those subordinate areas are actually just as vital, as they produce the norm against which the dominant parts are contrasted.

Regarding dominance, artists have two problems. First, they must see that each part has the necessary degree of importance; and second, they must incorporate these parts, with their varying degrees of importance, into the rhythmic movement and balance of the work. In doing this, artists often find that they must combine different methods to achieve dominance. One significant area might derive importance from its change in value, whereas another might rely on its busy or exciting shape (figs. 2.53, 2.54, and 2.55).

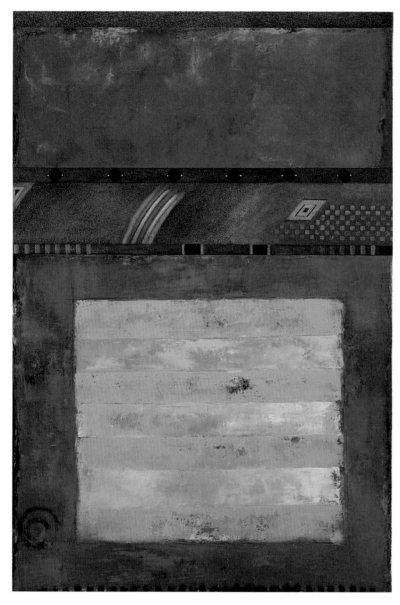

2.54 Poteet Victory, *Symbols of Manifest Destiny*, 1999. Oil and mixed media on canvas, 60 × 40 in. (152.4 × 101.6 cm). In this work, the yellow-orange striped rectangle becomes dominant because of the contrast of light against dark and warm color against cool color. Courtesy of the artist.

Movement

Many observers do not realize that in looking at artwork, they are being "taken on a tour." The tour director is, of course, the artist, who makes the eye travel comfortable and informative by providing visual pathways and areas of rest. The roadways leading to the rest stops have certain speed limits established by the artist, and the rest stops are of a predetermined duration.

The artist's roadways are, in fact, transitions between optical units, and the time required to negotiate them depends on the amount of harmony and variety applied to each. The eye movements dictated by these transitions are produced by the direction of lines, shapes, and shape edges (or contours) that seem to relate and "connect" to one another. The lines, shapes, and shape contours are generally pointed at one another or in the same general direction. They may be touching but are normally interrupted by gaps over which the eyes skip as they move about. Sometimes "leaps" are necessary, requiring strong directional thrusts and attractions.

The optical units that attract our attention contain vital information. In works that lack multiple areas of great emphasis, a single figure may be the dominant unit, as in the *Mona Lisa* (see fig. 5.12). Although extreme eye movement is not required throughout this composition, secondary material within the image may be of considerable inter-

2.55 Giambattista Tiepolo, *Madonna of Mt. Carmel and the Souls in Purgatory*, c. 1720. Oil on canvas, 82⅔ × 256 in. (210 × 650 cm). The movement weaves its way through this work because the lighting gives the figures dominance. © Scala/Ministero per i Beni e le Attivita culturali/Art Resource, New York.

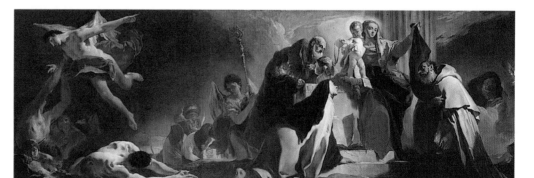

est and used to create its own pattern of **movement.** In other works, there may be several units of great interest that are widely separated, and it thus becomes critical that the observer's vision be directed to them. There is usually some hierarchy in these units, with some calling for more attention than others. Their degree of dominance usually determines the amount of time spent at each location.

The written word is read from side to side, but a visual image, whether two-dimensional or three-dimensional, can be read in any direction. The movement of one's eyes is dictated by the artist, who must ensure that all areas are exploited with no static or uninteresting parts. Carefully handled repetition and subtle variations both entice eye movement from one part of the composition to another. Areas of related values or colors may appear to move across a composition as a value pattern (fig. 2.56), while the pauses and beats of visual rhythms can create subtle changes that draw the eye along. By varying the negative space between individual shapes, movement can occur where groupings appear dense in one location and fade away in another. The movement should be self-renewing, constantly drawing the eye back into the work.

Artists not only can control eye movement across the surface of the composition but also direct movement into the depth of the pictorial space. Historically, the illusion of spatial positioning has been founded on linear perspective. Perspective is effective but not necessary. There is also "intuitive" space, which can suggest depth by using certain artistic devices—for example, overlapping, transparency, or simply a series of successively smaller objects that recede into the distance (see Chapter 8).

Some art, particularly kinetic (moving) sculpture, involves the physical movement of the work itself. As parts of the sculpture move about, the viewer stays to watch their changing relationships—this begins to incorporate the element of time into its movement (see Chapter 9, "Time and Motion"). However, most sculpture and picture surfaces are physically static, and movement must be developed through the artist's configuration of compositional parts.

Economy

As a work develops, the artist may realize that the solutions to various compositional problems are resulting in unnecessary complexity. This situation is frequently characterized by broad aspects of the work deteriorating into fragmentation, and it commonly results from the artist's working on one segment of the composition at a time. While this may be a necessary part of the developmental phase of the work, such isolated solutions may result in a lack of visual unity in the overall composition.

Sometimes order may be restored by returning to essentials, eliminating elaborate details, and relating the particulars to the whole. This sacrifice is not easily made or accepted because, in returning to essentials, interesting discoveries and effects must often be surrendered for legibility and a more direct expression. However, by applying the principle of economy, the work may regain a sense of unity.

Employing the principle of **economy** means composing with efficiency—

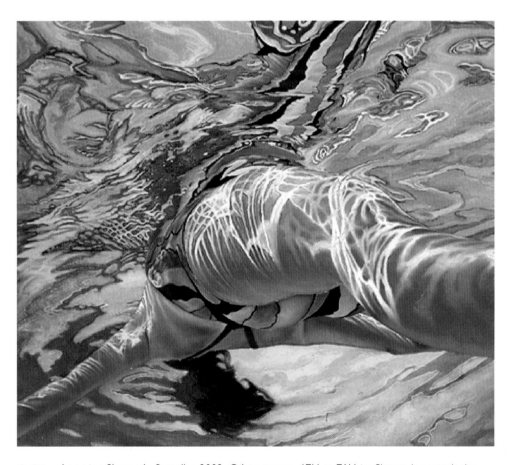

2.56 Lorraine Shemesh, *Propeller*, 2002. Oil on canvas, 67½ × 71½ in. Shemesh controls the movement through this painting with an interesting value pattern of light and dark colors. This movement is enhanced by an undulating repetition of shapes, the intersecting of curved lines, and the visual rhythms and patterns that they create. Private collection, courtesy Allan Stone Gallery, New York City.

The Principles of Organization   **85**

2.57 Tom Wesselmann, *1960 Judy Trying on Clothes,* 1997. Alkyd oil on cut-out aluminum, 58½ × 72½ in. Wesselmann has reduced the image to the few details he considers crucial, thereby practicing economy. Collection of the artist. Photograph by Jim Strong, Inc. © Estate of Tom Wesselmann/Licensed by VAGA, New York, NY.

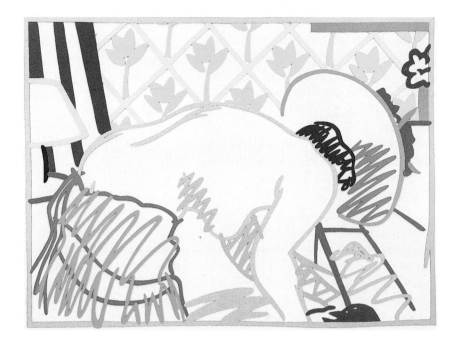

2.58 Milton Avery, *Seated Blonde,* 1946. Oil and charcoal on linen, 52 × 33¾ × 1 in. (132.1 × 85.7 × 0.4 cm). Avery has simplified the complex qualities of the surface structures of his two figures, reducing them to shapes and flat color. Through the use of economy, the artist abstracted the figures to strengthen their distance and isolation. Collection Walker Art Center, Minneapolis, Gift of Mr. and Mrs. Roy R. Neuberger, New York City, 1952. © 2008 Milton Avery Trust/Artists Rights Society (ARS), NY.

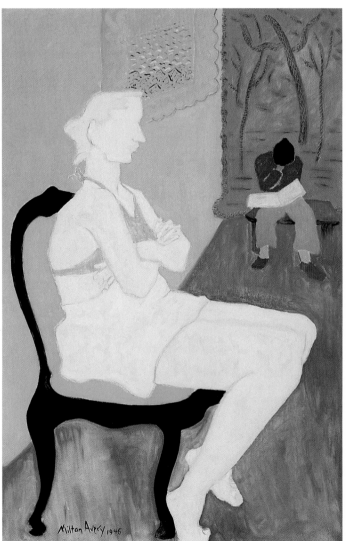

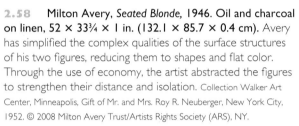

expressing an idea as simply and directly as possible with no arbitrary or excessive use of the elements. Economy has no rules but rather must be an outgrowth of the artist's instincts. If something works with respect to the whole, it is kept; if disruptive, it may be reworked or rejected.

Economy is sometimes associated with the term *abstraction.* Abstraction (simplification and rearrangement) implies an active process of selecting the essentials that strengthen both the conceptual and organizational aspects of the artwork. In some measure, the artistic style dictates the kind of abstraction, though all art requires abstraction to some degree.

While the early Modernists Pablo Picasso and Henri Matisse were among those most influential in the trend toward economical abstraction, economy is easy to detect in many contemporary art styles (figs. 2.57 and 2.58; see also figs. 4.1 and T.51). The hard-edged works of Ellsworth Kelly, the "field" paintings of Barnett Newman and Morris Louis, and the analogous color canvases of Ad Reinhardt all clearly feature economy (fig. 2.59; see also figs. 7.15 and T.78).

2.59 Barnett Newman, *Covenant,* 1949. Oil on canvas, 3 ft. 11¾ in. × 4 ft. 11⅝ in. (1.21 × 1.51 m). This example is characteristic of Newman, an early Color Field painter. Such works generally feature carefully placed stripes superimposed on a flat color. Hirshhorn Museum and Sculpture Garden, Smithsonian Institute, Washington, DC. Gift of Joseph H. Hirshhorn, 1972. Photo: Lee Stalsworth. © 2008 Barnett Newman Foundation/Artists Rights Society (ARS), New York.

The absence of elaboration results in a very direct statement.

In economizing, one flirts with monotony. Sometimes embellishments must be preserved or added to avoid this pitfall. But if the result is greater clarity, the risk (and the work) may be well worth it.

SPACE: RESULT OF ELEMENTS AND PRINCIPLES

The artist is always concerned about space as it evolves in an artwork. Some people regard space as an element (such as when working with sculpture), but for those working in a two-dimensional medium, it is a result of the elements as they are put into action and altered by the various principles of organization. In this section, we will only briefly cover some general aspects of spatial organization; Chapter 8 will explain in greater detail the different types of space and what the artist must do to achieve them.

In transferring nature's space to the canvas, the painter faces problems that have been dealt with in various ways in different historical periods. If the illusion of spatial phenomena is to be represented in the artwork, the artist must use the art elements to produce the effect sought. Quite often the artist uses the frame as a window into the space, terminating at some point or continuing to infinity. Such space is called *three-dimensional* or *plastic* because all of this seems to be condensed into the picture plane. These surfaces have their limits, but the illusion of depth gives a further dimension—a sense that actual 3-D space is involved. Artists *not* interested in developing the illusion of volume and depth may choose to work with a flat or shallow two-dimensional interpretation known as *decorative space*.

When considering space in a work, an artist usually looks for consistency of relationships. Nothing can throw an artwork so "out of kilter" as a jumbled spatial order. An artist who begins with one kind of space, say, a flat two-dimensional representation of a figure, should continue to develop 2-D concepts throughout the piece and in the succeeding stages of the artwork. Consistency contributes immeasurably to visual unity.

THREE-DIMENSIONAL FORM AND THE PRINCIPLES OF ORGANIZATION

The organizational principles used in three-dimensional art are the same as those used in two-dimensional art. However, three-dimensional forms, with their unique spatial properties, call for somewhat different applications of the principles.

Three-dimensional artists deal with forms that have multiple views (fig. 2.60). Composing is more complex. What might be a satisfactory solution for an arrangement with one view might be only a partial answer in the case of a work seen from many different positions. Adjustments of adjacent areas must be strong and intriguing enough to urge the viewer to move around the work, but not so strong that they destroy those areas in the new view. A series of calculated adjustments are required to totally unify a piece.

Compositionally, a three-dimensional work may be **tectonic** (closed, massive, and simple), with few and limited projections, as in figure 2.61, or **atectonic** (open, to a large degree), with frequent extensive penetrations and thin projections, as in figure 2.62. Both tectonic and atectonic arrangements can be found in nearly all 3-D art, and each of these arrangements can be used individually to achieve different expressive and spatial effects.

Harmony and Variety

Harmony and variety have been cited as indispensable concerns in the creation of two-dimensional artworks; this is equally true in the realm of the third

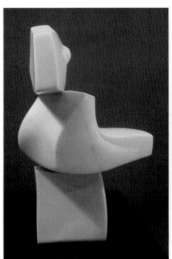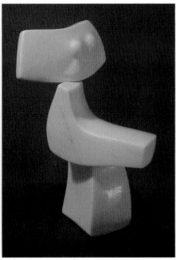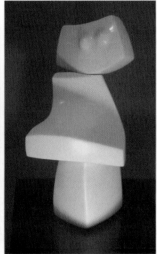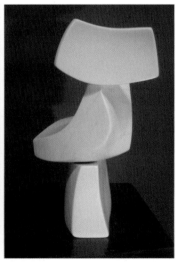

2.60   Shawn Morin, *Treasure Mountain Dove*, 2003. Colorado yule marble, 26 × 17 × 15 in. This sculpture encourages the viewer to move around the work. Relationships of shape and form are constantly changing with each new position. The change in the appearance from one view to the next represents the sculptor's challenge during creation—to make adjustments to the components in one view without destroying the structure of the next. Photos courtesy of the artist.

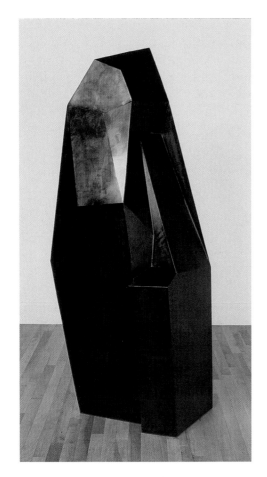

2.61 James DeWoody, *Big Egypt,* 1985. Black oxidized steel, 72 × 30 × 30 in. (182.9 × 76.2 × 76.2 cm). In this example of a tectonic arrangement, James DeWoody has cut planes that project in and out of his surfaces without penetrating voids or opening spaces. This is sometimes referred to as "closed" composition. Courtesy of the Arthur Roger Gallery, New Orleans, LA.

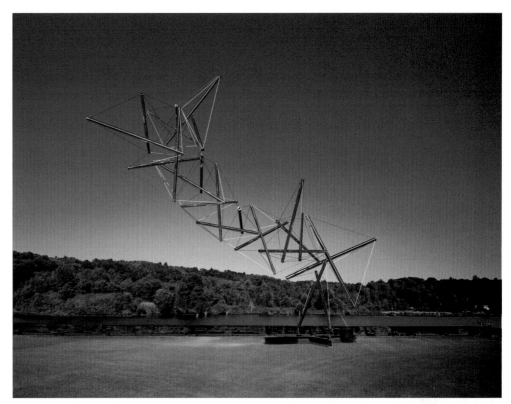

2.62 Kenneth Snelson, *Dragon,* 2000–3. Stainless steel, 30.5 × 31 × 12 ft. (9.3 × 9.5 × 3.65 m). Kenneth Snelson has developed sculptures that are "open," or atectonic. Based on technical principles related to the geometry of atoms, helixes, and weaving, his works are often referred to as "floating compression" or "tensegrity" installations. This work, *Dragon,* uses a steel cable to suspend individual steel tubes in the air with only minimal ground support. Courtesy of the artist. Photo © Jan Cook.

dimension, although its discernment is not always so obvious and its achievement somewhat different because it exists in the round. One must keep in mind that in order to fully view a three-dimensional work such as sculpture, the viewer must circumnavigate the work, which has an almost infinite number of viewpoints. The interest generated by the many views under the control of the sculptor produces a degree of variety, but this must be balanced by harmony for the benefit of the work's totality.

Extensions are an important consideration in producing harmony and in leading the viewer around a sculpture. These subjective edges, lines, and shapes suggest directions around the work in the same way extensions unify 2-D work. They imply connections with other such lines and shapes, thus creating a continuous movement encircling the work. The *repetition* of elements—line, shape, color, value, and texture—helps establish harmony and adds to the sense of visual flow (fig. 2.63).

The sculptor can calculate this movement to give a sense of rhythm that is either agitated or comparatively calm. Predictable rhythm incorporates proportional transitions that give flow to a work (fig. 2.64). If there are areas the sculptor considers significant, *closure*—employing the proximity of certain shapes or lines—may be used to draw attention to those passages. There are instances where the tension between close forms is emphasized and the work harmonized by the application of

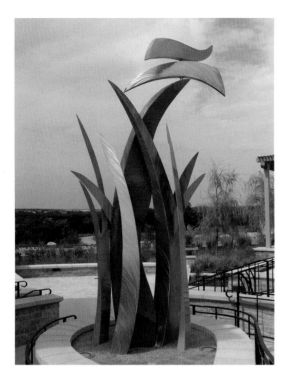

2.63 John Mishler, *Wind Seeker*, Stainless steel, paint, and bearings, 14 × 5 × 6 ft. (4.3 × 1.5 × 1.8 m). The repetition of the grasslike shapes, their graceful curves, and the shared markings of the polished surfaces help create harmony in this sculpture. In addition, the upward thrust and implied connection of the extended shape edges add to the unity and create visual movement within the piece. Commissioned for the Wolf Ranch Mall, Georgetown, TX. Courtesy of John Mishler.

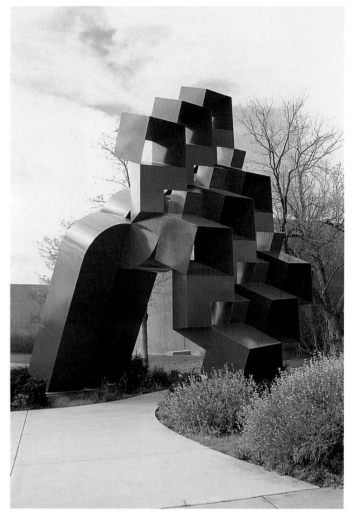

2.64 Sebastian, *Variación Nuevo Mexico*, 1989. Painted steel, **27 × 24 × 24 ft.** The rhythmical repetition of the stepping planes in Sebastian's sculpture creates an exciting, flowing movement. Funded by the City of Albuquerque 1% for Art Program and The Albuquerque Museum, 1987 General Obligation Bonds. In commemoration of the Sister City relationship between Albuquerque and Chihuahua, Mexico. Photograph © 2008 Jonathan A. Meyers.

interpenetration, with one form passing through another. Viewers must, however, be able to extricate themselves from these areas to facilitate the continuous movement sought.

Some sculptors make use of transparent materials, such as glass (fig. 2.65), rather than opaque media. The superimposition of such material creates genuine *transparency,* unlike the illusions of two-dimensional art. This also can suggest space, albeit usually in a limited way. Architects, who are increasingly sculptural in their vision,

sometimes make use of *overlapping* to produce harmony among the sections of their building structures. Additionally, in sculpture, there are instances of *interpenetration,* notably in large metal pieces or works with reflective surfaces.

Variety, as in 2-D works, is achieved by increasing the dissimilarities between areas or by reducing or reversing the means by which harmony is produced. Contrasts in shapes, textures, values, colors, and lines will all increase the amount of variety, even if there is

only a small change—the aim being, of course, to create greater interest.

The ultimate goal is an effective combination (sometimes a precarious balance) of both harmony and variety. This goal is a concern of all three-dimensional artists, whatever the nature of the work. It might be added that sculptural work in *low relief* (having shallow surface depth) is closely related to 2-D work, whereas *high-relief* sculpture is somewhat of a hybrid production, at times calling on some of the problems of harmony and variety encountered in *sculpture-in-the-round*

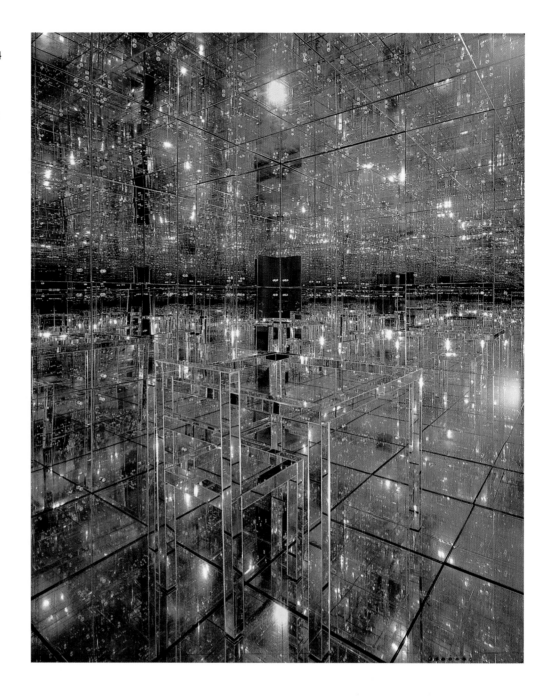

2.65 Lucas Samaras, *Mirrored Room*, 1966. Mirrors on wooden frame, 9 × 9 × 10 ft. (2.44 × 2.44 × 3.05 m). This is an example of Environmental Art, which, by its size and structure, may actually enclose the observer within the form of the work. Albright-Knox Art Gallery, Buffalo, NY. Gift of Seymour H. Knox, 1966.

(freestanding forms meant to be experienced from all sides).

Balance

When considering balance and the extension of spatial effects in three-dimensional art, we need to examine some special conditions. For example, when balancing a 3-D piece of work, the added dimension of depth affects its multiple views. While a sphere appears symmetrical from any view, a rectangular box may appear symmetrical only when one of its sides is seen straight-on. If the rectangular box is seen at an angle, the multiple views seen in depth may project other types of balance.

Three types of balance are possible in actual space: symmetrical (fig. 2.66), asymmetrical (fig. 2.67), and radial (fig. 2.68). Of the three, symmetrical and radial balance are considered formal and regular. Radial balance is spherical, with the fulcrum in the center. The parts that radiate from this point are usually similar in their formations. However, artists

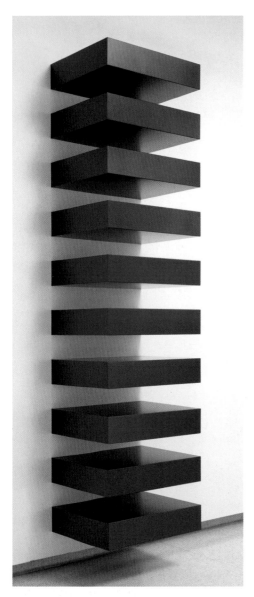

2.66 Donald Judd, *Untitled,* 1969/1982. Anodized aluminum, 6 × 27 × 24 in. (15.2 × 68.6 × 61 cm). In this minimal work, Judd is primarily interested in perceptually explicit shapes, reflective surfaces, and vertical interplay. There is a rhythm between shapes and negative space, and the work invites the eye to travel from one square to the next. Collection Walker Art Center, Minneapolis. Gift of Mr. and Mrs. Edmond R. Ruben, 1981. Art © Judd Foundation. Licensed by VAGA, New York, NY.

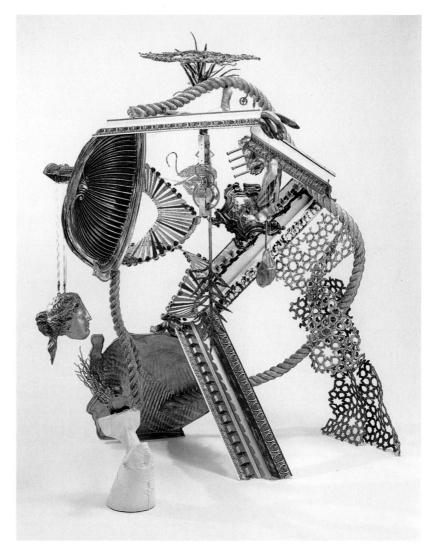

2.67 Nancy Graves, *Unending Revolution of Venus, Plants, and Pendulum,* 1992. Bronze, brass, enamel, stainless steel, and aluminum, 97 × 71½ × 56½ in. (2.46 × 1.82 × 1.44 m). In this sculpture, we see a variety of form parts. We also see an excellent example of an asymmetrically balanced sculpture. © Nancy Graves Foundation/ Licensed by VAGA, New York, NY. Photograph by Sam Kwong.

more commonly make use of asymmetrical balance because it provides the greatest individual latitude and variety.

Proportion

When we are viewing a three-dimensional work, the effect of proportion (the relationship of the parts to the whole) is fundamental in determining the basic form, for it sets the standard for relationships and permeates the other principles. Being in the presence of an actual 3-D work that can not only be seen but also touched or caressed, stood on, walked on, or passed through puts special emphasis on the relation of the parts to the whole. These proportional relations must apply continually in a 3-D work as we look at it from multiple views.

The actual size of a 3-D work when compared to the physical measurement of the human figure is referred to as its *scale*. Scale is most dramatic at the extremes, when 3-D pieces are small

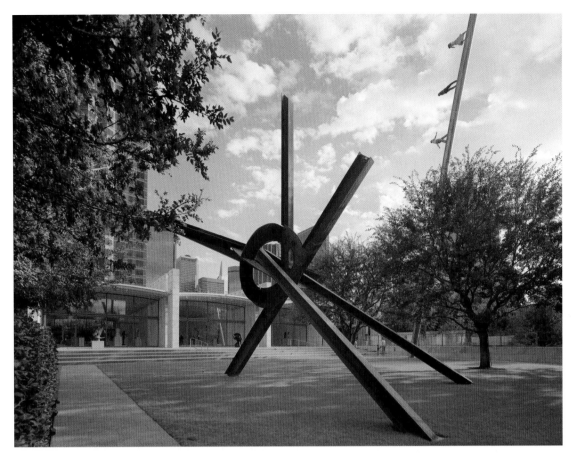

2.68 Mark di Suvero, *Eviva Amore*, 2001. Steel, Size unknown. The fulcrum of this sculpture is at the center of the work, identified by the circular shape, as the diagonal beams radiate in outwardly thrusting directions. Art © Mark di Suvero. Photo courtesy of Raymond and Patsy Nasher Collection, Dallas, Texas. Photographer: Tim Hursley.

enough to be held in the palm of the hand or when we stand in the presence of gigantic architecture, landscapes, or sculptures (see fig. 1.52). Small jewelry and miniaturized models (maquettes) are considered small scale. Larger works made for public places—like malls, parks, religious temples, mosques, or cathedrals—can be awe-inspiring in their size (see fig. 2.62).

Dominance

While developing a 3-D image, an artist strives for interest by creating differences through contrast that call attention to significant parts, making them dominant. As with 2-D organization, the emphasis or degree of contrast for the visual elements is varied to ensure that a hierarchy of importance is estab-

lished; some features are emphasized, and others are subordinated. This creates both primary focal points and secondary levels of interest that help move the eye around the work (see figs 2.63, 2.67, and 2.70). These differences result from compositional considerations within the medium.

Movement

Two types of movements are used by three-dimensional artists. Implied movement, the most common type, is illusionary (fig. 2.69; see also fig. 2.64), but actual movement—as with **kinetic** sculpture—involves the physical movement of the work itself. As parts of the sculpture move about, the viewer stays to watch their changing relationships. This infuses the element of time into

the composition and emphasizes those moving parts, thereby elevating their degree of dominance.

The actual movements found in kinetic art are set into motion by air, water, mechanical devices, or interactive computer-activated programs. Alexander Calder, an early innovator and the father of **mobile** sculptures, at first used motors to drive his pieces but later made use of air currents (fig. 2.70). Many contemporary sculptors also work with wind, water, and air propulsion. Jean Tinguely (see fig. 9.27), Arthur Ganson (see fig. 9.28), José de Rivera (see fig. 3.31), and Pol Bury (see fig. T.76) propel their sculptures with motor drives.

When properly combined, the principles of order produce vibrant three-dimensional forms. New conceptual

2.69 Ernst Barlach, *The Avenger,* 1914, later cast. Bronze, 17¼ × 22¾ × 8 in. (43.8 × 57.8 × 20.3 cm). This figure is not actually moving, but it does depict a powerful forward thrust. Movement is implied by the long, sweeping horizontal and diagonal edges of the robe, the projection of the head and shoulders, and the base plane.
© Ernst Barlach Lizenzverwaltung Ratzeburg. Photo Tate Gallery, London/Art Resource, NY.

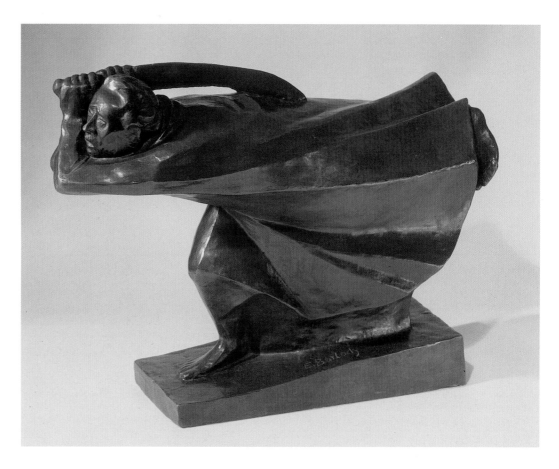

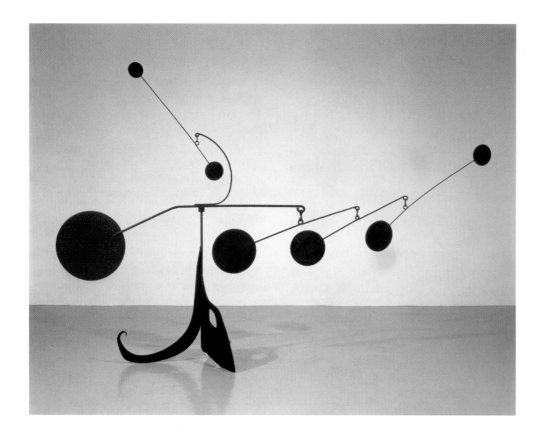

2.70 Alexander Calder, *Myxomatose,* 1953. Steel plate, rod, and paint, 101 × 161 × 52½ in. This noted artist introduced physically moving sculptures called *mobiles*. In this mobile, movement requires time for the observation of the changing relationships, thereby introducing a new dimension to art in addition to height, width, and depth. The result is a constantly altered, almost infinite series of views. Art © 2008 Calder Foundation, New York/Artists Rights Society (ARS), NY. Photo © Art Resource, NY.

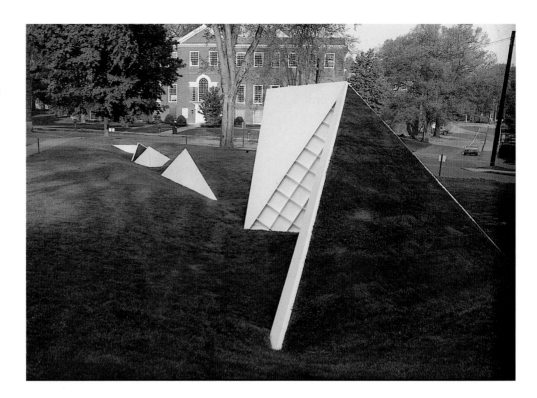

uses of time, space, and movement have brought three-dimensional work to the forefront so that it is no longer considered to be a stepchild of the graphic arts.

Economy

Artists working with 3-D form, like their counterparts working in 2-D form, are most successful when they express their ideas as simply and directly as possible. Examples in which the principle of economy is the primary focus are found within the group known as Primary Structurists or Minimalists. Like their fellow painters, the Minimalist sculptors want to create stark, simple, geometric shapes stripped of any emotional, psychological, or symbolic associations. They have renounced Illusionism, preferring instead to create large three-dimensional objects in actual space. Representative of this group, Beverly Pepper, Judy Chicago, and Donald Judd have reduced their shapes to simple geometric forms (figs. 2.71 and 2.72; see also fig. 2.66). In addition, the alignments of these shapes integrate economy with repetition and rhythm.

FORM UNITY: A SUMMARY

Artists select a picture plane framed by certain dimensions. They have their tools and materials and with them

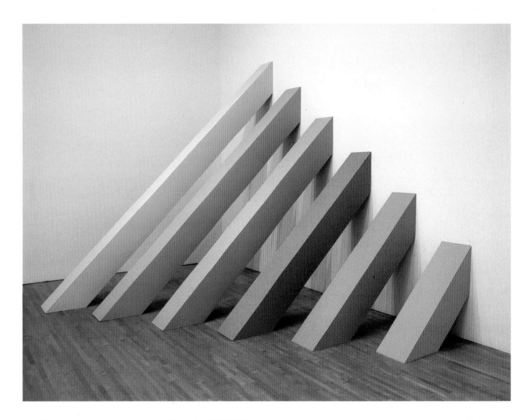

2.72 Judy Chicago, *Rainbow Pickett*, 1965/2004. Latex paint on canvas-covered plywood, 10 ft. 6 in. high × 10 ft. 6 in. wide × 9 ft. 2 in. deep. In this minimalist work, brightly colored surfaces heighten the basic visual relationship of the simplified nonobjective geometric volumes. In keeping with the desire to reduce the form to the barest essentials, Minimalists often prefer to work with the less sophisticated sculptural materials of plywood and canvas over the more technically demanding materials of cast bronze or welded metal. © 2008 Judy Chicago/Artists Rights Society (ARS), New York.

begin to create elements on the surface. As they do so, spatial suggestions appear that may conform to the artist's original conception; if not, a process of adjustment begins. The adjustment accelerates and continues as harmony and variety are applied to achieve balance, proportion, dominance, movement, and economy. As the development continues, artists depend on their intellect, emotions, and instincts in ratios varying from artist to artist and from work to work. The result is an artwork that has its own distinctive form. If the work is successful, its form has unity—all parts belong and work together.

A unified artwork develops like symphonic orchestration in music. The musical composer generally begins with a theme that is taken through a number of variations. Phrases are balanced by other phrases. Notations direct the tempo and dynamics for the perform-

ers. The individual instruments, in following these notations, play their parts in contributing to the total musical effect. In addition, the thematic material is woven through the content of the work, harmonizing its sections. The repetition and contrast of beats, rests, and accents help create layers of rhythm and movement. And yet, there is a sense of economy, as nothing is overdone. A successful musical composition sounds eloquent, with every measure perfected.

In every creative medium, be it music, art, dance, poetry, prose, or theater, the goal is unity. For the creator, unity results from the selection of devices peculiar to the medium and the use of certain principles to relate them. An understanding of the principles of form-structure is indispensable. In the first chapters of this book, we can begin to see the vast possibilities in the creative art realm. With further study,

we can develop an understanding that becomes, through persistent practice, natural and instinctive.

The art elements—line, shape, value, texture, and color—on which form is based can do little in isolation. They join forces in the total work as their development is guided by the principles of organization. The individual contributions of the elements can be studied separately, but in the development of a work, the ways in which they relate to one another are paramount. Because each element makes an individual contribution and has an intrinsic appeal, the elements are discussed separately in the following five chapters. As you study each element in turn, please keep the others in mind. In the end, you must consider all the elements both individually and collectively. The task is great but necessary for that one vital ingredient—unity.

Line

CHAPTER THREE

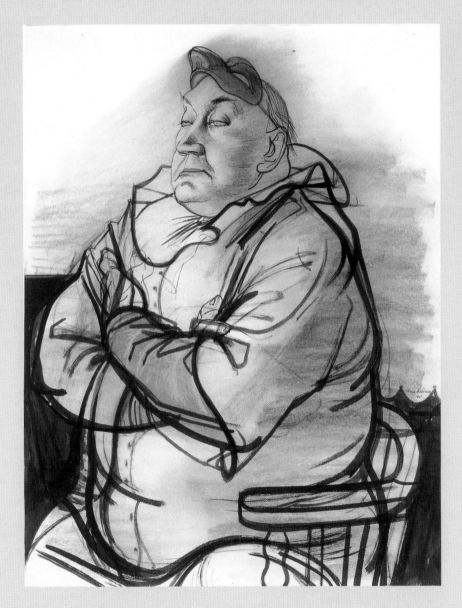

Rico Lebrun, *Seated Clown*, 1941. Ink and wash, with red and black chalk, 39 × 29 in.
Santa Barbara Museum of Art, gift of Mr. and Mrs. Arthur B. Sachs.

THE VOCABULARY OF
LINE

Line — The path of a moving point made by a tool, instrument, or medium as it moves across an area. A line is usually made visible because it contrasts in value with its surroundings. Three-dimensional lines may be made using string, wire, tubes, solid rods, and the like.

arris

On three-dimensional objects, the sharp edge or ridge formed by two surfaces meeting at an angle. Made visible by cast shadow, it is often interpreted as a line.

calligraphic lines

Lines that are generally flowing and rhythmical, like the qualities found in the kind of writing called *calligraphy*.

calligraphy

Elegant, decorative writing.

contour

In art, the line that defines the outermost limits of an object or a drawn or painted shape. It is sometimes considered to be synonymous with *outline*; as such, it indicates an edge that also may be defined by the extremities of dark, light, texture, or color.

cross-contour

A line that moves across a shape or object to define the surface undulations between the outermost edges.

cross-hatching

(See **hatching**.)

expression

1. The manifestation through artistic form of a thought, emotion, or quality of meaning. 2. In art, *expression* is synonymous with the word *content*.

gestural lines

Lines that are drawn freely, quickly, and seemingly without inhibition in order to capture the intrinsic spirit and animation seen in the subject. Gestural lines can imply the past, present, and future motion of the subject.

hatching

Repeated strokes of an art tool, producing clustered (usually parallel) lines that create values. In cross-hatching, similar lines pass over the hatched lines in a different direction, usually resulting in darker values.

implied line

A line that dims, fades, stops, and/or disappears. The missing portion of the line is implied to continue and is visually completed by the observer as the line reappears. Also known as a *subjective line*.

line

The path of a moving point made by a tool, instrument, or medium as it moves across an area. A line is usually made visible because it contrasts in value with its surroundings. Three-dimensional lines may be made using string, wire, tubes, solid rods, and the like.

LINE: THE ELEMENTARY MEANS OF COMMUNICATION

Line may be the most familiar element of art because we use it every day. As a graphic device, lines provide a means of sharing ideas. They are used by every literate culture to create ideograms (pictorial symbols of objects) or sound symbols (alphabets) that are the basis of written language. In art, line is the primary element in sketching and drawing, and it is often employed in preparation for larger works. Combined pictorially, lines can communicate difficult concepts where words alone fail. "A picture is worth a thousand words" is an old saying that points out the ease with which graphic images have long been understood.

The term *line* is also used in many other contexts: the checkout line, the football line, a police lineup, the line of sight, the gas line, and so on. These everyday expressions imply something that is strung out or stretched a certain distance. You have undoubtedly stood in line for something and felt impatience turn to relief as you reached the front. Your line may have been single file (narrow) or two abreast (wider). More than likely, the people in your line were irregularly spaced, and maybe the line even became straggly at some point. A standing line often exhibits differences in width because of the different sizes of the people in the line or because people are bunched together—although this had better not happen in a military parade, where a perfect formation is required.

Art lines and "people lines" have many characteristics in common. Theoretically, a line is an extension of a dot. When a standing line begins to form, the first person holds his or her place like a single dot. But as other people are added, with their different dimensions and positions, the line's characteristics change. In art, these line variations are called *physical characteristics*, and artists can use them to imply meanings as well as to produce the likeness of an object.

Lines can be seen everywhere: the lines the artist makes with instruments such as crayons, pens, and pencils have counterparts in nature. We can perceive lines in the cracks of a sidewalk, the rings of a tree stump, a row of pebbles, or bolts of lightning across the sky. Masses such as spider webs and tree limbs may also be seen as lines.

The artist can use line to represent complex ideas, record something observed, or simply document an activity or action (fig. 3.1). An objective use of line can describe simple measurements and surface characteristics and can indicate a sense of depth. Line can describe an edge, as on a piece of sculpture; it may mark a meeting of areas where value, texture, or color differences do not blend in a drawing (fig. 3.2); or it may define the outer limits of an object's shape (see fig. 3.11). However, line can be subjectively modified to suggest many emotional states and responses, including such complex feelings of anger, tension, calmness, energy, movement, weight, and the like. Thus, the artist uses line, whether objectively or subjectively, in a broadly communicative manner (fig. 3.3).

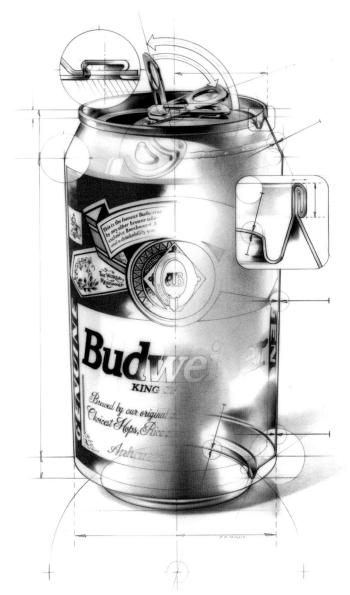

3.1 Bruce Morser, *Untitled (Beer Can)*, 1994. Colored pencil and plastic lead on film, 14 × 9 in. Morser uses line to communicate fine technical details and layers of visual instruction. Courtesy of Gerald & Cullen Rann.

THE PHYSICAL CHARACTERISTICS OF LINE

The physical characteristics of line are many. Lines may be short or long, thin or thick, straight or curved, direct or meandering, zigzag or serpentine, distinct or blurred. These characteristics have certain built-in associations that the artist may make use of. When we say that a person is a "straight arrow," we mean that he or she is straightforward and reliable; a "crooked" person, on the other hand, is devious and untrustworthy. In most cases, we have adjectives that fit the lines we see. And, like the word associations just cited, those meanings are part of line's subconscious power of suggestion.

Measure

Measure refers to the length and width of line—its measurable properties. A line may be of any length and breadth. An infinite number of combinations of long, short, thick, or thin lines can, according to their application, unify, divide, balance, or unbalance a pictorial area. This emotional dynamic is set up by line's measure. For example, thick lines tend to communicate more of a sense of stability than thinner lines. When applied to the development of typeface, a thick font seems more forceful than a thinner one

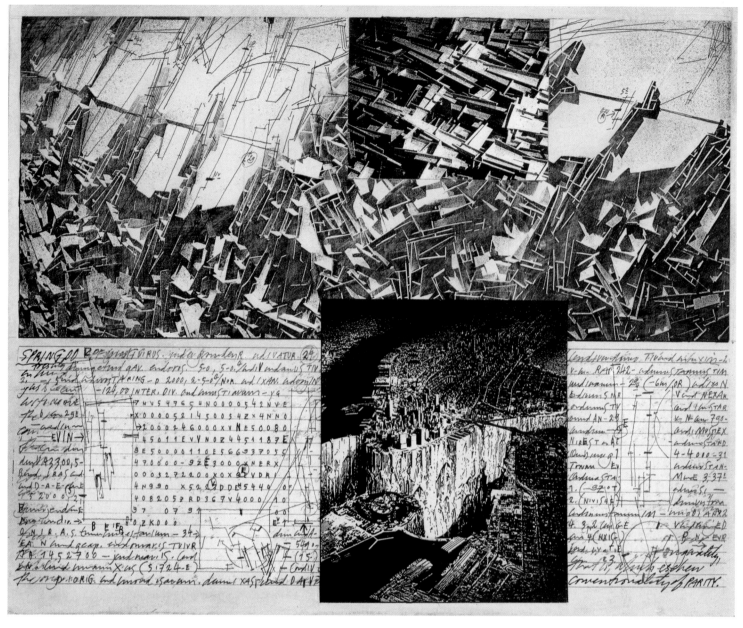

3.2 Lebbeus Woods, *Terrain 10,* 1999. Sanded paper collage with electrostatic print, ink, pencil, pastel, and colored pencil, 23⅜ × 19⅜ in. Woods combines abstract mark, text, and realistic rendering in this image. In the top half of the image, line is used to create the illusion of planes, alluding to natural and architectonic forms. In the top right and left of the image, the line disintegrates into mark where no modeling or value is used. The bottom half of the image employs writing/documentation and a realistic rendering of Manhattan in an altered landscape. The text functions as line and mark and balances the light areas on the top. The central positioning of the cityscape draws the viewer's attention by its realistic rendering, extreme dark and light values, and tightly rendered mark. Notice how this area is echoed in the top middle of the image to balance the white of the values. Courtesy Henry Urbach Architecture, New York.

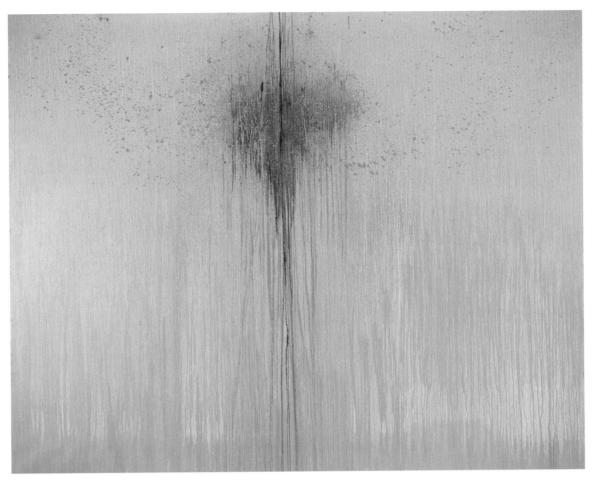

3.3 Pat Steir, *Summer Moon,* 2005. Oil on canvas, 109½ × 137 in. (278.1 × 348 cm). In this image, the artist presents a very personalized and subjective use of line, which makes the viewer aware of line's flowing movement across the canvas. Her application is reminiscent of the technique perfected in her waterfall series. Courtesy Cheim & Read, New York.

and provides a hierarchy for delivering information like titles, subtitles, and so forth. Thin lines are generally more elegant, gentle, or delicate. In figure 3.3 the repetition of fine fluid lines ties the image together and suggests movement. The measure of the line must be appropriate for the development of the image. A property of fragility in a flower like a translucent bougainvillea could be destroyed by a rendering using a bold wide line; but that same vigorous line quality could be used to convey strength in an architectural presentation.

Type

There are many different types of line. If the line continues in only one direction, it is straight; if changes of direction gradually occur, it is curved; if those changes are sudden and abrupt, an angular line is created. By joining the characteristics of *measure* and *type,* we find that long, short, thick, or thin lines can be straight, angular, or curved. A straight line, in its continuity, ultimately seems stiff and rigid and, if rendered thinly, may appear brittle. The curved line may form an

arc, reverse its curve to become wavy, or continue turning within itself to produce a spiral. Alterations of movement become visually entertaining and physically stimulating if they are rhythmical. A curved line is inherently graceful and, to a degree, unstable (see figs. 3.23 and 3.29). The abrupt changes of direction in an angular line create excitement and/or confusion (fig. 3.4). Our eyes frequently have difficulty adapting to an angular line's unexpected deviations of direction. Hence, the angular line is full of challenging interest.

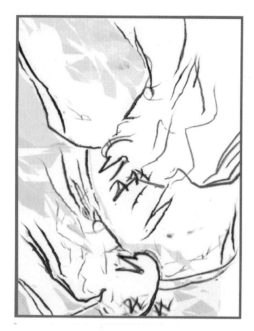

3.4 Clouret Bouchel, *Fight or Flight*, 2000. Mixed media, 9¼ × 12½ in. The abrupt changes of direction in the diagonal angular lines in this drawing create the excitement and tension of combat. Courtesy of the artist.

3.5 Mel Bochner, *Vertigo*, 1982. Charcoal, conté crayon, and pastel on canvas, 9 ft. × 6 ft. 2 in. (2.74 × 1.88 m). Line, the dominant element in this work, is almost wholly diagonal, imparting a feeling of intense activity and stress. Albright-Knox Art Gallery, Buffalo, NY. Charles Clifton Fund, 1982. © Mel Bochner.

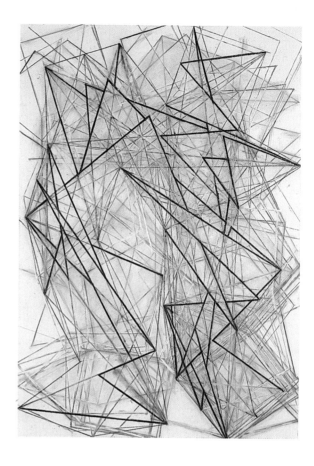

Direction

A further complication of line is its basic *direction;* this direction can exist irrespective of the component movements *within* the line. That is, a line can be a zigzag type but take a generally curved direction. Thus, the line type can be contradicted or flattered by its basic direction. A generally horizontal direction could indicate serenity and perfect stability, whereas a diagonal direction might imply agitation, motion, and instability (fig. 3.5). A vertical line generally suggests poise and aspiration.

The direction of line is very important, because in large measure it controls our eye movement within the composition (fig. 3.6). A slanted line could move our eyes in either direction, but when it becomes a line of type in a layout, it has a direction implied by the way it's read. Generally, when words or sentences slant upward, there is a sense of strength, expectation, or positive energy.

When slanted in a downward direction, the message delivers less energy. In addition, direction can facilitate a sense of continuity in a composition that contains lines with contrasting properties. For example, lines of various widths and lengths can be made to harmonize if they all share the same direction.

Location

The specific location of a line can enhance or diminish the visual weight and our psychological response to the other characteristics of the line. In Chapter 2 we saw that the location of an image on the picture plane, with regard to the effect of gravity, could create emotional responses ranging from excitement and anticipation to relief and calmness. Line is affected by its location in the same manner. A diagonal line high in the picture plane might appear to be soaring, while that same line placed in a low position might appear to be plunging.

Printmakers know of the importance of location and the development of line's visual weight. Having spent many hours developing a composition on a plate or woodblock with a left-to-right orientation, they find the image location reversed during printing. The feeling of balance within the composition is often so disturbed by the new location of the linear image that it requires adjustment. The same line in a new location appears to assume a new visual weight. As with any other characteristic of line, location should be carefully considered, since a line's placement can serve to unify or divide, balance or unbalance a composition.

A line's location is also important because it can affect the way in which we perceive the line. In the work of Ann Jonas, noted children's illustrator, the line's location has a bearing on the interpretation of what image the line is suggesting. In figure 3.7, you will find lines depicting people in a movie

3.6 Janice Lessman-Moss, *#305-703,* 2003. Cotton, stainless steel, Jacquard tapestry, power-loom-woven, Beljen Mills, NC, 71 × 70 in. The curving lines in this woven tapestry guide our eyes throughout the work while creating both harmony and variety. Many of the dark lines seem to imply circular shapes before they fade and disappear into other lines, while the patterns in light values act as a background, providing additional rhythm and movement. The image and ground seem to be in constant motion. © 2003 Janice Lessman-Moss. Photo: Gerry Simon.

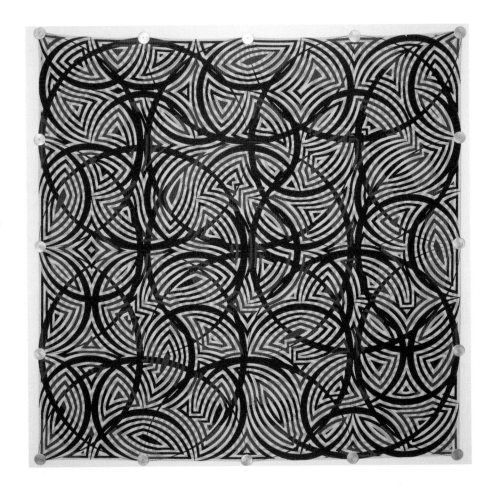

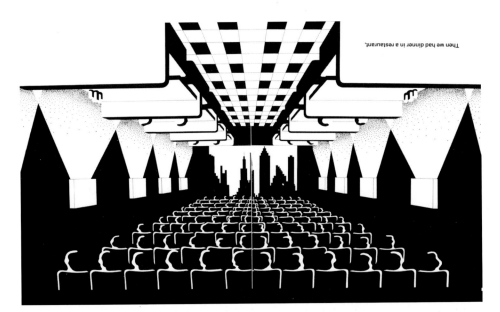

3.7 Ann Jonas, illustration from *Round Trip,* 1983. Printed illustration, 10 × 15 in. Ann Jonas has designed this illustration to be viewed from two directions. In the current orientation, the lines at the bottom appear to be people in a movie theater. However, by turning the illustration upside down, those lines appear to be ceiling tiles in a diner. This shows how the location of a line can influence how we interpret it. Illustration © 1983 by Anne Jonas. Used by permission of HarperCollins Publishers.

3.8 Line character of various media and techniques. (A) *Lines on smooth (left) and rough (right) paper, made with (top to bottom)*: 6B pencil; 3B pencil; HB pencil; 2H pencil; ebony pencil; black conté; sepia conté on its end; sepia conté on its side; Prussian blue crayon; blue oil pastel; blue-green pastel; wide charcoal stick; thin charcoal stick; blue chalk; and graphite powder applied by chamois, finger, and cotton ball. (B) *Lines on dry (left) and wet (right) paper, made with (top to bottom)*: eye dropper; narrow-nib Speedball; medium-nib Speedball; wide-nib Speedball; glass pen; medium bamboo-reed pen; narrow bamboo-reed pen; matt board, using its flat surface; matt board on its edge; finger; foam brush, wet with ink; dry foam brush, dragged through ink; brush of rosewood fiber in red watercolor; Japanese brush in blue watercolor; toothbrush spatter in red watercolor; ochre medium felt-tip marker; ochre wide-felt-tip marker; ochre fine-felt-tip marker. (C) *Examples of tools: (on left, top to bottom)* 6B pencil; 3B pencil; HB pencil; 2H pencil; ebony pencil; black conté next to graphite stick; sepia conté; blue crayon; oil pastel; charcoal sticks; blue chalk; and powdered graphite on cotton ball; *(on right, top to bottom)* eyedropper; narrow-nib Speedball; medium-nib Speedball; wide-nib Speedball; glass pen; medium bamboo-reed pen; narrow bamboo-reed pen; foam brush; matt board; rosewood brush; bamboo brush; Japanese brush; toothbrush; and felt-tip marker. *Lines made with additional media*: (D) graphite stick applied with varied pressure; (E) pencil on very rough paper; (F) string and cardboard in collage; (G) felt-tip pen; (H) reticulating inks and tusche washes; (I) watercolor paint; (J) oil and enamel scraped with razor blades; (K) engraving and mezzotint rockers on copper printing plate; (L) linoleum block cut with chisels and gouges; (M) scratches on the sculptural surface and lines caused by the meeting of adjacent planes; (N) wax resist and two glazes on a ceramic bowl.
Close-up sections of artworks courtesy of the artists.

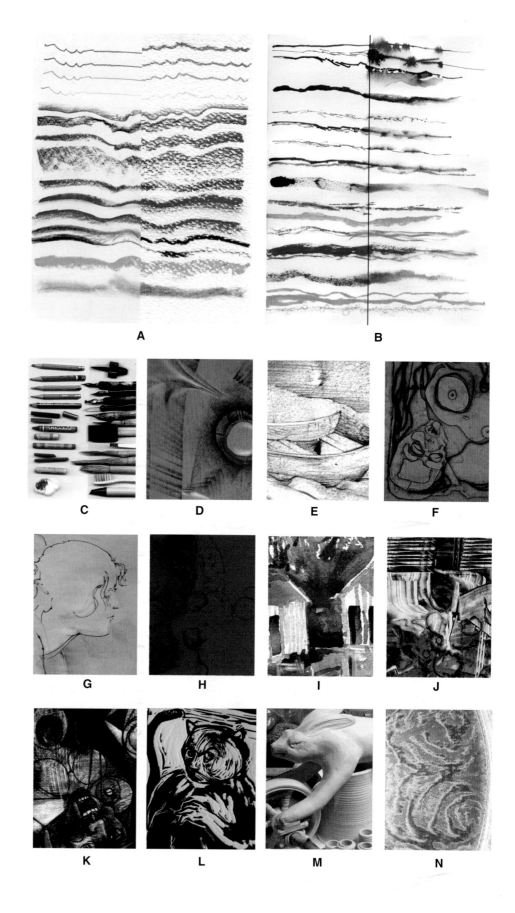

A

B

C

D

E

F

G

H

I

J

K

L

M

N

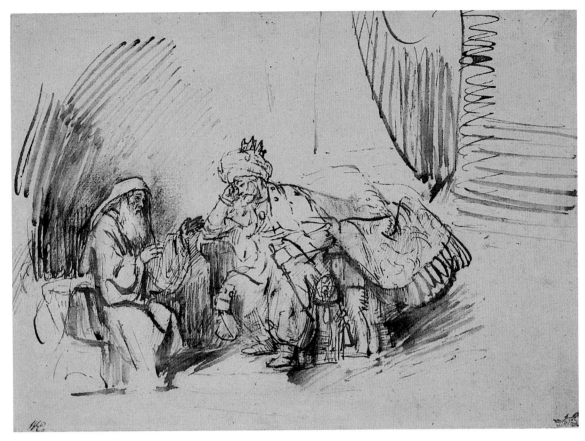

3.9 Rembrandt Harmenszoon van Rijn, *Nathan Admonishing David,* no date. Pen and brush with bistre, 7⁵⁄₁₆ × 9⁵⁄₁₆ in. (18.6 × 23.6 cm). The crisp, biting lines of the pen contrast effectively with the broader, softer lines of the brush. The Metropolitan Museum of Art, H. O. Havemeyer Collection, Bequest of Mrs. H. O. Havemeyer, 1929 (29.100.934) Image © The Metropolitan Museum of Art.

theater. However if the illustration is rotated 180 degrees, the image becomes something completely different; what we previously saw as people now become ceiling tiles. The way we interpret the line is greatly influenced by its location on the picture plane.

Character

Along with measure, type, direction, and location, line possesses *character*—a visual surface quality related to the medium with which the line is created. Each instrument—brush, burin, stick, pencil, finger, and so forth—has its distinctive characteristics that respond in different ways to different surfaces. As such, the character of a line can vary from chalk's grainy dots of vary-

ing density to the feathery reticulated edge of an ink line bursting across a wet surface. Some media, like ink, can provide a wide range of textures and edge qualities, from soft and blurred to sharp and crisp, while other media, like an assortment of pencils or conté crayons, have a wide range of potential values depending on the pressure applied and the hardness of the drawing material (fig. 3.8).

The personality or emotional quality of the line is rooted in the nature of the medium chosen. In Rembrandt's sketch *Nathan Admonishing David,* the expressive qualities created by the soft brush lines of ink, juxtaposed with the precise and firm lines of pen and ink, can be clearly seen (fig. 3.9). As artists become familiar with materials and

the range of their **expression,** they will quickly discover the formal properties and expressive possibilities of each.

To create visual interest, the artist can exploit all the individual characteristics of a medium or use an assortment of different media in the same work. A consistent use of lines of the *same* character could result in monotony, unless the unity so gained were balanced by the variation of other physical properties. The artist, who is the real master of the situation, controls whether the viewer sees lines of uniformity or accent, certainty or indecision, tension or relaxation. It is the artist's ability, experience, intention, and mental and physical condition that determine the effectiveness of line character.

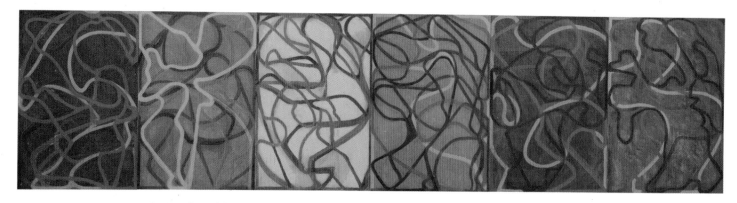

3.10 Brice Marden, *The Propitious Garden of Plane Image, Third Version*, 2000–2006. Oil on linen, 6 panels overall; 72 × 288 in. (183 × 732 cm). Brice Marden presents a weblike network of lines that seem to wander in space. This artist, however, works, reworks, and calculates the lines as he engages in spatial exploration using subtle changes in value, color, width, and direction. © 2008 Brice Marden/Artists Rights Society (ARS), New York, Courtesy Matthew Marks Gallery, New York.

LINE AND THE OTHER ART ELEMENTS

The physical characteristics of line are closely related to and dependent on the other elements. Line can possess value, texture, and color, and it can create value, texture, and shape. Some of these factors are essential to the very creation of line, while others are introduced as needed or may be the result of the line's application.

It is often difficult to make a completely arbitrary and absolute distinction between the elements, but it is still possible to recognize and analyze the linear components of a work of art. The elements cooperate in such a way as to give line an intrinsic appeal that allows it to be admired for its own sake. Artists often exploit this appeal by creating pictures where the lines are dominant while the other el-

ements are subordinate (fig. 3.10). On the other hand, there are some works that are line-free, consisting entirely of other elements.

Line and Shape

In visual art, lines can indicate the outer edges (outlines) of shapes and can also describe the surface undulations of the shapes between those edges. The line that defines the outermost limits of a drawn or painted figure, object, or mass is known as a **contour** (fig. 3.11). This outline may be a continuous, intentional mark, or it can be created by contrasting areas of value, texture, or color that do not blend together. When a series of closely placed lines creates textures and toned areas, the ends of these linear areas establish the boundaries that transpose the areas into shapes. Contour lines also have the capacity to separate

shapes, values, textures, and colors (see figs. 4.14 and 5.24). Without modulation in width or value, contours often create flat, articulated outlines that indicate various shapes' two-dimensional aspects; contours with modulation may generate a feeling of depth in addition to length and width.

Cross-contours, on the other hand, are lines that seem to follow the rise and fall of a shape's surface to create a sense of three-dimensionality. Instead of describing just the extremities of a shape or mass, cross-contours provide information about the nature of the surfaces contained within those edges, somewhat in the manner of a topographical map (fig. 3.12). Imagine an ant, saturated with ink, making several trips crawling up and down and across a face—leaving a colored path. The ink trail would describe the features of that face by cross-contour (fig. 3.13). One

3.11 Ellsworth Kelly, *Briar*, 1963. Graphite on paper, 22⅜ × 28⅜ in. (57 × 72 cm). Line becomes contour as it encircles an object, giving it a distinctive, and often recognizable, shape. Whitney Museum of American Art, New York. Purchase, with funds from the Neysa McMein Purchase Award. 65.42. Photograph by Geoffrey Clements © 2000: The Whitney Museum of American Art.

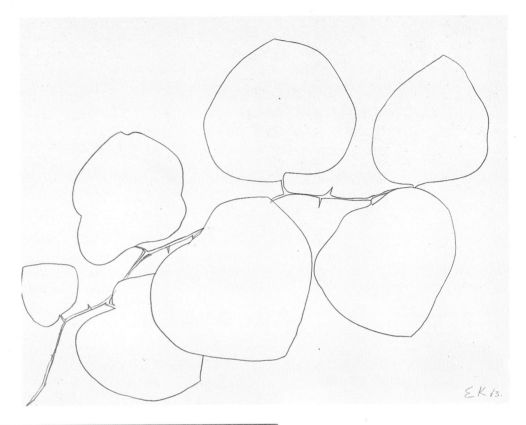

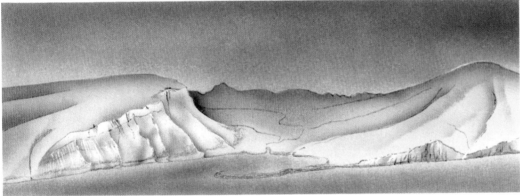

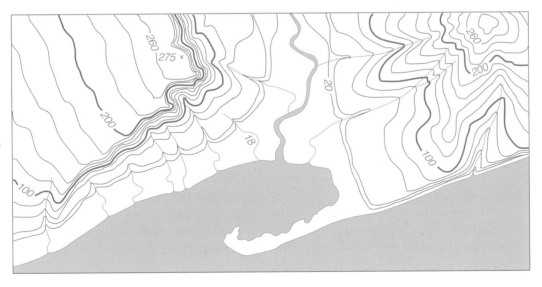

3.12 The lines on a topographical map indicate the various elevations of the earth's surface. In a similar way, the artist uses cross-contours to show the configuration of the subject.

Line and the Other Art Elements **107**

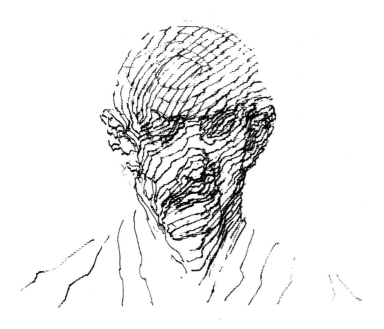

3.13 Harold Tovish, *Contour Drawing*, 1972. Pencil, 19 × 25 in. (48.3 × 63.5 cm). The cross-contours illustrate the dips and swells of features. This technique can be used to describe the surface of any subject being interpreted. Courtesy of the artist.

can use modulated lines (thick and thin, irregular and curved) to enhance cross-contours; one can even vary the pressure when producing the lines so that their darkest portions would seem to advance and the lightest to recede. Massed together, lines can be varied in spacing from narrow to wide to produce a similar advancing and/or receding effect.

Line and Value

The degree of lightness or darkness that a line exhibits against its background is called *value*. A change in value helps a line stand out from its surroundings—the greater the contrast, the more visible the line. Value differences can result from layers and mixtures of media, the amount of pressure exerted on a tool, or line characteristics (wide, heavy lines appear dark in value, while narrow lines appear lighter in value).

Groups of parallel lines can also create areas that differ in value. Value changes within those areas can be controlled by varying the *thickness* of the lines (wide lines appear dark, and narrow lines appear light) or by changing the *spaces between* the lines (widely spaced lines appear light, and closely spaced lines appear dark). These line variations often make interesting transitions between areas of contrasting value or color (fig. 3.14).

A common way of creating value with parallel lines is called **hatching**. These clustered lines not only produce value but can also be used to define the direction of the surface at any given point. Darker values can also be created by **cross-hatching**—passing a group of parallel lines across another group of lines, in a different direction (fig. 3.15). This helps create the sensation of shading (cast shadows) and three-dimensionality. The relationships of the ends of those linear areas establish boundaries that transpose the areas into shapes.

Line and Texture

Groups of lines can combine to produce *textures* that suggest a visual feeling for the character of the surface. Visual textures can indicate degrees of roughness or smoothness that simulate our

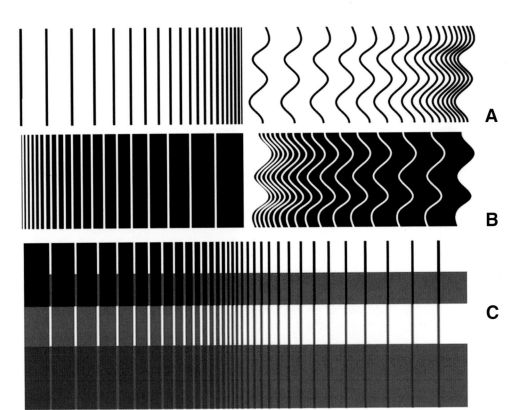

3.14 Group lines produce value and transition. (A) Darker areas are created when the black lines (straight or irregular) are drawn more closely together. (B) Darker areas appear when the black lines increase in width but remain constant in spacing. (C) Changes in line spacing and width act as a transition between areas of dark and light, black and a color, a color and white, and two different colors.

A

B

C

3.15 Andres Zorn, *The Toast,* 1893. Etching, 12⅝ × 10⁷⁄₁₆ in. (32 × 26.5 cm). In this work, Andres Zorn used hatching and cross-hatching to create degrees of value—darks where lines are densely drawn and lighter values where more paper can be seen. Kupferstichkabinett, Staatliche Kunstsammlungen, Dresden. Photo Deutsche Fotothek, Dresden.

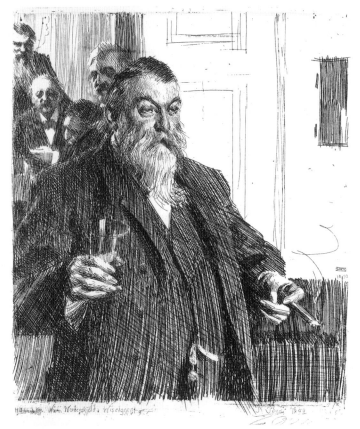

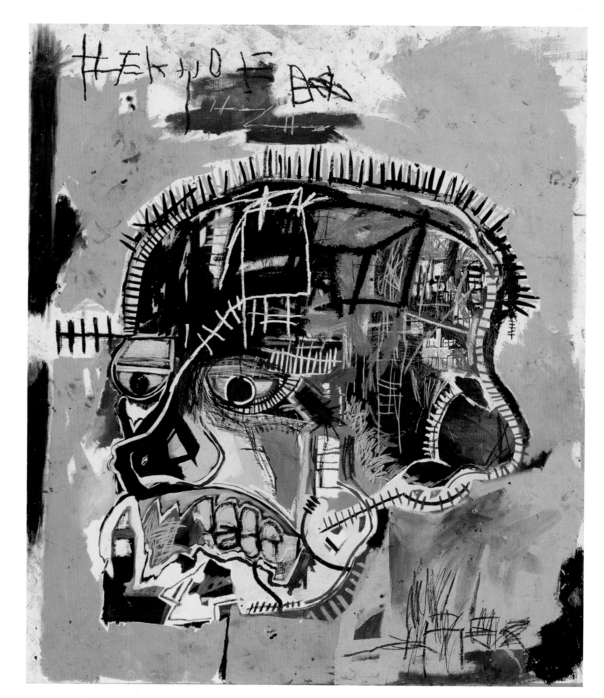

3.16 Jean-Michel Basquiat, *Untitled (skull)*, 1981. Acrylic and mixed media on canvas, 205.7 × 175.9 cm. Basquiat, first known for his poetic graffiti in New York during the 1970s, translated his emotional and personal expression onto canvas. In this work, Basquiat is not trying to duplicate textures in nature but is inventing his own textural surfaces with his many line combinations. The Eli and Edythe L. Broad Collection, Los Angeles. Photo: Douglas M. Parker Studio, Los Angeles. Art © 2008 The Estate of Jean-Michel Basquiat/ ADAGP, Paris/Artists Rights Society (ARS), New York.

sensation of touch (fig. 3.16). Regardless of whether the texture is invented or based on something seen, the inherent characteristic can be enhanced by the distinctive qualities of the medium and the manner of its handling (fig. 3.17). The texture of marks made by hard-bristled brushes can range from sharp to rough, depending on the pressure applied and the type of paint medium used. Soft-haired brushes can produce smooth textured lines with thin paint and thick blotted lines with heavy, viscous paint. When line is translated into any new medium, it has its own unique textural quality. Compare the texture of etched line (see fig. 3.15) to the linear texture of brushwork (see fig. 3.16) or the textural lines created on a woodcut (fig. 3.18). All tools and media will impose their distinctive textural fingerprints on the lines they create.

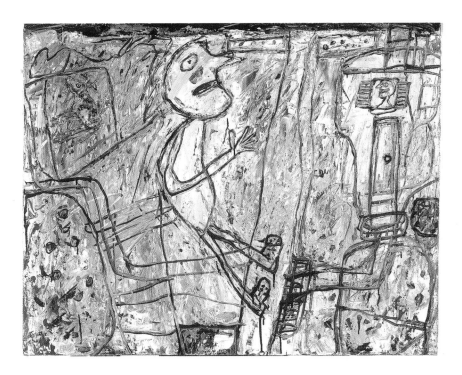

3.17 Jean Dubuffet, *Villa sur la route (Villa by the Road)*, 1957. Oil on canvas, 81.3 × 100.3 cm. The thick, linear textures in this painting are created by direct application and by scratching into the surface. This deliberately primitive style was inspired in Dubuffet by his fascination with graffiti and art created by children and the mentally ill who have no formal art training. © ADAGP, Paris and DACS, London 2006/Scottish National Gallery of Modern Art.

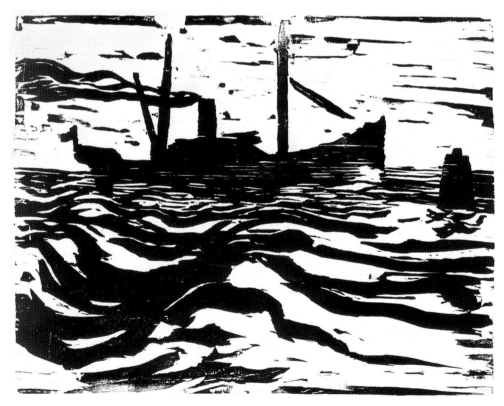

3.18 Emil Nolde, *Fischdampfer (Fishing Boat)*, 1910. Print (woodcut), 11¾ × 15⅜ in. (29.84 × 39.37 cm). When knives and gouges are used to cut the wood, the lines and textures created are different from those produced by another medium. Nolde-Stiftung Seebüll, Germany. Inventory number Ho41. Photograph by Kleinhempel, Hamburg.

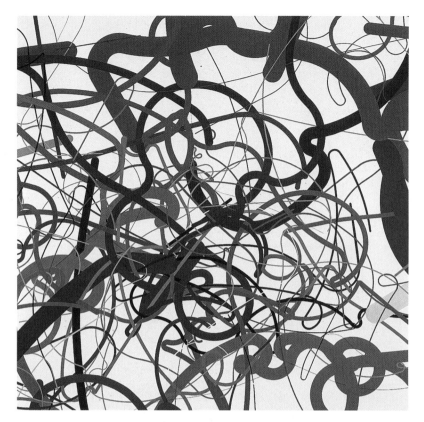

3.19 Zdenek Sykora, *Line No. 50*, 1988. Oil on canvas, 78.7 × 78.7 in. (200 × 200 cm). Variations in the continuous curvilinear lines within this painting create illusions of open space. These variations include changes in the physical properties of the measure, direction, location, and character of the lines, as well as changes in value and color. © National Gallery in Prague.

Line and Color

The introduction of *color* to a line adds an important expressive potential. Color can accentuate other line properties (see fig 3.10). A hard (crisp, sharp, or distinct) line combined with an intense color produces a forceful or even harsh effect. This effect would be considerably muted if the same line were created in a neutral color. In addition, colors have come to be identified with different emotional states. Thus, the artist might use red as a symbol of passion or anger, yellow to suggest cowardice or warmth, and so forth (see the "Color and Emotion" section in Chapter 7).

THE SPATIAL CHARACTERISTICS OF LINE

Depending on their application, the physical characteristics of graphic line can create a sense of space (fig. 3.19). Thick lines tend to advance forward spatially, while thinner lines in the same medium tend to recede by comparison. A line that modulates from thick to thin will become very active spatially, and when combined with changes of value, the darker thicker portions become even more dynamic. Value contrast alone can cause a line to advance and recede, and an individual line with varied values throughout its length may appear to writhe and twist in space. A line that curves and twists can even appear to move away from the viewer, especially if the width of that line varies. In addition, texture and color contribute to a line's spatial effect: a line with greater textural detail can suggest closeness, while less textural detail can suggest distance; and warm colors generally advance, while cool colors generally recede.

When a line indicates space that is flat or shallow, it is a *decorative line*. This two-dimensional quality is caused by a consistency in width, value, texture, color, and so on (see fig. 3.11). By comparison, a *plastic line*, having greater variation of the same elements, will advance and recede along its path and suggest an illusion of deeper plastic space (see fig. 3.9). Both are useful means, depending on the type of spatial feeling the artist wishes to employ for an image.

Whether isolated, modulated, grouped, or used in combination with other elements, every factor involved with line has something to say about its location in space. The artist's job is to use these factors to create spatial order (fig. 3.20).

LINE AS REPRESENTATION AND EXPRESSION

Line creates representation on both realistic and abstract levels. The lines drawn in an architect's plan for a

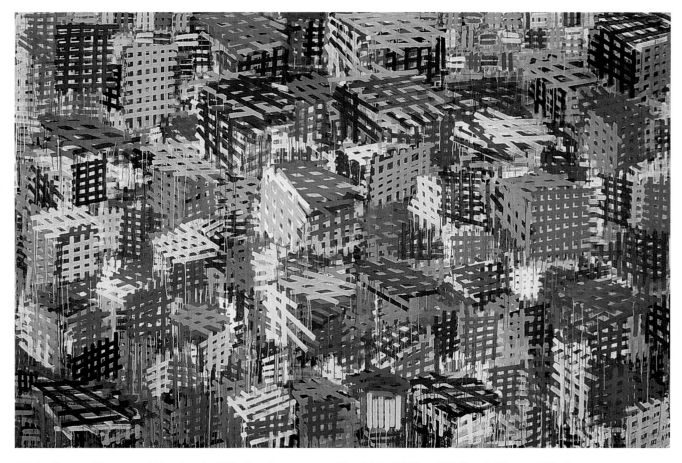

3.20 Denyse Thomasos, *Urban Jewels,* 1995. Acrylic on canvas, 10 × 16 ft. (304.8 × 487.68 cm). The spatial illusion, of such obvious importance in this example, is largely the product of the physical properties of the lines strengthened by contrasting areas of value and color. Lennon, Weinberg, NY.

building can symbolize walls or construction materials; the lines drawn on maps can represent rivers, roads, or contours; and the lines that form letters and words in a textbook can represent thoughts and concepts. Such use of line is primarily utilitarian, a convenient way of communicating ideas to another person.

Artists may indicate a wealth of factual information by employing a variety of line characteristics. The changes in the measure and direction of cross-contour lines, for example, might de-

scribe the three-dimensionality of an object's surface by appearing to advance and recede (fig. 3.21).

However, lines may also suggest certain emotional or psychological meanings. In a linear portrait of a person, the artist might use line properties to describe that person's physical details, but the artist's use of line quality might also be able to convey—either satirically or sympathetically—much information about the character of the sitter (fig. 3.22). In this way, the work becomes a subjective interpretation of

that subject. Artists who deal with typography also consider the expressive characteristics of line when selecting font or typeface—fonts composed of various thicknesses, length, direction, and so forth can reinforce or enhance the emotional impact of the words.

In addition to its ability to describe *facts* and *emotions,* line can express *action* in a "gestural" sense. The gesture in graphic work implies the past, present, and future motion of the drawn subject. **Gestural** drawing in any medium displays lines that are drawn freely,

3.21 Don Kirby, *Bluegrass, Jackson Rd. WA,* 1997. Gelatin silver print. The linear elements in this image act as cross-contour lines, revealing the undulation and contour of the field and helping to establish a sense of space. © Don Kirby, 8 Sonrisa Court, Santa Fe, NM, 87506.

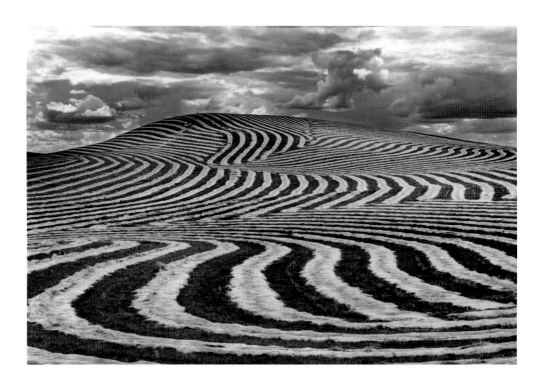

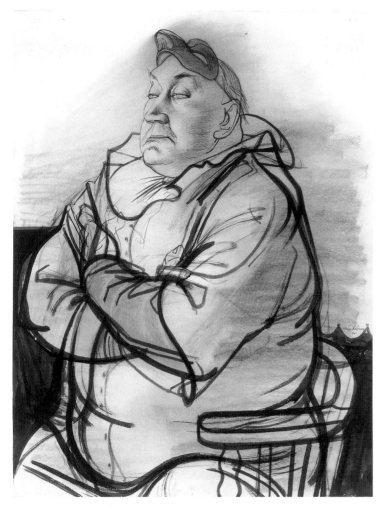

3.22 Rico Lebrun, *Seated Clown,* 1941. Ink and wash, with red and black chalk, 39 × 29 in. The power and fluid quality of the line used for the lower body gives the figure a solid, sturdy, and substantial presence, while the delicate rendering of facial features seems to reveal a complex personality. Santa Barbara Museum of Art, gift of Mr. and Mrs. Arthur B. Sachs.

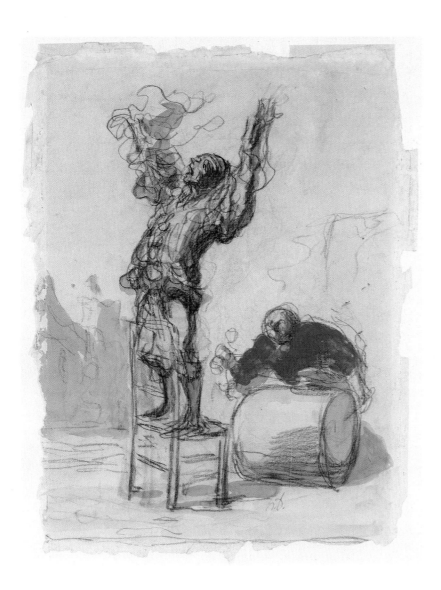

3.23 Honoré Daumier, *Street Show*, 1865–66. Black chalk and watercolor on laid paper, 14⅜ × 10¹/₁₆ in. (36.8 × 25.4 cm). Though subjects are often static and immobile, Daumier used the excitement of gestural line to interpret the gyrations of the dancer and the frenzied beating of the drummer. The Metropolitan Museum of Art, Rogers Fund, 1927. (27.152.2) Photograph © The Metropolitan Museum of Art.

quickly, and seemingly without inhibition. If preserved in the work, such lines capture the intrinsic spirit and animation seen in the subject. This spirit can pertain to both animate and inanimate subjects—a towel casually thrown over a chair has a unique "gesture," resulting from the way it falls, its weight and texture, and the surface it contacts. Obviously, this gestural concept applies even more conspicuously to those subjects that are capable of movement (figs. 3.23 and 3.24). Many paintings are preceded by and based on the artist's initial gestural response (fig. 3.25).

Whatever the approach, the energy suggested by the line, and even the act of making the line, is often related to the physics of body movement. Western artists tend to hold the brush on an angle like a writing pencil and easily make small circular strokes or arcs by pivoting the wrist. Asian cultures, on the other hand, have a rich tradition of writing with brushes rather than pencils. They hold the brush more vertically by using the first two fingers to pull the brush handle against the thumb and the back of the bottom fingers. This changes the subtle manner in which the wrist may move and relies more on the elbow as a pivot point. Such differences in body movements alter the expressive character of the lines.

Lines drawn with graceful curves that seem to flow effortlessly, swelling and suggesting movement, are known as **calligraphic lines.** Highly personal in nature, calligraphic lines are similar to

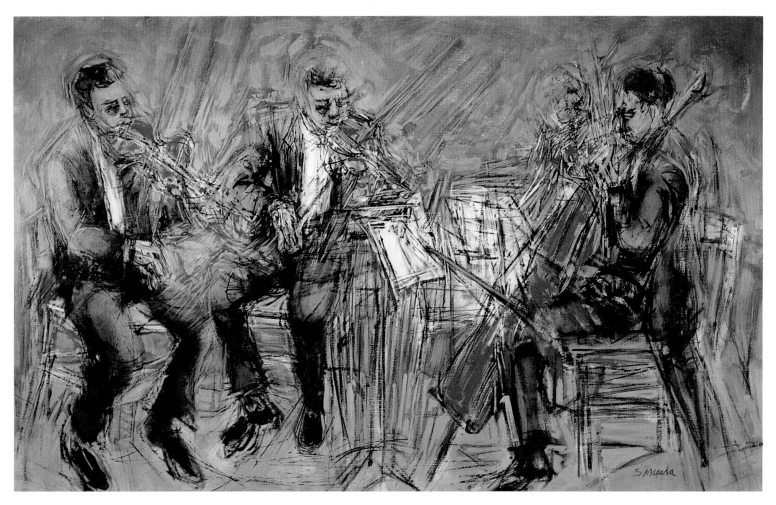

3.24 Steve Magada, *Trio,* c. 1966. Oil on canvas, size unknown. The gestural lines in this work successfully evoke the movements of the performers. Photograph courtesy of Virginia Magada.

3.25 Giovanni Battista Tiepolo, *Study for Figure of Falsehood on the Ceiling of the Palazzo Trento-Valmarana, Vicenza,* no date. Pen and brown ink, 6⅜ × 6 in. (16.2 × 15.4 cm). This gestural drawing clearly illustrates the dramatic motion of drawing as an activity. Artists often try to sustain this effect beyond the initial stage of a sketch. Princeton University Art Museum. Bequest of Dan Fellows Platt, Class of 1895 x1948-863.

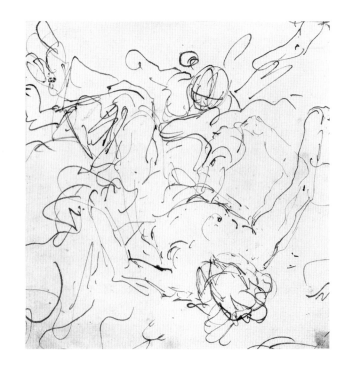

the individual qualities found in handwriting; they are fluid and rhythmical and intriguing to the eye as they enrich an artwork. In comparing the **calligraphy** of figure 3.26 with examples of the calligraphic lines drawn in figures 3.27 and 3.28, one can see the shared qualities of fluid movement and unique gesture. The written calligraphic line can be made to take on the quality of the object being described (see figure 3.28) or instill a sense of space, leaping upward and outward (see figure 3.27). This wide application of line includes the creation of value and texture, illustrating the impossibility of truly isolating the elements of art from one another.

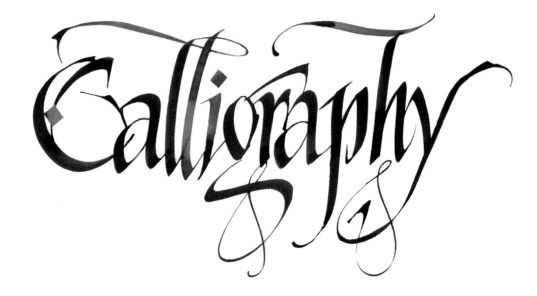

3.26 Annie Cicale, *Untitled,* 2001. Pen and ink drawing, 7 × 10 in. In the words of the artist, "Beautiful writing, called calligraphy, captures the power of the written word and elevates it so that the writing becomes an image as powerful as the words." Like the individual styles of painters or sculptors, such beautiful calligraphy evolves only after years of practice. Courtesy of the artist.

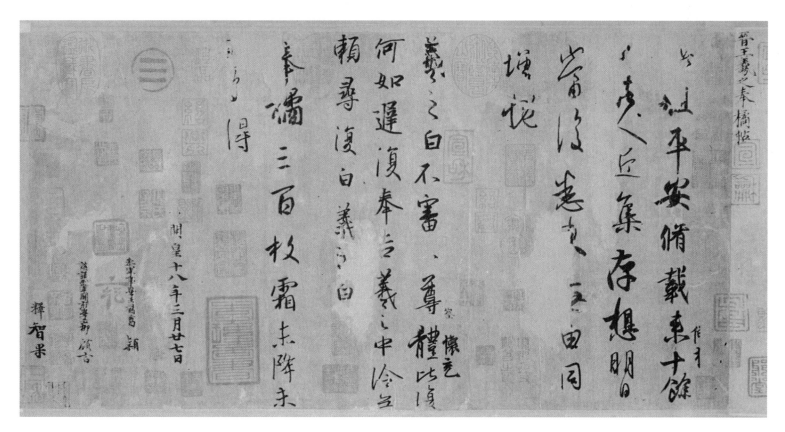

3.27 Wang Hsi-chih, from Three Passages of Calligraphy: "Ping-an," "Ho-ju," and "Feng-chu," Eastern Ch'in dynasty, fourth century (321–379 c.e.), *Calligraphy.* **Ink on paper.** Certain meanings intrinsic to line arise from its character. These meanings are the product of the medium, the tools used, and the artist's method of application. Calligraphy is esteemed in China as an art form equal to painting. Created with brush and ink on paper (the Chinese invented paper), the lively, abstract ideographs of Chinese calligraphy appear to leap upward and outward, "like a dragon leaping over heaven's gate." National Palace Museum, Taipei, Taiwan, Republic of China.

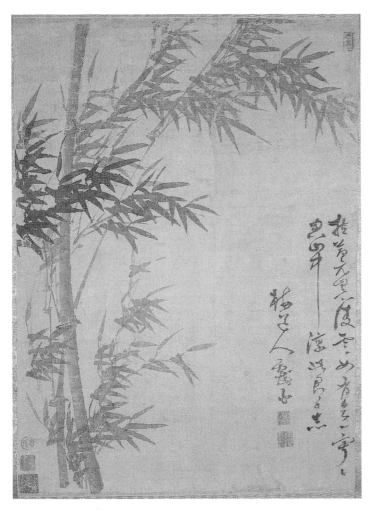

3.28 Wu Zhen (attributed to), *Bamboo in the Wind,* early-fourteenth-century hanging scroll, Yuan dynasty, China. Ink on paper, 29⅝ × 21⅜ in. (75.2 × 54.3 cm). Wu Zhen uses meticulous, controlled brushwork to describe the flowing linear (calligraphic) qualities of the bamboo tree. *Chinese and Japanese Special Fund. Courtesy of Museum of Fine Arts, Boston.*

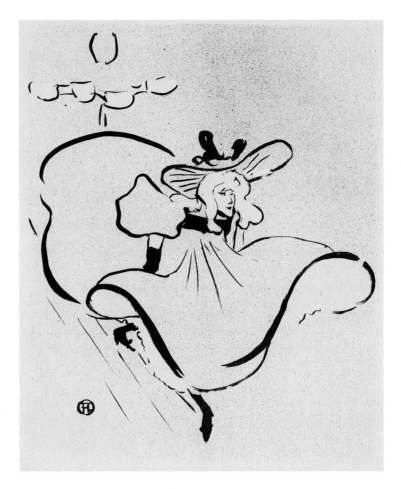

3.29 Henri de Toulouse-Lautrec, *Jane Avril,* first plate from *Le Café Concert,* 1893. Lithograph, printed in black, 10½ × 8⁷⁄₁₆ in. (26.7 × 21.4 cm). The lines in this image seem to have been drawn with great freedom, communicating the graceful action of the subject. *Gift of Abby Aldrich Rockefeller. (167.1946) The Museum of Modern Art/Licensed by SCALA/Art Resource, NY.*

In the lithograph *Jane Avril,* the artist Henri de Toulouse-Lautrec creates calligraphic lines with a gestural character that captures the spirit of the dance (fig. 3.29). The calligraphic line in this print also becomes a broken **implied line,** a variation in application that further suggests spatial change, movement, and animation. An implied line seems to fade, stop, and/or disappear and then reappear as a continuation or an extension of the same line, edge, or direction. This may be seen in figure 3.29 if one follows the line of the skirt around. It suggests movement and asks the viewer to complete missing sections (see the "Linking through Extensions" section in Chapter 2).

Line has many objective and subjective implications. In its role of signifying ideas and conveying feelings, line moves and lives, pulsating with significant emotions. It describes the edges or contours of shapes, it diagrams silhouettes, and it encompasses spaces and areas—all in such a way as to convey a variety of meanings. All are the direct result of the artist's manipulation of the physical properties.

The qualities of line can be described in terms of general states of feeling—somber, tired, energetic, brittle, alive, and the like. An infinite number of conditions of varying subtlety can be communicated by the artist. The various attributes of line can act in concert toward one goal or can serve separate roles of expression and design. Gently curving lines, long lines, thin lines, and lines placed low in the frame may all contribute to the feeling of calmness in a composition. However, in a work of art, as in the human mind, such feelings are rarely so clearly defined. The spectator's recognition of these qualities is a matter of feeling, which means that the spectator must be receptive and perceptive and have a reservoir of experiences to draw on.

For the artist an intuitively sensitive use of line evolves when one is empowered by a thorough understanding of line's physical properties and understands the relationship between line and the other elements. Such line, when used on a subconscious level, will become the catalyst for a creative response—an interaction between the intellect, the body, and the medium. Whether line is used to create a sketchy interpretation, express a deep emotion, reveal the gesture of an action, or record factual information, it remains a basic means of communication and one of the first elements employed.

THREE-DIMENSIONAL APPLICATIONS OF LINE

For the 3-D artist, line is a visual phenomenon that, for the most part, does not actually exist in nature or in the third dimension. What we visually interpret as line is primarily a change in value, color, or texture that indicates the meeting of planes or the outer edges of shapes. When two planes come together, they form a ridge, or an edge known as an **arris**. Whether we are looking at tree bark or cracks in the sidewalk, this edge can be perceived as a line when it is enhanced by a cast shadow (fig. 3.30). That line can fade away as the ridge, or arris, is softened and rounds over. In three-dimensional art, the spatial characteristics of line are physical, as they literally move in space with measurable distances between them. These three-dimensional lines may seem passive or

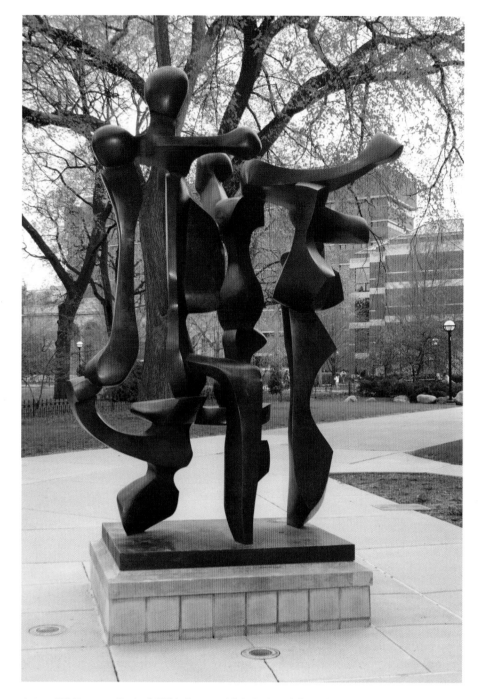

3.30 Bill Barrett, *Kindred*, 2001. Bronze, 10 ft. high × 9 ft. wide × 5 ft. deep. The contour lines in this sculpture come alive as it is "washed" with values ranging from highlights to deep shadows. Other internal lines occur along the arris (edge) where two planes meet abruptly and a contrasting shadow is cast. The sharper the edges, the greater the contrast. Where those edges are softened, the line becomes indistinct—dissolving completely in some locations. Just as line can be used to harmonize a graphic image, line used in 3-D work can control the eye movement and unify the form. Commissioned by the University of Michigan School of Social Work, Ann Arbor, MI. Photo by Tanya C. Hart Emley.

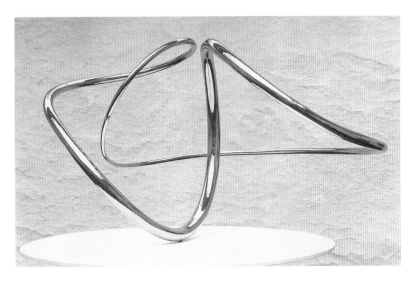

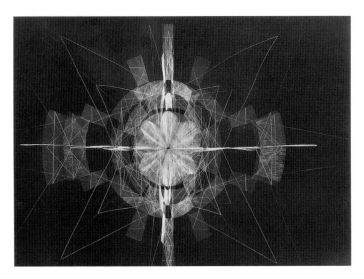

3.31 José de Rivera, *Brussels Construction*, 1958. Stainless steel, 3 ft. 10½ in. × 6 ft. 6¾ in. (1.18 × 2 m). The concept of attracting observers to a continuous series of rewarding visual experiences as they move about a static three-dimensional work of art led to the principle of kinetic, or mobile, art, as with this sculpture set on a slowly turning motorized plinth.

3.32 Richard Lippold, *Variation within a Sphere, No. 10, the Sun,* 1953–56. 22-karat gold-filled wire, 11 × 22 × 5½ ft. (3.35 × 6.70 × 1.68 m). The development of welding and soldering techniques for use in sculpture made the shaping and joining of thin linear metals possible, as in this work by Lippold.

actually swoop and swirl in that space (fig. 3.31).

The definition of line may also be broadened to include the main direction or axial thrust of a three-dimensional shape whose length is greater than its width. Materials like string, wire, tubes, solid rods, and the like have been used for their linear quality and have added to the repertoire of the plastic artist. Such linear explorations of space are a relatively new development, and complete works in these materials are unique to this time period. Artists like Richard Lippold (fig. 3.32), Alexander Calder (see fig. 2.70) and Kenneth Snelson (see fig. 2.62) have devoted their entire careers to creating such works.

Incising line in clay or in any other soft medium is similar to the graphic technique of drawing, but in addition to being made visible by cast shadows, line may be experienced tactilely because of the inscribed valleys and ridges. In three-dimensional art, incised lines are used to accent surfaces for interest and movement. Italian artist Giacomo Manzu employed such lines to add sparkle to relief sculpture (fig. 3.33).

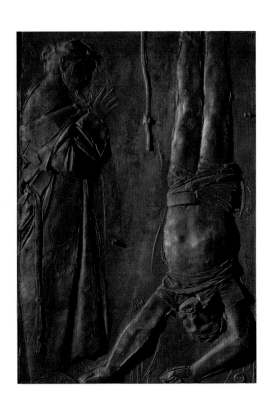

3.33 Giacomo Manzu, *Death by Violence,* 1950. Bronze cast from clay model, 36⅝ × 25¼ in. (93.5 × 64 cm). This is a study for one of a series of panels for the doors of Saint Peter's (Vatican, Rome). The confining spatial limitations of relief sculpture are evident. To create a greater feeling of mass, Manzu used sharply incised modeling that is similar to the engraved lines of the printmaker's plate. The crisp incising creates sharp value contrasts that accentuate movement as well as depth. © David Lees/Corbis.

Shape

CHAPTER FOUR

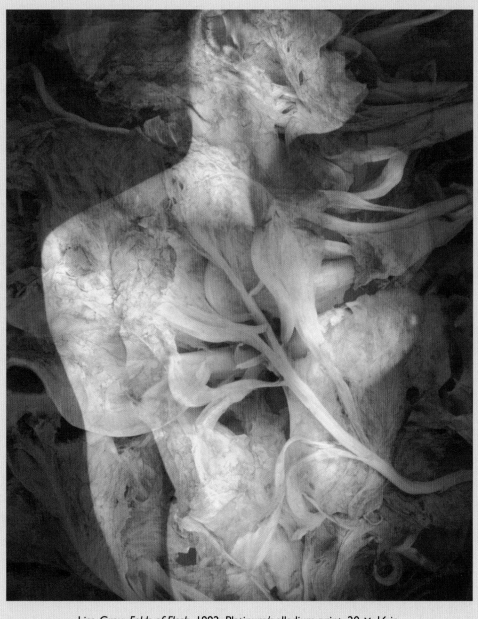

Lisa Gray, *Folds of Flesh*, 1992. Platinum/palladium print, 20 × 16 in.

Courtesy of Lisa Gray.

THE VOCABULARY OF
SHAPE

Shape — An area that stands out from its surroundings because of a defined
or implied boundary or because of differences of value, color, or texture.

actual shape

A positive area with clearly defined boundaries (as opposed to an implied shape).

amorphous shape

A shape without clear definition: formless, indistinct, and of uncertain dimension.

biomorphic shape

An irregular shape that resembles the freely developed curves found in living organisms.

Cubism

The name given to the painting style invented by Pablo Picasso and Georges Braque between 1907 and 1912, which uses multiple views of objects to create the effect of three-dimensionality while acknowledging the two-dimensional surface of the picture plane. Signaling the beginning of abstract art, Cubism is a semiabstract style that continued the strong trend away from representational art initiated by Cézanne in the late 1800s.

curvilinear shape

A shape whose boundaries consist of predominantly curved lines; the opposite of **rectilinear.**

decorative (shape)

Ornamenting or enriching but, more importantly in art, stressing the two-dimensional nature of an artwork or any of its elements. Decorative art emphasizes the essential flatness of a surface.

equivocal space

A condition, usually intentional on the artist's part, in which the viewer may, at different times, see more than one set of relationships between art elements or depicted objects. This may be compared to the familiar "optical illusion."

geometric shape

A shape that appears related to geometry; usually simple, such as a triangle, rectangle, or circle.

implied shape

A shape that does not physically exist but is suggested through the psychological connection of dots, lines, areas, or their edges. (See **Gestalt** in the Glossary.)

kinetic (art)

From the Greek word *kinesis,* meaning "motion"; art that includes the element of actual movement.

mass

1. In graphic art, a shape that appears to stand out three-dimensionally from the space surrounding it or creates the illusion of a solid body of material. 2. In the plastic arts, a physical bulk of material. (See **volume.**)

objective

That which is based, as closely as possible, on physical actuality or optical perception. Such art tends to appear natural or real; the opposite of **subjective.**

perspective

Any graphic system used to create the illusion of three-dimensional images and/or spatial relationships in which the objects or their parts appear to diminish as they recede into the distance. (See the discussion of atmospheric perspective and linear perspective in Chapter 8.)

planar (shape)

Having to do with planes; shapes that have height and width but no indication of thickness.

plane

1. An area that is essentially two-dimensional, having height and width. 2. A two-dimensional pictorial surface that can support the illusion of advancing or receding elements. 3. A flat sculptural surface.

plastic (shape)

1. Element(s) used in such a manner as to create the illusion of the third dimension on a two-dimensional surface. 2. Three-dimensional art forms, such as architecture, sculpture, and ceramics.

rectilinear shape

A shape whose boundaries consist of straight lines; the opposite of **curvilinear.**

shape

An area that stands out from its surroundings because of a defined or implied boundary or because of differences of value, color, or texture.

silhouette

The area between or bounded by the contours, or edges, of an object; the total shape.

subjective

That which is derived from the mind, instead of physical reality, and reflects a personal bias, emotion, or innovative interpretation; the opposite of **objective.**

Surrealism

A style of artistic expression, influenced by Freudian psychology, that emphasizes fantasy and whose subjects are usually experiences revealed by the subconscious mind through the use of automatic techniques (rubbings, doodles, blots, cloud patterns, etc.). Originally a literary movement that grew out of Dadaism, Surrealism was established by a literary manifesto written by André Breton in 1924.

three-dimensional

Possesses, or creates the illusion of possessing, the dimensions of depth, height, and width. In the graphic arts, the feeling of depth is an illusion, while in the plastic arts, the work has actual depth.

two-dimensional

Possesses the dimensions of height and width, especially when considering a flat surface or picture plane.

void

1. An area lacking positive substance and consisting of negative space. 2. A spatial area within an object that penetrates and passes through it.

volume

A measurable amount of defined, three-dimensional space. (See **mass.**)

INTRODUCTION TO SHAPE

Shapes are often referred to as the building blocks of art structure. Like the bricks, stones, and mortar used to construct architectural edifices, shapes in art build strength into the structure of the composition. With careful placement and treatment, shapes also create various illusions of depth and dimensionality and engage the viewer through their expressive nature.

As artists begin their work, they frequently have some preliminary vision of shape, whether planning composition-wide patterns or just thinking about individual subjects. The artist may have a clear concept in mind for an abstract image and know instinctively what shapes will give that idea substance and structure. Or he or she may prefer a responsive translation of visual experience and produce shapes with naturalistic contour lines.

Sketches that start with rambling lines or hatch marks may suggest ideas that evolve into more defined shapes.

As lines crisscross and connect to one another, spaces become enclosed and appear as shapes, while defined areas of contrast are perceived to emerge from their background and materialize into other shapes. With this progression, the act of doodling turns shapes with vague beginnings into refined images that capture the viewer's imagination.

Whatever the development, **shape** may be defined as an area distinguished from its surroundings by an outer edge or boundary. Whether explicitly precise or simply implied, that edge exists as either a contour line that encloses the area or as a contrast between the value, texture, or color of the shape and its surroundings (fig. 4.1).

SHAPE TYPES

The configuration of a shape's outer edge helps give it a character that distinguishes it from others. When the shapes used by an artist imitate observable phenomena, they may be described as **objective,** naturalistic, representational,

or realistic, depending on the context. However, when shapes are more imaginary or seem to have been contrived by the artist, they are often called **subjective,** abstract, nonobjective, or nonrealistic (see the "Abstraction" section in Chapter 1). Shapes may also belong to a number of other categories or families of shape type, according to the configuration of their edges.

Man, in his need to structure his existence, devised shapes that were ordered, mechanical in appearance, and often sharply defined. Known as **geometric shapes,** these include circles, ovals, squares, rectangles, triangles, hexagons, pentagons, and other mathematically derived shapes. Although geometric shapes may have a wide variety of configurations, they generally retain the character of being **curvilinear** (made of curved lines), **rectilinear** (straight-lined), or some combination thereof. Architecture, machinery, and other man-made technologies abound with standardized geometric shapes. However, these very precise shapes are not just the result of man imposing order

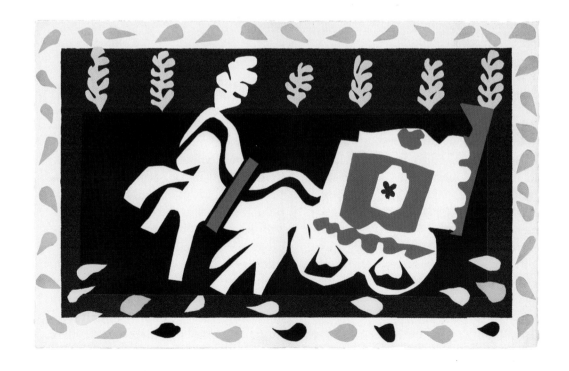

4.1 Henri Matisse, *The Burial of Pierrot,* Plate VIII from *Jazz,* 1947. Pochoir (stencil printing), 16¼ × 25⅛ in. (41.2 × 63.5 cm). Matisse's biomorphic shapes, which are abstracted from organic forms, stand out from the background area due to the contrasts in color and value. Though decorative in nature, the shapes give the composition a sense of energy and movement. © 2008 Succession H. Matisse/Artists Rights Society (ARS), New York. Photo: Archives Matisse.

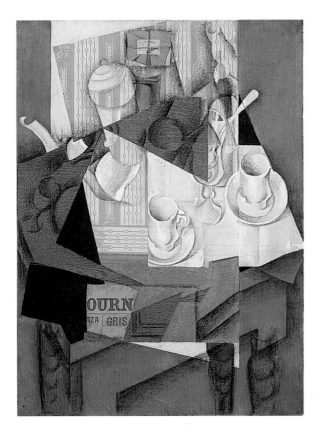

4.2 Juan Gris (José Victoriano González), *Breakfast*, 1914. Cut-and-pasted paper, crayon, and oil over canvas, 31⅞ × 23½ in. (80.9 × 59.7 cm). Gris, a Cubist, not only simplified shapes into larger, more dominant areas but also gave each shape a characteristic value, producing a carefully conceived light-dark pattern. He also made use of open-value composition, where the value moves from one shape into the adjoining shape, as we see in this example. The Museum of Modern Art, New York, NY. U.S.A. Acquired through the Lillie P. Bliss Bequest. Digital image © The Museum of Modern Art/Licensed by SCALA/Art Resource, NY.

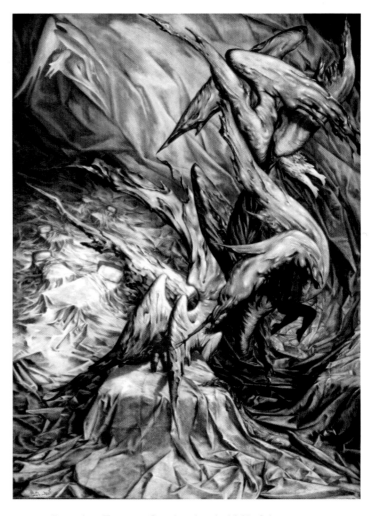

4.3 Dorothea Tanning, *Guardian Angels*, 1946. Oil on canvas, 35 × 57½ in. Here, Tanning combines a realistic rendering of form with the fantastic. Like other Surrealists, Tanning was interested in the inner psychic life of human beings. Courtesy New Orleans Museum of Art: Museum Purchase, Kate P. Jourdan Memorial Fund, 49.15 © 2008 Artists Rights Society (ARS), New York/ADGP, Paris.

on his surroundings through human invention, for they are commonly found in the natural world in spiral shells, honeycombs, snowflakes, and crystalline structures like quartz and other minerals. Visual artists often use geometric shapes to creatively interpret something seen or imagined and to give embodiment to those ideas in an orderly fashion (fig. 4.2; see also figs. 4.23, and T.77).

In contrast to the regulated, mechanistic qualities of geometric shapes are the flowing qualities of **biomorphic shapes.** Biomorphic shapes display edges of a rounded, curving, and sometimes undulating nature that suggests living organisms or natural forces (figs. 4.3 and 4.4). We commonly see these irregular shapes in the elemental organs and organisms encountered in biological studies as well as in stones, leaves, puddles, plant life, and clouds. Such shapes may also be referred to as *organic* or *natural*, since the term *biomorphic* was only coined in the early twentieth century. Sculptors and pictorial artists often use biomorphic, or organic shapes, in their respective media to represent the human—as well as the plant and animal—form. In addition, biomorphic shapes may symbolize various abstract thoughts or simply give a decorative quality to flat surfaces (fig. 4.5; see also figs. 3.11, 4.1, and 4.22).

Although the most obvious shapes are created by distinct and continuous boundaries, such unequivocal contours are not absolutely necessary for a shape to be seen. Instead, the edges only need to be suggested. We know from our study of closure (a Gestalt concept

4.4 Joan Miró, *The Painting,* 1933. Oil on canvas, 68½ in. × 6 ft. 5¼ in. (174 × 196.2 cm). Some shapes in this work seem to be veiled references to unlikely creatures and deserve the term *biomorphic* because of their organic configuration. Loula D. Lasker Bequest (by exchange). (229.1937) The Museum of Modern Art, New York, NY, U.S.A. Digital image © The Museum of Modern Art/Licensed by SCALA/Art Resource, NY. © 2008 Artists Rights Society (ARS), New York/ADGP, Paris.

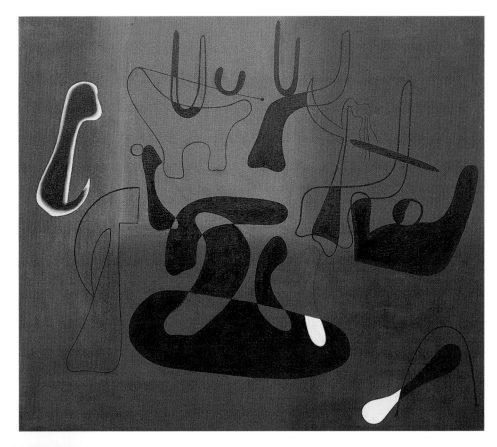

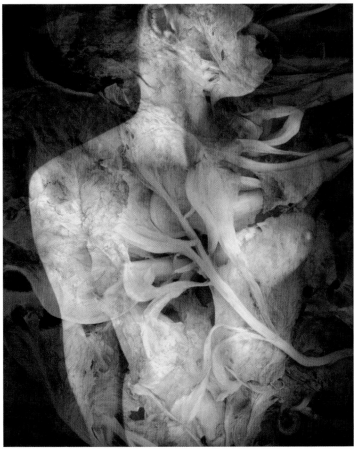

4.5 Lisa Gray, *Folds of Flesh,* 1992. Platinum/palladium print, 20 × 16 in. Lisa Gray's careful layering of undulating organic forms adds a decorative enrichment to the surface and suggests metaphors that communicate the inseparable connection of humanity to the natural world. Courtesy of Lisa Gray.

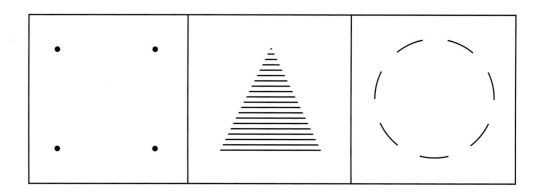

4.7 Yvonne Jacquette, *Lower Manhattan—Brooklyn Bridge View II*, 1976. Pastel monotype on off-white wove paper, 45.8 × 58.6 cm. This pastel by Jacquette is similar to Monet's paintings from the nineteenth century. She notes that Van Gogh and Seurat have influenced her soft, atmospheric style. A winter landscape, seen through flurries of snow, lends itself well to the blurred contours and high-key palette in this drawing. Gift of Anne Marie Davidson, 1989.482.12. Reproduction, The Art Institute of Chicago.

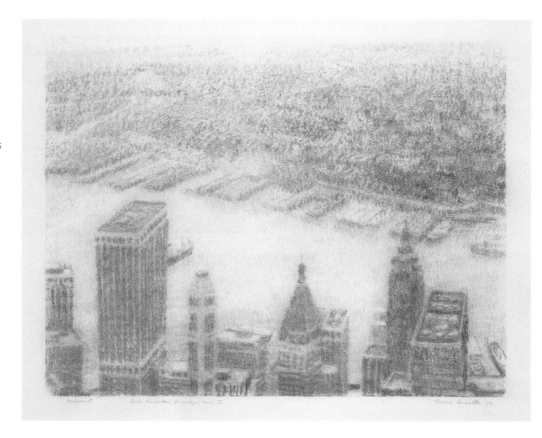

explained in Chapter 2) that the mind tries to see completed wholes and group relationships rather than just individual parts. So eager is the human mind to interpret pieces as whole images that it will even fill in missing information and impose shape identity in places where shapes don't actually exist. As illustrated in figure 4.6, the mind can perceive four dots as a square, parallel lines as a triangle, and dashes as a circle. Although we intuitively experience these shapes, they are not **actual shapes,** for none of them have clearly defined outer contours. Instead, each is an **implied shape,** created by the psychological connection of the dots or lines.

This ability to "see" shapes may be due, in part, to the insatiable need to impose meaning on what we experience. Once an area is surrounded by a boundary, it often transforms from negative background into positive shape, which allows us to see the shape as a figure, whether or not it can be recognized as something familiar. Thus, our minds can sense shapes when we cannot determine exactly where its edge exists. Even on a foggy day, we can sense blurred, fuzzy, and indistinct trees or buildings long before we can see them clearly. This vague shape is known as an **amorphous shape** (figs. 4.7 and 4.8). The name is rather an oxymoron, for the "image" is more of a promise of something yet to be—a subtle suggestion of shape without definition or certain dimensions—a shape without shape. One group of painters,

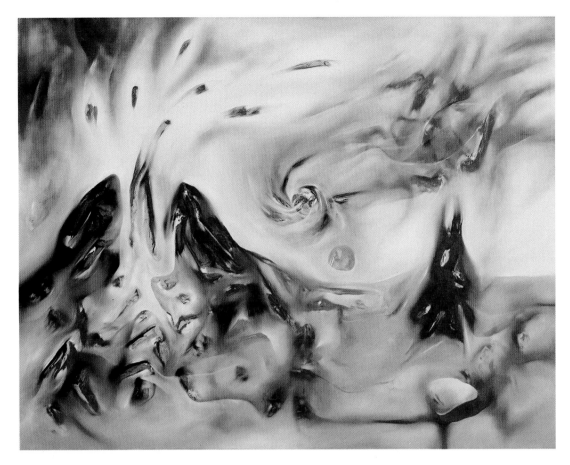

the Impressionists, often created amorphous shapes as they explored the atmospheric effect of sunlight on their imagery. From haystacks to cathedrals to bridges, the impression of light's effect on the surface of the object was more important than a naturalistic rendering of the object itself (see figs. 7.27, 7.28, and T.40).

In some works, the classification of an individual shape is not always easily made, due to the fact that shapes often share multiple properties. For example, a shape may be clearly defined as geometric or biomorphic on one side only to become amorphous on the other and blend into the background. Shapes can vary endlessly, ranging in type from objective to subjective, from geometric to biomorphic, from actual to implied, and so forth. Shapes with shared qualities may be seen in a vast number of works, including the energetic brushwork of Franz Kline (see fig. 1.24) and the delicately sculpted shapes of Lynda Benglis (see fig. T.81).

SHAPE DIMENSIONS

Shapes may also have either **two-dimensional** or **three-dimensional** identities. In pictorial artwork, shapes are created on the two-dimensional picture plane; however, artists may create the illusion of mass, volume, and space on their flat working surfaces through the careful juxtaposition and treatment of two-dimensional shapes. When we use the term **mass** to describe shapes on the picture plane, we mean that they have the appearance of solid three-dimensional bodies. The term **volume,** on the other hand, describes what appears to be a three-dimensional **void,** or an amount of measurable space. Rocks and mountains are masses, while holes and valleys are volumes; cups are masses, while the amounts of space they contain are volumes (fig. 4.9A and B). (In the **plastic** arts, shapes that physically exist in three dimensions are commonly referred to as masses or volumes.)

Shapes that have width and height but no indication of thickness are referred to as **planar shapes,** or **planes.** Depending on their configuration and juxtaposition, these planes range from having a flat, or **decorative,** appearance to one that seems to occupy deeper space. When a planar shape seems to lie flat on the surface of the picture plane,

4.9 Masses and volumes: Arches and Canyonlands National Parks, Utah. (A) The mountainous rock formations and their valleys represent mass and volume. (B) A close-up view illustrates a gigantic rock formation (mass) with an enormous hole (volume).

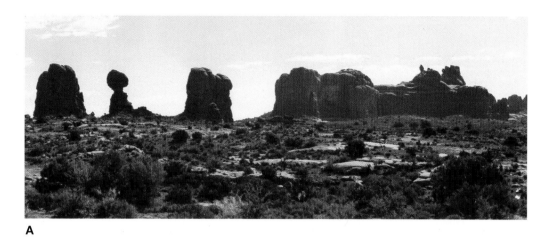

A

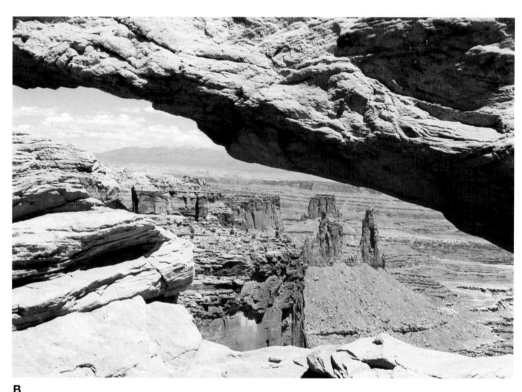

B

it has a decorative or shallow appearance (fig. 4.10, column A). However, a simple overlapping of two or more planar shapes can convert the flat working surface into a "window" through which shapes can be seen at different distances beyond the picture plane (fig. 4.10, column B). Contrasts in size, color, value, or texture can further establish this impression of depth. Of course, planar shapes do not have to appear parallel to the picture plane. When they appear to tilt in space and have a foreshortened appearance, they make an even stronger visual statement of depth (fig. 4.10, column C). The addition of gradient color, value, or texture can further enhance the illusion of receding planes, especially when used in combination with overlapping or interpenetration.

To produce the illusion of mass or volume on the picture plane, two or more planes must be arranged in relation to one another to give them an appearance of three-dimensionality (fig. 4.11). First, however, the artist must identify parts of the subject that can be represented by planar shapes. On masses such as cubes and rectangular solids, it is fairly obvious that their flat sides can be recognized as planes. However, rounded masses like spheres and ovoidal solids have no flat surface

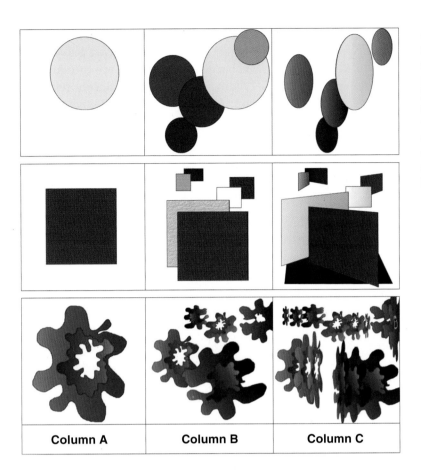

4.10 The spatial illusions of planar shapes. (Column A) Curvilinear, rectilinear, and biomorphic planar shapes can appear flat or shallow in depth. (Column B) Overlapping and contrast in size, value, color, or texture can create an impression of deeper depth. (Column C) Shapes can also appear tilted in space with adjustments in length and gradation in value, texture, or color.

| Column A | Column B | Column C |

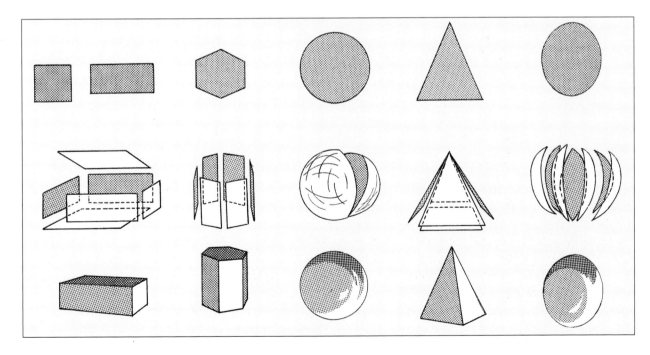

4.11 Planes and their three-dimensional equivalents.

facets, so identifying their planar shapes presents a special challenge—the artist must find areas of value or color change that can be interpreted as flat shapes (fig. 4.11, bottom row). When put together, these newly identified shapes will indicate reflected light and shadow on the three-dimensional surface and create the illusion of depth (fig. 4.12).

There is no limit to the number of shapes that can be shown three dimensionally on the picture plane, although geometric shapes may be the easiest. Squares, triangles, circles, hexagons, and ovoids all have their counterparts in three dimensions: cubes, pyramids, spheres, hexagonal solids, and ovoidal solids. The planes that constitute these 3-D objects do not even have to be closed or joined at the corners to suggest three-dimensionality. As seen in figure 4.11 in the middle row, the planes could be detached and tilted back at an angle. Although detaching the planes makes the 3-D objects less substantial, it shows their development more clearly and allows greater flexibility in the pictorial exploration of volume and space.

Presenting the planes in this way highlights the importance of the edges' function in creating the illusion of mass and depth. In figure 4.13A, the diagram shows planes that have parallel, angled edges. Because the angles lead away from the front edge or corner of the cube, they establish a directional movement into space. This combination of planes seems to provide three-dimensional solidity, whereas any plane on its own would appear relatively flat. In figure 4.13B, the angled edges of each plane are not parallel; in fact, if they continued, they would *converge* at some distant point. As a result, the planes appear to tilt or tip into space and *recede away from* the spectator. When several of these receding planes are juxtaposed and touching, the spatial illusion of mass and depth is greater than that provided by the use of parallel-edged planes. This is because the appearance of planes receding in depth more closely relates to our optical perception of images growing smaller as they move deeper into space.

However, planes with converging edges may not always provide the illusion of solid mass. If the edges seem to converge *toward the viewer* instead of toward a distant point, the solidity of the object becomes more ambiguous. At first glance, figure 4.13C appears to show the outside surface of a cube. After further inspection, the front vertical edge becomes the back of an empty nook, and the white plane that was originally seen from above is now seen from below, as a "ceiling." Figure 4.13C may even seem to switch back and forth from a hollow corner to a strangely formed solid block. This is a situation of ambiguous or uncertain depth, known as **equivocal**

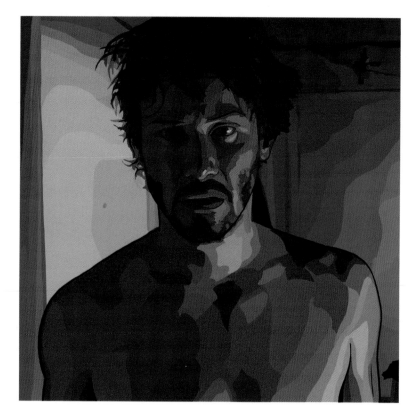

4.12 A scene from *A Scanner Darkly*, 2006 film by Richard Linklater (based on the novel of the same name by Philip K. Dick). Actor Keanu Reeves is pictured here as a cartoon image, which was created through the use of a technique called interpolated rotoscope. Areas of value or color are interpreted as planar shapes that, when put together, indicate light and dark and create the appearance of a three-dimensional image. Warner Bros./Photofest.

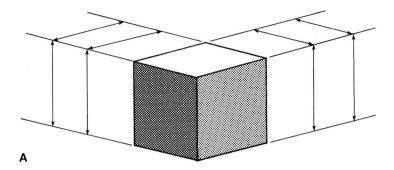

A

A combination of planes that show parallel edges in depth creates the illusion of mass (shape).

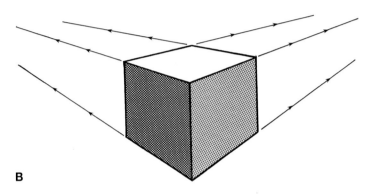

B

4.13B A combination of planes that show converging edges in depth (moving *away* from the viewer) creates the illusion of mass (shape).

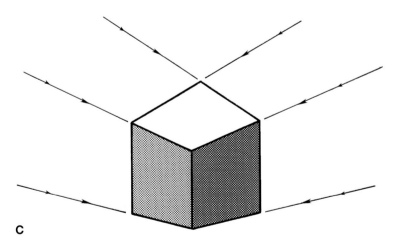

C

4.13C A combination of planes with edges converging *toward* the viewer creates the illusion of equivocal mass (shape). (This is the reverse effect of the shape in figure 4.13B.)

space—an optical illusion that can be described as "now you see it and now you don't," or more accurately, "now you see it and now you see it another way." Such ambiguities can add challenge, spice, and interest to the viewing of a composition. They exaggerate and distort shape definitions and impart some decorative qualities to the image.

Shapes with parallel and converging edges have been instinctively used by artists to create an *intuitive space*. Sometimes appearing shallow or decorative, this sense of space is created by layering, overlapping, and manipulating (aiming) the planes within the picture. Examples may be found in the early church work of the thirteenth and fourteenth centuries. However, with the arrival of the Renaissance and the interest in the sciences, the "felt" or intuitive spatial relationships were replaced by the invention of *linear perspective*. With this graphic system, artists could create a sense of deeper space in which objects diminish in size at a predictable rate as they recede.

While work employing linear perspective has remained popular, many contemporary artists have returned to the use of intuitive space. For them, the methodical systems of **perspective** are too predictable. They enjoy the freedom of creating imaginative three-dimensional shapes that are unencumbered by the restrictions of formulas and mechanical processes. Ron Davis, in his painting *Parallelepiped Vents #545*, employs flat planes, shapes with parallel edges, shapes with converging edges receding, and shapes with converging edges advancing (fig. 4.14). Al Held creatively employs the same types of shape-edge development in his painting *B/WX* (see fig. 8.40).

For more information on mechanical drawing systems used to create intuitive and plastic space, refer to the discussion on linear perspective and related mechanical systems in Chapter 8, "Space."

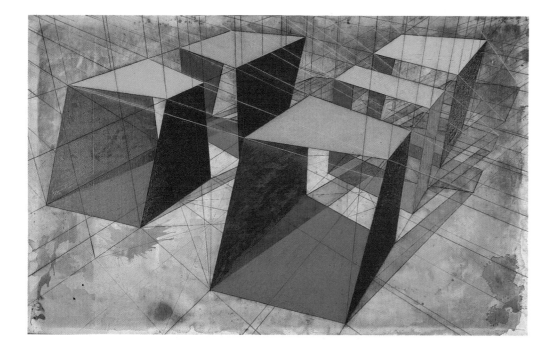

4.14 Ron Davis, *Parallelepiped Vents #545*, 1977. Acrylic on canvas, 9 ft. 6 in. × 15 ft. (2.90 × 4.57 m). While the strict order of linear perspective is not observed here, a sense of space is achieved by other means under the control of the artist's instincts. Los Angeles County Museum of Art, CA. Gift of the Eli and Edythe Broad Fund. Photography © 2001 Museum Associates/LACMA.

SHAPE AND COMPOSITION

Like the components of a building's foundation wall, shapes often become a key element in the structural footprint of a unified composition. Their placement and physical characteristics help establish a sense of harmony, variety, balance, and so forth. So important are shapes to composition that the contour of the picture frame is among the first considerations an artist must make, and that choice affects the relationship of all images and elements developed within. For example, a horizontal frame shape relates well to the establishment of horizontal images, shapes, or linear movements within the frame and allows shorter vertical shapes to provide relief and become accents (see figs. 4.1 and 4.23). The repetition of general directional forces thus becomes a factor for harmonizing the inside with the outside. For this reason, landscapes, reclining figures, or invented images whose major shapes and compositional move-

ments work across the image are more easily developed within a horizontal rather than a vertical frame shape. Likewise, vertical picture frames encourage the emphasis of vertical components and the use of horizontal marks or shapes as accents (see figs. 4.2 and 4.20). Obviously portraits, tall still lifes, and stained-glass windows are candidates for this type of development within a vertical frame shape. There are, however, always exceptions that can be found for every convention (see fig. 4.19, which shows a horizontal landscape in a vertical frame shape), so these observations are offered only as general guidelines.

When artists wish to create order or unity and increase the viewer's attention span as they work with shape, they have to apply the principles of organization to their designing process. In their search for significant order and expression, artists modify developing shapes and the elements until:

- An appropriate ratio of harmony and variety results

- The observer's attention is controlled both in terms of direction (movement) and duration (dominance)
- The desired degree and type of balance is achieved
- The space concept achieves consistency throughout
- An appropriate sense of proportion and economy is established

The principles determining the ordering of shapes are common to the other elements of form. However, shape is such a primary element that the concepts of harmony, variety, dominance, and so forth warrant specific review as they apply to it.

Harmony and Variety

The repetition of similar shapes is an easy way to create a sense of harmony in most compositions (see fig. 2.7). When shapes share similar edge characteristics, they seem to belong to a related group and may be referred to as a "shape family." As with members of a human family, the likeness need not always be identical but merely enough to see their relationship. By using the same number of sides on each shape or by using similar contour qualities (such as rectilinear, curvilinear, or amorphous edges), the shapes will appear to belong together. Their similarity in structure can then be enhanced by common applications of value, texture, or color.

An emphasis on shape harmony can result in a relatively peaceful interaction between shapes. However, overstressing harmony may curtail our interest; repeating the exact same shape over and over can lead to monotony and boredom. Enough differences must exist to make for challenging viewing. When trying to develop shapes within a composition, it is important for the artist to recognize how to make the shapes harmonize and still maintain enough variety to retain interest. Accent and excitement are created by dissimilarity—but how much change can be tolerated by the viewer's eye while still keeping the shapes within the original family of shapes?

To discover this, try changing a rectangle into a circle through a series of morphed shapes. First, draw the rectangle on a piece of paper. Then, by drawing on top of the previous image, gradually change the outer contour of the shape—change the number of sides and the length or angle of the sides, let the outer edges swell out or become indented, and so on. After drawing twenty or thirty new shapes, you should eventually end with a circle. The shapes in that progression will be related up to the point where the outer contour changes enough to make the additional shapes part of a different family grouping. You may have developed a couple of shape families in your long progression of shapes—try to spot the point of transition from one to the other. Try the same experiment with biomorphic shapes or purely invented shapes. To individually examine each shape in the

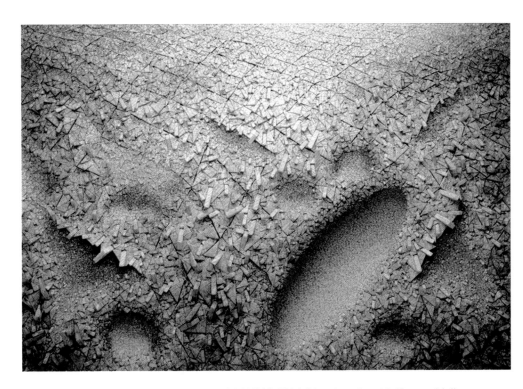

4.15 Kwang-Young Chun, *Aggregation 06-AU044*, 2004. Mixed media with Korean Mulberry paper, 86 × 123 in. (218.4 × 312.4 cm). The work is constructed of thousands of triangles wrapped in century-old mulberry paper to produce variations of surface texture and composition. It depends on a variation of trompe l'oeil using a range of tones from gray to black to create the illusion of deep depressions or craters and the patterns of drying earth. For those familiar with Korean culture, there is an additional layer of meaning. Evocative of childhood memories, the triangles suggest herbal medicine bundles wrapped in paper and hung in clusters from the ceilings of the family-run pharmacy. Courtesy of the Kim Foster Gallery, New York.

progression, draw the shapes on a stack of tracing paper, putting a fresh sheet down for each new shape.

Dominance

Artists develop dominance intuitively as they respond to each area and shape within a composition and as they establish all the principles of organization, from harmony and variety to economy. Obviously, the relative dominance of a shape may be altered by contrasts in size, color or value, visual detail, textural emphasis, directional force, and so forth (fig 4.15). But on a more basic level, simply changing the design of one shape can make it the dominant member of a grouping of similar shapes. Because the degree of dominance is established

by the degree of contrast, the amount of change within the shape family helps establish the amount of dominance given to each new shape. The more any shape looks like its neighbors, the less dominance it may have simply because of its design.

Shape dominance can also be a matter of association. Each shape must be appreciated purely for the aesthetic quality of its form, but when the design of a shape begins to take on the appearance of something familiar to the viewer, the relative dominance of that area is increased (fig. 4.16). For example, when a shape begins to suggest the letter *B*, it demands our attention in a new way with multiple levels of association: (1) the pure design of the shape; (2) any subconscious association with

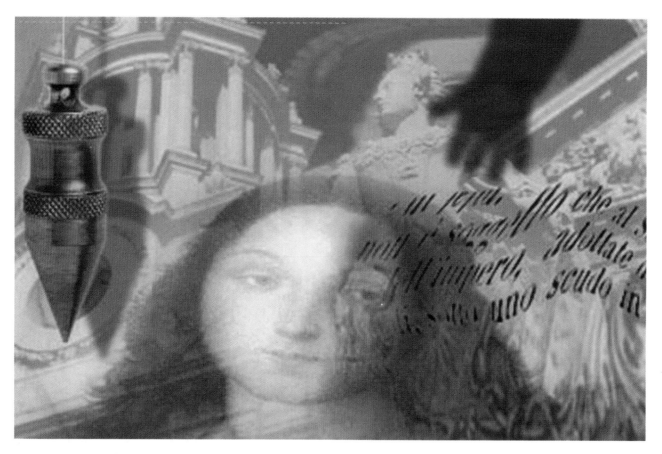

4.16   Fred Birchman, *Plum*, 1998. **Digital image.** Birchman uses dominance in this digital image in an interesting way. The plumb bob in the foreground is highly focused and casts a shadow. Even though the images behind the plumb bob are distorted and unfocused, they maintain their place because they remain recognizable and form a planar and scalar relationship to the plumb bob. Courtesy of Fred Birchman.

the symbol in the alphabet; and (3) the related sound accompanying the letter. If the letter is grouped with other letters to become a word—such as *bat*—there is another layer of meaning that could bring up memories of baseball or an animal flying into your hair. Although contrasts of size, color, value, clarity of focus, texture, and so on remain the principal devices for creating dominance, artists can use the innate appeal of associative factors to their advantage and force shape association to benefit the total organization.

Movement

Artists can use shape, along with the other elements of form, to generate visual forces that direct our eyes as we view the work. In some instances the movement is subtle. Some shapes like circles and squares, which are excellent at anchoring or holding a location in a composition, are also important in establishing tension and a subconscious movement. When other shapes are located close enough to these focal points, the eye bounces back and forth, trying

to make them join together or become part of a group relationship (see figs. 2.15 and 2.16).

Many shapes, such as the triangle, have a general body movement that points in one specific direction or another, based on the design of the shape. Obviously, not all shapes are equally important in contributing to movement, for some provide more of a directional force than others. Compare, for example, the "forceful" rectangle to the "stable" but less directional square. As a general rule, the longer the shape, the

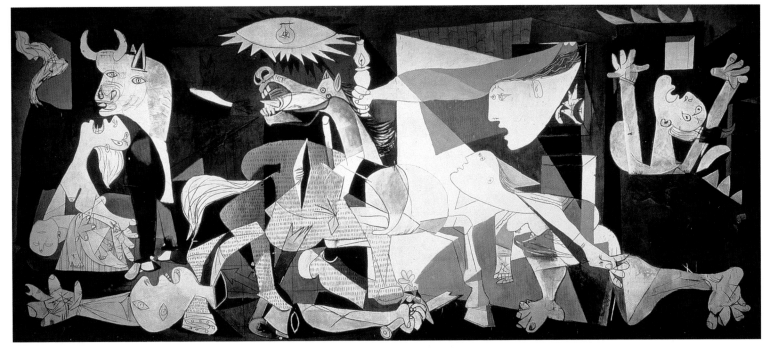

A

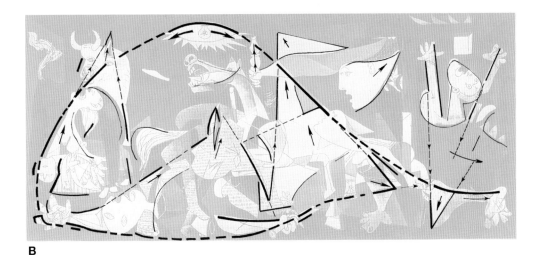

B

4.17 Pablo Picasso, *Guernica*, 1937. Oil on canvas, 11 ft. 5½ in. × 25 ft. 5¼ in. (3.49 × 7.75 m). The linear diagram (B) overlaying Picasso's *Guernica* is one of several possible interpretations of the way shape is used as a directional device. The arrows in the middle of the shapes indicate their major directional thrust. The thick solid lines show the edges where a perceived direction seems to line up with a corresponding shape edge across a space (indicated by broken lines). These create the major shape directions in overall composition. Secondary shapes, related in a similar way, are shown by middleweight lines. The lighter lines show curving shape edges counteracting the straighter and more broadly arced edges of the design. Museo Nacional Centro de Arte Reina Sofía, Madrid, Spain/SuperStock. Art © 2008 Estate of Pablo Picasso/Artists Rights Society (ARS), New York.

greater the directional force. Sometimes the directional device is a function of the shape's edges rather than the bulk of the shape. Contours can be "aimed" so that they imply a linkage with the edges of other shapes elsewhere in the composition. In this manner, eye movement may be encouraged in a certain direction by "joining" distant shapes through their related contours (fig. 4.17A and B).

Whether an artist is using shapes to create movement through shallow or deep space, the movement of the eyes along these paths should be rhythmic, providing pleasurable viewing and unification of the work. The character of the rhythm produced depends on the artist's intentions—jerky, sinuous, swift, or slow (fig. 4.18). The control of direction helps us see things in the proper sequence and according to the degree of importance planned for them.

The unifying and rhythmic effects provided by eye paths are modified by the number and length of the pauses in

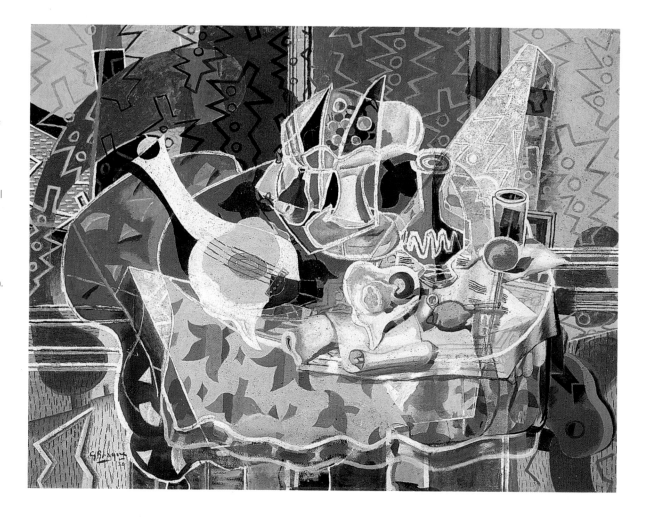

4.18 Georges Braque, *Still Life with Fruit and Stringed Instrument*, 1938. Oil and sand on canvas, 32 × 39⅜ in. (114.3 × 147.3 cm). The shapes of white line or light value define the designed pathways of eye travel. The visual tension and rhythmic movement result from the placement, size, soft accent, and general character of the shapes involved. Gift of Mrs. Albert D. Lasker in memory of her husband, Albert D. Lasker, 1959.505. Photo © The Art Institute of Chicago. Art © 2008 Artists Rights Society (ARS), New York/ADAGP, Paris.

the eye journey. In figure 4.19, the duration of a pause is determined by the visual importance of the area or shape—often a focal point in the artwork. When the planned pauses are of equal duration, the viewing experience is more monotonous. The artist, therefore, organizes pauses so that their lengths are related to the importance of the areas or images on the journey—a hierarchy of increasing importance or interest as the figures come to the foreground.

In a depiction of the Crucifixion, for example, we would expect an artist to make the figure of Christ particularly significant. In the case of Ismael Rodriguez Rueda's painting *El Sueño de Erasmo* (fig. 4.20), this emphasis is achieved by the accentuated size of the shape created by Christ's body; by making that shape more clearly defined than other shapes;

by its central location; and by accenting the color, value, and brushwork in that area. The shorter pauses within the composition are also brought about by contrasting the rectilinear quality of Christ's T-shape with the ovals in the right and left foreground, the arch tops in the background, and the differences in value and color. Playing a diminished role, but adding to the organized coherence of the painting through placement, is the repetition of the similar head shapes of the figures and the touches of yellow, red, and green throughout the painting.

Balance

In the search for compositional balance, artists work with the knowledge that a shape's visual weight is a result of how

the shape is used, the development of the negative area around it, and what properties are inherent to the art elements composing both. The placement, size, accent or emphasis, and general shape character all affect the amount of visual weight a shape has. A dark value adds weight to a shape; substituting a narrow contour line for a wider contour line reduces the shape's visual weight; and an amorphous edge can reduce the sense of focus on that shape and thereby reduce its visual weight and degree of dominance.

Shapes of various visual weights are found in all types of pictorial balance (symmetrical, radial, asymmetrical, etc.). No single shape family is restricted to the development of any specific type of balance—geometric shapes, for example, are not the only configuration

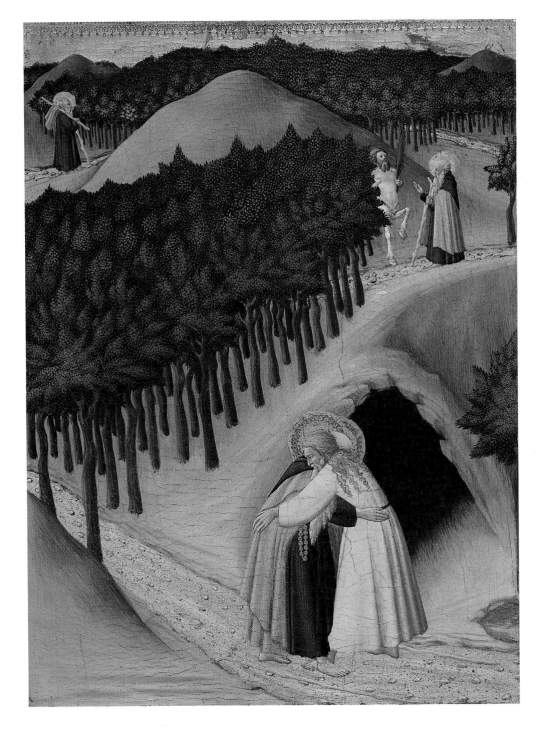

that can be used in asymmetrical balance (see fig. 4.5).

Choices in location and physicality of the shapes will affect how the artist wants to treat the shapes' surfaces, which then affects the visual weight of the shapes as well as other areas and may lead to subsequent adjustments throughout the composition. The artist manipulates the shapes and the elements involved with their creation until the relationships result in the desired equilibrium.

This also means that the artist must balance the spatial forces developed within the work. With decorative shapes, the balance only occurs on the surface of the picture plane. With three-dimensional appearances, the thrusting and recession

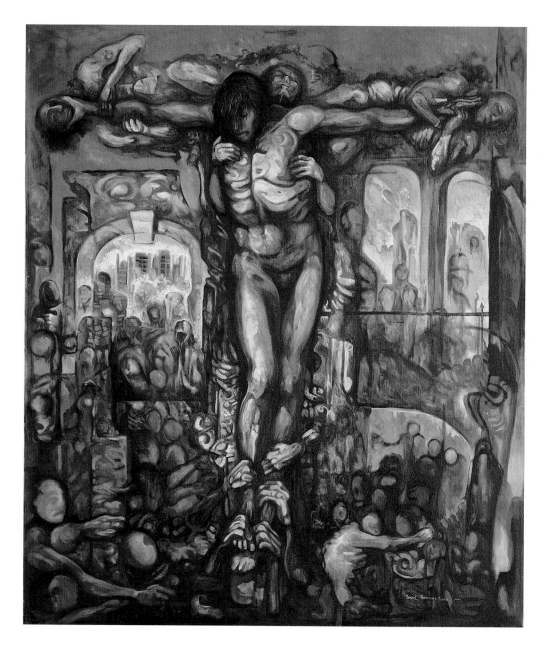

4.20 Ismael Rodriguez Rueda, *El Sueño de Erasmo (The Dream of Erasmus)*, 1995. Oil on canvas, 39⅓ × 47½ in. (100 × 120 cm). The figure of Christ is made dominant by its size and central location. In the creation of varied visual pauses, the artist has skillfully played opposites of differing contrasts against each other—sometimes strongly accented, sometimes subdued: blues against oranges, reds against greens, yellow against violets, light against dark, and biomorphic shapes against the geometric shapes of architectural settings.
Courtesy of Ismael Rodriguez Rueda.

of shapes in deeper "space" must also balance; otherwise, the picture plane can appear twisted. Regardless of the degree of depth involved, equalization of the spatial forces depends on adjustments in shape size and position, as well as variations in the application of the other elements.

Proportion and Economy

When trying to develop appropriate proportions and a sense of economy, an artist may benefit from breaking down the subject into simple planar shapes (fig. 4.21A and B). This allows the vastness and intricacies of a subject to be simplified for easy translation onto the picture plane and provides a method for studying the compositional arrangement of those shapes. Working from light to dark, general planar shapes are blocked in, one layer at a time. In each succeeding step, the lighter shapes become more defined as their contours are articulated by the darker shapes that surround and overlap them. In the end, as shown in figure 4.21A, shape layers indicate not only the overall tree shape but also individual clumps of foliage, and the image becomes quite refined.

This "planar analysis" is a way of learning to see information. By breaking down the complexities of an image, it is easier to distinguish the relationship of the parts to each other and to the whole with respect to proportion and overall value. This use of planar shapes creates economical, stable, and ordered units that are useful for preliminary sketches and for developing the work's final organization. Such a study helps the

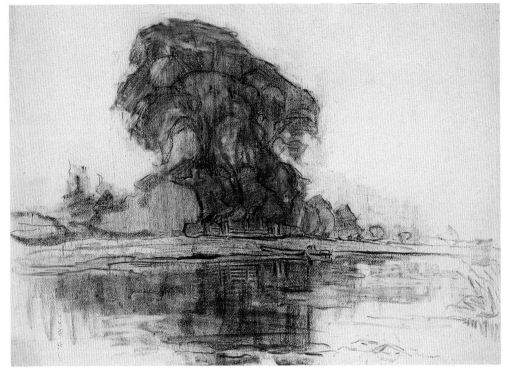

A

4.21A Piet Mondrian, *Landzicht Farm: Compositional Study,* c. 1905. Charcoal on blue/gray paper, 18⅜ × 24½ in. (46.7 × 62.2 cm). In this work, Piet Mondrian used outer contours to establish the larger simplified planar shapes. They, in turn, are broken into smaller organic planes that provide more and more detail. Edward E. Ayer Endowment, in memory of Charles L. Hutchinson, 1962.105., The Art Institute of Chicago © 2008 Mondrian/Holtzman Trust, c/o HCR International, Warrenton, Virginia

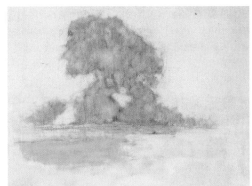

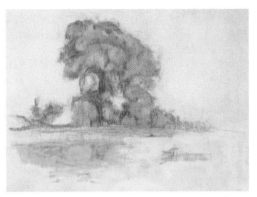

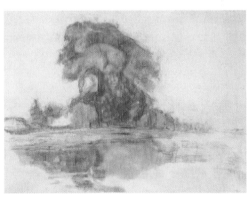

4.21B The four smaller illustrations are not the work of Mondrian. They simply suggest how his image may have progressed. The lightest generalized areas are drawn as planes. Then with each succeeding step, darker shapes and details are added. The work concludes with the final accents as seen in figure 4.21A.

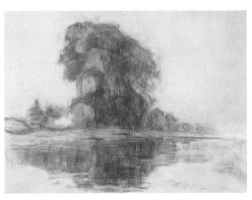

B

artist establish appropriate proportions within an image, work from the general to the specific, introduce continually refined detail, and create a sense of space. Although these examples focus on responsive drawing (which uses physical references as subjects), planar development is also a good approach for working nonobjectively.

SHAPE AND EXPRESSIVE CONTENT

While a shape's physical characteristics may be easily defined, its expressive character is rather difficult to pinpoint, because viewers react to the configuration of shape on many different emotional levels. In some cases, our responses to shapes are commonplace; in others, our reactions are complex because our own personality traits and experiences influence our interpretation of a shape's meaning. Our emotional sensitivity to shape is demonstrated by the familiar Rorschach (inkblot) test, which was designed to aid psychologists in evaluating emotional stability. The test indicates that shapes provoke emotional responses on different levels. Thus, the artist might use specific abstract or representational shapes to provoke a desired response. By using the knowledge that some shapes are inevitably associated with certain objects and situations, the artist can set the stage for a pictorial or sculptural drama. The full meaning of any shape, however, can only be revealed through the relationships developed throughout the entire composition.

Whether viewing inkblots or artwork, our reaction to shape is often quite primal and subconscious. Some shapes convey relatively standard meanings. Squares, for instance, commonly express perfection, stability, solidity, symmetry, self-reliance, and monotony. Similarly, circles may suggest self-possession, independence, and/or confinement; ovals

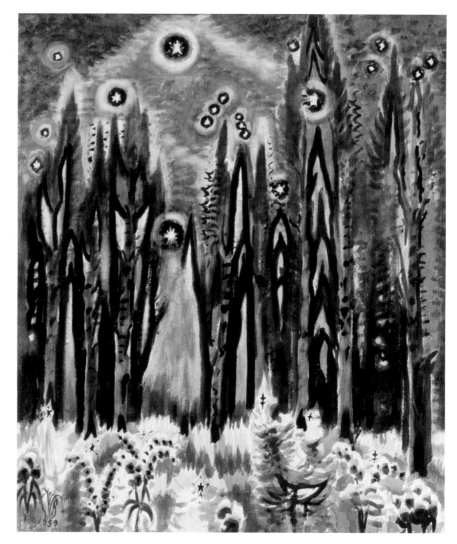

4.22 Charles Burchfield, *Orion in December*, 1959. Watercolor and pencil on paper; sheet: 39⅞ × 32⅞ in. Burchfield believed that an artist must paint not what he sees in nature but what is there. To do this, he invented his own symbols, drawing from the sights and sounds around him to represent the force and beauty of nature. In this wonderful scene, the primeval forest soars—perhaps as a Gothic cathedral—stars symbolize ecstasy, and Orion, the hunter in Greek mythology, hovers, merging heaven and earth. Along the bottom, crackling ice-covered shrubs twist and move as if in a frigid breeze and repeat the patterns of the starlit sky. Smithsonian American Art Museum, Washington, DC/Art Resource, NY.

may suggest fruitfulness and creation; stars could suggest reaching out.

The psychological association of abstract shapes may be especially appealing to certain artists. Particularly in the twentieth century, numerous movements were based on the use of specific abstract configurations. The Surrealists of the early 1900s, for example, were interested in the mystic origins of being and in the exploration of subconscious revelations, such as in dreams. With the increasing awareness of the microscopic world, the growth of Freudian psychology, and the revival of interest in pure abstraction (in which shapes function symbolically), biomorphic shapes became a key component in the work of **Surrealism** (see fig. T.66). Such shapes may be seen in the paintings by Burchfield (fig. 4.22) and Miró (see fig. 4.4). Other artists, like Matisse and Braque, worked with abstracted organic forms in a less symbolic manner (see figs. 4.1 and 4.18).

In contrast, the precise, machinelike quality of geometric shapes appealed to artists working with **Cubism,** who used them in their analytical dissection and reformulation of the natural world (see fig. 4.33A and B). Following the Cubists, the Futurists were influenced by the stylization of machinery and created pristine, clear-cut shapes and shape relationships that expressed the power and speed of the mechanized world (see fig. T.59). Later, the Minimalists and the Conceptualists of the 1970s and 80s also used simple geometric shapes to further reduce images to their basic elements of meaning (see figs. 2.71 and 2.72).

While the configuration of a shape greatly affects our interpretation of it, additional characteristics of the shape can also affect its psychological impact. Color, value, texture, spatial depth, and the application of particular media can affect whatever feeling we intuit in such works of art. Depending on how they are treated by the artist, shapes may feel static, stable, active, or lively or seem to contract or expand. For example, the work of Charles Sheeler (fig. 4.23), Dorothea Rockburne (fig. 4.24), and Joseph

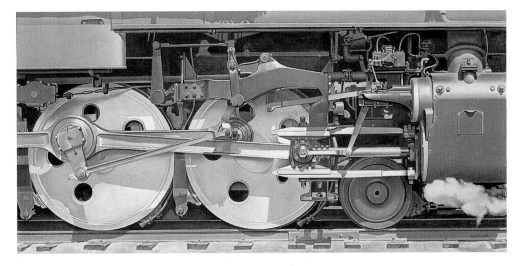

4.23 Charles Sheeler, *Rolling Power*, 1955. Oil on canvas, 15 × 30 in. (38.1 × 72.6 cm). While commenting on the abstract quality of his images, Sheeler remarked, "I had come to feel that a picture could have incorporated in it the structural design implied in abstraction and be presented in a wholly realistic manner." Smith College Museum of Art, Northampton, MA. Purchased, Drayton Hillyer Fund, 1940. Courtesy of Smith College Museum, Northampton, MA.

4.24 Dorothea Rockburne, *Mozart and Mozart Upside Down and Backward*, 1985–87. Oil on gessoed linen, hung on blue wall, 89 × 115 × 4 in. (226.06 × 292.1 × 10.16 cm). In this painting, Dorothea Rockburne is representative of the Neo-Abstractionist painters, who leaned toward the geometric abstraction of the 1950s. Though based on a seemingly simple scheme, on closer examination, this piece reveals a labyrinth of interlocking rectilinear shapes. Courtesy of André Emmerich Gallery, a Division of Sotheby's, on behalf of the artist. © 2008 Dorothea Rockburne/Artists Rights Society (ARS), NY.

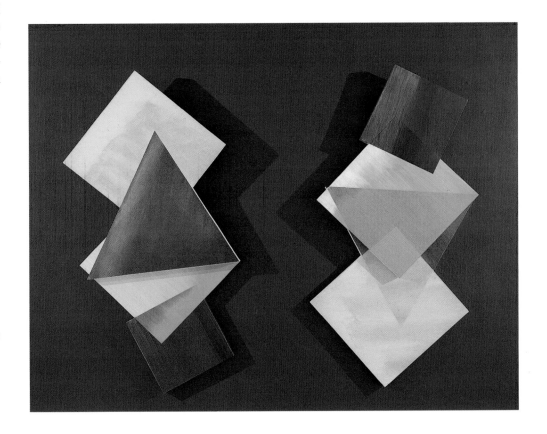

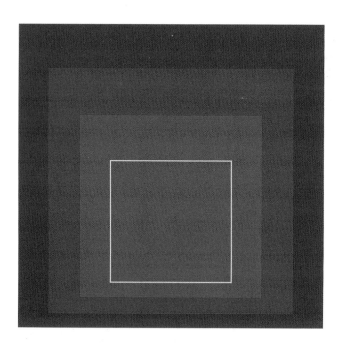

Josef Albers, *White Line Square IX,* from the series *Homage to the Square,* 1966. Colored lithograph, 21 × 21 in. (53.3 × 53.3 cm). The meaning of the squares in this picture lies not in their resemblance to a real object but in their relationship to one another. © 1966 Josef Albers and Gemini G.E.L., Los Angeles, CA. © 2008 the Josef and Anni Albers Foundation/Artists Rights Society (ARS), New York.

4.26 Helen Frankenthaler, *Madame Butterfly,* 2000. Woodcut print, triptych, 41¼ × 79 in. (104.8 × 200.7 cm). Many shapes are not meant to represent or even symbolize. Here, for example, the shape extremities, the softly changing values of the larger shapes, and the brown wood-grained ground act against the horizontal violet and white components and the outer frame shape. The artist provokes a momentary feeling of excitement within an otherwise quiet mood.
Printed and published by Tyler Graphics Ltd., 2000. © Helen Frankenthaler/Tyler Graphics Ltd. Photograph by Steven Sloman.

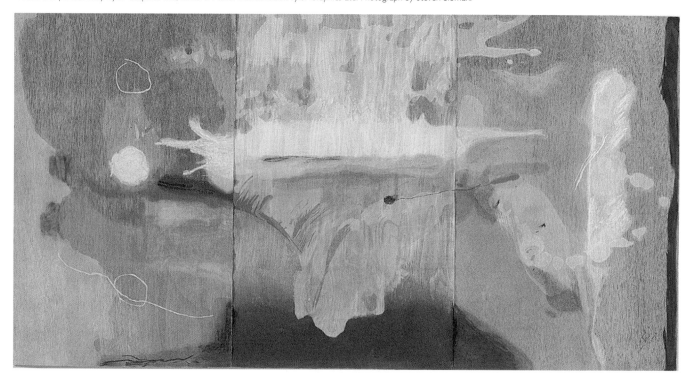

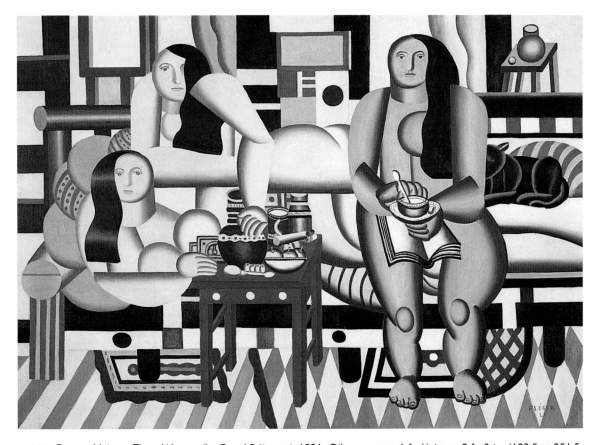

4.27 Fernand Léger, *Three Women (Le Grand Déjeuner)*, 1921. Oil on canvas, 6 ft. ¼ in. × 8 ft. 3 in. (183.5 × 251.5 cm). The Cubist painter Léger commonly used varied combinations of geometric shapes in very complex patterns. Here, because of his sensitive design, he not only overcomes a dominant, hard-edged feel but also imbues the painting with an air of femininity. © 2008 Artists Rights Society (ARS), New York/ADGP, Paris. The Museum of Modern Art, New York, NY, U.S.A. Mrs. Simon Guggenheim Fund. Digital image © The Museum of Modern Art/Licensed by SCALA/Art Resource, NY.

Albers (fig. 4.25) all use similar geometric shapes, but differences in color, value, and their application change the shapes' meanings and create a different type of space. In figures 4.23 and 4.24, shapes imply spatial depth through the use of blended colors and values. However, in figure 4.25, the sense of space is achieved in a different manner; although Albers's shapes appear flat, that flatness is contradicted by the contrast of color and value, which make various squares advance or recede, and a tunneling effect is made by placing the squares closer to the bottom edge of the picture frame. In other examples,

the quality of the shape's edge is important; the terms *soft edge* and *hard edge* are used to indicate the degree of clarity or sharpness used to define the image (figs. 4.26 and 4.27).

Our reactions to abstraction and/ or representation also affect how we interpret any work of art. Many people accept Sheeler's artwork, even when the abstraction is more pronounced, because the subject is still recognizable (see figs 1.13 and 4.23). However, other people react adversely to simple, non-objective shapes like those in Albers's paintings (see fig. 4.25). Unfortunately, viewers who value representational art-

work because they can easily interpret the subject matter often fail to see the intellectual metaphor and visual effects of the shape relationships; they don't appreciate how *form itself* may be the subject matter.

Conception and imagination have always been part of artistic expression. It is usually a matter of degree as to how much artists use their imagination and how much they use their perceptual vision in the selection and creation of their shapes (figs. 4.28 and 4.29). Artists, therefore, go beyond literal copying and transform shapes into their personal style or language of

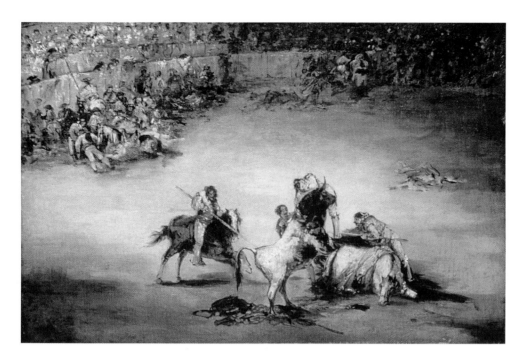

4.28 Francisco Goya, *The Bullfight*, c. 1824. Oil on canvas, 24¾ × 36½ in. (63 × 93 cm). While it is a straightforward exercise to recognize the picador in this painting, this should only be a starting point for understanding the blood and tragedy that Goya found in the bullring. Toledo Museum of Art, Toledo, Ohio. Purchased with funds from the Libbey Endowment. Gift of Edward Drummond Libbey.

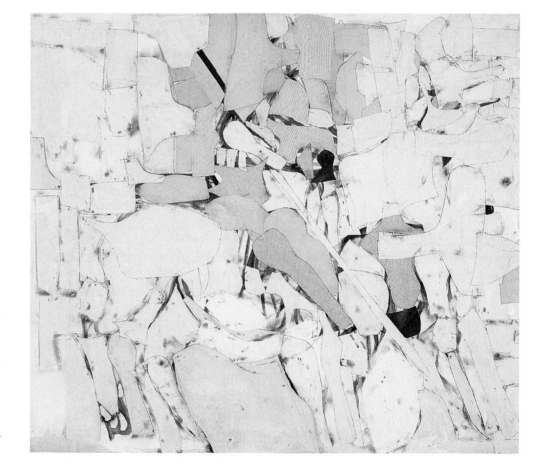

4.29 Conrad Marca-Relli, *The Picador*, 1956. Oil and fabric collage on canvas, 3 ft. 11¼ in. × 4 ft. 5 in. (1.20 × 1.35 m). Artists differ in their responses to subject matter. It is often a matter of degree as to how much artists use their imaginations and how much their visual perceptions vary. Such differences are apparent if one contrasts the use of the picador here and in figure 4.28. Hirshhorn Museum and Sculpture Garden, Smithsonian Institution, Washington, DC. Gift of Joseph H. Hirshhorn, 1966. Photograph by Lee Stalsworth.

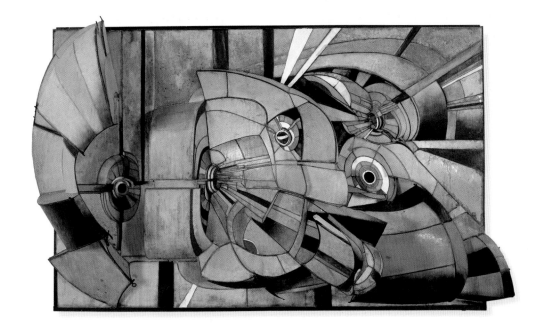

4.30 Lee Bontecou, *Untitled*, 1966. Welded steel, canvas, epoxy, leather, wire, and light, 78½ × 119 × 31 in. (199.4 × 302.3 × 78.7 cm). Lee Bontecou is known for her personal sculptural relief images—the art of assemblage that brings sculpture and painting together. Web-like arrangements of canvas strips that have been attached to metal frames create related shape families which unify the work, create visual movement, and suggest a combination of natural metaphors from landscape to wildlife to space. The introduction of circular forms could imply variously holes, thresholds, voids, or even birdlike eyes. The power and mystery of her chosen shapes seem to fuse natural forms with the abstract becoming unsettling or even surreal for many viewers. Photo: Courtesy of Museum of Contemporary Art, Chicago. Gift of Robert B. Mayer Family Collection, 1991.85. Art © Lee Bontecou/ courtesy Knoedler & Company, New York.

form (figs. 4.30 and 4.31). The student only has to glance around the classroom to see the diverse ways people work on a similar exercise.

From these examples, it is clear that each shape (or combination of shapes) can display a particular personality according to its physical employment and our responses to it. The artist's challenge is to use the infinitely varied presentation of shape to make believable the illusion inherent in all art. In other words, an artwork is never the real thing, and the shapes producing the image are never real animals, buildings, or people; they are the artist's subjects, if indeed the artist uses those subjects at all. Capable artists, whatever the degree of fantasy they employ, are able to convince us that the fantasy is a possible reality. Any successful work of art, regardless of medium, leads the sensitive observer into the persuasive world of the imagination.

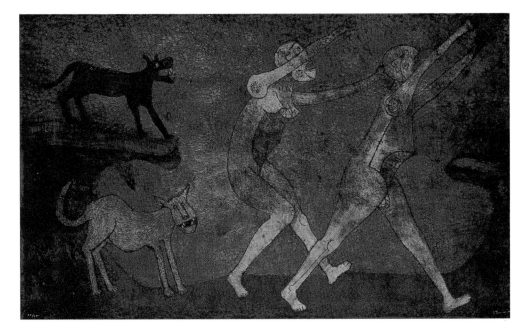

4.31   Rufino Tamayo, *Dos Personajes Atacados por Perros*, 1983. (Edition of 75) Mixografia on handmade paper, 60 × 90 in. (152.4 × 228.6 cm). Tamayo has created an air of fantasy by semiabstracting the people and dogs, creating an image of distance and ritualized terror. Courtesy of Mixografía®, Los Angeles, printers of fine art prints since 1968.

THREE-DIMENSIONAL APPLICATIONS OF SHAPE

In the plastic arts, shape has greater significance and usage than the other elements, as the artist working in three dimensions instinctively begins with shape. Due to the added physical dimension of the media, the definition of *shape* takes on expanded meaning in the plastic arts. It encompasses the totality of the mass or volume lying between its contours, including any projections and depressions. It may also include interior planes—relatively flat areas on the three-dimensional form (see fig. 3.30). In trying to describe 3-D shapes, we can speak of the overall space-displacing shape of a piece of sculpture or architecture, the flat or curved shape that moves in space, or the negative shape that is partially or totally enclosed (see fig. 1.40).

Like many shapes in the graphic arts, 3-D shapes are generally measurable areas that are limited by (and/or contrasted with) other shapes, values, textures, and colors. Those contrasts greatly help define shape edges (fig. 4.32). (Such contrasts are often heightened by or even dependent on the effects of light and shadow—to be discussed in Chapter 5.) When boundaries are clearly defined, the shapes are more easily understood, whereas ill-defined edges often lead to confusing or monotonous viewing. Shape edges guide the eye through, around, and over the 3-D surface, creating a desire to experience the entire work. However, the visible shape depends on the viewer's position. A slight change in viewpoint results in a change in the perceived shape and its contour.

A major contour is the outer limit (or **silhouette**) of the total 3-D work as seen from one position (fig. 4.33A and B). Secondary contours are perceived

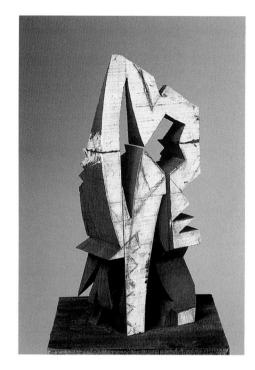

4.32 Mel Kendrick, *White Wall*, 1984. Basswood, Japan paint, 16 × 5 × 6½ in. (40.6 × 12.7 × 16.5 cm). The shape of this three-dimensional piece has edges that have been clearly defined. Courtesy of the artist.

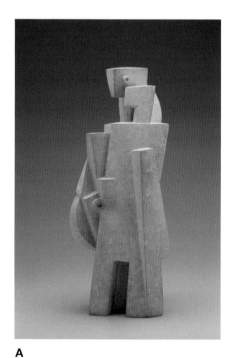

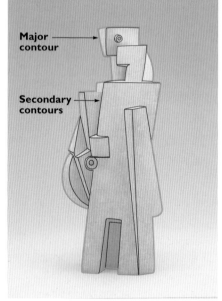

Major contour

Secondary contours

4.33 Jacques Lipchitz, *Man with Mandolin*, 1917. Limestone, 29¾ in. (75.6 cm) high. Exploring Lipchitz's work in the round from every position reveals the changing contours and makes the three-dimensional work exciting. (B) In an isolated view of the image, the major contour surrounds the silhouette or the total visible area of the work. Secondary contours occur on internal edges. (A) Photo: Gift of Collection Société Anonyme. 1941.547. Photo © Yale University Art Gallery/Art Resource, NY. Art © The Marlborough Gallery, NY

A   **B**

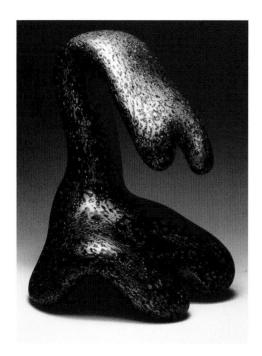

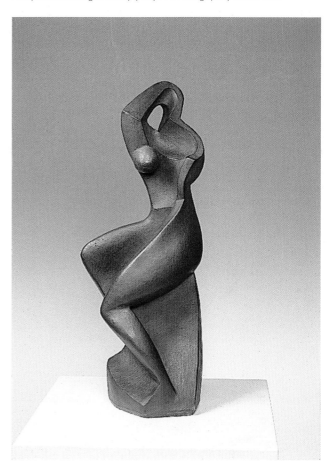

4.35 Alexander Archipenko, *Woman Doing Her Hair,* c. 1958. Bronze casting from plaster based on original terracotta of 1916, 21⅝ in. (55 cm) high. This is a significant example of sculptural form where the shape creates negative space, or a void. Archipenko was one of the pioneers of this concept. Courtesy of the Kunst Museum, Düsseldorf, Germany. © 2008 Estate of Alexander Archipenko/Artists Rights Society (ARS), NY. Photograph by Walter Klein.

4.34 Ken Price, *Sweets,* 2001. Fired and painted clay, 12¼ × 8¾ in. The major contour of *Sweets* is its outermost edge. Secondary contours are nonexistent or, at best, minimal. © Ken Price, Courtesy Matthew Marks Gallery, New York.

edges of shapes or planes that move across and/or between the major contours. Some 3-D works are constructed so that the secondary contours are negligible (fig. 4.34). Contours can be "aimed" so that they imply a linkage with the edges of other shapes elsewhere in the composition. This is particularly true of atectonic work or pieces containing several items in a group setting. In this manner, eye movement may be encouraged subconsciously in a certain direction by "joining" distant shapes through their related contours (see fig. 3.30). When other shapes are located close enough to these focal points, the eye bounces back and forth, trying to make them join together or become part of a group relationship.

A shape might also be a negative space or void—a three-dimensional open area that seems to penetrate through or be contained by solid material. These open shapes can surround solid masses and also extend between them. Alexander Archipenko and Henry Moore, prominent twentieth-century sculptural innovators, pioneered the use of void shapes (figs. 4.35 and 4.36). Voids provided new spatial extensions for these artists and others who followed. The use of voids revealed interior surfaces, opened direct routes to the back sides of a sculpture, and reduced excessive weight (fig. 4.37). Void shapes should be considered integral parts of the total

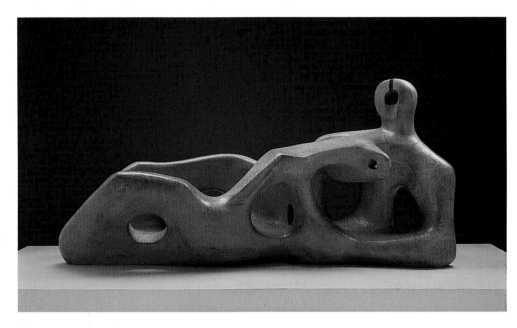

4.36 Henry Moore, *Reclining Figure*, 1939. Carved elm wood, 37 × 79 × 30 in. (94 × 201 × 76 cm). Moore's work is a synthesis of influences from primitive sculpture, Surrealism, and a lifelong study of the forms of nature. Detroit Institute of Arts. Founders Society Purchase with funds from the Dexter M. Ferry, Jr., Trustee Corporation. Reproduced by permission of the Henry Moore Foundation.

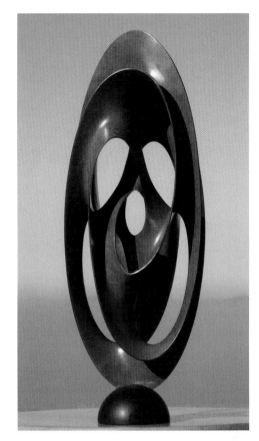

4.37 Carlo Sequin, *Totem 3*, 2004. Bronze, 5 × 3 × 13 in. tall. Our eyes are drawn around this work not only by the revolving edges of the shape but also by the voids, which serve to draw our attention through the piece and reveal the interior surface. Courtesy of Carlo H. Sequin, University of California, Berkeley.

form. In linear sculpture, enclosed void shapes become so important that they often dominate the width, thickness, and weight of the materials that define them (see fig. 3.31).

Like their two-dimensional counterparts, three-dimensional shapes also play a large role in establishing dominance (emphasis) within sections of a work. The relative dominance of a shape may be altered by contrasts in size, color, value, visual detail, or textural emphasis (see figs. 2.63 and 4.30). A shape may be made the dominant member of a group by making it different from those around it. Because the degree of dominance is established by the degree of contrast, the amount of change within the shape family helps to establish the amount of importance given to each shape. Less difference makes them more easily harmonized. With **kinetic** forms (mobiles), the length of time an observer concentrates on the work may also be increased through the physical motion of various portions of the sculpture—the constantly changing relationship of shapes may hold the viewer's attention longer than immobile works of art.

The sculptor, whose work involves actual space, may have an advantage over the graphic artist when it comes to spatial design. However, when sculptors (plastic artists) do their initial planning using graphic means, they must be aware that the picture plane is a contradiction to their three-dimensional intentions and in reality offers only one view of the proposed three-dimensional work.

Value

CHAPTER FIVE

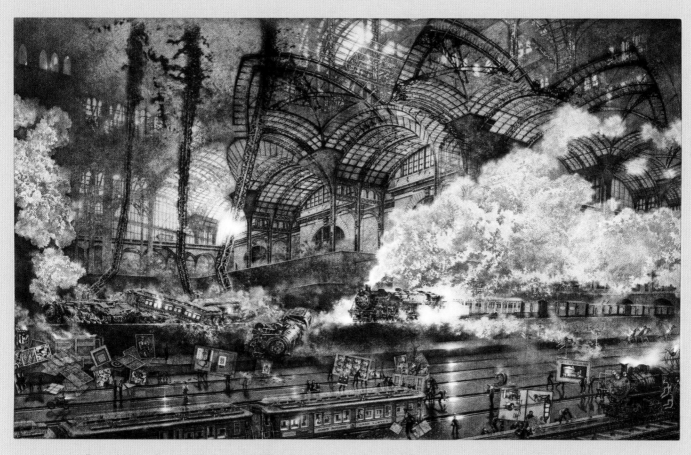

Peter Milton, *Points of Departure III: Twentieth Century Limited,* 1998. Etching and engraving, 24½ × 38½ in.
© Peter Milton. Courtesy of Davidson Galleries.

Value — **1.** The relative degree of lightness or darkness. **2.** The characteristic of color determined by the degree of lightness or darkness or the quantity of light reflected by the color.

achromatic value
Relating to differences of lightness and darkness, without regard for hue and intensity.

cast shadow
The dark area that occurs on a surface as a result of something being placed between that surface and a light source.

chiaroscuro
1. The distribution of lights and darks in a picture, usually in an attempt to develop the illusion of mass, volume, or space. 2. A technique of representation that blends light and shadow gradually to create the illusion of three-dimensional objects in space or atmosphere.

chromatic value
The value (relative degree of lightness or darkness) demonstrated by a given color.

closed-value composition
A composition in which values are contained within the edges or boundaries of shapes. The value pattern reveals the subject(s) and is dependent upon the positioning of the subject(s).

decorative (value)
Ornamenting or enriching but, more importantly in art, stressing the two-dimensional nature of an artwork or any of its elements. Decorative value stresses the essential flatness of a surface.

high-key value
A value that has a level of middle gray or lighter.

highlight
The portion of an object that, from the observer's position, receives the greatest amount of direct light.

local value
The relative lightness or darkness of a surface, seen in the objective world, that is independent of any effect created by the degree of light falling on it.

low-key value
A value that has a level of middle gray or darker.

open-value composition
A composition in which values are not limited by the edges of shapes and therefore flow across shape boundaries into adjoining areas. The value pattern created is unrelated to the location of the subject(s).

plastic (value)
Value used to create the illusion of volume and space.

sfumato
A technique devised by Leonardo da Vinci of softly blending areas from light to dark, creating subtle transitions. Images often have vague outlines and a hazy or smoky appearance. *Sfumato* is derived from the Latin *fumo*, meaning "smoke." Leonardo described sfumato as "without lines or borders, in the manner of smoke beyond the focus plane."

shadow
The darker value on the surface of an object that suggests that a portion of it is turned away from or obscured by the source of light.

shallow space
The illusion of limited depth. With shallow space, the imagery moves only a slight distance back from the picture plane.

silhouette
The area between or bounded by the contours, or edges, of an object as defined by a contrast of value; the total shape.

tenebrism
A technique of painting that exaggerates or emphasizes the effects of chiaroscuro. Larger amounts of dark value are placed close to smaller areas of highly contrasting lights—which change suddenly—in order to concentrate attention on important features.

value
1. The relative degree of lightness or darkness. 2. The characteristic of color determined by the degree of lightness or darkness or the quantity of light reflected by the color.

value pattern
The arrangement or organization of values that control compositional movement and create a unifying effect throughout a work of art.

INTRODUCTION TO VALUE RELATIONSHIPS

From the rising of the sun to the soft glow of the moon, we see images as light against dark or dark against light. The greater the contrast, the easier the image can be seen—although an extreme contrast of light and dark is not always necessary for an object to be understandable.

In the visual arts, an area's relative lightness or darkness is referred to as its **value**. Contrasts in value allow us to see lines and shapes, sense depth and dimensionality, and perceive surface textures. Our eyes are also guided through a composition by the patterns of those value contrasts, which encourage us to focus on particular locations

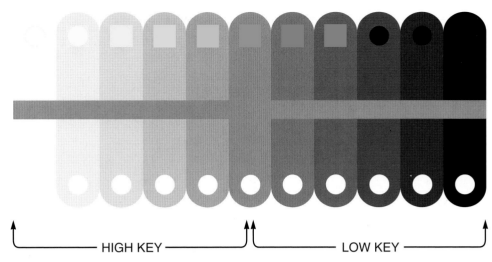

in the work. Careful value choices even affect our psychological or emotional reactions. This means value not only has compositional function but great expressive capability as well. Clearly, an understanding of value is basic to the study of art, because all the other art elements incorporate it and are brought to life by its application.

This chapter is primarily concerned with **achromatic values**, which consist of white, black, and the limitless degrees of gray without color. The achromatic value scale in figure 5.1 illustrates the change from white to black in evenly gradated steps. Although there could be an infinite number of steps between any two values, the chart has the same number of steps from middle gray to white and from middle gray to black.

Many beginning artists do not realize that when they are working with color, they are working with value as well. The comparative lightness or darkness of a color is its **chromatic value**. A standard yellow, for example, is of far greater lightness than a standard violet, although both colors may be modified to the point that they become virtually equal in value. (Chapter 7, "Color," covers this in more detail.) The relative values of various colors are often easier to compare after they have been translated into their corresponding achromatic values. The value scale in figure 5.1 can be a useful tool for finding the appropriate level of gray for any color.

In order to harmonize a piece, an artist often chooses to work with values that are closely related. The artist selects values within a limited range rather than use the full value spectrum. A work that uses predominantly dark values, ranging from middle gray to black, may be said to have **low-key values** (figs. 5.2 and 5.3). When a work contains mostly light values, ranging from white to middle gray, it is said to have **high-key values** (fig. 5.4). With both

HIGH KEY — **LOW KEY**

5.1 This scale shows a value gradation from light to dark against middle gray. To use the scale, make a colored photocopy, and remove the black and white circles in each gray stripe using a paper punch. To find the achromatic value for any color, slide the photocopy back and forth over the color, comparing the value of the gray stripes to the color seen through the punched holes. Search until you find the stripe where the value of the gray and the color appear to be the closest—neither being darker or lighter. That will be the correct achromatic value for that color. The location of the stripe relative to middle gray will also indicate if the color's value is high key or low key. Note: it is often easier to compare value and color while squinting.

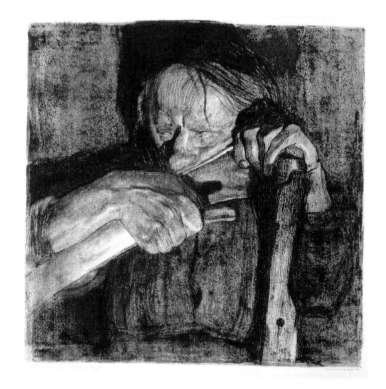

5.2 Käthe Kollwitz, *Whetting the Scythe* (K1.90x/xiib), original 1905. Edition published by Otto Felsing in 1921. Plate 3 of the *Peasants' War* series. Etching, 11¾ × 11¾ in. (298 × 298 mm). Käthe Kollwitz brilliantly used low-key values—middle gray to black—to create a dramatically menacing mood in her composition, which is quite appropriate for the subject matter: peasants preparing for revolt. Notice how the lightest of those values is reserved for small areas of highlight, while the majority of the work consists of darker tones. Art © 2008 Artists Rights Society (ARS), New York/VG Bild-Kunst, Bonn. Photo © Whitworth Art Gallery, The University of Manchester, UK/The Bridgeman Art Library.

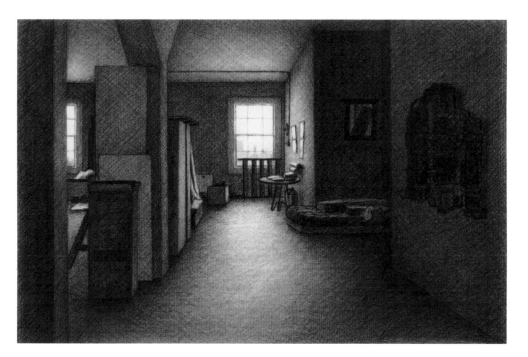

5.3 Susan Kraut, *Untitled*, 1979. Charcoal, with stumping and erasing, on ivory laid paper, 325 × 459 mm. The degree of line concentration indicates the value of the subject; where tightly bunched shadows are suggested, the forms of the interior are defined. Though defined with strong contrasts and refined shapes, the overall darkness and minimal use of highlights create a low-key composition and establish a very thoughtful mood. Jalane and Richard Davidson Collection, 2001.689. Photograph by Robert Lifson. Reproduction, The Art Institute of Chicago.

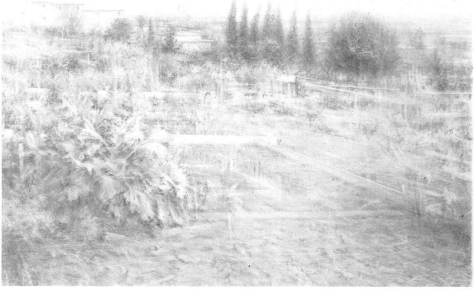

5.4 Robert Bauer, *Centinela III*, 2004. Graphite on gessoed paper, 15 × 18¼ in. In this image the artist has developed what appears at first glance to be quite a full and broad array of value. But a closer examination reveals that the range of value is limited to the lightest values on the achromatic scale—from white to middle gray. Known as high-key composition, it holds the viewer's attention by the skillful organization of areas of related value and juxtaposing extremes of the limited value range employed. © Robert Bauer, courtesy of Forum Gallery, New York and Los Angeles.

approaches, a limited amount of the opposite values may be introduced for accents, but those contrasting accents should not destroy the dominant feeling of lightness or darkness. The "key" selected can be used to establish a gen-eral mood for the work—a preponder-ance of dark (low-key) areas creates an atmosphere of gloom, mystery, drama, or menace, whereas a composition that is basically light (high-key) will pro-duce quite the opposite effect.

VALUE AND ART MEDIA

Although rich darks, a complete range of grays, and sparkling highlights are possible with any medium, some

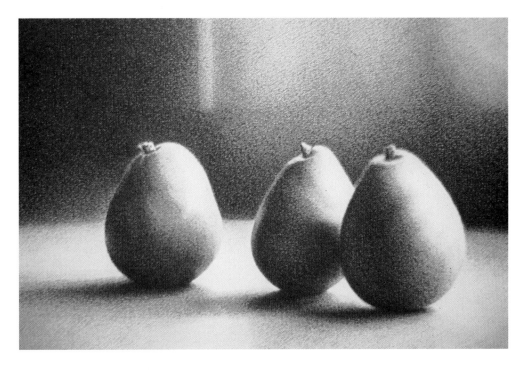

5.5 Martha Alf, *Pears Series II #7*, 1978. 4B pencil on bond paper, 11 × 14 in. At a casual glance, these values appear blended by rubbing drawing materials, but close examination reveals that Martha Alf created this image using delicately drawn lines so fine that they are not recognized as individual lines. Rather, the marks combine to produce areas of strong highlights and shadows that define the pears and their surroundings. This results in crisp and sparkling surfaces. Newspace Gallery, Los Angeles. Photograph by George Hoffman.

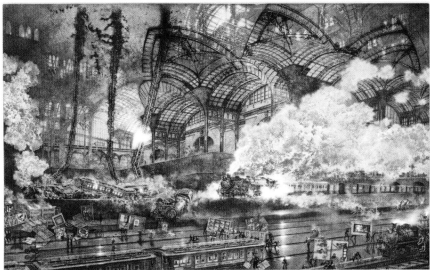

5.6 Peter Milton, *Points of Departure III: Twentieth Century Limited*, 1998. Etching and engraving, 24½ × 38½ in. This very large and complex intaglio print uses a full range of achromatic values to capture the essence of another era. As seen here, etching and engraving techniques can create quite a wide range of line qualities, as well as sharp value contrasts and more subtle gradations of light to dark. © Peter Milton. Courtesy of Davidson Galleries.

media lend themselves more naturally than others to the development of a full range of value. Graphic artists working in drawing, printmaking, or photography, for example, have long explored the value ranges inherent to the tools, materials, and techniques of each medium.

For the *draftsman,* the range of value for a drawn line could be the result of the medium used or the pressure exerted on the medium by the artist. In a pencil line, for example, the degree of value could be determined by the hardness of the graphite, the force with which it is used, or the surface quality of the paper (see fig. 3.8D). Value can also be created by placing lines of the same or different qualities (wet or dry, pencil or chalk, direct or blended) alongside or across each other to produce generalized areas of value. These marks may be so delicate that they are barely noticeable (fig. 5.5) or so aggres- sive that they reveal the energy driving the artist. In addition to hatching and cross-hatching, a wide range of grays and gradual changes in value can also be created using small dots of black and diluted black inks.

Intaglio prints, or *etchings,* are also able to generate strong contrasts of light and dark, as well as many ranges in between (fig. 5.6). Intaglio printing involves a metal plate that the artist has cut into or etched using acid. Ink

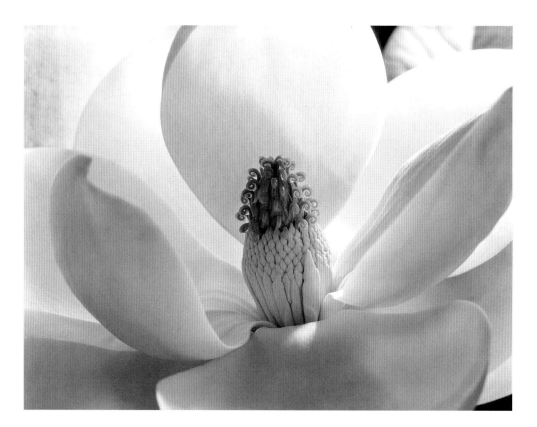

is rubbed into the crevices of the plate, which is then wiped so that only those crevices contain the ink. Under the pressure of a press, the ink is then forced out of the plate onto the printing paper. Value is determined by the depth and texture of the crevices, as well as their closeness to each other (see 3.15).

Woodcuts, or *relief prints,* are printed from blocks of material cut with gouges or knives. Printing a single block produces an image with high contrasts (like black and white). Here, the middle ranges of value are optical effects due to cutting lines (printed as white areas) on the block; the number and the width of the lines cut determine the amount of optical gray until the area becomes a solid white (see fig. 3.18). Even subtler shading effects can be created by printing gray tones from multiple blocks that are cut with slightly different images, with the final block printed in black ink. Early relief prints were achromatic;

however, experimentation soon began with colored blocks, and the use of color in printmaking remains popular today (see fig. 4.26).

In *lithography,* a full range of achromatic value is drawn by oil crayon on limestone (or metal plates). After being chemically treated and washed in water, the stone allows the application of ink in only the drawn areas. When the inked stone is covered with paper and passed through a press with a scraper bar, the pressure of the press forces the ink to transfer to the paper (see figs. 1.14 and 3.29).

Screen printing, also known as *silkscreen* or *serigraphy,* became popular because of the speed of printing. It is capable of black-and-white images but has been more often used to develop colored images. With screen printing, ink is forced through a screen onto the printing paper by pressure applied to a squeegee. The preparation of the screen

determines the ink pattern—various areas of the screen can be made to block passage of the ink. After printing the lightest value, additional areas of the screen can be blocked out in order to print subsequent layers of darker values, or multiple screens may be used.

Photography has been exceptionally adept at capturing the effects of light playing on the surface of an object. Without interpretation, the camera records **highlights** and **shadows** in a full range of values (fig. 5.7). Although the use of color photography is widespread, many contemporary photographers prefer to work with achromatic values, due to their ability to powerfully express an idea. In addition, black-and-white photography can also be a tool for organizing the value structure and setting up the general mood of a work. When colored objects are photographed on black-and-white film, they are automatically converted into corresponding

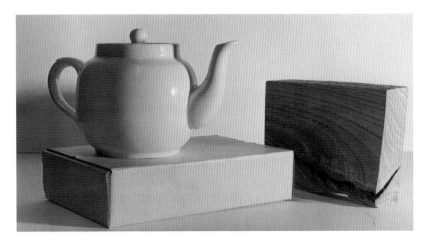

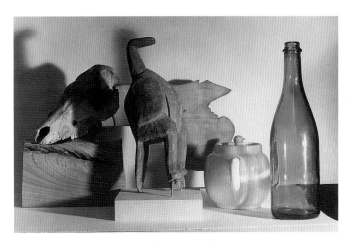

5.8 Russell F. McKnight, *Light and Dark,* 1984. Photograph, size unknown. A solid object receives more light on one side than the other because of its proximity to a light source. As the light is blocked out, shadows occur. Curved surfaces exhibit a gradual change of value, whereas angular surfaces show sharp changes: (A) highlight, (B) light, (C) shadow edge, (D) shadow core, (E) cast shadow, and (F) reflected light. Courtesy of the artist.

5.9 Russell F. McKnight, *Shadows,* 1984. Photograph, size unknown. Light can cast overlapping shadows that tend to break up and hide the true character of object forms. When the shapes of shadows are not factored into a composition, results are often disorganized, as in this experiment. Courtesy of the artist.

shades of gray, and artists can often use such photos to study the range of values used in colorful works of art, instead of translating the colors by hand with an achromatic value scale (see fig. 5.1).

PLASTIC VALUE

Artists have long been concerned with the problem of using value to translate the effect of light playing on their subject matter. An object's surface, before being affected by strong lighting, has a naturally occurring value known as its **local value.** However, as the object is exposed to more light on one side than another, additional values can be seen. The appearance of the local value may seem to be affected by those areas that intercept the light and create shadows elsewhere. In the highlighted areas, the value appears lighter than normal; in the shadowed areas, darker than normal (fig. 5.8).

Light and shadow patterns vary according to the shape of the object receiving the light. A spherical surface will

demonstrate an even gradation from light to dark, while a surface with intersecting planes will show a sudden contrast in value. Each basic form has its own highlight and shadow pattern. Thus, as seen in figure 5.8, an evenly flowing gradation of value evokes a sense of a gently curved surface, and an abrupt change of value generally indicates a sharp or angular surface. These lights and darks that create the appearance of depth are referred to as **plastic** value (see fig. 5.5).

Cast shadows are the dark areas that occur on an object or a surface when another shape is placed between it and the light source. The nature of the shadow created depends on the size and location of the light source, the size and shape of the interposed body, and the character of the surfaces where the shadow falls. Although cast shadows offer clues to the circumstances of a given situation, they only occasionally give a true indication of the nature of the forms involved (fig. 5.9).

The location of the light source is always an important consideration; it aids in describing the dimensionality

of an object and its spatial setting, and the intense lights and darks created by spotlights and shadows also contribute to a work's psychological and emotional impact. Side lighting emphasizes an object's mass and helps develop the contours of its form (fig. 5.10A); however, a light placed directly in front of the object (or multiple lights evenly spaced on either side) will seem to flatten the object by centering the highlight, restricting the shadow area, and limiting the range of value that can define the object (fig. 5.10B). By moving the light to a location beside or slightly behind the object, such qualities as the translucency of delicate flower petals or the juiciness of fruit will be enhanced (see figs. 5.7 and 6.1). Lighting placed directly behind an opaque object, on the other hand, can make the image dark, distorted, and mysterious, with interesting foreground shadows and a halo around the outer edge of the subject. Hiding the light source behind an object in the foreground is a clever way of establishing such drama (see fig. 5.16). Changes in the viewer's emotional

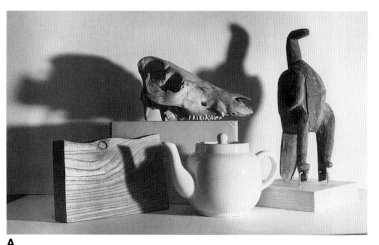

A

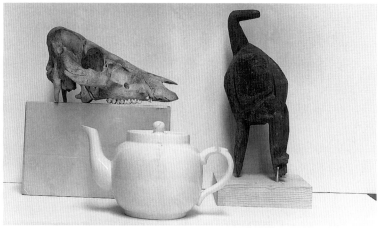

B

5.10 Russell F. McKnight, *Effect of Light on Objects*, 1984. Photograph. (A) Light from one source emphasizes the three-dimensional qualities of an object and gives an indication of depth. The cast shadows also give definite clues to the descriptive and plastic qualities of the various objects. (B) The group of objects is under illumination from several light sources. This form of lighting tends to flatten object surfaces and produces a decorative effect. Courtesy of the artist.

response can be adjusted by raising or lowering the light source, which will affect the location and strength of the darks and the intensity and size of any halos or highlights.

Not to be overlooked, of course, is the strength of the light source itself. Extreme drama often requires the greatest contrasts possible. Soft and diffused lighting, however, can be used to help harmonize dissimilar components, create an atmospheric spatial development, and generally establish high-key images devoid of harsh contrasts (see fig. 5.4).

Although lights and shadows exist in nature as the by-products of strict physical laws, artists often adjust them to enhance the three-dimensional effect of an image and/or provide greater compositional interest. Artists aren't bound to an exact duplication of cause-and-effect in light and shadow, because a series of shapes with shadows on the same side may become a monotonous image. The shapes of highlights and shadows are often altered or even reversed to produce the desired degrees of unity and contrast with adjacent areas in the composition. By taking liberties with lights and shadows, artists may create their own visual language (see fig. 5.15).

Chiaroscuro

As early painters explored ways of making their images more believable, they eventually developed the technique of gradually blending contrasting lights and darks in a picture to develop the illusion of mass or volume. This technique is known as **chiaroscuro**. The term also alludes to the way that artists handle atmospheric effects to create the illusion that the objects are surrounded on all sides by space; the grayer and less distinct the objects become, the farther away they appear.

Chiaroscuro developed mainly in painting, beginning with Giotto (1266–1337), who began to use darks and lights to give some three-dimensionality (*modeling*) to shapes developed by linear contours (fig. 5.11). Later, the early Florentine masters Masaccio, Fra Angelico, and Fra Filippo Lippi used the blended transitions to express further structure and volume in space (see fig. 8.16A). Leonardo da Vinci employed even bolder contrasts in lights in darks, but always with a soft transition between values; his method of subtle blending (called **sfumato**) created vague outlines and gave a smoky appearance to the image but allowed for a broader value range (fig. 5.12). Thereafter, the great Venetian painters, such as Titian, completely subordinated line and created an enveloping atmosphere of dominant *tonality* by using certain ranges of value more than others (fig. 5.13).

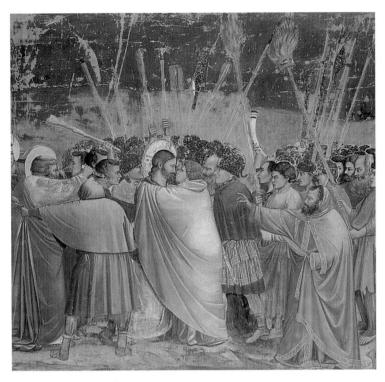

5.11 Giotto, *The Kiss of Judas*, Scrovegni Chapel, Padua, 1304–6. Fresco, 7 ft. 7 in. × 6 ft. 7½ in. (2.31 × 2.02 m). Although line and shape predominate in Giotto's works, some early attempts at modeling with chiaroscuro value can be seen. Church of the Twelfth Century/SuperStock.

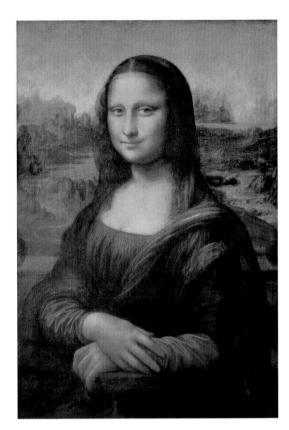

5.12 Leonardo da Vinci, *Mona Lisa*, 1503–6. Oil on panel, 30½ × 21 in. (76.2 × 52.5 cm). While exploring chiaroscuro, Leonardo extended the value range set by previous artists; he also developed a technique known as *sfumato*, which featured soft blending and subtle transitions from light to dark. Louvre, Paris, France/The Bridgeman Art Library.

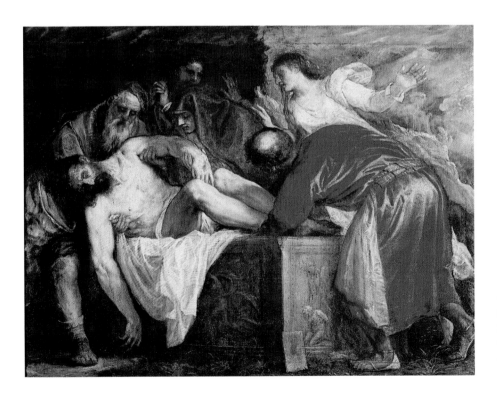

5.13 Titian (Tiziano Vecellio), *The Entombment of Christ*, 1559. Oil on canvas, 4 ft. 6 in. × 5 ft. 8⅞ in. (1.37 × 1.75 m). The Venetian master Titian subordinated line (contrasting edges with value) and enveloped his figures in a total atmosphere that approaches tenebrism. Museo del Prado, Madrid, Spain. Photo: Scala/Art Resource, NY.

5.14 Caravaggio (Michelangelo Merisi), *David Victorious over Goliath*, 1599–1600. Oil on canvas, 44 × 36 in. (110 × 91 cm). Caravaggio was essentially the leader in establishing the dark manner of painting in the sixteenth and seventeenth centuries. Several of the earlier northern-Italian painters, however, such as Correggio, Titian, and Tintoretto, show a strong tendency toward compositions using darker values. The Prado Museum, Madrid, Spain/The Bridgeman Art Library.

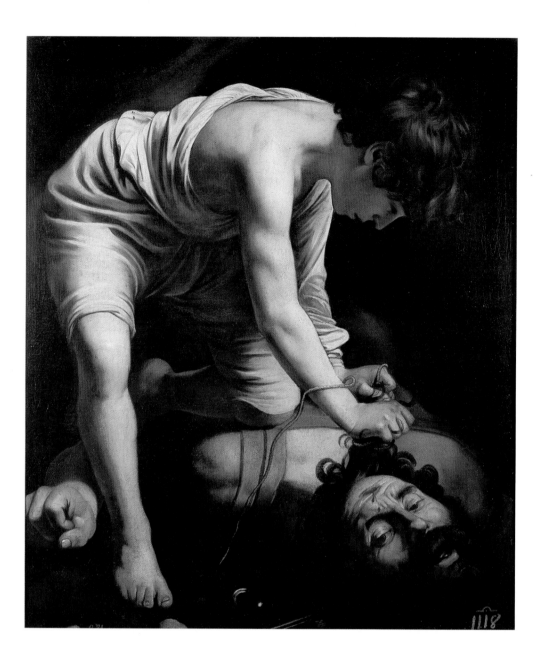

Tenebrism

Extreme or exaggerated chiaroscuro is called **tenebrism**. By increasing the percentage of dark values and the level of contrasts in their work, artists exaggerate or emphasize the effects of chiaroscuro. Large amounts of dark value are placed close to small areas of highly contrasting lights; the values blend but seem to change more suddenly. This quick and extreme transition concentrates attention on important features in the work.

The first tenebrists were an international group of painters who, early in the seventeenth century, were inspired by the work of Michelangelo Merisi da Caravaggio (fig. 5.14). Caravaggio based his approach on the work of earlier northern-Italian painters and instituted this so-called dark manner of painting in Western Europe. The tenebrists and their followers were fascinated by the peculiarities of lighting, particularly the way that lighting affected mood or emotional expression. They deviated from standard light conditions by placing the implied light sources in unexpected locations, thereby creating unusual visual and spatial effects (fig. 5.15). Rembrandt continued to adapt and perfect the techniques of this dark manner, which he learned from migratory artists from Germany and southern Holland (fig. 5.16). The strong contrasts lent

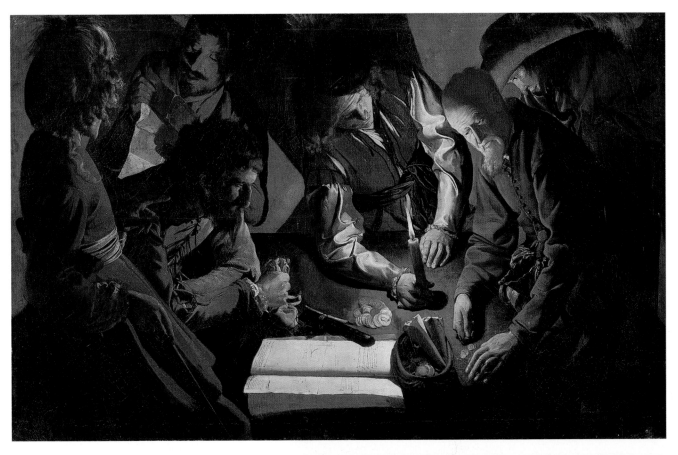

5.15 Georges de La Tour, *The Payment of Taxes*, c. 1618–20. Oil on canvas, size unknown. In a complex composition, La Tour has used strong candlelight and its highlights and shadows to produce the atmosphere of a quiet drama. Multiple figures provide the opportunity for combining natural and invented shadows, which reinforce the structural movement. Lviv State Picture Gallery, Ukraine/The Bridgeman Art Library.

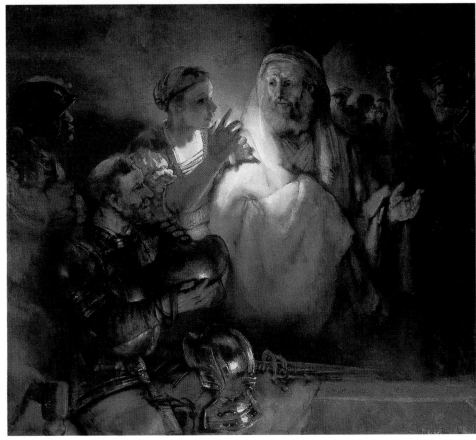

5.16 Rembrandt Harmenszoon van Rijn, *The Denial of St. Peter*, 1660. Oil, 154 × 169 cm. Rembrandt often used invented and hidden light sources that deviated from standard conditions to enhance the mood or emotional expression. The spotlight effect predates the invention of dramatic stage lighting. Collection Rijksmuseum Amsterdam.

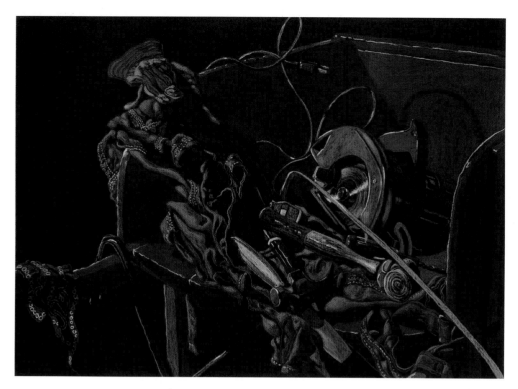

5.17 Jack Beal, *Still Life with Tools*, 1979. Pastel on black wove paper, 75.9 × 101.7 cm (sheet). Beal transforms ordinary tools into mysterious objects with his tenebristic use of pastel. The objects in the wheelbarrow seem to glow, elevated from their prosaic origins. Jalane and Richard Davison Collection, 1990.511.2. Reproduction, The Art Institute of Chicago.

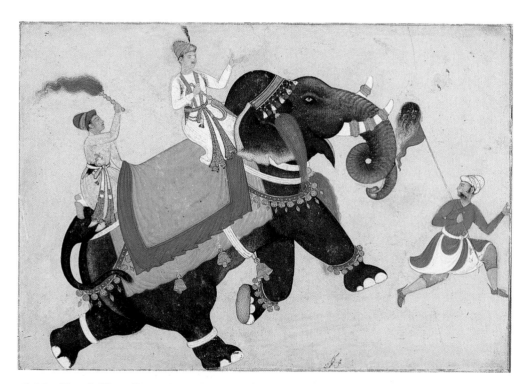

5.18 Signed: Khem Karan, *Prince Riding an Elephant*, Mughal, period of Akbar, c. 1600. Opaque watercolor and gold on paper, 12¼ × 18½ in. (31.2 × 47 cm). Historically, South Asian artists have usually disregarded the use of light (illumination) in favor of decorative-value compositions. The Metropolitan Museum of Art, Rogers Fund, 1925. (25.6B.4) Photograph © 1988 The Metropolitan Museum of Art.

themselves well to highly dramatic—even theatrical—work, and *value* became an instrument of the characteristic exaggeration found in Baroque painting. Later, the dark manner evolved into the pallid, muddy monotone that pervaded some nineteenth-century Western painting. However, contemporary artists like Jack Beal have revived interest in these techniques for their expressive properties (fig. 5.17).

DECORATIVE VALUE

Art styles that stress **decorative** or **shallow space** usually ignore conventional light sources or neglect representation of light altogether. If lighting effects appear, they are incorporated based on their contribution to the total form of the work rather than the appearance of an object. The lack of lighting effects—either natural or "staged"—is characteristic of the artwork of children. It is also notably absent from the work of primitive and prehistoric tribes and traditional East Asians and from certain periods of Western art, notably the Middle Ages. In addition, the work of many contemporary artists is completely free of illusionistic lighting; instead, such artists concentrate on pictorial invention, imagination, and formal considerations. Emotional impact is not necessarily sacrificed (as witnessed in medieval art), but the emotion speaks primarily through the form and is consequently less extroverted.

The trend away from illumination values (lights and darks from a single light source) gained strength in the nineteenth century, partly because of growing interest in Middle Eastern and East Asian art forms (fig. 5.18). The interest in nondramatic lighting was also given a scientific, Western interpretation when the naturalist Édouard Manet observed that multiple light sources tend to flatten object surfaces and neutralize

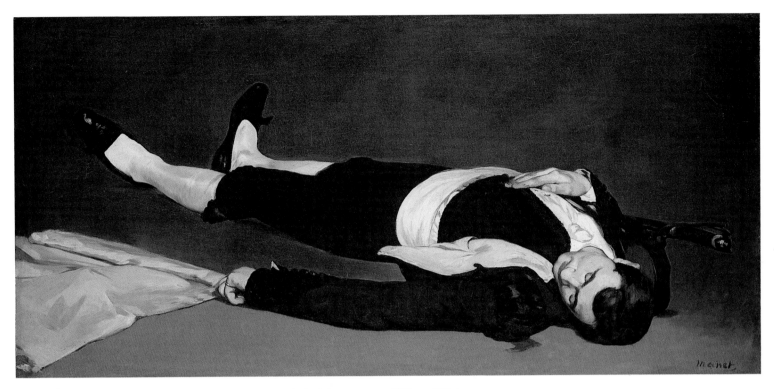

5.19 Édouard Manet, *The Dead Toreador*, probably 1864. Oil on canvas, 29⅞ × 60⅜ in. (75.9 × 153.4 cm). Manet, a nineteenth-century naturalist, was one of the first artists to break with traditional chiaroscuro, making use, instead, of flat areas of value. These flat areas meet abruptly, unlike the blended edges used by artists before Manet. This was one of the great technical developments of nineteenth-century art. Widener Collection. © 1998 Board of Trustees, National Gallery of Art, Washington DC.

the plastic qualities of objects, thereby minimizing gradations of value (see fig. 5.10B). As a result, he laid his colors on canvas in flat areas, beginning with bright, light colors and generally neglecting shadow (fig. 5.19). Some critics have claimed this to be the basic technical advance of the nineteenth century, because it paved the way for nonrepresentational uses of value and helped revive interest in the shallow-space concept.

The idea of carefully controlled shallow space is well illustrated in the works of the early Cubists and their followers (see fig. T.51). In those paintings, space is given its order by the arrangement of flat planes abstracted from the subject matter. In the initial stages of this trend, the planes were shaded individually and semi-naturalistically, al-though giving no indication of any one light source. Later, each plane took on a characteristic value and, in combination with others, produced a carefully conceived shallow space. Eventually, this shallow spatial effect was developed through attention to the advancing and receding characteristics of value (see fig. 4.2). The explorations of these early-twentieth-century artists helped focus attention on the intrinsic significance of each and every element. Value was no longer forced to serve primarily as a tool of superficial transcription, although it continued to be of descriptive usefulness. Most creative artists should think of value as a vital and lively participant in pictorial organization (fig. 5.20). An artist can strengthen underlying compositional structure by controlling contrasts of value; it is instrumental

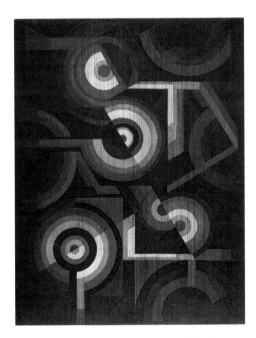

5.20 Jisik Shin, *Lunar Image I*, 1990. Print (etching), 11⅞ × 15¾ in. (30 × 40 cm). Absent of the need for any three-dimensional illusion of imagery, the light and dark contrasts in this etching create a dynamic two-dimensional value pattern. Courtesy of the artist.

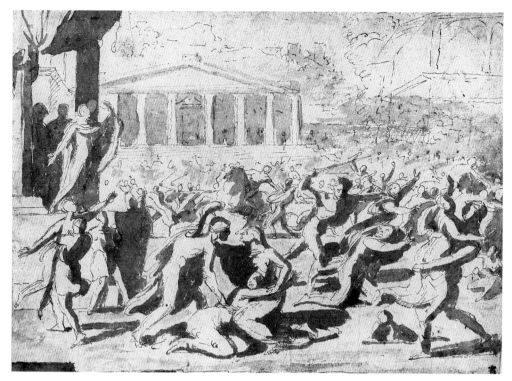

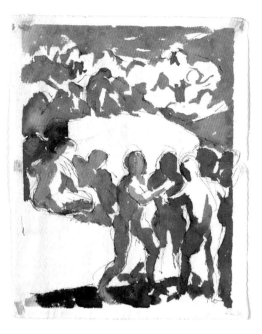

5.22 Barry Schactman, *Study after Poussin,* 1959. Brush and ink with wash, 10 × 7⅞ in. (25.4 × 20 cm). Loose, rapid sketches can also be used to explore value patterns, color structure, and movement. Yale University Art Gallery, New Haven, CT. Transfer from Yale Art School.

5.21 Nicolas Poussin, study for *Rape of the Sabines,* c. 1633. Pen and ink with wash, 6½ × 8⅞ in. (16.4 × 22.5 cm). Preparatory, or "thumbnail," sketches give the artist the opportunity to explore movement, ground systems, value structure, and compositional variations. In Poussin's sketch, it seems likely that the artist was striving for rhythmical movement within the horizontal thrust of the composition. Devonshire Collection, Chatsworth. Reproduced by permission of the Duke of Devonshire and the Chatsworth Settlement Trustees. Photograph: Photographic Survey Courtauld. Institute of Art.

in creating relative dominance, indicating deep or two-dimensional space, establishing mood, and producing spatial unity.

VALUE PATTERN AND COMPOSITION

Although most viewers recognize the importance of the subject in an artwork, they often overlook the importance of the areas of value that are strategically woven through the composition. These organized areas of light and dark create a **value pattern,** which becomes the compositional skeleton that supports the image. The value pattern provides the underlying movement, tension, and ground system on which the subject is built. When properly integrated into the final work, the value pattern reinforces the subject. It should neither distract from the image nor separate itself as an overpowering entity or isolated component.

Before starting the final image, many artists explore possible variations for a composition's value pattern by making small studies known as *thumbnail sketches*. These small-scale preliminary value studies allow artists to see multiple variations of the relationship between the subject and its ground before selecting a final solution. In figures 5.21 and 5.22, for example, Nicolas Poussin and Barry Schactman develop large rhythmical dark shapes across the bottom of the composition while intermingling smaller receding toned shapes in the middle areas.

Although small studies are beneficial in compositional planning, they may be difficult to relate to the final work because of their scale. Small drawings may look exciting because of the way the areas of value are drawn—with rapid, sketchy strokes full of textural detail. But when enlarged many times, these small strokes may become flat shapes that no longer have the same visual appeal. The new enlarged shapes of value will then require a refinement of detail before the proper relationship of value and mood can be established.

Artists who embrace the use of value pattern can benefit from its subconscious movement and direction. This is true regardless of whether the work is black-and-white or uses color. Unfortunately, pure, intoxicating color often "blinds" people from seeing how chromatic val-

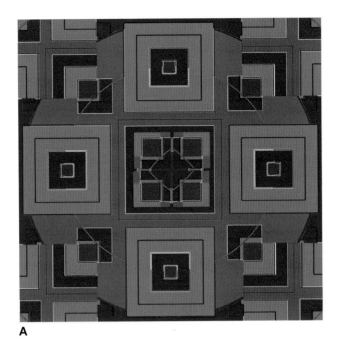

A

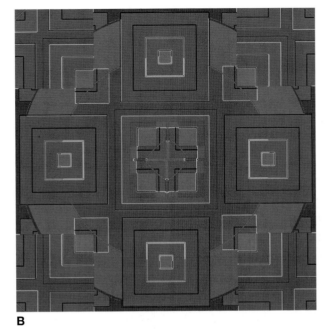

B

5.23 A common weakness when using color is a lack of awareness of the pattern created by the colors' values. Black-and-white photographs of artwork can reveal this problem very clearly. When figure A is translated into achromatic values (B), it becomes apparent that the range of lights and darks is quite limited. While this may be exactly what is desired, it may also surprise the novice who thinks only in terms of color. Even a composition of closely related hues benefits from the careful consideration of its value pattern.

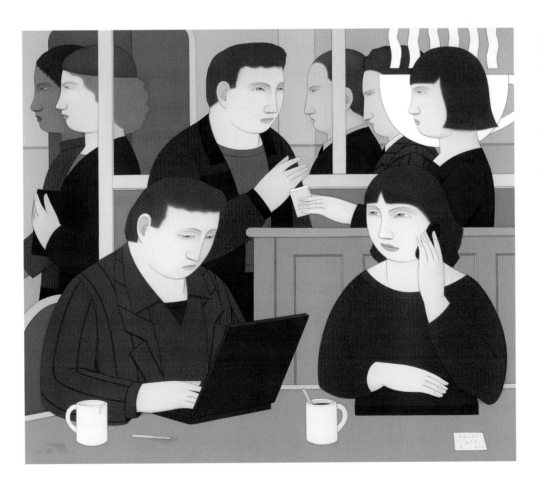

ues relate to the overall organization. Black-and-white photographs of colorful work may help reveal any related weaknesses (fig. 5.23A and B).

While integrating the value structure into the image, the artist should be aware of two approaches for developing the value pattern: closed-value and open-value compositions. In **closed-value compositions,** values are contained within the edges or boundaries of shapes. This sets those shapes apart from surrounding areas and often serves to clearly identify them. The pattern created by these values is dependent on the position of the subject(s) (fig. 5.24). In **open-value compositions,**

5.24 Andrew Stevovich, *Internet Café,* 2006. Oil on linen, 28 × 32 in. In this painting, a closed-value composition, the color values lie between prescribed and precise limits, primarily object edges and contours. Courtesy of Andrew Steovich and Adelson Galleries.

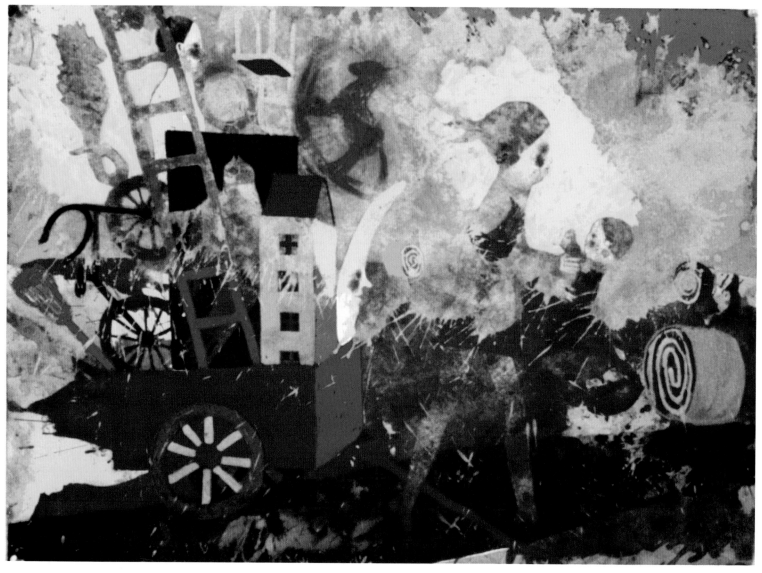

5.25 DeLoss McGraw, *Mother and Child "Bleak and Lonely Heights" in August Moving Sunlight,* 2002. Gouache on paper, 20 × 30 in. This is an example of what is basically an open-value composition. A light-valued yellow moves across the upper half, occasionally interrupted by a rocking horse, black rectangle, and ladder. A dark red shape moves across the lower third through the baby, the woman's dress and legs, the wagon, and the background. A linear accent or subtle change of color defines the subject in those areas. A few closed areas—like the wheels and ladders—are strategically placed for contrast. Courtesy of ACA Galleries, New York.

values cross over shape boundaries into adjoining areas, and a line or subtle change in texture or color is often necessary to make the shapes visible. The pattern made by these values is not in any way dependent on the location of the subject(s); this independent patterning of lights and darks helps integrate the shapes and unify the composition (fig. 5.25; see also fig. 4.2).

With both open-value and closed-value compositions, the emotive possibilities of value schemes are easy to see. The artist may employ closely related values to generate hazy, foglike effects (see figs. 5.4 and 8.4). Sharply crystal-lized shapes are enhanced by dramatically contrasting values (see figs. 5.5 and 5.14). Thus, value can run the gamut from decoration to vivid expression. It is a multipurpose tool for establishing contrasts, controlling eye movement, creating the illusion of space, and conveying a vast range of emotion.

THREE-DIMENSIONAL APPLICATIONS OF VALUE

Although artists working with three-dimensional forms do not have to deal with creating the illusion of mass through the rendering of light and dark surfaces, they are certainly aware of the relationship between lighting and dimensionality. As the artist physically manipulates three-dimensional shapes, contrasting lights and shadows are produced on the forms. The appearance of light and dark is the result of the quantity of light actually reflected by the object's surfaces, although 3-D masses do also have their own local values. Areas that are high and face a source of illumination appear to be lighter, while surfaces that are low, penetrated to any degree, or facing away from the light source appear to be darker. Each basic form reacts differently to the light. As we see in figure 5.26, gently curved surfaces reveal an evenly flowing value gradation, whereas an abrupt change of value occurs on a sharp edge. Any angular change of two juxtaposed surfaces, however slight, results in contrasts of value. The sharper the angular change, the greater the contrast (see figs. 3.30, 4.33, 4.35, and 5.8).

When any part of a 3-D work blocks the passage of light, shadows result. (This includes an area that has been heavily textured, although shadows cast by the textures themselves will make the area appear darker when compared to smoother passages.) The pattern of lights and darks changes as the position of the viewer, the work, or its source of illumination changes. If a work has substantial high and low shape variations and/or penetration, the shadow patterns are more likely to define the work, regardless of the position of the light source. For most 3-D work, the light source is relatively constant, and the highlights and shadows only change as the viewer moves positions. However, the relationship of light and shadow continuously changes with kinetic sculpture (such as mobiles), since the intensity of light markedly changes the shadow effect as the object itself moves (see fig. 2.70). Many sculptors are interested in creating these kinds of relationships.

Value changes can also be achieved by painting a 3-D work. It is much easier to see shadow patterns that are cast on an object painted with light values than on a piece that has been painted with dark values (see fig. 1.40). The lighter values work best on pieces that depend on secondary contours; darker values are most successful in emphasizing the major contour, or **silhouette** (see figs. 4.33A and B and 4.37). Strong contrasts between image and background also create the silhouettes that define thin linear 3-D structures (see figs. 3.31 and 3.32).

For the three-dimensional artist, a good light source and the value range created by it are an important compositional tool. Light and shadows aid in describing a work's dimensionality and spatial setting; enhance the effectiveness of the design pattern; and contribute to the psychological, emotional, and dramatic expression of the artist.

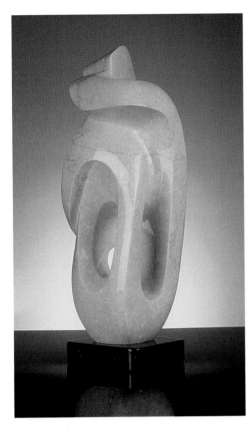

5.26 Julie Warren Martin, *Marchesa*, 1988. Italian Botticino marble, 28 × 12 × 10 in. (71.1 × 30.5 × 25.4 cm). A piece of sculpture "paints" itself with values. The greater the projections and the sharper the edges, the greater and more abrupt the contrasts. From the Collection of Kirby and Priscilla Smith.

Texture

CHAPTER SIX

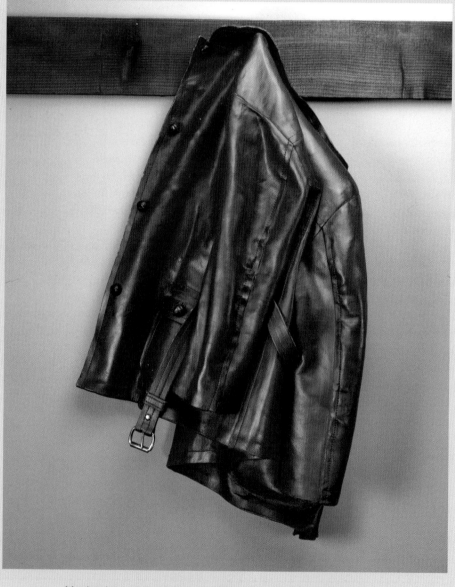

Marilyn Levine, *Anne's Jacket*, 1999. Ceramic, 36 × 20½ × 7¼ in.
Courtesy of Frank Lloyd Gallery, Collection of the Museum of Arts and Design.

THE VOCABULARY OF
TEXTURE

Texture — The surface character of a material that can be experienced through touch or the illusion of touch. Texture is produced by natural forces or through an artist's manipulation of the art elements.

abstract texture

A texture derived from the appearance of an actual surface but rearranged and/or simplified by the artist to satisfy the demands of the artwork.

actual texture

A surface that can be experienced through the sense of touch (as opposed to a surface visually simulated by the artist).

assemblage

A technique that involves grouping actual items (three-dimensional objects) in a display. The items may be found or specially created, and they are often displayed "in situ"—that is, in a natural position or in the middle of a room rather than on a wall.

atmospheric perspective

The illusion of depth produced in graphic works by lightening values, softening details and textures, reducing value contrasts, and neutralizing colors in objects as they recede.

collage

A technique of picturemaking in which real materials possessing actual textures are attached to the picture-plane surface, often in combination with painted or drawn passages.

genre paintings

Paintings with subject matters that concern everyday life, domestic scenes, family relationships, and the like.

invented texture

A created texture whose only source is the artist's imagination. It generally produces a decorative pattern and should not be confused with **abstract texture.**

paint quality

The intrinsic character of a painting medium—thickness, glossiness, and so forth—which can enrich a surface through its own textural interest.

papier collé

A visual and tactile technique in which scraps of paper having various textures are pasted to the picture surface to enrich or embellish those areas. The printing of text or images on those scraps can provide further visual richness or decorative pattern.

pattern

1. Any artistic design (sometimes serving as a model for imitation). 2. A series of repeated elements and/or designs that are usually varied and produce interconnections and obvious directional movements.

simulated texture

A convincing copy or translation of an object's texture in any medium. (See **trompe l'oeil.**)

tactile

A quality that refers to the sense of touch.

texture

The surface character of a material that can be experienced through touch or the illusion of touch. Texture is produced by natural forces or through an artist's manipulation of the art elements.

trompe l'oeil

Literally, "deceives the eye"; the copying of nature with such exactitude as to be mistaken for the real thing. (See **simulated texture.**)

INTRODUCTION TO TEXTURE

Texture is a universal experience that often occurs on a subconscious level. Whether running your toes through grass or putting on a sweater, you feel the unique tactile quality of those materials, even if you are not overtly aware of it. Even while holding this book, you gather specific information about the feel of its surface. Place your fingers against the open edge, and sense the sharp corners or the ridged effect of the stacked pages; feel the slippery smoothness of the page's surface. Look around, and you will see many other textures—some that warn you of danger, others that entice and invite exploration. In fact, everything has a texture, from the rough surface of tree bark to the soft fluffiness of a carpet, from the hard glossiness of a window pane to the jagged edge of broken glass. Look a little further, and there may even be a painting or an art reproduction full of textures. Although that artwork has a texture when touched, it most likely also gives the appearance of a different texture than what can actually be felt. Our world is full of varied tactile experiences.

THE NATURE OF TEXTURE

Texture may be unique among the art elements because it immediately activates two sensory processes. It is more intimately and dramatically known through the sense of touch, but we can also *see* texture and, thus, predict

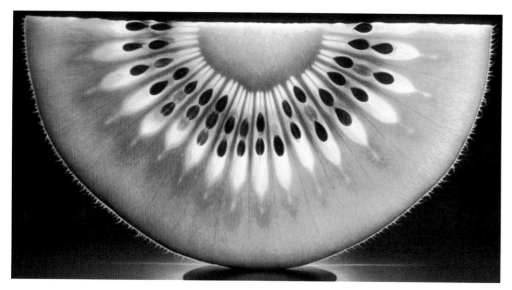

6.1 Dennis Wojtkiewicz, *Kiwi Series #1*, 2005. Oil on canvas, 36 × 66 in. (91.4 × 167.6 cm). This painting is an excellent example of our sight being able to activate other senses. Here, the presentation of the translucent fruit and fuzzy skin is so convincing that we have a visual and a tactile reaction—and for some, a sensation of taste. Courtesy J. Cacciola Gallery, New York, NY.

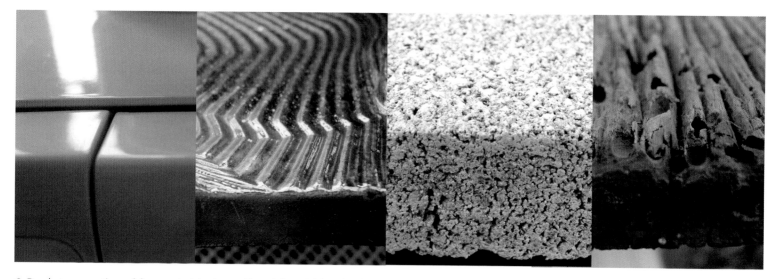

6.2 A cross section of four materials shows (*from left to right*): a hard, smooth, glossy surface; a rippled metallic surface; rough cinderblock; and weathered wood. The textures of these objects can be clearly seen due to the highlights and shadows formed by the light shining on each surface, suggesting how the actual objects would feel if they were stroked. The far left, being flat, produces no shadows but shows reflections. The middle left texture produces both shadow and reflection. In the cinderblock, shadows are cast among the small stones, and in the wood, alongside the weathered undulations.

its feel. In viewing a picture or a piece of sculpture, we may recognize objects through the artist's use of characteristic shapes, colors, and value patterns—but we may also react to the artist's rendering of the surface character of those objects. In such a case, we have both visual and **tactile** experiences (fig. 6.1).

Whether the artist is working with 2-D or 3-D media, our tactile response to the work is always a concern, and an understanding of the nature of texture is of vital importance. The feel of an object's surface—its physical texture—depends on the degree to which it is broken up by its composition or treatment. The

more broken, the rougher the texture. This not only determines how we feel it but also how we see it. Rough surfaces intercept light rays, producing an often irregular pattern of lights and darks; glossy surfaces reflect the light more evenly, giving a less broken appearance (fig. 6.2). As we see these patterns of different values, our memory of touching surfaces with similar characteristics then triggers a tactile response or sensory reaction. Thus, we can predict an object's feel without ever touching its surface.

TYPES OF TEXTURE

The artist can use four basic types of texture: actual, simulated, abstract, and invented.

Actual Texture

Actual texture is the "real thing"—a surface that can be experienced through the sense of touch. It is not an illusion created by drawing or painting. Historically, actual texture has been a natural part of three-dimensional art; wood, glass, and fibers, for example, have inherent textures that are incorporated into the work, although those textures may be manipulated. For many works of art, the design depends heavily on the actual texture of the medium, especially in the textile arts as well as in ceramics, jewelry, and so forth (see figs. 1.53, 1.54, and 1.56). Architects, for example, often rely on the feel of the materials and balance the varying textures through careful composition (see figs. 1.51 and 1.52).

Graphic artists, too, can utilize the actual texture of their materials, and quite often their work seems to cross the boundary from two- into three-dimensionality. As artists begin to paint or draw on canvas, they change the textural quality of that surface. In some cases, as with charcoal or graphite, the change is subtle—little is done to the "feel" of the surface. In other cases, like *impasto* painting, the thickness and texture of the applied paint can be quite heavy and modeled. This buildup of material alters the way the surface "feels" to the touch, and often, the paint is textured enough to create its own highlights and shadows. The textural enrichment can be

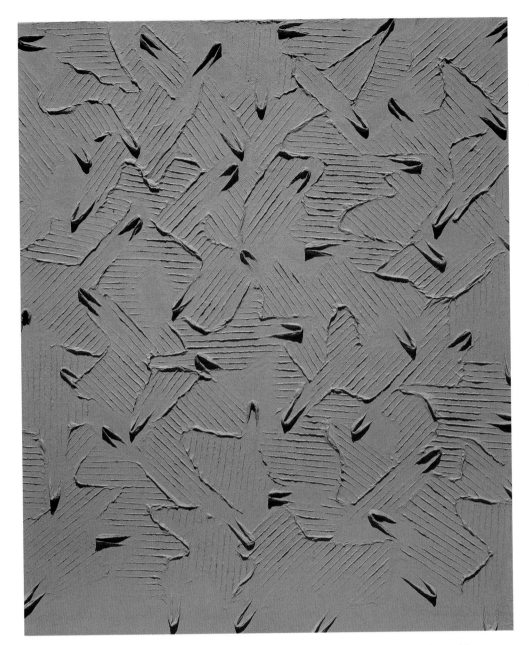

6.3 Seo-Bo Park, *Ecriture No. 940110*, 1994. Mixed media with Korean paper, 26 × 18 in. (65.3 × 46 cm). The massing of paint is clearly evident, particularly in the central portion. Some shapes seem to have been effected by a comblike instrument. Courtesy of Jean Art Gallery, Seoul, Korea.

employed in the creation of specific subject matter, but many times it is used to simply enliven an area with interesting visual detail. In Seo-Bo Park's *Ecriture No. 940110*, the paint is applied in projecting mounds and ridges that begin to create their own patterns (fig. 6.3). Other artists, like Van Gogh in his *Starry Night*, apply the pigment in heavy ribbons directly from the tube of paint, with the furrows of paint reinforcing the subject matter in the picture (see fig. 1.19). The creation of actual texture in both cases is enhanced by the **paint quality,** which is the intrinsic character of the painting medium. The artist controls the paint's thickness, glossiness, and textural richness through the addition of various varnishes, binders, and aggregates in the form of sand or marble dust (fig. 6.4).

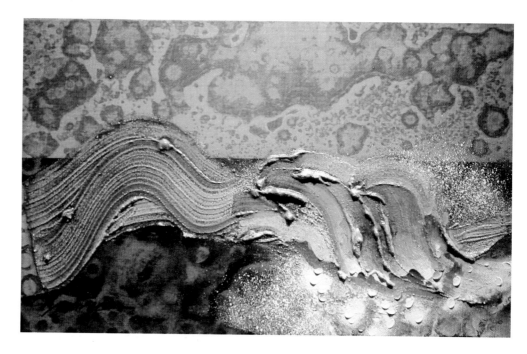

6.4 Robert Mazur, *Nightwave*, 2007. Acrylic on canvas, 18 × 30 in. (45.7 × 76.2 cm). In this painting, invented textures are used to suggest the subject matter. Wet-on-wet resists symbolize sky and water, while heavily aggregated paint textures applied by fingers, brush, and modified palette knife represent crashing waves. Collection of Mr. and Mrs. Edward Plocek. Courtesy of the artist.

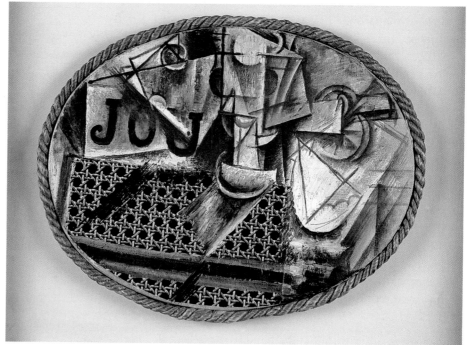

6.5 Pablo Picasso, *Still Life with Chair Caning*, 1912. Oil on pasted oilcloth, rope, oval, 10⅝ × 13⅜ in. (27 × 34.9 cm). With this work, Picasso pioneered the development of the papier collé and collage forms—art created by fastening actual materials with textural interest to a flat working surface. These art forms may be used to simulate real textures but are usually created for decorative purposes. Musée Picasso, Paris, France. © 2008 Estate of Pablo Picasso/Artists Rights Society (ARS), NY. Bridgeman-Giraudon/Art Resources, NY.

In the early twentieth century, the concept of actual texture was expanded to include the addition of various textural materials along with the application of paint. In 1908, Picasso pasted a piece of paper to a drawing. This is the first known example of **papier collé,** a practice that was later expanded to include the use of tickets, portions of newspapers, menus, and the like (see fig. 4.2). Papier collé soon led to **collage,** an art form in which actual textures, in the form of rope, chair caning, and other articles of greater substance than paper, were employed. Sometimes these were used in combination with printed pictures of textures, which were used more for decorative purposes than for simulating real objects (fig. 6.5).

The problem created by mixing objects and painting is: what is real—the objects, the artistic elements, or both? Do the painted objects have the same reality as the genuine objects? Whatever the answers, the early explorations of the Cubists (the style of Picasso and Braque, about 1907–1912) stimulated other artists to explore new attitudes toward art and made them more

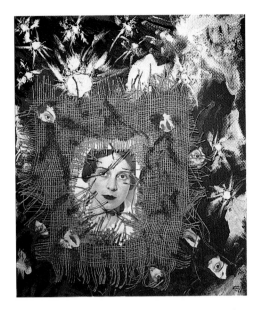

6.6 Ilse Bing, *My World*, 1985. Mixed media, 14 × 17 × 3¾ in. (35.6 × 43.2 × 9.5 cm). The inspiration behind the use of burlap in this artwork stems ultimately from the first collages of Picasso and Braque—then a revolutionary, but now a fairly commonplace, technique. © Ilse Bing, courtesy of Edwynn Houk Gallery, New York.

conscious of surface (fig. 6.6). Today, many artists use actual textures created from combining paint with a wide range of materials other than aggregate, ranging from nails to paintbrushes (fig. 6.7; see also fig. 9.13).

Simulated Texture

Every surface has characteristic light and dark features as well as reflections. When these are skillfully reproduced in an artist's medium, the imitations may be mistaken for the surfaces of real objects. The surface character that looks "real" but in fact is not is said to be a **simulated texture** (fig. 6.8).

Simulated textures are useful for making things identifiable; moreover, we experience a rich tactile enjoyment when viewing them. The Dutch and Flemish artists produced amazing naturalistic effects in still-life and **genre paintings.** Their work shows the evident relish with which they moved

from one simulated texture to another. Interior designers employ this concept when painting faux (fake) surface treatments imitating stone or veined marble. Simulated textures are often associated with **trompe l'oeil** paintings, which attempt to "fool the eye" with photographic detail convincing enough that it might be mistaken for the real thing (fig. 6.9; see also fig. 6.1). Simulation is a copying technique, a skill that can be quite impressive in its own right. However, those viewers who can't see past the richness of detail miss everything else the composition has to offer.

Abstract Texture

Instead of trying to reproduce or exactly imitate the textures of their subjects, many artists prefer to abstract them. **Abstract textures** usually display some hint of the original texture, but they have been modified to suit the artist's particular needs. The result is often a

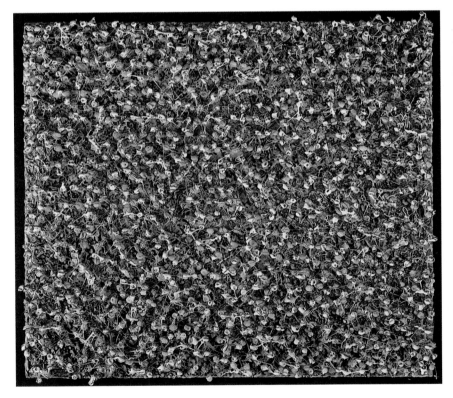

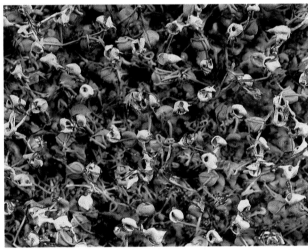

6.7 Gary Lawe, *I Remember Being Free*, 1998. Lucite, acrylic, encaustic, and nails, 24 × 30 in. (61 × 76 cm). The admixture of nails with the varied paint media creates an actual textured surface that is rich in its inherent visual and tactile qualities. Courtesy of the artist Gary Lawe and the Don O'Melveny Gallery, West Hollywood.

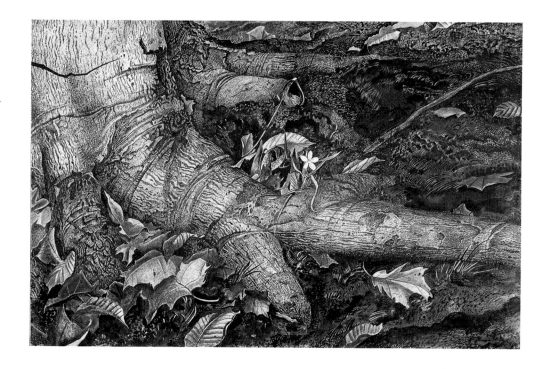

6.8 Andrew Newell Wyeth, *Spring Beauty*, 1943. Drybrush watercolor on paper, 20 × 30 in. (50.8 × 76.2 cm). Skillful manipulation of the medium can effectively simulate actual textures. Sheldon Memorial Art Gallery, University of Nebraska, Lincoln, Nebraska. The F. M. Hall Collection 1944. H-247.

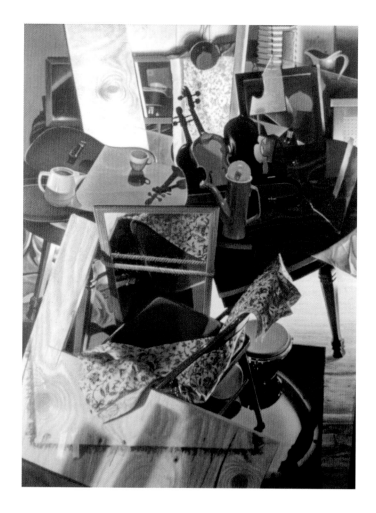

6.9 Gary Schumer, *Split Table Still Life*, 1992. Oil on canvas, 64 × 76 in. (162.6 × 193 cm). In this painting, the artist is concerned with the simulation of textures ranging from plywood and plexiglass to cloth, ceramic, and metal. As with all trompe l'oeil painting, the wealth of detail can obscure other compositional offerings—such as the compelling value pattern and the Cubist-like twisting and layering of spatial planes. Courtesy of the artist, Private Collection.

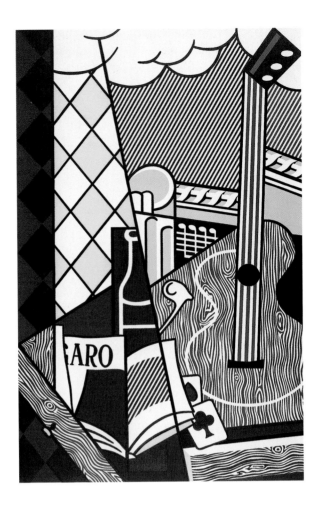

6.10 Roy Lichtenstein, *Cubist Still Life with Playing Cards*, 1974. Oil and magna on canvas, 96 × 60 in. (243.8 × 152.4 cm). The wood grain in this work is not abstracted beyond recognition; it is clearly derived from wood, though simplified and stylized. © Estate of Roy Lichtenstein.

simplified version of the original, emphasizing the pattern or design (fig. 6.10). Abstract textures normally appear in works where the degree of abstraction is consistent throughout. In these works, the textures function in a decorative way; obviously there is no attempt to "fool the eye," but they serve the role of enrichment in the same way that simulated textures do. Besides helping the artist to simplify his or her material, abstract textures can be used to accent some areas or diminish others (i.e., to achieve relative dominance) and to control eye movement. Thus, they can be a potent compositional tool.

Invented Texture

Invented textures are textures without precedent; they do not simulate, nor are they abstracted from reality. They are purely the creation of the artist's imagination and usually appear in abstracted and nonobjective works (fig. 6.11).

6.11 Brian Fridge, *Vault Sequence No. 10*, 2000. Black-and-white silent video, four minutes, DVD, edition 2 of 5. *Vault Sequence* is a seven-minute video of the inside of the artist's refrigerator freezer. Through the medium of video, the artist creates invented texture. The time-based aspect of this medium creates images that would otherwise not be seen. The video camera's eye reveals mini-universes. Courtesy of Brian Fridge, the Modern Art Museum of Fort Worth, and Dunn & Brown Contemporary.

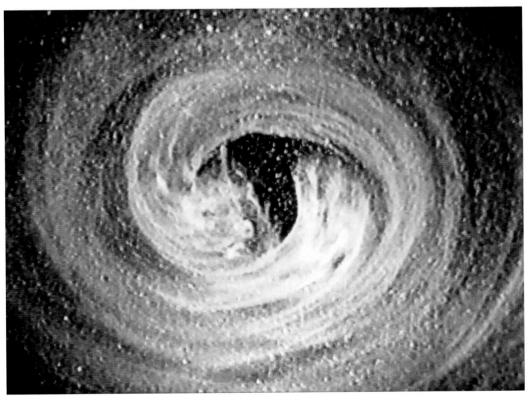

It is sometimes difficult to distinguish abstracted from invented textures, because a skilled artist (seeking something a little more unique than simulation or abstraction) can invent a texture and make it appear to have a precedent where none exists. In such a case, it is difficult to know how to classify the texture; although the texture is created, not re-created, it still seems to be derived from some source. Invented textures, in some settings, may also suggest textures familiar to the observer, although such references to the objective world are not intended by the artist. These textures would most likely show up in abstract works in which the viewer might not know whether they were invented or abstracted.

Usually, the uses of invented textures are the same as those cited for abstract textures—decorative enrichment, relative dominance or emphasis, and movement. In the hands of a Surrealist artist, it is also possible that invented textures could be inserted in an unlikely context for a surprise or shock effect (see figs. 6.18 and T.66).

TEXTURE AND PATTERN

Because both texture and pattern are developed through lights and darks, the difference between the two can be confusing. As defined in Chapter 2, **pattern** is a decorative design, normally thought of in two-dimensional (or flat) terms. It generally involves repetition—sometimes rather random, sometimes more controlled—and often serves as ornament (fig. 6.12A). Pattern is not concerned with surface texture but with appearance.

Texture, on the other hand, is normally associated with a three-dimensional disruption of surface. Lights and darks indicate the various

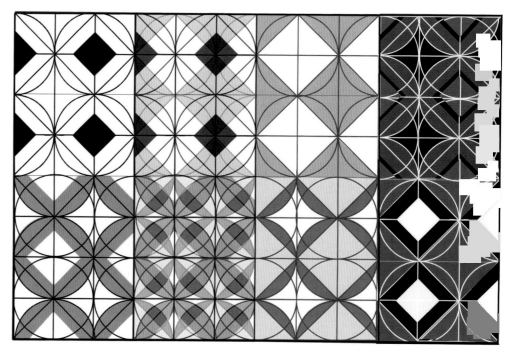

6.12A This illustration shows several pattern variations. As with most patterns, these are made up of repeated motifs and appear as basically flat designs of light and dark.

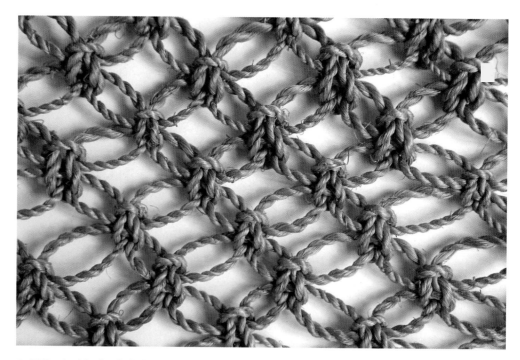

6.12B In this detailed photograph of fiber art, one can see repeated motifs that create pattern, but in this case, the pattern of lights and darks is the product of three-dimensional textures that create highlights and shadows. Even as a flat photo, the knotted fibers clearly appear textural in addition to containing pattern.

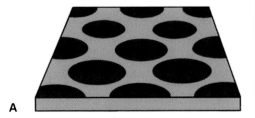

A

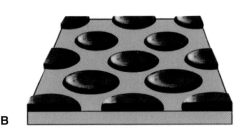

B

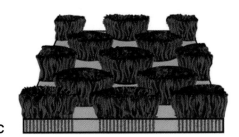

C

6.13 **Three different combinations of pattern and texture.** (A) The circle motif dyed onto this portion of a silk tie creates a pattern but no illusion of texture on the surface. The pattern comes from the variations in value and color of the dye against the background of the silk tie. (*The pattern is independent of texture.*) (B) A circle motif embossed on paper creates both pattern and textural change on the surface. The pattern comes from the organization of the circles, the embossing, and the highlights and shadows of the raised surface areas. (*The three-dimensional surface helps create the pattern.*) (C) The tufts of fiber woven into a rug produce a pattern of circles and create a rather pronounced change in surface texture. The pattern comes from the organization of value and color change in conjunction with the highlights and shadows seen around and within the tufted areas. (*Texture creates the larger pattern, while smaller patterns may be seen within the textural shapes.*)

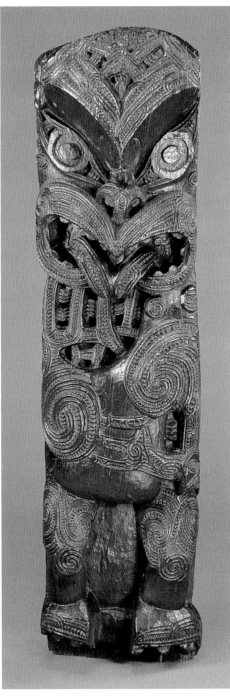

6.14 *Ancestral Figure from House Post,* Maori, New Zealand, c. 118–29. Wood, 43 in. (109.22 cm) high. The Maori shallow-relief figure from New Zealand, representing a tribal ancestor, is decorated with curving or spiral bands. They are enhanced by the application of abstracted textual pattern based on the tattooing that embellished the tribal members' bodies. The carving functioned as one of the wall planks in their meeting house. © Boltin Picture Library.

reflections and shadows created by high and low dimensions of the object in relation to the light source (fig. 6.12B). When viewing a work of art, the basic difference between texture and pattern rests on whether the surface stimulates a tactile response or simply contains an organization that engages the eye.

Imagine a silk tie with a dyed pattern of circles (fig. 6.13A). There is no textural change or any illusion of it on the surface of the silk, and the repeating pattern serves as ornamentation. However, when the design of circles is embossed on paper or woven into a rug (fig. 6.13B and C), changes in the surface texture create changes in value due to shadows and highlights. These textural variations, along with the lights and darks seen on the surface, help create the pattern. An interest in pattern arising out of texture can be found in every culture. In the Maori *Ancestral Figure from House Post,* the spiral bands of pattern are also made visible because of a change in the texture on the surface of the sculpture (fig. 6.14).

Artwork may require viewing from several distances to be fully understood, as viewing distance can affect the appearance of textural density. From a significant distance, the observer will see a general textural field—a generalized area or shape appearing as subtle changes in color or value. Up closer, the patterned relationships become more noticeable. When extremely close, the texture becomes the focal point, obscuring the larger pattern. An analogy might be drawn to a field of corn. Distant areas of the field appear as a blanket of color. Mid-range areas show the overall pattern of the rows. Close up, the texture of the plants is visible, as are new patterns such as the veining of the leaves or the kernels of corn (fig. 6.15). Discovering relationships at various distances depends on how we focus our attention and may be a little like finding a world in a drop of water.

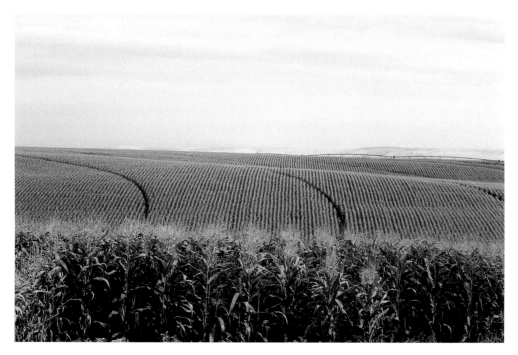

6.15 The individual cornstalks, with their leaves and tassels, can be clearly seen in this low-altitude view of a field. In the foreground, the corn, taken as a whole, appears as a huge three-dimensional texture. In the distant view over the top of the field, the corn forms patterned rows. © Royalty-Free/Corbis.

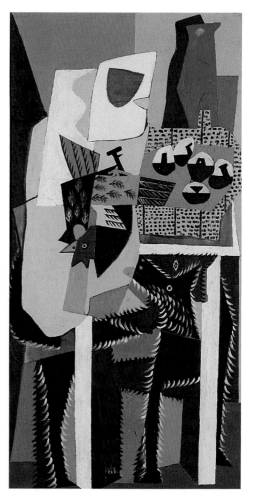

6.16 Pablo Picasso, *Dog and Cock*, 1929. Oil on canvas, 60⅞ × 30⅛ in. (154.6 × 76.5 cm). Abstract texture can be a compositional tool that is important for capturing and directing attention. Clearly the abstracted white fur of the dog attracts us and creates movement. Gift of Stephen Carlton Clark, B.A. © Yale University Art Gallery/Art Resource, NY. © 2008 Estate of Pablo Picasso/Artists Rights Society (ARS), New York.

TEXTURE AND COMPOSITION

Aside from their ability to stimulate our sense of touch, texture's variations of light and dark are often exciting and, with the added emphasis and emotional associations of texture, influence composition as a whole. In concert with the other art elements and subject to the principles of organization, similarities between textural areas can harmonize while contrasts can provide variety and interest.

Our attention is constantly being maneuvered about the surface of an artwork by (among other things) the degree of emphasis given to the various areas of that surface. The movement of our eyes is directed from one attractive area to another, passing over, or through, the "rests" (or deemphasized areas). If an area is visually dead, or not attractive enough, a texture can be added or emphasized to make it come to life. On the other hand, in engaging our attention, textural areas may compete with other parts of the artwork; if a textural area is too strong in its hold on the spectator, other areas (possibly more important ones) may not get the attention they deserve, and the texture must then be diminished.

The control of textures, subject to the other elements, helps create the directional thrusts that move through the work. The abstract textures in Picasso's *Dog and Cock*, for example, draw our eyes to the more significant parts of the painting (fig. 6.16).

TEXTURE AND SPACE

Texture can also help define space. When textures appear blurred and lack strong contrasts, they make objects seem distant, but if they are sharp and have strong contrasts, the objects appear

6.17 Thomas Hill, *Yosemite Valley (from below Sentinel Dome as Seen from Artist's Point)*, 1876. Oil on canvas, 72 × 120 in. (182.88 × 304.8 cm). The foreground areas move forward because of their greater textural contrasts and clarity, while other areas are thrust into space by grayness and only the faint suggestion of details. The Oakland Museum Kahn Collection 68.133.1. Photograph by M. Lee Fatherree.

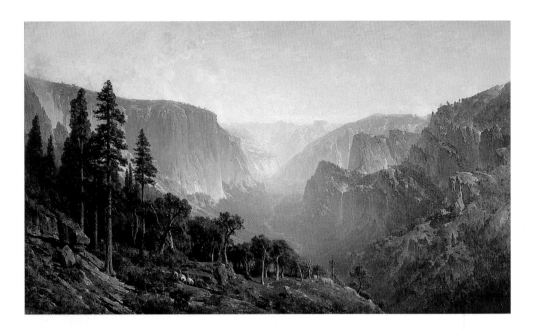

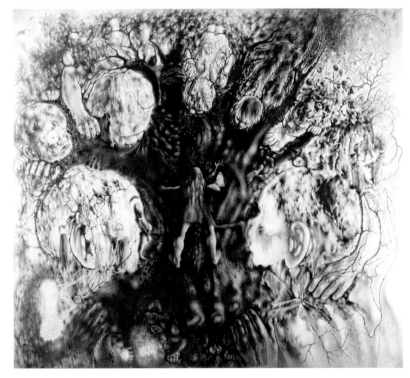

6.18 Pavel Tchelitchew, *Hide-and-Seek [cache-cache]*, 1940–42. Oil on canvas, 6 ft. 6½ in. × 7 ft. 3 in. (1.99 × 2.15 m). A personal textural style is greatly responsible for much of the emotional quality of this painting. Here, along with the invented textures and biomorphic shape patterns, we find the suggestion of an organic presence that evokes a feeling of biological mystery. © SuperStock, Inc./SuperStock.

to move forward. This reflects how the character of texture differs with great distance and is one of the principles of **atmospheric perspective,** a commonly used technique in representational painting (fig. 6.17; see also fig. 8.4). A less traditional artist might use textures from far to near and produce controlled variations or surprising contradictions.

TEXTURE AND EXPRESSIVE CONTENT

Textures tend to have symbolic or associative meanings, and they can provoke psychological or emotional responses that may be pleasant or unpleasant. In doing this, the textures are usually associated with environments, experiences,

objects, or persons from our experience. When we say a person is "slippery as a snake" or "a roughneck," tactile sensations are being linked to personality traits. In this way, textures can be used as supplementary psychological devices that enhance and alter the expressive content of the artwork on a subconscious level (fig. 6.18). The artist

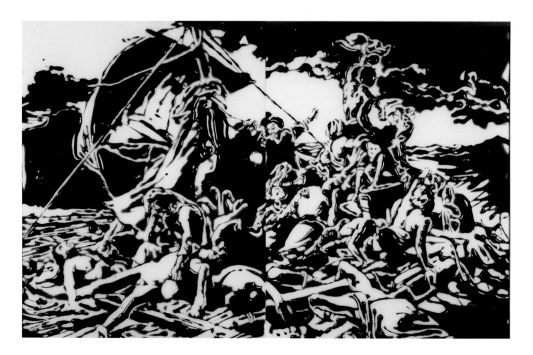

6.19 Vik Muniz, *The Raft of the Medusa,* 1999. Pictures of chocolate, two chromogenic color prints, overall 80 × 125 in. (203.2 × 317.5 cm), panel (each) 80 × 62½ in. (203.2 × 158.8 cm). In *The Raft of the Medusa,* Muniz photographed a painting from 1819 by the French Romantic painter Théodore Géricault. The original painting was based on an event of Géricault's time. Muniz then drew over his initial photograph with chocolate syrup and photographed it again for the final image. The medium used to create the texture of the photograph obscures Géricault's original imagery. The resultant image and the visceral quality of the medium cause the viewer to question and analyze the layers of meaning presented by Muniz. Whitney Museum of American Art, New York; Purchase, with funds from Anne and Joel Ehrenkranz 2000.144a-b. © Vik Muniz/Licensed by VAGA, New York, NY.

can also use textures to stimulate our curiosity, shock us, or make us reevaluate our perceptions. Vik Muniz does this with the use of chocolate syrup as a drawing medium in figure 6.19.

THREE-DIMENSIONAL APPLICATIONS OF TEXTURE

Most of the discussion in this chapter has dealt with the graphic arts and the types of texture that graphic artists create, but textural possibilities are perhaps more pronounced in the making of 3-D artworks. The architect balances the smoothness of steel and glass with the roughness of stone, concrete, and brick (see fig. 1.52). The ceramist works with glazes, aggregates in the clay, and various incised and impressed textures (see fig. 1.55). Jewelers, using different techniques, show concern for texture when making raised ware, pins, brooches, or bracelets (see fig. 1.53). Sculptors manipulate the textures of clay, wood, metal,

and other natural and artificial materials (see fig. 1.40). From this we can see that texture is involved in all art forms, as it is in many life experiences—however unconscious of it we may be.

When working with three-dimensional materials, textures enrich a surface, complement the medium, and enhance expression and content. Textured surfaces range from the rough feel of rusted metal or tree bark to the contrasting smoothness of glass or polished marble. Certain surfaces are inherent to certain media, and traditionally, these intrinsic textures are respected. The artist usually employs certain textures to characterize the distinctive qualities of the subject. The sleek suppleness of a seal, for example, seems to call for a polished surface, whereas the character of a rugged, forceful person calls for a rough-hewn treatment. However, artists sometimes surprise us with a different kind of treatment.

All of the types of texture available to the graphic artists are also available to plastic artists and are developed from the textures inherent in the materials

being used. Actual textures, which are experienced in the plastic arts through touch as opposed to a visual graphic illusion, are the immediate domain of 3-D artists. Their work is created with material that has its own innate tactile quality. In figure 6.20, Nari Ward employs the actual texture of brick, soda cans, and other found objects. Other artists like Patrick Dougherty take their cues from nature's nest builders and weave sticks, branches, and twigs into mammoth environmental sculptures (fig. 6.21). The use of actual texture also plays a role in the fairly recent development called **assemblage,** which blurs the boundaries between two-dimensional and three-dimensional work. Growing out of the earlier experiments with collage, assemblage combines 2-D and 3-D objects of various sorts—some found, others specially made. Although assemblage may seem similar to collage, the distinction is that assemblage brings together items that are larger and bulkier. Further difference is evidenced in their presentation; many works with assemblage are

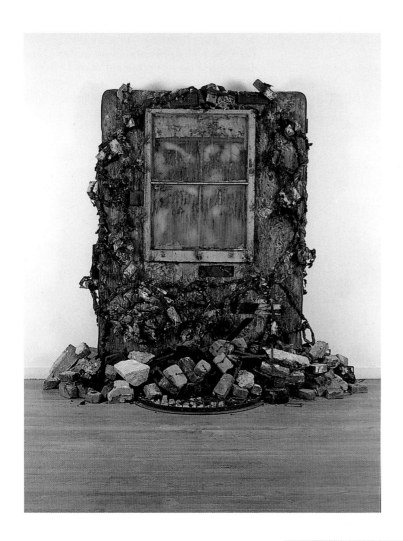

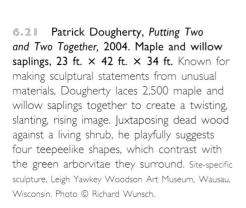

6.20 Nari Ward, *Blue Window Brick Vine*, 1993. Mixed media, size unknown. Ward uses the texture of found objects (mattress, window, soda cans, bricks) to create a feeling of nature's reclamation of a human habitation. Because of its shallow depth (three inches), it functions much like a stage flat used for theater. © Nari Ward.

6.21 Patrick Dougherty, *Putting Two and Two Together*, 2004. Maple and willow saplings, 23 ft. × 42 ft. × 34 ft. Known for making sculptural statements from unusual materials, Dougherty laces 2,500 maple and willow saplings together to create a twisting, slanting, rising image. Juxtaposing dead wood against a living shrub, he playfully suggests four teepeelike shapes, which contrast with the green arborvitae they surround. Site-specific sculpture, Leigh Yawkey Woodson Art Museum, Wausau, Wisconsin. Photo © Richard Wunsch.

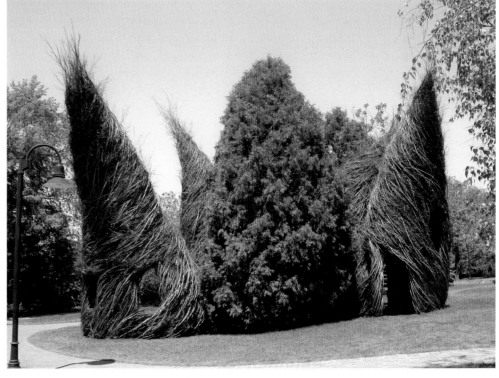

Three-Dimensional Applications of Texture

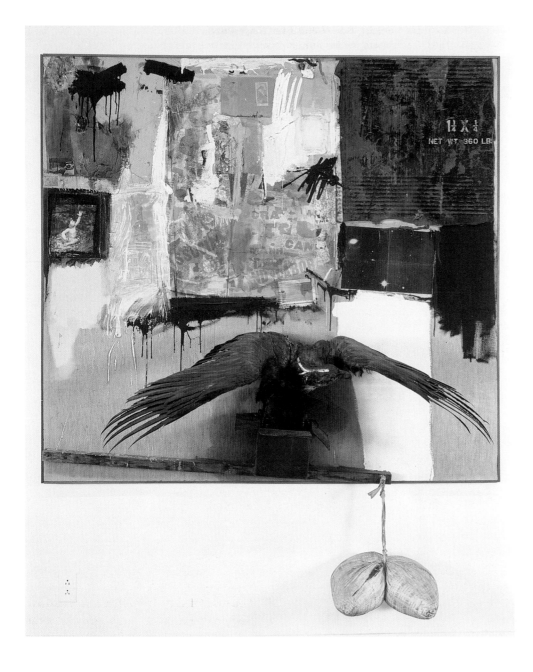

6.22 Robert Rauschenberg, *Canyon*, 1959. Combine painting: oil, pencil, paper, fabric, metal, cardboard box, printed reproductions, photograph, wood, and objects on canvas, with a bald eagle, cord, and pillow, 81¾ × 70 in. (207.65 × 177.8 cm). The technique of assemblage clearly blurs the traditional boundaries between two-dimensional and three-dimensional work. Using actual, abstracted, and invented texture, the artist combines painting and collage with three-dimensional bulky items and brings them off the wall into the viewer's space. © Robert Rauschenberg/Licensed by VAGA, New York, NY.

intended for display on the floor, standing alone in their own space. But even when assemblages include painting formats, their objects project significantly off the wall. Each of the assembled objects, of course, possesses actual texture in its own right (fig. 6.22; see also fig. T.73).

Although we might think of simulated texture as only a graphic device, sculptors can recreate the textures that are characteristic of the subject being interpreted; by cutting into the surface of their chosen material, they can closely simulate the exterior qualities of hair, cloth, skin, and other textures (fig. 6.23). Sometimes the treatment of materials can even trick the senses into experiencing another medium. Through careful manipulation of the surface and with the proper finish, the surfaces of clay, wood, metal, and other natural and artificial materials can appear so naturalistic that they literally fool the eye—three-dimensional trompe l'oeil (fig. 6.24; see also figs. 1.40 and 7.50).

Abstracted texture and invented texture are also available to the plastic artist. Both types of texture can enrich a specific area, change the value of an area

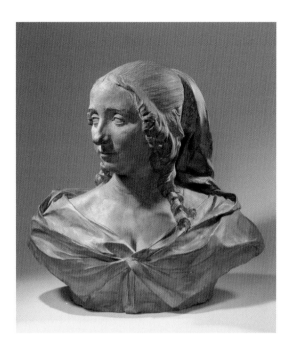

6.23 Rombout Verhulst, *Bust of Maria van Reygersberg,* Leiden, 1663. Terra-cotta, 45 cm high. In this work, Rombout Verhulst has united the sober realism of the period to the skillful rendering of details such as hair and clothing. The sensitivity of his modeling of flesh brings out the expressive and malleable qualities of the clay. Courtesy of Rijksmuseum, Amsterdam.

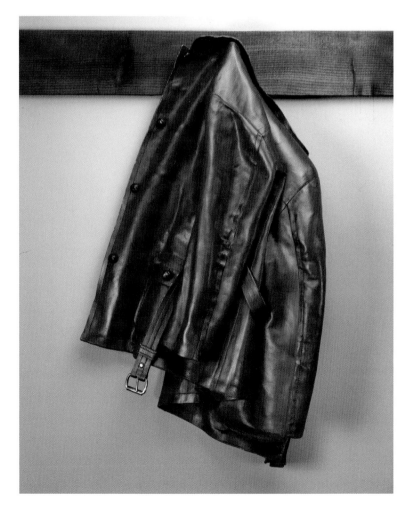

6.24 Marilyn Levine, *Anne's Jacket,* 1999. Ceramic, 36 × 20½ × 7¼ in. For this masterful work of trompe l'oeil, Levine has used clay to simulate the texture of a leather jacket, right down to the scratches and wear marks of well-loved leather. Courtesy of Frank Lloyd Gallery, Collection of the Museum of Arts and Design.

(because of the way light and shadow play on the texture's surface), and alter the flow and tempo of a viewer's eye travel (see fig. 6.14).

Quite certainly, careful observation and skill are required to capture a realistic texture while still controlling its pattern (for compositional integrity); however, incorporating a more subjective or even unnatural texture into a composition involves just as much ingenuity. Regardless of whether a work involves 2-D or 3-D media, or some combination thereof, texture is an inherent part of every surface, and its impact on the organization and expression of the piece should never be overlooked.

Color

CHAPTER SEVEN

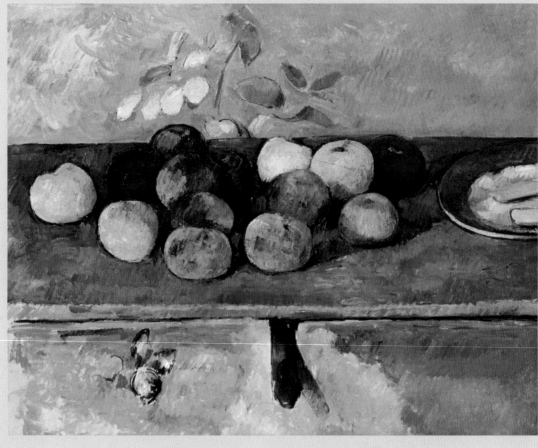

Paul Cézanne, *Apples and Biscuits*, c. 1879–1882. Oil on canvas, 46 x 55 cm.
Musée de l'Orangerie, Paris, France/Lauros-Giraudon, Paris/SuperStock.

THE VOCABULARY OF
COLOR

Color — The visual response to different wavelengths of sunlight identified as red, green, blue, and so on; having the physical properties of hue, intensity, and value.

academic
Art that conforms to established traditions and approved conventions as practiced in formal art schools. Academic art stresses standards, set procedures, and rules.

achromatic
Relating to color perceived only in terms of neutral grays from light to dark; without hue.

additive color
Color created by superimposing light rays. Adding together (or superimposing) the three primary colors of light—red, blue, and green—will produce white. The secondaries are cyan, yellow, and magenta.

analogous colors
Colors that are closely related in hue. They are usually adjacent to each other on the color wheel.

chroma
1. The purity of a hue, or its freedom from white, black, or gray (and wavelengths of other color). 2. The intensity of a hue. 3. Computer programs often refer to chroma as *saturation*.

chromatic
Pertaining to the presence of color.

chromatic value
The relative degree of lightness or darkness demonstrated by a given color.

color
The visual response to different wavelengths of sunlight identified as red, green, blue, and so on; having the physical properties of hue, intensity, and value.

color tetrad
Four colors, equally spaced on the color wheel, containing a primary and its complement and a complementary pair of intermediates. This has also come to mean any organization of color on the wheel forming a rectangle that could include a double split-complement.

color triad
Three colors, equally spaced on the color wheel, forming an equilateral triangle. The twelve-step color wheel is made up of a primary triad, a secondary triad, and two intermediate triads.

complementary colors
Two colors directly opposite each other on the color wheel. A primary color is complementary to a secondary color, which is a mixture of the two remaining primaries.

high-key color
Any color that has a value level of middle gray or lighter.

hue
The generic name of a color (*red, blue, green,* etc.); also designates a color's position in the spectrum or on the color wheel. Hue is determined by the specific wavelength of the color in a ray of light.

intensity
The saturation, strength, or purity of a hue. A vivid color is of high intensity; a dull color is of low intensity.

intermediate color
A color produced by a mixture of a primary color and a secondary color.

intermediate triad
A group of three intermediate colors that are equally spaced on the color wheel and form an equilateral triangle; two groups of intermediate triads are found on the color wheel: red-orange/yellow-green/blue-violet and red-violet/blue-green/yellow-orange.

local (objective) color
The color as seen in the objective world (green grass, blue sky, red barn, etc.).

low-key color
Any color that has a value level of middle gray or darker.

monochromatic
Having only one hue; may include the complete range of value (of one hue) from white to black.

neutralized (color), neutralization (of color)
Color that has been grayed or reduced in intensity by being mixed with any of the neutrals or with a complementary color (so that the mixture contains all three primaries, in equal or unequal amounts).

neutrals
1. The inclusion of all color wavelengths will produce white, and the absence of any wavelengths will be perceived as black. With neutrals, no single color is noticed—only a sense of light and dark or the range from white through gray to black. 2. A color altered by the addition of its complement so that the original sensation of hue is lost or grayed.

patina
1. A natural film, usually greenish, that results from the oxidation of bronze or other metallic material. 2. Colored pigments and/or chemicals applied to a sculptural surface.

pigment
A color substance that gives its color property to another material by being mixed with it or covering it. Pigments, usually insoluble, are added to liquid vehicles to produce paint and ink. They are different from dyes, which are dissolved in liquids and give their coloring effects by staining or being absorbed by a material.

primary color
A preliminary hue that cannot be broken down or reduced into component colors. Primary colors are the basic hues of any color system that in theory may be used to mix all other colors.

primary triad
The three primary colors on the color wheel (red, yellow, and blue), which are equally spaced and form an equilateral triangle.

secondary color
A color produced by a mixture of two primary colors.

secondary triad
The three secondary colors on the color wheel (orange, green, and violet), which are equally spaced and form an equilateral triangle.

shade (of color)
A color produced by mixing black with a hue, which lowers the value level and decreases the quantity of light reflected.

simultaneous contrast
When two different colors come into direct contact, the contrast intensifies the difference between them.

spectrum
The band of individual colors that results when a beam of white light is broken into its component wavelengths, identifiable as hues.

split-complement(s)
A color and the two colors on either side of its complement.

subjective color
1. That which is derived from the mind, instead of physical reality, and reflects a personal bias, emotion, or interpretation. 2. A subjective color tends to be inventive or creative.

subtractive color
The sensation of color that is produced when wavelengths of light are reflected back to the viewer after all other wavelengths have been subtracted and/or absorbed.

tertiary color
Color resulting from the mixture of all three primaries, two secondary colors, or complementary intermediates. Tertiary colors are characterized by the neutralization of intensity and hue. A great variety of tertiary colors, created by mixing differing amounts of the parent colors, are found on the inner rings of the color wheel, which lead to complete neutralization.

tint (of color)
A color produced by mixing white with a hue, which raises the value level and increases the quantity of light reflected.

tonality, tone (color)
1. A generic term for the quality of a color, often indicating a slight modification in hue, value, or intensity—for example, yellow with a greenish tone. 2. The dominating hue, value, or intensity; for example, artwork containing mostly red and red-orange will have an overall tonality of red (the dominant *hue*), and areas of color might have a dark tonality (indicating the dominant *value*) or a muted tonality (indicating the dominant *intensity* level).

value (color)
1. The relative degree of lightness or darkness. 2. The characteristic of color determined by its lightness or darkness or the quantity of light reflected by the color.

value pattern
The arrangement or organization of values that control compositional movement and create a unifying effect throughout a work of art.

THE CHARACTERISTICS OF COLOR

Color, the most universally appreciated element, appeals to children and adults instantly. Infants reach out for brightly colored objects, and older children watch in fascination as yellow mixed with blue magically becomes green. The average person finds color exciting and attractive. This person may question art for many other reasons but seldom objects to the use of color, provided that it is harmonious in character. In fact, a work of art can frequently be appreciated for its color style alone.

Color is one of the most expressive elements because it affects our emotions directly. When we view a work of art, we do not have to rationalize what we are supposed to feel about its color; instead, we have an immediate emotional reaction to it. Pleasing rhythms and harmonies of color satisfy our aesthetic desires. We like certain combinations of color and reject others. In representational art, color identifies objects and creates illusionistic space. The study of color is based on scientific theory—principles that can be observed and easily systematized. In this chapter, we will examine these basic characteristics of color relationships to see how they help give form and meaning to the subject of an artist's work.

LIGHT: THE SOURCE OF COLOR

Color begins with and is derived from light, either natural or artificial. Where there is little light, there is little color; where the light is strong, color is likely to be intense. When the light is weak, such as at dusk or dawn, it is difficult to distinguish one color from another. Under strong sunlight, as in tropical climates, colors seem to take on additional intensity.

Every ray of light coming from the sun is composed of waves that vibrate at different speeds. The sensation of color is aroused in the mind by the way our sense of vision responds to the different

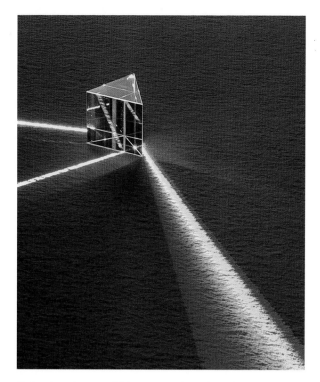

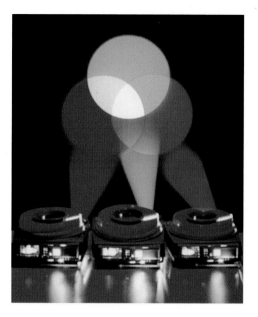

7.1 As a beam of light passes through a glass prism, the rays of light are bent, or refracted, at different angles according to their wavelengths. The rays of red have the longest wavelengths and are bent the least; those of violet have the shortest wavelengths and have the greatest refraction. In this rainbow array of hues, called the *spectrum,* we see bands of red, orange, yellow, green, blue, blue-violet (or indigo), and violet. © David Parker/Photo Researchers, Inc.

7.2 The projected additive primary colors—red, blue (a color named by industry and scientists that is actually closer to violet), and green—create the secondary colors of cyan, yellow, and magenta when two are overlapped. When all three primaries are combined, white light is produced. © Eastman Kodak Company.

wavelengths. This can be demonstrated by observing the way a beam of white light passes through a glass prism and then reflects off a sheet of white paper. The rays of light bend, or refract, as they pass through the glass at different angles (according to their wavelengths) and then reflect off the white paper as different colors. We see these colors as individual stripes in a narrow band called the **spectrum.** The colors easily distinguishable in this band are red, orange, yellow, green, blue, blue-violet, and violet (scientists use the term *indigo* for the color artists call *blue-violet*). These colors also blend gradually; thus, we can discern several intermediate colors between them (fig. 7.1).

Additive Color

The colors of the spectrum are pure, and they represent the greatest intensity (brightness) possible. If we could reverse the process mentioned in the previous paragraph and combine all these spectrum colors back together, we would again have white light. When artists or physicists work with rays of colored light, they are using **additive color,** and by mixing only a select few of the spectrum colors, they may produce various other colors of light. Red, blue, and green are known as the *additive primaries.* These three colors of light are so basic that they themselves cannot be created from other mixtures, but

when they are combined, they form the *additive secondaries*—magenta, yellow, and cyan. As seen in figure 7.2, magenta is produced where red and blue light overlap; yellow is produced where red and green light overlap; and cyan is produced where green and blue light overlap. In the center of that figure, white light is created where the red, blue, and green light rays overlap (magenta, yellow, and cyan thereby also overlap)—demonstrating once again that white light may be created by the presence of all color wavelengths.

The television and computer industries both use this additive-color mixing process. Most modern TVs and color monitors consist of small pixel

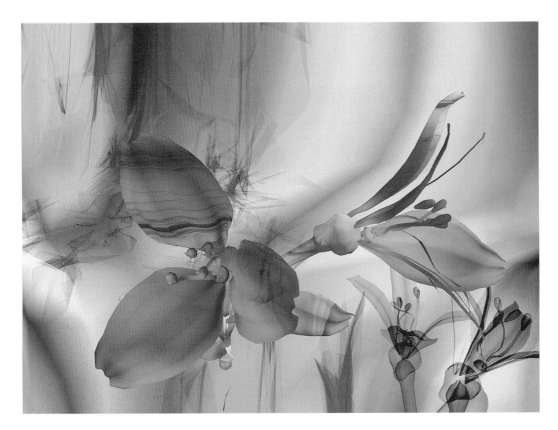

7.3 Charles Csuri, *Wondrous Spring*, 1992. Computer image, 48 × 65 in. (121.9 × 165.1 cm). In Csuri's computer-generated image, floral forms are used to explore the transparency and intensity of color as light. When printed on paper, the inks attempt to simulate the illumination of the pixels on the screen. Courtesy of Charles Csuri.

groups that emit red, blue, and green light. Arranged in nearly imperceptible horizontal and vertical lines, these units can illuminate each color singly or in various combinations to produce the sensation of every color possible. At viewing distance, the eye merges the glowing pixels to perceive one complete image every one-thirtieth of a second. Numerous technologies (including the cathode ray tube, liquid crystal display, plasma display, and digital light projection) offer innovative methods for transmitting images, but all use additive color in their methodology. Some quickly flash the colored lights to make an image; some use a steady stream of constantly changing lights. In general, the more frames displayed per second, the smoother the movement appears on screen. The image may seem jumpy at 18 frames per second but smooth at 30 frames per second—although as many as 120 frames may be needed in high-end video rendering to make the image seem more realistic for computer games and special effects. Normally, our brains can process only about 75 frames per second; the extra information is coalesced to make each image more complete.

The computer can be employed as an important tool in additive-color mixing. Not only can software programs allow the artist to create color images, many with the illusion of three-dimensional space and scale (fig. 7.3), but they also assist the artist in developing ideas. Computer-generated models let the user move about in the image, trying multiple spacing and color relationships. The artist is even able to explore the additive-color effects of stage lighting on characters and props before building the actual sets. This is an extremely valuable technology, because with additive-color stage lighting, things are not always what they initially seem. A reddish stage light will often make the object take on that color, and if green is projected on the opposite side, interesting qualities may be created by the highlights and shadows of the natural contours. Where the two spotlights overlap, a new color (yellow tones) may be seen. Though a bit garish in this instance, additive-color stage lighting that is appropriate to the image can do much to heighten the emotional response of the audience. With complex custom programming, colored spotlights and projected images can even entice the viewer into a unique sense of three-dimensional space (fig. 7.4).

Increasingly, an artist needs to be familiar with the additive-color system. In addition to computer art, it is used in theater, video production, computer animation graphics, the neon-sign industry,

7.4 Jennifer Steinkamp, *Stiffs*, 2000. Light/space/sound installation using six Epson-5350 1500-lumen projectors, six iMacs, two G3s, 24-track sound, one Icube; each monolith 3 × 17 × 1 ft., room 70 × 38 × 17 ft. Soundtrack by Jimmy Johnson. Programming by Sarah Rosenbaum. This installation carefully incorporates sight, sound, and the spatial architecture of the room to draw the viewer into the work. Its integrated computer animation, video projection, and electronic music create an interactive environment that challenges viewers' preconceptions about art. As viewers approach each monolith, the color patterns arc upward and the animation increases in speed. The sound is also designed to encompass the viewer upon approach. Even the shadows cast by onlookers help viewers become part of the work. The additive color used in this work is only one example of the creative ways artists can incorporate the power of color for heightened expressive effects. Photo credit: Steven Heller, courtesy ACME, Los Angeles and greengrassi, London. Courtesy of the artist and Williamson Gallery, Art Center College of Design.

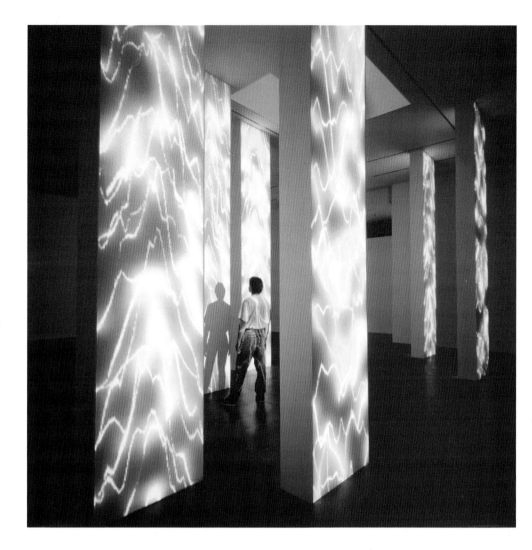

digital billboards, slide and multimedia presentations, laser light shows, and landscape and interior lighting. In each case, artists and technicians work with light and create color by mixing the light primaries—red, blue, and green.

Subtractive Color

Since all the colors are present in a beam of sunlight (white light), you may be wondering how certain objects can appear to be one color or another. Any colored object has certain physical properties, called *pigmentation* or *color quality*, that enable it to absorb some color waves and reflect others. The wavelengths that are reflected back to our eyes allow us to perceive that object as a particular color. A green leaf, for example, appears green to the eye because the leaf *reflects* only the green waves in the ray of light; the other wavelengths are absorbed, or subtracted, by the pigments in the leaf. An artist's **pigments** have this same property and when applied to the surface of an object, give it the same characteristic. The artist may also modify the surface pigmentation of an object through the use of dyes, stains, and chemical treatments, such as those applied to sculpture.

Regardless of how the surface pigmentation is applied or altered, the sensation of color is created when the object's surface reflects certain wavelengths; the surface absorbs all wavelengths *except* those of the color perceived. When color is experienced through *reflected* light, we are dealing with **subtractive color** rather than actual light rays and additive color. With an area of white, all the light wavelengths of color are reflected back to the viewer—none is subtracted (or absorbed) by the white. However, when a color pigment covers the surface, only the wavelengths of that color are reflected back to the viewer—all others are subtracted (or absorbed) by the pigment. As a result, the sensation of that specific color is experienced.

If all the pigment colors were to be blended together, they would (in theory) cancel each other out, and the mixture would *absorb all* wavelengths. In theory, the mixture would appear black—no color reflected. However, in actual practice on the palette, the combination of all pigment colors results not in black but in dark gray, which hints at some color presence but feels rather "muddy." This occurs because of adulterants and imperfections in pigments, inks, and dyes and the fact that the surface may not perfectly absorb all wavelengths. As a result, the area may reflect a mixture of various colors and/or a certain amount of white.

The theory of subtractive color, then, helps explain how we perceive most colored objects and images; the colors we see are reflected wavelengths, as all others have been absorbed. The following sections, therefore, will be concerned with the artist's typical palette of pigments and the color made visible by subtraction (reflected light).

ARTISTS' PIGMENTS AND THE TRIADIC COLOR SYSTEM

As previously mentioned, the spectrum contains red, orange, yellow, green, blue, blue-violet, and violet, with hundreds of subtle color variations. This range of color is available in pigments as well. Beginning artists are likely to use only a few simple, pure colors. They may not realize that simple colors can be varied or that mixing them can create an even wider range of color.

In traditional processes (using pigments and subtractive color), three colors cannot be created from mixtures: these are the hues red, yellow, and blue, known as the **primary colors** (fig. 7.5). When two or more of these primaries are mixed, in equal or unequal amounts, they can produce all of the possible colors.

Mixing any *two* primaries in more or less equal proportions produces a **secondary color**: red and yellow result in orange; yellow and blue create green; and blue and red produce violet (see fig. 7.5).

Intermediate colors are mixtures of a primary color with a neighboring secondary color. Combining yellow and green, for example, will create the intermediate color yellow-green (fig. 7.6). Because a change in the proportion of primary or secondary color used will

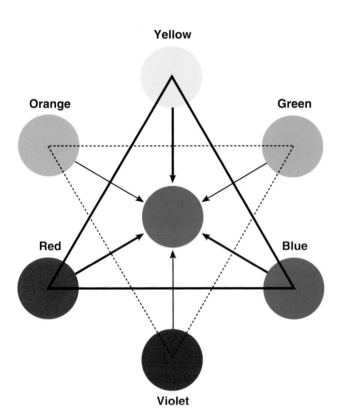

7.5 Primary and secondary colors. A primary triad is shown by solid lines. When the yellow, red, and blue of the primary triad are properly mixed together, the resulting color is a neutralized gray. A secondary triad is connected by dotted lines. When secondary colors are also properly mixed together, the resulting color is gray.

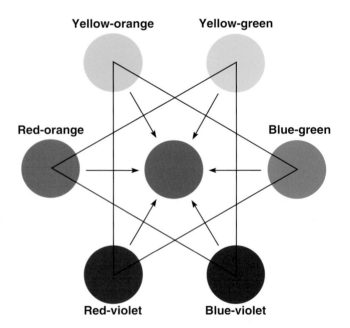

7.6 Intermediate colors. Intermediate colors are created by mixing a primary with a neighboring secondary color (see fig. 7.5). As illustrated here, intermediate colors form two intermediate triads. When the colors of an intermediate triad are mixed together in appropriate proportions, the resulting color is usually a neutralized gray. Unbalanced mixtures produce tertiary colors, which are found in the center rings of figure 7.7.

change the resultant color, many subtle variations are possible; the yellow-green can be made to lean more toward yellow or more toward green.

If we study the theoretical progression of mixed color from yellow to yellow-green to green and so on, we discover a natural order that may be presented as a color wheel (fig. 7.7). Our ability to differentiate subtle variation allows us to see a new color at each position. Note that the primaries, secondaries, and intermediates are found on the outermost ring, where the hues are at spectrum intensity.

Although the number of possible colors is actually infinite, we generally recognize the wheel (or its outermost ring) as having twelve colors, which can be divided and organized into **color triads.** This system of organization is known as the *triadic color system.* The three primary colors are spaced equally apart on the wheel, with yellow usually on the top because it is lightest in value. These colors form an equilateral triangle called a **primary triad** (see fig. 7.5). The three secondary colors are placed between the primaries from which they are mixed; evenly spaced, they create a **secondary triad** composed of orange, green, and violet (see fig. 7.5). Intermediate colors placed between each primary and secondary color create equally spaced units known as **intermediate triads** (see fig. 7.6). The placement of all the colors results in the twelve-step color wheel.

As we move around the color wheel, there is a change in the wavelengths of the light rays that produce the colors. The closer together colors appear on the color wheel, the closer their relationships are; the farther apart, the more contrasting in character they are. The colors directly opposite each other afford the greatest contrast and are known as **complementary colors** (see fig. 7.17). The complement of any color—based on the triadic system—is the combination of the other two colors in its triad.

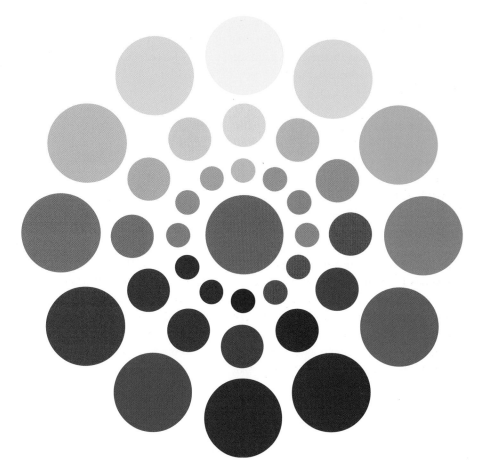

7.7 The outermost ring of the color wheel includes the primary, secondary, and intermediate colors at their greatest intensity (brightness); only twelve steps are shown here, although the number of possible hues is actually infinite. The inner rings contain the tertiary colors, which result from the mixture of one primary with its complement. As each color progresses from the outermost ring toward the center of the wheel (and toward its complement), it loses intensity and becomes more neutralized (grayed). Complete neutralization occurs in the center circle. Only two steps are shown between the outermost ring and complete neutralization, but the number of possible steps is actually infinite.

For example, the complement of red (a primary color) is green—a theoretical mixture of equal parts of the remaining points of the primary triad (in this case, yellow and blue). Thus, the color and its complement are made up of the three triadic colors; the complement of yellow is violet—a mixture of blue and red. The complement of any secondary color may be found by knowing what primaries created that secondary; for example, orange is created from red and yellow, so the remaining member of the primary triad (blue) will be orange's complement.

When a color is mixed with its complement, it becomes **neutralized** (grayed), and a **tertiary** color is produced. Tertiary colors are also created by mixing any two secondary colors or by combining non-analogous intermediate colors. In practical terms, this involves the intermixing of all three primaries in varying proportions and creates the browns, olives, maroons, and so on found on the inner rings of the color wheel (see fig. 7.7). Between the initial color in the outermost ring and complete neutralization in the center, there are actually an infinite number of possible steps, but, for the sake of space, we have presented only two inner rings in our illustration. This will be more fully explained in the coming section called "Intensity."

It should be noted that the color illustrations presented here are created by inks and should be used as guides rather than absolutes. The actual mixing of pigments will reveal, for instance, that each manufacturer's "red" is different and that the color of your mixed "green" depends on what you use as primaries; lemon yellow mixed with ultramarine blue will create a different green than one that uses cadmium yellow and cobalt blue. Color-mixing experiments will disclose much about opacity, staining power, and the adulterants mixed in by manufacturers.

We will see later in this chapter that photographers, printers, and some other artists use alternate systems for organizing color (see "The Evolution of the Color Wheel"). Those systems involve a different set of primaries and secondaries from those mentioned here. However, for the majority of this chapter when we discuss color, we will be concerned with the triadic color system of the painter's palette.

Neutrals

Not all pigments, of course, contain a perceivable color. Some, like black, white, or gray, do not look like any of the colors of the spectrum. No color quality is found in these examples; they are **achromatic.** They differ merely in the quantity of light they reflect. Because we do not distinguish any one color in black, white, and gray, they are also called **neutrals.**

Even though we may not realize it, neutrals actually do reflect varying amounts of the color wavelengths. One

neutral, white, could be thought of as the presence of *all* color, because it occurs when a surface reflects all of the color wavelengths to an equal degree. Black, then, could be thought of as the *absence* of color, because it results when a surface absorbs all of the color rays equally and reflects none of them. Absolute black is rarely experienced except in such places as deep caves or ocean depths. Therefore, most blacks will contain some trace of reflected color, however slight.

Any gray is an impure white, because it is created by only partial reflection of all the color wavelengths. If a great amount of light is reflected, the gray is light; if very little light is reflected, the gray is dark. The neutrals are concerned with the *quantity* of light reflected, whereas color involves the *quality* of light reflected.

THE PHYSICAL PROPERTIES OF COLOR

Regardless of whether the artist works with **chromatic** paints, dyes, or inks, every color used must be described in terms of three physical properties: hue, value, and intensity (figs. 7.8 and 7.9).

Hue

Hue is the generic color name—*red, blue, green,* and so on—given to the visual response for each range of identifiable wavelengths in visible light (fig. 7.10; see also fig 7.1); it also designates a color's position in the spectrum or on the color wheel. Each hue actually exists in many subtle variations, although the differences in wavelengths are so small that they can still bear the same simple color name. Many reds, for example, differ in character from the theoretical red of the spectrum, yet we recognize the hue "red" in all of them. A color's hue can be changed by adding it to another hue;

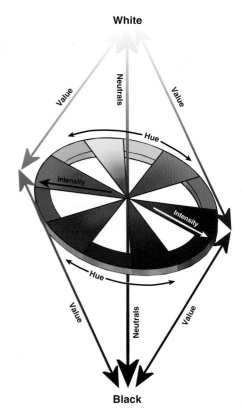

7.8 This diagram demonstrates the relationship between the three physical properties of color: hue, value, and intensity. Based on this, we can imagine all the color variations existing on a three-dimensional solid (a double cone). As the colors move circularly around the solid, they change in hue. When the hues move upward or downward on the solid, they change in value. As the colors on the outside move towards the center, they become more neutralized (closer to the achromatic neutrals) and lose their intensity.

this actually changes the wavelength of light. There are an unlimited number of steps (variations) that may be created by mixing any two hues—many steps exist between yellow and green, for example. Yet, for the sake of clarity, artists recognize the hues as those identified on the twelve-step color wheel.

Value

The second physical property of color, known as **chromatic value,** indicates the lightness or darkness of a color—or the quantity of light a color reflects. A

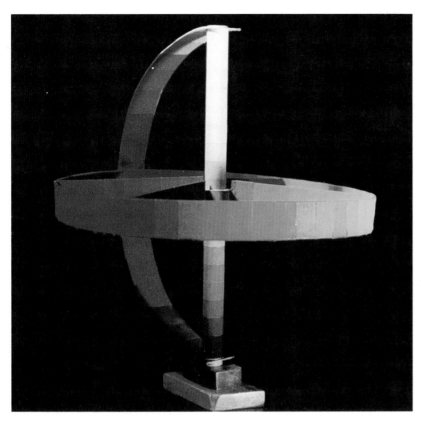

large amount of light is reflected from yellow, whereas a small amount of light is reflected from violet. Each color at its maximum intensity has a normal value that indicates the amount of light it reflects. It can, however, be made lighter or darker than normal by adding white or black. When a hue is mixed with varying amounts of white, the colors produced are known as **tints.** When a hue is mixed with varying amounts of black, the resulting colors are called **shades.** Many value steps can exist between the lightest and darkest appearance of any one hue.

Although a wide range of chromatic values can be produced by simply adding black or white, value changes can also be made by mixing a pigment of one hue with a pigment of another hue that is darker or lighter; this mixing will also alter both the color's value and hue. The only dark or light pigments available that would change the value *without* altering the hue are black, white, or a gray. (For example, red mixed with white will become the color *pink*, but the hue will remain *red*.)

7.9 This three-dimensional model illustrates the three main characteristics of color. The center wheel could also be slightly tilted to indicate that yellow (at maximum intensity) is lighter in value than violet (at maximum intensity). See also figure 7.8. Photograph courtesy of Ronald Coleman.

7.10 **The electromagnetic spectrum.** The sun, being the most efficient source of light, sends radiation to the earth in a series of waves known as electromagnetic energy. This may be likened to throwing a pebble into the middle of a pond. Waves radiate from that point and can be measured from the crest of one ripple to the crest of the next ripple. Similarly, waves from the sun range from mere atmospheric ripples—gamma rays, which measure no more than six quadrillionths of an inch (0.000000000000006 in.)—to the long, rolling radio waves, which stretch 18½ miles from crest to crest. The wavelengths visible to the human eye are found in only a narrow range within this electromagnetic spectrum; their unit of measure is the nanometer (nm), which measures one-billionth of a meter from crest to crest. The shortest wavelength visible to mankind measures 400 nm—a light violet. The sensations of yellow, orange, and red are apparent as the waves lengthen to between 600 and 700 nm. Contained in a ray of light but invisible to the human eye are infrareds ("below reds") and ultraviolets ("above violets"). See figure 7.1.

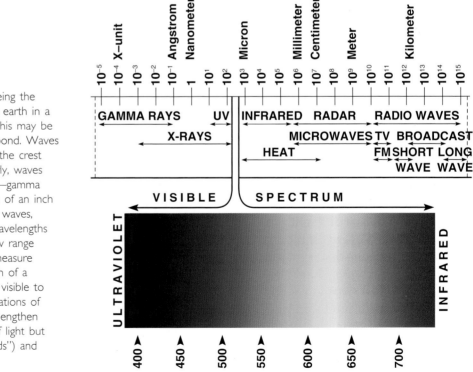

We should know the normal value of each of the colors in order to use them effectively. This normal value can be most easily seen when the colors of the wheel are placed next to a scale of neutral values from black to white, where the colors can be matched with their equivalent achromatic values (fig. 7.11). All colors that are above middle gray are called **high-key colors.** All colors that are below middle gray are referred to as **low-key colors.**

Whether a color remains low or high key is up to the artist. As noted, a low-key violet may be lightened with white. That adjustment will raise violet's value level, which can be increased until it corresponds to the value level for any color along the neutral scale; violet could even be made equal in value to yellow-orange on the gray scale. Similarly, a high-key color such as yellow may be adjusted with enough black that it becomes a low-key color (fig. 7.12).

Regardless of how the value level is obtained, *color* can be used to create a **value pattern** in the organization of a work. A wise artist once said, "Color gets all the glory . . . but value does all the work!" While many artists work intuitively using only color and its brilliance, the most insightful also understand and employ color's value as a compositional tool (see figs. 2.55 and 5.25).

Intensity

The third property of color, *intensity* (also sometimes called brightness, saturation, or **chroma**), refers to the quality of light in a color. Intensity distinguishes a brighter appearance from a duller one of the same hue; that is, it differentiates a color that has a high degree of saturation or strength from one that is grayed (neutralized) or less intense. The saturation point, or the purist color, is actually found in the spectrum produced by a beam of light passing through a prism. The artist's pigment that comes closest

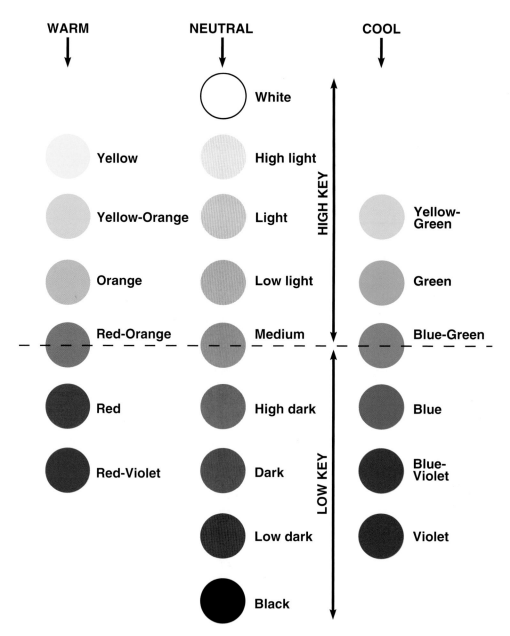

7.11 **Color values.** This chart indicates the relative normal values of the hues at their maximum intensity (purity or brilliance). The broken line identifies those colors and neutrals at the middle (50 percent) gray position. All neutrals and colors above this line are high key; those below it are low key. Warm colors are found on the yellow and red side, while cool colors are found with the greens and blues.

to resembling this color is said to be at maximum intensity.

The purity of the light waves reflected from the pigment produces the brightness or dullness of the color. For example, a pigment that reflects only the red rays of light is an intense red, but if any of the complementary green rays are also reflected, the red's brightness is dulled or neutralized. If the green and red rays are *equally* absorbed by the surface, the resulting effect is a neutral gray. Consequently, as a color loses its intensity, it tends to approach gray.

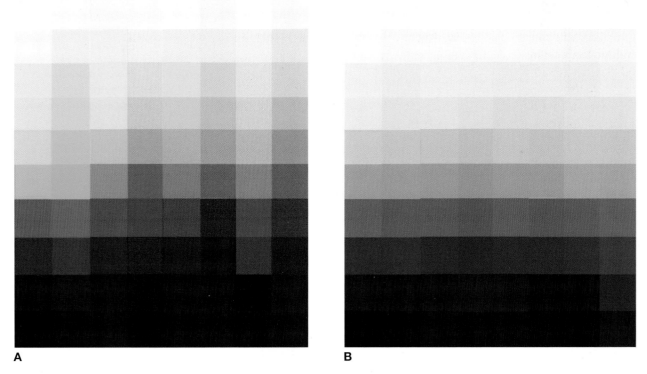

A　　　　　　　　　　　　　　　　　　　**B**

7.12 **Color value chart.** Chart A shows how colors that are high key or low key at maximum intensity can be adjusted until they cover a wide range of values; chart B shows those colors at their equivalent achromatic gray levels. The use of chromatic value is an important component in creating effective color and value patterns.

There are several ways to alter the intensity of a color. One common approach is to place the color next to its complement. The extreme contrast between the two will make the intensity of both colors appear to increase. (This will be discussed more thoroughly in the section "Simultaneous Contrast.") Other methods usually involve the mixing of pigments—a physical blending of two or more colors—which will automatically decrease the intensity of the color.

Figure 7.13 shows the alteration of a hue (pigment) by adding neutrals (black, white, or gray). When white is added to any hue, the color loses its brightness or intensity as it becomes lighter in value. In the same way, when black is added to a hue, the intensity diminishes as the value darkens. We cannot change value without lowering intensity, although

these two properties are not the same. We can, however, lower the intensity without altering the value. By mixing the hue (pigment) with a neutral gray of the same value (as illustrated in the middle of fig. 7.13), the resulting mixture is a variation in intensity *without* a change in value. The color becomes less bright as more of that same gray is added, but it will not become lighter or darker in value.

The most efficient way to decrease the intensity of any hue is to add the complementary hue (fig. 7.14). Mixing two hues that occur exactly opposite each other on the color wheel (such as red and green, blue and orange, or yellow and violet) actually results in the intermixing of all three primaries. In theory, the two complements would cancel each other out and a black should theoretically be

created, which would absorb all wavelengths and not allow any colors to be reflected. However, because of impurities and an inability of the surface to absorb all the wavelengths, a neutral gray is actually produced. In the studio, the combination of some complements—blue with orange, for example—may produce "better" grays than others. Note: the gray ink in these diagrams may appear darker and characterless when compared to your experiments.

When complements are mixed together, the three primaries are combined, and a *tertiary color* is produced. If the mixture has uneven proportions, the dominating hue creates the resulting color character, or **tonality.** Although the hue and intensity are neutralized to varying degrees relative to the amount of complement used, the resulting color

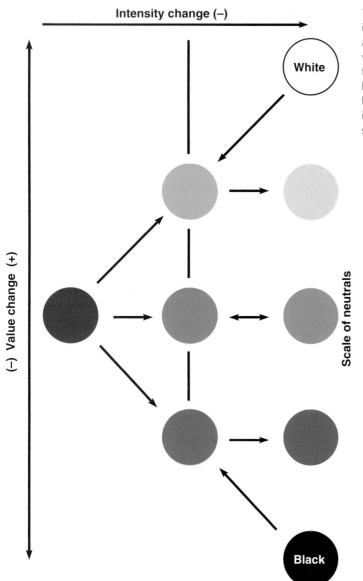

Intensity change (–)

(–) Value change (+)

White

Scale of neutrals

Black

7.13 This diagram illustrates the way neutrals may be used to change the intensity of a color. When a neutral gray of the same value level is added to a bright red, the color character is changed, the intensity is lowered, but the value level is neither raised nor lowered. When white is added to the red, the value level of the color is raised, but the intensity level is lowered. When black is added to the red, the new color will have a lower value level and a lower intensity level. This suggests that any color's hue may be altered and its intensity lowered without altering the value level by adding a neutral of the same shade of grayness to the original color.

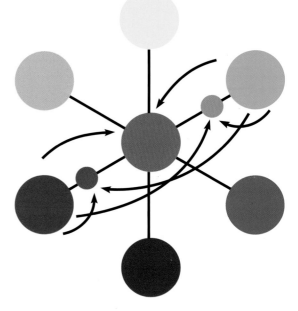

7.14 This diagram indicates the change of intensity that results from adding to a color a little of its complement. For instance, adding a small amount of green to red produces a gray-red. In the same way, a small amount of red added to green results in a gray-green. When the two colors are balanced (not necessarily in equal amounts), the resulting mixture is a neutral gray.

will have a certain liveliness of character not present when a hue is neutralized with a *gray* pigment. Hundreds of tertiary colors may be observed between one color and its complement. A neutralization scale will show incremental steps as the color is mixed with more and more of its complement until complete neutralization occurs (see figs. 7.7 and 7.14).

Of course, tertiary colors may also be created by mixing two secondary colors or by mixing two non-analogous intermediate colors that share a common color—for example, yellow-orange

and red-violet both contain the hue *red*. When certain colors are combined, they will have about the same character and appearance as those colors created by the (incomplete) neutralization of a color by its complement. This neutralization also occurs with the mixing of any combination of colors that contain the three primaries. For example, mixing yellow-orange (y+y,r) with yellow-green (y+y,b) and red-violet (r+r,b) would, in theory, mix about four yellows with three reds and two blues. Here, the four yellows are neutralized by two reds and two blues (the equiva-

lent of four violets), which leaves behind an extra red part. As a result, the tertiary color has a muddy reddish tone. (The "math" in this example is only theoretical, of course; in actual practice, the proportions may differ due to variations in the color, grade, and opacity of materials.)

On the color wheel in figure 7.7, the tertiary colors are placed between the outermost ring and the completely neutralized center circle. Tertiary colors of the same degree of neutralization create inner rings and appear as the browns (neutralized oranges), olives (neutral-

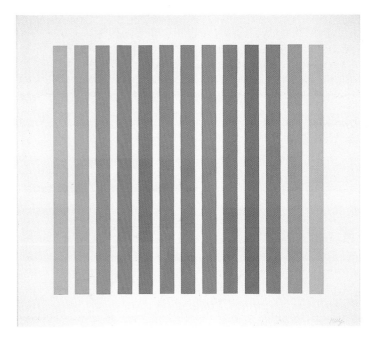

7.15 Ellsworth Kelly, *Spectrum*, 1972. Collage on paper, 45 × 48 in. (114.3 × 121.9 cm). In this color study, Kelly has employed all the contrasting colors in the spectrum. The addition of white to each color brings them into a harmonious relationship by raising their value level and lowering their intensity. © Ellsworth Kelly. Private collection.

ized greens), and so on. They are characterized by a change of value, a loss of intensity, and an alteration of hue. They are not to be found on the outermost ring with the primary, secondary, and intermediate colors.

When mixing a color with its complement, it must be pointed out that it is difficult to change the color's intensity without *also* changing its value level (see fig. 7.14). If a small amount of green (lighter value) is added to red (darker value), the result is a loss of intensity and a *lightening* of value for the neutralized red. Conversely, when a small amount of red (darker value) is added to the green (lighter value), the green loses some of its intensity and becomes *darker* in value. This dual relationship

involving intensity and value is perhaps more easily seen with yellow and violet. However, it occurs with every pair of complements except one—red-orange and blue-green. They are the only pair of complements that may be used to lower each other's intensity *without* changing the value level. This occurs because they begin with the same value level—middle gray.

DEVELOPING AESTHETIC COLOR RELATIONSHIPS

When listening to music, we find a single note played for a long period of

time rather boring. Once the composer begins to combine notes in chords, however, harmonic relationships of sound are created. Sounds combine in different ways, and some are better than others at creating harmonic effects. The same is true for an artist's colors. No color is important in itself; each is seen on the picture surface in a dynamic interaction with other colors. Because of the way it is presented, any organization of color—in an objective or nonobjective format—can play on our emotions and evoke content or meaning (see figs. 7.35 and 7.38).

To develop a discerning eye for those combinations that are pleasing, study the colors found in nature—which range from the vibrant golds, greens, blues, and violets found on a peacock's feather to the soft muted browns and grays on the surface of a rock. Study the percentage of colors in those objects, and try applying that same correlation to the color schemes in your own work. There are no exact rules for creating pleasing color relationships, only some guiding principles.

The successful use of color depends on an understanding of some basic color relationships. A single color by itself has a certain character, creates a mood, or elicits an emotional response, but that character can change when the color is seen with other colors. Just as the musician can vary combined tones to form different harmonies, so too can the artist create different relationships (harmonies) among colors that may be closely allied or contrasting (figs. 7.15 and 7.16).

Complements and Split-Complements

Color organizations that result in the greatest contrast in hue occur when two colors that appear directly opposite each other on the color wheel (complementaries) are placed next to each other in

7.16 Pictured here are nine variations of a composition, each containing a different color scheme: (A) monochromatic, (B) analogous, (C) primary triad, (D) secondary triad, (E) tetrad, (F) complements, (G) split-complements, (H) warm, (I) cool. The scales beneath each block display some of the hues, values, and intensities available for use within each color scheme.

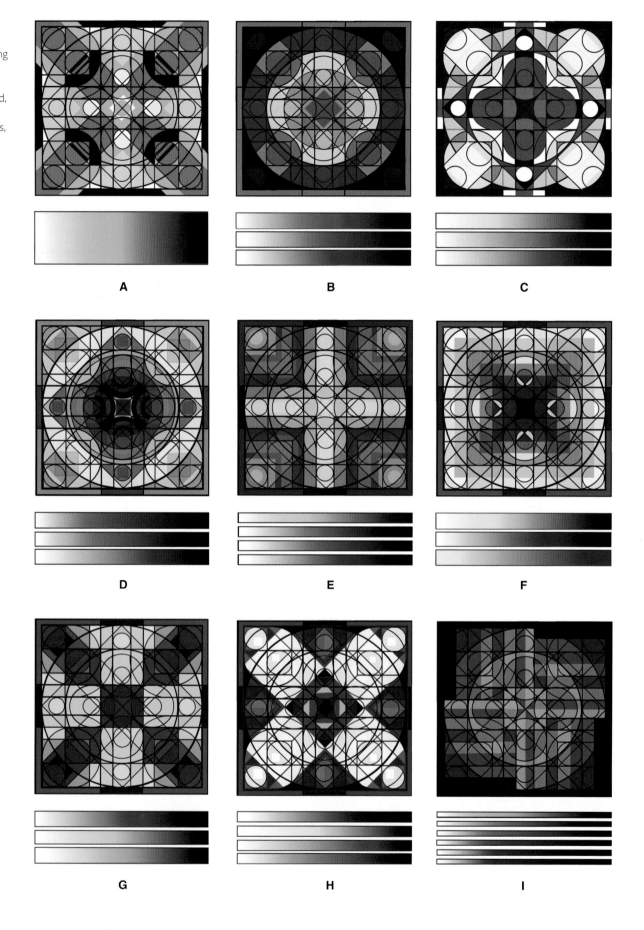

the composition (fig. 7.17). When a color is seen, only that wavelength is being reflected; the other wavelengths not reflected equal the color's complement. Therefore, when two complements are placed nearby, a vibrancy occurs because of the great contrast. Each color tends to increase the apparent intensity of the other color, and when used in equal amounts, they are difficult to look at for any length of time (see the section "Simultaneous Contrast"). This is overcome by reducing the amount of one of the colors or by introducing changes in the intensity or value level of one or both colors (see figs. 7.15 and 7.16F).

A subtle variation with slightly less contrast would be the **split-complement** system, which incorporates a color and the two colors on either side of its complement (see figs. 7.16G and 7.17). This color scheme provides a more complex palette than the straight complementary system, especially when incorporating changes of intensity or value from the complete range of colors available in this color scheme. The color bars below the illustration 7.16G show the range of values and colors available for use in that split-complement composition. Color schemes in which the colors are fairly close to spectrum intensity are relatively easy to identify, but, as the colors become altered by neutralization or change of value (as indicated on the color bars), color schemes become more difficult to categorize. For example, the colors in figure 7.18 have all been adjusted in value or intensity. As a result, the image would probably not be readily identified as a split-complement composition, but its general tonality is based on the relationship of yellow-orange, red-orange, and blue as shown in the color bars.

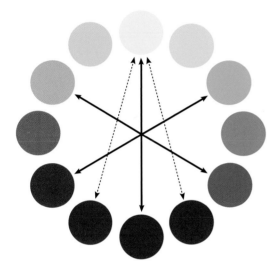

7.17 Complementary colors. In this diagram, complementary colors are connected by solid lines. They are of extreme contrast. An example of split-complementary colors (yellow, red-violet, and blue-violet) is shown by dotted lines. Though yellow is the example used here, the idea may be applied to any color and would include the color on either side of the hue's complement. Split-complements are not as extreme in contrast as complements.

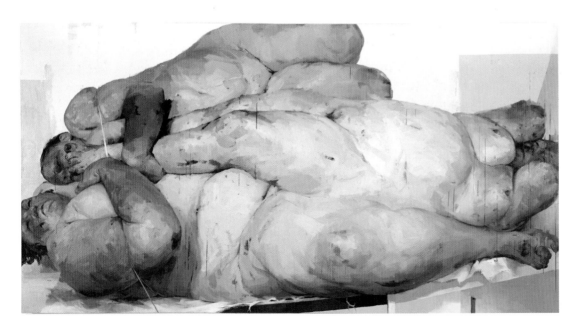

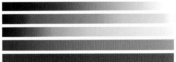

7.18 Jenny Saville, *Fulcrum*, 1999. Oil on canvas, 103 × 192 in. (261.6 cm × 487.7 cm). While developing a very painterly surface, Saville confronts our traditional view of beauty regarding the female body. The color scheme, though not easily recognizable, makes use of hues altered in value or intensity. It seems to be based on a split-complementary organization of blue, yellow-orange, and red-orange. The color bars show the range of color available with such a color scheme.
© Jenny Saville. Courtesy Gagosian Gallery.

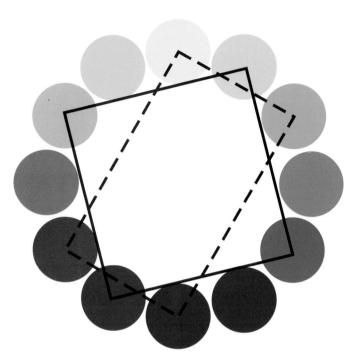

7.19 Color tetrad intervals (squares and rectangles). The color tetrad is composed of four colors equally spaced to form a square. A more casual relationship would have a rectangle formed out of two complements and their split-complements. The rectangle or square may be rotated to any position on the color wheel to reveal other tetrad color intervals.

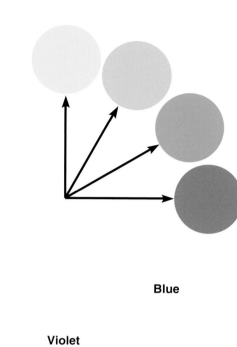

Orange

Red   Blue

Violet

7.20 Analogous colors (close relationships).

Triads

A triadic color organization is based on an even shorter interval between colors, giving less contrast between the colors. Here, three equally spaced colors form an equilateral triangle on the color wheel; these *color triads* are used in many combinations. A *primary triad*, using only primary colors, creates striking contrasts (see figs. 7.5 and 7.16C). With the *secondary triad*, composed of orange, green, and violet, the interval between hues is the same, but the contrast is softer (see figs. 7.5 and 7.16D). This effect occurs because any two hues of the triad share a common color: orange and green both contain yellow; both orange and violet contain red; and green and violet both contain blue. Intermediate color schemes may be organized into two *intermediate triads* (see fig. 7.6). Here,

too, as we move farther away from the purity of the primaries, the contrast between the two triads is softer.

Tetrads

Another color relationship is based on a square rather than an equilateral triangle. Known as a **color tetrad**, this system is formed when four colors are used in the organization. They are equally spaced around the color wheel and contain a primary, its complement, and a complementary pair of intermediates (fig. 7.19; see also fig. 7.16E). A tetrad has also come to mean, in a less strict sense, any organization of color forming a "rectangular structure" that could include a double split-complement. This system of color harmony is potentially more varied than the triad because of the additional

colors present, depending on which colors are selected for use and in what proportions. Avoiding the temptation to use all the colors in equal volumes will add interest.

Analogous and Monochromatic Colors

Analogous colors are those that appear next to each other on the color wheel. They have the shortest interval and therefore an extremely harmonious relationship, because three or four neighboring hues always contain one common color that dominates the group (fig. 7.20, see also fig. 7.16 B). Analogous colors not only are found at the spectrum intensity levels (the outermost ring of the color wheel) but may also include the variety of colors made by neutralization (intensity changes) and

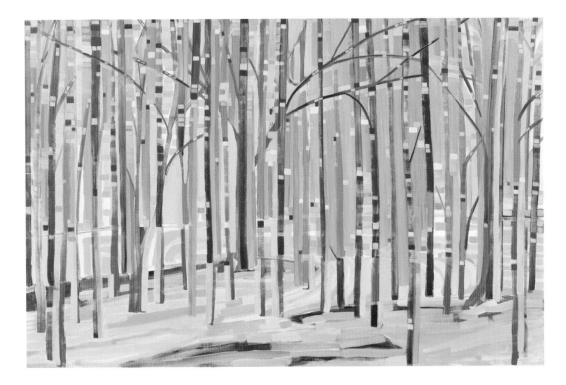

7.21 Benjamin Butler, *In the Forest*, 2005. Oil on canvas, 48 × 72 in. In this work, Benjamin Butler has created a composition using analogous colors, featuring yellow-greens, greens, and blue-greens. For greater variety, he has added complementary colors in the form of browns (low-key oranges), pinks, and red-violets. Courtesy of the artist.

value changes of any of these related hues (fig. 7.21).

On the other hand, **monochromatic** color schemes use only one hue but explore the complete range of tints (value levels to white) and shades (value levels to black) for that hue (see figs. 7.33 and 7.16A). Even with thousands of variations of tints and shades of one hue, this scheme is also potentially the most monotonous. Nonetheless, monochromatic studies are a useful test of the artist's understanding of a given hue's value range.

Warm and Cool Colors

Color "temperature" is another way to organize color schemes. All of the colors can be classified into one of two groups: "warm" colors or "cool" colors. Red, orange, and yellow are associated with the sun or fire and thus are considered warm (see fig. 7.16H). Any colors containing blue (such as green, violet, and blue-green) are associated with air, sky,

plants, and water; these are called cool (see fig. 7.16I). This quality of warmth or coolness in a color may be affected or even changed by the hues around or near it. For example, the coolness of blue, like its intensity, may be heightened by locating it near a touch of its complement, orange.

Tertiary colors can also have a sense of color temperature based on their tonality. Brown, earthy tones generally feel warm, while olives are cool. In addition, artists working with neutral grays can introduce a hint of warmth or coolness to the grays in order to extend the palette; the gray changes from achromatic to chromatic, creating a subtle increase in variety and interest (see fig. 5.4).

Plastic Colors

Colors may also be organized according to their ability to create compositional depth. Artists are able to create the illusion of an object's volume or flatten an area using color. This ability to model

a shape comes from the advancing and receding characteristics of certain colors. For example, a spot of red on a gray surface seems to be in front of that surface; a spot of blue, similarly placed, seems to sink back into the surface. In general, warm colors advance, and cool colors recede (fig. 7.22). The character of such effects, however, can be altered by differences in the value and/or intensity of the color.

These spatial characteristics of color were fully developed by the French artist Paul Cézanne in the late nineteenth century. He admired the sparkling, brilliant color of the Impressionist artists of the period but thought their work had lost the solidity of earlier painting. Consequently, he began to experiment with expressing the bulk and weight of forms by modeling with color.

Before Cézanne's experiments, the traditional **academic** artist had modeled form using a technique known as *grisaille*, or *dead painting*. With this technique, the object was first painted in

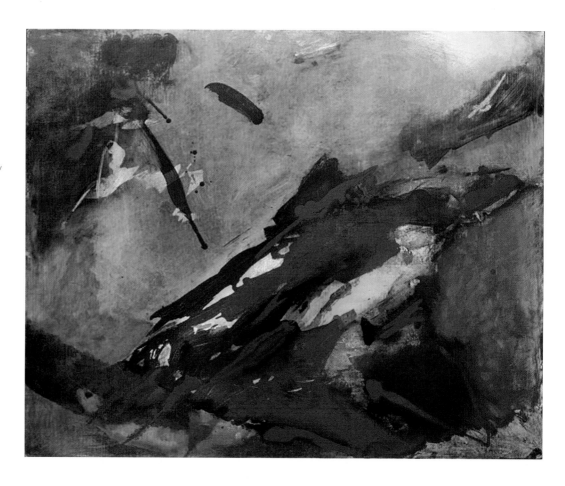

differing neutral values and later over-glazed with a thin layer of the object's local (natural) color. Cézanne, however, discovered that a change of hue on a form could serve the purpose of a change of value, while imparting new effectiveness of expression. He modeled the form by placing warm color on the part of the subject that was to advance and adding cool color where the surface receded (fig. 7.23). Cézanne felt that this rich color and its textural application expressed the actual structure of a solid object. Later, modern artists realized that Cézanne's advancing and receding colors could also create those backward and forward movements in space that give liveliness and interest to the picture surface (see fig. 7.30). However, this is only a tool, and there is no single correct way to employ it.

Paul Gauguin, for example, often applied the same principles *in reverse* to flatten the spatial qualities in a pictorial organization. By placing cool colors in the foreground, he made it appear to recede. By painting the background in warm colors, he caused it to advance. This combination flattened the pictorial space, making it more decorative than plastic (fig. 7.24). Likewise, abstract artists use the relationships of balance, movement, and space, giving content to a painting although no actual objects are represented (fig. 7.25). Line, value, shape, and texture are greatly aided by the ability of color to create space and meaning.

Simultaneous Contrast

While trying to match colors, an artist may mix a color on a palette only

to find that it appears entirely different when juxtaposed with other colors on the canvas. Why does a red-violet appear to change color when placed beside a violet? During the early nineteenth century, a French chemist, M. E. Chevreul, wanted to discover why the Gobelin tapestry works was receiving complaints about the color stability of certain blues, browns, light violets, and blacks. As director of tints and dyes, Chevreul discovered that the problem was not a question of the dyestuffs but rather a phenomenon of color contrast. The appearance of these colors varied depending on which color they were placed beside.

These discoveries were the starting point for the *Law of Simultaneous Contrast of Colors*, published in 1839. With this publication, Chevreul became the

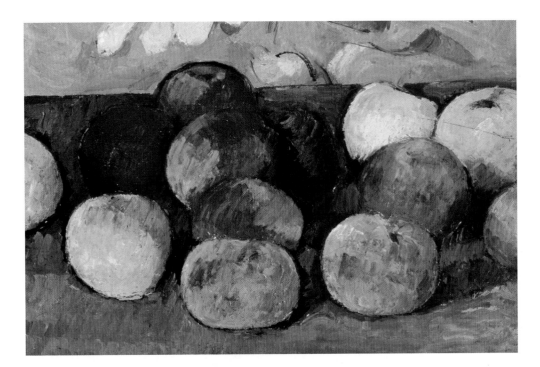

7.23 Paul Cézanne, *Apples and Biscuits,* c. 1879–1882. Oil on canvas, 46 × 55 cm. Cézanne used block-like brushstrokes and change of color as a means of creating volume and modeling form. Rather than merely indicating an adjustment in value, warm colors made the apples come forward while blended cooler tones forced their outer edges to recede. In addition, warm browns were used to pull the table front forward while cool blues made the background recede. Musée de l'Orangerie, Paris, France/Lauros-Giraudon, Paris/SuperStock.

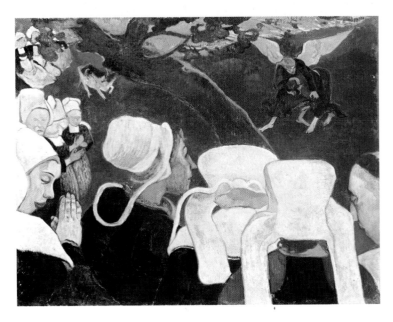

7.24 Paul Gauguin, *Vision after the Sermon (Jacob Wrestling with the Angel),* 1888. Oil on canvas, 28¾ × 36½ in. (73 × 92 cm). Gauguin has used the nature of plastic color to reverse a normal spatial order. Instead of items in the foreground advancing toward the viewer and objects in the background receding to create a deep illusionistic space, he made the pictorial space shallow. Cool blues and blue-blacks pushed the foreground figures back, while warm reds and oranges pulled the background forward, flattening the space within the image. National Gallery of Scotland, Edinburgh, Scotland/SuperStock.

"technical prophet" of two schools of painting that followed—Impressionism and Post-Impressionism. Both groups of painters often juxtaposed complements that increased the intensity of each other through simultaneous contrast. Another early student of these principles, Eugène Delacroix, once said, "Give me mud and I will make the skin of a Venus out of it, if you will allow me to surround it as I please."

The effect of one color on another is explained by the rule of **simultaneous contrast.** According to this rule, whenever two different colors come into direct contact, their similarities seem to decrease, and their dissimilarities seem to increase. In short, contrast intensifies the difference between colors. This effect is most extreme, of course, when the colors are directly contrasting in hue, but it occurs even if the colors have some degree of relationship. For example, a yellow-green surrounded by green appears more yellow, but if surrounded by yellow it seems more green. The contrast can be in the characteristics of intensity and value as well as in hue. A grayed blue looks brighter if placed against a gray background and will tend to make the gray take on an orange cast; however, the same grayed blue looks even grayer or more neutralized against a bright blue background. The most striking effect occurs when complementary hues are juxtaposed: blue is brightest when seen next to orange, and green is brightest when seen next to red. When a warm color is seen in simultaneous contrast with a cool color, the warm hue appears warmer and the cool color cooler. A color always tends to bring out its complement in a neighboring color. If a green rug is placed against a white wall, the eye may make the white take on a very light red or warm cast. A touch of green in the white may be necessary to counteract this. When a neutral gray made of two complementary colors is placed next to a strong intense color, it tends to take on a hue that is opposite the intense color. When a person wears a certain color of clothing, the complementary color in that person's complexion is emphasized.

Some of these conditions of imposed "color" may be explained by the theory that the eye (and mind) seeks a state of balanced involvement with the three light primaries. More than a psychological factor, this seems to be a physiological function of the eyes' receptors and their ability to receive the three light primaries—some combination of all three is involved in most mixed colors. As our eyes flash unceasingly about our field of vision, all the light primaries are experienced, and the corresponding receptors are repeatedly activated. The mind seems to function with less stress when all three receptor systems are involved concurrently (although not necessarily in equal proportions). If one or more primaries are continually missing, the eye seems to try to replace the missing color or colors because of receptor fatigue. For example, if we stare at a spot of intense

7.25 Mark Rothko, *Number 10*, 1950. Oil on canvas, 7 ft. 6⅜ in. × 4 ft. 9⅛ in. (2.30 × 1.45 m). Using apparently simple masses of color on a large scale, the artist is able to evoke emotional sensations in the observer. Rothko was one of the American artists who worked in the pure abstract idiom. © 1998 Kate Rothko Prizel & Christopher Rothko/Artists Rights Society (ARS), New York. The Museum of Modern Art, New York, NY. U.S.A. Gift of Philip Johnson. Digital image © The Museum of Modern Art/Licensed by SCALA/Art Resource, NY.

red for several seconds and then shift our eyes to a white area, we see an afterimage of the same spot in green, its complement. The phenomenon can be noted with any pair of complementary colors (fig. 7.26).

Although we seem to desire the three primaries visually, our optic function may get overstimulated under certain conditions. Large volumes of clashing full-intensity complements can make us uneasy (see fig. T.77). Museum guards at an Op Art show were said to

have asked for reassignment, complaining of visual problems ranging from headaches to blurred focus.

The condition of balanced stimulation of the color receptors is much easier to experience when the three primaries are physically mixed together. The colors produced are less saturated or intense and seem easier to experience physically. This would explain why tertiary colors—neutralized sometimes nearly to the loss of hue—are thought of as being more

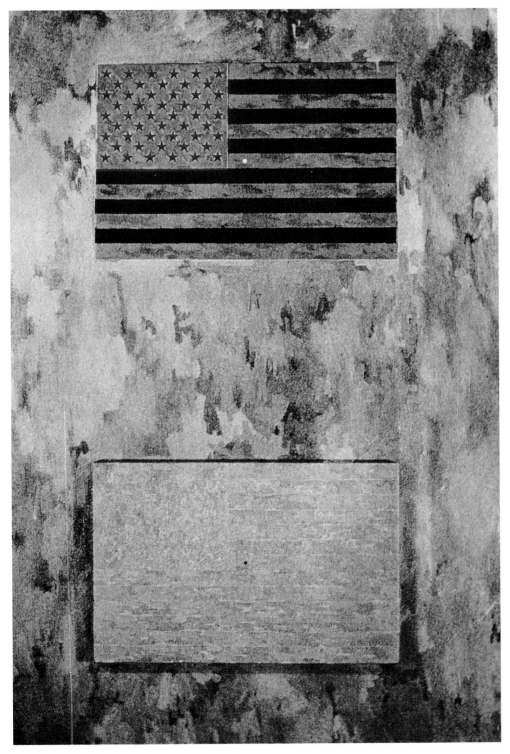

relaxing. Hues such as blues and greens seem to be easier on the eye and mind when lightened with white; white would add more wavelengths to the reflected light and thus stimulate additional combinations of receptors. Hues that have been muted, neutralized, or lightened in value will appear to recede compared to their most saturated or intense states. Intense blue walls will make a room appear smaller than a very light tint of the same blue.

Try some experiments to see the principles of simultaneous contrast in practice. See if the same color placed in the center of two related colors can be made to appear as two different hues, however subtle or different. Further, try making two subtle variations in color appear to be the same by changing their surrounding colors. Investigate the eye's battle to focus or find edges when adjoining shapes or areas are closely related in value level or intensity and become difficult to see. Black lines will give greater clarity to the image but may also tend to flatten the areas. This may also work for "pulsating" edges that occur when the eye has the greatest struggle for edge definition—when complements are placed together. Greater contrast in value or intensity levels will also help with the visual problem of edge resolution or separation of image.

All these changes in appearance make us realize that no one color can be experienced in isolation, but each must be considered in relation to the other colors present. For this reason, many artists find it easier to develop a color composition globally rather than try to finish one area completely before going on to another.

Color and Emotion

Color may also be organized or employed according to its ability to create mood, symbolize ideas, and express emotions. Color, as found on the canvas, can express a mood or feeling

7.26 Jasper Johns, *Flags*, 1965. Oil on canvas with raised canvas, 6 × 4 ft. (1.83 × 1.22 m). With this painting, Johns wanted the viewer to experience an afterimage. This occurs when the retina's receptors are overstimulated and are unable to accept additional signals. They then project the wavelengths of the complementary colors. Stare at the white dot on the upper flag for forty seconds. Then shift your focus to the dark dot on the lower flag, and you will see an afterimage in red, white, and blue. © Jasper Johns/Licensed by VAGA, New York, NY.

in its own right, even though it may not be descriptive of the objects represented. Reds are often thought of as being cheerful and exciting, whereas blues can impart dignity, sadness, or serenity. Also, different values and intensities in a color range affect emotional impact. A wide value range (strongly contrasting light or dark hues) gives vitality and directness to a color scheme; closely related values and low intensities create feelings of subtlety, calmness, and repose (figs. 7.27 and 7.28).

Colors can evoke emotions that are personal and reinforced by everyday experiences. For example, some yellows look acidic and bitter, almost forcing a pucker like a sour lemon. Other colors carry with them cultural associations. Our speech is full of phrases that associate abstract qualities like virtue, loyalty, and evil with color: "true blue," "dirty yellow coward," "red with rage," "seeing red," "virgin white," "green with envy," and "gray gloom." In some cases, these feelings seem to be universal because they are based on shared experiences. Every culture understands the danger of fire (reds) and the great vastness, mystery, and consistency of the heavens and the seas (blues). Blues can imply reliability, fidelity, loyalty, and honesty, while reds suggest danger, bravery, sin, passion, or violent death. However, not all color has the same meaning in every culture. On pre-Columbian artifacts, priest-kings are shown in self-bloodletting rituals, and victims are sacrificed to the sun, with red symbolizing renewal and rebirth by allowing the life of the sun to continue. For other cultures, green rather than red is the sign of regeneration, hope, and life. Numerous color associations can be traced back historically. For example, purple has signified royalty since the ancient Greek and Roman civilizations, because only the royalty could afford the expense of extracting a purple dye from 10,000 tiny shellfish—

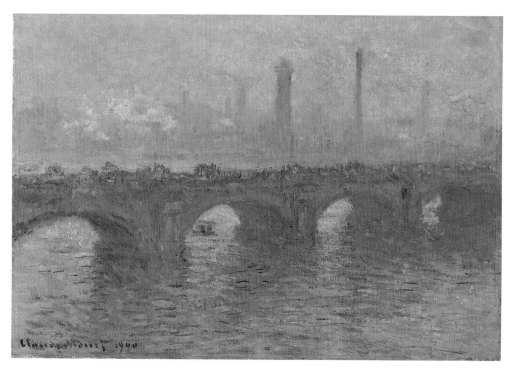

7.27 Claude Monet, *Waterloo Bridge, Grey Weather*, 1900. Oil on canvas, 65.4 × 92.4 cm. The Impressionist Monet painted almost 100 views of the Waterloo Bridge during three trips to London. Painting the view from his room in the Savoy Hotel, he studied the characteristics of light at different times of the day and in differing weather conditions. As a result, the hues, values, and intensities are markedly affected, as we can see by comparing this painting with figure 7.28.

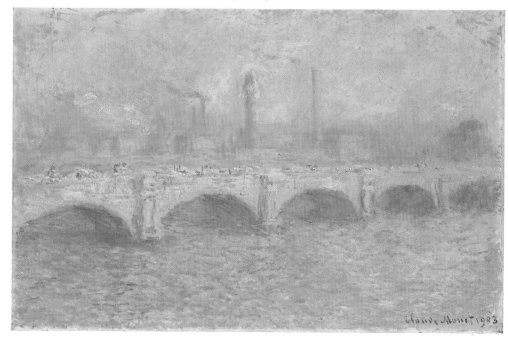

7.28 Claude Monet, *Waterloo Bridge, Sunlight Effect*, 1903. Oil on canvas, 65.7 × 101 cm. In giving the impression of a passing moment, the artist has deliberately sacrificed detailed architectural information for the effect of sunlight, color, and atmosphere playing on that form. This also applies to figure 7.27.

which is what was required to produce a gram of color. However, even when dye became more affordable, the tradition (and the significance) remained. In China, ancient potters created very unusual glazes for their ware. Among the glazes was a very deep copper red that was so beautiful that the very best ware in every kilnload was immediately carried away to the emperor himself.

Psychological Application of Color

Research has shown that light, bright colors make us feel joyful and uplifted; warm colors are generally stimulating; cool colors are calming; and cool, dark, or somber colors are generally depressing. Medical facilities, trauma centers, and state correctional facilities are often painted in light blues or "institutional greens" because of these colors' calming effect. Winter skiing lodges are adorned in warm yellows, knotty pine, oranges, and browns to welcome those coming in from subzero temperatures. Stories abound of the use of motivating color and sports programs. One visiting team was furious and refused to use the assigned locker room because the powder-puff pink walls implied they were sissies. In another incident, the home team's locker room was painted bright red to keep the players keyed up and on edge during halftime, while light blue surroundings in the visitors' locker room encouraged the opponents to let down and relax. It has been shown in some work situations that bright, intense colors encourage worker productivity, whereas neutralized or lighter hues slow down the workforce.

We are continually exposed to the application of color's emotive power. In a supermarket, the meat section is sparkling white to assure us of its cleanliness and purity. To encourage us to purchase the products, the best steaks are

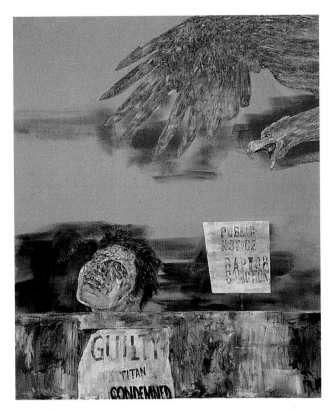

7.29 Leon Golub, *Prometheus II*, 1998. Acrylic on linen, 119 × 97 in. (302.3 × 246.4 cm). Leon Golub often dealt with psychological color, expressing personal issues through metaphors. A bloody red announces the daily vulture attack, while deep gloomy colors remind us of death and pain. Prometheus, a Titan, was chained to a rock by the Greek god Zeus for stealing fire from Mount Olympus. © Estate of Leon Golub/Licensed by VAGA, New York, NY. Courtesy Ronald Feldman Fine Arts.

garnished with parsley or green plastic trim to make them appear redder and more irresistible. Bright yellow and orange cereal boxes use contrasting lettering (often complementary) to scream for our attention. Extremely small spaces are rarely painted in dark or bright warm colors, which would make them feel even smaller. Instead, the space is made to appear larger by light cool colors.

With artists, an angry exchange, a love letter, a near miss in traffic may all subconsciously influence a choice of color. The power of color to symbolize ideas becomes a tool. It enriches the metaphor and makes the work stronger in content and meaning. Many artists have evolved a personal color style that comes primar-

ily from their feelings about their subjects rather than being purely descriptive. John Marin's color is essentially suggestive, with little concern for naturalistic form or solidity (see fig. 8.44). Frequently delicate and light in tone, his colors are in keeping with the medium in which he worked (watercolor). The color in the paintings of Vincent van Gogh is often vivid, hot, intense, and applied in snakelike ribbons of pigment. His uses of texture and color express the intensely personal style of his work (see figs. 1.15 and 1.19). In the work of Leon Golub, color becomes a personal symbol. Anything but delicate and saccharin, Golub's color sets a gloomy mood and helps express his feelings about the inevitability of pain, aging, indignity, and

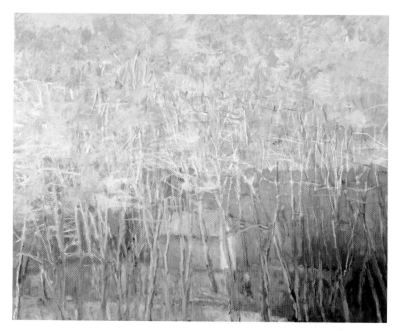

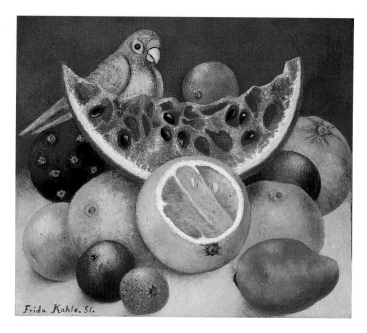

7.30 Wolf Kahn, *Web of Trees*, 2003. Oil on canvas, 64 × 78 in. (162.6 × 198.1 cm). Wolf Kahn is one contemporary painter who uses his subject—landscape—to express a personal joy found in color. The vibrant, even risky use of color structure is a hallmark of his later work, making it instantly recognizable. Courtesy of Ameringer & Yohe Fine Art. Art © Wolf Kahn/Licensed by VAGA, New York, NY.

7.31 Frida Kahlo, *Still Life with Parrot*, 1951. Oil on masonite, 9½ × 10¼ in. (24.1 × 26 cm). This still life is painted in local color—color that simulates the hues of the objects in nature. Art Collection, Harry Ransom Humanities Research Center, University of Texas at Austin. Reproduction authorized by National Institute of Fine Art and Literature of México and Banco de México. © 2008 Banco de México Diego Rivera & Frida Kahlo Museums Trust. Av. Cinco de Mayo No. 2, Col. Centro, Del. Cuauhtémoc 06059, México, D.F.

death (fig. 7.29). An emotional approach to color appealed particularly to the Expressionist painters, who used it to create entirely subjective treatment having nothing to do with objective reality (see fig. T.56). Contemporary artists like Wolf Kahn continue to interpret their environment in terms of personal color selection (fig. 7.30).

Even filmmakers recognize the power of color and use it to change the feel and impact of their work; movies are dramatically affected by using specific colorization or altering the color tonality of the scenes. For example, in the film *O Brother, Where Art Thou?* (released in 2000), the colors were digitally altered—some more neutralized than others—so that sepia tones transmit the feeling of the Dust Bowl era. In *Pitch Black* (2000), many scenes consist only of shades of blue to indicate the overex-

posure of sunlight on an alien planet. In the film *300* (2006), the majority of colors are neutralized, but a select few—like the scarlet robes or yellow embers—are made more intense for dramatic effect. From these numerous examples, it is clear that we cannot avoid the emotional effects of color—they impact our senses directly as a psychological and physiological function of sight itself.

THE ROLE OF COLOR IN COMPOSITION

When painting was seen as a purely illustrative art, the description of appearances was considered color's most important function. Thus, for a long period in the history of Western art, color was seen as arising from the

object being represented. In painting, color used to indicate the natural appearance of an object is known as **local (objective) color** (fig. 7.31; see also fig. 6.1). Yet a much different (if not more) expressive quality is achieved when the artist depicts objects in colors other than their local color. When an entirely **subjective color** treatment is substituted for local color, the colors used and their relationships are invented by the artists for purposes other than mere representation (fig. 7.32; see also figs. 7.30 and 7.41). This style of treatment may even deny color as an objective reality; that is, we may have blue cows, green faces, or purple trees. When colors are subjectively applied, as in much contemporary art, an understanding of their use becomes critical to an understanding of their meaning.

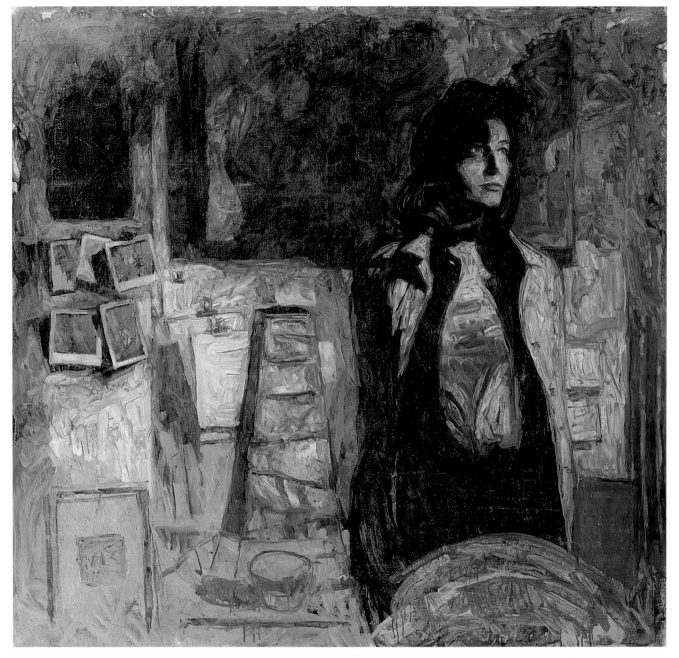

7.32 Gilles Marrey, *1997*, 1998. Oil on canvas, 55 × 56 in. (140 × 142 cm). The subjective colors in this painting may not be as obviously invented as a "blue horse," but they effectively set up the mood and mystery within this painting. © Caldwell Snyder Gallery, NY.

Regardless of whether color is used objectively or subjectively, it serves several purposes in artistic composition. These purposes are not separate and distinct but instead frequently overlap and interrelate. As we have discussed throughout this chapter, color can be used in the following ways:

1. To give spatial quality to the pictorial field.
   a. Color can supplement, or even substitute for, value differences to give plastic quality.
   b. Color can create interest through the counterbalance of backward and forward movement in pictorial space.
2. To create mood and symbolize ideas.
3. To serve as a vehicle for expressing personal emotions and feelings.

4. To attract and direct attention as a means of giving organization to a composition.
5. To accomplish aesthetic appeal by a system of well-ordered color relationships.
6. To identify objects by describing the superficial facts of their appearance.

Color Balance

Whether an artist chooses to work with color combinations that are extremely bold (even offensive) or chooses colors that are subtler and more psychologically soothing, all effective color combinations have at their root the consideration of similarity and contrast. The unity of the composition relies on harmonious relationships between the various colors, but these relationships must also be made alive and interesting through variety. This basic problem is the same one encountered in all aspects of form organization: finding an appropriate sense of equilibrium between similarity and contrast.

Color combinations are brought into a harmonious relationship when they have properties in common, including hue, intensity, and value; the more they share, the more harmonious the relationships become. However, any attempt to harmonize the interaction of colors must be balanced by the need to keep the relationships interesting—at times, even exciting. This is accomplished through the introduction of *variety* in hue, value, or intensity—and the resulting contrasts those variations create. Therefore, successful interaction of color is a matter of balancing the need for harmony with the natural desire for variety. Of course, the degree that color relationships are brought into accord must be regulated according to the expressive needs of the concept being explored.

Color schemes that contain hues in close proximity on the color wheel

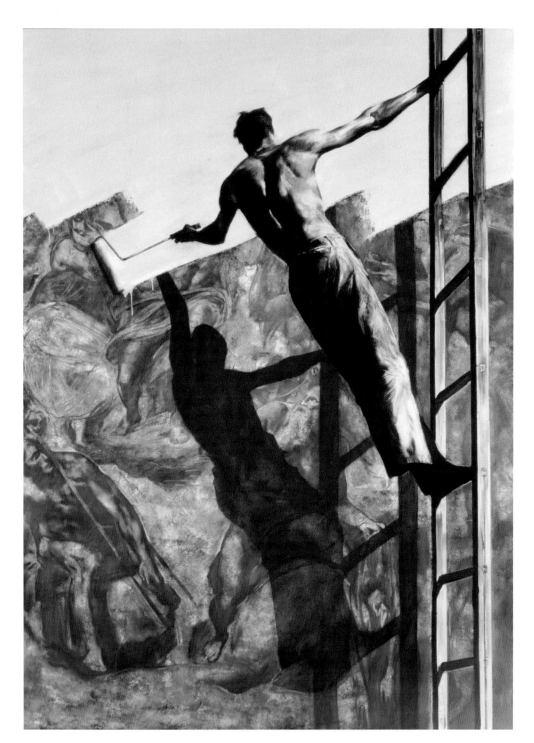

7.33 Mark Tansey, *Triumph over Mastery II*, 1987. Oil on canvas, 98 × 68 in. The harmony and serenity of Tansey's monochromatic palette is deceptive for the viewer. Only close inspection reveals its picture-within-a-picture structure. The figure in the image is rolling paint over Michelangelo's *Last Judgment*. © Mark Tansey.

(and closely related in wavelength frequency) tend to create harmonious compositions, while colors that are farther apart have stronger contrasts and create a color scheme with more variety. As a general rule, a monochromatic color scheme is the most harmonious, followed by analogous colors, tetrads,

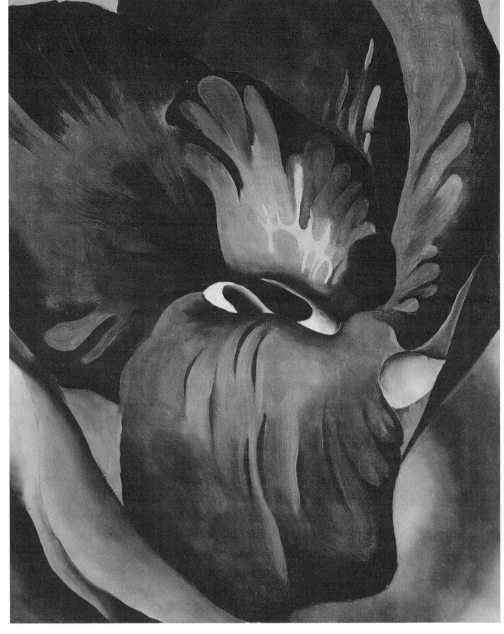

7.34 Georgia O'Keeffe, *Canna Red and Orange*, 1922. Oil on canvas, 10 × 16 in. (50.8 × 40.6 cm). Inspired by light, this Precisionist artist stripped away most features of reality to create her colorful, semiabstract images. Georgia O'Keeffe Museum, Santa Fe/Art Resource, NY. © 2008 The Georgia O'Keeffe Foundation/Artists Rights Society (ARS), New York.

of the colors used, as well as their location in the composition, affect the overall success of the color choices.

Color and Harmony

Let us look first at how to harmonize a composition through its color relationships. The pleasing quality of a color pattern frequently depends on the amount or proportion of color used, and in general, compositions in which one color or one kind of color predominates are more easily harmonized than color arrangements with equal amounts of different colors. A simple way to create harmony is to repeat a color in differing values and intensities while controlling its placement in different parts of the composition (figs. 7.33 and 7.34). These new areas will collectively contribute to an increase in volume of that hue and to the general harmonic tonality for the image.

Even when many varied colors are used in a composition, a single hue can be a harmonizing factor if a little of it is physically mixed with every color used in the composition (see fig. 7.15). This tends to lower the intensity of all the colors involved and give them a hint of the tonality of the shared hue. A similar effect can be created by glazing over a varicolored pattern with a single transparent color, which becomes the harmonizing hue.

Unified patterns may also be created by adjusting color temperature—so that all the colors of a composition are made to share a hint of warmth or coolness. However, there are often times when it is desirable to encourage color relatedness without sacrificing the range of hue. In these situations, diverse colors may be harmonized by bringing them all to a similar value level or making their intensity levels correspond (see figs. 5.4 and 7.30). As we can see in figure 7.35, Ellen Phelan applies this concept by adding a dark neutral to all the colors involved, which lowers their intensity and value. Not only does this

triads, split-complements, and finally, complementary colors, which offer the most variety and are least harmonious (see fig. 7.16).

However, any attempt to base the aesthetic appeal of color pattern purely on fixed theoretical color harmonies will probably not be very successful. Effective color combinations depend as much on how we *distribute* our colors as on the relationships among the hues themselves. The *amounts* or *proportions*

7.35 Ellen Phelan, *Peonies, Roses and Books,* 2004. Watercolor and gouache on paper, 27.5 × 20.8 in. (72.4 × 52.8 cm). In this composition, muted and dark colors hint at the developing floral shapes. These amorphous forms could have been brought into harmony by mixing dark neutrals with all of the colors involved. However, the artist accomplishes the same thing by applying dark color washes over the forms which effectively lowers their value and neutralizes their intensity. This creates an unusual and exciting low-key composition of suggested shape and color. © Ellen Phelan/ Artists Rights Society (ARS) New York.

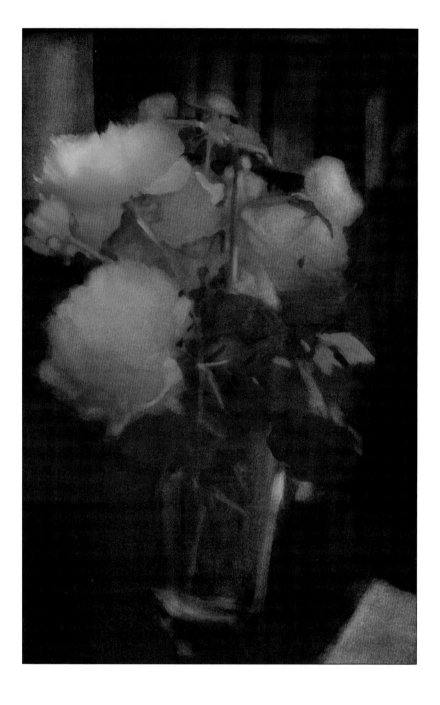

tie all the areas together, but it creates a low-key composition that aids in the development of amorphous shapes. Sharing a high or low key or sharing a similar loss of brilliance can make even unusual combinations have some degree of harmony relative to the amount of change involved.

Even complementary colors, which of course vie for our attention through simultaneous contrast, can be made more unified if one of them is softened or neutralized.

When color predominance is not enough to pull an organization together, the image can be made more harmonious by changing the character of the surrounding areas. In such cases, an image that is hard to visually understand or distinguish may become more readable, in addition to becoming more unified. In figure 7.36, Romare Bearden makes a whole series of diversely modeled and expressive images easier to

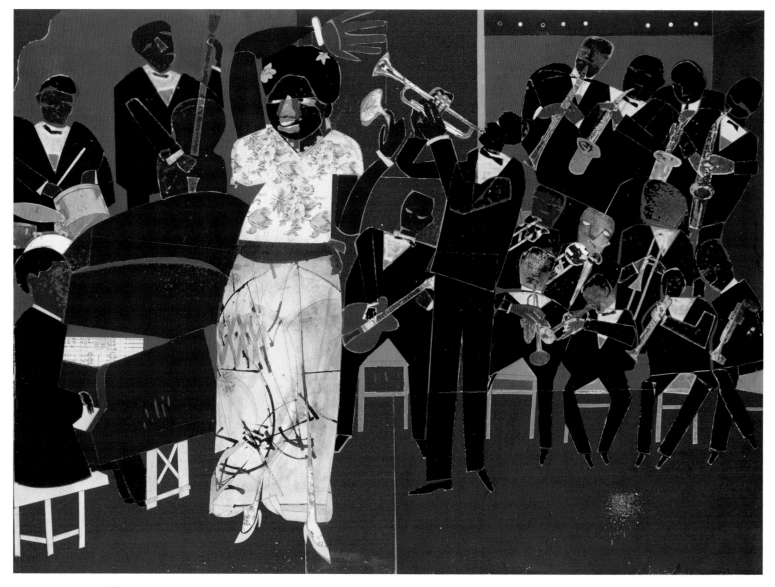

7.36 Romare Bearden, *Empress of the Blues,* 1974. Paper collage, **36 × 48 in.** Bearden has created figures that are very active in their complexity of shape and visual detail and made them readable by contrasting them against a very uncomplicated and decorative background of slightly neutralized color. Photo © Smithsonian American Art Museum, Washington, DC/Art Resource, NY © Romare Bearden Foundation/Licensed by VAGA, New York, NY.

recognize by introducing a very simple and decorative background.

Another commonly used method of relating colors of extreme contrasts is to separate all or part of the colors by a neutral line or area. Absolute black or white lines are the most effective neutrals for this purpose because they are so positive in character (have a strong presence) themselves. They not only tie together the contrasting hues but also enhance their color character because of value contrast (see fig. 7.15). Georges Rouault often found a black line effective in separating highly contrasting colors (fig. 7.37). The neutral black leading between the brilliant colors of stained-glass windows is another example of this unifying character. A similar unifying effect can be brought about by using a large area of neutral light gray or a neutralized color as a background to clashing contrasts of color (fig. 7.38).

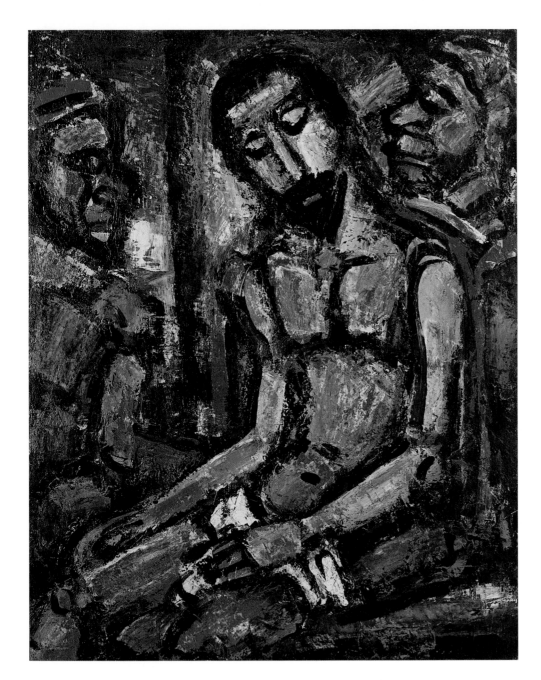

7.37 Georges Rouault, *Christ Mocked by Soldiers,* 1932. Oil on canvas, 36¼ × 28½ in. (92.1 × 72.4 cm). In this Expressionist contrast of clashing complements, the pattern is stabilized by heavy neutralizing lines of black, reminiscent of medieval stained glass. © 2008 Artists Rights Society (ARS), New York/ADGP, Paris. The Museum of Modern Art, New York, NY. U.S.A. Given anonymously. Digital image © The Museum of Modern Art/Licensed by SCALA/Art Resource, NY.

Color and Variety

In any color scheme, the basic problem is to create unified color relationships without destroying the general strength and intensity of expression found in their contrasts. There is often the danger that the composition may become too harmonious during the attempt to unify color—resulting in a level of visual monotony. In those situations, more va-riety can be introduced back into the work through greater contrasts in hue, value, or intensity. Sometimes this is a matter of simply reversing or softening some of the techniques that made the colors harmonize. In other words, if colors were related because of a close interval (as revealed on the color wheel), then creating a wider separation would introduce more variety and greater interest into the color organization (e.g., a scheme of red and red-violet could be changed to red and violet); in addition, colors related by lowered intensity or value levels could benefit from stronger contrasts of either or both. Selecting the widest array of hue, value, and intensity will imbue the relationships with even greater variety and interest.

Where the basic unity of a color pattern has already been established, strong contrasts of color hue, value, or

7.38 Joan Mitchell, *Untitled*, 1992. Oil on canvas, 110¼ × 78¾ in. (280 × 200 cm). Characterized by aggressive brushwork, Joan Mitchell's painting has a variety of highly contrasting colors and values: large areas of dark are balanced by even larger areas of light value; blues are countered by smaller oranges, green by pink, and yellowish white by touches of violet. Reference MITC–0436. Courtesy of the artist's estate and the Robert Miller Gallery.

intensity can be used as accents; the size of these accents, then, prevents them from disturbing the basic unity of the color theme. Small amounts of complementary color or neutrals of contrasting value can add subtle variety to the color pattern (fig. 7.39; see also fig. 4.14). Low-key or high-key compositions benefit greatly from such contrasting accents, which add interest to what might otherwise be a monotonous composition (see figs. 4.20 and 4.29).

Controlling the amount of contrasting color used also allows the area of interest to have more focus (fig. 7.40; see also fig. 7.23). A small dark spot of color, through its lower value, can draw more attention than the larger lighter area surrounding it. Likewise, a spot of intense color, though small, can often balance a larger amount of a grayer, more

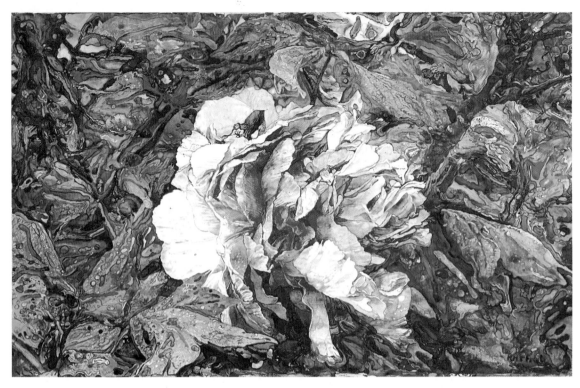

7.39 Joseph Raffael, *Spirit Like the Wind II,* 2007. Watercolor on paper, 43½ × 66½ in. (110.5 × 168.9 cm). Having established a color pattern of dark blues and greens against a lighter pink, the artist uses small accents of contrasting value and color to provide detail and enliven those areas. Private collection, Courtesy of Nancy Hoffman Gallery, New York.

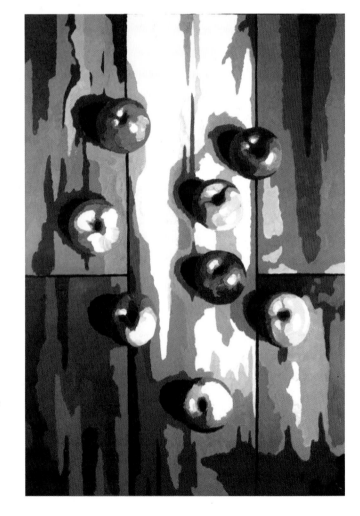

7.40 Norman Sunshine, *Equilibrium,* 2007. Oil on canvas, 72 × 48 in. (182.8 × 121.9 cm). This work is appropriately titled. Try covering any portion of the composition, and you will discover that it feels incomplete. Related in analogous tones (from red to violet to blue), the smaller contrasting areas of neutralized yellows and changes in value and hue keep the image interesting. © Norman Sunshine. Courtesy of Morrison Gallery.

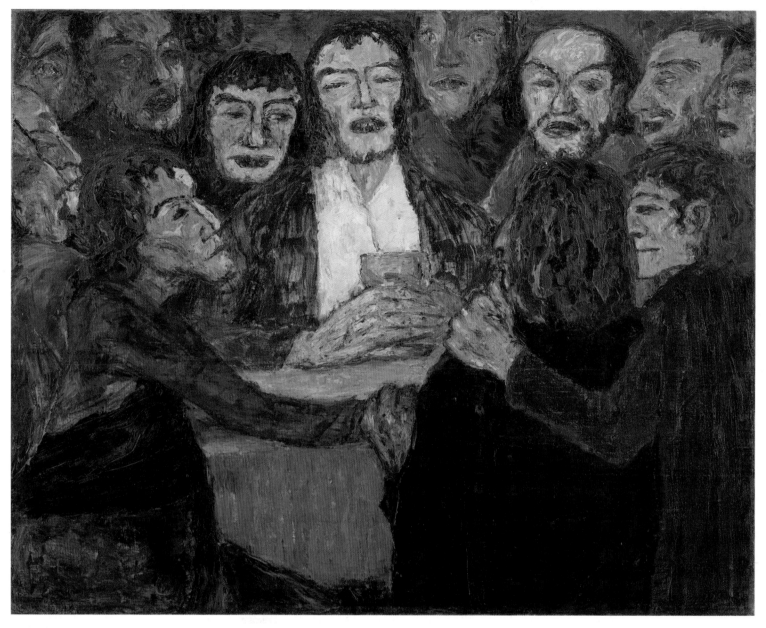

7.41 Emil Nolde, *The Last Supper*, 1909. Oil on canvas, 33⅞ × 42⅛ in. (86 × 107 cm). The Expressionists usually employed bold, clashing hues to emphasize their emotional identification with a subject. Intense feeling is created by the use of complementary and near-complementary hues. © Nolde Stiftung Seebüll, Courtesy of the Statens Museum for Kunst, Copenhagen.

neutralized color (see fig. 7.32). In addition, a small amount of warm color usually dominates a larger amount of cool color, although both may be of the same intensity (see figs. 7.22 and 7.24). If all of the areas in a composition were made equally important, however, it would be difficult to find a spot on which to fix our attention; this would probably create a rather chaotic viewing experience.

Finally, we should remember that artists frequently produce color combinations that defy these guiding principles but are still satisfying to the eye. Artists use color as they do the other elements of art structure—to give highly personalized meaning to the subjects of their work. We must realize that there can be brutal color combinations as well as refined ones. The more extreme or

turbulent combinations are appropriate if they accomplish the artist's purpose of exciting us rather than calming us. Some of the German Expressionist painters have proven that these clashing color schemes can have definite aesthetic value when used purposefully (fig. 7.41). There are no exact rules for arriving at pleasing effects in color relationships—only the guiding principles that we have discussed. With this foundation, every artist must build his or her own language of color as it is used in dynamic interaction in each work.

THE EVOLUTION OF THE COLOR WHEEL

In this book, the circular arrangement of the twelve-step color wheel is based on a subtractive system of artist-pigmented colors that uses red, yellow, and blue as primaries. This triadic primary system has evolved over many centuries. With the growth of ideas and technology, additional systems of color organization have developed along the way.

The Origins of Color Systems

Sir Isaac Newton investigated the physical nature of color around 1660. Having separated color into the spectrum—red on top and violet on the bottom—he was the first to conceive of it as a color wheel. Ingeniously, he twisted what was a straight-line spectrum, joined the ends, and inserted purple, a color leaning to red-violet and not found in the spectrum. This red-violet he saw as a transition between violet and red. Newton's wheel contained seven colors, which he related to the seven known planets and the seven notes of the diatonic scale in music (the standard major scale without chromatic half steps)—red corresponding to note C, orange to D, yellow to E, green to F, blue to G, indigo to A, and violet to B.

The Discovery of Pigment Primaries

Around 1731, J. C. Le Blon recognized the primary characteristic of the pigments of red, yellow, and blue and their ability to create orange, green, and vio-

let. To this day, his discovery remains the basis of pigment color theory.

The First Triadic Color Wheel

The first wheel in full color and based on the three-primary system (for pigments) was published around 1766. It appeared in a book titled *The Natural System of Colours* by Moses Harris, an English engraver. In the first decade of the nineteenth century, Johann Wolfgang von Goethe began placing the colors, with their triangular arrangements, around a circle. In addition, Philipp Otto Runge created the first color solid (a three-dimensional color organization) by exploring tints, tones, and shades of color.

In the United States, many educators advanced the red, yellow, and blue primary color wheels. Most noted among them was Louis Prang, who published *The Theory of Color* in 1876. Modern-day scholars like Johannes Itten, Faber Birren, and Joseph Albers have done much to explore the relationship between color and expression. Their research has also clarified the historical development of the triadic color system and how colors interact, each affecting the perception of the other.

The Discovery of Light Primaries

The discovery of red, green, and blue light primaries (see fig. 7.2) was actually discovered around 1790, paralleling early developments with pigment. These concepts of light were explored by scientists Hermann von Helmholtz of Germany and James Clerk Maxwell of Great Britain. Some additive-light primary systems have been represented as circles, but they should not be confused with color systems designed for artists' pigment.

The Ostwald Color System

A distinguished German chemist and physicist, Wilhelm Ostwald, developed a color system around 1916 related to psychological harmony and order. Created from pigment hues technically available at the time, it used red, yellow, sea green, and blue, with the secondaries of orange, purple, turquoise, and leaf green. The colors were placed in a circle and expanded by mixing neighboring colors into a twenty-four-hue system—capable of further expansion. Complements were placed opposite each other—blue opposite yellow, for example. Strict rules for standardizing colors for industrial application were used. A three-dimensional model placed each color on the apex of a triangle and black and white on the other two points. The color harmonies were based on mathematical relationships that doubled the tonal color change at each step from white to black, providing an even progression in the steps. This system concentrated on value changes, with intensity being controlled by and limited to the initial point of the triangle. The system was never fully adopted for industrial application.

The Munsell Color System

Around 1936, the American artist Albert Munsell formulated a system to show the relationships between different color tints and shades based on hue, value, and intensity. This system was an attempt to give names to the many varieties of hues that result from mixing different colors with each other or with the neutrals. American industry adopted the Munsell system in 1943 as its material standard for naming different colors. The system was also adopted by the United States Bureau of Standards in Washington, DC.

In the Munsell system, the five basic hues on the color wheel are red, yellow,

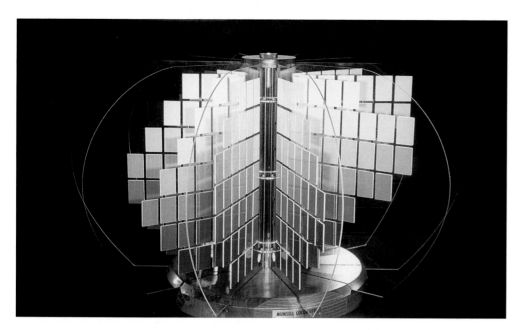

7.42 Munsell color tree, 1972. Clear plastic chart 10½ × 12 in. (26.7 × 30.5 cm), base size 12 in. (30.5 cm) diameter, center pole size 12⅝ in. (32.1 cm) high, chip size ¾ × 1⅜ in. (1.9 × 3.5 cm). The Munsell system in three dimensions. The greatest intensity of each hue is found in the color vane farthest from the center trunk. The value of each vane changes as it moves up and down the tree. The center trunk changes only from light to dark. The colors change in hue as they move around the tree. Courtesy of X-Rite, Incorporated and GretagMacbeth AG/LLC USA.

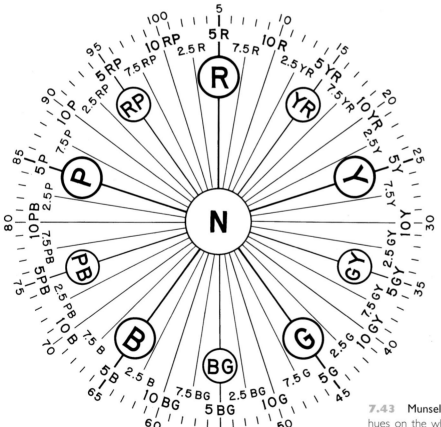

green, blue, and purple (violet). The mixture of any two adjacent colors on this color wheel is called an *intermediate color*. For example, the mixture of red and yellow is the intermediate color yellow-red. The other intermediate hues are green-yellow, blue-green, purple-blue, and red-purple.

To clarify color relationships, Munsell devised a three-dimensional color system that classifies the different shades or variations of colors according to the qualities of hue, value, and intensity (or chroma). His system is in the form of a tree. The many different-color tones are adhered to transparent plastic vanes that extend from a central trunk like tree branches. The column nearest the center trunk shows a scale of neutral tones that begin with black at the bottom and rise through grays to white at the top. The color tone at the outer limit of each branch represents the most intense hue possible at each level of value (fig. 7.42).

The most important part of the Munsell color system is the color notation, which describes a color in terms of a letter and numeral formula. The hue is indicated by the notation found on the inner circle of the color wheel, shown in figure 7.43. The value of the colors is indicated by the numbers on the central trunk. The intensity, or chroma, is shown by the numbers on the vanes that radiate from the trunk. These value and intensity relationships are expressed by fractions, with the number on top representing the value and the number on the bottom indicating the intensity (chroma). For example, *5Y 8/12* is the notation for a bright yellow.

It is interesting to compare the Munsell color wheel with the triadic color wheel used in this book (see figs. 7.7 and 7.43). Munsell places blue opposite

7.43 Munsell color wheel. This diagram shows the relationships of the hues on the wheel in terms of a specific type of notation (as explained in the text). Courtesy of X-Rite, Incorporated and GretagMacbeth AG/LLC USA.

yellow-red and red opposite blue-green, whereas we place blue opposite orange and red opposite green.

The Process Color System (Four-Color Printing Process)

We have already discussed how we experience color by reflected light. A colored object reflects only the wavelengths of that color while absorbing all others (see the section "Subtractive Color"). By taking the reflected wavelengths and passing them through specific camera filters, photographers and printers have learned how to isolate and photograph individual wavelengths.

When light passes through a sheet of clear glass, all the color wavelengths pass through. However, when a red-colored glass is used, only the wavelengths of red are allowed to pass; all other wavelengths are absorbed and essentially blocked from going any farther. The absorbed wavelengths equal red's opposite, or the additive (light) complement of red, which is cyan (see fig 7.2).

Thus, a red glass camera filter blocks all exposure on black-and-white film except for the shades of red that pass through the filter, which are recorded on the negative as gray to black shapes. The wavelengths blocked by the filter (which equal red's complement, cyan) are also recorded on the negative, but as transparent areas.

When a photosensitive printing plate is exposed through the negative film, the transparent areas allow exposure of the plate, making it printable—and revealing the various values of cyan. Where the negative is opaque black (from recording the red wavelengths), the unexposed printing plate remains white and unprintable. In this manner, a red filter produces a printing plate for its complement—cyan.

When this process is completed using a green filter, a printing plate for the value levels of magenta is created.

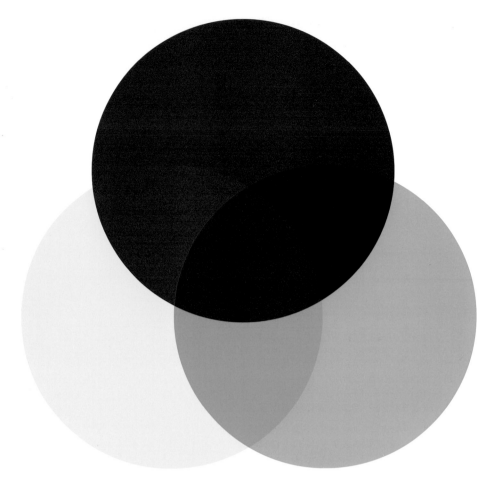

7.44 The primary colors of the process-printing system include yellow, cyan, and magenta. Where they are mixed, they produce red, blue (a color named by industry and scientists that is actually closer to violet), and green. When all three are combined, they produce "black." Notice that the process-printing primaries are the additive secondary colors and that the process-printing secondary colors are the additive primary colors.

Similarly, photographing through a filter named "blue"—actually on the violet side—produces a plate for printing the value ranges of yellow.

Using these techniques, printers and photographers have created a special color organization in which magenta, yellow, and cyan serve as the primary colors (fig. 7.44). Notice that these primaries are the secondary colors in the additive (light) system (illustrated in figure 7.2), and they aren't the primary colors of red, yellow, and blue familiar to the studio artist (illustrated in fig. 7.5). In the process color system for printing, red is a mixed color!

When the printing plates for magenta, yellow, and cyan are printed together, all the colors and value ranges possible may be created (fig. 7.45). Where the magenta and yellow overlap, red is created as a secondary color; where the magenta is decreased and the yellow increased, the color swings more toward orange; and so on, depending on the adjustment of the two colors. Similarly, the other secondary colors are created by overprinting the remaining primaries: cyan plus magenta produces blue, and cyan plus yellow produces green. Overprinting all three primaries (cyan, magenta, and yellow) creates something close to black, but that is usually heightened by printing a fourth plate in black to add definition (fig. 7.45D–F).

With this four-color printing process, the printing industry has made great advances in color reproduction. Of course, several techniques came together to make this process possible:

1. Monochrome photography provided images in black, white, and a full value range of unbroken grays.
2. Halftoning was invented, which allowed all the shades of gray to be printed with only one shade of ink—black—on white paper. With this technique, the gray areas of an image were translated into networks of tiny black-and-white dots of differing sizes and spacing for different values. It then became much easier for the printing industry to commercially reproduce the range of gray values found in the photograph.
3. After it was discovered that an image could be photographed through colored filters, halftoning was incorporated to create a printing plate with the proper range of value for each of the primaries—magenta, yellow, and cyan. The layering and juxtaposition of these tiny dots optically creates the thousands of colors and values possible. Our eyes just blend the dots together to see a complete image with smooth transitions and continuous color (see fig. 7.45 E and F).

Quite clearly, artists who work with dyes, color printing for photography, transparent inks, and the printing industry will all need to become very familiar with the process color system and its primaries of magenta, yellow, and cyan.

Color Photography

Color photographers also use magenta, cyan, and yellow. Instead of artists' pigment, they develop color using dyes and gelatin emulsions. Colored film contains three layers of emulsion that respond to the light primaries of blue,

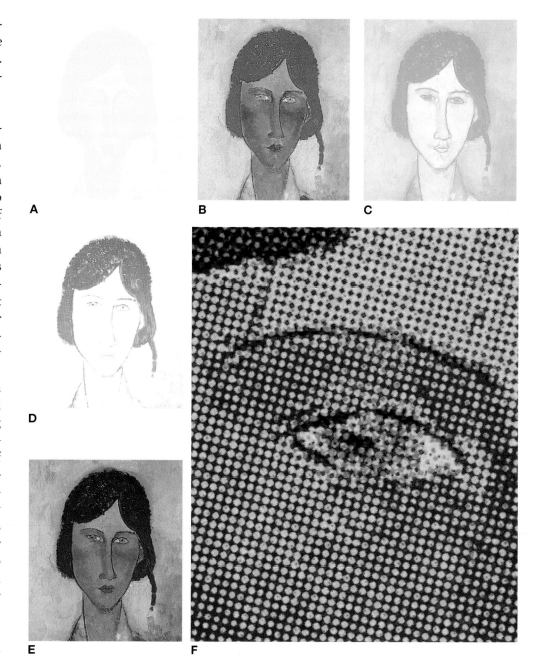

7.45 These illustrations show the yellow (A), magenta (B), cyan (C), and black (D) printing plates used in the four-color printing process. When layered together, they produce the full-color image (E), a detail of Modigliani's *Gypsy Woman with Baby.* An enlargement (F) shows the dots printed from each plate and the colors created where the yellow, magenta, cyan, and black inks overlap.
© National Gallery of Art, Washington/SuperStock.

red, and green light. When the exposed film is developed, a multilayered negative results. Light-sensitive silver halide compounds are converted to metallic compounds by the developer. In the process, they oxidize and combine with "coupler" compounds to produce dyes. Each layer forms one of the three dyes that are the primaries for process printing—yellow, magenta, and cyan. A yellow image is formed on the blue-sensitive layer; a magenta image forms on the green-sensitive layer; and a cyan image is created on the red-sensitive layer. Next, the silver is bleached out of each layer, leaving only the appropriate-colored dye on the correct layer. Color negatives, positive color transparencies (slides), and color printers all involve this same basic process (fig. 7.46).

Color Computer Printing

Electronic imagery—drawn by hand, imported by scanning, or created by digital camera—requires a computer to produce a paper image. Most printers use a CYMK ink system, which is an acronym for cyan, yellow, magenta (the process-printing primaries in ink form), and black. *K* is used to denote black to avoid confusing *black* with *blue* (*B* commonly stands for blue). Because the computer images are created on the color monitor, each of the colors printed on paper must be made to simulate the illumination of the pixels on the monitor. An almost infinite number of colors can be created by printing cyan, yellow, and magenta either alone or in various combinations. "Black" may either be a product of combining all the primaries with black ink or the black ink alone. "White" is a result of the color of the paper stock being used. Cyan and magenta produce "blue" (a color closer to violet); yellow and cyan produce green; and magenta and yellow produce red.

Printers now have the capacity of printing colored detail so fine that it is difficult to see even with magnification.

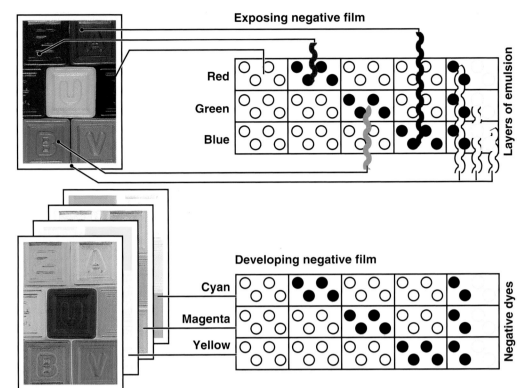

7.46 When color negative film is exposed, the blue-, green-, and red-sensitive layers of emulsion (color spots) record latent images (gray dots) that can be developed into black-and-white negatives. Colors that are mixtures of the primaries are recorded on several layers. Blacks do not expose any of the emulsion, while white light is recorded in all layers. Each color thus leaves a corresponding negative black-and-white impression.

When exposed color negative film is developed, a black-and-white negative image is produced in each emulsion layer (black dots). During this development, a colored dye is combined with each black-and-white negative image. The dyes are cyan, magenta, and yellow. Once the silver is bleached out, the three layers (colored dots) show the subject in superimposed negative-dye images.
Photograph by Bob Coyle/© McGraw-Hill Higher Education.

This is determined by the size of the dot pattern. Most color printers are capable of more than 300 dots per inch; some are even able to spray small droplets by the millions onto the paper. They can even project bursts of droplets from multiple nozzles that combine before striking the paper as a single dot. In this manner, such printers are capable of generating images with over a million color possibilities per dot. Considering the closeness of the dots of color, the variety of colors printed, and their concentration in an area, color printers can produce virtually any color and/or value the artist desires.

Many color printers now have programs that allow the artist to edit the image before printing—greatly altering the image's mood and appearance. Artists may explore adjustments to brightness and/or contrast, color balance (which separates shadow, midtones, and highlights by changing the levels of cyan, magenta, and yellow), and color mixing (which adjusts overall tonality through changes in the percentage of red, green, and blue used). Such color experiments can be very addicting, as global changes are seen instantly.

As artists begin to explore how they may employ computer-printing technol-

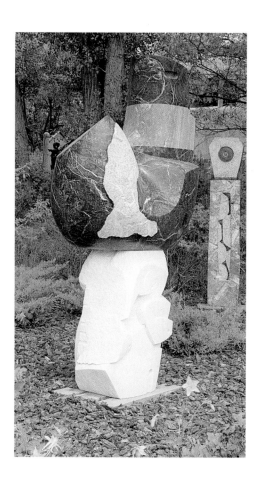

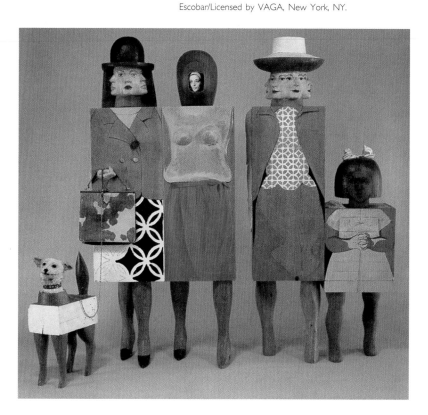

ogy, many are experimenting with printing on alternative media. Images have been printed on canvas, wearable silks, specialty films and plastics, and even archival and exotic papers like kinwashi and Japanese mulberry. Other artists are using the printed image as a starting point for embellishment, creating a kind of digital mixed media. They often start by sealing the surface with Krylon sprays or other acrylic sealers, followed by applications of paint, crayons, melted wax, and collaged images. Many also distress the surface by gouging, grinding, or embossing it or burning it with a torch. Whatever the final application, the combination of digital image and computer printing allows the artist to quickly create multiple variations of a concept and to evaluate the tonality, mood, and the spirit of the presentation in various surroundings. It can become an exciting tool in an artist's development of a personal and expressive color palette (see fig. 7.3).

THREE-DIMENSIONAL APPLICATIONS OF COLOR

Color is also an inherent feature of sculpture materials. Sometimes it is pleasantly diverse, as in the variegated veining of wood or stone; in *Nurse Log* (fig. 7.47), Michael Braden takes full advantage of such natural color—often altering it subtly by playing highly polished (bright local color) against unpolished or even roughened sections (dulled local color). However, the intrinsic color of some sculptural material can be bland, as in the flat chalkiness of plaster. Paint can be added when the material needs enrichment or when the surface requires color to bring out the form more efficiently. Painted surfaces can also add expression and provide additional two-dimensional detail to the three-dimensional form as abstract or simulated texture (fig. 7.48; see also fig. 4.34).

Many times, the application of color is an attempt to capture the richness and form-flattering quality of the **patina** found on bronzes oxidized by exposure to the atmosphere (fig. 7.49; see also fig. 3.30). Artists often speed up the aging process and control color development with the application of chemical washes. This surface patina can help relate all surfaces and textures while establishing harmony within a piece. More recently, the term *patina* has come to refer to any surface-color development and is not limited in application to bronze sculpture. An expanded palette of color is offered to three-dimensional work by the application of clay slips, acrylic and oil paints, enamels, salt fuming, stains, dyes, and electroplating, which allows the artist to simulate the color and texture of one material in another (fig. 7.50; see also figs. 1.40 and 6.24). As a result, color schemes can be created from analogous to tetrads; in addition, all of the properties of color—from developing space to creating emotional responses—are relevant to three-dimensional applications.

Obviously, color cannot be considered in isolation. The elements of value and color are so interwoven in sculpture that artists often use the two terms interchangeably. Thus, an artist may refer to value contrasts in terms of color, actually thinking of both simultaneously. This approach subordinates color to the structure of the piece. On the other hand, in certain historical periods (for example, early Greek art) the application of bright color was commonplace. Some revival of this technique is evident in contemporary works. In every case, the basic criterion for the use of color is compatibility with the form of the work.

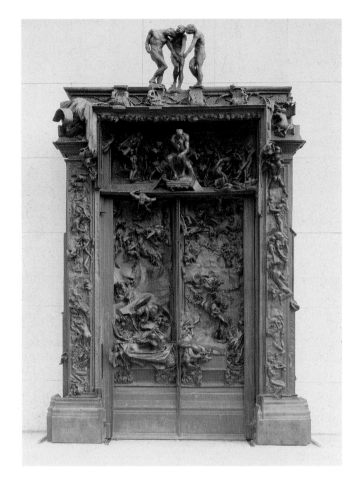

7.49 Auguste Rodin, *The Gates of Hell,* 1880–1917. Bronze, 20 ft. 8 in. × 13 ft. 1 in. (6.3 × 3.99 m). The forms in this high relief nearly break loose from the underlying surface. The entire work is made to harmonize by a surface patina, which can serve to flatten the appearance of an image. In this instance, however, the active images and their three-dimensional quality are enhanced by the cast shadows. Musée Rodin, Paris, France. Peter Willi/The Bridgeman Art Library.

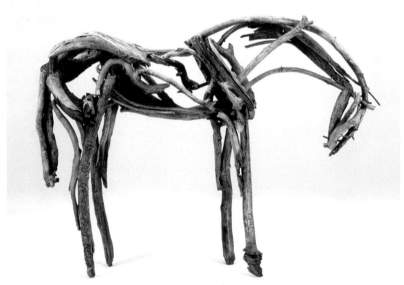

7.50 Deborah Butterfield, *Not Yet Titled (#2891.1),* 2005. Unique cast bronze with patinated surface, 37 × 48 × 13 in. This piece appears to be made of wood, but it is actually bronze that has been chemically colored (patinated) to resemble weathered wood. The three-dimensional artist has access to an unlimited range of color, which may be used to create this kind of trompe l'oeil effect or present textures and patterns that are completely invented. Courtesy of the artist.

Space

CHAPTER EIGHT

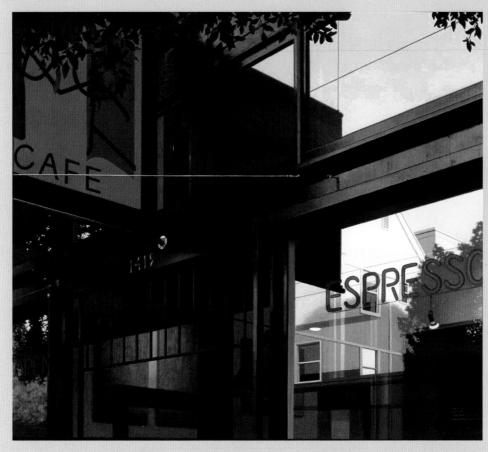

Gus Heinze, *Espresso Cafe*, 2003. Acrylic on gessoed panel, 32 × 35½ in.
Courtesy of the artist and Bernarducci.Meisel.Gallery, NY.

223

THE VOCABULARY OF
SPACE

Space — The interval, or measurable distance, between points or images; can be actual or illusionary.

atmospheric perspective
The illusion of deep space produced in graphic works by lightening values, softening details and textures, reducing value contrasts, and neutralizing colors in objects as they recede (see **perspective.**)

decorative (space)
Ornamenting or enriching but, more importantly in art, stressing the two-dimensional nature of an artwork or any of its elements. Decorative art (space) emphasizes the essential flatness of a surface.

four-dimensional space
An imaginative treatment of forms that gives a sense of intervals of time or motion.

fractional representation
A pictorial device (used notably by the Egyptians) in which several spatial aspects of the same subject are combined in the same image.

infinite space
A concept in which the picture frame acts as a window through which objects can be seen receding endlessly.

installations
Interior or exterior settings of media created by artists to heighten the viewers' awareness of the environmental space.

interpenetration
The positioning of planes, objects, or shapes so that they appear to pass through each other, which locks them together within a specific area of space.

intuitive space
The illusion of space that the artist creates by instinctively manipulating certain space-producing devices, including overlapping, transparency, interpenetration, inclined planes, disproportionate scale, fractional representation, and the inherent spatial properties of the art elements.

isometric projection
A technical drawing system in which a three-dimensional object is presented two-dimensionally; starting with the nearest vertical edge, the horizontal edges of the object are drawn at a 30-degree angle, and all verticals are projected perpendicularly from a horizontal base.

linear perspective
A system used to depict three-dimensional images on a two-dimensional surface; it develops the optical phenomenon of diminishing size by treating edges as converging parallel lines that extend to a vanishing point or points on the horizon (eye level) and recede from the viewer. (See also **perspective.**)

oblique projection
A technical drawing system in which a three-dimensional object is presented two-dimensionally; the front and back sides of the object are parallel to the horizontal base, and the other planes are drawn as parallels coming off the front plane at a 45-degree angle.

orthographic drawing
Graphic representation of two-dimensional views of an object, showing a plan, vertical elevations, and/or a section.

perspective
Any graphic system—including atmospheric perspective and linear perspective—used in creating the illusion of three-dimensional images and/or spatial relationships in which the objects or their parts appear to diminish as they recede into the distance.

plastic (space)
1. The use of the elements to create the illusion of the third dimension on a two-dimensional surface. 2. Three-dimensional art forms, such as architecture, sculpture, and ceramics.

relief sculpture
An artwork, graphic in concept but sculptural in application, that utilizes relatively shallow depth to establish images. The space development may range from very limited projection, known as "low relief," to more exaggerated space development, known as "high relief." Relief sculpture is meant to be viewed frontally, not in the round.

reverse perspective
A graphic system for depicting three-dimensional images, commonly seen in traditional East Asian art, in which the "parallel" lines of objects or their parts seem to converge toward the viewer, rather than away into the distance. (See **perspective.**)

shallow space
The illusion of limited depth. With shallow space, the imagery appears to move only a slight distance back from the picture plane.

space
The interval, or measurable distance, between points or images; can be actual or illusionary.

structured ambiguity
A condition in which the positive figure and the negative background seem to reverse roles, fluctuating back and forth between the two functions to create an ambiguous sense of space. Structured ambiguity is often employed as a transition between contrasting values or colors and is a valuable tool for creating optical illusions, denying space, and blending an image into its background.

three-dimensional
Possesses the dimensions of (or illusions of) height, width, and depth. In the graphic arts, the feeling of depth is an illusion, while in the plastic arts, the work has actual depth.

transparency
A visual quality in which a distant image or element can be seen through a nearer one.

two-dimensional
Possesses the dimensions of height and width, especially when considering the flat surface, or picture plane.

void
1. An area lacking positive substance and consisting of negative space. 2. A spatial area within an object that penetrates and passes through it.

INTRODUCTION TO SPACE

Today, the mention of **space** makes us think of spaceships, a space station, the solar system, and the infinite cosmos beyond. Artists, too, have been interested in an unending deep space, but one, paradoxically, to be found right here on earth. As we will discuss in this chapter, artistic devices can give the illusion of this kind of infinite space. On the other hand, the artist may choose to limit the degree of space we see. Space can be shrunk almost to the level of the picture plane, but not quite, because any element placed in a pictorial area immediately takes on some apparent depth in space. All of this is, of course, pure illusion in pictorial art, but it is not illusion for three-dimensional artists, who produce objects that have their own space. Space, thus, concerns all artists, and they must find ways of dealing with it in a consistent manner.

The understanding and use of space has greatly evolved over the years. The earliest images, from the caves of southern Europe, reveal a minimal concern for the illusion of space, with many images superimposed randomly over each other. In the ancient Near East, however, a flat and hierarchical order became important and was used to emphasize significant events or individuals through size variations. Over the centuries, the need to present images in a more realistic spatial context led to discoveries like mechanical perspective, photography, and the use of film to capture moving objects; images were usually created with a singular point of view and in a **two-dimensional** presentation with these techniques. Today, however, contemporary artists dealing with television and computer images have the capability to create things unthinkable even thirty years ago. Artists now design environments that allow the viewer to interact with the image—to move about in the setting in real time.

For an artist, the importance of space lies in its function. A basic understanding of its implications and use is essential.

Space, as discussed in this chapter, will not be limited to the graphic fields of drawing, painting, printmaking, and so forth, because the basic concepts can also be applied to the individual cells of storyboard presentations, video frames, computer-generated images, and traditional sculpture. Because space is an illusion in pictorial art, it will be presented as a "product" of the elements. However, in the **three-dimensional** arts—such as sculpture, ceramics, jewelry, architecture, and much installation work—space actually exists and will be treated as an element.

SPATIAL PERCEPTION

Our conceptions of space are conditioned by our experience of the world. Vision is perceived through the eyes but experienced by the mind. Visual experience involves the whole pattern of nerve and brain response to what we see. As our eyes perceive the world around us, we continually shift our focus of attention. In the process, we use two different types of vision: stereoscopic and kinesthetic. Having two eyes set slightly apart from each other, we receive two slightly different views of our visual field at the same time. The term *stereoscopic* refers to our ability to mentally combine these two slightly different views into one image. This process enables us to experience vision three-dimensionally and to judge distances. With *kinesthetic* vision, we experience space through the movements of our eyes and bodies. We explore an object's surface(s) with our eyes in order to recognize it; our eyes travel as we attempt to organize its separate parts into a whole. Objects close to us require more ocular movement than those farther away, and this kinesthetic eye activity adds to the spatial perception of our visual experience.

MAJOR TYPES OF SPACE

Two types of space can be suggested by the artist: decorative space and plastic space.

Decorative Space

Decorative space involves height and width but very little depth. It results from the very flat surface treatment of images or elements, which appear confined to the flatness of the picture plane without any concern for a deep spatial environment. As these images are developed, they seem to remain flat, enriching and embellishing the picture plane without creating the illusion of depth. In fact, a truly decorative space is difficult to achieve; any art element, when used in conjunction with others, will seem to advance and recede. However, when those areas or objects remain basically flat and limited to the picture plane, the space is said to be decorative (fig. 8.1).

Plastic Space

The term **plastic** refers to that which has been modeled or made to have the illusion of a three-dimensional presence. In this context, plastic space pertains to the environment in which those objects appear. Artists locate their images in plastic space according to their needs and feelings for each situation. An infinite range of space is available to the artist and may be categorized into the following general areas based on the depth of the space employed.

Shallow Space

Shallow space occurs when the artist wants to create some depth but, at the same time, limit the viewer's penetration into the pictorial space. Interior views, still-life images, and various nonobjective works are often presented in varying degrees of limited or shallow

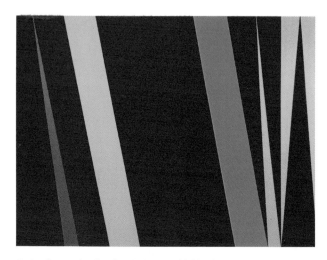

8.1 James Little, *Sneak-Attack*, 2003. Oil, wax, canvas, 78 × 102 in. (198.1 × 259.1 cm). Although the colors and other line qualities may seem to advance or recede in this painting, the images appear relatively flat on the pictures surface as a decorative treatment rather than creat an illusion of specific spatial depths. Courtesy of James Little and June Kelly Gallery NY.

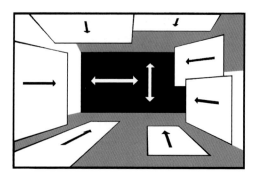

8.2 **Shallow space.** As a variation on the concept of shallow space, artists occasionally define the planes that make up the outer limits of a hollow boxlike space behind the picture plane. The diagram shows this concept, although in actual practice, a return to the picture plane would be made through objects occupying the space defined. The back plane acts as a curtain that prevents penetration into deep space.

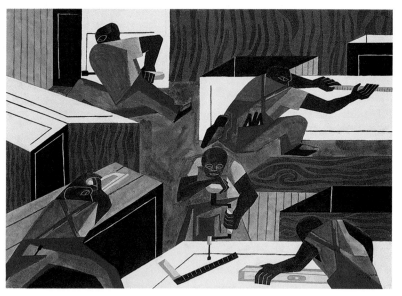

8.3 Jacob Lawrence, *Cabinet Makers*, 1946. Gouache with pencil underdrawing on paper, 21¾ × 30 in. (55.2 × 76.2 cm). The use of shapes with solid colors and values, generally lacking in traditional shading, creates an overall feeling of flatness. In addition, a stagelike effect arises from the shallow space. © Hirshhorn Museum and Sculpture Garden, Smithsonian Institution, Washington, DC. Gift of Joseph H. Hirshhorn, 1966. Photograph by Lee Stalsworth. Art © 2008 The Estate of Gwendolyn Lawrence/Artists Rights Society (ARS), New York.

formats. Shallow space may be compared to the views one might experience when observing a box or stage. The space is limited by the placement of the sides and back wall. For consistency, any compositional objects or figures that might appear in such stagelike confines are usually narrowed in depth or flattened (fig. 8.2). In the painting *Cabinet Makers,* by Jacob Lawrence, the figures have been flattened and placed in a confined room (fig. 8.3).

Asian, Egyptian, and European medieval painters used comparatively shallow space in their art. Early Renais-sance paintings were often based on the shallow sculptures that were popular then. Many modern artists also elected to use shallow space because it allowed more positive control than deep space and was more in keeping with the flatness of the working surface. Gauguin, Matisse, Modigliani, and Beckmann were typical advocates of the concepts of limited space (see figs. 4.1 and 7.24). For these artists, not having to create the illusion of deep plastic space allowed more control of the placement of decorative shapes as purely compositional elements.

Deep and Infinite Space

An artwork that emphasizes deep space starts with the picture plane and creates a spatial perception (feeling) that extends beyond and into that surface. The viewer's eye seems to move into the far distances of the picture field. This spatial feeling is similar to looking through an open window over a landscape that rolls on and on into infinity. This infinite quality is produced by certain relationships of art form: size, position, overlapping images, sharp and diminishing details, converging parallels, and perspective are traditional methods of indicating deep spatial penetration (see 6.17).

Infinite spatial concepts, allied with **atmospheric perspective,** dominated Western art from the beginning of the Renaissance (about 1350) to the middle of the nineteenth century. During this period, generations of artists such as Botticelli, Ruisdael, Rembrandt, and Beirstadt, to name only a few, developed and perfected the deep-space illusion that seems to accord with visual reality (fig. 8.4).

Although there have been periods in the history of art when one spatial treatment or another seemed dominant, works of contemporary artists range from decorative space to profoundly infinite space without showing a prejudice toward any particular approach. Any space concept can be valid as long as its elements are consistent in relation to the spatial field chosen.

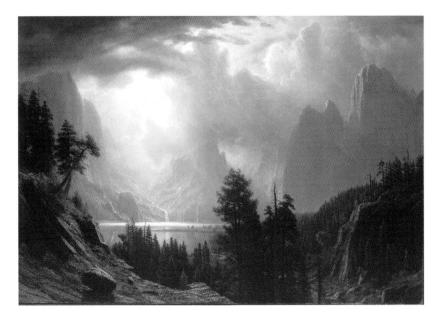

8.4 Albert Bierstadt, *King Lake, California*, early 1870s. Oil on canvas, 27¾ × 38½ in. (70.5 × 97.8 cm). Nineteenth-century American landscape painting, which aimed at the maximum illusion of visual reality, emphasized the concept of infinite space. The foreground areas move forward because of their greater textural contrasts and clarity, while the diminishing sizes of objects and hazy effects of atmospheric perspective give the viewer a sense of seeing far into the distance. Columbus Museum of Art, Ohio: Bequest of Rutherford H. Platt, 1929.003.

SPATIAL INDICATORS

Artistic methods of representing space are so interdependent that attempts to isolate and examine all of them here would be impractical and inconclusive. In addition, such attempts might leave the reader with the feeling that art is based on a formula. Thus, we will confine this discussion to basic spatial concepts.

Our comprehension of space, which comes to us through objective experiences, is enlarged, interpreted, and given meaning by the use of our intuitive faculties. Spatial order develops when the artist senses the right balance and the best placement, then selects vital forces to create completeness and unity. Obviously, then, this process is not a purely intellectual one but rather a matter of instinct or subconscious response (see figs. 4.13A and B, 5.17, 8.37, and 8.38).

Because the subjective element plays so large a part in controlling space, we can readily see that emphasis on formula here, as elsewhere, can quell the creative spirit. Art is a product of human creativity and is always dependent on individual interpretations and responses. Space, like other qualities in art, may be either spontaneous or premeditated, but it is always the product of the artist's will. If an artist has the impassioned will to make things so, they will usually be so, despite inconsistency and defiance of established principles. Therefore, the methods of spatial indication discussed in the following pages are presented merely as examples that have been used frequently and that guarantee a spatial effect.

Sharp and Diminishing Detail

Because we do not have the eyes of eagles, and because we view things through the earth's atmosphere, we are not able to see near and distant planes with equal clarity at the same time. A glance out the window confirms that close objects appear sharp and clear in detail, whereas those far away seem blurred and lack definition. Artists have long known of this phenomenon and have used it widely in illusionistic work—presenting sharply defined images in the foreground but decreasing the clarity as the pictorial space recedes. In recent times, they have used this method and other traditional methods of space indication in works that are otherwise quite abstract. Thus, in abstract and nonobjective conceptions, sharp lines, clearly defined shapes and values, complex textures, and intense colors are associated with foreground, or near, positions. Hazy lines, indistinct shapes, grayed values, simple textures, and neutralized colors are identified with background, or distant, locations. These characteristics are often included in the definition of *atmospheric perspective* (see figs. 8.4 and 8.6).

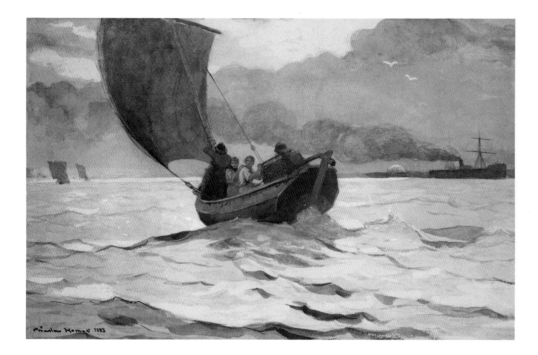

8.5 Winslow Homer, *Returning Fishing Boats*, 1883. Watercolor and white gouache over graphite on white paper, 13 × 19⅝ in. (40.3 × 62.9 cm). The horizon line in this painting separates the space into a ground plane below and a sky plane above. The smaller size and higher position of the distant boats help achieve the spatial effect. Courtesy of the Fogg Art Museum, Harvard University Art Museums, Anonymous Gift. Photograph by Katya Kallsen. © President and Fellows of Harvard College, Harvard University.

Size

We usually interpret largeness of scale as nearness. Conversely, a smaller scale suggests distance. If two sailboats are several hundred feet apart, the nearer boat appears larger than the other. Ordinarily, we would interpret this difference in scale not as one large and one small boat (although this could play a part in our perception) but as vessels of approximately the same size placed at varying distances from the viewer (fig. 8.5). Therefore, if we are to use depth scale as our guide, an object or a human figure assumes a scale that corresponds to its distance from us, regardless of all other factors (fig. 8.6; see also fig. T.45). This concept of space has not always been prevalent. In some styles of art, largeness indicates importance, power, and strength rather than spatial location (see figs. 2.50 and 8.12).

Position

Artists and observers customarily assume that the horizon line, which provides a point of reference, is at eye level. Thus, the position of objects is judged in relation to that horizon line. The bottom of the picture plane is seen as the closest visual point, and the eye's rise up to the horizon line indicates the receding of space (see fig. 8.5). Evidence suggests that this manner of seeing is instinctive (resulting from continued exposure to the objective world), for its influence persists even when viewing greatly abstracted and nonobjective work (fig. 8.7; see also figs. 2.17 and 3.7). The alternative, of course, is to see the picture plane as entirely devoid of spatial illusion and to register the distances between visual elements as simply what is actually measurable across the flat surface. It is difficult to perceive a picture in this way even when we discipline ourselves to do so, because it requires us to divorce ourselves entirely from all the intuitions about space we form through our experience.

Overlapping

Another way of suggesting space is by overlapping planes or volumes. If one object covers part of the visible surface of another, the first object is assumed to be nearer. Overlapping is a powerful indicator of space, because once used, it takes precedence over other spatial indicators. For instance, a ball placed in front of a larger ball appears closer than the larger ball, despite its smaller size (fig. 8.8). Color, value, and textural choices can then exaggerate or minimize the spatial effect of the overlapped shapes. If the colors, values, or textures are of minimal contrast, the overlapped areas tend to unite and create a shallow or ambiguous (unequivocal) space (see fig. 2.18C). The Futurists often presented shallow or ambiguous space by overlapping multiple images of the same object in different positions (see fig. 9.9).

Transparency

The overlapped portion of an object is usually obscured from our view. If, however, that portion is visible through the overlapping plane or object, the effect of **transparency** is created. Transparency, which tends to produce a close spatial relationship, is clearly evident in the triangles in Leonardo Nierman's

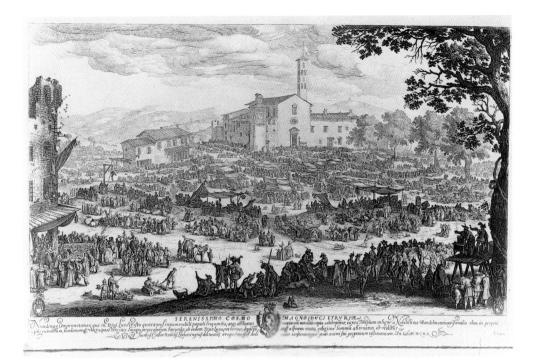

8.6 Jacques Callot, *The Great Fair at Imprunita,*1620. Etching, 16¹⁵/₁₆ × 26 in. In Callot's print, note how the figures gradually get smaller as they recede into the background areas. This, combined with the artist's use of linear perspective with the buildings, gives the viewer a strong sense of depth. The Metropolitan Museum of Art, Harris Brisbane Dick Fund, 1917 (17.3.2645). Photograph, all rights reserved, The Metropolitan Museum of Art.

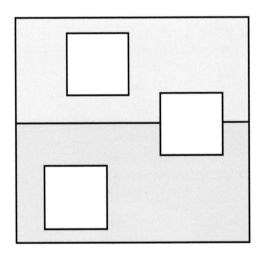

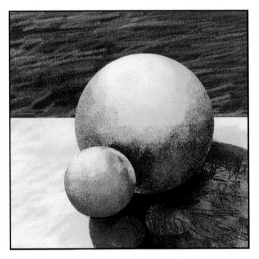

8.7 **Placement of squares.** A line across the picture plane reminds us of the horizon that divides ground plane from sky plane. Consequently, the lower shape seems close and the intermediate shape more distant, while the upper square is in a rather ambiguous position as it touches nothing and seems to float in the sky.

8.8 Larger objects usually advance more than smaller ones, but as an indicator of space, overlapping causes the object being covered to recede regardless of size.

painting *Broken Star* (fig. 8.9). It is also found in the works of the Cubists and other artists who are interested in exploring shallow space (see figs. 4.2 and T.51).

Interpenetration

Interpenetration occurs when planes or objects appear to pass through each other, emerging on the other side. This generally provides a very clear statement of the spatial positioning of the planes and objects involved, and it can create the illusion of either shallow or deep space (figs. 8.10 and 8.11; also see fig. 2.21).

Fractional Representation

Fractional representation can best be understood by studying the treatment of the human body by Egyptian mural artists. Here we can find, within one figure, the profile of the head with the frontal eye visible, the torso seen front-on, and a side view of the hips and legs—a combination of the most representative aspects of the different parts of the body (figs. 8.12 and 8.13). Fractional representation is a spatial device revived in the nineteenth century by Cézanne, who used its principles in his still-life paintings (see the section "Multiple Viewpoints" in Chapter 9). It was also employed by many twentieth-century artists, most conspicuously Picasso. The effect is flattening in Egyptian work but plastic in the paintings by Cézanne because it is used to move us "around" the subjects (see fig. 9.5).

Converging Parallels

The space indicated by converging parallels can be illustrated using a rectangular plane such as a sheet of paper or a tabletop. By actual measurement, a rectangle possesses one set of short parallel edges and one set of long parallel edges (fig. 8.14). If the plane is arranged so

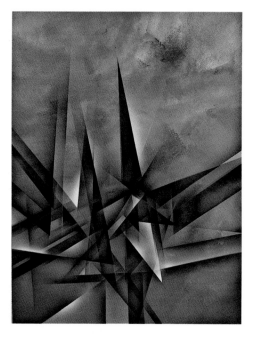

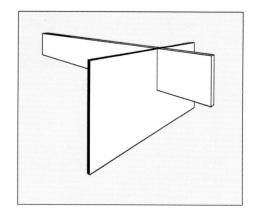

8.10 **Interpenetrating planes.** The passage of one plane or volume through another automatically gives depth to a picture.

8.9 Leonardo Nierman, *Broken Star,* 1991. Mixed media on masonite, 32 × 24 in. The precise, hard-edged geometric shapes in this work are a legacy of Cubism. However, notice that the implied triangular shapes overlap, remain transparent, and create a shallow space that contrasts with the deeper space behind. Courtesy of the artist.

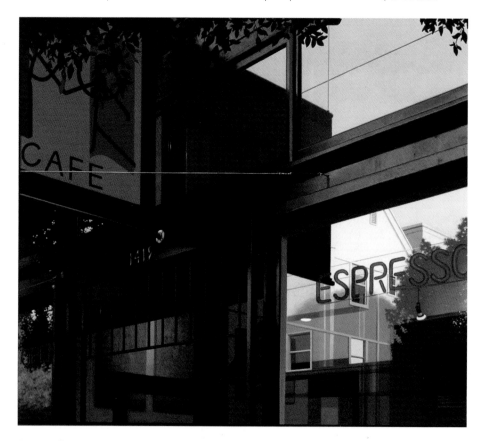

8.11 Gus Heinze, *Espresso Cafe,* 2003. Acrylic on gessoed panel, 32 × 35½ in. Object and reflection merge to create the illusion of interpenetrating planes and a sense of depth that goes beyond the building's structural beams and wall of glass. Courtesy of the artist and Bernarducci.Meisel.Gallery, NY.

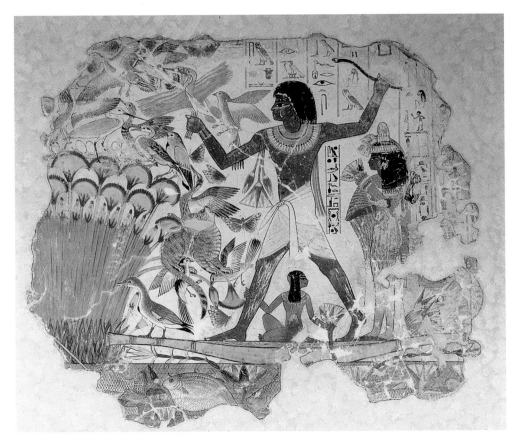

8.12 Nebamun hunting birds, from the tomb of Nebamun, Thebes, Egypt, c. 1400 B.C.E., size unknown. This work illustrates the Egyptian concept of pictorial plasticity: various representative views of Nebamun are combined into one image (fractional representation) and are kept compatible with the flatness of the picture plane. The arbitrary positioning of the figures and their disproportionate scale add to this effect. Fragment of a fresco secco. Courtesy of the British Museum, London.

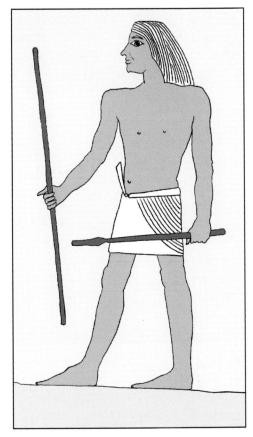

8.13 This drawing illustrates the Egyptian technique of fractional representation of the human figure. The head is in profile but the eye full-face. The upper body is frontal, gradually turning until the lower body, from the hips down, is seen from the side. This drawing combines views of parts of the body in their most characteristic or easily seen positions. In order to see all these views, one would have to move around the body.

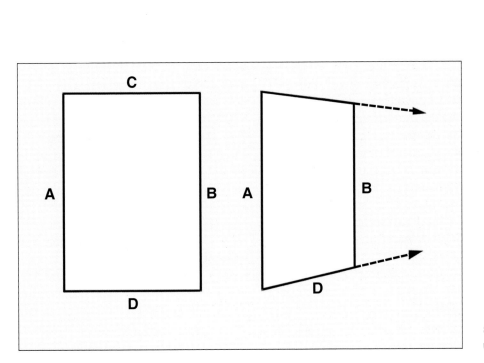

8.14 Converging parallels can make a shape appear to recede into the pictorial field.

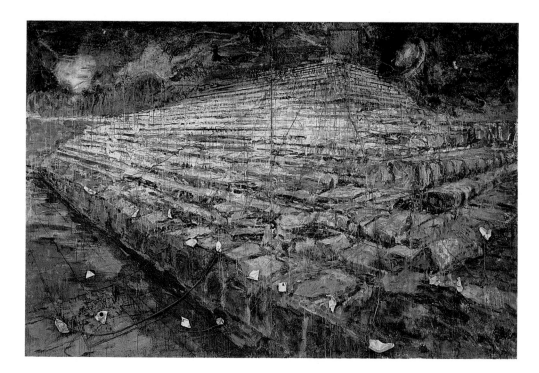

8.15 Anselm Kiefer, *Osiris und Isis/Bruch und Einung*, 1985–87. Mixed media, 150 × 220½ in. (381 × 560 cm). Kiefer uses perspective to help him intensify the viewer's confrontation with scale in his enormous canvas. San Francisco Museum of Modern Art. Purchased through a gift of Jean Stein, by exchange, the Mrs. Paul L. Wattis Fund, and the Doris and Donald Fisher Fund. © Anselm Kiefer.

that one of the long edges (A) is viewed head-on, its corresponding parallel edge (B) will appear to be much shorter. Because these edges appear to be of different lengths, the pair of parallel edges (C and D) that connect them must seem to converge as they move back into space. Either set of lines (A-B or C-D), even in the absence of the other set, would continue to indicate space quite forcefully. This principle of converging parallels is found in many works of art that do not necessarily abide by the rules of **perspective.** The principle is closely related to perspective, but the degree of convergence is a matter of subjective or intuitive choice by the artist. It need not be governed by fixed vanishing points and other systematic rules governing the rate of convergence (fig. 8.15).

Linear Perspective

Linear perspective is a system for accurately representing sizes and distances of known objects in a unified visual space. This helps develop the illusion of three-dimensional images as they recede into the distance. Based on optical perception, it incorporates the artist's (and viewer's) judgments about concepts of scale, proportion, placement, and so on by applying spatial indicators such as size, position, and converging parallels. A general understanding of perspective occurred in Renaissance Italy with the revival of interest in ancient Greco-Roman literature, philosophy, and art. This spirit swept Europe during the fourteenth and fifteenth centuries—the era that brought this spatial system to a point of high refinement. Linear perspective focuses attention on one view—a selected portion of nature as seen from one position at a particular moment in time. The use of eye level, guidelines, and vanishing points gives this view mathematical exactitude (fig. 8.16A and B).

It is generally believed that perspective was developed by the Florentine architect Filippo Brunelleschi (1377–1446) and was quickly adapted to painting by his contemporary, Masaccio (1401–1428; see fig. 8.16A). Employing their knowledge of geometry (an important subject in classical education), Renaissance artists conceived a method of depicting objects, both animate and inanimate, in a space more realistic than any other that had appeared in Western art since the Romans.

In their concept, the perspective drawing of shapes makes the picture plane akin to a view through a window, the picture frame acting as a window frame (fig. 8.17A). As seen in figure 8.17B, imaginary sightlines, called *guidelines,* are extended along the edges of the room's architectural planes to a point behind the angel's head. The guidelines converge at a point on the eye level that is called the *vanishing point* (infinity). By convention, the eye level is synonymous with the *horizon line* (where the sky and ground meet), which is often clearly seen in landscapes (see figs. 8.4 and 8.5). While the eye level reveals the elevation of the observer's/painter's eyes, it also demarcates upper and lower divisions called *ground plane* (floor) and *sky plane*

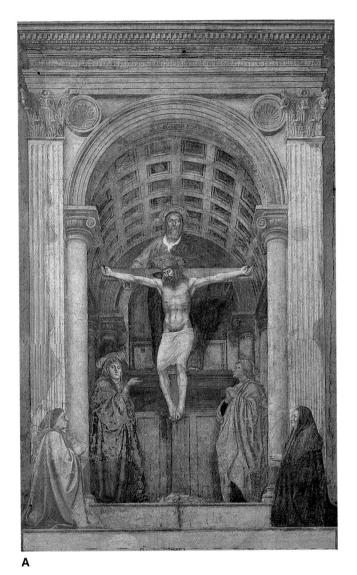

A

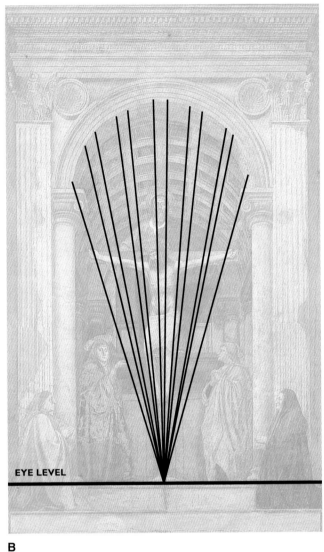

B

EYE LEVEL

8.16 Masaccio, *Trinity with the Virgin, St. John and Donors*, 1427. Fresco at Santa Maria Novella, Florence, Italy, 21 ft. 10 in. × 10 ft. 5 in. (6.65 × 3.18 m). According to some art history experts, Masaccio's fresco is the first painting created in correct geometric perspective. The single vanishing point lies at the foot of the cross, as indicated by the overlay (B). Photo SCALA/Art Resource, New York.

(ceiling). A vertical axis that passes through the vanishing point establishes the location of the artist or viewer. This is known as the *viewer's location point*. Changing this point will drastically alter the view of the room (fig. 8.18A and B).

Major Types of Linear Perspective

There are three major types of linear perspective: one-point, two-point, and three-point. Each system is related to the way the artist views the subject or scene. Perspective is based on the theoretical assumptions that the artist maintains a fixed position and views the subject with one eye. The Renaissance painter's approach was to imagine rays of light emanating from one fixed point (the artist's eye) to every point on the object being drawn. These rays passed through a grid or glass screen that was placed between the artist and the object, and the points where the lines passed through the grid were then transferred to the artist's canvas (see fig. 8.19 on page 236). This type of device helped the artist draw more accurate foreshortening and achieve the naturalistic view he wanted to re-create on the canvas. (This device is also similar in concept to the "camera obscura," which actually projects the image through a small hole onto a dark wall.)

In reality, most viewers casually move their eyes and heads as their focus travels from object to object within the image. While these movements increase the viewers' ability to understand the

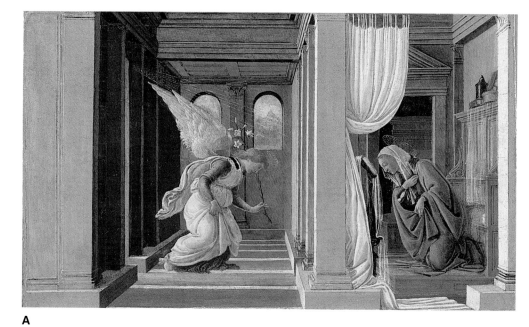

A

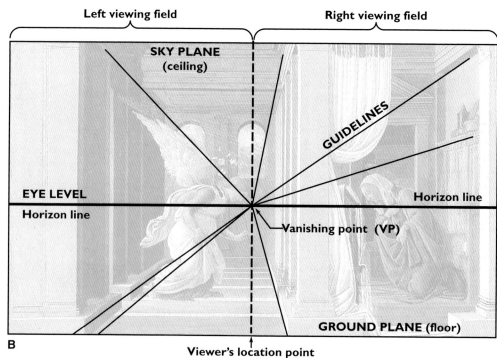

B

subject, such changes of viewpoint to some extent violate the concepts of linear perspective.

Assuming a minimum of movement, the artist can view his or her subjects in one of three ways:

1. By taking a position directly in front of the image; the whole front plane of the subject is made to appear flat, or parallel, to the picture plane (one-point perspective).

2. By moving so that an edge—instead of the whole flat plane—is closest and centrally located; all planes will then appear to recede, because the top and bottom edges converge to vanishing points on either side (two-point perspective).

3. By assuming a position very much above or below the subject; the sides as well as the top and bottom edges will converge to distant points (three-point perspective).

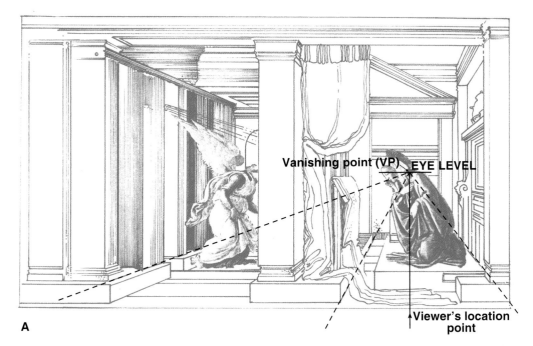

A

Vanishing point (VP)　EYE LEVEL

Viewer's location point

8.18 These illustrations show how the interior might have changed if Botticelli had moved his location point left or right and up or down (see fig. 8.17A). Figure A indicates what Botticelli would have seen by moving to the right and standing directly in front of the Madonna. Figure B depicts the view he would have had by moving to the left, past the angel, and moving up a ladder one or two steps. Notice how the architectural elements change with each view, obscuring important parts of the image.

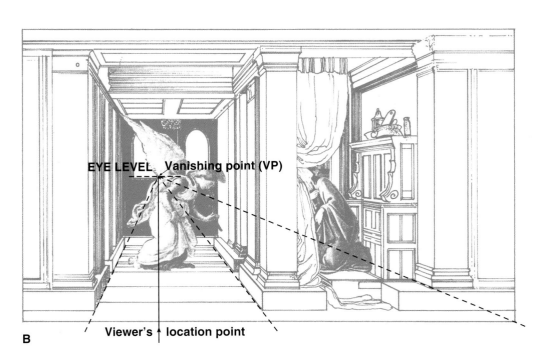

EYE LEVEL　Vanishing point (VP)

B　Viewer's ↑ location point

In each of these examples, the subject is thought of as stationary and the artist as changing position. But the same concepts could be applied to still-life material that is altered or repositioned while the artist's location point remains stationary.

One-Point Perspective

One-point perspective is used when the artist views a flat surface or facing plane directly, or front-on. This flat plane will be drawn parallel to the picture plane and the horizon line. In this system, the artist first establishes the horizon line, which represents the eye level (fig. 8.20). The horizon line is placed low on the page if the artist is close to the ground, high on the page if the artist is on a ladder, or centered if the artist is standing. Next, the artist chooses a vanishing point (VP), usually centered on the

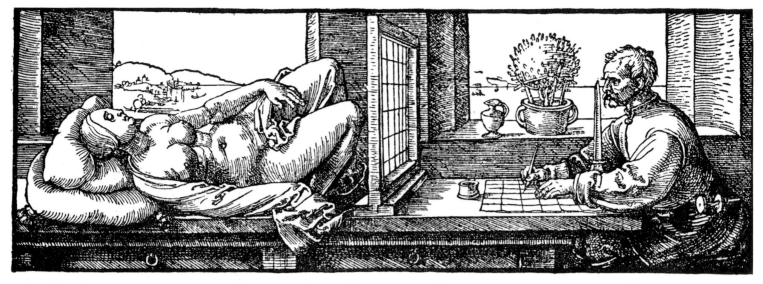

8.19 Albrecht Dürer, *Draftsman Drawing a Nude*, c. 1525. Woodcut, size unknown. This woodcut illustrates an early approach to recording the effects of perspective and foreshortening from a fixed view. In "Underweysung der Messing (Instruction in Proportion)" (Nurenberg, 1527) (appeared only 3rd ED., 1538). Private collection/Foto Marburg/Art Resource, New York.

8.20 With one-point perspective, the whole front or back plane of the subject is made to appear flat or parallel to the picture plane.

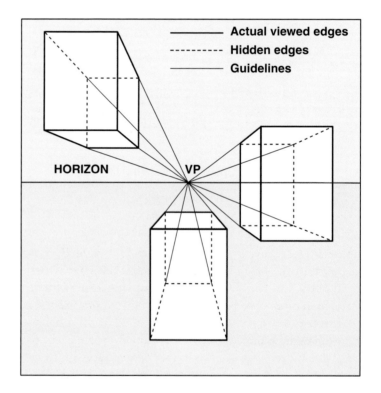

horizon line. To make the composition less static, the vanishing point can be placed slightly to the right or left of center, so that the picture is not divided too symmetrically. In either case, the vanishing point represents a position directly in front of the viewer and at eye level.

After the vanishing point on the horizon line is established, the artist begins with the frontal plane of the geometric solid—that portion closest to the viewer. Guidelines drawn from the four corners of the frontal plane to the vanishing point will establish the theoretical position of the solid's side planes. The length of these planes is established by drawing horizontal or vertical lines that are parallel to the front edges. The solid's sides will appear to diminish in size as they recede in depth toward the horizon.

In one-point perspective, all lines that are not horizontal or vertical will return to the same vanishing point. The horizontal and vertical lines, which define the original flat plane or any planes behind and parallel to it, are at right angles to each other; they remain constant and geometrically stable (measurable). The horizontal and vertical lines are also either parallel or perpendicular

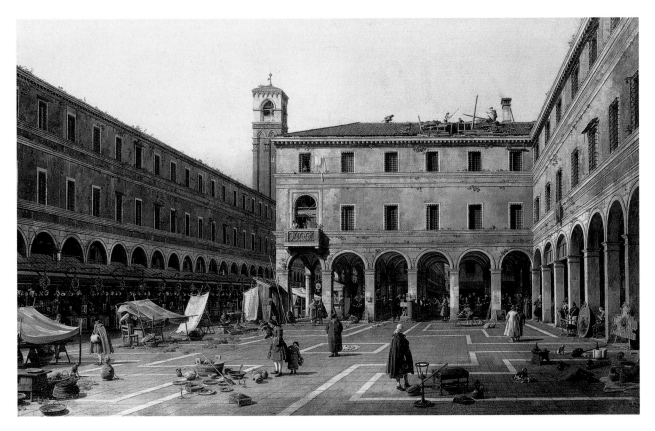

8.21 Antonio Canaletto, *Campo di Rialto*, c. 1756. Oil on canvas, 119 × 186 cm. The appearance of planes and volumes in space determined by the systematic procedures of linear perspective is well illustrated in this painting by an eighteenth-century Venetian artist. It is in one-point perspective and shows the day-to-day business of Venice's center. Bildarchiv Preussicher Kulturbesitz/Art Resource, NY.

to the ground plane and establish the object's spatial location.

Notice that the three geometric solids in figure 8.20 are located fairly close to the vanishing point. In reality, when viewing such solids, one sees the sides as foreshortened. The farther from the vanishing point the solids are, the more distorted their side planes should seem to appear. Solids that are placed to the extreme far left or right in one-point perspective compositions become so distorted that they would be more accurately drawn in two-point perspective. However, artists often employ such distortions for their compositional and/or conceptual advantages.

Subjects with a flat frontal view, like the end of a room, hallways, long frontal views of the interior and exterior of buildings, streets, and lines of trees, all lend themselves well to one-point per-

spective pictures, as seen in Canaletto's *Campo di Rialto* (fig. 8.21).

Two-Point Perspective

Two-point perspective is most often employed when the artist views a leading edge instead of a flat plane. The geometric solid will appear to be at an angle to the lines of sight. In other words, it will seem to be in an angular position at some depth beyond the surface of the picture plane (figs. 8.22 and 8.23).

As in one-point perspective, the artist begins by establishing the horizon line relative to the height of the artist's viewing position. Next, two vanishing points are located along the horizon line, at the extreme left (LVP) and right (LVR) ends. In reality, the vanishing points are out at the very edges of our field of vision, but for the convenience of drawing, they are commonly located just beyond the outer edges of the pic-

ture plane. Then, the artist draws the closest portion of the box—the vertical edge—as a vertical line. From the top and bottom corners of this line, guidelines are extended back to both vanishing points; these will be used to establish the side, top, and/or bottom planes of the geometric solid. The other vertical edges of the box are then defined by drawing vertical lines from one guideline to the next.

With two-point perspective, all lines except those that are vertical will return to the vanishing points, and each of the planes will appear to diminish as they recede. The verticals indicate the height of the volumes, remain parallel, and are perpendicular to the ground plane. Only the verticals may be accurately measured, and they never converge.

If the artist chooses to exaggerate or distort the image beyond what is naturally observed, the location of the

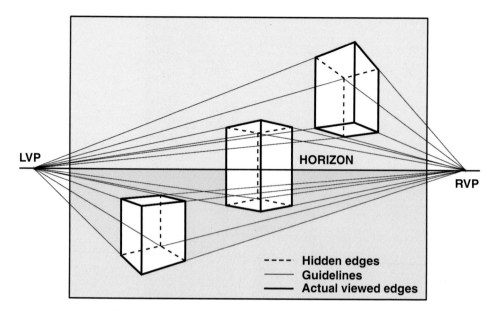

8.22 With two-point perspective, one vertical edge is closest, and all top and bottom edges recede and converge at the left or right vanishing point.

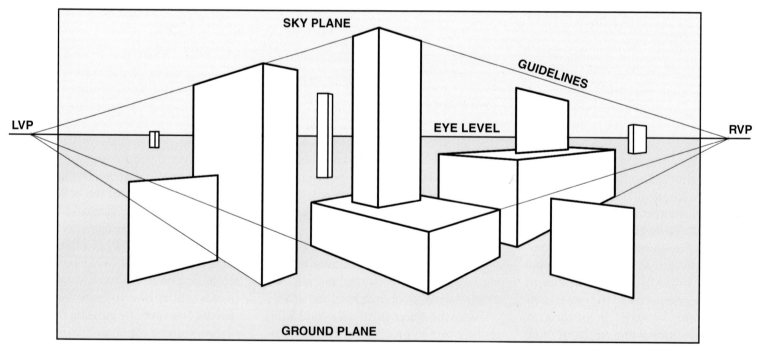

8.23 This example of two-point perspective illustrates planes and solids at multiple depths. Notice how the edges on the objects further in the distance differ from those closer to the viewer—the angles of the receding lines become more horizontal. In this illustration, the vanishing points are located outside the edges of the pictorial plane. The horizon line, which is at eye level, represents infinity and divides the picture plane into areas that stand for the ground and sky. Object edges are shown as heavy lines, while guidelines are lighter lines.

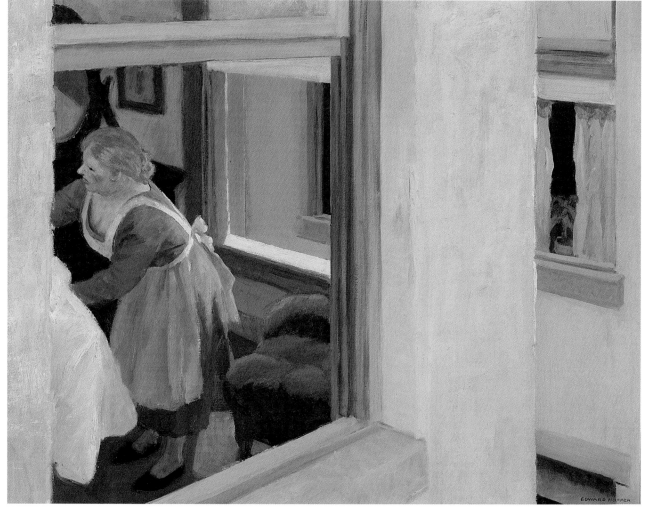

8.24 Edward Hopper, *Apartment Houses,* 1923. Oil on canvas, 25½ × 31½ in. (64.8 × 80 cm). This unusual interior with layers of space revealed through windows is painted in two-point perspective. The perspective is used to direct the viewer back and forth into the picture plane. Pennsylvania Academy of the Fine Arts, Philadelphia. John Lambert Fund. Acc. No. 1925.5.

vanishing points may be changed as suited. Fixing them closer together will often exaggerate the receding quality of the shapes. Placing the vanishing points farther apart will reverse this distortion. If the length of the horizon line on the picture plane is meant to represent our entire visual field, the vanishing points are located just beyond the outer edges of the picture plane. For compositional reasons, however, an artist might choose to work with only a portion of the complete field of view—maybe for a close-up image; in this case, the vanishing points would need to be located much

farther beyond the edge of the picture plane (fig. 8.24). In any case, the location of the vanishing points depends on the perception and instinct of the artist.

Two-point perspective is most often employed to depict objects or architecture set at an angle to the line of sight. These angular positions may occur at any depth in the picture plane, as can be seen in the painting by Hopper (see fig. 8.24) and also in Callot's etching (see fig. 8.6).

Three-Point Perspective

Three-point perspective is used when an artist views an object from an exag-

gerated position—such as lying on the ground and looking up at a tree or looking down from a skyscraper into the center of the city. These perspectives are sometimes referred to as a "frog's-eye view" (fig. 8.25) and a "bird's-eye view" (fig. 8.26), respectively.

The artist begins by locating the horizon line that indicates the location of the viewer's eyes—either relatively high or low in the picture—and fixing the left vanishing point (LVP) and the right vanishing point (RVP) at the appropriate locations (fig. 8.27). As with two-point perspective, the closer

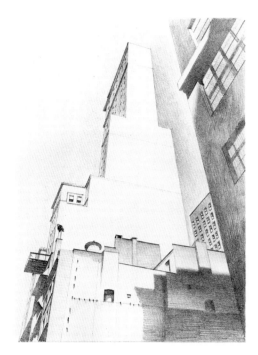

8.25 Charles Sheeler, *Delmonico Building*, 1926. Lithograph, 9¾ × 6⅞ in. (24.7 × 17.4 cm). This painting makes use of three-point perspective—a "frog's-eye view." Fogg Art Museum. © President and Fellows, Harvard University Art Museums, Boston, MA. Gift of Paul J. Sachs.

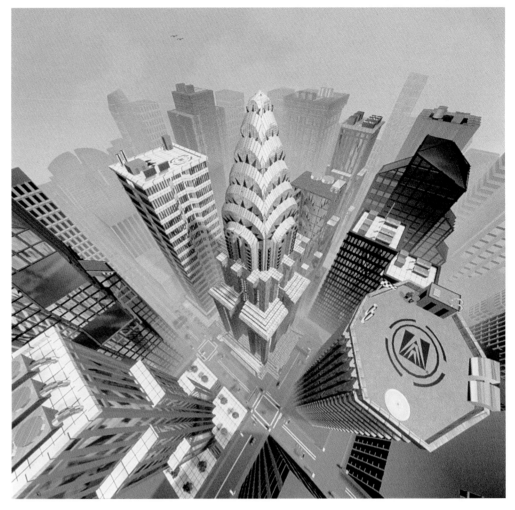

8.26 Gene Bodio, *New City*, 1992. Computer graphic created using Autodesk 3D Studio– Release 2. This is a "bird's-eye view" generated by a computer. Though not strictly in three-point perspective, the picture is an unusual variation in the depiction of three-dimensional objects in space. Courtesy of the artist. San Rafael, CA.

together the vanishing points are placed, the greater the exaggeration or distortion of the image. Next, the artist determines the viewer's location and extends an imaginary vertical line upward on the page, perpendicular to the horizon line. A third point, called the vertical vanishing point (VVP), is then located at an appropriate location on this vertical axis (see fig. 8.27). The location of the VVP helps control the distortion of the object; the farther away from the horizon line the third point is located, the less exaggerated the image will be.

Instead of starting with the nearest flat plane (as in one-point) or the nearest edge (as in two-point), three-point perspective begins with the nearest corner. In figure 8.27, the image (a rectangular solid that seems to be floating overhead) is started by establishing the nearest corner (a). From this point, guidelines are extended to the RVP and to the LVP. These locate the leading front edges of the bottom plane. The width of both edges should then be marked (b and c). From those points, new guidelines should be extended to the RVP and LVP. This completes the bottom plane and locates all four of its corners.

The "verticals" should now be drawn up and away from the three closest cor-

ners (marked a, b, and c); but because there are no true verticals in three-point perspective, these lines will have to converge to the VVP. Once the "verticals" are drawn, the height of the rectangular solid can be established on the center "vertical" edge. After marking this point (d), guidelines are extended from it to the RVP and to the LVP. This completes the drawing of the edges and fully defines the geometric solid as seen from below in three-point perspective. In certain cases, such as when the object walls are meant to be transparent, the hidden back edges (extended from the corners labeled e, f, and g) could also be added.

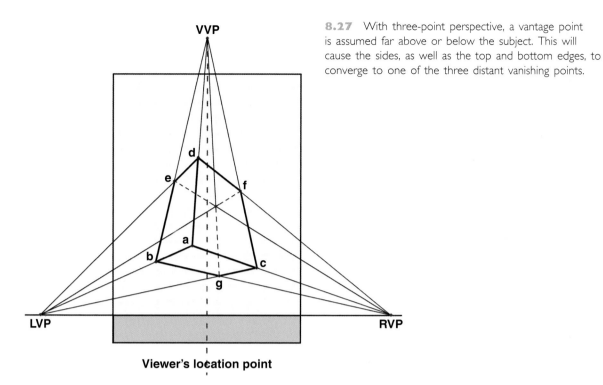

VVP

LVP

RVP

Viewer's location point

8.27 With three-point perspective, a vantage point is assumed far above or below the subject. This will cause the sides, as well as the top and bottom edges, to converge to one of the three distant vanishing points.

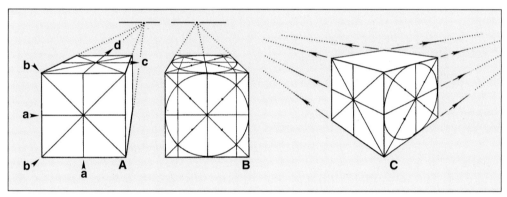

8.28 **Subdividing a plane.** These diagrams illustrate how to find the perspective center of a plane by crossing diagonals from corner to corner (A). To draw a circle on the same plane, divide each half of the diagonals into thirds. Draw the circle so that it passes through the outside "third" marks (closest to the corners) on the diagonals. The circle should also touch the middle points on the sides of the square. This concept may be applied to one- and two-point perspective (B and C).

Only in three-point perspective are the vertical (height) lines, as well as those receding to the left and right vanishing points, drawn as receding in space. All three sets of guidelines converge at vanishing points. They are neither perpendicular nor parallel to one another but at oblique angles (see fig. 8.25).

Perspective Concepts Applied

Whether using one-, two-, or three-point perspective, the artist is working with a system that helps establish items of known size at various distances into the picture plane. Based on the angle and orientation of the receding plane, dimensions decrease at a predictable rate. But in order for the artist to project items at the proper rate of recession, he or she must first be able to find the midpoints, or centers, of various planes.

As illustrated in figure 8.28A, a cube shown in one-point perspective has a frontal plane, a receding top, and a receding side plane. The center of any frontal plane—square or rectangular— may be found by physically measuring the horizontal and vertical lengths and dividing them in half. Lines (a) drawn from those points parallel to the verticals and horizontals will divide the plane into quarters. However, this type of subdividing works on *only* flat frontal planes (which are found exclusively in one-point perspective—not two- or three-point perspective). It will *not* work on any plane with converging sides (regardless of whether one-, two-, or three-point) because the sides get smaller as they move away from the viewer, and their changing ratio is not measurable on a ruler.

Notice on the frontal plane, that the diagonals (b) drawn from corner to corner pass through the exact center found by measurement. The same type of diagonal lines drawn from corner to corner on a receding plane will pass through and reveal the *perspective center* of the receding plane. Lines drawn

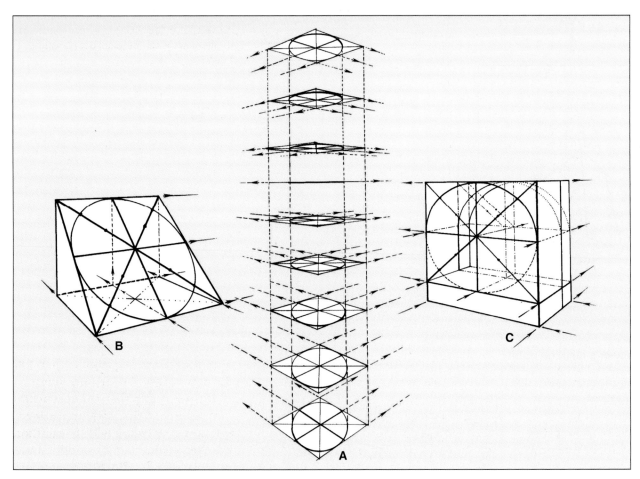

8.29 When seen from the side, a perfect circle looks like an ellipse. The ellipse flattens as it moves closer to the horizon line (A). It may be applied to an inclined plane (B) or used to create arches, tunnels, and so on (C).

through this center point, parallel to the front edge (c) and to the vanishing point (d), then create an equal division of the four edges of the receding plane. This concept of corner-to-corner diagonals may be applied to cubes or rectangles in one-, two-, and three-point perspective to locate the perspective centers on *any receding plane.*

Using the center point of a cube's *front* square, a circle can be drawn with a compass to fit perfectly into that frontal plane (fig. 8.28B). Notice that when the diagonals are divided in thirds between the center and each corner, the circle crosses the diagonal lines on approximately the outer third mark. When a *receding* plane is meant to contain a circle, the circle will actually appear as an ellipse and cannot be drawn using a compass. The appropriate ellipse can be drawn on the top receding plane when it passes through the third marks on the diagonals and touches the square on the center points of each side. This system may be applied to *any receding plane—* vertical or horizontal—in one-, two-, or three-point perspective (fig. 8.28C).

Occasionally, an artist must draw appropriate ellipses for the top and bottom of anything cylindrical, relative to their positions above or below the horizon line. Figure 8.29A shows how ellipses change as they rise and fall; notice that the ellipses flatten as they get closer to the horizon line but become more circular the farther they are away from the horizon line. Of course, ellipses do not always have to be horizontal or vertical—observe the ellipse drawn on the diagonal plane (fig. 8.29B). It is drawn using the same corner-to-corner diagonals used in finding the center of the diagonal plane. The same concept may also be applied to drawing arches, bridges, and so on (fig. 8.29C). Although only the upper half of the ellipses are seen in an arch, it will be necessary to know the basic cube or rectangle they were found in and the perspective centers of their shapes.

Once a square or rectangle is created, it may be easily turned into a pyramid, cylinder, or cone by finding the perspective center for the top and bottom planes of the new shapes. For a pyramid (fig. 8.30A), simply draw lines from the top plane's perspective center to the four corners on the bottom plane. For the cylinder (fig. 8.30B), it will be necessary to first draw the proper ellipse on the top

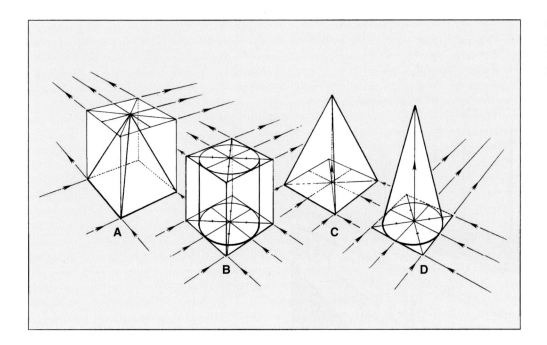

8.30 The concept of locating a plane's perspective center and the correct ellipse to indicate a circle can be extended to create pyramids, cylinders, and cones.

and bottom planes—as described earlier. Then draw vertical lines from the outermost limits of both ellipses. Also note that a second pyramid (fig. 8.30C) and cone (fig. 8.30D) can be drawn with only the establishment of the bottom plane. From the perspective center of the bottom plane, draw a vertical line at any desired length. Then from the end of this line, draw lines to the four corners (for a pyramid) or to the outer-edge points on an ellipse (for a cone).

The system for finding the perspective center of a receding plane can also be used to project known distances back or sideways into space at the proper diminishing rate or ratio. If a telephone company plants seven poles equally spaced down the road, how does an artist know exactly where they should be drawn on the picture plane? Study figure 8.28A, covering up either the top half or the bottom half of the illustration. Note that the diagonal lines (b) stop at the center point. In the portion covered up, they continue on toward the upper and lower corners. Therefore, if the perspective center (vertical or horizontal plane) can be found, a known shape (half a unit) can be projected into a space on the opposite side of the cen-

ter mark by continuing the diagonals until they cross an extension of the top or bottom edge.

To draw equally spaced telephone poles in perspective, simply draw the first pole and extend guidelines from the top and bottom to the vanishing point (fig. 8.31). Draw the second pole touching the top and bottom guidelines at any distance from the first. The two poles should be parallel. Next, find the center of the second pole either by measuring or by finding the perspective center between poles (by intersecting diagonals) and running a guideline from that midpoint to the vanishing point—the guideline will run through the center of the second pole. Then draw a line from the top or bottom of the first pole through the midpoint found on the second pole, extending it until it touches the top and bottom guidelines. Where the extended line touches the guideline, draw another vertical; this will become the next pole at a perspective unit equal to the one just projected. A single diagonal line may be used to project through the center point on the new pole to find the location of the next pole. This process may be repeated as often as necessary until the number of poles desired has been reached.

Spacing may be projected horizontally as well as vertically. The same procedure has been applied to the guardrail poles (and their shadows) in the lower right corner of figure 8.31. In addition, linear projection may be applied to locate floor tiles, windows, or any architectural components with consistent spacing (fig. 8.32).

A perspective drawing may also have several vanishing points other than those located on the horizon line (fig. 8.33). Multiple vanishing points are often used when it is desirable to show multiple objects set at different angles, such as on a gable, a truss-roofed house, a door opening at an angle, or an open box lid. In such cases, the edges of the angular planes are extended to vanishing points separate from the LVP, RVP, or VVP, and any additional images on those planes (like shingles or window panes) would be extended to those new points. A separate vanishing point may also be located to represent a source of light, with all cast shadows being indicated by guidelines projected from it to the ground plane. As a further complication, an artist may encounter situations where houses and other objects are not parallel to each other. As a result, one-, two-, and

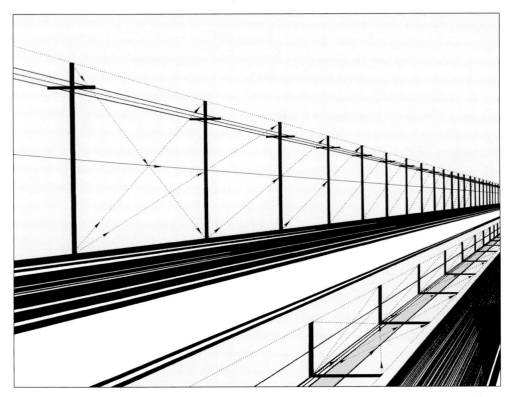

8.31 **Telephone poles showing vertical projection systems.** A given unit—the distance between two telephone poles—may be projected. Extending a diagonal guideline from a corner through the midpoint of the next pole to the appropriate top or bottom guideline reveals the location of the next pole. Units may be projected on a vertical or horizontal plane.

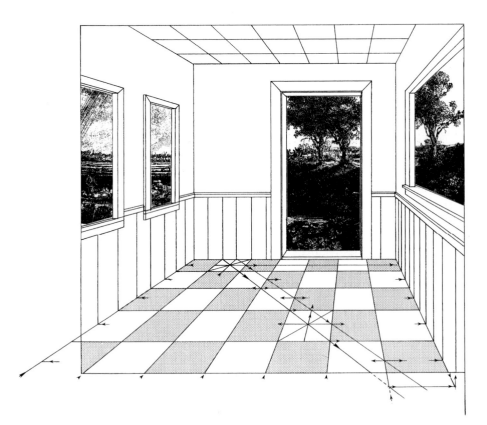

8.32 **A room interior.** Because horizontals and verticals in one-point perspective may be measured, all tile spacing was marked on the back edge of the floor. From the vanishing point, floor lines were extended through each of these points toward the viewer. After establishing the first row of tiles, a diagonal line was extended from corner to corner of one tile and beyond. Where the diagonal crossed each floor line, a horizontal line was drawn, thereby defining a new row of tiles. A second line, passing through the center of the edge of each tile, located points that were projected onto both walls to identify wallboard spacing and window widths.

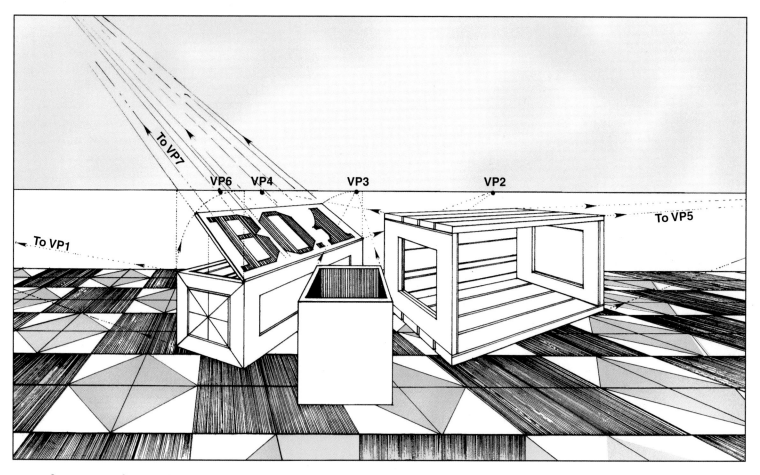

8.33 **Seven in one.** Seven vanishing points (VPs) were used to create this drawing. VPs 1 and 2 were used for the left box. VP 3 was used to create the center cube. VPs 4 and 5 were used for the open crate on the right. VP 6 was used for the floor tiles. VP 7 was used to define the inclined plane of the box lid and its lettering.

possibly three-point perspective systems may all be used in the same drawing.

The Disadvantages of Linear Perspective

Linear perspective has been a traditional drawing device used by artists for centuries. During that time, the system has evolved and undergone modifications in attempts to make it more flexible or more realistic in depicting natural appearances. Some of these include the use of multiple perspectives, with more than three vanishing points, and, at other times, the use of multiple eye levels. Linear perspective was most popular during periods of scientific inquiry and reached its culmination in the mid-nineteenth century. Despite its seeming virtue of accurately depicting natural appearances,

the method has certain disadvantages that, in the opinion of some artists, outweigh its usefulness. Briefly, the liabilities of linear perspective are as follow:

1. It can never depict a shape or mass as it is known to be.
2. It can portray appearances from only one position in space.
3. The necessary recession of parallel lines toward common points readily leads to monotonous effects.
4. The reduction of scale within a single object, resulting from the convergence of lines, is a type of distortion (see fig. 8.14; this diagram indicates that a rectangular shape depicted in perspective becomes a trapezoid and leaves spatial vacuums above C and below D).

These disadvantages are mentioned only to suggest that familiar modes of vision are not necessarily best in every work of art. At times, an intuitive use of perspective can be more expressive than systematic formulas for indicating pictorial depth (see fig. 8.38).

To a certain extent, artists can become prisoners of the system they use. Because of its inflexible rules, perspective emphasizes accuracy of representation—an emphasis that tends to make the presentation more important than what is being represented. If, however, artists see perspective as an aid rather than an end in itself, as something to be used when and if the need arises in creating a picture, it can be very useful (see fig. 8.15). Many fine works of art ignore perspective or show "faults" in the use

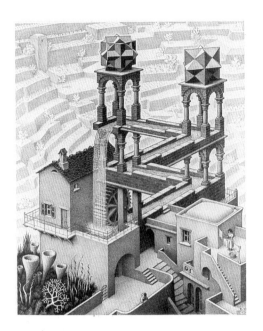

spective, for both present a flat frontal view that is always parallel to the picture plane (fig. 8.35A). However, with oblique projection, all the left- or right-side edges are drawn parallel and come off the frontal plane at a 45-degree angle. (They would have converged at a singular vanishing point, if drawn in one-point perspective.) For engineering and architectural applications, the frontal plane is always drawn at full scale. This use of nonconverging parallel edges on receding planes is also seen in Asian art.

Isometric projection may be compared to two-point perspective in appearance. Both begin with a vertical front edge. However, isometric work does not have any converging receding edges (fig. 8.35B). All edges that intersect at the vertical move away at a 30-degree angle, both to the left and to the right. For ease of drawing, all three dimensions of the object use the same measurement system (scale); there is no diminishing ratio on the receding planes. Hence, this system is used for technical illustration and drafting to illustrate and convey accurate dimensions. Artists often prefer this system to oblique perspective because all three faces are visible at the same time with less apparent distortion. No side of the image is drawn parallel to the viewer (picture plane).

Orthographic drawing is perhaps less understood as a system for identifying objects in a spatial setting, but artists, engineers, industrial designers, and architects use it to present blueprints and schematic layouts (see fig. 9.6). With this system (which presents plan, elevation, and section views), all sides of the rectangular (geometric) object are drawn parallel or perpendicular to a base line, and the measurements are scaled to an exact ratio.

Reverse perspective, as seen in traditional East Asian art, is a dramatic contrast to the linear perspective of the West. Ancient canons prescribed the convergence of "parallel" lines as they *approach* the spectator, rather than

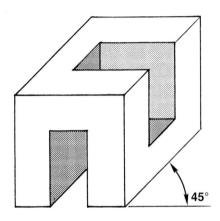

8.35A Oblique projection. This system for showing spatial relationships makes use of a flat frontal shape with nonconverging side planes drawn at a 45-degree angle from the front plane.

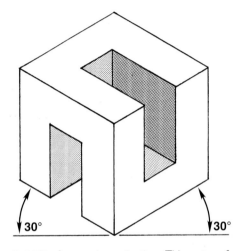

8.35B Isometric projection. This system for showing spatial relationships features a vertical front edge and nonconverging side planes, which are drawn at a 30-degree angle to the left and right.

of the system. In such cases, the type of spatial order created by traditional perspective is not compatible with the aims of the artists (fig. 8.34). However, like any tool, perspective should be learned by artists because it extends the range of conceptual expression.

Other Projection Systems

The spatial position of objects may also be depicted using other graphic systems such as oblique projection, isometric pro-

jection, orthographic projection, and reverse perspective. Most of these methods use nonconverging parallel projecting lines, and because they present a stable and consistently measurable image that does not diminish as it recedes, designers, architects, and technical engineers use them for ease of drawing. These systems do, however, tend to flatten out objects when compared to traditional perspective systems that use vanishing points.

Oblique projection looks, at first glance, to be related to one-point per-

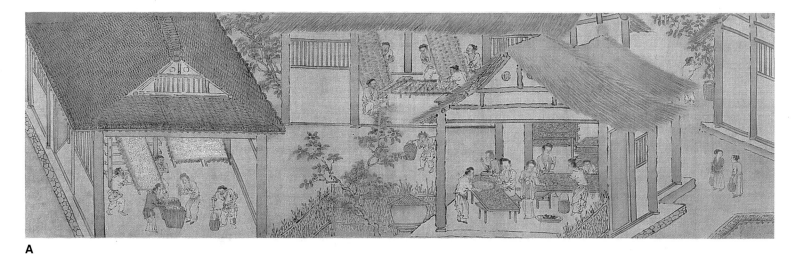

A

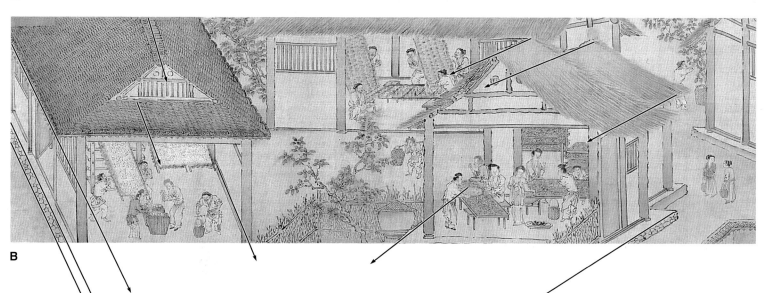

B

8.36 Attributed to Liang Kai, *Sericulture* (detail), Chinese, early thirteenth century, Southern Song dynasty. Handscroll, ink, and light color on paper, 26.5 × 98.5 cm. (A) This Chinese artist, following his own (Asian) concept of space as moving forward toward the observer, employs—from a Western point of view—a kind of reverse perspective. (B) A simple analysis of the *Sericulture* detail shows that if the lines defining the buildings are extended back toward the horizon line, they will never meet as they would in the linear perspective of Western artists. However, if they are extended forward, following the Asian concept of space, they seem to converge. As a result, the front of the buildings is narrower than the back—which is characteristic of East Asian perspective. © The Cleveland Museum of Art, John L. Severance Fund, 1977.5.

as they recede. This type of presentation closes the spatial depth so that the picture becomes a stage and the spectator becomes an actor-participant in an active spatial panorama that rarely loses its identification with the picture plane (fig. 8.36A and B). Similar space concepts have been employed in the West during various historical periods. Ideas on pictorial space usually agree with the prevailing mental climate of the society that produces the art. In this sense, space itself is a form of human expression.

Intuitive Space

The same planes and volumes that create illusions of space in linear perspective can also be used to produce **in-tuitive space**, which is independent of strict rules and formulas. Intuitive space is thus not a system but a product of the artist's instinct for manipulating certain space-producing devices. The devices that help the artist control space include overlapping, transparency, interpenetration, inclined or receding planes (converging parallels), disproportionate scale, and fractional representation.

In addition, the artist may exploit the inherent spatial properties of the art elements. The physical properties of the art elements tend to thrust forward or backward and thus can be used to define items spatially. By marshaling these spatial forces in any combination as needed, the artist can impart a sense of space to the pictorial image while adjusting relationships (fig. 8.37). The space derived from this method is readily sensed by everyone; if judged by the standards of linear perspective, however, it may seem strange, even distorted. Nevertheless, intuitive space has been the dominant procedure during most of the history of art; it rarely implies great depth, but it makes for tightly knit imagery within a relatively shallow spatial field (fig. 8.38).

THE SPATIAL PROPERTIES OF THE ELEMENTS

The spatial effects that arise from using the elements of art structure must be recognized and controlled. Each of the elements possesses inherent spatial qualities, but the interrelationship between elements yields the greatest spatial feeling. The artist can achieve many types of spatial experiences by manipulating the elements—that is, by varying their position, number, direction, value, texture, size, and color. The resultant spatial variations are endless (see fig. 3.19).

Line and Space

Line, by its physical structure, implies continued direction of movement. Thus line, whether moving across the picture plane or deep into it, helps indicate spatial presence. Because, by definition, a line must be greater in length than in width (or else it would be indistinguishable from a dot or a shape), it tends to emphasize one direction. The extension of this dominant direction in a single line creates continu-

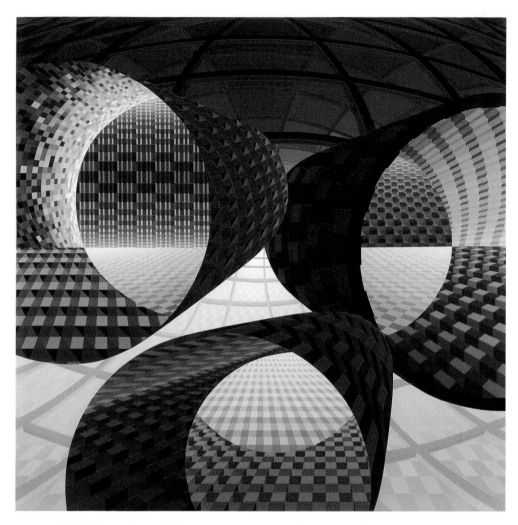

8.37 Al Held, *Bionuclear II*, 2000. Acrylic on canvas, 84 × 84 in. Certain contemporary artists employ individualistic devices to create unusual spatial effects. In this painting, Al Held creates an intuitive sense of space by combining three-dimensional geometric shapes with fragmented planes and surface patterns that do not follow the same "rules" of linear perspective. As a result, what appear to be tunnels soon begin to turn inside out to become multidirectional "wormholes" that transport the viewer to another location or view. © Al Held Foundation/Licensed by VAGA, New York, NY.

ity, moving the eye of the observer from one unit or general area to another. Line can be a transition that unifies the front, middle, and background areas.

In addition to direction, line contains other spatial properties. Long or short lines, thick or thin lines, and straight, angular, or curved lines take on different spatial positions and movements in contrast with one another. The indications of three-dimensional space mentioned earlier in this chapter are actively combined with the physical properties of line. A long thick line, for instance, appears larger (a spatial indication)

and hence closer to the viewer than a short thin line. Overlapping lines establish differing spatial positions, especially when they are set in opposite directions (e.g., vertical against horizontal). A diagonal line may be made to move from the picture plane into deep space, whereas a vertical or horizontal line generally appears comparatively static (fig. 8.39). In addition, the plastic qualities of overlapping lines can be increased by modulating their values. Lines can be lightened to the point that they disappear or become "lost," only to reappear (be-

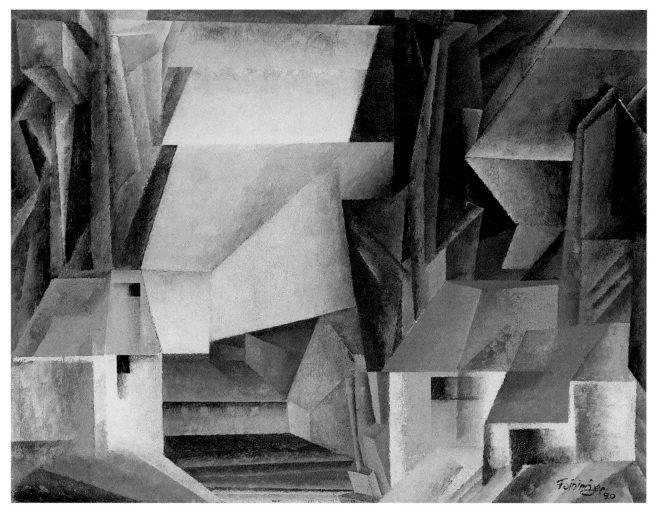

8.38 Lyonel Feininger, *Hopfgarten,* 1920. Oil on canvas, 25 × 32¼ in. In this painting, the artist has used intuitive methods of space control, including overlapping planes and transparencies, as well as planes that interpenetrate one another and incline into space. The Minneapolis Institute of the Arts. Given in memory of Catharine Roberts Seybold by her friends and family.

come "found") and grow darker across the composition. This missing section, or *implied line,* can also help control compositional direction or movement. The modulated plastic illusion invariably suggests change of position in space.

The spatial indication of line convergence that occurs in linear perspective is always in evidence wherever a complex of lines occurs. The spatial suggestions arising out of this principle are so infinitely varied that particular effects are usually the product of the artist's intuitive explorations. Wavy, spiral, serpentine, and zigzag line types adapt to all kinds of space through their un-

expected deviations of direction and accent. They seem to move back and forth from one spatial plane to another. Unattached single lines define their own space and may have plastic qualities within themselves. Lines also clarify the spatial dimensions of solid shapes (fig. 8.40).

Shape and Space

Shape may refer to planes, solids, or volumes, all of which occupy space and are therefore entitled to consideration in this chapter. A planar shape, although physically two-dimensional, may create the illusion of three-dimensional space

(see fig. 4.10). The space appears two-dimensional when the plane seems to lie on the picture surface (see fig. 4.1). The space appears three-dimensional when its edges seem to converge at a point toward the front or the back of the picture plane (see figs. 2.21 and 8.23).

Solids, volumes, and masses automatically suggest three dimensions. Such shapes express the space in which they must exist and become an actual part of it (figs. 8.41 and 8.42). The spatial position of planes, solids, and volumes can be made distant by diminishing their size in comparison to others in the foreground and by neutralizing their

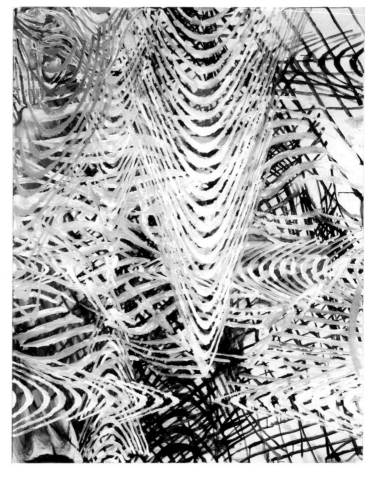

8.39 Terry Winters, *Untitled (Indigo)*, 2003. Oil on linen, 77 × 59½ in. The physical characteristics and properties of each line contribute to the development of the space within this painting. Individual lines overlap, converge, and define their own space while collectively creating a relatively deep visual labyrinth. © Terry Winters, Courtesy Matthew Marks Gallery, New York.

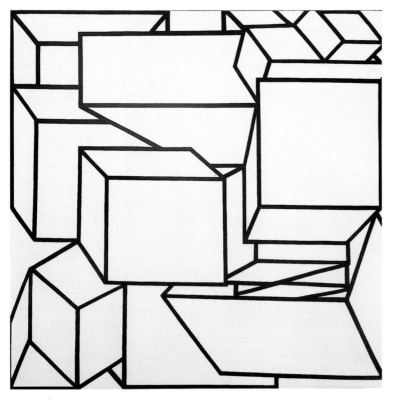

8.40 Al Held, *B/WX*, 1968. Acrylic on canvas, 9 ft. 6 in. × 9 ft. 6 in. (2.90 × 2.90 m). Although the physical properties of the lines in this work are consistent throughout, their arrangement causes the enclosed shapes to be seen in different spatial positions. This is somewhat similar to the program of Op Art. Albright-Knox Art Gallery, Buffalo, NY. Gift of Seymour H. Knox, 1969. © Al Held/Licensed by VAGA, New York, NY.

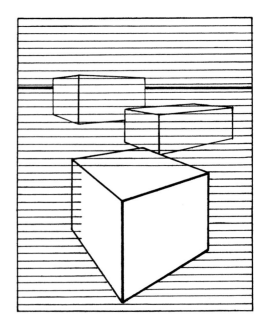

8.41 Planes and solids in space. The relationship of planes in this diagram describes an effect of solids or volumes that in turn seem to occupy space. The size, overlapping, and placement of these volumes further increase the effect of solidity. The horizontal shaded lines indicate an imaginary position for the picture plane, causing the near volume to project into the observer's space, or in front of the picture plane.

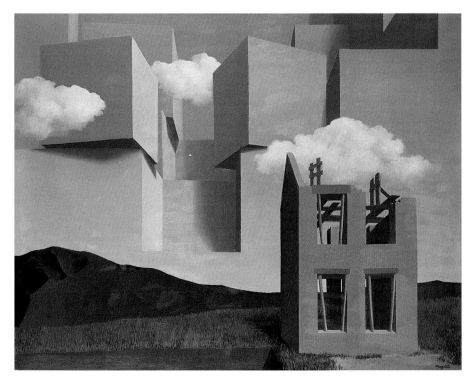

8.42 René Magritte, *The Unmasked Universe*, 1932. Oil on canvas, 29.5 × 35.8 in. (75 × 91 cm). On close inspection, one can see that this work is deliberately inconsistent in its use of space. As a Surrealist, Magritte often created ambiguous and unexpected effects to titillate our senses. Art © 2008 C. Herscovici, London/Artists Rights Society (ARS), NY. © Photo Herscovici/Art Resource.

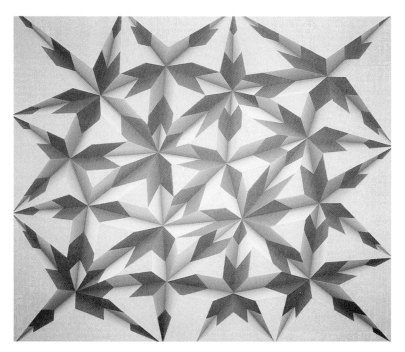

8.43 Tony King, *Map: Spirit of '76*, 1976. Acrylic and newspaper on canvas, 7 × 8 ft. (2.13 × 2.44 m). The format, with its papier collé surface, is perfectly flat, but the use of light and dark values creates a strongly three-dimensional illusion. Courtesy of Owens Corning Collection, Toledo, OH.

value, color, intensity, and detail (see fig. 8.38). This treatment relates back to the indications of space outlined earlier in this chapter.

Value and Space

The plastic effect of value can be used to control pictorial space. When a light source is assumed to be in front of a work, the objects in the foreground appear light. The middle and background objects become progressively darker as they move away from the picture plane (see fig. T.27). When the light source is located at the back of the work, the order of values is reversed (see fig. 6.17). The order of value change is consistent in gradation from light to dark or dark to light.

In the natural world, foreground objects are seen with clarity and great contrast, while distant objects are ill defined and gray. Therefore, neutral grays, when juxtaposed with blacks or whites, generally take a distant position (see fig. 8.4).

Cast shadows are sometimes helpful in describing plastic shape (see figs. 5.10A and 5.15), but they may be spatially confusing and even injurious to the design if not handled judiciously (see fig. 5.9). Shapes that are defined by multiple light sources, however, may appear flattened and decorative (see fig. 5.10B).

Value-modeling can be abstract in the sense that it need not follow the objective natural order of light and dark. Many artists totally ignore this natural order, using instead the inherent spatial position that results from the contrast of dark and light (fig. 8.43).

Texture and Space

Because of the surface enrichment that texture produces, it is tempting to think of this element purely in terms of decorative usefulness. However, texture can also have the plastic function of describing the depth position of surfaces. Sharp, clear, and bold textures generally advance, while fuzzy, dull, and minuscule textures generally recede (see fig. 6.17). When modified through varied use of value, color, and line, texture significantly contributes to the total pictorial unity.

Texture is one of the visual signs used to produce the decorative surface so valued in contemporary art. The physical character of texture is related to allover patterned design and therefore operates effectively on decorative surfaces. When patterned surfaces are repeated and distributed over the entire pictorial area, the flatness of the picture plane becomes vitally important. Many works by Pablo Picasso utilize surface textures to preserve the flatness of the picture plane (see fig. 6.16).

Color and Space

One of the outstanding contributions of modern artists has been their reevaluation of the plastic potentials of color. Color is now integrated directly into the picture in a positive and direct manner in order to model the various spatial planes of surface areas (see the "Plastic Colors" section in Chapter 7). Since the time of Cézanne, a new awareness of the spatial characteristics of color has arisen in art. Prior to that, space was considered as deriving from the picture plane and receding from it. Later, John Marin and others dealt with the spaces on or in front of the picture plane chiefly through the use of color (fig. 8.44). Hans Hofmann, the abstractionist, often used colors to advance shapes seemingly beyond the picture plane. He controlled the degree to which they advanced or receded by contrasts of value, intensity, and hue (fig. 8.45).

Analogous colors, because they are closely related, create limited spatial movement; contrasting colors enlarge the space and provide varied accents or focal points of interest. Changes in value and intensity also contribute to the spatial differences. All exploit the limitless dimensions of space.

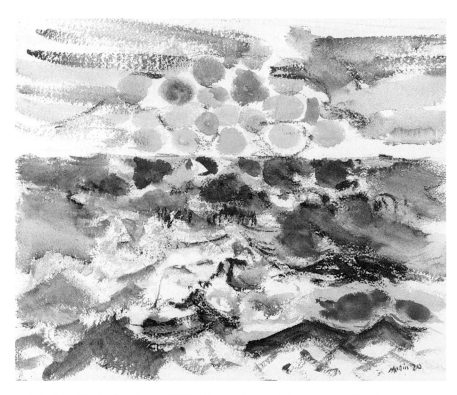

8.44 John Marin, *Sun Spots*, 1920. Watercolor and charcoal on off-white wove paper, 16½ × 19¾ in. (41.9 × 50.2 cm). Marin used the watercolor medium to exhibit a free, loose style of painting. His play of color—sea against sunspots—helps create tremendous spatial interaction. The Metropolitan Museum of Art, Alfred Stieglitz Collection, 1949 (49.70.121). Photo © The Metropolitan Museum of Art.

8.45 Hans Hofmann, *The Gate*, 1959–60. Oil on canvas, 6 ft. 3⅛ in. × 4 ft. ½ in. (1.9 × 1.23 m). The large receding areas of cool greens and blues in this painting unify the color scheme. The smaller areas of warm yellows and reds give balance to the total color pattern. Spatial contrast is softened and the composition is harmonized by the lower intensity of the colors used. Solomon R. Guggenheim Museum, New York, NY. 62.1620. Photograph by David Heald. © Estate of Hans Hofmann/ Licensed by VAGA, New York, NY.

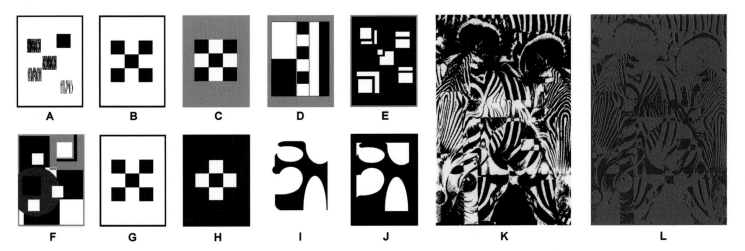

8.46 Structured ambiguity versus stable figure/ground relationships.

STRUCTURED AMBIGUITY

We have studied the graphic development of three-dimensional space and have looked at the common spatial indicators like size, position, overlapping, clarity of detail, and so forth. In the process, we have seen that pictorial space often depends on the viewer's ability to recognize a line, a group of marks, or a shape. Once identified, the line, marks, or shape become the positive figure(s) within a spatial reference relative to the surrounding area or ground.

Now, however, we would like to consider for a moment a different type of space—albeit an ambiguous or uncertain space—called **structured ambiguity.** This space occurs when a mark, a group of marks, or a shape seems vague or unreadable—appearing to be positive (figure) at one moment but negative (background) at the next. It may even fluctuate back and forth between the two states. This is a situation that denies a clear shape identity and thus prevents a clear sense of space.

As a spatial condition, even though uncertain, structured ambiguity can be a very important tool in the development of optical illusions and softening spatial effects; it also functions as a valuable transition between areas of contrasting values or opposing colors, which makes for interesting value patterns (see figs. 2.19 and 3.14C). For these reasons alone, it is important to understand how structured ambiguities may be created. However, it's also important to know when to avoid them. Images will likely be more readable without ambiguous spatial references and confusing figure/ground identity. So, if structured ambiguity is introduced where needed and avoided where inappropriate, the resulting images will have the best of both worlds: smooth transitions between opposing grounds, recognizable shapes, interesting value patterns, and convincing pictorial space.

How, then, is a structured ambiguity created, and what conditions cause it to occur? When the artist's pen, pencil, or brush touches the white picture plane, two things happen. First, the resulting mark defines a location and divides, to some extent, the picture plane. Generally, the mark is seen as a positive image, while the remaining area is perceived as negative. Second, the mark may seem to take a position in front of or at some distance behind the picture plane. Each of these results will continue to be important as the work develops.

As marks accumulate and become shapes, the artist begins to design these shapes into an organized pattern. In figure 8.46A, the shapes are seen as black positive figures on a white negative ground. When the shapes are drawn close together, as in figure 8.46B, the black pattern still reads as positive and the white as the negative ground. But, when the areas of black and white are relatively equal in volume—neither surrounding the other—or when they are surrounded by a third value or color (fig. 8.46C), the figure/ground relationship between the black and white areas is much less obvious, even impossible to distinguish. One moment the black shapes are perceived as positive, making a pattern on a white ground, and the next moment the reverse—the spatial relationship between the black areas and the white areas has been lost.

The primary cause of this ambiguity is a state of *equivalency*. Equal amounts of any or all of the following elements may cause the unstable figure/ground condition:

- The size of the positive and negative areas involved
- The volume of black and white or opposing color used to define the shapes
- The size of the marks made and the spaces between them
- The character of the marks and the character of the negative areas (including direction, width, and length)
- The shape type
- The application or general quality of any of the elements used to define the positive and negative areas (texture, color, value, intensity, and so forth).

Ambiguous space also occurs when one shape or color is not allowed to surround another (fig. 8.46D, see also fig. 2.8) or when all shapes run off the edges of the composition (see fig. 1.37). In both of these situations, the viewer cannot tell where the shapes begin or end, which adds instability to the spatial condition. Because the shapes in figure 8.46A, B, and E are surrounded, they have a greater probability of functioning as figures, or positive areas; the surrounding color becomes an area of background because of the *difference* in the amount of black and white along with the variation in size of those shapes.

It is interesting to note that there are times when a positive area can act as a negative *without* necessarily creating a sense of ambiguous space. This can be seen in figure 8.46F, where a large red circle (seen as a positive against the black) can also function as a background for smaller black and white squares (see also fig. 2.24). The smaller shapes remain positive while the red circle fluctuates between positive and negative, depending upon where we focus our attention.

Beginning artists are often advised not to mat with black mats, because doing so can destroy the pattern of the original figure/ground relationship. For example, in figure 8.46G, positive black shapes create a design on a white background. But when closely cropped with a black mat, as in figure 8.46H, the planned pattern of the black shapes becomes part of the background and the white background becomes the positive pattern—this unplanned shift could greatly alter the effectiveness of the original design. This may occur even with multisided shapes, as in figures 8.46I and 8.46J. The same concept also applies to colored mats on work with colored shapes.

In addition to denying clear spatial references in a work, the creation of structured ambiguity can make some drawn images nearly impossible to recognize. It can even make typeface difficult to read when the size of the type and the space around it are too closely related. Quite clearly, the inclusion or exclusion of structured ambiguity will greatly influence the designing process.

Although simplified geometric shapes were used for the sake of clarity in these illustrations, the same principles apply to more complicated studio work. In figures 8.46K and 8.46L, structured ambiguity allows the Zebras to be more difficult to discover, as if camouflaged within the elements of the composition. Shapes run off the edges of the composition. Implied edges create additional floating shapes that seem both positive and negative. Because it is unclear where the shapes truly begin or end, entire areas of the work fluctuate between figure and ground. The image is also filled with similar shape type, direction, length, width, texture, color, and intensity. All of these factors contribute to the viewer's inability to find the animals.

To fully understand the changing ground conditions inherent in a structured ambiguity, it must be experienced firsthand. There is an exercise to help an artist discern the moment when developing forms reverse their ground relationships or become ambiguous. It requires a source of interesting typeface and a pair of cropper bars. The objective will be to slide the cropper bars around until shapes lose the identity of the typeface and create uncertainty about whether they function as figure or background. The exercise is illustrated in figure 8.47 A through L.

In figure 8.47A, the letters definitely read as yellow figure on a black background. As you slide the cropper bars around, reducing the amount of background, there will be a moment when the identity of the letters is destroyed and the relationship between what is positive and what is negative is lost (fig. 8.47B and C). When that moment occurs, try to discern the relationship of the volume of both colors. Figure 8.47D illustrates the same solution but with multiple colors.

With letters that have distinct shapes, it may be more difficult to lose the letter's identity, as demonstrated in figure 8.47F through I. In order to create structured ambiguity in those cases, it may help to change the angle or work upside down; seeing the shape in a new context will probably help it lose its old identity (in fig. 8.47, compare H to I and C to E).

If you continue to crop in closer after reaching a state of structured ambiguity, you will experience the figure/ground relationship reversing again. In figure 8.47J, the green letter has been cropped so close that it has become the background—and the red background has now become the positive figure.

In figure 8.47K, this exercise is applied to a woodcut print with black lines on white and white lines on black. By cropping in, an area is located where the marks do not have a stable figure/ground relationship (fig 8.47L). This is an area of structured ambiguity that is functioning as a transition between the two ground systems. As you experiment, try compositions made with one, two, and three letters; compositions involving different frame shapes (rectangles, circles, ovals, diamonds, or multisided formats); compositions using color; and images consisting of differing types of balance (from radial to symmetrical to asymmetrical).

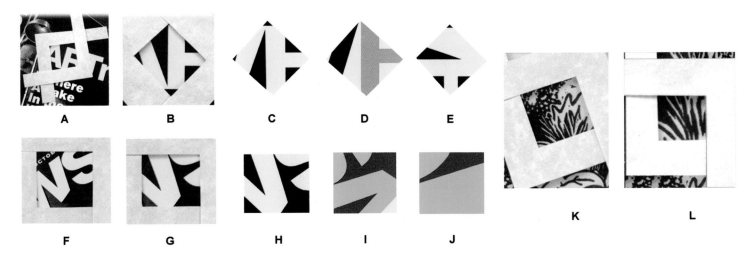

8.47 A structured ambiguity exercise.

Once an artist understands what creates structured ambiguity, he or she can choose to incorporate it or avoid it. Images can be made to read clearly with the subtlest of adjustments to the relationship between the positive or negative areas; whether or not this is beneficial depends on the work and the artist's intention. Since the positive area gets the most attention by its very function, it is even more important to grow sensitive to how the negative areas are being planned and how they affect the compositions. Creating structured ambiguities will help establish optical illusions, create compositions in which you wish to deny space, transition between areas of contrast, or make an area or image softly blend into its surrounding area. Both structured ambiguity and stable figure/ground relationships are useful in the right setting, and both, when grasped, are valuable tools at the disposal of the artist.

THREE-DIMENSIONAL APPLICATIONS OF SPACE

In pictorial art, space is an illusion and has been presented as a *product* of the elements. However, in the three-dimensional arts—such as sculpture, ceramics, jewelry, architecture, and much installation work—space actually exists and must be treated as an element. For artists working in those three-dimensional areas, space may be characterized as a boundless extension of area in all directions. In so far as pure space has no visual qualities, a medium is necessary to define and limit the boundaries of the space that is to be used.

When artists use space, they tend to limit its vastness. They may mark off extensions in one, two, or three dimensions or use measurable distances between preestablished elements. Objects are used to displace space and to control spatial intervals while manipulating depth. Rectangular and ovoidal shapes control space effectively, because their weight is felt and established by the flat or rounded dimensions of the surfaces (fig. 8.48). Although these two solids are three-dimensional, their spatial indications are minimal. Greater interest and, in turn, greater spatial qualities could be added to the two shapes by manipulating their surfaces. If material were cut away, the space would move inward, and if material were added, the space would move outward. The two shapes seen together create a spatial interval. This, too, could be manipulated to create varied interest.

The increasing complexity of three-dimensional organization may be see in figure 8.49, using bricks as simple sculptural objects. In figure 8.49A, four bricks have been arranged in a very restricted manner to form a large, minimal rectangular solid. The individual bricks are distinguished only by the cracklike edges visible in the front and side planes. These linear edges are reminiscent of graphic linear renderings—decorative and without much physical or spatial presence. This minimalist approach is evident in the individual forms seen in the work of Donald Judd (see fig. 2.66) and Judy Chicago (see fig. 2.72).

The four bricks illustrated in figure 8.49B are separated by indentations similar to the mortar joints used by masons. These gaps, though relatively shallow, nevertheless produce distinctively clearer and darker edges than those shown in figure 8.49A. Although the darker edges indicate greater three-dimensional variation than in the first stack of bricks shown, they still have decided spatial limitations. Many low-**relief sculptures** (sometimes known as *bas-relief*) function in a similar way (see fig. 3.33).

The bricks in figure 8.49C utilize even more space. They are positioned so that the planes moving in depth are contrasted with the front and top planes,

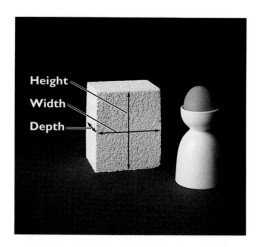

8.48 The rectangular and ovoid solids are examples of two minimal objects that can be formed from displaced, boundless space. The flat and rounded planes in these positions define their special characteristics and spatial intervals. Photograph: Lynn Whitney.

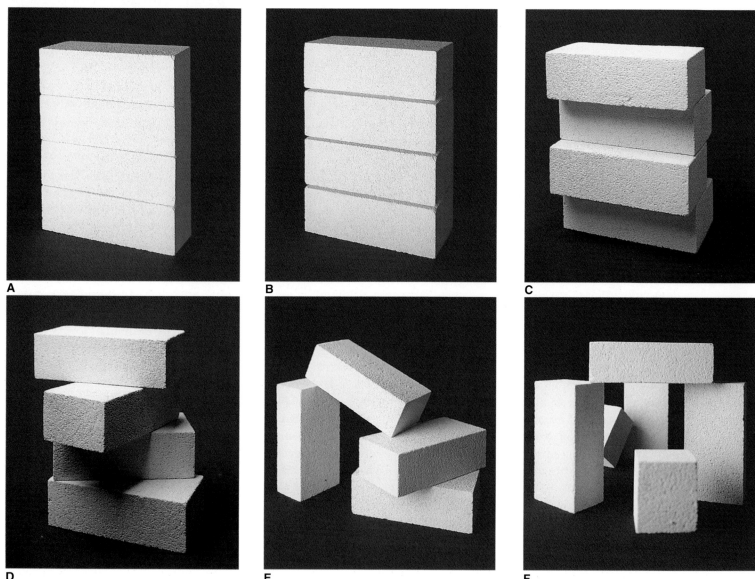

8.49 These figures show bricks that have been arranged and rearranged to illustrate an increasing level of visual complexity within the third dimension—this is achieved by interactions between the *positive* objects and *negative* sculptural spaces. (A) Closely stacked bricks, (B) separated bricks, (C) alternated bricks, (D) rotated bricks, (E) crossed and slanted bricks, (F) greatly separated bricks. Photographs: Lynn Whitney.

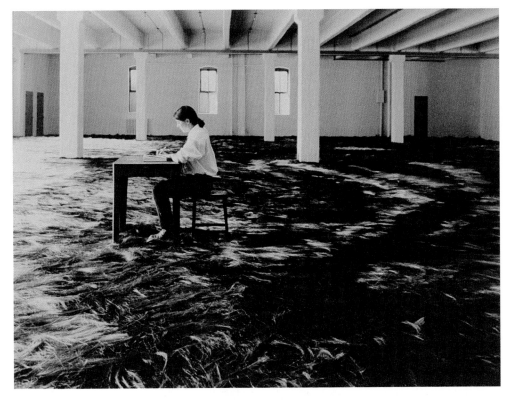

8.50 Ann Hamilton, *tropos,* 1993. Installation. Hamilton's installations seem to provide an imaginative, strangely moving, sensuous world beyond verbal or logical apprehension. They offer a direct bodily sensation or experience that is at the core of human instincts, as the title of this work implies. Courtesy of Sean Kelly Gallery, New York. Photo courtesy of Dia Center for the Arts. Photographer Thibault Jenson.

which move toward and away from the viewer. The light that strikes the grouping produces stronger shadows and more interesting value patterns than are found in figure 8.49B. This arrangement can be compared to the qualities of *high-relief* sculpture, in which the sculpted figures almost seem to free themselves from their supporting panel. The play of deep shadows against the lights on projecting parts of a high-relief sculpture can increase the work's expressive or emotional qualities, as seen in *The Gates of Hell* by Rodin (see fig. 7.49).

Although the bricks are still in a compact and closed arrangement, their rotation in figure 8.49D makes possible new directions and spatial relationships. The work is becoming more spatially interesting as contrasts of movement, light, and shadow increase. In a way, this inward and outward play of bricks

is similar to what the sculptor creates in a freestanding form (sometimes referred to as *sculpture-in-the-round*—meaning 3-D work not attached to a wall surface). Such works are no longer concerned with simple front and side views but with multiple axes and vantage points; this instills the viewer with a desire to move about the piece (see figs. 2.60 and 5.26).

The variety of brick positions in figure 8.49E, particularly that of the diagonally tipped brick, creates far greater exploitation of space than the previous groupings. The **void,** or open space, emphasizes the three-dimensional quality of the arrangement by producing a direct link between the space on each side. This approach is found in John Goforth's *Untitled* (see fig. 1.43), John Mishler's *Wind Seeker* (see fig. 2.63), and Bill Barrett's *Kindred* (see fig. 3.30).

In figure 8.49F, the bricks are separated and achieve even greater spatial independence. They represent the sculptural images seen in architectural settings or **installations,** which invite us to walk into and around them to experience the expanded sense of space. In *The Gates* Project for Central Park, New York, Christo and Jeanne-Claude created a saffron environment using fabric-covered gates. To appreciate its ever-changing relationships and multiple views, the viewer had to stroll the miles of covered walkway (see fig. 1.28). Patrick Daugherty's twisting and tilting woven structures also invite us to change our perceptions of the environment (see fig. 6.21). Sandy Skoglund appeals to our sense of exploration in a different way with her surreal space; not allowed entry, viewers had to study the relationships between fox and environment as visitors in a dream in *Fox Games* (see fig. 1.31). Sometimes the space between units can be threatening, as in the work of Rebecca Horn, who presents a piano hanging overhead and questions the viewer's willingness to tempt fate (fig. 1.29). However, Ann Hamilton uses the space to confront the viewer with an oddly sensuous experience (fig. 8.50). And finally, in the interactive video/sound/space installations by artists like Jennifer Steinkamp (see fig. 7.4), the activity of the viewer within the space directs the creation of the ongoing image. This integration of time and motion expands the work beyond three dimensions—and develops what may be thought of as **four-dimensional space** (this will be fully discussed in Chapter 9, "Time and Motion").

Thus, we have seen the understanding and application of spatial concepts grow increasingly more complex. Regardless of whether one incorporates these concepts in clay, silver, cast bronze, or mixed media, the challenge for the artist is the same—to define the space, limit its boundaries, and give it significance through an expression of form.

Time and Motion

CHAPTER NINE

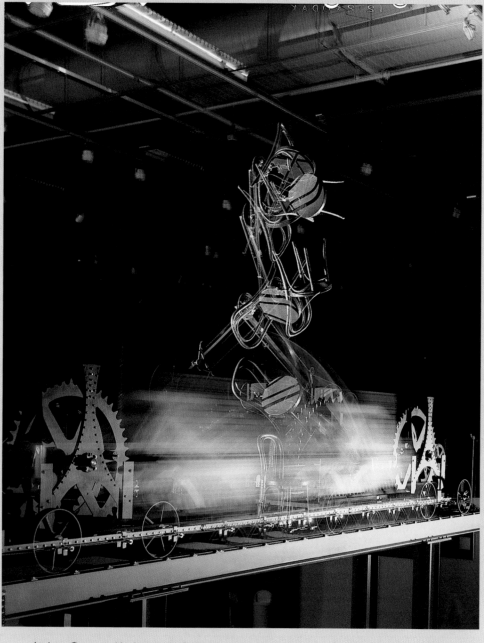

Arthur Ganson, *Machine with Chair* (time-lapse photograph of 1995 version), 1995.
Arthur Ganson is a sculptor at the Massachusetts Institute of Technology. Photograph by Henry Groskinsky.

THE VOCABULARY OF
TIME AND MOTION

Time — A system or way of measuring the interval between events or experiences.
Motion — The process of moving, or changing place or position in space.

actual motion
The movement found in art forms like kinetic art, where bodies physically change their location during a period of time.

animation
The rapid succession of a sequence of drawings, computer-generated images, or pictures of objects such as clay figures that create the illusion of a moving image.

cell (or single cell)
One image from a series of related images that presents an idea. Cells are commonly found in comic strips, graphic novels, or storyboard presentations, which tend to isolate the images from each other by an outline in the shape of a rectangle. Cells also refer to the individual frames of animated cartoons.

close-up
A cinematic technique in which the subject fills the camera frame; used to focus the viewer's attention on specific imagery or detail.

crosscutting
A cinematic technique that abruptly shifts from one event or character to another and is often used to allow the viewer to move between characters and change points of view as the dialogue or action evolves.

dissolve
An aesthetic technique, used as a film or video transition between images or scenes, in which one shot disappears as another slowly appears.

duration
The length of time in which an activity takes place.

fade
An aesthetic technique, used as a film or video transition between scenes, in which the image slowly darkens to black.

flashback
A cinematic technique of jumping to a sequence of events in the story that are meant to have taken place in the past.

flash-forward
A cinematic technique of jumping to a sequence of events in the story that are meant to take place in the future.

four-dimensional space
An imaginative treatment of forms that gives a sense of intervals of time or motion.

frame
A single static image as applied to cartoons, storyboards, animation, films, videos, or computer-generated graphics.

Futurism
An early-twentieth-century movement that sought to express the fourth dimension through the speed, power, and motion of the industrial age.

implied motion
The sense or illusion of movement given to a static object.

installations
Interior or exterior settings of media created by artists to heighten the viewer's awareness of the environmental space.

kinetic
Derived from the Greek word *kinesis,* meaning "motion." Kinetic art includes the element of actual motion.

long shot
A cinematic technique in which the filmmaker provides a distant view with a broader perspective of image; often used to imply a larger conceptual context.

medium shot
A cinematic technique in which the filmmaker provides a view that seems to lie somewhere between a close-up and a long shot.

mobile
A three-dimensional moving sculpture.

motion
The process of moving, or changing place or position in space.

motion picture
The illusion of a moving image created by showing a series of still pictures in rapid sequence.

multimedia
The combination of many different groups of media such as text, still and moving graphics, and spoken and instrumental sounds; also often integrated with communication technologies involving television, video, telephones, and computers.

multiple exposures
A photographic technique that shows a figure in motion by displaying a rapid series of exposures within the same image.

slow motion
1. A cinematic technique that slows down the movement and time in a film; created by shooting a high number of frames per second and showing them at a much slower speed.
2. The sense that time and movement are progressing more slowly than normal.

still frame
One frame (or full-screen image) from a series of frames normally seen in a film or video presentation that when viewed in sequence present the illusion of a moving picture. Related to **cell.**

superimposing, superimposed images
A technique in which various views of the same subject are placed on top of each other in the same image.

time
A system or way of measuring the interval between events or experiences.

video
A recording of visual images that are stored in an electronic format (digital or videotape) and viewed on a television, computer monitor, or projection screen. The sensation of motion is an illusion created by the rapid sequence of images.

THE SEARCH FOR A NEW SPATIAL DIMENSION

Every great period in the history of art has espoused a particular concept of space. These spatial preferences reflect basic conditions within the civilization that produced them. When a new spatial approach is introduced, it is at first resisted by the public. Eventually, however, it becomes the standard filter through which people view things. During the periods of their influence, these conventions become the norms of vision.

Artists of the Renaissance, for example, conditioned by the outlook of the period, sought to accomplish the optical, scientific mastery of nature by reducing it part-by-part to a static geometric system. By restricting their attention to one point of view, artists were able to develop perspective and represent some of the illusory distortions of actual shapes as seen by the human eye. Modern artists, however, equipped with new scientific and industrial materials and technology, have extended the search into nature initiated during the Renaissance. The acceleration of change prompted by the cataclysmic revelations of modern science has produced new concepts that are without precedent. Nature's inner and outer structures have been probed with microscope, camera, and telescope. Automobiles, airplanes, and spacecraft have given us the opportunity to see more of the world than our early predecessors knew existed. The radically changed environment of the artist has brought about a new awareness of space. It has become increasingly evident that space cannot always be described from one point of view, and the search continues for a new graphic vocabulary to describe visual discoveries.

Because one outstanding feature of the modern world is **motion,** it has become a motivating factor in much contemporary artistic expression. Motion and the resulting passage of **time** have both become a part of space, and they are represented by artists in ways that reflect the speed and pace of the contemporary world. Hence, a new dimension is added to spatial conception—the *fourth dimension:* time and space. Whether the goal is to represent moving images or to create real-time interactive artwork, the power and energy of **four-dimensional space** continues to captivate. And as our methods of personal communication and entertainment change to incorporate the wonder of technological advancements, there is no doubt that artistic expressions of space, time, and motion will also continue to evolve.

PICTORIAL REPRESENTATIONS OF MOVEMENT IN TIME

Writers and musicians have some control over the amount of time their audiences must devote, from beginning to end, to a written or musical piece. By contrast, the work of graphic artists has nearly always been immediate and comprehendible at a glance. In an effort to capture their audience for longer amounts of time, many graphic artists have explored ways of slowing the viewing experience by manipulating the sense of space and movement within the work.

As discussed in Chapter 2, various treatments and combinations of the elements will alter the viewer's eye movement across and through the composition. This entices the viewer to spend time looking at the work, although it does not necessarily express the ideas of movement and time as concepts themselves. In fact, visual artists have always struggled with the problem of depicting movement and the passage of time within the boundaries of the two-dimensional picture plane. How does one represent the movement of the subject? the movement of the viewer? The search is not just about how to direct the amount of time spent looking at the image but also how to capture the sense of time through the appearance of physical motion, the expectation of motion, and/or the sensation of being moved.

Implied Motion through Line Direction or Shape Position

From time immemorial, artists have grappled with the problem of representing movement on the stationary picture surface. In the works of prehistoric and primitive cultures, the efforts were not organized but instead were isolated attempts to show a limited phase of observed activity (such as moving animals or ritualistic kills). Then, as now, when the subject seems paused in the midst of action, and relatively imbalanced, the threat of gravity creates an almost tangible sense of impending movement (see fig. 2.6).

The subject's motion can also be implied through the general direction and repetition of lines and shapes (see figs. 1.19, 2.10, and 2.56). This applies even more so to nonobjective images, which do not have the power of suggestion so inherent in recognizable shapes (see figs. 2.8 and 3.19); here, movement is created by the direction of shapes, edge quality, and color placement. The feeling of motion is further enhanced when the elements create an optical illusion—contrasting colors and shapes can make the image pop out toward the viewer or create an undulating spatial movement (see fig. 9.1; see also fig. T.77). In figurative work, gestural line is often used to capture the excitement and activity of the characters that are portrayed (see figs. 3.23, 3.24, and 3.25); although, in

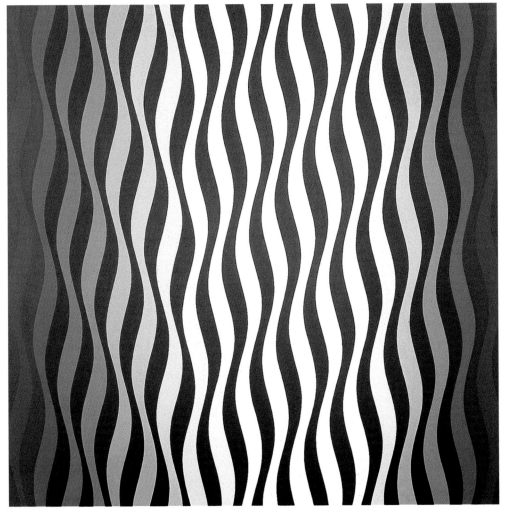

9.1 Bridget Riley, *Drift No. 2*, 1966. Acrylic on canvas, 7 ft. 7½ in. × 7 ft. 5½ in. (2.32 × 2.27 m). Op artists generally use geometric shapes, organizing them into patterns that produce fluctuating, ambiguous, and tantalizing visual effects very similar to those observed in moire patterns, such as in door or window screens. Albright-Knox Art Gallery, Buffalo, NY. Gift of Seymour H. Knox, 1967.

the nonobjective works of artists like Jackson Pollock, the gestural lines capture the very movement and energy of the artist himself (see fig. T.71).

Sequenced Images

The artists of the medieval and early-Renaissance periods illustrated biblical stories by repeating a series of still pictures. The representation of the different phases of the narrative (either in a sequence of several pictures or a sequence within a single work) created a visual synopsis of the subject's movement within a designated space and over a given period of time (figs. 9.2 and 9.3). These pictures are antecedents of the modern comic strip and graphic novel. They are also the forebears of **animation,** in which individual **frames** are presented in rapid sequence to make the image appear to move on the screen (see fig. 9.15).

Some contemporary artists, such as Lanna Pendleton Hall, instill the sense of time's passage by creating subtly changing **cells** within a single image.

Together, these segments seem to capture a fuller experience of the time spent lingering at that scene (fig. 9.4).

Multiple Viewpoints

In the nineteenth century, Paul Cézanne, a Post-Impressionist painter, tried another approach to introduce the concepts of movement, time, and space—and in turn, extended the viewer's involvement with a painting. His aim was to render objects in a manner more "true to nature." This nature, it should be pointed out, was not the Renaissance world of optical appearances; instead, it was a world of forms in space, conceived in terms of a plastic image. His images emphasized the mass and volume of forms by presenting them in a way that included many vantage points rather than a single one, as had been the traditional approach. In addition, he also often saw them as abstracted to basic cones, cubes, and squares.

In his still-life paintings, Cézanne frequently shifted the viewpoint within the same work from the right side to the left side and from the top to the bottom, creating the illusion of looking around an object. He changed the eye levels, split the individual object planes, and combined all of these views in the same painting, creating a composite view of the group (fig. 9.5). It was almost as if the viewer had been invited to bring in a ladder and view part of the material from a low position and then climb far up the ladder to see other sections before moving the ladder and continuing to search for new views of the objects. This presentation of multiple views essentially reflects our typical experience of the volume and mass of actual objects—we move around them or revolve them in front of us. However, all of the vantage points—as well as the time necessary to discover them—are represented in a single painting.

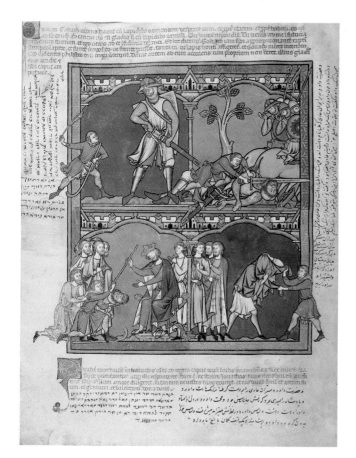

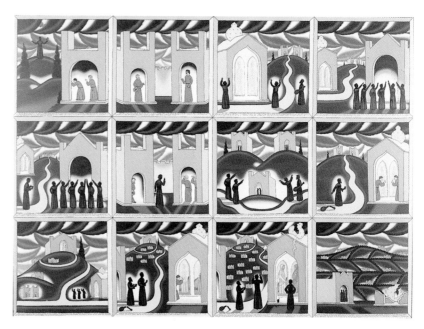

9.3 Roger Brown, *Giotto and His Friends (Getting Even),* 1981. Oil on canvas, 6 ft. × 8 ft. ⅜ in. (1.83 × 2.45 m). Contemporary artist Roger Brown has used the historical technique of segmental narrative. Each segment of the work is a portion of an unfolding story. © The School of the Art Institute of Chicago and the Brown Family.

9.2 Unknown, *David and Goliath,* c. 1250. Manuscript, 15⅜ × 11¾ in. (39 × 30 cm). The element of time passing is present here but in a conventional episodic manner. The order of events proceeds in a style similar to that of a comic strip. Pierpont Morgan Library, New York, M.638 f.28v./Art Resource, New York.

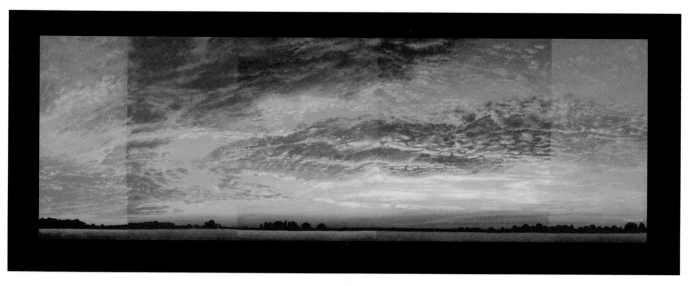

9.4 Lanna Pendleton Hall, *Spectacular Sunrise,* 2006. Oil on linen, 24 × 72 in. (61 × 182.9 cm). This contemporary painting uses a sequence of images to create the sense of passing time. The subtle changes between segments capture the various lighting and atmospheric conditions found during the progression of a sunrise. Courtesy of the artist.

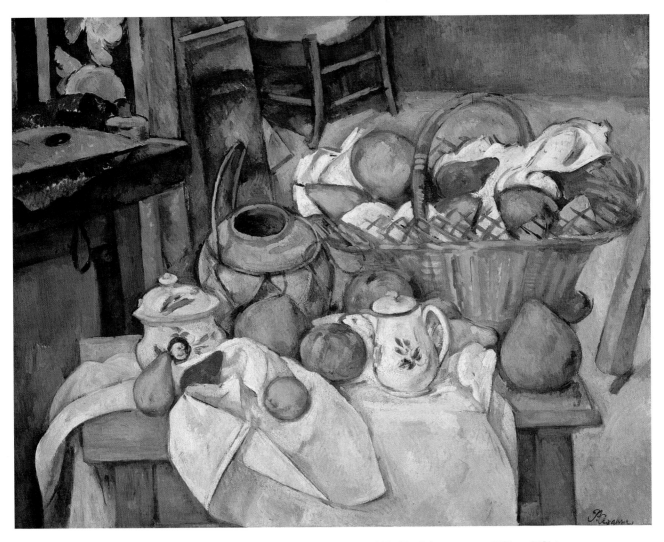

9.5 Paul Cézanne, *Still Life with Basket of Fruit (The Kitchen Table)*, c. 1888–90. Oil on canvas, 25⅝ × 31⅞ in. (65.1 × 81 cm). Cézanne was concerned with the plastic reality of objects as well as with their organization into a unified design. Although the pitcher and sugar bowl are viewed from a direct frontal position, the rounded jar behind them is painted as if it were being seen from a higher location. The handle of the basket is shown as centered at the front, but it seems to become skewed into a right-sided view as it proceeds to the rear. The left and right front table edges do not line up and are thus viewed from different vantage points. Cézanne combined these multiple viewpoints in one painting in order to present each object with a more profound sense of three-dimensional reality. Musée d'Orsay, Paris, France. Photo © Erich Lessing/Art Resource, New York.

When table edges failed to align across the picture, tops of bottles and baskets seemed to tilt at different angles, or the bottoms of chairs seemed to set on floor planes that couldn't exist under normal circumstances, early viewers thought of Cézanne as a bad draftsman. Many failed to understand that he was trying to establish a new visual vocabulary—one introducing volumes and their space through multiple views.

In the early twentieth century, the Cubists working in a style known as "analytic" Cubism adopted many of the pictorial devices used by Cézanne. They, too, usually showed an object from as many views as suited them, except the subject matter was first broken down into faceted planes and shapes for each of the views. Objects were rendered in a type of orthographic drawing, divided into essential views that

could be drawn in two dimensions, not unlike the Egyptian technique cited in Chapter 8 (see figs. 8.12 and 8.13). The basic view (the top view) is called a *plan*. With the plan as a basis, the *elevations* (or *profiles*) were taken from the front and back, and the *sections* were taken from the right and left sides (fig. 9.6). The superimposing and juxtaposition of all this information showed much more of the object than would actually

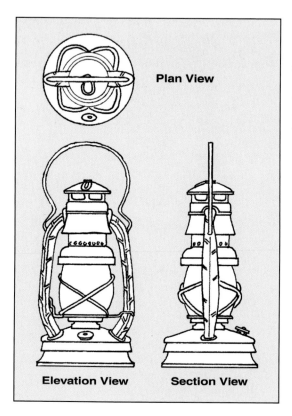

Plan View

Elevation View   **Section View**

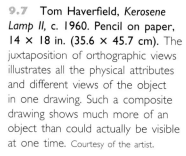

9.6 Tom Haverfield, *Kerosene Lamp*, c. 1960. Pen and ink, 9 × 12 in. (22.9 × 30.5 cm). In this work, objects are rendered in a type of orthographic drawing that divides them into essential views able to be drawn in two dimensions. Courtesy of the artist.

9.7 Tom Haverfield, *Kerosene Lamp II*, c. 1960. Pencil on paper, 14 × 18 in. (35.6 × 45.7 cm). The juxtaposition of orthographic views illustrates all the physical attributes and different views of the object in one drawing. Such a composite drawing shows much more of an object than could actually be visible at one time. Courtesy of the artist.

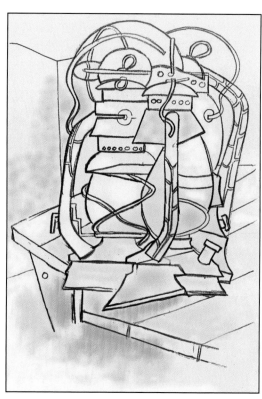

be visible at one time. The technique seems a distortion to the lay spectator conditioned to a static view, but within the limits of artistic selection, everything is present that we would ordinarily expect to see (fig. 9.7).

In the works of the Cubists, we find that a picture can have a life of its own and that the creation of space is not essentially a matter of portrayal or rendering. The Cubists worked step-by-step to illustrate that the more a painted object departed from straightforward optical resemblance, the more systematically the full three-dimensional nature of the object could be explored. Eventually, they developed the concept of the "synthetically" designed picture. Instead of analyzing a subject into planes and shapes, they began by developing large, simple geometric shapes, divorced from a model. Subject matter suggested by the shapes was then imposed, or synthesized, into this spatial system (see fig. 4.2).

Contemporary artists like David Hockney have revived the interest in the Cubists' sense of multiple viewpoints and viewer movement. Working from a different approach, Hockney has made composite images from multiple photographs, each taken at a slightly different angle. In this manner, the small jumps in position and misalignments between prints make the viewer continually adjust his or her viewpoint. These small segments must then be joined in the mind to form a single portrait (fig. 9.8).

Superimposed and Blurred Images

Another representational means to suggest the movement of an image involves **superimposing** (overlapping) a series of altered positions of the same figure or its parts within a single pictorial arrangement; as a result, the image may seem blurred or have indistinct contours. This technique, in essence, catalogs a moving

body's sequence of positions and indicates the visible changes.

Twentieth-century artists explored the possibility of fusing these changing figure positions by filling out the pathway of their movement. As a result, figures are not seen in fixed positions but as abstract moving paths of action (figs. 9.9 and 9.10). The subject in Marcel Duchamp's *Nude Descending a Staircase* is not the human body but the type and degree of energy the human body emits as it passes through space. This painting signified important progress in the pictorialization of motion, in which the plastic forces are functionally integrated with the composition. The energy of motion was also captured and explored with the use of photography, which created superimposed images through **multiple exposures** of the film (fig. 9.11).

The **Futurists,** motivated by the power and speed of the industrial age, machines, flight, and warfare, were

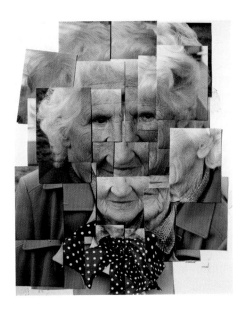

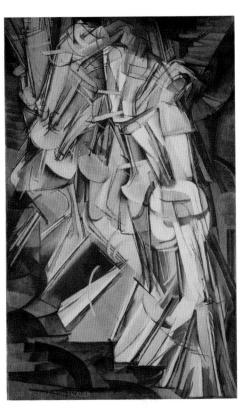

9.8 David Hockney, *Mother I, Yorkshire Moors, August 1985 #1,* 1985. Photographic collage, 18½ × 13 in. (47 × 33 cm). By layering multiple photos of an image, each taken at a slightly different angle, the viewer is forced to continually adjust his or her viewpoint to see a complete image. This provides a potentially more rounded and realistic understanding of the subject. Photographic composites like this also allow for the creation of an image that has more width and depth than the view normally seen with a camera lens. © David Hockney

9.9 Marcel Duchamp, *Nude Descending a Staircase, No. 2,* 1912. Oil on canvas, 58 × 35 in. (147.3 × 88.9 cm). The subject of Duchamp's painting is not the human body but rather the type and degree of energy a body emits as it passes through space. Philadelphia Museum of Art, PA. Louise and Walter Arensberg Collection. Photo: Corbis Media. © 2008 Artists Rights Society (ARS), New York/ADAGP, Paris/Succession of Marcel Duchamp.

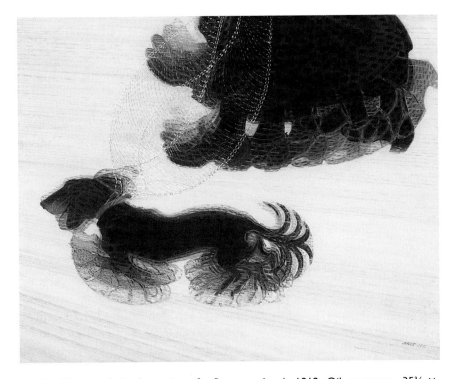

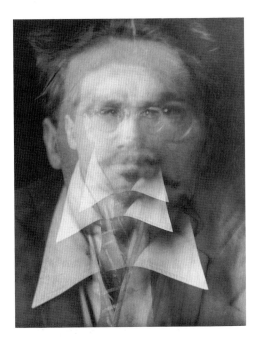

9.10 Giacomo Balla, *Dynamism of a Dog on a Leash,* 1912. Oil on canvas, 35⅜ × 43¼ in. (89.9 × 109.9 cm). To suggest motion as it is involved in time and space, Balla invented the technique of repeated contours. This device was soon imitated in newspaper comic strips, thereby becoming a mere convention. Albright-Knox Art Gallery, Buffalo, NY. Bequest of A. Conger Goodyear and Gift of George F. Goodyear, 1964. © 2008 Artists Rights Society (ARS), New York/SIAE, Rome.

9.11 Alvin Langdon Coburn, *Portrait of Ezra Pound,* 1916. Photograph, size unknown. Strongly influenced by Cubism, the diversely talented photographer Coburn produced this multiple image of the poet Ezra Pound. Courtesy George Eastman House, Rochester, NY.

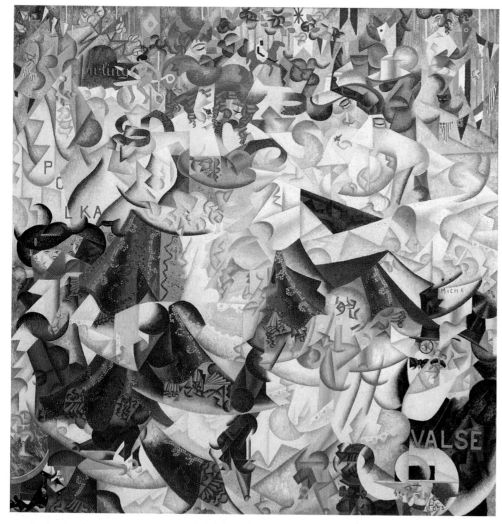

9.12 Gino Severini, *Dynamic Hieroglyphic of the Bal Tabarin*, 1912. Oil on canvas with sequins, 63⅝ × 61½ in. (161.6 × 156.2 cm). The works of the Futurists were devoted to motion for its own sake. They included not only the shapes of figures and objects and their pathways of movement but also their backgrounds. These features were combined in a pattern of kinetic energy.
© 2008 Artists Rights Society (ARS), New York/ADGP, Paris. The Museum of Modern Art, New York, NY. U.S.A. Acquired through the Lillie P. Bliss Bequest. Digital image © The Museum of Modern Art/Licensed by SCALA/Art Resource, NY.

devoted to motion for its own sake. Their works included not only the shapes of figures and objects and their pathways of movement but also their backgrounds. These features were combined in a pattern of kinetic energy. Although this form of expression was not entirely new, it provided a new type of artistic adventure—simultaneity of figure, object, and environment (fig. 9.12; see also fig. T.59). Contemporary artists continue to experiment with the concept of movement, subject, and surroundings (figs. 9.13 and 9.14).

MOTION PICTURES: FILM AND VIDEO

Modern scientific study of the optics of an object in motion began around 1824 (with the Thaumatrope, a toy that alternated two different images to create the illusion of a moving object) and paralleled the discovery and development of photography. Among the pioneers to link photography with the study of motion were Coleman Sellers and Eadweard Muybridge. Sellers was an engineer who, in 1861, patented the Kinematoscope—a device that contained photographs mounted on a turning paddle wheel, which flashed the pictures in sequence so rapidly that the images appeared animated. Eadweard Muybridge was a photographer who was known for his photographs of animals and people in motion, as well as experiments using multiple cameras to capture the first series of split-second movements (fig. 9.15). In the late 1870s, Muybridge presented his individual images in sequence inside a Zoetrope (known as the "wheel of life"), which was basically a cylinder with regularly spaced vertical slots. As the images were viewed through the slots of the spinning Zoetrope, the animals appeared to come alive, running and jumping (fig. 9.16). By 1879, Muybridge was presenting his moving images using a Zoetrope that had been modified for projection. Muybridge, a leader in the study of objects in motion, drew worldwide acclaim from his extensive public lectures and book publications.

From this point onward, scientists and artists in many countries seemed to be in a desperate race to alter still photography into an art form that could depict motion in a new way. Rather quickly, glass-plate images were replaced by materials that could bend and flex, and by 1887 Thomas Alva Edison commissioned W. K. L. Dickson to invent a **motion-picture** camera. In 1891, Edison presented his first motion picture and patented a Kinetoscope (often called a "peep show"), in which a film loop, run on spools, passed between an incandescent lamp and a shutter to present moving images for individual viewing. By 1895 short documentary

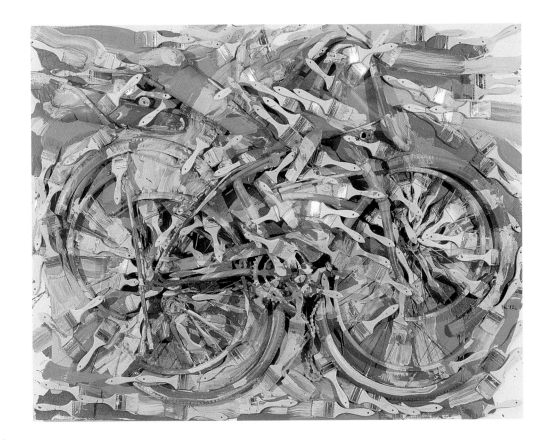

9.13 Arman, *Lava Bike*, 1991. Bicycle, brushes, acrylic paint on canvas, 48 × 60 × 12½ in. (121.9 × 152.4 × 31.8 cm). Fluid motion, speed, and environment are presented in new ways with modern materials and in a new, shallow three-dimensional format. Courtesy of the artist. © 2008 Artists Rights Society (ARS), New York/ADAGP, Paris.

9.14 Harold E. Edgerton, *Baseball hit-fly ball*, 1950s– 1970s. Gelatin silver print, size unknown. Harold Edgerton used stroboscopic and ultrahigh-speed photography to present scenes that were impossible to see with the naked eye. © Harold and Esther Edgerton Foundation, 2008, courtesy of Palm Press, Inc.

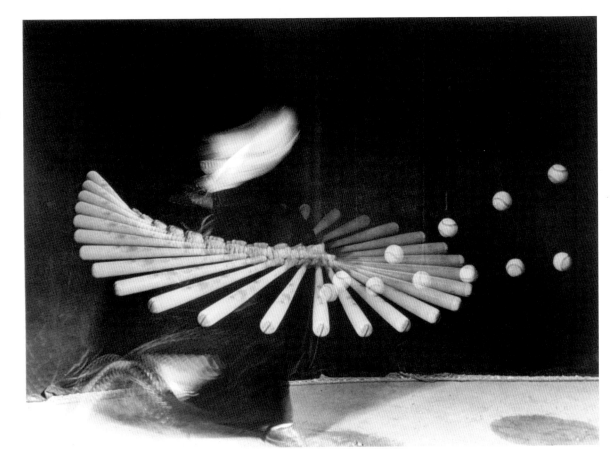

9.15 Eadweard Muybridge, *A Horse's Motion Scientifically Considered*, c. 1875. Engravings after photographs, size **unknown.** An American rancher friend and supporter of Muybridge encouraged his studies of horses in motion, which proved that at some point in midgallop all four hooves leave the ground (note the top row, numbers 2, 3, and 4). The photographer took the series with some of the earliest fast-action cameras and went on to influence Manet, Degas, and later artistic students of motion. Hulton Deutsch Collection/Corbis.

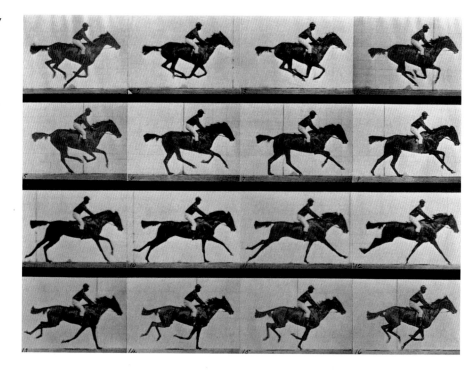

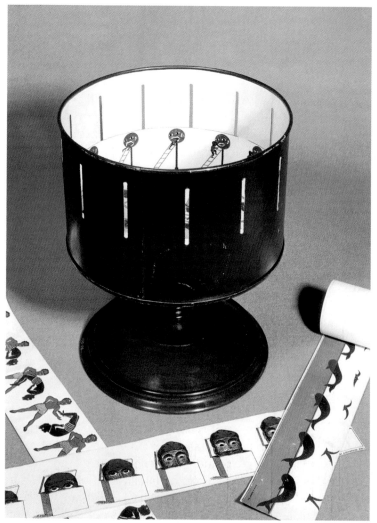

9.16 **The Zoetrope.** Also known as the "wheel of life," the Zoetrope was invented in 1834 in England by William Horner. As shown here, a strip of paper displaying a sequence of images was placed in the center of the cylinder. When the viewer looked through the vertical slots to the inside, the images appeared to move as the wheel was spun. © NMPFT/SSPL/The Image Works.

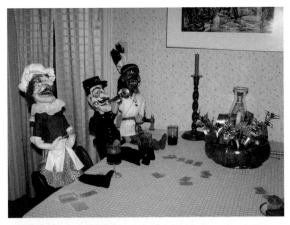

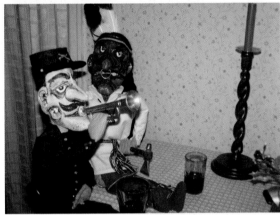

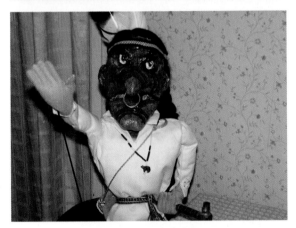

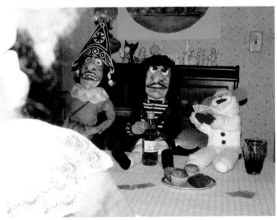

9.17 These still frames are examples of an evolving student work created with puppets and stop-motion photography. They illustrate some of the cinematic techniques that help tell a story even without dialogue or sound: (*from top to bottom*) long shot, medium shot, close-up, and crosscut.

films were being made in the United States, Germany, France, and the Netherlands; by 1900 film production had expanded to include Czechoslovakia, Italy, Japan, Russia, and Scandinavia. Projection systems began appearing, which made screenings for larger audiences possible. Soon film theaters appeared, like the Nickelodeon in Pittsburgh. Though the theaters were often set up in storefronts, the realism of the narrative and the excitement of the action of the new movie medium led the industry through many phases—from the silent-film era to the "talkies"—including melodramas, westerns, slapstick comedies, serialized episodes, fully animated feature films, and epics like David O. Selznick's *Gone With the Wind* (1939) and MGM's *The Wizard of Oz* (1939).

Although the film industry in general was preoccupied with filling the public's appetite for action, color, and sound, the early work by film artists like D. W. Griffith had systematized many aesthetic techniques, which helped focus the viewer's attention and capture their interest. The sense of space, movement, and time could all be controlled by altering the closeness of images, their sequencing, and the transitions in between. **Close-ups** drew attention to the character and their delivery; **crosscutting** allowed the viewer to move back and forth from one character to another as the dialogue evolved. In this manner, a single conversation or parallel and often diverse storylines could be developed at the same time. When combined with **medium** and **long shots,** the viewer could experience the facial expressions and body language of the actors and yet also see them in the context of a general setting or in a much broader conceptual context in a long shot (fig. 9.17). To aid in the change from one scene to another, certain transitions were also devised that have become standard fare. **Fades** allowed a scene or image to softly blur and fade away; **dissolves** allowed the image to disappear while another slowly appeared—keeping the images or concepts from being completely isolated. With the camera's ability to change viewpoints, not only was the image moving but the viewer was effectively changing position as well. And for the first time, observers had to spend a relatively defined amount of their time experiencing an artistic representation of time. In fact, the use of time was something that could now be manipulated—shifting slowly from face to face or flashing between cars or horses in a chase.

The use of actual time management, or **duration** of a scene, became an important tool in developing viewer emotion and involvement. Time could be sped up by photographing at 1 frame per second, instead of the standard 24 frames per second (which was the speed of the projector); if the subjects were already in great motion, this technique emphasized the speed of their action, or, it could present in a few minutes what might have evolved over several days, like the opening and closing of a flower. This compression of time demanded attention from the viewers and could be used to set up their emotional response. On the other hand, a sense of **slow motion** could be created by increasing the number of frames photographed per second and spreading an action over several minutes that may have taken place in a moment. With this technique, a cowboy flying off a horse would be able to express several types of emotion before hitting the ground, whereas normal speed might present the whole scene as a blur and not even allow any time for contemplation of the rider. Action in slow motion was developed by photographing at 100 frames per second instead of 24 frames per second. This provided a sense of detail and emphasized the impact of specific scenes. The presentation of time could be further manipulated with the use of **flashbacks** and **flash-**

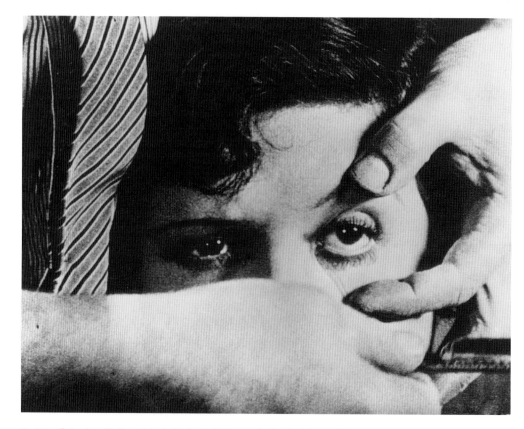

9.18 Salvador Dalí and Luis Buñuel (Director), *An Andalusian Dog,* 1929. Black-and-white silent film, sixteen minutes. This still frame from the film shows the moment just before a woman's eye is cut open, which is one of a series of events meant to shock the audience. © The Everett Collection. © 2008 Salvador Dali, Gala-Salvador Dali Foundation/Artists Rights Society (ARS), New York.

forwards, which could be inserted at any junction to present the audience with a past episode, provide a glimpse into the future, or develop a parallel storyline.

While the exploration of these techniques and other practices like controlled lighting all hinted at the possibilities of the new medium for individual self-expression, the scale of studio projects and the necessary equipment created financial obstacles. Smaller-scale work, however, often shown in art houses, provided more of an outlet for aesthetic or conceptual self-expression. *An Andalusian Dog* (1929), for example, created by the painter Salvador Dalí and director Luis Buñuel, was a personal and emotional accomplishment that provided an exploration of dreams and the subconscious mind; some, however, viewed it as escapism from the

Hollywood-type productions. Disjointed in chronology, the sixteen-minute black-and-white silent film showed scenes like the scrambled sequences of a nightmare: the night sky, a wispy cloud, the full moon, an eye being sliced by a razor, ants in the palm of a hand, a severed hand in the street. As illustrated by the **still frame** in figure 9.18, these components were meant to provoke, shock, and horrify, much in keeping with the spirit of the Surrealists' revolution.

The potential for film as a personal art medium was greatly enhanced when Eastman Kodak developed fireproof celluloid film and, later, introduced the 8-mm film in the 1960s. At the same time, the introduction of portable cameras, projectors, and other user-friendly equipment provided an affordable means by which artists, designers, teachers, students, home users,

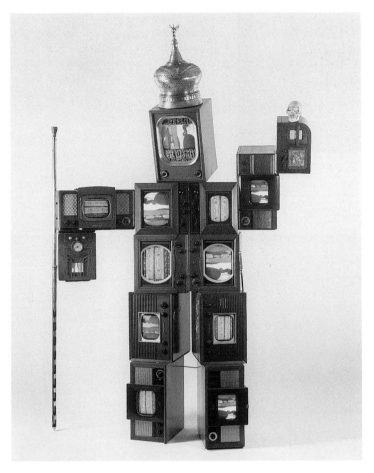

9.19 Nam June Paik, *Hamlet Robot,* 1996. Two radios, twenty-four TVs, transformer, two laser disc players, laser discs, crown, scepter, sword, and skull, 144 × 88 × 32 in. Nam June Paik's portrait of Hamlet is a video sculpture programmed with a kaleidoscopic mix of contemporary audio and visual technology. Courtesy Carl Solway Gallery, Cincinnati, OH, from the collection of The Chrysler Museum of Art, Norfolk, VA. Photograph by Chris Gomien.

and professionals could view, produce, and create films.

With the development of the computer and its resulting miniaturization, new technology has allowed a transformation of the general film industry. Instead of having to use cumbersome equipment and specially dedicated film, handheld cameras and camcorders can record still and moving images as digital information on a memory chip. When the images are transported to a computer, they may be easily altered and saved in many formats. Personal computers also provide access to user-friendly home-editing programs that allow the creation of quality images

that were available only to the professional studio a few years ago. The sequences of scenes and camera shots can be altered with relative ease; sounds can be changed or lined up with different scenes; and the viewer's experience of time can be generally manipulated. Special effects can also be added (like snow patterns, lighting changes, or altered colors) and computer-generated images can be seamlessly inserted onto shots of real objects and people—all of which may add emotional emphasis or place focus on a particular idea.

The motion-picture or **video** camera in the hands of a creative person can lead to fantastic developments.

Look to the careers of Steven Spielberg and George Lucas. They have dazzled the public with stunts and special effects and captivated popular imagination with films like *Star Wars* (1977), *E.T.: The Extra-Terrestrial* (1982), *Jurassic Park* (1993), and *War of the Worlds* (2005). Artists like Andy Warhol, working with traditional fixed-camera positions, have used motion pictures to study reality in a new way by presenting everyday activities such as sleeping. Brian Fridge even challenges our understanding of four minutes in a freezer (see fig. 6.11). Movies like *The Blair Witch Project* (1999) also manage to cross truth with fiction by presenting their stories in such a way as to seem like private reality—more like a personal documentary or video diary than a fictional, scripted film—sometimes even speaking directly to the viewer as if an interactive, intimate participant.

Clearly, video recording has given individual artists a practical means for offering the direct action of human thoughts and movements, and when combined by way of the computer with TV receivers or other monitors, it provides a powerful new medium for artists to explore. Art museums and galleries have featured **installations** with TV receivers, monitors, and motion-picture screens that glow with artistic images of every imaginable human expression or action. The receivers and screens are positioned for the utmost viewing and, in some installations, appear as if they were paintings, drawings, prints, or sculptures. Their size and scale are varied for compatible viewing.

The Korean-born artist Nam June Paik is considered to be the first video artist. He often synchronized video images and music with a live performance. Paik also assembled video screens, radios, and TV receiver cabinets into sculptured forms that were as much works of art as the videos (fig. 9.19). He produced numerous performance works, along with rewired TVs

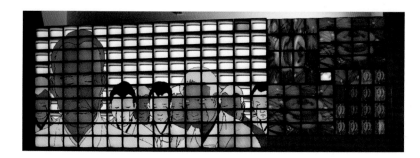

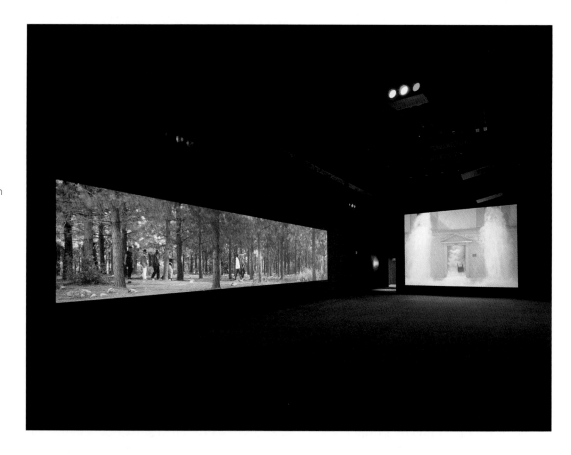

9.21 Bill Viola, *Going Forth by Day*, 2002. Video and sound installation with seven projectors, ten speakers, subwoofer, seven amps, six equalizers, cables, speakers, projector mount, and two servers; dimensions vary with installation. *Going Forth by Day* is a video installation inspired by the Egyptian Book of the Dead and the great fresco paintings of the Italian Renaissance. It comprises five panels that examine cycles of birth, death, and rebirth. The "panels"—actually state-of-the-art high-definition video projections seen directly on the walls of a space—are approximately thirty-five minutes long and play simultaneously on continuous loops. The suite of works is an epic about nature's cycles and the flow of time. Commissioned by the Deutsche Bank in consultation with the Solomon R. Guggenheim Foundation for the Deutsche Guggenheim Berlin, 2004, 2004.59. Photograph by David Heald © The Solomon R. Guggenheim Foundation, New York.

and multimonitor sculptures in almost every possible arrangement—even giant walls of television sets: *Information Wall* in 1992 featured 429 monitors; *Megatron* in 1995, included 215 monitors with eight-channel color video and two-channel color video and two-channel sound (fig. 9.20); and a blinking, flashing light show used laser beams, TV sets, and a waterfall at the Guggenheim in 2000.

Early contact with Paik and other sound and video artists encouraged an-

other artist, Bill Viola, to continue creating video artworks and installations in the 1970s. Viola has since become a pioneer in the use of video and the exploration of the moving image in artworks that reflect art history, spirituality, and conceptual issues. The work illustrated in figure 9.21, commissioned by a museum in Berlin, is a culmination of this expertise. Viewers enter the work architecturally, with all five image-sequences playing simultaneously on every wall of one large gallery. Once inside, they stand at the center of

an image-sound world. Each panel tells a story that is part of a larger narrative cycle. Viewers are free to move around and watch each panel individually or to experience the piece as a whole.

COMPUTERS AND MULTIMEDIA

Viola's work is a good example of the degree to which the computer has become a tool in the field of art today. In his case, the computer undoubtedly aided in the conceptualizing during the planning phase, the scriptwriting, the editing of audiovisuals, and the control of the presentation. But we do not call it "computer art" as such.

Computer art can be traced back to 1962, when Ivan Sutherland introduced Sketchpad, a computer-based drawing program utilizing a light pen and a mainframe computer. During the course of the 1960s, other computer scientists—engineers and mathematicians—demonstrated various properties of computer programming by creating drawings using the computer in conjunction with ink plotters and other printing devices. George Nees's 1965 show in Stuttgart of his computer-generated drawings is often credited with being the first exhibition of "computer art." A 1968 exhibition in London titled "Cybernetic Serendipity" is considered to be the first to draw widespread international attention to the potentials of computer-based applications in art.

After the introduction of the personal computer around 1979, the focus of computer art shifted from printed output to the animation of graphics onscreen. In order to represent 3-D perspective pictures realistically in films, hardware and software developers had to find ways to achieve high resolution and the realistic lighting of moving scenes. What resulted are now common effects seen in films and advertisements, such as the penetration, melting away, or shape changing (morphing) of objects. This development and improvement of computer graphics during the past generation rivals or even exceeds in scope the transformation of painting during the Italian Renaissance.

In its early stages, computer art was looked down on as the hobby of technicians. But the boundaries of science, technology, and art are blurring, and now more artists are engaging in computer art. In the 1990s, artists began using computing power to try new

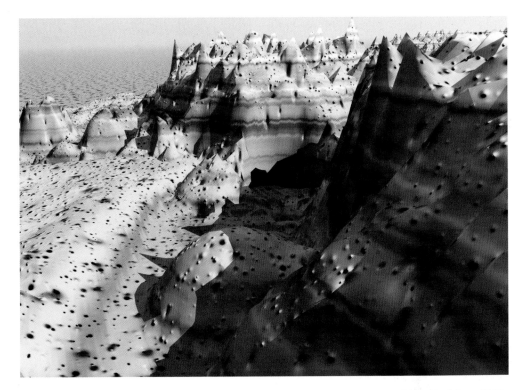

9.22 Yael Kanarek, digital landscape in the sunset/sunrise desert terrain of *World of Awe*, 2000. *World of Awe* is a Web-based, imaginary reality combining text and imagery. The graphical user interface evolves continuously, presenting a journal that includes landscape drawings, love letters, travelogs, and unique navigation features. © Yael Kanarek.

procedures and practices, including interactive installations and the programming of art over networks. One such new media artist is Yael Kanarek. Since 1995, Kanarek has maintained an online journal called *World of Awe* (www .worldofawe.net), a **multimedia** narrative about a traveler in search of a lost treasure. This Web-based artwork has expanded over the years, evolving into a network of projects and collaborations online, in galleries, and in performance spaces (fig. 9.22).

Indeed, computers have opened a new era of multimedia for communications, information gathering, processing, education, and entertainment—and they are changing the world like nothing before them. Not only do computers provide users access to research and entertainment resources, but they function as tools for creative artistic de-

velopment, including motion explorations. Multimedia may already be one of the most powerful educational and entertainment tools that a computer facilitates. First, as its name suggests, multimedia combines many different groups of media—such as text, still and moving graphics (animation), and spoken and instrumental sounds—into a single unifying force. Second, multimedia may be integrated with the communication technologies of television, telephone, Internet, film, and video. Because computers have become powerful enough to process almost any type of data, programmers have added a seemingly endless group of software titles, among which many are quite user friendly and available for ready use by artists and designers. Some of the most frequently used software programs include paint programs (drawing and painting), image manipulation, 3-D modeling, animation, audio editing and authoring, and digital video (motion sequences). Many artists create their own software so that they can control the most implicit specialized areas. Some programs are even made to accept feedback from the spectator, which then alters the projection of sound and visual information to allow the viewer to directly interact with the artwork (see fig. 7.4).

Multimedia, because it involves combinations of various art forms, naturally leads to collaboration between artists of different disciplines. Jack Ox and David Britton, for example, began working together in 1998 to create visualizations that interpret complex interactive data (fig. 9.23). Ox had twenty years of experience producing 2-D work, and Britton came to the project with software experience in animation and computer gaming. Together, they created a "virtual color organ" capable of visualizing musical compositions.

For centuries, the work of artists was flat and restricted to a single point of view. Now, because of concepts made possible by the computer, artists are able to design with images never possible before. Artists now have the capability to enter an image and control the exploration within that space—flying over, around, and through objects on command. Images can also be created in real time and real space. These concepts have become commercially viable, being adopted for training films and video games and for specific applications like medical diagnostic imaging and architectural design. Clients can now take a virtual tour of a prospective new home; they can move freely about in the structure, to see it and all the furnishings from every possible angle—even rearrange the contents of the space. With this technology, artists can turn over to the audience the control for experiencing a work of art.

Today, image manipulation and 3-D modeling are commonplace, and

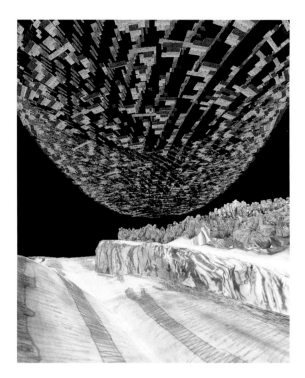

9.23 Jack Ox and David Britton, Visualization of *Im Januar am Nil*, composed by Clarence Barlow, 1984, 2001. *Im Januar am Nil* is a visualization of a Clarence Barlow composition for small chamber orchestra. Barlow's unusual spiraling temporal pattern, although difficult to apprehend by ear, becomes visible when translated into 3-D computer images. After the music is finished, viewers can move through the image and interact with different parts that evolved during the course of the musical performance. © Jack Ox and David Britton. It was realized in the 21st C. Virtual Color Organ™. For the full story: www.jackox.net.

new ideas about Web space, real time, and virtual reality are starting to take hold. For artists around the world, the use of technology and the computer are well-embedded in artistic practice, and the digital workbench has become a place where art is made.

THREE-DIMENSIONAL APPLICATIONS OF TIME AND MOTION

As we have seen, the contemplation of time and motion has been an important concept for two-dimensional artists. Methods of involving the viewer have evolved from creating areas of visual interest and eye travel to graphically presenting elapsed time and multiple points of view. Though these techniques often result in complicated images, the work as a totality requires only a moment for reflection and contemplation. In contrast, the use of time can play an even greater role in the work of three-dimensional artists—becoming an el-

ement that can be manipulated. In a plastic work, the viewer is enticed to move about the piece, constantly being drawn from one set of relationships to the next.

Some sculptures also create the illusion of movement. In those cases we have **implied motion.** In an early attempt to add movement to otherwise static figures, Greek sculptors organized the lines in the draperies of their figures to accent a continuous flowing direction. By following these linear accents, the eye of the observer readily moves smoothly over the figure's surface. The stance or position of the subject can also produce an expectation of movement. For example, the viewer can feel Ernst Barlach's figure *The Avenger* charging through space, about to deliver a blow with the uplifted sword (see fig. 2.69). In *Unique Forms of Continuity in Space,* a sculptural work by the Futurist artist Umberto Boccioni, movement is implied by the shape and directionality of the faceted planes that make up this abstracted figure (fig. 9.24). The sculptures shown in figures 9.25 and 9.26 are even

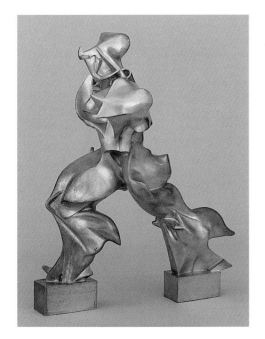

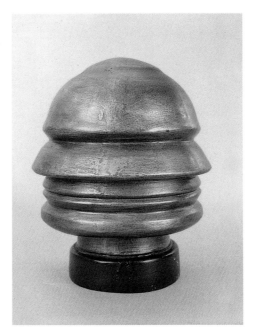

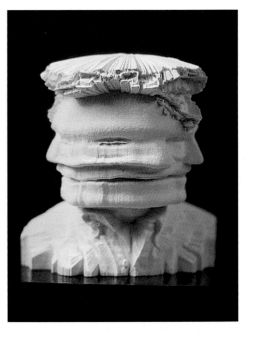

9.24 Umberto Boccioni, *Unique Forms of Continuity in Space,* 1913. Bronze (cast 1931), 43⅞ × 34⅞ × 15¾ in. (111.4 × 88.6 × 40 cm). Boccioni was a leading founder and member of the Futurist group. An accomplished painter and sculptor, he was preoccupied for much of his career with the dynamics of movement. Acquired through the Lillie P. Bliss Bequest. (231.1948) The Museum of Modern Art, New York, NY. U.S.A. Digital image © The Museum of Modern Art/Licensed by SCALA/Art Resource, NY.

9.25 Renato Bertelli, *Continuous Profile of Mussolini,* 1933 (later manufactured by Ditta Effeffe, Milan, with Mussolini's approval). Bronzed terra-cotta, 11¾ in. high × 9 in. in diameter (29.8 cm. high × 22.9 cm in diameter). Bertelli, following the influence of the Futurists, explored the concepts of simultaneity and continuous movement in portraiture. Mussolini recognized the appeal to "modernity" and organized the mass distribution of the sculpture. Courtesy of The Mitchell Wolfson Jr. Collection, The Wolfsonian–Florida International University, Miami Beach, Florida. Photograph by Bruce White.

9.26 Dan Collins, *Of More Than Two Minds,* 1994. Three-dimensional laser digitizing, cast hydrocal from CNC wax original, 3¾ × 3⅝ × 2½ in. Though inspired by timeless concepts of the body in motion, current technology has opened new means of exploration and expression. Courtesy of the artist.

able to capture the energy of blurred and superimposed images found in two-dimensional artwork.

While all types of motion may be implied and understood rather quickly, some three-dimensional work employs **actual motion** that is distinctive and involves the entire work. It requires longer periods of time to experience, as compared to work that creates the illusion of movement. In the case of **kinetic** sculpture, the artwork itself, not the observer, moves. **Mobiles,** for example, present a constantly changing, almost infinite series of views (see figs. 2.7 and 2.70). Water, wind currents, motors, and vibrating or rotating pedestals

can all provide a source of movement for work. With José de Rivera's *Brussels Construction,* the work rotates on its base, and time is a planned element. The viewer must wait for the piece to assume its original orientation in order to experience all the compositional aspects of the work (see fig. 3.31). In the work of Calder and de Rivera, there is a feeling of spontaneity and unpredictability, which is even further developed in the work of artists like Jean Tinguely (fig. 9.27), whose work was planned to be presented as it self-destructed—flying apart in all directions. In some cases, the memory of the event by those who were present is the only record of the

work's existence. Other artists like Arthur Ganson use time-lapse photography to record the duration, path, and energy of the presentation (fig. 9.28).

Just as the boundaries between sculpture and painting are blurred by artists working with assemblages (see fig. 6.22), so too are the boundaries between sculpture-in-the round and multimedia presentations. As artists create installations that combine audio, computer-generated animation, and sculptural constructions in self-directed interactive experiences, the viewer must spend a somewhat designated amount of time experiencing the work—listening, watching, exploring, interacting.

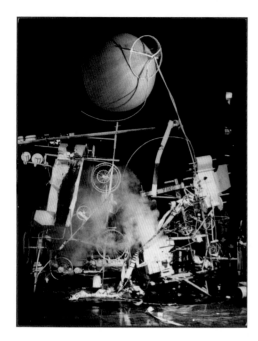

9.27 Jean Tinguely, *Homage to New York,* 1960. Scrap metal, bicycle parts (eighty bicycle, tricycle, and baby-carriage wheels), washing machine drum, bathtub, piano, several electric fans, old Addressograph, baby bassinet, bells, car horn, playing cards, American flag scraps, many bottles of chemical stinks, apparatus to make smoke, fire extinguishers, orange meteorological sounding balloon, radio, oil canister, hammer, and saw—all powered by fifteen engines—8 m high. Time and motion were definite composites in this piece. Constructed of wheels, pulleys, and motors, the work was designed to self-destruct over a period of twenty-seven minutes in homage to the energy of a city that keeps rebuilding itself. Courtesy of Museum Tinguely. Photo: David Gahr.

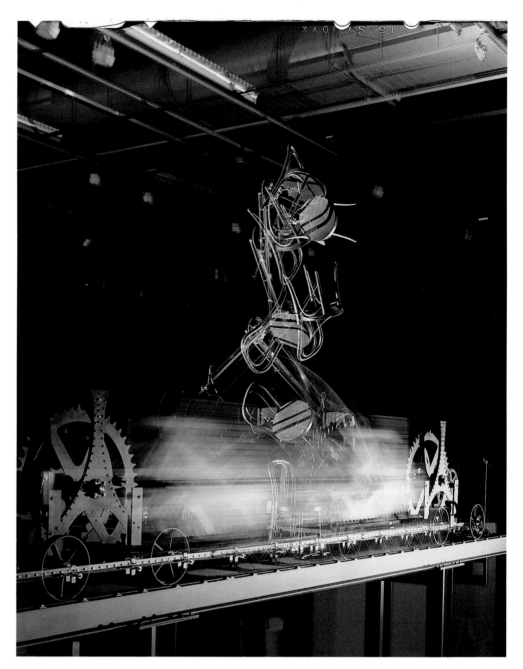

9.28 Arthur Ganson, *Machine with Chair* (time-lapse photograph of 1995 version), 1995. Steel (machine), fiberglass over foam (chair), motor, electronic switches and circuits, rubber; track 30 ft. long, machine 5 ft. high, chair at highest point 13 ft. from track. Like Jean Tinguely, Arthur Ganson has found the machine to be an instrument for the poet/artist. He produces some machine-driven sculptures that involve kinetic ironies, mechanical awareness, and a sense of time, space, and motion. Arthur Ganson is a sculptor at the Massachusetts Institute of Technology. Photograph by Henry Groskinsky.

In the process, the viewer may change position, and the work may physically move. At the same time, the work may also present the illusion of movement through sequenced images and flashing lights. In addition, the sense of time may be altered even though there is real-time interaction.

The exploration of space in terms of the four-dimensional space-time continuum is in its infancy. As technology advances and research reveals more of the mysteries of the natural world, artists will continue to absorb and interpret them according to their individual experiences (fig. 9.29). It is reasonable to assume that even more revolutionary concepts will emerge in time, producing

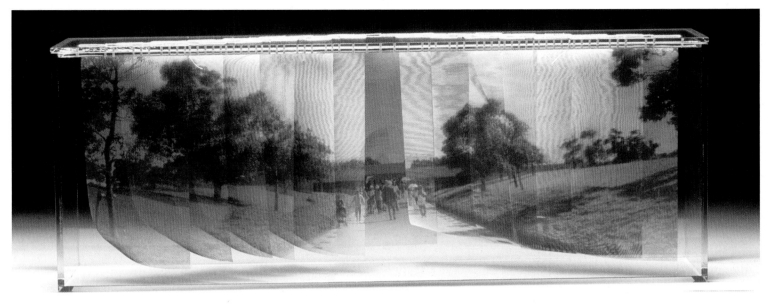

9.29 Katherine D. Crone, *Tokyo Sunday*, 2004. Digitally altered photograph printed on silk organza, linen thread, and acrylic-plastic box, 8¾ × 23½ × 4¾ in. While encouraging the evolution of innovative graphic directions, the newest digital technology aids Katherine Crone in the investigation of texture, pattern, transparent layering, and the integration of the visual complexities within those surfaces. In this work, the layered prints almost read like pages of a book, overlapping like individual memories to create a temporal experience of time and space. Courtesy of Katherine D. Crone, Photo by D. James Dee.

great changes in art styles. The important point to remember is that distortions and unfamiliar forms of art expression do not occur in a vacuum; they usually represent earnest efforts to comprehend and interpret our world in terms of the latest frontiers of understanding.

Regardless of what technologies the future may present—be it rapid prototyping, laser definition, or holographic imaging—artists must learn to use time as a tool in establishing appropriate levels of emphasis within the work, providing spatial harmonies among the compositional elements, and developing sufficient contrasts within the work to maintain visual interest. By these means, the human scene—in whatever way it may evolve in time, space, and action—will become an inspiration for study and creativity in many exciting forms.

AFTER IMAGES

A Visual Timeline of
Artistic and Stylistic Comparisons

*"The arts have a development which comes not only from the individual,
but also from an accumulated strength, the civilization which precedes us."*

— *Henri Matisse, 1936* [*]

"After Images" presents a visual and historical timeline of art with thumbnails of works of art that illustrate particular styles and side-by-side works of art that connect visually so clearly that students cannot mistake their actual connection historically as well. The title "After Images" comes from the fairly common practice among artists to title their works as "after" the work of another artist, such as Picasso's *Portrait of a Painter, after El Greco,* 1950. Many of the works of art in the timeline follow this description and were selected because of the direct visual connections between them.

Students studying art are often visual learners, and this timeline taps into that learning style. The intent of the image comparisons is to grab students' attention and encourage them to become engaged firstly with the image comparisons alone with minimal text. Secondly, the timeline attempts to employ visual learning in order to encourage textual learning by piquing students' curiosity about the connections they see so that they will want to learn more and begin their own research projects.

The side-by-side comparisons should aid in making memorable associations between periods of Western art history via clear visual connections of form, line, shape, value, texture, color, space, and so on. When students study closely how these fun-damental art elements were used by a Renaissance "old master" such as Titian in *Allegory on the Theme of Prudence* (c. 1565–1570) and then compare that to the American modernist Ben Shahn's *After Titian* (1959), they will immediately see how the modern artist transformed, reduced, and abstracted Titian's form, line, shape, value, texture, and so on from a naturalistic and modeled rendering of three human faces and three animal heads into a stylized and flattened space where the background and foreground elements merge into an overall composition of colors. The change from one style to the other teaches students about those concepts and those two different periods efficiently and effectively.

VOCABULARY OF CONTENT AND STYLE

Abstract Expressionism   An American art movement that grew out of Surrealism in the mid- to late-twentieth century, with an emphasis on spontaneity or subconscious creation.

Action painting   A term coined by Harold Rosenberg to describe a subgroup of Abstract Expressionist painters who worked with gestural lines, movements, and sometimes rapid and fluid image constructions as opposed to large blocks or "fields" of pure color as with the Color Field painters.

Classicism   A reference to ancient Greek and Roman civilizations, but also any art that encompasses or stresses order, balance, and unity.

Color Field   An abstract style of painting following Abstract Expressionism that is characterized by a canvas with areas of solid colors.

Conceptual Art   Art that focuses on a concept or idea over materials and aesthetics.

Constructivism   A movement, founded by Vladimir Tatlin between 1913 and 1922, associated primarily with three-dimensional spatial concepts in sculpture and architecture.

content   The expression, essential meaning, significance, or aesthetic value of a work of art.

Cubism   The name given to the painting style invented by Pablo Picasso and Georges Braque between 1907 and 1912, which incorporates multiple views of objects to simulate their three-dimensionality while acknowledging the two-dimensional surface of the picture plane. Signaling the beginning of abstract art, Cubism is a semiabstract style that continued a trend away from representational art initiated by Cézanne in the late 1800s.

Dadaism   The earliest style of Fantastic Art to appear in the 1900s that opened modern art to a new freedom of humorous expression, creative imagination, contradictory tendencies, and intentional provocation.

[*]Henri Matisse, "Statements to Tériade," 1936, in *Art in Theory 1900–2000*, eds. Charles Harrison and Paul J. Wood (Oxford: Blackwell, 2002), p. 384.

Environmental Art   Art that deals with the natural environment but can also be applied to historical, political, and social contexts of a particular environment. Environmental Art usually addresses issues of natural phenomena and environmental awareness and uses natural materials that do not cause further harm to the environment.

Expressionism   Starting in France and Germany around 1905, the style allowed young artists to paint a subject in non-naturalistic colors in accord with their feelings. It is a form of art that tries to reveal the emotional essence rather than to show external appearance or resemblance.

Fantastic Art   A trend that occurred at the beginning of World War II which opened up experimentation and was impelled by the war, its horrors, and a gathering sense of alienation from society in an age of technology.

Futurism   An early-twentieth-century movement in art and literature that refashioned Cubism in light of its own desire to glorify the dynamic character of the machine age.

Happenings   A form of participatory art in which spectators, as well as artists, were engaged. It brings together the basic concepts of motion, time, and space.

Impressionism   A movement of art that initiated new ideas about color, light, finish, and, to a lesser degree, dynamic movement. It became the preoccupation of early modernist painters.

installations   Interior or exterior settings of media created by artists to heighten the viewers' awareness of the environmental space.

Les Fauves   Artist members of the earliest Expressionist group in France that used unnaturally bold coloring and exaggeratedly distorted figures, which gave their paintings the look of "wild beasts."

Minimalism   A movement that not only included art but also, music, dance, and literature and was a precedent for non-

objective abstraction in the early twentieth century. Minimalism relied only on the basic elements for meaning—without any trace of the artistic process.

Naturalism   The approach to art that attempts a description of things as they appear in nature. Pure naturalism would contain no personal interpretation introduced by the artist.

Neoclassicism   Originating in France in the 1700s, the style grew from the discovery of the ancient Roman ruins of Herculaneum and Pompeii and the publication of Johann Joachim Winckelmann's *The History of the Art of the Ancients*.

Neo-Expressionism   The return, in the early 1980s, to figurative art and a more personalized expression. The movement satisfied the growing appetite for recognizable images and meaningful content by producing monumental dramatic figures with broad gestures, painted in broad brushstrokes.

New Realism   Art that emphasized the human figure and portraiture extensively and strove for a matter-of-fact kind of verisimilitude, but without the sly humor of Pop Art.

Op Art   A form of art that is primarily optical and highly graphic, although it can merge into three-dimensionality when used in paintings that include an element of relief. It is an extension and modification of the geometric abstraction that developed in the early twentieth century.

Performance Art   An expanded category of participatory art that can include theater, dance, music, cinema, video, and computer.

Pictorialism   An especially later-nineteenth-century to early-twentieth-century movement of European and American photographers who wanted to enhance photography's perceived lack of subjectivity and creativity by emphasizing a softer-focus negative and a highly manipulated print process in the darkroom.

Pop Art   The term stands for "popular art," which was prompted by the dissatisfaction of younger artists with their position or prospects in relation to the dominance of abstract art.

Post-Impressionism   A movement started by some painters associated with Impressionism who sought a return to the structural organization of pictorial form, an increased emphasis on the picture surface for the sake of pictorial unity and the unique patterns and textures that might result, and a more-or-less conscious exaggeration of natural appearances for emotionally suggestive effects.

Postmodernism   A movement resulting from artists' reactions to high-modernist abstract art and dogma (especially to Minimalism and the International Style in architecture), the increasing financial disparity between rich and poor, cynicism about politics and society (some of which resulted from the Vietnam War and Watergate), and so forth. Resulted in the reintroduction of the human figure; decoration; literary subjects; the appropriation of earlier artists' styles, works, or parts thereof; the reuse of older media; and mixed techniques along with newer methods.

Post-Painterly Abstractionism   Art on large, flat planes painted in a more traditional manner.

Realism   The style of art that creates an impression of visual, political, and economical actuality without going into extremes of detail while also attempting to relate and interpret universal meanings that lie beneath surface appearances. As a movement, it relates to painters like Honoré Daumier in nineteenth-century France and Winslow Homer in the United States in the 1850s.

representational art   A type of art in which the subject is presented through the visual art elements so that the observer is reminded of actual objects. (See **naturalism** and **Realism**.)

Romanticism   The style of art that focuses on the emotional as opposed to the rational. The macabre, the fantastic, the stormy, and the lyrical moods of nature, animals, and humans became fit subjects for artistic expression. The style grew out of the literary trends that affected all of eighteenth-century Europe and gave more emphasis to form, artists' materials, and processes.

simultaneity   A cubist technique developed by Pablo Picasso that showed the structure of objects in space by portraying many different facets of them at the same time.

Straight photographers   A number of especially early- to mid-twentieth-century American photographers, often associated with the reaction against Pictorialism, who wanted to locate the creativity of their medium within the sharp focusing and selective framing of the camera and within the unmanipulated print from the negative.

style   A specific artistic character or dominant trend of form noted during a period of history or during an art movement. Style also refers to the expressive use of media that gives an artwork individual character.

Surrealism   A style of art, influenced by Freudian psychoanalysis, that emphasizes fantasy and is said to be revealed by the subconscious mind through the use of automatic techniques (rubbings, doodles, blots, cloud patterns, etc.). Originally a literary movement that grew out of Dadaism, Surrealism was established by a literary manifesto written by André Breton in 1924.

Symbolism   A style that sought to achieve an ultimate reality through intuitive or inward spiritual experiences of the world.

CHRONOLOGICAL OUTLINE OF
WESTERN ART

TIMELINE

PREHISTORIC ART (c. 35,000–3000 B.C.E.)

35,000 B.C.E.	**Upper Paleolithic:** *Late Stone Age:* Stone tool industries
28,000	**Art begins:** Cave painting and fertility goddesses (Europe)
10,000	**Mesolithic:** *Middle Stone Age:* End of last Ice Age
6000–3000	**Neolithic:** *New Stone Age:* Begins in the Middle East; spreads to Europe; settled agricultural communities; pottery, architecture begin

ANCIENT ART (c. 4000 B.C.E.–146 C.E.)

4000 B.C.E.	**Egyptian Art:** Old Kingdom
3000	**Sumerian Art:** Iraq; invention of writing
2800	**Aegean Art:** Minoan I and II, Crete
2300	**Akkadian Art:** Syria and Iraq
2000	**Aegean Art:** Mycenaean Age, Greece; Minoan III, Crete
1700	**Babylonian Art:** Syria and Iraq
1600	**Egyptian Art:** New Empire
1500	**Neolithic:** Ends in Europe
1100	**Aegean Art:** Homeric Age, Greece, Turkey
	Etruscan Art: Italy

1000	**Egyptian Art:** Decadence
900	**Assyrian Art:** Middle East
750	**Greek Art:** Archaic Age, Greece and southern Italy
	Etruscan Art: Northern Italy
600	**Neo-Babylonian Art:** Middle East
550	**Achaemenid Persian Art:** Iran, Middle East
470	**Greek Art:** Classical Age, Greece
330	**Greek Art:** Ptolemaic Age, Egypt
320	**Greek Art:** Hellenistic Age, Greece and Middle East (Seleucid Empire)
280	**Roman Art:** Roman Republic, Italy
140	**Graeco-Roman Art:** Italy to Greece and Middle East
30 B.C.E.–146 C.E.	**Imperial Roman Art:** Italy, parts of Europe and Middle East

EARLY CHRISTIAN AND MEDIEVAL ART (c. 200–1300 C.E.)

500 B.C.E.–400 C.E.	**Migratory Period Art in Europe:** Celts, Goths, Slavs, Scandinavians
200	**Iranian (Persian) Art:** Sassanid Empire
	Late Imperial Roman Art and Early Christian Art: Italy and Europe
330	**Early Byzantine Art:** Centers at Constantinople (Istanbul), Turkey, and part of Middle East
	Coptic Christian Art: Egypt
	Early Christian Art: Western Europe and Italy
476	**Roman Art ends**
493	**Early Byzantine Art:** Introduced at Ravenna and Venice
570–632	**Mohammed founds Islamic religion**
650	**Islamic Art:** Beginning in Syria, Palestine, and Iraq
760	**Carolingian Art:** France, Germany, and northern Italy
800	**Developed Byzantine Art:** Middle East, Greece, Balkans, and parts of Italy
950	**Ottonian Art:** Mostly in Germany
1000	**Romanesque Art:** France, England, northern Spain (Moslems in southern Spain), Italy, and Germany
1150	**Gothic Art:** France, Italy, northern Spain, Germany, and England

TIMELINE

NOTE: From here on, listed artists are painters unless otherwise indicted in parentheses.

1300

Proto-Renaissance Italy: Duccio, Giotto, Pisano (sculptor)

1400

Early Renaissance Italy: Donatello (sculptor), Masaccio, Francesca, Fra Angelico, Fra Filippo Lippi, Brunelleschi (architect), da Vinci

1503 Renaissance/1919 Dadaism

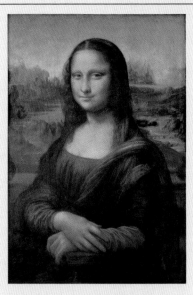

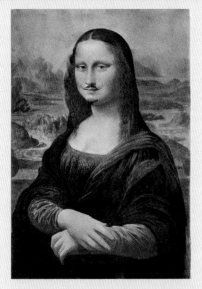

T.1 Leonardo da Vinci (1452–1519), *Mona Lisa,* 1503–06. Oil on panel, 30½ × 21 in. (76.2 × 52.5 cm). Louvre, Paris, France/The Bridgeman Art Library.

T.2 Marcel Duchamp (1887–1968), *Replica of L. H. O. O. Q.,* 1919. Color reproduction of Mona Lisa altered with a pencil, 8 × 5 in. Photo © Boltin Picture Library/The Bridgeman Art Library © 2008 Succession Marcel Duchamps/Artists Rights Society (ARS), New York/ADAGP, Paris.

1505 Renaissance/1927 Surrealism

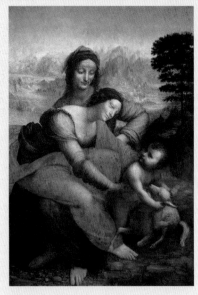

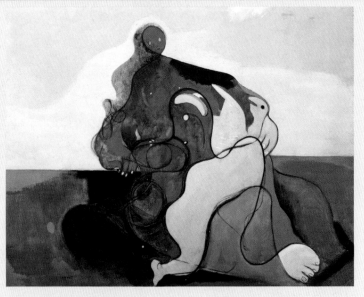

T.3 Leonardo da Vinci (1452–1519), *Virgin and Child with Saint Anne,* c. 1510. Oil on panel, 168.5 × 130 cm. Louvre, Paris, France/ Giraudon/The Bridgeman Art Library.

T.4 Max Ernst (1891–1976), *The Kiss (Le Baiser),* 1927. Oil on canvas, 50¾ × 63½ in. Art © 2008 Artists Rights Society (ARS), New York/ADAGP, Paris. Photo © The Art Archive/Peggy Guggenheim Collection Venice/Gianni Dagli Orti.

TIMELINE

Chronological Outline of Western Art

Early Northern Renaissance: Modified by vestiges of Medievalism
Netherlands: van Eyck, van der Goes, van der Weyden
France: Limbourg brothers, Fouquet
Germany: Dürer, Lochner, Moser, Witz, Pacher, Schongauer (printmaker)

High Renaissance Italy: Giorgione, Titian, Raphael, Michelangelo (sculptor), Tintoretto

1500

1505 Renaissance/1863 Realism

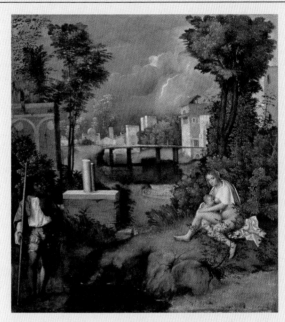

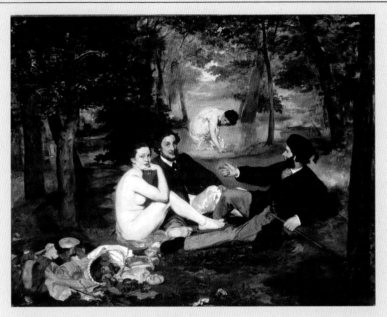

T.5 Giorgione (c. 1477–1511), *The Tempest*, c. 1505. Oil on canvas, 32¼ × 28¾ in. (82 × 73 cm). Galleria dell' Accademia, Venice, Italy/Bridgeman Art Library, London/SuperStock.

T.6 Édouard Manet (1832–1883), *Le Déjeuner sur l'Herbe*, 1863. Oil on canvas, 84¼ × 106¼ in. (214 × 269 cm). © Réunion des Musées Nationaux/Art Resource, NY.

1509 Renaissance/1857 Pictorialism

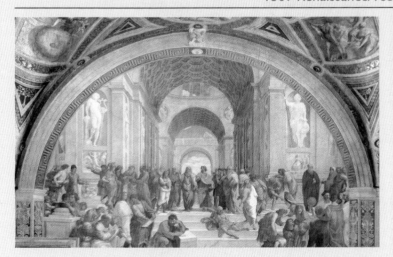

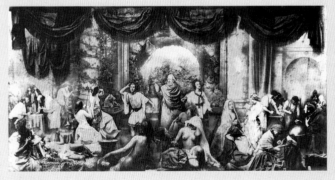

T.8 Oscar Rejlander (1813–1875), *Two Ways of Life*, 1857. Albumen silver print, 16 × 31 in. Courtesy George Eastman House, Rochester, NY, gift of the Royal Photographic Society of Great Britain, Bath, England.

T.7 Raphael (1483–1520), *The School of Athens*, 1509–11. Fresco, size unknown. © Scala/Art Resource, NY.

TIMELINE

High Renaissance in Western Europe (affected by Italy)

Netherlands: Bosch, Breughel
Germany: Dürer (printmaker), Grünewald
France: Master of Moulins

1515 Renaissance/1982 Postmodernism

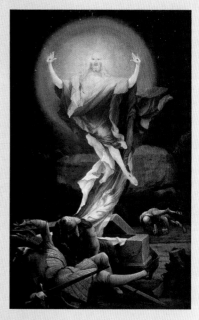 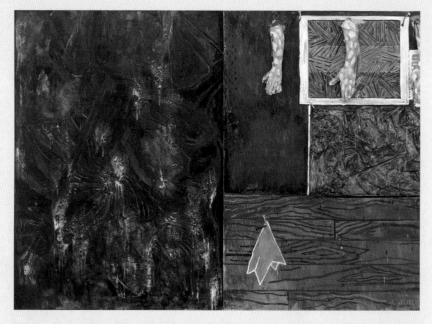

T.9 Matthias Grünewald (c. 1455–1528), *The Resurrection of Christ,* from the Isenheim altarpiece, c. 1515 (detail). Oil on wood, 105⅞ × 120⅞ in. © The Art Archive/Unterlinden Museum Colmar/Gianni Dagli Orti.

T.10 Jasper Johns (b. 1930), *Perilous Night,* 1982. Encaustic on canvas with objects, 67 × 96 × 5 in. Robert and Jane Meyerhoff Collection, image courtesy of the Board of Trustees, National Gallery of Art, Washington, DC, 1982. Art © Jasper Johns/Licensed by VAGA, New York, NY.

1518 Renaissance/1989 Postmodernism

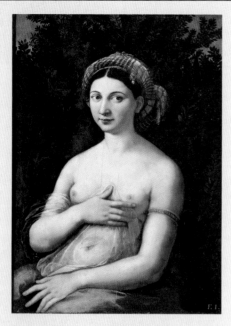 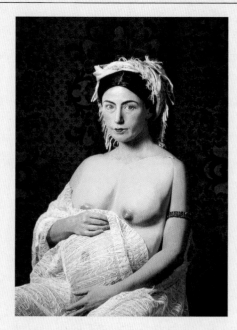

T.11 Raphael (1483–1520), *La Fornarina,* c. 1518. Oil on panel, 33 × 23 in. © Scala/Art Resource, NY.

T.12 Cindy Sherman (b. 1954), *Untitled #205,* 1989. Color photograph, 53½ × 40¼ in. Edition of six. Courtesy of the artist and Metro Pictures.

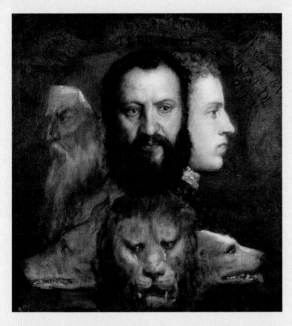

T.13 Titian (c. 1488–1576), *Allegory on the Theme of Prudence,* c. 1565–70. Oil on canvas, 76.2 × 68.6 cm. © Image Asset Management Ltd./SuperStock.

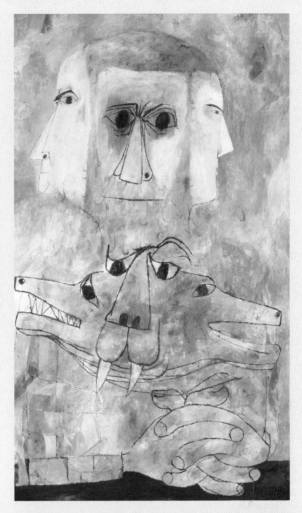

T.14 Ben Shahn (1898–1969), *After Titian,* 1959. Tempura on fiberboard, 53½ × 30½ in. Gift of the Sara Roby Foundation. Photo © Smithsonian American Art Museum, Washington, DC/Art Resource, NY. Art © Estate of Ben Shahn/Licensed by VAGA, New York, NY.

1520

Mannerism and Early Baroque Italy
Italy: Caravaggio, Bernini (sculptor), Borromini (architect)
Spain: El Greco

BAROQUE AND ROCOCO ART (c. 1600–1800)

1600

Baroque Art in Europe
Netherlands (Belgium, Holland): Rubens, Van Dyck, Hals
France: Poussin, Claude
Spain: Ribera, Velázquez

TIMELINE

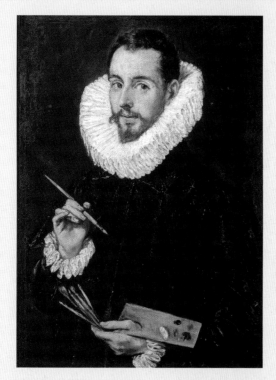

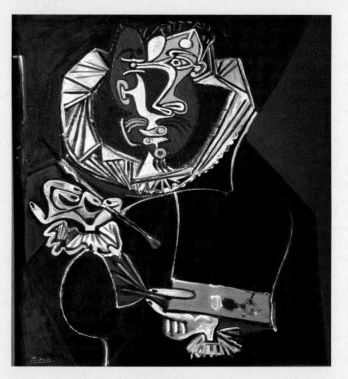

T.15 El Greco (1541–1614), *Portrait of Jorge Manuel,* c. 1603. Oil on canvas, 81 × 56 cm. © Scala/Art Resource, NY.

T.16 Pablo Picasso (1881–1973), *Portrait of a Painter, after El Greco,* 1950. Oil on wood panel, 39⅝ × 31⅞ in. Art © 2008 Estate of Pablo Picasso/Artists Rights Society (ARS), New York. Photo: Rosengart Coll., Lucern Galerie, Switzerland/Peter Willi/SuperStock.

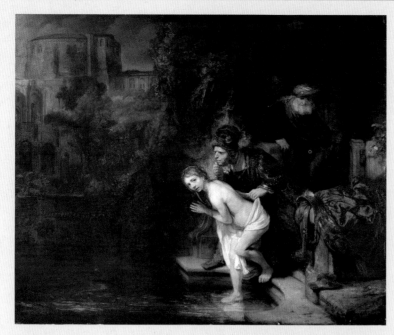

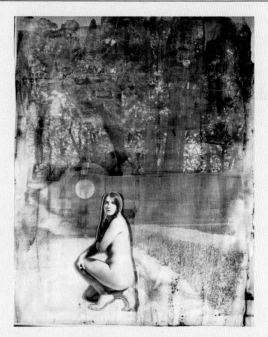

T.17 Rembrandt Harmenszoon van Rijn (1606–1669), *Susanna and the Elders,* 1647. Oil on mahogany panel, 30 × 36 in. © Bildarchiv Preussischer Kulturbesitz/Art Resource, NY.

T.18 Bea Nettles (b. 1946), *Suzanna . . . Surprised,* 1970. Photo emulsion on muslin, photolinen, stitching, 28 × 35 in. Courtesy of the artist.

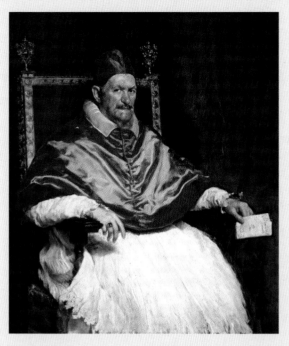

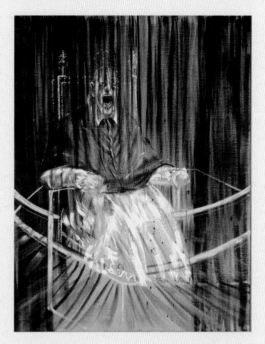

T.19 Diego Velázquez (1599–1660), *Innocent X*, c. 1650. Oil on canvas, 141 × 119 cm. © Alinari/Art Resource, NY.

T.20 Francis Bacon (1909–1992), *Study after Velázquez's Portrait of Pope Innocent X*, 1953. Oil on canvas, 5 × 4 ft. Photo © Bridgeman-Giraudon/Art Resource. Art © The Estate of Francis Bacon/ARS, New York/DACS, London.

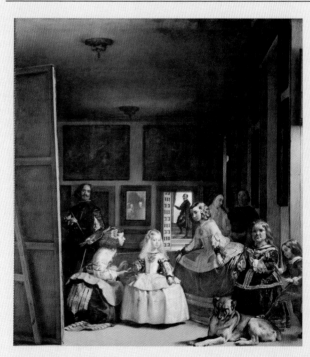

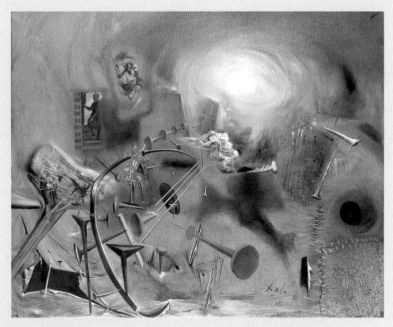

T.21 Diego Velázquez (1599–1660), *Las Meninas*, 1656. Oil on canvas, 10 ft. 5 in. × 9 ft. 1 in. © Erich Lessing/Art Resource, NY.

T.22 Salvador Dalí (1904–1989), *Portrait of Juan de Pareja, the Assistant to Velázquez*, 1960. Oil on canvas, 29¼ × 34¾ in. (74.3 × 88.27 cm). Minneapolis Institute of Arts, gift of Mrs. John Sargent Pillsbury, Sr. © 2008 Salvador Dali, Gala-Salvador Dali Foundation/Artists Rights Society (ARS), New York.

TIMELINE

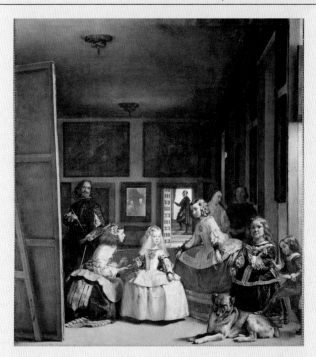

T.23 Diego Velázquez (1599–1660), *Las Meninas*, 1656. Oil on canvas, 10 ft. 5 in. × 9 ft. 1 in. © Erich Lessing/Art Resource, NY.

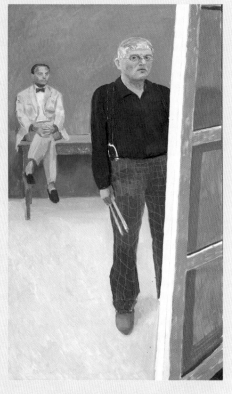

T.24 David Hockney (b. 1937), *Self-Portrait with Charlie*, 2005. Oil on canvas, 72 × 36 in. © David Hockney. Photography by Richard Schmidt.

1701 Baroque/1973 Neo-Figurative

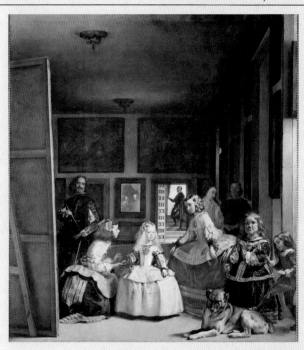

T.25 Diego Velázquez (1599–1660), *Las Meninas*, 1656. Oil on canvas, 10 ft. 5 in. × 9 ft. 1 in. © Erich Lessing/Art Resource, NY.

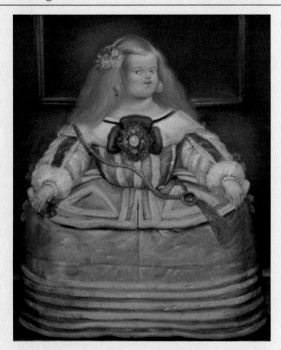

T.26 Fernando Botero, *After Velázquez*, 1976. Oil on canvas, 76 × 62½ in. Photo © Marianne Haas/CORBIS. Art © Fernando Botero. Courtesy of The Marlborough Gallery.

TIMELINE

Early Colonial Art in the Americas: Primarily limners (or primitive portraitists) in English colonies; church or cathedral art in Latin America

1700

Rococo Art: Primarily France but spreads to other European countries
France: Watteau, Boucher, Chardin, Fragonard
Italy: Canaletto, Guardi, Tiepolo
England: Gainsborough, Hogarth, Reynolds

Colonial Arts and Early Federal Art in the United States: Copley, Stuart, West

NINETEENTH-CENTURY ART (c. 1780–1900)

c. 1780

T.27

Neoclassicism
France: Ingres, David (see fig. T.27)
 T.27 Jacques-Louis David, *The Oath of the Horatii,* 1786. Oil on canvas, approx. 14 × 11 ft. (4.27 × 3.35 m). The Louvre, Paris, France. Photo: Lauros-Giraudon, Paris/SuperStock.)
Italy: Canova (sculptor)

1814 Romanticism/1989 Feminist Postmodernism

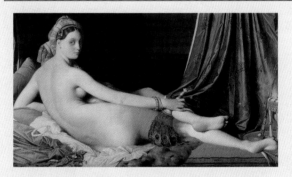

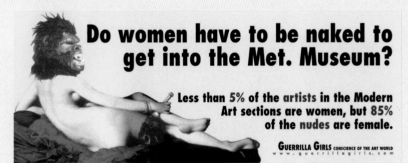

T.28 Auguste-Dominique Ingres (1780–1867), *La Grande Odalisque,* 1814. Oil on canvas, 91 × 162 cm. © Musée du Louvre, Paris/SuperStock.

T.29 Guerrilla Girls, *Do women have to be naked to get into the Met. Museum?,* 1989. Poster, 11 × 28 in. © Guerilla Girls, Inc., Courtesy of www.guerillagirls.com.

c. 1820

Romanticism
France: Barye (sculptor), Delacroix, Géricault, Niépce (first permanent camera image), Daguerre (photographic process), Rejlander (painter and photographer)
Spain: Goya
England: Turner, Fox Talbot (photographic process)
United States: Ryder

1850

Realism and Naturalism
France: Daumier (see fig. 1.22), Courbet (see fig. 1.21), Rodin and Claudel (Romantic/Realist sculptors)
England: Constable
United States: Eakins, Homer, Brady, Gardner, Jackson and O'Sullivan (photographers)

TIMELINE

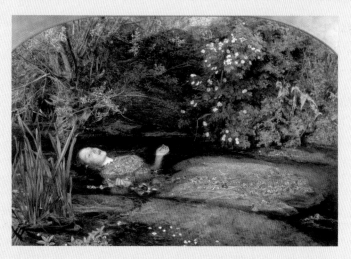

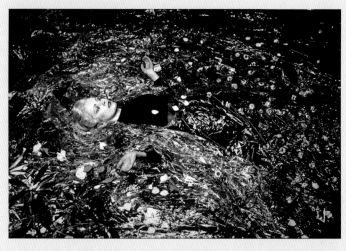

T.30 Sir John Everett Millais (1829–1896), *Ophelia*, 1851–52. Oil on canvas, 30 × 44 in. © Tate, London/Art Resource, NY.

T.31 Victor Burgin (b. 1941), *The Bridge—Venus Perdica*, 1984. Gelatin silver print with text panel, 112.3 × 76.6 cm. Courtesy of George Eastman House, Rochester, NY.

1857 Japanese Print/1887 Post-Impressionism

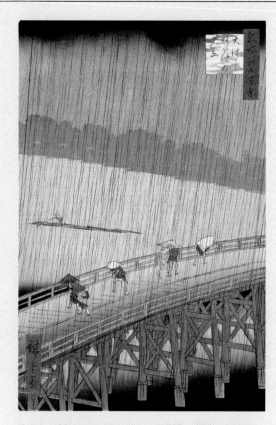

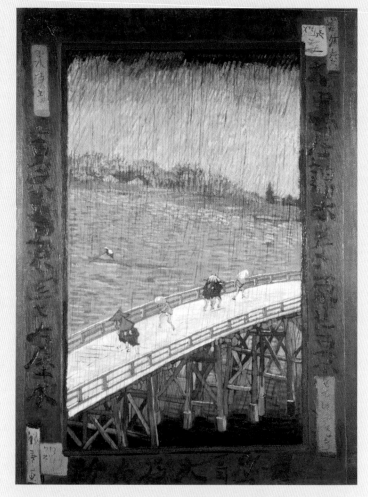

T.32 Utagawa Hiroshige (1797–1858), *Sudden Shower over Shin-Ohashi Bridge and Atake (Ohashi Atake no Yudachi)*, plate 58 from "One Hundred Famous Views of Edo." 1857. Woodcut print, size unknown. © Brooklyn Museum of Art, New York, USA/The Bridgeman Art Library.

T.33 Vincent van Gogh (1853–1890), *Japonaiserie: Bridge in the Rain (after Hiroshige)*, 1887. Oil on canvas, 73 × 54 cm. © Francis G. Mayer/CORBIS.

TIMELINE

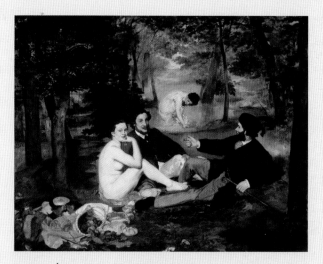

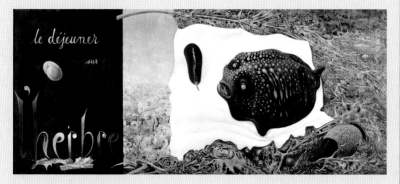

T.35 Max Ernst (1891–1976), *Le Déjeuner sur l'Herbe (Luncheon on the Grass)*, 1944. Oil on canvas, 68 × 150 cm. Photo © DACS/The Bridgeman Art Library. Art © 2008 Artists Rights Society (ARS), New York/ADAGP, Paris.

T.34 Édouard Manet (1832–1883), *Le Déjeuner sur l'Herbe*, 1863. Oil on canvas, 84¼ × 106¼ in. (214 × 269 cm). © Réunion des Musées Nationaux/Art Resource, NY.

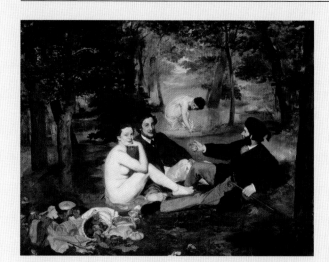

T.36 Édouard Manet (1832–1883), *Le Déjeuner sur l'Herbe*, 1863. Oil on canvas, 84¼ × 106¼ in. (214 × 269 cm). © Réunion des Musées Nationaux/Art Resource, NY.

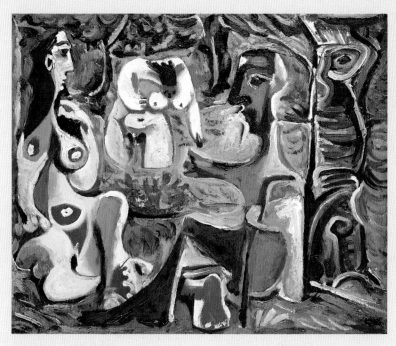

T.37 Pablo Picasso (1881–1973), *Les Déjeuners II*, 1961. Oil on canvas, 60 × 73 cm. Art © 2008 Estate of Pablo Picasso/Artists Rights Society (ARS), New York. Photo © DACS/The Bridgeman Art Library.

TIMELINE

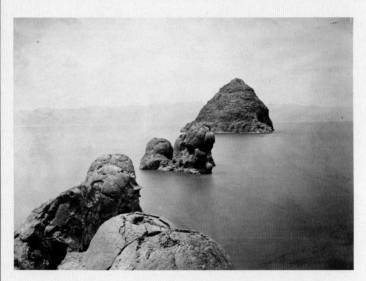

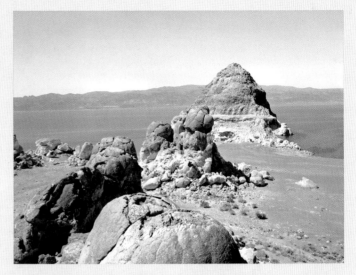

T.38 Timothy H. O'Sullivan (1840–1882), *"Pyramid," Pyramid Lake, Nevada,* 1868. Albumen print, 19.8 × 27.0 cm. © Gift of Harvard University, Courtesy of George Eastman House, Rochester, NY.

T.39 Mark Klett (b. 1952), for the Rephotographic Survey Project, *Pyramid Isle, Pyramid Lake, NV,* 1979. Gelatin silver print, size unknown. Courtesy of Mark Klett.

| 1870 |

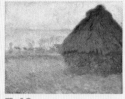

T.40

Impressionism

France: Monet (see fig. T.40), Pissarro, Renoir, Degas (some sculpture), Morisot
England: Sisley
United States: Cassatt, Hassam, Twachtman, Muybridge (Anglo-American photographer)
Italy: Medardo-Rosso (sculptor)

T.40 Claude Monet, *Haystack at Sunset,* 1880. Oil on canvas, 28⅞ × 36½ in. (73.3 × 92.6 cm.) Juliana Cheney Edwards Collection. Courtesy of Museum of Fine Arts, Boston.

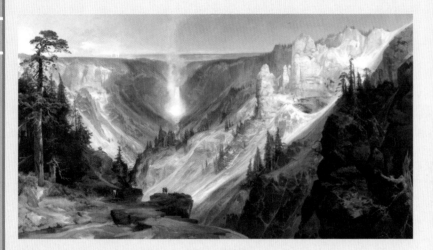

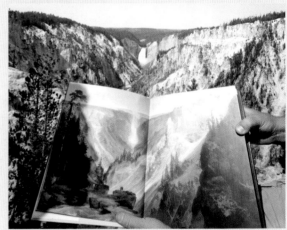

T.41 Thomas Moran (1837–1926), *Grand Canyon of the Yellowstone,* 1872. Oil on canvas, 84 × 144 in. Lent by the Department of the Interior Museum. © Smithsonian American Art Museum, Washington, DC/Art Resource, NY.

T.42 Mark Klett (b. 1952), *Viewing Thomas Moran at the Source, Artist's Point, Yellowstone National Park, NP 8/3/00,* 2000. Pigmented ink-jet print, 24 × 30 in. Courtesy of Mark Klett.

TIMELINE

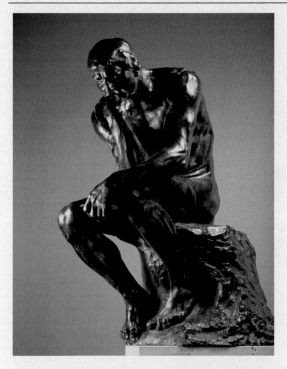

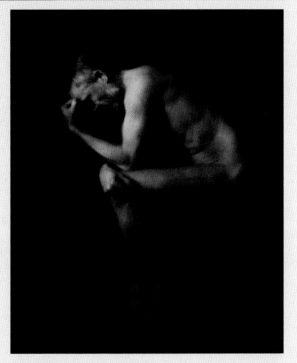

T.43 August Rodin (1840–1917), *The Thinker,* 1879–87. Bronze, 27½ in. © The Gallery Collection/Corbis

T.44 Alvin Langdon Coburn (1882–1966), *Le Penseur,* 1906. Gum-platinum print, 28.7 × 22.9 cm. Gift of Alvin Langdon Coburn, Courtesy of George Eastman House, Rochester, NY.

1880

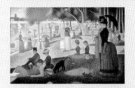

T.45

Post-Impressionism
France: Seurat (see fig. T.45), Cézanne (see figs. 7.23 and 9.5), Gauguin, Toulouse-Lautrec
Holland: Van Gogh (see fig. 1.19)
    T.45 Georges Seurat, *Sunday Afternoon on the Island of La Grande Jatte,* 1884–86. Oil on canvas, 81¾ × 121¼ in. Art Institute of Chicago. Helen Birch Bartlett Memorial Collection 1926.224. Photo © Art Institute of Chicago. All rights reserved.

Symbolism
France: Bonnard

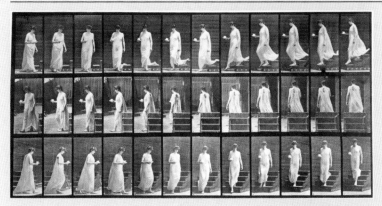

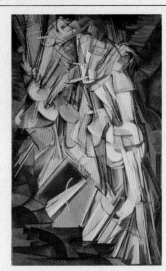

T.47 Marcel Duchamp (1887–1968), *Nude Descending a Staircase,* No. 2, 1912. Oil on canvas, 147.5 × 89 cm. Philadelphia Museum of Art, PA. Louise and Walter Arensberg Collection. Photo: Corbis Media. © 2008 Artists Rights Society (ARS), NY/ADGP, Paris/Estate of Marcel Duchamp.

T.46 Eadweard Muybridge (1830–1904), *Woman Descending a Stairway and Turning Around,* from *Animal Locomotion,* c. 1887. Collotype on paper, 7⅞ × 15¼ in. (20.1 × 38.6 cm). © Smithsonian American Art Museum, Washington, DC/Art Resource, NY.

TIMELINE

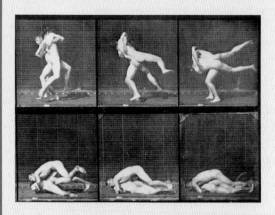

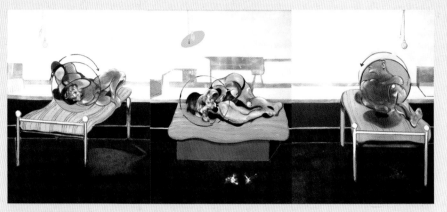

T.48 Eadweard Muybridge (1830–1904), *Two Men Wrestling*, plate 347 from *Animal Locomotion*, c. 1887. Collotype on paper, 7⅞ × 15¼ in. (20.1 × 38.6 cm). © Private Collection/The Stapleton Collection/ The Bridgeman Art Library.

T.49 Francis Bacon (1909–1992), *Three Studies of Figures on Beds*, 1972. Oil and pastel on canvas, triptych, each panel 6 ft. 6 in. × 4 ft. 10 in. © Private Collection/The Bridgeman Art Library © 2008 Estate of Francis Bacon/Artists Rights Society (ARS), New York/DACS, London.

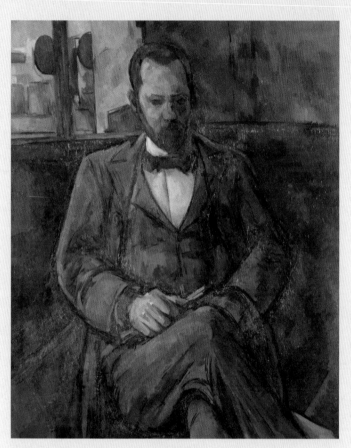

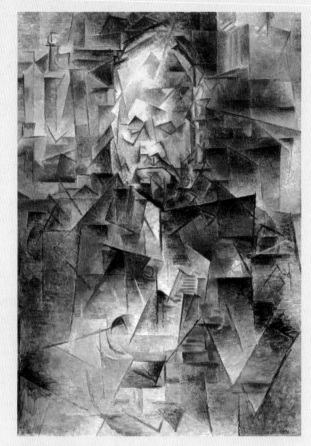

T.50 Paul Cézanne (1839–1906), *Portrait of Ambroise Vollard*, 1899. Oil on canvas, 39½ × 32 in. © Réunion des Musées Nationaux/Art Resource, NY.

T.51 Pablo Picasso (1881–1973), *Portrait of Ambroise Vollard*, 1909. Oil on canvas, 36 × 26 in. Art © Estate of Pablo Picasso/Artists Rights Society (ARS), New York. Photo: Scala/Art Resource, NY.

TIMELINE

Chronological Outline of Western Art

NOTE: Artists often change styles and media, so some names appear under more than one category. Note Pablo Picasso in particular.

1900

Sculpture in the Early 1900s
France: Maillol
United States: Lachaise
Germany: Lehmbruck, Kolbe

1905–1908

Fauvism (Early Expressionism)
France: **Les Fauves (Wild Beasts)** Matisse (see fig. 4.1), Derain, Dufy, Vlaminck, Modigliani (**Italian**), Rouault, Utrillo, Picasso (**Spanish**: Blue, Rose, and Negro periods).

1903 Pictorialism/1930 Modernism

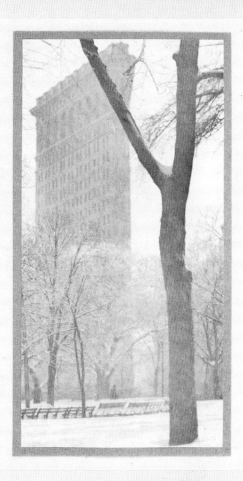

T.52 Alfred Stieglitz (1864–1946), *The "Flat-Iron,"* c. 1903. Photogravure, 6⅝ × 3¼ in. © 2008 Georgia O'Keefe Museum/Artists Rights Society (ARS), New York. Photo: Réunion des Musées Nationaux/Art Resource, NY.

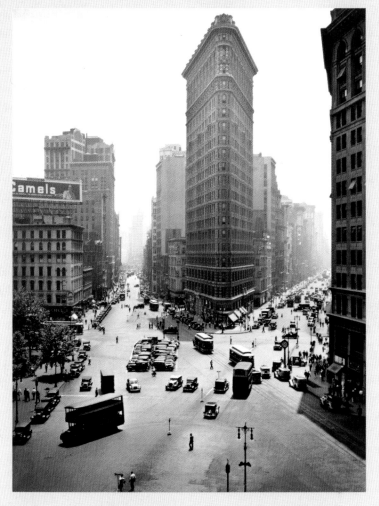

T.53 Berenice Abbott (1898–1991), *Flatiron Building, Manhattan,* c. 1930s. Gelatin silver print, 23¼ × 17⅝ in. Minneapolis Institute of Arts, Gift of the William R. Hibbs Family. © Berenice Abbott/Commerce Graphics Ltd., Inc.

TIMELINE

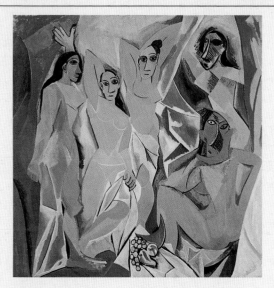

T.54 Pablo Picasso (1881–1973), *Les Demoiselles D'Avignon,* 1907. Oil on canvas, 8 ft. × 7 ft. 8 in. (243.9 × 233.7 cm). © 2008 Estate of Pablo Picasso/Artists Rights Society (ARS), New York. The Museum of Modern Art, New York, NY. USA. Acquired through the Lille B. Bliss bequest. Digital image © The Museum of Modern Art/Licensed by SCALA/ Art Resource, NY.

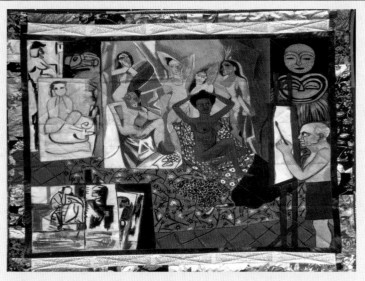

T.55 Faith Ringgold (b. 1930), *Picasso's Studio,* 1991, French Collection #7. Acrylic on canvas with fabric border, 73 × 68 in. Wooster Museum of Art. Faith Ringgold © 2001.

1905–1913

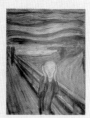

T.56

German Expressionism

Die Brücke (The Bridge): Munch (**Norwegian**; fig. T.56) Kirchner, Nolde, Schmidt-Rottluff
T.56 Edvard Munch, *The Scream,* or *The Cry,* 1893. Oil and tempera on board, 35¼ × 28 in. (89.5 × 73.7 cm). National Gallery, Oslo, Norway. Photo: Bridgeman Art Library, London/ SuperStock. © 2008 The Munch Museum/The Munch-Ellingsen Group/Artists Rights Society (ARS), New York.

Der Blaue Reiter (The Blue Rider): Jawlensky (**Russian**), Kandinsky (**Russian**), Macke, Kuehn (photography)

1905–1917

Stieglitz and Steichen found 291 Gallery in New York City to advance acceptance of photography and avant-garde art

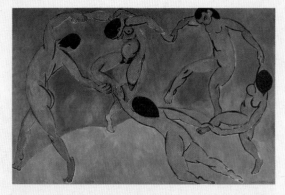

T.57 Henri Matisse (1869–1954), *Dance,* 1910. Oil on canvas, 8½ × 12 ft. Hermitage Museum, St. Petersburg. Art © 2008 Succession H. Matisse/Artists Rights Society (ARS), New York. Photo: Archives Matisse.

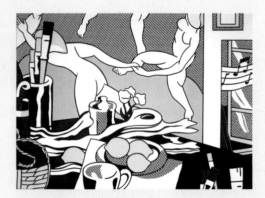

T.58 Roy Lichtenstein (1923–1997), *Artist's Studio: "Dancers,"* 1974. Oil and synthetic polymer (paint) on canvas, 8 ft. × 10 ft. 8 in. © Estate of Roy Lichtenstein. Gift of Mr. and Mrs. S. I. Newhouse, Jr. (362.1990) Photo © The Museum of Modern Art/Licensed by SCALA/Art Resource, NY.

TIMELINE

1907

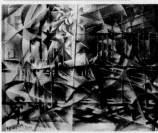

T.59

Cubism
France: Picasso (**Spanish** painter, sculptor, potter), Braque, Léger, Gris (**Spanish**; see fig. 4.2)

Futurism
Italy: Balla (see fig. T.59), Severini, Carra, Boccioni (painter and sculptor; see fig. 9.24), Bragaglia (photographer)
France: Duchamp (see fig. T.47)
> **T.59** Giacomo Balla, *Speeding Automobile,* 1912. Oil on wood, 21⅞ × 27⅛ in. (55.6 × 68.9 cm). © 2008 Artists Rights Society (ARS), New York/SIAE, Rome. The Museum of Modern Art, New York, NY. U.S.A. Purchase. Digital image © The Museum of Modern Art/ Licensed by SCALA/Art Resource, NY.

1910–1920

Abstract Art
Germany: Albers, Hofmann, Kandinsky (**Russian**; see fig. 1.23), Archipenko (**Russian** sculptor), Feininger (**American**)

1913–1922

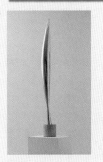

T.60

Constructivism
Russia: Tatlin, Malevich, Larionov, Gabo and Pevsner (sculptors)
Holland: Mondrian (see fig. 1.8)
France: Delaunay, Brancusi (**Romanian** sculptor; see fig. T.60), Arp (sculptor)
England: Nicholson
United States: Dove, Marin, O'Keeffe, Sheeler, Davis, Stieglitz (photographer), Steichen (photographer), Strand (photographer), Coburn (**English** photographer)
> **T.60** Constantin Brancusi, *Bird in Space,* 1928. Bronze (unique cast), 54 × 8½ in. (137.2 × 21.6 × 16.5 cm). © 2008 Artists Rights Society (ARS), New York/ADGP, Paris. The Museum of Modern Art, New York, NY. U.S.A. Given anonymously. Digital image © The Museum of Modern Art/Licensed by SCALA/Art Resource, NY.

Fantasy in Art—Individual Fantasists
France: Chagall (**Russian**), Rousseau (primitive painter)
Italy: de Chirico
Germany: Schwitters, Klee (**Swiss**)

1913

Armory Show, New York: Helped introduce avant-garde art to the United States

1914

Dadaism
France: Arp, Duchamp (see fig. T.47), Picabia
Germany: Schwitters, Ernst
United States: Man Ray (photographer, painter)

c. 1918/19–1924

Die Neue Sachlichkeit (The New Objectivity)
Germany: Dix, Grosz, Heckel, Schlemmer, Sander (photographer)

Independent German Expressionists: Beckmann, Kokoschka (**Austrian**)

TIMELINE

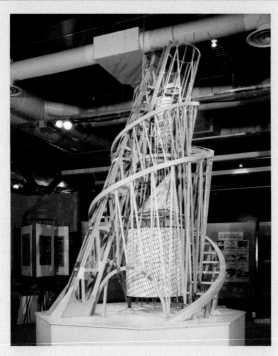

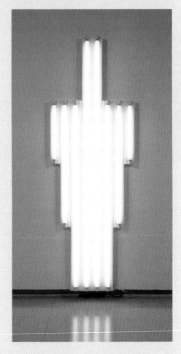

T.61 Vladimir Tatlin (1855–1953), *Model for Monument to the Third International, 1919–20,* replica 1968. Wood, metal, and motor, 15 ft. high. © Jacques Faujour/Réunion des Musées Nationaux/Art Resource, NY.

T.62 Dan Flavin (1933–1996), *"Monument" for V. Tatlin,* 1969. Fluorescent tubes and fixtures, 96⅟₁₆ × 32⅟₁₆ × 4¾ in. Collection Walker Art Center, Minneapolis. Gift of Leo Castelli Gallery, 1981 2008 Stephen Flavin/Artists Rights Society (ARS), New York.

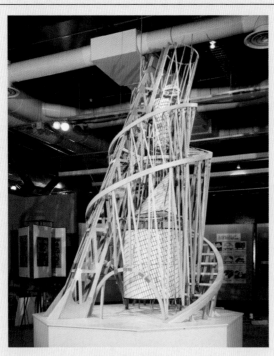

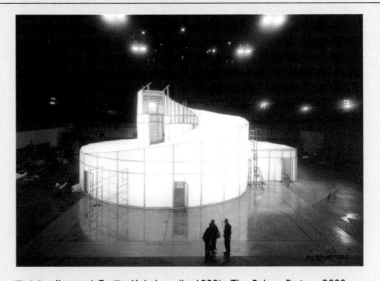

T.64 Ilya and Emilia Kabakov (b. 1933), *The Palace Project,* 2000. Installation, exterior view, London, 24 × 54 × 77 ft. Photo by Dirk Powels. Organized by the Public Art Fund. © Ilya and Emilia Kabakov. Photography: Gil Amiaga. Courtesy Sean Kelly Gallery, New York.

T.63 Vladimir Tatlin (1855–1953), *Model for Monument to the Third International, 1919–20,* replica 1968. Wood, metal, and motor, 15 ft. high. © Jacques Faujour/Réunion des Musées Nationaux/Art Resource, NY.

TIMELINE

Later Expressionism
France: Soutine, Buffet, Balthus, Dubuffet
United States: Avery, Baskin, Broderson, Lawrence, Levine, Shahn, Weber
Mexico: Kahlo, Orozco, Rivera, Siqueiros

1924

Surrealism
France: Arp (sculptor), Cartier-Bresson (photographer), Delvaux (**Belgian**), Magritte (**Belgian**), Masson, Miró (**Spanish**), Picasso (**Spanish**), Tanguy, González (**Spanish** sculptor)
Switzerland: Giacometti (sculptor, painter; see fig. T.65)
England: Bacon
Germany: Ernst
United States: Dalí (**Spanish** painter; Surrealist cinemas with Luis Buñuel; see fig. T.66), Man Ray (photographer, painter)

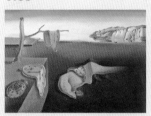

T.65

T.65 Alberto Giacometti, *Three Walking Men*, 1948–49. 29½ in. (74.9 cm) high. Art Institute of Chicago. Edward E. Ayer Endowment in memory of Charles L. Hutchinson, 1951.256. Photo © Art Institute of Chicago. All rights reserved. © 2008 Artists Rights Society (ARS), New York/ADAGP, FAAG, Paris.

T.66 Salvador Dalí, *Persistence of Memory*, 1931. Oil on canvas, 9½ × 13 in. (24.1 × 33 cm). © 2008 Salvador Dalí, Gala-Salvador Dalí Foundation/Artists Rights Society (ARS), New York. The Museum of Modern Art, New York. NY, U.S.A. Given anonymously. Digital image © The Museum of Modern Art/Licensed by SCALA/Art Resource, NY.

T.66

1936 Surrealism/1955 Postmodernism

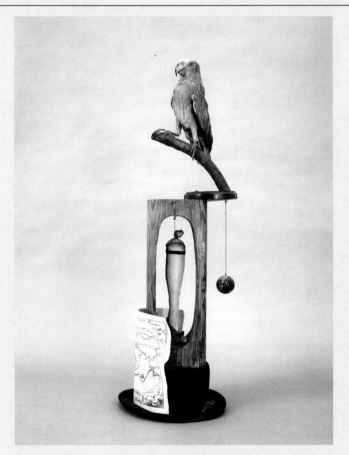

T.67 Joan Miró (1893–1983), *Poetic Object*, 1936. Assemblage, 32 × 12 × 10 in. Gift of Mr. and Mrs. Pierre Matisse. © 2008 Successió Miró/Artists Rights Society (ARS), New York/ADAGP, Paris. Photo © The Museum of Modern Art/Licensed by SCALA/Art Resource, NY.

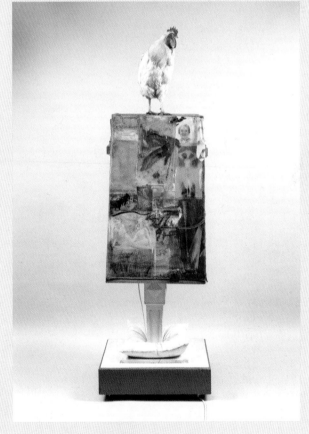

T.68 Robert Rauschenberg (b. 1925), *Odalisk*, 1955–58. Mixed media, 6 ft. 9 in. × 2 ft. 1 in. × 2 ft. 1 in. Photo © Rheinisches Bildarchiv Köln. Art © Estate of Robert Rauschenberg/Licensed by VAGA, New York, NY.

1930–1940

Realist Painting and Photography (Straight) in the United States: Wyeth, Wood, Benton, Burchfield

F-64 Group of photographers: Weston, Adams, Cunningham

1936 Farm Security Administration Photography/1981 Postmodernism

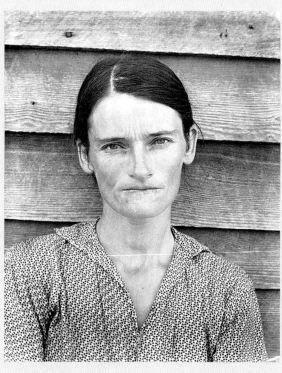

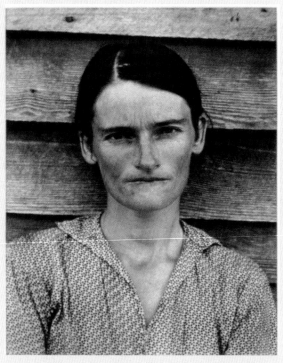

T.69 Walker Evans (1903–1975), *Allie Mae Burroughs, Wife of a Cotton Sharecropper, Hale County, Alabama,* **1936.** Gelatin silver print, 9½ × 7 9/16 in. Minneapolis Institute of Arts, The William Hood Dunwoody Fund. © The Metropolitan Museum of Art.

T.70 Sherrie Levine (b. 1947), *After Walker Evans,* **1981.** Gelatin silver print, 6¼ × 5 in. (15.9 × 12.7 cm). © S. Levine. Courtesy of the artist and the Paula Cooper Gallery, New York. © Walker Evans Archive, The Metropolitan Museum of Art.

LATE-TWENTIETH-CENTURY INTO TWENTY-FIRST-CENTURY ART

1920s–1950s

Kinetics and Light Sculpture: (Early 1900s examples)
France: Duchamp (1920s)
United States: Calder (U.S. Wire Circus, c. 1928), Wilfred (Clavilux color organ, 1930–63)

c. 1951–1965

Abstract Expressionist Painting

Action or Gestural Group (predecessors from abroad)—Albers (**German**), de Kooning (**Dutch**), Gorky (**Armenian**), Hofmann (**German**), Matta (**Chilean**), Mondrian (**Dutch**), Tamayo (**Mexican**)

U.S. New York School—Frankenthaler (see fig. 4.26), Kline (see fig. 1.24), Louis, Mitchell, Pollock (see fig. T.71), White (photographer)

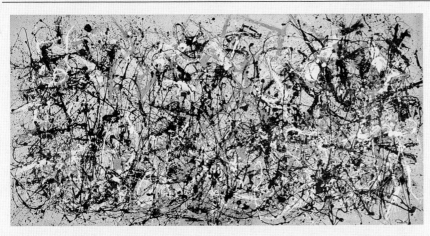

T.71 Jackson Pollock (1912–1956), *Autumn Rhythm (Number 30)*, 1950. Oil on canvas, 8 ft. 9 in. × 17 ft. 3 in. (2.67 × 5.26 m). The Museum of Modern Art, New York. George A. Hearn Fund, 1957 (57.92). Image © The Metropolitan Museum of Art. Art © The Pollock-Krasner Foundation/Artists Rights Society (ARS), New York.

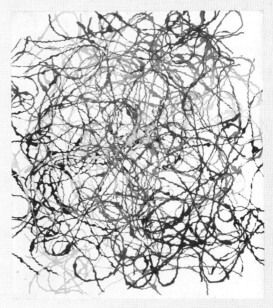

T.72 Andy Warhol (1928–1987), *Yarn*, 1983. Synthetic polymer paint and silkscreen on canvas, 101.6 × 101.6 cm. Art © 2008 The Andy Warhol Foundation for the Visual Arts/Artists Rights Society (ARS), New York. Photo © The Andy Warhol Foundation, Inc./Art Resource, NY.

Color Field Painting Group (Hard-Edge)
United States: Diebenkorn, Callahan (photographer), Kelly, Newman (see fig. 2.59), Noland, Stella, Rothko (**Russian**; see fig. 7.25)

Painters elsewhere similar to Abstract Expressionism
France: Mathieu, Manessier, Soulages
Portugal: Vieira da Silva
Spain: Tapies

Surreal Abstract or Abstract Expressionist Sculptors
England: Moore (see fig. 4.36), Hepworth, Chadwick
France: Richier, Lipchitz (**Latvian**)
United States: Calder, Smith, Noguchi

c. 1958–1965

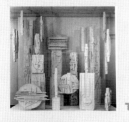

T.73

T.74

Pop Art and Assemblage Predecessors
England: Hamilton, Kitaj (**American**)
United States: Johns, Rauschenberg, Chamberlain (assembler), Dine, Frank (**Swiss** photographer), Friedlander (photographer), Hockney (**English**), Indiana, Kienholz (assembler), Lichtenstein, Marisol (**Venezuelan** sculptor, assembler), Nevelson (sculptor or assembler; see fig. T.73), Oldenburg (sculptor, assembler; see fig. 2.48), Samaras (**Greek** assembler), Segal (sculptor), Stankiewicz (assembler), Warhol (see fig. T.74), Wesselman, Winogrand (photographer).
T.73 Louise Nevelson, *American Dawn*, 1962. Painted wood, 18 × 14 × 19 ft (5.49 × 4.27 × 3.05 m) in situ. Grant J. Pick Purchase Fund 1967.387, The Art Institute of Chicago. Photography © The Art Institute of Chicago. © 2008 Estate of Louise Nevelson/Artists Rights Society (ARS), New York.
T.74 Andy Warhol, *100 Cans*, 1962. Oil on canvas, 6 ft. × 4 ft. 4 in. (1.83 × 1.32 m). Albright-Knox Art Gallery, Buffalo, NY. Gift of Seymour H. Knox, 1963. © 2008 Andy Warhol Foundation for the Visual Arts/Artists Rights Society (ARS), New York.

TIMELINE

c. 1958–1970

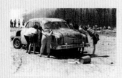

T.75

Happenings, Performance or Action Art

United States: Kaprow (earliest Happening 1958; see fig. T.75), most Pop artists involved
Germany: Beuys

T.75 Allan Kaprow, *Household,* May 1964. One photograph of a series taken of a Happening commissioned by Cornell University, Ithaca, NY. Courtesy of the artist, Allan Kaprow. Photograph © Sol Goldberg.

1960s–1970s

T.76

Abstract Expressionism in the United States

United States: Rickey, Bury (**Belgian**; see fig. T.76), Chryssa (**Greek**), Flavin, Lippold, Samaris and Takis (**Greek**), Tinguely (**Swiss** 1930–63)

T.76 Pol Bury, *The Staircase,* 1965. Wood with motor, 78⅝ × 27 × 16¼ in. (200 × 68.6 × 41.3 cm). Collection, the Solomon R. Guggenheim Foundation, New York; 65.1765. © 2008 Artists Rights Society (ARS), New York/ADAGP, Paris

1960s–1980s

New Realism (Photorealism)
United States: Estes, Fish, Perlstein, Close, Hanson (sculptor)

Feminist Art Movement: Historical Precedents; begins in acknowledgment of women's domestic art as significant achievements
United States: Chicago, Schapiro, Ringgold, Sherman

c. 1964–1970s

T.77

Op Art: Extremely limited abstract style depending primarily on the observer's visual perception for content; derives from earlier scientific investigations into color theory.
France: Vasarely (see fig. T.77)
United States: Anuskiewicz
Germany: Riley (**English**)

T.77 Victor Vasarely, *Vega Per,* 1969. Oil on canvas, 64 × 64 in. Honolulu Academy of Arts. Gift of the Honorable Clare Boothe Luce, 1984 (5311.1). © 2008 Artists Rights Society (ARS), New York/ADAGP, Paris

c. 1964–1975

T.78

Minimalism: Climax of abstract/nonobjective art, informed by Color Field painting and all types of abstract sculpture
United States: Bell (sculptor, assembler), Flavin (light sculptor, assembler), Judd (sculptor; see fig. 2.66), Katzen (sculptor), LeWitt (painter), Martin (sculptor), Pepper (sculptor), Reinhardt (see fig. T.78), di Suvero (sculptor), Caro and Smith (**English** sculptors)

T.78 Ad Reinhardt, *Blue 1953,* 1953. Oil on canvas, 50 × 28 in. (127 × 71.1 cm). Collection of the Whitney Museum of American Art, New York. Gift of Susan Morse Hilles 74.22, © 2008 Estate of Ad Reinhardt/Artists Rights Society (ARS), New York

1965–1990s

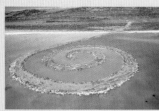

T.79

Environmental and Installation Art: Forerunners—Schwitters (**German**) and Duchamp (**French**)

Environmental Art
United States: Christo and Jeanne-Claude, Oldenburg, Smithson (see fig. T.79), Heizer, Samaras (**Greek**; see fig. 2.65)

T.79 Robert Smithson, *Spiral Jetty,* Great Salt Lake, Utah, 1970. Rock, salt crystals, earth, algae, coil, 1,500 ft. (457 m). © Estate of Robert Smithson/Licensed by VAGA, New York, NY

Installation Art: Paik (**Korean**), Pfaff (**English**), Hamilton (**American**), Skoglund (**American**)

c. 1965–1990s

Postmodernism
United States: Johnson (architect), Kruger (collage and installation artist), Levine (photographer), Venturi (architect)

c. 1965–1980s

Process and Conceptual Art
Germany: Beuys
United States: Hess (**German**), early exemplars (1965): Kosuth (see fig. T.80), Morris

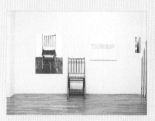

T.80 Joseph Kosuth, *One and Three Chairs*, 1965. Wooden folding chair, photographic copy of a chair, and photographic enlargement of dictionary definition of a chair; chair, 32⅜ × 14⅞ × 207 in. (82 × 37.8 × 53 cm); photo panel, 36 × 24⅛ in. (91.5 × 61.1 cm); text panel, 24 × 24⅛ in. (61 × 61.3 cm). © 2008 Joseph Kosuth/Artists Rights Society (ARS), New York. The Museum of Modern Art, New York, NY. U.S.A. Larry Aldrich Foundation Fund. Digital Image © The Museum of Modern Art/Licensed by SCALA/Art Resource, NY

T.80

1980s

Introduction to Computer Arts

1980s–1990s

Neo-Expressionism
Germany: Kiefer (see fig. 8.15), Baselitz, Fetting
Italy: Cucchi, Chia
United States: Schnabel, Rothenberg, Sherman (photographer, painter)

c. mid-1980s–2000s

Neo-Abstraction
United States: Benglis (sculptor, painter; see fig. T.81), Graves (sculptor; see fig. 2.67), Marden (sculptor, painter), Puryear (sculptor), Jensen, Scully (**Irish**), Rockburne (**Canadian**), Rothenberg

T.81 Lynda Benglis, *Tossana*, 1995–96. Stainless steel, wire mesh, zinc, aluminum, and silicone bronze, 49 × 63 × 14 in. (1.24 × 1.6 × .36 m). © Lynda Benglis/Licensed by VAGA, New York, NY

T.81

Late 1990s–2000s

Film Stills (Pictorialism in Photography): Use of staging, including special lighting effects, with photographic artists often acting and directing; strong influence of movies and Sherman (photographic method)

Photography: Exploration of objectivity by making precise photographs on a very large scale

New Global Art Related to Neo-Expressionist Art of the 1980s: Use of multimedia and art installation to express human diversity and differences while addressing humanity as a whole

New-New Painters: Use of synthetic materials to produce three-dimensional paintings; information unavailable yet; no historical perspective established

TIMELINE

Abstract Expressionism
An American art movement that grew out of Surrealism in the mid- to late-twentieth century, with emphasis on spontaneity or subconscious creation.

abstract texture
A texture derived from the appearance of an actual surface but rearranged and/or simplified by the artist to satisfy the demands of the artwork.

abstraction
A process or visual effect characterized by the simplification and/or rearrangement of the image.

academic
Art that conforms to established traditions and approved conventions as practiced in formal art schools. Academic art stresses standards, set procedures, and rules.

accent
Any stress or emphasis given to the elements of a composition that brings them more attention than other features that surround or are close to them. Accent can be created by a brighter color, darker value, greater size, or any other means by which a difference is expressed.

achromatic
Relating to color perceived only in terms of neutral grays from light to dark; without hue.

achromatic value
Relating to differences of lightness and darkness, without regard for hue and intensity.

Action painting
A term coined by Harold Rosenberg to describe a subgroup of Abstract Expressionist painters who worked with gestural lines, movements, and sometimes rapid and fluid image constructions as opposed to large blocks or "fields" of pure color, as with the Color Field painters.

actual motion
The movement found in art forms like kinetic art, where bodies physically change their location during a period of time.

actual shape
A positive area with clearly defined boundaries (as opposed to an implied shape).

actual texture
A surface that can be experienced through the sense of touch (as opposed to a surface visually simulated by the artist).

addition
A sculptural term that means building up, assembling, or putting on material.

additive color
Color created by superimposing light rays. Adding together (or superimposing) the three primary colors of light—red, blue, and green—will produce white. The secondaries are cyan, yellow, and magenta.

aesthetic, aesthetics
1. Sensitive to art or beauty. "Aesthetically pleasing" implies intellectual or visual beauty (i.e. creative, eloquent, or expressive qualities of form, as opposed to the mere recording of facts in visual, descriptive, or objective ways.) 2. The study or theory of beauty—traditionally a branch of philosophy but now a compound of the philosophy, psychology, and sociology of art—dealing with the definition, inspiration, intent, forms, and psychological effects of art and beauty.

allover pattern
A design that is formed through the systematic repetition of smaller designed units over an entire surface.

amorphous shape
A shape without clear definition: formless, indistinct, and of uncertain dimension.

analogous colors
Colors that are closely related in hue. They are usually adjacent to each other on the color wheel.

animation
The rapid succession of a sequence of drawings, computer-generated images, or pictures of objects such as clay figures that create the illusion of a moving image.

approximate symmetry
The use of similar imagery on either side of a central axis. The visual material on one side may resemble that on the other but is varied to prevent visual monotony.

arris
On three-dimensional objects, the sharp edge or ridge formed by two surfaces meeting at an angle. Made visible by cast shadow, it is often interpreted as a line.

art
"The formal expression of a conceived image or imagined conception in terms of a given medium" (Sheldon Cheney).

assemblage
A technique that involves grouping found or created three-dimensional objects, which are often displayed "in situ"—that is, in a natural position or in the middle of a room rather than on a wall.

asymmetry
"Without symmetry"; having unequal or noncorresponding parts. An example: a two-dimensional artwork that, without any necessarily visible or implied axis, displays an uneven distribution of parts throughout.

atectonic
Three-dimensional work characterized by considerable amounts of space; open, as opposed to massive (or tectonic), and often with extended appendages.

atmospheric perspective
The illusion of depth produced in graphic works by lightening values, softening details and textures, reducing value contrasts, and neutralizing colors in objects as they recede.

balance
A sense of equilibrium between areas of implied weight, attention, attraction, or moments of force; one of the principles of organization.

Bauhaus
Originally a German school of architecture that flourished between World War I and World War II. The Bauhaus attracted many leading experimental artists of both two- and three-dimensional fields.

biomorphic shape
An irregular shape that resembles the freely developed curves found in living organisms.

calligraphic lines
Lines that are generally flowing and rhythmical, like the qualities found in the kind of writing called *calligraphy*.

calligraphy
Elegant, decorative writing.

casting
A sculptural technique in which liquid materials are shaped by being poured into a mold. This technique is also known as **substitution.**

cast shadow
The dark area that occurs on a surface as a result of something being placed between that surface and a light source.

cell (or single cell)
One image from a series of related images that presents an idea. Cells are commonly

found in comic strips, graphic novels, or storyboard presentations, which tend to isolate the images from each other by an outline in the shape of a rectangle. Cells also refer to the individual frames of animated cartoons.

chiaroscuro
1. The distribution of lights and darks in a picture, usually in an attempt to develop the illusion of mass, volume, or space. 2. A technique of representation that blends light and shadow gradually to create the illusion of three-dimensional objects in space or atmosphere.

chroma
1. The purity of a hue, or its freedom from white, black, or gray (and wavelengths of other color). 2. The intensity of a hue. 3. Computer programs often refer to chroma as *saturation.*

chromatic
Pertaining to the presence of color.

chromatic value
The value (relative degree of lightness or darkness) demonstrated by a given color.

Classicism
A reference to ancient Greek and Roman civilizations, but also any art that encompasses or stresses order, balance, and unity.

closed-value composition
A composition in which values are contained within the edges or boundaries of shapes. The value pattern reveals the subject(s) and is dependent on the positioning of the subject(s).

close-up
A cinematic technique in which the subject fills the camera frame; used to focus the viewer's attention on specific imagery or detail.

closure
A concept from Gestalt psychology in which the mind perceives an incomplete pattern or information to be a complete, unified whole; the artist provides minimum visual clues, and the observer brings them to final recognition.

collage
A technique of picturemaking in which real materials possessing actual textures are attached to the picture plane surface, often in combination with painted or drawn passages.

color
The visual response to different wavelengths of sunlight identified as red, green,

blue, and so on; having the physical properties of hue, intensity, and value.

Color Field
An abstract style of painting following Abstract Expressionism that is characterized by a canvas with areas of solid colors.

color tetrad
Four colors, equally spaced on the color wheel, containing a primary and its complement and a complementary pair of intermediates. This has also come to mean any organization of color on the wheel forming a rectangle that could include a double split-complement.

color triad
Three colors equally spaced on the color wheel, forming an equilateral triangle. The twelve-step color wheel is made up of a primary triad, a secondary triad, and two intermediate triads.

complementary colors
Two colors directly opposite each other on the color wheel. A primary color is complementary to a secondary color, which is a mixture of the two remaining primaries.

composition
The arranging and/or structuring of all the art elements, according to the principles of organization, that achieves a unified whole. Often used interchangeably with the term **design.**

concept
1. A comprehensive idea or generalization. 2. An idea that brings diverse elements into a basic relationship.

Conceptual Art
Art that focuses on a concept or idea over materials and aesthetics.

Conceptual artists
Artists who focus on the idea, or "concept" of the work and are much more concerned with conveying a message or analyzing an idea than with the final product.

conceptual perception
Creative vision derived from the imagination; the opposite of **optical perception.**

Constructivism
A movement founded by Vladimir Tatlin between 1913 and 1922 associated primarily with three-dimensional spatial concepts in sculpture and architecture.

content
The expression, essential meaning, significance, or aesthetic value of a work of art.

Content refers to the sensory, subjective, psychological, or emotional properties we feel in a work of art, as opposed to our perception of its descriptive aspects alone.

contour
In art, the line that defines the outermost limits of an object or a drawn or painted shape. It is sometimes considered to be synonymous with *outline;* as such, it indicates an edge that also may be defined by the extremities of dark, light, texture, or color.

craftsmanship
Aptitude, skill, or quality workmanship in the use of tools and materials.

cross-contour
A line that moves across a shape or object to define the surface undulations between the outermost edges.

crosscutting
A cinematic technique that abruptly shifts from one event or character to another and is often used to allow the viewer to move between characters and change points of view as the dialogue or action evolves.

cross-hatching
(See **hatching.**)

Cubism
The name given to the painting style invented by Pablo Picasso and Georges Braque between 1907 and 1912, which uses multiple views of objects to create the effect of three-dimensionality while acknowledging the two-dimensional surface of the picture plane. Signaling the beginning of abstract art, Cubism is a semiabstract style that continued the strong trend away from representational art initiated by Cézanne in the late 1800s.

curvilinear shape
A shape whose boundaries consist of predominantly curved lines; the opposite of **rectilinear.**

Dadaism
The earliest style of Fantastic Art to appear in the 1900s that opened modern art to a new freedom of humorous expression, creative imagination, contradictory tendencies, and intentional provocation.

decorative
1. The two-dimensional nature of an artwork or any of its elements (shape, space, value, etc.). Decorative art and/or its elements emphasize the essential flatness of a surface. 2. Has generally referred to the ornamentation or enrichment of a surface.

descriptive (art)
A type of art that is based on adherence to actual appearances.

design
The organizing process or underlying plan on which artists base their total work. In a broader sense, *design* may be considered synonymous with the terms **form** and **composition.**

dissolve
An aesthetic technique, used as a film or video transition between images or scenes, in which one shot disappears as another slowly appears.

dominance
The principle of organization in which certain visual elements assume more importance than others within the same composition or design. Some features are emphasized, and others are subordinated. Dominance is often created by increased contrasts through the use of isolation, placement, direction, scale, and character.

duration
The length of time in which an activity takes place.

economy
The distillation of the image to the basic essentials for clarity of presentation; one of the principles of organization.

elements of art
Line, shape, value, texture, and color—the basic ingredients the artist uses separately or in combination to produce artistic imagery. Their use produces the visual language of art.

Environmental Art
Art that deals with the natural environment but can also be applied to historical, political, and social contexts of a particular environment. Environmental Art usually addresses issues of natural phenomena and environmental awareness and uses natural materials that do not cause further harm to the environment.

equivocal space
A condition, usually intentional on the artist's part, in which the viewer may, at different times, see more than one set of relationships between art elements or depicted objects. This may be compared to the familiar "optical illusion."

expression
1. The manifestation through artistic form of thought, emotion, or quality of meaning. 2. In art, *expression* is synonymous with the term **content.**

Expressionism
Starting in France and Germany around 1910, the style allowed young artists to paint a subject in non-naturalistic colors in accord with their feelings. It is a form of art that tries to reveal the emotional essence rather than to show external appearance or resemblance.

fade
An aesthetic technique, used as a film or video transition between scenes, in which the image slowly darkens to black.

Fantastic Art
A trend that occurred at the beginning of World War I, which opened up experimentation and was impelled by the war, its horrors, and a gathering sense of alienation from society in an age of technology.

flashback
A cinematic technique of jumping to a sequence of events in the story that are meant to have taken place in the past.

flash-forward
A cinematic technique of jumping to a sequence of events in the story that are meant to take place in the future.

form
1. The total appearance, organization, or inventive arrangement of all the visual elements according to the principles that will develop unity in the artwork; composition. 2. In sculpture, form can also refer to the three-dimensional shape of the work.

four-dimensional space
An imaginative treatment of forms that gives a sense of intervals of time or motion.

fractional representation
A pictorial device (used notably by the Egyptians) in which several spatial aspects of the same subject are combined in the same image.

frame
A single static image as applied to cartoons, storyboards, animation, films, videos, or computer-generated graphics.

Futurism
An early-twentieth-century movement in art and literature that refashioned Cubism in light of its own desire to glorify the dynamic character of the machine age.

genre paintings
Paintings with subject matters that concern everyday life, domestic scenes, family relationships, and the like.

geometric shape
A shape that appears related to geometry; usually simple, such as a triangle, rectangle, or circle.

Gestalt, Gestalt psychology
A German word for "form"; an organized whole in experience. Around 1912, the Gestalt psychologists promoted the theory that explains psychological phenomena by their relationships to total forms, or *Gestalten,* rather than their parts. In other words, our reaction to the whole is greater than our reaction to its individual parts or characteristics, and our minds integrate and organize chaotic stimuli so that we see complete patterns and recognizable shapes.

gestural lines
Lines that are drawn freely, quickly, and seemingly without inhibition in order to capture the intrinsic spirit and animation seen in the subject. Gestural lines can imply the past, present, and future motion of the subject.

glyptic
1. The quality of an art material like stone, wood, or metal that can be carved or engraved. 2. An art form that retains the color, tensile, and tactile qualities of the material from which it was created. 3. The quality of hardness, solidity, or resistance found in carved or engraved materials.

golden mean, golden section
1. Golden mean—"perfect" harmonious proportions that avoid extremes; the moderation between extremes. 2. Golden section—a traditional proportional system for visual harmony expressed when a line or area is divided into two sections so that the smaller part is to the larger as the larger is to the whole. The ratio developed is 1:1.6180, or roughly 8:13.

graphic (art)
Two-dimensional art processes such as drawing, painting, photography, printmaking, and so on that generally exist on a flat surface and can create the illusion of depth. Commercial applications include posters, newspapers, books, and magazines.

Happenings
A form of participatory art in which spectators, as well as artists, were engaged. It brings together the basic concepts of motion, time, and space.

harmony
A principle of organization in which parts of a composition are made to relate through commonality—repeated or shared characteristics, elements, or visual units. Harmony is the opposite of **variety.**

hatching

Repeated strokes of an art tool, producing clustered (usually parallel) lines that create values. In cross-hatching, similar lines pass over the hatched lines in a different direction, usually resulting in darker values.

high-key color

Any color that has a value level of middle gray or lighter.

high-key value

A value that has a level of middle gray or lighter.

highlight

The portion of an object that, from the observer's position, receives the greatest amount of direct light.

hue

The generic name of a color (*red, blue, green,* etc.); also designates a color's position in the spectrum or on the color wheel. Hue is determined by the specific wavelength of the color in a ray of light.

implied lines

Implied lines (subjective lines) are those that dim, fade, stop, and/or disappear. The missing portion of the line is implied to continue and is visually completed by the observer as the line reappears.

implied motion

The sense or illusion of movement given to a static object.

implied shape

A shape that does not physically exist but is suggested through the psychological connection of dots, lines, areas, or their edges. (See **Gestalt**.)

Impressionism

A movement of art that initiated new ideas about color, light, finish, and, to a lesser degree, dynamic movement. It became the preoccupation of early modernist painters.

infinite space

A concept in which the picture frame acts as a window through which objects can be seen receding endlessly.

installations

Interior or exterior settings of media created by artists to heighten the viewers' awareness of the environmental space.

intensity

The saturation, strength, or purity of a hue. A vivid color is of high intensity; a dull color is of low intensity.

intermediate color

A color produced by a mixture of a primary color and a secondary color.

intermediate triad

A group of three intermediate colors that are equally spaced on the color wheel and form an equilateral triangle; two groups of intermediate triads are found on the color wheel: red-orange/yellow-green/blue-violet and red-violet/blue-green/yellow-orange.

interpenetration

The positioning of planes, objects, or shapes so that they appear to pass through each other, which locks them together within a specified area of space.

intuitive space

The illusion of space that the artist creates by instinctively manipulating certain space-producing devices, including overlapping, transparency, interpenetration, inclined planes, disproportionate scale, fractional representation, and the inherent spatial properties of the art elements.

invented texture

A created texture whose only source is the artist's imagination. It generally produces a decorative pattern and should not be confused with **abstract texture.**

isometric projection

A technical drawing system in which a three-dimensional object is presented two-dimensionally; starting with the nearest vertical edge, the horizontal edges of the object are drawn at a 30-degree angle, and all verticals are projected perpendicularly from a horizontal base.

kinetic (art)

From the Greek word *kinesis,* meaning "motion"; art that involves an element of random or mechanical movement.

Les Fauves

Artist members of the earliest Expressionist group in France that used unnaturally bold coloring and exaggeratedly distorted figures, which gave their paintings the look of "wild beasts."

line

The path of a moving point made by a tool, instrument, or medium as it moves across an area. A line is usually made visible because it contrasts in value with its surroundings. Three-dimensional lines may be made using string, wire, tubes, solid rods, and the like.

linear perspective

A system used to depict three-dimensional images on a two-dimensional surface; it develops the optical phenomenon of diminishing size by treating edges as converging parallel lines that extend to a vanishing point or points on the horizon (eye level) and recede from the viewer. (See **perspective.**)

local (objective) color

The color as seen in the objective world (green grass, blue sky, red barn, etc.).

local value

The relative lightness or darkness of a surface, seen in the objective world, that is independent of any effect created by the degree of light falling on it.

long shot

A cinematic technique in which the filmmaker provides a distant view with a broader perspective of the image; often used to imply a larger conceptual context.

low-key color

Any color that has a value level of middle gray or darker.

low-key value

A value that has a level of middle gray or darker.

manipulation

The sculptural technique of shaping pliable materials by hand or with the use of tools—also known as **modeling.**

mass

1. In graphic art, a shape that appears to stand out three-dimensionally from the space surrounding it or that appears to create the illusion of a solid body of material. 2. In the plastic arts, the physical bulk of a solid body of material.

medium, media (pl.)

The material(s) and tool(s) used by the artist to create the visual elements perceived by the viewer.

medium shot

A cinematic technique in which the filmmaker provides a view that seems to lie somewhere between a close-up and a long shot.

Minimalism

A movement that not only included art but also, music, dance, and literature and was a precedent for nonobjective abstraction in the early twentieth century. Minimalism relied only on the basic elements for meaning—without any trace of the artistic process.

mobile
A three-dimensional, moving sculpture.

modeling
A sculptural term for shaping a pliable material.

moments of force
The direction and degree of energy implied by the art elements in specific compositional situations; amounts of visual thrust produced by such matters as dimension, placement, and accent.

motif
A designed unit or pattern that is repeated often enough in the total composition to make it a significant or dominant feature. Motif is similar to "theme" or "melody" in a musical composition.

monochromatic
Having only one hue; may include the complete range of value (of one hue) from white to black.

motion
The process of moving, or changing place or position in space.

motion picture
The illusion of a moving image created by showing a series of still pictures in rapid sequence.

movement
Eye travel directed by visual pathways in a work of art; one of the principles of organization. Movement is guided by harmonious connections, areas of variety, the placement of visual weights, areas of dominance, choices in proportions, spatial devices, and so on.

multimedia
The combination of many different groups of media such as text, still and moving graphics, and spoken and instrumental sounds; also often integrated with communication technologies involving television, video, telephones, and computers.

multiple exposures
A photographic technique that shows a figure in motion by displaying a rapid series of exposures within the same image.

Naturalism
The approach to art that is essentially a description of things visually experienced. Pure naturalism would contain no personal interpretation introduced by the artist.

negative area
The unoccupied or empty space left after the positive images have been created by the artist. Consideration of the negative areas is just as important to the organization of form as the positive areas.

Neoclassicism
Originating in France in the 1700s, the style grew from the discovery of the ancient Roman ruins of Herculaneum and Pompeii and the publication of Johann Joachim Winckelmann's *The History of the Art of the Ancients*.

Neo-Expressionism
The return, in the early 1980s, to figurative art and a more personalized expression. The movement satisfied the growing appetite for recognizable images and meaningful content by producing monumental dramatic figures with broad gestures, painted in broad brushstrokes.

neutralized (color), neutralization (of color)
Color that has been grayed or reduced in intensity by being mixed with any of the neutrals or with a complementary color (so that the mixture contains all three primaries, in equal or unequal amounts).

neutrals
1. The inclusion of all color wavelengths will produce white, and the absence of any wavelengths will be perceived as black. With neutrals, no single color is noticed—only a sense of light and dark or the range from white through gray to black. 2. A color altered by the addition of its complement so that the original sensation of hue is lost or grayed.

New Realism
Art that emphasized the human figure and portraiture extensively and strove for a matter-of-fact kind of verisimilitude, but without the sly humor of Pop Art.

nonobjective, nonrepresentational art
A type of art that is completely imaginative, in which the elements, their organization, and their treatment are entirely personalized and the image is not derived from anything visually perceived by the artist.

objective
That which is based on the physical reality of the object and reflects no personal interpretation, bias, or emotion; the opposite of **subjective.**

oblique projection
A technical drawing system in which a three-dimensional object is presented two-dimensionally; the front and back sides of the object are parallel to the horizontal base, and the other planes are drawn as parallels coming off the front plane at a 45-degree angle.

Op Art
A form of art that is primarily optical and highly graphic, although it can merge into three-dimensionality when used in paintings that include an element of relief. It is an extension and modification of the geometric abstraction that developed in the early twentieth century.

open-value composition
A composition in which values are not limited by the edges of shapes and therefore flow across shape boundaries into adjoining areas. The value pattern created is unrelated to the location of the subject(s).

optical perception
A purely visual experience with no exaggeration or creative interpretation of that which is seen; the opposite of **conceptual perception.**

organic unity
A condition in which the components of art (subject, form, and content) are completely interdependent. Though not a guarantee of "greatness," the resulting wholeness is vital to a successful work.

orthographic drawing
Graphic representation of two-dimensional views of an object, showing a plan, vertical elevations, and/or a section.

paint quality
The intrinsic character of a painting medium—thickness, glossiness, and so forth—which can enrich a surface through its own textural interest.

papier collé
A visual and tactile technique in which scraps of paper having various textures are pasted to the picture surface to enrich or embellish those areas. The printing of text or images on those scraps can provide further visual richness or decorative pattern.

patina
1. A natural film, usually greenish, that results from the oxidation of bronze or other metallic material. 2. Colored pigments and/or chemicals applied to a sculptural surface.

pattern
1. Any artistic design (sometimes serving as a model for imitation). 2. A repeating element and/or design that can produce a new set of characteristics or organization.

Performance Art
An expanded category of participatory art that can include theater, dance, music, cinema, video, and computer.

perspective

Any graphic system used to create the illusion of three-dimensional images and/or spatial relationships in which the objects or their parts appear to diminish as they recede into the distance.

Pictorialism

An especially later-nineteenth-century to early-twentieth-century movement of European and American photographers who wanted to enhance photography's perceived lack of subjectivity and creativity by emphasizing a softer-focus negative and a highly manipulated print process in the darkroom.

picture frame

The outermost limits or boundary of the picture plane.

picture plane

The actual flat surface on which the artist executes a pictorial image. In some cases, the picture plane acts merely as a transparent plane of reference to establish the illusion of forms existing in a three-dimensional space.

pigment

A color substance that gives its color property to another material by being mixed with it or covering it. Pigments, usually insoluble, are added to liquid vehicles to produce paint and ink. They are different from dyes, which are dissolved in liquids and give their coloring effects by staining or being absorbed by a material.

planar (shape)

Having to do with planes; shapes that have height and width but no indication of thickness.

plane

1. An area that is essentially two-dimensional, having height and width. 2. A two-dimensional pictorial surface that can support the illusion of advancing or receding elements. 3. A flat sculptural surface.

plastic

1. Three-dimensional art forms such as architecture, sculpture, and ceramics. 2. The use of the elements (shape, space, value, etc.) to create the illusion of volume and space—the third dimension—on a two-dimensional surface.

Pop Art

The term stands for "popular art," which was prompted by the dissatisfaction of younger artists with their position or prospects in relation to the dominance of abstract art.

positive area

The subject—whether representational or nonrepresentational—which is produced by the art elements (shape, line, etc.) or their combination. (See **negative area.**)

Post-Impressionism

A movement started by some painters associated with Impressionism who sought a return to the structural organization of pictorial form, an increased emphasis on the picture surface for the sake of pictorial unity and the unique patterns and textures that might result, and a more-or-less conscious exaggeration of natural appearances for emotionally suggestive effects.

Postmodernism

A movement resulting from artists' reactions to high-modernist abstract art and dogma (especially to Minimalism and the International Style in architecture), the increasing financial disparity between rich and poor, cynicism about politics and society (some of which resulted from the Vietnam War and Watergate), and so forth. Resulted in the reintroduction of the human figure; decoration; literary subjects; the appropriation of earlier artists' styles, works, or parts thereof; the reuse of older media, and mixed techniques along with newer methods.

Post-Painterly Abstractionism

Art on large, flat planes painted in a more traditional manner.

primary color

A preliminary hue that cannot be broken down or reduced into component colors. Primary colors are the basic hues of any color system that, in theory, may be used to mix all other colors.

primary triad

The three primary colors on the color wheel (red, yellow, and blue), which are equally spaced and form an equilateral triangle.

principles of organization

Concepts that guide the arrangement and integration of the elements in achieving a sense of visual order and overall visual unity. They are harmony, variety, balance, proportion, dominance, movement, and economy.

Process artists

Artists who focus on the execution, or "process," of the work and are much more concerned with the technique they employ in creating the work than with the final product.

proportion

The comparative relationship of size between units or the parts of a whole. For example, the size of the Statue of Liberty's hand relates to the size of her head. (See **scale.**) Proportion is one of the principles of organization.

radial

Emanating from a center.

realism, Realism (art movement)

A style of art that emphasizes universal characteristics rather than specific information (e.g., a generalization of all "motherhood" rather than an extremely detailed portrait of a specific woman). As a movement, it relates to painters like Honoré Daumier in nineteenth-century France and Winslow Homer in the United States in the 1850s.

rectilinear shape

A shape whose boundaries consist of straight lines; the opposite of **curvilinear.**

relief sculpture

An artwork, graphic in concept but sculptural in application, that utilizes relatively shallow depth to establish images. The space development may range from very limited projection, known as "low relief," to more exaggerated space development, known as "high relief." Relief sculpture is meant to be viewed frontally, not in the round.

repetition

The use of the same visual effect—and/or similar visual effects—a number of times in the same composition. Repetition may produce the dominance of one visual idea, a feeling of harmonious relationship, an obviously planned pattern, or a rhythmic movement.

representational art

A type of art in which the subject is presented through the visual art elements so that the observer is reminded of actual objects (see **naturalism** and **Realism**).

reverse perspective

A graphic system for depicting three-dimensional images, commonly seen in traditional East Asian art, in which the "parallel" lines of objects or their parts seem to converge toward the viewer, rather than away into the distance. (See **perspective.**)

rhythm

A continuance, a flow, or a sense of movement achieved by the repetition of regulated visual units; the use of measured accents.

Romanticism
The style of art that focuses on the emotional as opposed to the rational. The macabre, the fantastic, the stormy, and the lyrical moods of nature, animals, and humans became fit subjects for artistic expression. The style grew out of the literary trends that affected all of eighteenth-century Europe and gave more emphasis to form, artists' materials, and processes.

scale
The association of size relative to a constant standard or specific unit of measure related to human dimensions. For example, the Statue of Liberty's scale is apparent when she is seen next to an automobile. (See **proportion.**)

sculpture
The art of shaping three-dimensional materials to express an idea.

secondary color
A color produced by a mixture of two primary colors.

secondary triad
The three secondary colors on the color wheel (orange, green, and violet), which are equally spaced and form an equilateral triangle.

sfumato
A technique devised by Leonardo da Vinci of softly blending areas from light to dark, creating subtle transitions. Images often have vague outlines and a hazy or smoky appearance. *Sfumato* is derived from the Latin *fumo,* meaning "smoke." Leonardo described sfumato as "without lines or borders, in the manner of smoke beyond the focus plane."

shade (of color)
A color produced by mixing black with a hue, which lowers the value level and decreases the quantity of light reflected.

shadow
The darker value on the surface of an object that suggests that a portion of it is turned away from or obscured by the source of light.

shallow space
The illusion of limited depth. With shallow space, the imagery moves only a slight distance back from the picture plane.

shape
An area that stands out from its surroundings because of a defined or implied boundary or because of differences of value, color, or texture.

silhouette
The area between or bounded by the contours, or edges, of an object; the total shape.

simultaneity
A cubist technique developed by Pablo Picasso that showed the structure of objects in space by portraying many different facets of them at the same time.

simultaneous contrast
When two different colors come into direct contact, the contrast intensifies the difference between them.

simulated texture
A convincing copy or translation of an object's texture in any medium. (See **trompe l'oeil.**)

slow motion
1. A cinematic technique that slows down the movement and time in a film; created by shooting a high number of frames per second and showing them at a much slower speed. 2. The sense that time and movement is progressing more slowly than normal.

space
The interval, or measurable distance, between points or images; can be actual or illusionary.

spectrum
The band of individual colors that results when a beam of white light is broken into its component wavelengths, identifiable as hues.

split-complement(s)
A color and the two colors on either side of its complement.

still frame
One frame (or full-screen image) from a series of frames normally seen in a film or video presentation that when viewed in sequence present the illusion of a moving picture. Related to **cell.**

Straight photographers
A number of especially early- to mid-twentieth-century American photographers, often associated with the reaction against Pictorialism, who wanted to locate the creativity of their medium within the sharp focusing and selective framing of the camera and within the unmanipulated print from the negative.

structured ambiguity
A condition in which the positive figure and the negative background seem to reverse roles, fluctuating back and forth between the two functions to create an ambiguous sense of space. Structured ambiguity is often employed as a transition between contrasting values or colors and is a valuable tool for creating optical illusions, denying space, and blending an image into its background.

style
The specific artistic character and dominant trends of form noted during periods of history and art movements. Style may also refer to artists' expressive use of media to give their works individual character.

subject
1. In a descriptive approach to art, refers to the persons or things represented. 2. In more abstract applications, refers to visual images that may have little to do with anything experienced in the natural environment.

subjective
That which is derived from the mind, instead of physical reality, and reflects a personal bias, emotion, or innovative interpretation; the opposite of **objective.**

substitution
In sculpture, replacing one material or medium with another. (See also **casting.**)

subtraction
A sculptural term meaning the carving or cutting away of material.

subtractive color
The sensation of color that is produced when wavelengths of light are reflected back to the viewer after all other wavelengths have been subtracted and/or absorbed.

superimposing, superimposed images
A technique in which various views of the same subject are placed on top of each other in the same image.

Surrealism
A style of artistic expression, influenced by Freudian psychology, that emphasizes fantasy and whose subjects are usually experiences revealed by the subconscious mind through the use of automatic techniques (rubbings, doodles, blots, cloud patterns, etc.). Originally a literary movement that grew out of Dadaism, Surrealism was established by a literary manifesto written by André Breton in 1924.

Symbolism
A style that sought to achieve an ultimate reality through intuitive or inward spiritual experiences of the world.

symmetry
The exact duplication of appearances in mirrorlike repetition on either side of a (usually imaginary) straight-lined central axis.

tactile
A quality that refers to the sense of touch.

technique
The manner and skill with which artists employ their tools and materials to achieve an expressive effect.

tectonic
The quality of simple massiveness; three-dimensional work lacking any significant extrusions or intrusions.

tenebrism
A technique of painting that exaggerates or emphasizes the effects of chiaroscuro. Larger amounts of dark value are placed close to smaller areas of highly contrasting lights—which change suddenly—in order to concentrate attention on important features.

tertiary color
Color resulting from the mixture of all three primaries, two secondary colors, or complementary intermediates. Tertiary colors are characterized by the neutralization of intensity and hue. A great variety of tertiary colors, created by mixing differing amounts of the parent colors, are found on the inner rings of the color wheel, which lead to complete neutralization.

texture
The surface character of a material that can be experienced through touch or the illusion of touch. Texture is produced by natural forces or through an artist's manipulation of the art elements.

three-dimensional
Possesses the dimensions of (or illusions of) height, width, and depth. In the graphic arts, the feeling of depth is an illusion, while in the plastic arts, the work has actual depth.

time
A system or way of measuring the interval between events or experiences.

tint (of color)
A color produced by mixing white with a hue, which raises the value level and increases the quantity of light reflected.

tonality, tone (color)
1. A generic term for the quality of a color, often indicating a slight modification in hue, value, or intensity—for example, yellow with a greenish tone. 2. The dominating hue, value, or intensity; for example, artwork containing mostly red and red-orange will have an overall tonality of red (the dominant *hue*), and areas of color might have a dark tonality (indicating the dominant *value*) or a muted tonality (indicating the dominant *intensity* level).

transparency
A visual quality in which a distant image or element can be seen through a nearer one.

trompe l'oeil
Literally, "deceives the eye"; the copying of nature with such exactitude as to be mistaken for the real thing. (See **simulated texture**.)

two-dimensional
Possesses the dimensions of height and width, especially when considering the flat surface, or picture plane.

unity
The result of bringing the elements of art into the appropriate ratio between harmony and variety to give a sense of oneness.

value
1. The relative degree of lightness or darkness. 2. The characteristic of color determined by its lightness or darkness or the quantity of light reflected by the color.

value pattern
The arrangement or organization of values that control compositional movement and create a unifying effect throughout a work of art.

variety
Differences achieved by opposing, contrasting, changing, elaborating, or diversifying elements in a composition to add individualism and interest. Variety is an important principle of organization; the opposite of **harmony**.

video
A recording of visual images that are stored in an electronic format (digital or videotape) and viewed on a television, computer monitor, or projection screen. The sensation of motion is an illusion created by the rapid sequence of images.

visual unity
A sense of visual oneness—an organization of the elements into a visual whole. Visual unity results from the appropriate ratio between harmony and variety (in conjunction with the other principles of organization).

void
1. An area lacking positive substance and consisting of negative space. 2. A spatial area within an object that penetrates and passes through it.

volume
The measurable amount of defined or occupied space in a three-dimensional object.

ADAM, MICHAEL. *Womankind.* New York: Harper and Row, 1979.

AGOSTON, GEORGE A. *Color Theory and Its Application in Art and Design.* Berlin: Springer Verlag, 1987.

AIKEMA, BERNARD, and MARGUERITE TUIJN. *Tiepolo in Holland: Works by Giambattista Tiepolo and his Circle in Dutch Collections.* Rotterdam: Museum Boijmans Van Beuningen, 1996.

ALBERS, JOSEF. *Interaction of Color.* New Haven, CT: Yale University Press, 1963.

ANDERSON, MAXWELL L., et al. *2000 Biennial Exhibition.* New York: Abrams, 2004.

ARMSTRONG, TOM. *200 Years of American Sculpture.* Catalog for Whitney Museum of American Art. Boston: Godine Press, 1976.

ARNHEIM, RUDOLPH. *Art and Visual Perception.* Berkeley: University of California Press, 1966.

Art in America (periodical). 575 Broadway, New York City, NY.

Art News (periodical). W. 38th Street, New York City, NY.

BAIGELL, MATHEW. *Charles Burchfield.* New York: Watson-Guptil, 1976.

BARASS, GORDON S. *The Art of Calligraphy in Modern China.* Berkeley: University of California Press, 2002.

BATCHELDER, ANN, and NANCY ORBAN. *Fiberarts Design Book Five.* Asheville, NC: Lark Books, 1995.

BETHERS, RAY. *Composition in Pictures.* New York: Pitman, 1956.

BETTI, CLAUDIA, and TEEL SELE. *A Contemporary Approach: Drawing.* New York: Holt, Rinehart and Winston, 1980.

BINDMAN, DAVID. *William Blake.* New York: Thames and Hudson, 1982.

BIRREN, FABER. *Color Perception in Art.* New York: Van Nostrand Reinhold, 1976.

———. *Creative Color.* New York: Van Nostrand Reinhold, 1961.

———. *Principles of Color.* New York: Van Nostrand Reinhold, 1969.

BLOOMER, CAROLYN M. *Principles of Visual Perception.* New York: Van Nostrand Reinhold, 1976.

BRO, L. V. *Drawing: A Studio Guide.* New York: Norton, 1978.

BUENDIA, J. R., et al. *Paintings of the Prado.* Boston: Little, Brown, 1994.

CANADAY, JOHN. *What Is Art?* New York: Knopf, 1980.

CARPENTER, JAMES M. *Visual Art: An Introduction.* New York: Harcourt Brace Jovanovich, 1982.

CHADWICK, WHITNEY. *Women Artists and the Surrealist Movement.* New York: Thames and Hudson, 1991.

CHAET, BERNHARD. *The Art of Drawing.* New York: Holt, Rinehart and Winston, 1970.

CHEVREUL, M. E. *The Principles of Harmony and Contrasts of Colors and Applications to the Arts.* New York: Van Nostrand Reinhold, 1981.

CHILVERS, IAN, HAROLD OSBORNE, and DENNIS FARR. *The Oxford Dictionary of Art.* New York: Oxford University Press, 1988.

CLEAVER, DALE G. *Art: An Introduction.* New York: Harcourt Brace Jovanovich, 1972.

COLEMAN, RONALD. *Sculpture: A Handbook for Students.* Dubuque, IA: Brown, 1990.

The Complete Letters of Vincent Van Gogh. Boston: New York Graphic Society, 1978.

COMPTON, MICHAEL. *Pop Art.* London: Hamlyn, 1970.

CRAWFORD, WILLIAM. *The Keepers of the Light: A History and Working Guide to Early Photographic Processes.* New York: Dobbs Ferry, 1979.

DANOT, ARTHUR C., and CHRISTOPHER SWEET. *Mark Tansey: Visions and Revisions.* New York: Abrams, 1992.

DAVIS, PHIL. *Photography.* Dubuque, IA: Brown, 1990.

DIAMOND, DAVID G. *Art Terms.* Boston: Bulfinch Press Book / Little, Brown, 1992.

EDWARDS, BETTY. *Drawing on the Right Side of the Brain.* Los Angeles: Tarcher, 1979.

ELIOT, ALEXANDER. *Myths.* New York: McGraw-Hill, 1976.

ELSEN, ALBERT E. *Origins of Modern Sculpture.* New York: Braziller, 1974.

FAINE, BRAD. *The Complete Guide to Screen Printing.* Cincinnati: Quartu, 1989.

FAULKNER, RAY, HOWARD SMAGULA, and EDWIN ZIEGFELD. *Today: An Introduction to the Visual Arts.* New York: Holt, Rinehart and Winston, 1987.

FINE, RUTH E., ET AL. *Contemporary American Realist Drawings.* Manchester, UK: Hudson Hills, 2000.

FRIEDMAN, MARTIN, et al. *Walker Art Center: Painting and Sculpture from the Collection.* New York: Rizzoli, 1990.

GERDEMAN, DAN. *Big Ideas for Small Movies: A Short Film Idea Book for Filmmakers, Artists, and Teachers.* Hilliard, OH: Gerdy Art Entertainment, 2006.

GOGH, VINCENT VAN. *Dear Theo: The Autobiography of Vincent van Gogh.* Edited by Irving Stone and Jean Stone. New York: Grove, 1960.

GUY, JOHN, DEBORAH SWALLOW, ROSEMARY CRILL, ET AL. *Arts of India 1550–1900.* London: Victoria and Albert Museum, 1990.

HAMMACHER, ABRAHAM MARIE. *The Evolution of Modern Sculpture.* New York: Abrams, 1969.

HELD, JULIUS S. *Rembrandt Studies.* Princeton, NJ: Princeton University Press, 1991.

HELLER, NANCY. *Women Artists: An Illustrated History.* New York: Abbeyville, 1981.

HIBBARD, HOWARD. *The Metropolitan Museum of Art.* New York: Harper and Row, 1980.

HUNTER, SAMUEL. *American Art of the 20th Century.* New York: Abrams, 1972.

ITTEN, JOHANNES. *The Art of Color.* New York: Van Nostrand Reinhold, 1970.

———. *Design and Form.* New York: Van Nostrand Reinhold, 1975.

JAFFE, HANS L. C. *Piet Mondrian.* New York: Abrams, 1985.

JENKINS, DONALD. *Images of a Changing World.* Portland, OR: Portland Art Association, 1983.

KNAPPE, KARL-ADOLF. *Dürer.* New York: Abrams, 1965.

KNOBLER, NATHAN. *The Visual Dialogue.* New York: Holt, Rinehart and Winston, 1980.

KUEPPERS, HARALD. *The Basic Law of Color Theory.* New York: Barron's Educational Series, 1982.

———. *Color Atlas*. New York: Barron's Educational Series, 1982.

LANE, R. *Images from the Floating World*. Secaucus, NJ: Cartwell Books, 1978.

LERNER, ABRAM, ET AL. *The Hirshhorn Museum and Sculpture Garden*. New York: Abrams, 1974.

LEWIS, R. L., and S. I. LEWIS. *The Power of Art*. Orlando, FL.: Harcourt Brace, 1994.

Life Library of Photography. New York: Time-Life, 1971.

LOCKER, J. L. *The World of M. C. Escher*. New York: Abrams, 1971.

LOTHROP, SAMUEL K. *Treasures of Ancient America: The Arts of the Pre-Colombian Civilizations from Mexico to Peru*. Cleveland, OH: Skira, 1964.

LOWE, SARAH M. *Frida Kahlo*. New York: Universe, 1991.

LUCIE-SMITH, EDWARD. *Late Modern: The Visual Arts since 1945*. New York: Praeger, 1969.

———. *The Thames and Hudson Dictionary of Art Terms*. New York: Thames and Hudson, 1984.

MACAULAY, DAVID. *The New Way Things Work*. Boston: Houghton Mifflin/Lorraine Books, 1988.

MEISEL, L. K. *Photorealism since 1980*. New York: Abrams, 1993.

MENDELOWITZ, DANIEL M., and DUANE A. WAKEMAN. *A Guide to Drawing*. Orlando, FL: Harcourt Brace Jovanovich, 1993.

MYERS, JACK FREDRICK. *The Language of Visual Art*. Orlando, FL: Holt, Rinehart and Winston, 1989.

National Gallery of Art. *Johannes Vermeer*. Washington, DC: Author, 1995.

POIGNANT, R. *Oceanic Mythology*. London: Hamlyn, 1967.

Rendezvous: Masterpieces from the Centre Georges Pompidou and the Guggenheim Museums. Paris: Centre Georges Pompidou; New York: Guggenheim Museum, 1998.

RUBIN, W. *Primitivism in 20th Century "Art."* 2 vols. New York: Museum of Modern Art, 1984.

RUSSELL, STELLA PANDELL. *Art in the World*. Orlando, FL: Holt, Rinehart and Winston, 1978.

SAFF, DONALD, and DELI SACILOTTO. *Printmaking*. New York: Holt, Rinehart and Winston, 1978.

SMITH, BRADLEY. *Mexico: A History in Art*. New York: Doubleday, 1968.

SMITH, B., and W. WENG. *China: A History in Art*. New York: Harper and Row, 1972.

SPARKE, PENNY, FELICE HODGES, EMMA DENT, and ANNE STONE. *Design Source Book*. Secaucus, NJ: Chartwell, 1982.

STRUPPECK, JULES. *The Creation of Sculpture*. New York: Holt, 1952.

SUTTON, P. *Dreamings: The Art of Aboriginal Australia*. New York: Braziller, 1988.

TERUKAZU, AKIYAMA. *Japanese Painting*. New York: Rizzoli, 1977.

THORP, R. L. *Son of Heaven: Imperial Arts of China*. Seattle: Son of Heaven Press, 1988.

TOMASSONI, ITALO. *Mondrian*. London: Hamlyn, 1970.

TOWNSEN, CHRIS. *The Art of Bill Viola*. New York: Thames and Hudson, 2004.

TROYEN, CAROL, and ERICA E. HIRSHLER. *Charles Sheeler: Paintings and Drawings*. Boston: Little, Brown, 1987.

VERITY, ENID. *Color Observed*. New York: Van Nostrand Reinhold, 1980.

VINCENT, GILBERT T., SHERRY BRYDON, and RALPH T. COE, EDS. *Art of the North American Indians: The Thaw Collection*. Cooperstown: New York State Historical Association; Seattle: University of Washington Press, 2000.

WAX, CAROL. *The Mezzotint*. New York: Abrams, 1996.

WEISS, HILLARY. *The American Bandanna*. San Francisco, CA: Chronicle, 1990.

WESTERMANN, MARIT. *Rembrandt*. London: Phaidon, 2000.

WINGLER, M. HANS. *The Bauhaus*. Cambridge, MA: M. I. T. Press, 1986.

WONG, WUCIUS. *Principles of Color Design*. New York: Van Nostrand Reinhold, 1987.

———. *Principles of Form and Design*. New York: Van Nostrand Reinhold, 1993.

———. *Principles of Three-Dimensional Design*. New York: Van Nostrand Reinhold, 1977.

YENAWINE, PHILIP. *How to Look at Modern Art*. New York: Abrams, 1991.

ZEMEL, CAROL. *Van Gogh's Progress*. Berkeley: University of California Press, 1997.